D1210562

A
Karamazov
COMPANION

*Commentary on the Genesis, Language,
and Style of Dostoevsky's Novel*

Victor Terras

THE UNIVERSITY OF WISCONSIN PRESS

DEER PARK PUBLIC LIBRARY
44 LAKE AVENUE
DEER PARK, N. Y. 11729

Published 1981

The University of Wisconsin Press
114 North Murray Street
Madison, Wisconsin 53715

The University of Wisconsin Press, Ltd.
1 Gower Street
London WC1E 6HA, England

Copyright © 1981
The Board of Regents of the University of Wisconsin System
All rights reserved

First printing

Printed in the United States of America

019981 ✓
12.50 PB

Library of Congress Cataloging in Publication Data
Terras, Victor.
A Karamazov companion.
Bibliography: pp. 447–56
Includes index.
1. Dostoevskiĭ, Fedor Mikhaĭlovich, 1821–1881. BroThers Ka
Brat'ia Karamazovy. I. Title.
PG3325.B73T47   891.73'3   80-5117
ISBN 0-299-08310-1
ISBN 0-299-08314-4 (pbk.)

Contents

COMMENTARY

Contents

Preface

THIS companion volume to *The Brothers Karamazov* refers to the recent Academy edition (F. M. Dostoevskii, *Polnoe sobranie sochinenii v tridtsati tomakh* [Leningrad: Nauka, 1976], vols. 14 and 15) for the Russian original, and to the Garnett-Matlaw translation (Fyodor Dostoevsky, *The Brothers Karamazov* [New York: W. W. Norton, 1976]) for the English text. The present volume consists of two parts: an Introduction, which discusses briefly the background, ideas, and techniques of *The Brothers Karamazov;* and the Commentary, or reader's guide, to the novel. The notes of the Commentary are keyed to the texts by page and line number (and by volume in the case of the Russian text), with the page and line number of the English text given first.

The novel appeared almost exactly a hundred years ago. Hence, historical events which were making newspaper head-lines then (Bismarck's *Kulturkampf,* for example) have receded into the limbo of expert historical erudition. Since they are important for an understanding of the novel, they are pointed out in the Commentary when referred to in the novel. The novel is set in mid-nineteenth-century Russia, a setting removed from the American reader of today geographically, culturally, and chronologically. The Commentary will draw the reader's attention to facts with which he is unlikely to be familiar, but which are important for an understanding of the text. For example, a divinity student (Russ. *seminarist*) in nineteenth-century Russia was not the social equivalent of an American divinity student of the same period, or of today.

Dostoevsky was a "tricky" writer who often delivered his message through more or less subtle allusions. Since events and individuals alluded to are often outside the scope of even an educated American reader's knowledge, they are pointed out in the Commentary. Also, important details which are lost in the English translation are pointed out.

The Garnett-Matlaw translation is an admirable achievement. It is, however, based on what I believe to be a flawed notion of what Dostoevsky was trying to do. Dostoevsky was trying to create an individualized "amateur" narrator, remarkable more for a certain ingenuous bonhomie and shrewd common sense than for sound logic, an elegant style, or even correct grammar. The translation has smoothed out many rough edges, eliminating illogicalities and tautologies, deleting repetitions, and introducing *le mot juste* where Dostoevsky's narrator had obviously missed it. I have pointed out some of the more striking instances where the English translation has "corrected" Dostoevsky, usually destroying a nuance in the process. I have also pointed out simple mistranslations, of which there are very few indeed.

The Garnett-Matlaw translation does not by and large try to duplicate Dostoevsky's stylistic patterns, in particular that which Roman Jakobson has called "the poetry of grammar." I have inserted some observations on stylistic effects—such as emphatic repetition and parallelism, "key words," accumulation of modal expressions, paradox, and catachresis—just to remind the reader that these and other active stylistic patterns are ever-present in the original. I have also tried to draw attention to verbal leitmotifs and symbols, particularly where the translation does not bring them out properly. For example, the title and leitmotif of Book Four is *Nadryvy,* translated "Lacerations" in Garnett-Matlaw (I propose to translate *nadryv* by "rupture"). The word appears throughout Book Four in various nominal, verbal, and adjectival forms, clearly as a result of conscious "orchestration" by Dostoevsky. The translation does not duplicate this detail, and I have drawn attention to it in the Commentary.

The Brothers Karamazov is a novel with a message (or several messages; religious, moral, and political). Dostoevsky's strategy in delivering his message is rarely straightforward and often well camouflaged. At the risk of spoiling the reader's pleasure of recognizing Dostoevsky's stratagems by himself, I have pointed out the key junctures in the development of the principal theses of the novel.

The Brothers Karamazov is a novel with an involved plot and a very large number of characters (a list, in alphabetic order, is provided). For a reader who reads the novel for the first time it is not easy to separate important characters and events from dead ends (there are a few) and secondary developments. Attention will be drawn to these and some other features of Dostoevsky's novelistic technique, such as polyphonic development of characters, foreshadowing, and "variations on a theme." The Commentary contains a considerable number of cross-references which are revealing of Dostoevsky's control of his work and of his novelistic strategy.

The novel contains hundreds of biblical and literary quotations and allusions. Inasmuch as this feature plays an important role in the ideological argument as well as in the narrative texture of the novel, they will have to be pointed out to the reader.

Finally, the Commentary contains a large number of references to the Introduction, where a general outline of the ideological content, structure, and texture of the novel is given.

The Russian text on which this commentary is based is the first and only complete critical edition of Dostoevsky's works. I shall refer to this work (henceforth *PSS*) frequently in the introduction and Commentary. In addition to the text of the novel, *PSS* contains (1) variants to the text (15:377–96), whose sources (extant manuscripts, proofs, the author's notes on the margins of a printed copy of the novel, etc.) are listed in 15: 397–99; (2) all of Dostoevsky's manuscripts and notes relating to *The Brothers Karamazov* (15:199–374); (3) a detailed introduction concerning the literary and historical background, genesis, and reception of the novel (15:399–523); and (4) a commentary containing explanatory as well as critical notes, with particular emphasis on identification of literary sources and social as well as literary echoes and allusions in the text (15:523–619). I have utilized much of this material, the fruit of many years of research by a collective of dedicated scholars.

Research into the text and into the historical and literary back-

ground of *The Brothers Karamazov* can be conducted only by
scholars who read Russian. At the writing of this introduction
even Dostoevsky's correspondence is unavailable in English, except for some selections.[1] While the notebooks to *The Brothers
Karamazov* are available in translation,[2] a large body of books,
articles, reviews, letters, and memoirs by Dostoevsky's Russian
contemporaries, which are crucial to an understanding of the
genesis and reception of the novel, have never been translated.
Therefore, I shall have to refer to Russian sources frequently. As
far as genesis, literary and historical background, as well as contemporary reception are concerned, my work presents merely
the bare essentials of a subject whose vastness is obvious to
anyone who has read the introduction in *PSS*. The function of
my own introduction and commentary is not so much to introduce the reader to the philological, historical, or biographical
problems involved in the study of *The Brothers Karamazov* as to
help him understand the novel as the expression of a philosophy
of life and as a work of art.[3]

1. Dostoevsky's letters will be quoted in my own translation from the Russian
edition: F. M. Dostoevskii, *Pis'ma,* ed. A. S. Dolinin, 4 vols. (Moscow and Leningrad, 1928–59). The full English text of many of the letters quoted here may be
found in the following selections: S. S. Koteliansky and J. Middleton Murry,
eds. and tr., *Dostoevsky: Letters and Reminiscences* (New York, 1923); Ethel
Colburn Mayne, ed. and tr., *Letters of Fyodor Michailovitch Dostoevsky to His
Family and Friends,* 2nd ed. (New York, 1961); Jessie Coulson, *Dostoevsky: A
Self-Portrait* (London, 1962); Fyodor Dostoevsky, *The Brothers Karamazov,*
The Constance Garnett Translation Revised by Ralph E. Matlaw, Backgrounds
and Sources, Essays in Criticism, ed. Ralph E. Matlaw (New York: A Norton
Critical Edition, 1976), pp. 751–69.

2. The notebooks for *Crime and Punishment, The Idiot, The Possessed, A
Raw Youth,* and *The Brothers Karamazov* have appeared under the editorship of
Edward Wasiolek (Chicago and London, 1967, 1967, 1968, 1969, and 1971).
Furthermore: Carl R. Proffer, ed., *The Unpublished Dostoevsky: Diaries and
Notebooks, 1860–81,* 3 vols. (Ann Arbor, 1973–76).

3. For a reconstruction of the genesis of *The Brothers Karamazov,* see *PSS*
15:411–50. In English, see Edward Wasiolek, ed. and tr., *The Notebooks for
"The Brothers Karamazov"* (Chicago and London, 1971).

Transliteration

А а	A a	С с	S s
Б б	B b	Т т	T t
В в	V v	У у	U u
Г г	G g	Ф ф	F f
Д д	D d	Х х	Kh kh
Е е	E e	Ц ц	Ts Ts
Ё ё	Io io	Ч ч	Ch Ch
	(Yo yo in	Ш ш	Sh sh
	Garnett-Matlaw)	Щ щ	Shch shch
Ж ж	Zh zh	ъ	"
З з	Z z	ы	y
И и	I i	ь	'
Й й	I i	Э э	E e
К к	K k	Ю ю	Iu iu
Л л	L l		(Yu yu in
М м	M m		Garnett-Matlaw)
Н н	N n	Я я	Ia ia
О о	O o		(Ya ya in
П п	P p		Garnett-Matlaw)
Р р	R r		

In the English text the established spelling of some Russian words and names has been retained (*Herzen* rather than *Gertsen*). Russian names ending in *-ii* and *-yi* are spelled with a *-y* (*Dostoevsky* rather than *Dostoevskii*, *Liagavy* rather than *Liagavyi*). Some names which are anglicized in the Garnett-Matlaw translation are given in regular transliteration (*Marfa* rather than *Martha*).

xiii

Abbreviations and Short Titles

The following abbreviations and short titles are used for works by Dostoevsky:

BK Notebooks	*The Notebooks for "The Brothers Karamazov,"* ed. and tr. Edward Wasiolek (Chicago and London, 1971).
Diary of a Writer	*The Diary of a Writer,* tr. and ed. Boris Brasol, 2 vols. (New York and London, 1949).
Pis'ma	*Pis'ma,* ed. A. S. Dolinin, 4 vols. (Moscow and Leningrad, 1928–59).
PSS	*Polnoe sobranie sochinenii v tridtsati tomakh,* 17 vols. (Leningrad, 1972–76).

INTRODUCTION

I

Genesis and Background

1. *The Brothers Karamazov* in Dostoevsky's Life

The Brothers Karamazov is Dostoevsky's last novel, completed the year before his death on 28 January 1881. It is intimately linked with the biographical facts of the last years of his life. Thus, Dostoevsky's involvement in current public and political affairs, while it found a more direct expression in the articles of his *Diary of a Writer* (1876–78) and in his "Discourse on Pushkin" (1880), is present in *The Brothers Karamazov* as well. Hence, the former two provide a natural commentary to the latter (see sect. 5.b. *Diary of a Writer*). The topography of Skotoprigonievsk ("Cattle Run"), the provincial town which provides the setting for the novel, is that of Staraia Russa, a town about 150 miles to the southeast of St. Petersburg (now Leningrad), where Dostoevsky used to spend his summers with his family and where he had bought a house in 1877. The house itself is rather faithfully reproduced as the house of Fiodor Pavlovich Karamazov.

The death of Dostoevsky's son Aleksei (Aliosha) on 16 May 1878 caused an interruption of his work on the novel and led to his pilgrimage to the monastery of Optina Pustyn' (near Kozelsk, about 150 miles southwest of Moscow) 23–29 June. Both events are of crucial importance to the genesis of the novel.

During the last years of his life Dostoevsky was a major public figure within the conservative ranks of the Russian intelligentsia. His personal friendship with the even then powerful Konstantin

3

Pobedonostsev (1827–1907, a member of the Council of the Empire since 1872, appointed chief procurator of the Holy Synod in 1880) was significant. Dostoevsky discussed his work with Pobedonostsev while it was in progress and received some help from him (Pobedonostsev had some of his subordinate clerics do re-research on details of monastic life for Dostoevsky).[1] Dostoevsky's correspondence with Pobedonostsev and with Nikolai Liubimov, editor of the conservative journal *Russkii vestnik* [The Russian herald], in which the novel initially appeared, shows the writer quite pointedly professing the political (antisocialist and antiliberal) and religious (apologetical) tendencies of the novel.[2] A. Boyce Gibson is demonstrably right when he says that in writing *The Brothers Karamazov* Dostoevsky "felt he was executing some kind of a Christian commission and was responsible to his fellow-believers for its success or failure."[3]

On the other hand, *The Brothers Karamazov* is also a recapitulation and a summing-up of Dostoevsky's entire career, a work in which themes and motifs from even his earliest works and echoes from his whole past life are once more brought into focus. (See 5.a. Fiction.)

Themes, types, and ideas which play a role in *The Brothers Karamazov* appear in Dostoevsky's letters and notebooks years before the actual inception of this novel (see 3. Early Versions). Nevertheless, the first notebook entry which can be directly linked to the inception of *The Brothers Karamazov* was made by Dostoevsky on 13 September 1874, while he was working on *A Raw Youth*. It is a sketch for a drama along the lines of the Il'inskii story in *Notes from the House of the Dead* (1859–60) and contains some elements of the plot of *The Brothers Karamazov*.

1. Leonid Grossman, "Dostoevskii i pravitel'stvennye krugi 1870-kh godov" [Dostoevsky and government circles of the 1870s], *Literaturnoe nasledstvo* 15:135.

2. For instance, "But my socialist (Ivan Karamazov) is a sincere man who admits outright that he agrees with the 'Grand Inquisitor's' view of mankind, to the effect that the faith of Christ (allegedly) elevated man much higher than he is, in fact, worth. The question is asked point-blank: 'Do you despise humanity, or do you respect it, you, its would-be saviors?' " (Letter to N. A. Liubimov, 11 June 1879, *Pis'ma* 4:58).

3. A. Boyce Gibson, *The Religion of Dostoevsky* (Philadelphia, 1974), p. 169.

(For details, see 6.b. Il'inskii and Dmitry Karamazov.) The character of the brother who though innocent is convicted of the murder of his father is obviously Dmitry Karamazov's. But in many ways the plot outlined in this sketch is quite different from that of *The Brothers Karamazov.*[4]

The actual history of the creation of *The Brothers Karamazov* begins in 1876, when several letters, notebook entries, and passages in *Diary of a Writer* suggest that Dostoevsky was thinking of a new novel. A letter of 7 June 1876, addressed to one V. A. Alekseev, who had asked Dostoevsky to explain to him a passage in the May issue of *Diary of a Writer,* contains the essence of the argument of "The Grand Inquisitor" (*Pis'ma* 3:2₁1-13). But as late as a letter of 17 December 1877 Dostoevsky can merely say: "There is a novel in my head and in my heart, asking to be expressed."[5] It is only in the early part of 1878 that we find Dostoevsky working intensively on a plan for a new novel.[6] A note from mid-April suggests a fusion of Dostoevsky's longtime preoccupation with a novel "about children" (see 3. Early Versions) with the resuscitated Il'inskii theme. Dostoevsky's early drafts and notes for *The Brothers Karamazov* remain undiscovered. Extant notes and manuscript versions reflect a relatively late stage in the development of the novel (see 7. Notebooks).

2. The Story of the Writing of *The Brothers Karamazov*

The actual writing of *The Brothers Karamazov* begins some time after Dostoevsky's return from Optina Pustyn', still in the summer of 1878. Late in October Anna Grigorievna, the writer's wife—who was also his secretary, stenographer, and copyist—copied Books One and Two, which were then submitted to *The Russian Herald* on 7 November. Book Three followed on 31

4. See Robert L. Belknap, "The Sources of Mitja Karamazov," in *American Contributions to the Seventh International Congress of Slavists,* 2 (The Hague and Paris, 1973): 44–46.

5. Letter to S. D. Ianovskii, 17 December 1877, *Pis'ma* 3:284.

6. See Anna Dostoevsky, *Dostoevsky: Reminiscences,* tr. and ed. Beatrice Stillman (New York, 1975), pp. 293–95.

January 1879. Part I of *The Brothers Karamazov* appeared in the January and February issues of *The Russian Herald*. At this stage only a vague outline of the whole novel existed in Dostoevsky's mind. In a letter to Liubimov, his editor, dated 30 January 1879, Dostoevsky suggests that the novel will consist of three parts, each to be divided into an unspecified number of books, and the books into chapters (*Pis'ma* 4:45). As it turned out, the novel was to consist of four parts, each divided into three books, and an epilogue.

Dostoevsky was unable to deliver the next installment in time for the March issue, and so Book Four appeared in the April issue. The next two books—"Pro and Contra" and "The Russian Monk"—were in Dostoevsky's own opinion crucial to the success of the whole novel. As for Book Five, Dostoevsky feared that Ivan Karamazov's rebellious eloquence might be judged excessive by the censors (or even by *The Russian Herald*). Hence, he took great pains to explain to his editor (whom he knew to be in touch with the publisher, Mikhail Katkov), as well as his powerful friend Konstantin Pobedonostsev, that Ivan Karamazov's arguments were being advanced only to be refuted later in the novel.[7] Dostoevsky's apprehensions as regards Book Six were of a different order. A relatively minor difficulty lay in the circumstance that Dostoevsky, a layman who, though always a practicing Christian, had never been particularly close to the Orthodox church, might lack the knowledge to describe Russian monastic life and its ideals truthfully. (There were, in fact, some

7. In a letter to Liubimov, dated 11 June 1879 (two days after Dostoevsky had mailed the conclusion of Book Five to him), Dostoevsky takes care to detach himself from Ivan Karamazov and his ideas: "Here is the completion of that which 'a mouth speaking great things and blasphemies' [Rev. 13:5] has to say. A contemporary *negator,* of the most rabid sort, openly declares himself in favor of the devil's counsel, asserting that this is more likely than Christ's to ensure mankind's happiness" (*Pis'ma* 4:58). Dostoevsky's letter to Pobedonostsev, dated 19 May 1879 (*Pis'ma* 4:57) has been interpreted by Dolinin as an oblique request that Pobedonostsev help Book Five ("Pro and Contra") to withstand the censor or overcome the veto of M. N. Katkov, Dostoevsky's reactionary publisher. See A. S. Dolinin, "K istorii sozdaniia *Brat'ev Karamazovykh,*" in *F. M. Dostoevskii: Materialy i issledovaniia,* ed. A. S. Dolinin (Leningrad, 1935), p. 68.

negative reactions along these lines.) The major difficulty lay in the formidable problems involved in the *realistic* presentation (Dostoevsky insisted all along that his Father Zosima was to be a "real-life" character) of a moral and religious *ideal*. Dostoevsky, who ordinarily refrained from interpreting or analyzing his own works, had a great deal to say about Father Zosima and was somewhat diffident about his creation even as he mailed the complete manuscript of Book Six to Liubimov on 7 August 1879.[8] Books Five and Six were printed in the May (Five, chap. i–iv), June (Five, chaps. v–vii), and August (Book Six) issues of *The Russian Herald*.

Dostoevsky wrote much of Book Seven (which he initially proposed to call "Grushen'ka," but eventually called "Aliosha") in August at Bad Ems, a German resort town where he went a number of times for his health, and completed it at Staraia Russa in September. As he sent off the first three chapters on 16 September, he wrote to Liubimov: "The last chapter (which I shall send you), 'Cana of Galilee,' is the most essential in the whole book, and perhaps in the whole novel" (*Pis'ma* 4: 113). Book Seven made the September issue.

The first four chapters of Book Eight appeared in the October issue, and a letter of Dostoevsky's, dated 8 November 1879 and written in response to a reader, E. N. Lebedev, who had asked that he explain to her the meaning of chapter iv ("In the Dark"), shows that Dostoevsky had by this time worked out the circumstantial and psychological outline of the novel: Smerdiakov is the killer, Ivan is guilty by virtue of having allowed the murder to happen, and Dmitry is innocent (*Pis'ma* 4:117). But a letter dated 16 November, to Liubimov, suggests that Dostoevsky was still working out the details of the story line as he was going

8. "I have entitled this sixth book 'A Russian Monk'—a bold and provocative title, since all our hostile critics will cry out: 'Is this what a Russian monk is like? How dare he place him on such a pedestal?' But it is all the better if they do cry out, isn't it? (And I'm sure they will.) As far as I am concerned, I believe that I have not sinned against reality: it is true not only as regards the ideal, but it is also true as regards reality" (*Pis'ma* 4:91). See also Sven Linnér, *Starets Zosima in "The Brothers Karamazov": A Study in the Mimesis of Virtue* (Stockholm, 1975), pp. 21–22 et passim.

along (*Pis'ma* 4:118). In particular, the decision to introduce a separate book, "The Preliminary Investigation," was made at this late stage, in connection with Dostoevsky's research into the legal aspect of a murder case.[9]

After chapters v–viii of Book Eight had appeared in the November issue, Dostoevsky had to apologize to Liubimov once more, as Book Nine turned out longer than originally planned and was not ready for the December issue. Instead of it, *The Russian Herald* printed Dostoevsky's letter of apology, in which recurrent poor health is given as the reason for his failure to meet his deadlines. Extant drafts of this letter suggest that Dostoevsky was on the verge of starting a polemic with his critics even before the novel had been completed (it was being heatedly discussed and often violently attacked after each new installment), but thought better of it. Book Nine appeared in the January 1880 issue.

After having granted himself a brief rest, Dostoevsky began Part Four of the novel. An extant "Plan of Part Four" (*BK Notebooks,* p. 184) shows three sections, corresponding more or less to Books Ten, Eleven, and Twelve, but no Epilogue, and suggests an organization and emphasis rather different from what is found in the definitive text. The idea to devote the entire tenth book to "The Boys" came to Dostoevsky at this late stage. Thus, his long-time project of a "novel about children" was at least partly realized (see 3. Early Versions). Book Ten was sent off about 1 April 1880. A letter to Liubimov, dated 9 April, contains an afterthought characteristic of Dostoevsky: he asks the editor to inquire whether secondary school pupils such as he had described in Book Ten were obliged to wear a uniform in the 1860s (the period in which the novel is set) and, if so, to make the necessary corrections in the text (*Pis'ma* 4:135). There is ample evidence of such active concern for specific details of realistic description scattered throughout Dostoevsky's notebooks and

---

9. A. A. Stakenschneider, a jurist who had at one time been a public prosecutor in the provinces, was Dostoevsky's main source of information on legal details, trial procedure, and the like. A. F. Koni, another well-known jurist and judge, was another. See *PSS* 15:432, 437, 445.

correspondence.[10] In a letter of 13 April, Dostoevsky responds to Liubimov's suggestion that Kolia ought to be at least a year older: fourteen, not thirteen. He agrees with Liubimov and authorizes him to make the necessary changes (*Pis'ma* 4:137–38). Book Ten appeared in the April issue of *The Russian Herald*.

Dostoevsky's plans to publish Book Eleven in June were derailed by his stay in Moscow 23 May to 10 June, on the occasion of the unveiling of a monument to Alexander Pushkin. In the course of the festivities Dostoevsky delivered his celebrated "Discourse on Pushkin." Book Eleven appeared in two installments: chapters i–v in the July issue, and chapters vi–x in the August issue. Dostoevsky's initial plan did not provide for what now became chapter ix of Book Eleven, "The Devil: Ivan Fiodorovich's Nightmare." In a letter dated 10 August, which accompanied the completed manuscript of Book Eleven, Dostoevsky wrote to Liubimov: "Although I believe myself that *I could have done without* chapter ix, I wrote it with pleasure and I am certainly not going to renounce it myself" (*Pis'ma* 4:190). The rest of the letter is an apology of this fantastic chapter, in which Dostoevsky mentions, among other things, that he has consulted medical authorities regarding the clinical verisimilitude of Ivan Karamazov's nightmare.

Dostoevsky completed his novel with an incredible outburst of energy, with the last five installments appearing in consecutive issues of *The Russian Herald*. In several letters from those months, the writer complained that he was working "like a galley slave." But he also emphasized that he "had been redoing and rewriting the manuscript as many as five times, for he couldn't possibly complete his novel in slipshod fashion, thus ruining the whole idea and the whole plan.[11] Book Twelve was finished 6 October and the epilogue 8 November. As Dostoevsky sent the Epilogue to *The Russian Herald,* he wrote to Liubimov: "There it is, the novel is finished! I have worked on it for three

10. See *PSS* 15:457–58 for instances in which Dostoevsky went out of his way to consult experts in various fields (education, medicine, the church, law, administration).

11. Letter to M. A. Polivanov, 18 October 1880, *Pis'ma* 4:205.

years, printed it for two years—this is an important moment for
me'' (*Pis'ma* 4:212).

A separate edition of the novel, in two volumes, appeared in
December 1880, with the title page giving 1881 as the year of
publication. The text of *PSS* is based on it. Deviations from it
are listed *PSS* 15:398–99.

3. Early Versions of Aspects of *The Brothers Karamazov*

Dostoevsky's notebooks and correspondence contain references
to a good many works which he planned at one time, but never
wrote. Some eventually became parts of other works. A few of
these abortive efforts deserve to be mentioned in connection
with *The Brothers Karamazov*. The first of these is a plan for a
novel to be entitled *Atheism,* which occupied Dostoevsky in
1868 and 1869, while he was still working on *The Idiot*. In a letter to his friend the poet Apollon Maikov, dated 11/23
December 1868, Dostoevsky gives this outline of his plan:

> I have in mind now: (1) A big novel, to be called *Atheism* (for God's
> sake, this is *entre nous*), but before tackling which I'll have to read a
> whole library of atheists, Catholics, and Orthodox. . . . I have my hero:
> a Russian, one of our social set, getting on in years, not highly
> educated, but not uneducated either, and not unsuccessful in his
> career—*suddenly,* well on in life, he loses his faith in God. He has been
> concerned all his life with his career, he has never done anything uncon-
> ventional, and until he is forty-five there is nothing very special about
> him. His loss of faith has a colossal effect on him. . . . He seeks among
> the new generation, the atheists, the Slavs and the Europeans, Russian
> fanatics and hermits, Catholic priests; he comes under the strong in-
> fluence, among others, of a Jesuit proselytizer, a Pole, and from there
> descends into the abyss of the Russian flagellants—and finally dis-
> covers Christ and the Russian soil, the Russian Christ and the Russian
> God.[12]

Dostoevsky's correspondence suggests he felt that he had a great
personal stake in the realization of this plan, in that it was going
to resolve his own searchings, doubts, and errors. The novel
never materialized, although the loss of faith in God and its con-

12. For details on *Atheism,* see *PSS* 9:500–504.

sequences are an important theme in virtually all of Dostoevsky's novels. *The Brothers Karamazov* comes closer to a realization of this plan than do any of the preceding novels.

Even more interesting is *The Life of a Great Sinner,* a plan for which Dostoevsky sketched between 20 December 1869 and 15 May 1870.[13] Another letter to Maikov, dated 25 March/6 April 1870, contains this sketch of the planned work:

> The general title of the novel is *The Life of a Great Sinner,* but each story will have a separate title of its own. The main problem which will be dealt with in all the parts is one that has tormented me consciously or unconsciously all my life—the existence of God. The hero in the course of his life is now an atheist, now a believer, then a fanatic and sectarian, and then an atheist again. The second story will take place in a monastery. I have concentrated all my hopes on this second part. Perhaps at last people will say that not all of what I have written is trivial. (I will confess to you, Apollon Nikolaevich, that I hope to introduce Tikhon of Zadonsk as the main character of the second story, under a different name, of course. . . . A thirteen-year-old boy who has taken part in the commission of a crime, mature and depraved (I know this type), the future hero of the whole novel, has been placed in custody at the monastery by his parents. . . . This young wolf and child-nihilist meets Tikhon. . . . There in the monastery I shall place Chaadaev (also under a different name, of course). Why should Chaadaev not have been confined in a monastery for a year? . . . Others might also come as Chaadaev's guests, Belinsky, for example . . . or even Pushkin. . . . But the main thing is Tikhon and the boy. . . . Perhaps I shall produce an imposing, *positive,* saintly figure. . . . Perhaps Tikhon is precisely the *positive* Russian type our literature is seeking. (*Pis'ma* 2:261)

It is not difficult to recognize an echo of this plan in Book Two of *The Brothers Karamazov.* Tikhon of Zadonsk is one of the prototypes of Father Zosima (see 6.c. Father Zosima and Other Monks). The westernizer Piotr Chaadaev (1794–1856) is not too far removed from Miusov. The boy-hero of *The Life of a Great Sinner,* however, is very different from Aliosha, hero of *The*

13. See *Notebooks for "The Possessed,"* ed. Edward Wasiolek, tr. Victor Terras (Chicago, 1968), pp. 54–68. Cf. Komarowitsch's remarks in *Die Urgestalt der "Brüder Karamasoff": Dostojewskis Quellen, Entwürfe und Fragmente* (Munich, 1928), p. 68.

Brothers Karamazov. Hence, any projection from *The Life of a Great Sinner* upon a possible sequel to *The Brothers Karamazov* (see III.3.e. Expository Novel)—which would mean that Aliosha would experience the depths of sin, become an atheist, etc.—is inherently problematic.

"A novel about children, and only about children, with a boy-hero,"[14] occupied Dostoevsky in 1874, during the early stages of his work on *A Raw Youth.* A character who is also identified as "the idiot" acts as a counsellor to a "children's empire." Since some early entries in Dostoevsky's notebooks to *The Brothers Karamazov* refer to the character who will later be Aliosha as "the idiot," there seems to be a connection here. Alongside the theme of a "children's empire," there also shows up a sketch of three brothers, one of whom is an atheist, the other a fanatic, and the third "the generation of the future, a living force, new man."[15] This corroborates the notion that, of the three brothers in *The Brothers Karamazov,* only Dmitry is a truly new type: Ivan and Aliosha have their predecessors (see 5.a. Fiction), and versions of them existed in Dostoevsky's mind long before he started his last novel. The basic idea which appears in these sketchy notes—namely, that the psychology of children is as complex as that of adults and that children are as capable of great good and great evil as any adult—reappears in *The Brothers Karamazov.*

Another theme which is explicitly identified by Dostoevsky as the title of a new novel is *Disorder* (*Besporiadok*). It appears throughout the notebooks to *A Raw Youth,*[16] which novel is in part a treatment of this theme. The same theme, however, also appears in *The Brothers Karamazov,* where the social panorama presented is one of a society adrift and in disarray, of "accidental families," a prevalent lack of firm convictions, no honor or honesty, and widespread cynicism.

In 1876 Dostoevsky was considering writing a novel entitled *Fathers and Children.* His notebooks of that period contain a

14. *Notebooks for "A Raw Youth,"* ed. Edward Wasiolek, tr. Victor Terras (Chicago, 1969), p. 25. Cf. *PSS* 15:406, 438.
15. *Notebooks for "A Raw Youth,"* p. 37.
16. Ibid., p. 120, et passim.

number of entries which deal with critical situations involving father-son relationships, such as this: a father abandons his son to freeze to death after having found out that he is not the real father.[17] In *The Brothers Karamazov* the father-son theme is, of course, raised to a wholly new, metaphysical level (see II.3. Fathers and Children).

4. Literary Sources of *The Brothers Karamazov*

More than any other novel of Dostoevsky's, *The Brothers Karamazov* is a work "written in the margins of other books." In many of its aspects it is a more or less explicit reaction to readily identifiable works of Russian and world literature. In addition, it contains a very large number of casual literary quotations and allusions. Only literary correspondences which are functional in either an ideological or aesthetic sense will be mentioned here. The sources of less significant quotes and allusions will be pointed out in the Commentary.

4.a SECULAR SOURCES

Shakespeare's is a strong presence in *The Brothers Karamazov*.[18] Cox has suggested some very deep and basic analogies between Shakespeare and Dostoevsky,[19] and it may well be that Dostoevsky sensed these himself. Nevertheless, whenever Shakespeare appears on the pages of *The Brothers Karamazov*, the connection seems casual, even with an element of travesty. Thus, as Matlaw indicates, "neither the physical setting nor the mental state of the woman correspond to Ophelia's"[20] when a young Russian lady is reported to have flung herself into a river "to be like Shakespeare's Ophelia" (Book One, chap. i, p. 3). The same can be said of the passage in Book Eight (chap. iii, p.

17. See *The Unpublished Dostoevsky: Diaries and Notebooks, 1860–81*, ed. Carl R. Proffer, 2 (Ann Arbor, 1975): 149.

18. See Ralph E. Matlaw, *"The Brothers Karamazov": Novelistic Technique* (The Hague, 1957), pp. 6–9.

19. Roger L. Cox, *Between Earth and Heaven: Shakespeare, Dostoevsky, and the Meaning of Christian Tragedy* (New York, 1969), esp. chap. 9 ("The Grand Inquisitor"), pp. 192–214.

20. Matlaw, *"The Brothers Karamazov,"* p. 7.

358) in which Dmitry is likened to Othello, or of that in which he quotes Hamlet's "Alas, poor Yorick!" (chap. v, p. 383)

Voltaire is brought in to be refuted.[21] Ivan Karamazov's arguments have a great deal in common with Voltaire's attacks against a Leibnizian "best of all possible worlds" in *Candide*. (Dostoevsky, only a year before *The Brothers Karamazov*, planned to write "a Russian *Candide*.") Voltaire is discredited by presenting his ideas as trivial (Kolia, a thirteen-year-old schoolboy, quotes Voltaire) and old-fashioned (Ivan Karamazov's devil, shabby and middle-aged, is a Voltairean). Diderot, whose works Dostoevsky had been rereading as late as 1869),[22] is likewise downgraded by association: we meet him as the butt of a silly anecdote told by Fiodor Pavlovich Karamazov (Book Two, chap. ii, p. 34).

Komarowitsch has pointed out some striking parallels between George Sand's novel *Mauprat* (1837) and *The Brothers Karamazov*.[23] Specifically, the hero of that novel, Bernard, has a great deal in common with Dmitry Karamazov. Komarowitsch suggests that Dostoevsky actually acknowledges his debt by having Dmitry repeat the name "Bernard" several times (Book Eleven, chap. iv). While Komarowitsch's arguments are quite convincing, this particular connection is not necessarily relevant to an interpretation of *The Brothers Karamazov*.[24]

The influence of Victor Hugo is deeper and more varied. As early as 1879 a Russian critic likened Father Zosima to Bishop Myriel in *Les misérables*.[25] Hugo, too, incorporated into his novel two chapters entitled "What He Believed" and "What He Thought." Some French Catholic critics found Myriel objectionable for reasons not dissimilar to those advanced by Russian Orthodox critics of Zosima's "rose-colored Christianity."[26]

21. See L. P. Grossman, "Russkii Kandid: K voprosu o vliianii Vol'tera na Dostoevskogo," *Vestnik Evropy*, no. 5 (1914): 192–203.

22. See Leonid Grossman, *Biblioteka Dostoevskogo po neizdannym materialam* (Odessa, 1919), p. 122.

23. Komarowitsch, pp. 167–235.

24. Cf., however, Belknap, "The Sources of Mitja Karamazov," p. 47.

25. E. Markov, in his eighth "critical discourse" (*kriticheskaia beseda*) in *Russkaia rech'*, no. 12 (1879): 268. Cf. Linnér, pp. 123–24.

26. Linnér, pp. 129–30.

There is proof that Dostoevsky was impressed with the figure of Myriel (see, e.g., his letter to S. E. Lur'e, 17 April 1877, *Pis'ma* 3:264). Javert from the same novel is considered by some to have been the prototype of Smerdiakov.[27]

There is a striking parallel between a scene in Hugo's novel *Quatrevingt-treize* (Pt. III, Bk. Seven, chap. v, "Le cachot") and "The Grand Inquisitor." It shows Cimourdain (the master) visiting Gauvain (the disciple) in his prison cell the night before his execution. They engage in a discussion of mankind's future. Cimourdain looks for a bourgeois *Rechtsstaat;* Gauvain dreams of an ideal republic of equal citizens. Here is the highlight of their dialogue:

> "You are losing yourself in your pipedreams."
> "And you in your calculations."
> "Harmony is made of dreams."
> "But so is algebra, too."
> "I wish man were made by Euclid."
> "And I," said Gauvain, "I would prefer him made by Homer."

Christ and the Grand Inquisitor are involved in a similar antinomy. Christ and Gauvain advocate a higher humanity and freedom; Cimourdain and the Grand Inquisitor, "reality" controlled by reason.

Victor Hugo's poetry, with which Dostoevsky may have been familiar, contains a number of pieces whose theme is that of a conflict between the ideal of Christ and the practices of the Church, also featured by "The Grand Inquisitor." The theme of a meeting between Christ, returned to earth, and his vicar, the Pope, appears in "La voix de Guernsey" (1867) and "Le Pape" (1878).[28]

The importance of Schiller for *The Brothers Karamazov* was first pointed out compellingly by Dmitry Chizhevsky.[29] Fiodor

---

27. Konstantin Mochulsky, *Dostoevsky: His Life and Work,* tr. Michael A. Minihan (Princeton, 1967), p. 579.

28. See *PSS* 15:463–65 for further possible sources of "The Grand Inquisitor." A lengthy satirical poem, "Le Christ au Vatican" (1864), originally attributed to Victor Hugo, has often been mentioned as one of the sources of "The Grand Inquisitor," but it is hardly worthy of such attention.

29. D. Čyževs'kyj, "Schiller und die *Brüder Karamazov,*" *Zeitschrift für slavische Philologie* 6:1–42.

Pavlovich Karamazov recognizes at one point that the plot of which he is a part resembles that of Schiller's drama *The Robbers* (Book Two, chap. vi, p. 61). He then promptly proceeds to quote from another drama of Schiller's, *Cabal and Love* (p. 64). In both instances the old buffoon grossly perverts the meaning of his source. Not so his son Dmitry, who quotes Schiller not only profusely (including several stanzas from the "Ode to Joy" and "The Eleusian Festival") but also meaningfully: Dmitry is himself an incarnation of Schiller's idea of the moral regeneration of man through the development of his aesthetic sensibility.[30] In antithesis to Schiller, Dmitry discovers that aesthetic sensibility is ambivalent: there is "the ideal of the Madonna" and "the ideal of Sodom" (Book Three, chap. iii, p. 97). Nevertheless, Dmitry's sensuous passion is less of an obstacle to eventual salvation than Ivan's intellectual passion. As Chizhevsky has shown, Ivan, too, quotes Schiller and precisely in the key passage of his "revolt" (Book Five, chap. iv, p. 226), when he says: "And so I hasten to give back my entrance ticket. . . . It's not God that I don't accept, Aliosha, only I most respectfully return Him the ticket." Zhukovsky's Russian translation of lines 3-4, stanza iii, of Schiller's poem "Resignation" reads: "The entrance letter to an earthly paradise / I return to Thee unopened";[31] and the context is comparable to that in Dostoevsky's passage. In Schiller's drama *Don Carlos,* the Grand Inquisitor—a character very similar to Dostoevsky's—offers King Philip virtually the same alternative as that presented by Dostoevsky's Grand Inquisitor: freedom and exposure to sin, or giving up freedom and ridding oneself of responsibility and sin (which the Grand Inquisitor will assume).[32] Further Schilleriana will come up in the Commentary.

Goethe's importance for *The Brothers Karamazov* is considerable. Ivan Karamazov was soon dubbed "the Russian Faust."[33] Dostoevsky was rereading *Faust* while working on

30. Robert L. Jackson, "Dmitrij Karamazov and the 'Legend,' " *Slavic and East European Journal* 9:263.

31. Čyževs'kyj, p. 11. The German original is not quite this close.

32. *Don Carlos,* Act V, scene x. Cf. Čyževs'kyj, pp. 26–29.

33. A. L. Bem, "*Faust* v tvorchestve Dostoevskogo," fasc. 5 of *Russkii Svobodnyi Universitet v Prage* (Prague, 1937), p. 132.

The Brothers Karamazov (*PSS* 15:466) and was familiar with the second part of *Faust*. Ivan Karamazov's dialogue with the devil is in some ways a response to Goethe's *Faust*. Friedrich Mucker-mann has suggested that the devil's refusal to speculate on things metaphysical and his insistence on Euclidean reasoning may be a direct echo of *Faust,* Pt. II, lines 11441-46.[34] In his notebooks, Dostoevsky emphasizes "the Word" repeatedly, and in the text of the novel he lets it appear in its full Johannine power (Book Eleven, chap. IX, p. 614): this may very well be a response to Faust's challenge to the primacy of the Word (*Faust,* Pt. I, lines 1225-37). For further Goetheana see the Commentary.

Of the many sources of "The Grand Inquisitor," *The Life of Jesus* (1835) by David Friedrich Strauss (1808-74) is one of those explicitly acknowledged by Dostoevsky. In reducing Christ to an historical—albeit sublime—personage, Strauss had also given a "mythic" interpretation to the three temptations of Christ. In a passage of his *Diary of a Writer,* Dostoevsky suggests that Strauss may have had the noblest intentions when he replaced Christianity with humanism, but also that "if these contemporary higher teachers were given a full chance to destroy old society and build from the bottom up," a horrible nightmare would be the result.[35]

Dostoevsky's dialogue with Russian authors encompasses a long list of works. Here only those which emerge from Dostoevsky's text as distinct entities will be mentioned. Others will come up in the Commentary.

Russian folklore is noticeably present in *The Brothers Karamazov,* and we have it on Dostoevsky's own evidence that he himself had written down several of these items. This is true of the legend of the onion told by Grushen'ka (Book Seven, chap. iii, p. 330), as well as of the songs in Book Eight, chapter viii.[36] Of Smerdiakov's song, Dostoevsky relates that it is "not his own composition, but a popular song."[37]

34. Friedrich Muckermann, *Goethe* (Bonn, 1931), as paraphrased by Bem, p. 120.

35. *Diary of a Writer,* 1873, "One of the Contemporaneous Falsehoods," 1:151.

36. Letters to Liubimov, 16 September and 16 November 1879, *Pis'ma* 4:114, 119.

37. Letter to Liubimov, 10 May 1879, *Pis'ma* 4:54.

Pushkin, naturally, is quoted and alluded to more often than any other Russian author. The presence of Pushkin's "little tragedies," in particular, is felt in the background almost throughout the novel.[38] *The Brothers Karamazov* share with them the theme of man's usurpation of divine power and the eventual collapse of that rebellion, which proves to have been a futile gesture of self-delusion in the first place. Dostoevsky acknowledges his debt to Pushkin by eliciting the recognition of a scene from *The Covetous Knight* when Fiodor Pavlovich challenges his son Dmitry to a duel (Book Two, chap. vi, p. 64), or by letting Ivan quote (inaccurately) a line from *The Stone Guest* (Book Five, chap. v, p. 230). Numerous other Pushkiniana will be treated in the Commentary. It has been pointed out that Pushkin's voice is the most "authoritative" of all the secular voices in the novel.[39] Thus, a little detail such as that Kolia Krasotkin has read Belinsky, but has not read Pushkin's *Eugene Onegin* (Book Ten, chap. vi, p. 524), acquires a special significance.

While Dostoevsky loved and revered Pushkin, he never developed a similar deep feeling for Gogol. Yet his contemporaries generally saw him as a writer entirely in the Gogolian tradition. Thus, Mikhail Saltykov-Shchedrin, a serious critic, felt that Mme. Khokhlakov was merely an unsuccessful variation on Gogol's two ladies in *Dead Souls,* chapter ix, one of whom is "simply pleasant" and the other "pleasant in every respect."[40] While this is unfair and incorrect, there are some authentic echoes of *Dead Souls* in *The Brothers Karamazov.* The public prosecutor's oration (Book Twelve, chap. ix, p. 686) ends in a most infelicitous quotation of the famous troika passage (*Dead Souls,* chap. xi), which sounds pompous and ridiculous in the context, yet is genuinely prophetic. The "landowner" Maksimov claims at one point to be that same landowner Maksimov who suffered a flogging at the hands of Nozdriov (*Dead Souls,*

38. Pushkin wrote his "little tragedies" in 1830. They are *The Covetous Knight, Mozart and Salieri, A Feast during the Plague,* and *The Stone Guest.*

39. Nina M. Perlina, "Quotation as an Element of the Poetics of *The Brothers Karamazov*" (Ph.D. diss., Brown University, 1977), pp. 166–71.

40. See *PSS* 15:494. For other, similar opinions on Gogol and Dostoevsky, see *PSS* 15:496.

chap. iv). Maksimov's ingenuous little conceit is characteristic of Dostoevsky's quoting technique at large.

Miusov's anecdote (Book Two, chap. v, pp. 57–58) is apparently from Alexander Herzen's *My Past and Thoughts,* Pt. V, chap. xxxix ("Money and the Police"), a detail which enhances the impression, aimed at by Dostoevsky, that Miusov is typical of all Russian liberal westernizers. Another liberal westernizer in the novel is Ivan Karamazov's devil, whose ideas, opinions, and mannerisms bear a strange resemblance to Dostoevsky's arch-enemy Ivan Turgenev.[41] Turgenev is also quoted at least twice, by Mme. Khokhlakov (Book Two, chap. iv, p. 47, and Book Eight, chap. iii, p. 363), in contexts which bring out Turgenev's pessimism and atheism.

The references to Nikolai Nekrasov (1821–78), another old friend and ideological adversary of Dostoevsky's, are related to the theme of innocent suffering. Ivan Karamazov quotes Nekrasov outright, referring to an unnamed poem of his about "how a peasant lashes a horse . . . on its meek eyes.'"[42] But to Dostoevsky's contemporaries, who knew their Nekrasov by heart, Dmitry was likewise "quoting" Nekrasov when he asked, "Why is the babe weeping?" (Book Nine, chap. viii, p. 479), and so was Father Zosima when he deplored the horrors of child labor (Book Six, chap. iii[f], p. 294), Nekrasov's poem "Children Weeping" (1861) being recognized in both instances.[43] The fact that Dostoevsky links the most formidable argument against his own theodicy to Nekrasov, a leader of the radicals, is another acknowledgement of the polemic character of the novel.

The political and religious views presented in *The Brothers Karamazov* coincide significantly with the ideas of various conservative Russian thinkers contemporary to Dostoevsky. The

41. See Victor Terras, "Turgenev and Ivan Karamazov's Devil," *Canadian Slavic Studies* 6:265–71.

42. Book Five, chap. iv, p. 221. The poem in question is "About the Weather" (1858–59).

43. First pointed out by Orest Miller in his articles "Deti v sochineniiakh F. M. Dostoevskogo" [Children in the works of F. M. Dostoevsky] (1882) and "Karamazovshchina i inochestvo" [Karamazovism and monkdom] (1885). See Orest Miller, *Russkie pisateli posle Gogolia,* 1 (St. Petersburg, 1913): 240, 246, et passim.

theological articles of Fiodor Tiutchev (whose poetry is also quoted) and Aleksei Khomiakov, both vigorous apologists of Orthodoxy against Catholicism and Protestantism,[44] have left a mark on "The Grand Inquisitor," particularly so far as its anti-Catholic message is concerned. The ideas expressed in "The Grand Inquisitor" have a more abstract, philosophic equivalent in Vladimir Soloviov's *Discourses on Godmanhood* (1877–81), with which Dostoevsky was well acquainted, being a personal friend of Soloviov's and having attended some of his lectures.

The influence of Nikolai Fiodorov (1828–1902) is well attested by notebook entries, Dostoevsky's correspondence, and a passage in *Diary of a Writer*.[45] Fiodorov's mystic positivism proposes to replace modern individuation by integrating every aspect of being in a concerted effort of all humanity. The universal task of humanity is seen as "resurrecting the fathers" by all conceivable means, science included. The energy needed for this effort is to be channeled into the "common cause" from the many destructive and wasteful pursuits now serving individual needs. Fiodorov's philosophy is fantastic, archaist (he agrees with some primitive folk beliefs), utopian (it bears some resemblance to Fourier's utopian socialism), and heretical. Dostoevsky, while fascinated by it, was also skeptical. But Fiodorov's persistent emphasis on a reorganization of human life on the principle of sonhood (which implies a denial of "progress," since that would contradict the principle of "sonhood") drew Dostoevsky's attention to the metaphysical and religious aspect of the father-son relationship, which others had seen merely in social, historical, or psychological terms.[46]

44. Tiutchev's "Encyclica" (1865) and "Two Unities" (1870) as well as Khomiakov's "A Few Words by an Orthodox Christian on the Western Confessions" (1855) are the main texts Dostoevsky must have had in mind. Khomiakov's influence is well documented in Dostoevsky's notebooks. See, e.g., *The Unpublished Dostoevsky*, 3:158. Cf. R. V. Pletniov, "Serdtsem mudrye: O startsakh u Dostoevskogo," in *O Dostoevskom*, ed. A. L. Bem, 2 (Prague, 1933): 80.

45. See a letter to N. P. Peterson, 24 March 1878, *Pis'ma* 4:9–10; and *Diary of a Writer*, 1876, "Segregation," 1:247–49.

46. Regarding Dostoevsky and Fiodorov, see Linnér, pp. 199–202;

4.b. SACRED SOURCES

The importance of secular sources pales before the all-pervading presence of the Bible and religious literature in *The Brothers Karamazov*. In fact, the novel may be seen as an attempt of Dostoevsky's to translate the evangelic vision of man and his destiny into modern Russian terms. Nor is Rosen's suggestion that the Book of Job is the structural model of *The Brothers Karamazov* to be rejected.[47]

Every major position of the central argument of the novel is anchored in the New Testament. Sandoz has pointed out, almost certainly correctly, that 2 Thessalonians 2:6–12 is Dostoevsky's "ultimate frame of reference" for "The Grand Inquisitor."[48] Sandoz has also pointed out that the key phrase "All things are lawful" is a biblical quotation (1 Cor. 6:12). Linnér has drawn attention to the importance of the epigraph (John 12:24) for the whole novel.[49] That the importance of Christ's temptation by the devil (Matt. 4:1–11, Luke 4:1–13) extends to the whole argument of the novel is clear. For a further discussion of the religious content of *The Brothers Karamazov*, see II.2. *The Brothers Karamazov* as a Theodicy, and 5. Moral and Religious Philosophy.

In addition to the Bible, Dostoevsky refers to a host of religious works, some of which are identified in the text. Among them we find Fathers of the Eastern church (John Damascene, Ephraim Syrus, and Isaac of Niniveh) and of the Russian church

---

Mochulsky, pp. 567–69; and Komarowitsch, pp. 3–58. For an English version of some excerpts from Fiodorov's work, see James Edie et al., eds., *Russian Philosophy*, 3 vols. (Chicago, 1965), 3:40.

47. Nathan Rosen, "The *Book of Job* in the Structure of *The Brothers Karamazov*" (ms.). I thank Professor Rosen for having allowed me to read his manuscript before its publication. See also Harry Slochower, "The Pan-Slavic Image of the Earth Mother: *The Brothers Karamazov*," in *Mythopoesis: Mythic Patterns in the Literary Classics* (Detroit, 1970), pp. 258–60. Certainly Dostoevsky's emphasis on the importance of the Book of Job in this novel (and elsewhere) is most remarkable.

48. Ellis Sandoz, *Political Apocalypse: A Study of Dostoevsky's Grand Inquisitor* (Baton Rouge, 1971), p. 96.

49. Linnér, pp. 185–86.

(Saint Theodosius, Saint Sergius of Radonezh, Saint Nilus of Sorsk, and Saint Tychon [Tikhon] of Zadonsk).[50] Tikhon is also among the prototypes of Father Zosima, who is a composite image of several holy men of the Russian church (see 6.c. Father Zosima and Other Monks). The style and structure of Book Six, devoted to him, are modeled on Russian sacred literature (see III.2.b. Religious Content as Subtext). Aliosha Karamazov's image is designed on the pattern of a saint, specifically Saint Alexis. These correspondences are made quite explicit in the novel.[51] The resemblance of Dmitry Karamazov's fate to the vita of Ephraim Syrus is also striking, though not explicit (*PSS* 15: 476).

Saint Isaac of Niniveh (Russ. Isaak Sirin), anchorite and bishop towards the end of the sixth century, seems to have had a more than casual influence on the religious doctrine expressed in Father Zosima's exhortations. A new Slavonic translation of Isaac's sermons and wisdom had been prepared by Paisy Velichkovsky in 1787 (from the Greek, rather than from the original Syriac), and Dostoevsky owned an 1858 edition of this

50. See George P. Fedotov, ed., *A Treasury of Russian Spirituality,* vol. 2 of *The Collected Works of George P. Fedotov* (Belmont, Mass., 1975), for texts on and by Theodosius, Sergius, Nilus, and Tychon. In some instances outright echoes from the writings of Saint Tychon can be found in *The Brothers Karamazov.* See Pletniov, pp. 78–82; and A. V. Chicherin, "Rannie predshestvenniki Dostoevskogo," in *Dostoevskii i russkie pisateli: Traditsii, novatorstvo, masterstvo,* ed. V. Ia. Kirpotin (Moscow, 1971), pp. 361–64. For literature on Russian monasticism see Linnér, p. 94, n. 12.

51. See Jostein Børtnes, "Aleša," in *Dostoevskijstudier* (Oslo, 1968), and V. E. Vetlovskaia, "Literaturnye i fol'klornye istochniki *Brat'ev Karamazovykh:* Zhitie Alekseia cheloveka bozhiia i dukhovnyi stikh o niom," in *Dostoevskii i russkie pisateli* (Moscow, 1971), pp. 325–54. Vetlovskaia suggests that these correspondences relate specifically to the folk version of the life of Saint Alexis. Thus, Dmitry at one point calls Aliosha (a tall young man) "a little man," which is the epithet fondly given Saint Alexis in the folk legend. Grushen'ka calls Aliosha a "prince," which Saint Alexis is in the folk legend. The name of the saint's bride in the folk legend is either Katerina or Lizaveta. A girl named Lizaveta is mentioned at the same time that Saint Alexis first comes up in the novel (Book Two, chap. iii, p. 44)—while Aliosha and Liza Khokhlakov are also present. Vetlovskaia points out many other such details. There is direct evidence that Dostoevsky had a copy of the folk legend (Vetlovskaia, p. 333).

book.[52] Isaac distinguishes three levels of human faculties (those of the body, the soul, and the spirit [p. 251]), and three degrees of knowledge: there is knowledge which is anterior to faith (natural knowledge), there is knowledge born of faith (spiritual knowledge), and there is knowledge which rests with God (absolute knowledge; p. 212). A strong advocate of human free will, Isaac teaches that man has a natural faculty to discern good from evil; to lose this faculty is to sink lower than one's natural state (p. 213). A mystic, Isaac recognizes "the delight of the mysteries of the visible created things, which is the first summit of knowledge" (p. 34) and often speaks of the alternations of light and darkness, the deep dejection and sudden ecstasy, to which anchorites are subject (pp. 225–30). The main approach to God is love, with fear and divine discipline being the others. Love is universal, as "even those who are scourged in Hell are tormented with the scourgings of love" (p. 136). The worth of human actions is measured by the degree of love of God which inspires them (p. 256). In a statement that is important for the argument of *The Brothers Karamazov*, Isaac answers the question of why, if God be good, He created hell, death, and Satan, by asserting: "Sin, hell and death do not at all exist with God. For they are facts, not persons. Sin is the fruit of will. There was a time when it was not. And there will be a time, when it will not be. Hell is the fruit of sin; at some time or other it had beginning; but its end is not known. Death, however, is provided by the wisdom of the creator. It will rule a certain time only over nature; then it will vanish altogether. Satan is the name of the deviation of will from the truth, but it is not the designation of a natural being" (p. 128). Elsewhere, hell is defined as "ignorance and oblivion of God" (p. 351) and described thus: "There will be psychic weeping and grinding of teeth, which is a grief more hard than the fire" (p. 60). One recognizes these ideas in Father Zosima's exhortations "Of Prayer, of Love, and of Contact with Other Worlds" and "Of Hell and Hellfire, a Mystic Reflection" (Book Six, chap. iii[g] and [i], pp. 297–300 and 301–2).

52. Grossman, *Biblioteka Dostoevskogo,* p. 151. My references here are to *Mystic Treatises of Isaac of Niniveh,* tr. A. J. Wensinck (Wiesbaden, 1969).

Dostoevsky used some contemporary religious works, whose echoes in *The Brothers Karamazov* were recognized as such by contemporary readers. The most important of these is *The Tale of His Travels and Pilgrimages through Russia, Moldavia, Turkey, and the Holy Land by Parfeny, a Monk Tonsured at Holy Mount Athos,* Pts. I–IV (2nd rev. ed., Moscow, 1856). This work, belonging to the ancient and popular genre of the pilgrimage, was widely read in Dostoevsky's lifetime and was considered a classic of sorts. Dostoevsky took many details of monastic life, particularly those concerning elders and elderdom, from that work—a circumstance many contemporary readers would have been aware of. Indeed, Dostoevsky did not merely "use" Parfeny and other, similar sources, but actually transplanted their spirit and their style (or "voice") into the text of his novel.[53]

Zundelovich has pointed out the obvious contrast between "The Grand Inquisitor"—only ostensibly a "legend"—and its unsophisticated medieval counterpart, also related by Ivan Karamazov (Book Five, chap. v, p. 228).[54] Ivan, the scholar, quotes these "assorted ancient *mystères*" from various sources,[55] but always with a tinge of condescension. He is unaware of the irony of the situation: these simple legends contain the very truth which escapes him in "The Grand Inquisitor."

5. Connections with Earlier Works

5.a. Fiction

Readers who were familiar with Dostoevsky's preceding works recognized in *The Brothers Karamazov* familiar themes,

53. See Perlina, pp. 92–93.

54. Ia. O. Zundelovich, "Obraz mira Dostoevskogo v ego sotsial'no-filosofskom romane *Brat'ia Karamazovy,*" in *Romany Dostoevskogo: Stat'i* (Tashkent, 1963), p. 204.

55. Victor Hugo's *Notre-Dame de Paris,* N. S. Tikhonravov's edition of Old Russian apocryphs (*Pamiatniki otrechennoi russkoi literatury,* 2 vols. [Moscow, 1863]), or even Gustave Flaubert: Ivan's account of "John the Merciful" is based on Flaubert's "La Légende de saint Julien l'hospitalier," translated by Turgenev in 1877 (see Matlaw, *"The Brothers Karamazov,"* p. 14).

ideas, and characters. Dostoevsky's notebooks point at significant connections with the preceding major work, *A Raw Youth,*
and earlier works as well. Besides, Dostoevsky was preoccupied
with rather the same ideas all his life.[56] Thus, an interest in
children and a nagging pain at seeing children suffer are found
even in some of Dostoevsky's earliest works: *Poor Folk* (1846),
"A Christmas Party and a Wedding" (1848), and *Netochka
Nezvanova* (1848–49). The roots of the Grand Inquisitor theme
are found in "The Landlady" (1848), and Grushen'ka has been
linked with the heroine of that story.[57] The self-conscious buffoon (Fiodor Pavlovich Karamazov) is first met in the early
story "Polzunkov" (1848) and then in many other versions. The
lame girl is a recurring figure, of which Liza Khokhlakov is the
latest version.[58] Ivan Karamazov and his ideas remind one of
Raskol'nikov in *Crime and Punishment.* Aliosha is a new version of Prince Myshkin of *The Idiot.*[59] A contemporary critic
noticed the connection as early as April 1879 (*PSS* 15:490). Both
Aliosha and Zosima represent another of Dostoevsky's efforts
to create a "perfectly beautiful human being," whose ideal was
Christ. The early pages of the notebooks to *The Brothers Karamazov* also show a connection between Zosima and the pious
pilgrim Makary in *A Raw Youth.*[60]

Some ideas which are commonly associated with *The Brothers
Karamazov* were expressed, or at least hinted at, in earlier works.
The theme of the three temptations of Christ is brought up
by Lebedev in *The Idiot* (Pt. III, chap. iv) and by Shatov in *The
Possessed* (Pt. II, chap. vi). Ivan Karamazov's atheist utopia is
preceded by Stavrogin's and Versilov's dreams of a golden age
in *The Possessed* and *A Raw Youth,* respectively. The journal
version of *The Possessed* has a passage, deleted in the definitive
version, in which Stavrogin tells Dasha about a devil who has
visited him, thus anticipating Ivan Karamazov's interview with

56. See Mochulsky, pp. 596–97, for a discussion of earlier versions of the
main characters and themes of *The Brothers Karamazov.*

57. Komarowitsch, pp. 141–42.

58. See *PSS* 9:122–39, 497–524, and 15:404.

59. See *BK Notebooks,* pp. 22, 32–33, where the character who will be
Aliosha is called "the idiot."

60. See *BK Notebooks,* p. 25. Cf. Linnér, p. 83; Mochulsky, p. 575.

the devil (*PSS* 15:405). The motif of space travel in Ivan's nightmare had appeared in "Dream of a Ridiculous Man" (1877) and represents one of Dostoevsky's many links with utopian socialism.

5.b. *DIARY OF A WRITER*

Diary of a Writer has been called "the laboratory in which the ideology of the last novel is given its definitive form."[61] The number of correspondences between it and *The Brothers Karamazov* is large. Only a few examples can be given here. The episode told in "Vlas" (1873) about a peasant who shoots at the Eucharist[62] is advanced one step further by Fiodor Pavlovich (Book Three, chap. viii, p. 125). The martyrdom of Sergeant Danilov which is the subject of Smerdiakov's sarcasm (Book Three, chap. vii, p. 116) was the subject of an article in *Diary of a Writer* (1877, 2:569–74). The details of "Apropos the Kroneberg Case" (1873, 1:210–13) reappear in Ivan Karamazov's horror stories about the abuse of children by their parents (Book Five, chap. iv, pp. 222–24). Altogether, *Diary of a Writer* shows Dostoevsky much concerned with questions of education, child care, and parent-child relationships. Elements of "The Grand Inquisitor" show up often throughout *Diary of a Writer* (see *PSS* 15:463).

One must keep in mind, of course, that the emphasis and tendency of a given motif may be different in *Diary of a Writer* and *The Brothers Karamazov*. For example, Dostoevsky puts some of his most serious and concerned thoughts about the rootlessness of the young generation into the mouth of the bungling Ippolit Kirillovich (Book Twelve, chap. vi, pp. 659–60). *Diary of a Writer* also has a chapter entitled "Pro and Contra" (March 1877, 2:640–45) but it is devoted to "the Jewish question." Linnér (p. 40) has drawn attention to the fact that the real "elder" described in *Diary of a Writer* is rather different from

---

61. Mochulsky, p. 596. This is essentially how Dostoevsky saw it himself. See his letter to Kh. D. Alchevskaia, 9 April 1876, *Pis'ma* 3:205–8.

62. *Diary of a Writer* 1:34–35, henceforth cited by year, volume and page in the text.

Father Zosima. Generally speaking, *The Brothers Karamazov* does not repeat, or back up, the many obvious misconceptions, biases, and errors of Dostoevsky's journalism: the writer's artistic tact acts as a screen which eliminates or transforms most of the prejudices of his intellect.

6. Prototypes

6.a. AUTOBIOGRAPHIC ELEMENTS

The Brothers Karamazov contains more autobiographic elements than most of Dostoevsky's works (see 10. Personal Idiosyncrasies). Some of these elements may be discussed as prototypes. Anna Grigorievna, the writer's wife, reports that in her doubts, thoughts, and even words," as he described a mother grieving at the loss of her child. The words Zosima speaks to the grieving mother were those that Father Amvrosy of Optina Pustyn' had said to Dostoevsky to be passed on to Anna Grigorievna.[63] While Aliosha is, of course, connected with the figure of Saint Alexis (see 4.b. Sacred Sources), Anna Grigorievna was certainly right when she said that "together with the name, all of a father's tenderness, all the unrealized hopes for his son's brilliant future, were transmitted to the novel's young hero."[64]

At least since Sigmund Freud's famous essay "Dostoevsky and Parricide,"[65] many people have assumed that Mikhail Andreevich Dostoevsky, the writer's father, was the prototype for Fiodor Pavlovich Karamazov. But the only trait which connects them is the family tradition—never verified by Dostoevsky himself and quite possibly false—that Mikhail Andreevich was murdered by the peasants of his village, Chermashnia, who allegedly resented his carrying on with their women. Other than that, Dr. Dostoevsky bore little resemblance to Fiodor Pavlovich. He was not a colorful character, and he was by the standards of his

63. See Anna Dostoevsky, *Dostoevsky: Reminiscences,* p. 294.
64. See Mochulsky, pp. 571–72; *PSS* 15: 456.
65. In *Dostoevsky: A Collection of Critical Essays,* ed. René Wellek (Englewood Cliffs, N.J., 1962), pp. 98–111.

day a good father. The commentators of *PSS* quite properly reject this connection.[66]

6.b. IL'INSKII AND DMITRY KARAMAZOV

Dmitry Karamazov has a real-life prototype in a sublieutenant, Il'inskii, whom Dostoevsky had met in Omsk prison. The first sketches of this character still bear Il'inskii's name.[67] Il'inskii is mentioned, though not by name, in *Notes from the House of the Dead.* He was serving twenty years for parricide. Before the murder, he had led an altogether wild life and was deeply in debt. At his trial he had refused to admit any knowledge of the crime, although the evidence against him was overwhelming. In *Notes from the House of the Dead,* Pt. I, chap. i, Dostoevsky gives this sketch of his fellow convict's character: "The whole time I lived with him, he was in the most excellent, cheerful spirits. This was a self-willed, flighty, extremely irresponsible person, although far from a fool."[68] Dostoevsky concludes his sketch by saying that he, naturally, did not believe that the man was guilty. In Part II, chapter vii, written a year and a half later, Dostoevsky was able to report that he had received word from Siberia that the "parricide" mentioned in the first chapter of Part I had indeed been innocent: the true murderers had recently confessed to the crime, and the unfortunate convict had been freed after having served ten years. Thus, there is a good deal of Il'inskii in Dmitry Karamazov. Yet, as Robert L. Belknap has demonstrated in his study, this is only a nucleus, and only the literary connections and creative additions to this nucleus make Dmitry the unforgettable character he is.[69]

66. *PSS* 15:452–53. See also Joseph Frank, "Freud's Case-History of Dostoevsky," in *Dostoevsky: The Seeds of Revolt, 1821–1849* (Princeton, 1976), pp. 379–91, and N. Losskii, *Dostoevskii i ego khristianskoe miroponimanie* (New York, 1953), p. 74.

67. See *BK Notebooks,* pp. 30, 32. See also sect. 1. *The Brothers Karamazov* in Dostoevsky's Life, above.

68. For the full text, see Belknap, "The Sources of Mitya Karamazov," p. 40.

69. Ibid., pp. 39–51. Perlina suggests the poet and critic Apollon Grigor'ev (1822–64) and the poet A. I. Polezhaev (1805–38), two lines from whose poem "Coriolanus" are quoted by Ivan Karamazov (Book Five, chap. v, p. 229), as partial prototypes for Dmitry Karamazov, with some good arguments. See Perlina, pp. 32–33, 139–43.

6.c Father Zosima and Other Monks

The prototypes for Father Zosima have occupied scholars for a long time.[70] There is Father Amvrosy (1812–91), whom Dostoevsky had visited at Optina Pustyn' in 1878.[71] The monastery and Zosima's cell are patterned after Optina Pustyn' and Father Amvrosy's cell.[72]

Father Zosima of Tobolsk (1767–1835), whose secular name was Zakhary Verkhovsky, had a biography reminiscent of Zosima's.[73] A life of Zosima of Tobolsk, written by a disciple of his, had appeared in 1860.[74] Dostoevsky used it extensively. Even more important is Tikhon of Zadonsk (1724–83).[75] Linnér compares Zosima with the historical Tikhon and finds that, while Zosima has inherited many of Tikhon's traits, he is also different, particularly in that he lacks Tikhon's weaknesses. Zosima is lucid, relaxed, and cheerful. Tikhon was diffident and often tense. Zosima is therefore less of a "person," as Dostoevsky purposely refrained from using his psychological skills in delineating this character.[76]

There are a number of other possible prototypes for Father Zosima.[77] The image of the Russian elder as presented in Father Zosima was not accepted by the elders of Optina Pustyn' and was generally found to be too "rosy."[78] Fathers Varsonofy and

70. See *PSS* 15:456–58; Komarowitsch, pp. 59–118; Mochulsky, pp. 632–34; Linnér, passim.

71. See John B. Dunlop, *Staretz Amvrosy: Model for Dostoevsky's Staretz Zossima* (Belmont, Mass., 1972). Cf. Linnér, pp. 90–93.

72. Mochulsky, p. 631.

73. See M. S. Al'tman, "Proobrazy startsa Zosimy," in *Dostoevskii i ego vremia,* ed. V. G. Bazanov and G. M. Fridlender (Leningrad, 1971), p. 215; Pletniov, pp. 84–85.

74. *Zhitie i podvigi startsa skhimomonakha Zosimy* (Moscow, 1860).

75. See Nadejda Gorodetzky, *Saint Tikhon of Zadonsk: Inspirer of Dostoevsky* (New York, 1976); "St. Tychon: A Westernizing Kenotic," in Fedotov, pp. 182–241; Linnér, pp. 104–11; Komarowitsch, p. 61 (biography and bibliography).

76. Linnér, pp. 57–80, 110. Mochulsky, p. 635, comes to similar conclusions.

77. Perlina suggests that a popular legend, "The Pilgrimage of St. Zosima to the Land of the *rakhmany*" (a version of the legend of the land of the blest), probably one of the direct sources of Dostoevsky's "Dream of a Ridiculous Man," is also a part of the "subtext" of *The Brothers Karamazov.* See Perlina, pp. 91–92, and also Linnér, p. 122.

78. *PSS* 15:498; Mochulsky, p. 589.

Ferapont both have identifiable prototypes in the history of Optina Pustyn'.[79]

6.d. Ivan Karamazov and Other Characters

There has been a good deal of speculation regarding prototypes for Ivan Karamazov. Anna Grigorievna is reported to have named Vladimir Soloviov (*PSS* 15:471–72). M. S. Al'tman connects him with Ivan Nikolaevich Shidlovsky, a friend of Dostoevsky's youth.[80] Braun is probably right when he suggests that Ivan is "an independent, creatively formed personage, with the author himself, as well as some other individuals (Belinsky, for instance), serving as a model."[81]

Dostoevsky's brother Andrei Mikhailovich identifies a retarded girl named Agrafena as the prototype for Elizaveta Smerdiashchaia.[82] A young woman named Agrippina ("Grushen'ka") Men'shov, mentioned in Dostoevsky's letter to his wife of 25 July/6 August 1879 (*Pis'ma* 4:76), may be the prototype for Grushen'ka Svetlov, whose Polish ex-lover insists on calling her Agrippina, instead of Agrafena or Grushen'ka.

Some minor characters have definite prototypes. Rakitin is drawn after Grigory Eliseev (1821–91), a journalist whose biography was more or less that which Ivan projects for Rakitin (Book Two, chap. vii, p. 73). A staff member of the radical journal *The Contemporary,* Eliseev had graduated from Kazan divinity school and had authored a pious hagiographic work.[83]

79. See Komarowitsch, pp. 129–32.

80. M. S. Al'tman, "Etiudy po Dostoevskomu," *Izvestiia AN SSSR* 22, fasc 6 (1963): 489–90. This connection is based mainly on the fact that Shidlovsky was definitely the prototype of Ordynov, hero of "The Landlady" (1847), whose ideas anticipate some of Ivan Karamazov's ideas. Perlina suggests V. S. Pecherin (1807–85), a Russian nobleman who became a Jesuit, compelled by his vision of suffering humanity (Perlina, pp. 126–30).

81. Maximilian Braun, *Dostojewskij: Das Gesamtwerk als Vielfalt und Einheit* (Göttingen, 1976), p. 248.

82. *Vospominaniia Andreia Mikhailovicha Dostoevskogo,* ed. A. A. Dostoevskii (Leningrad, 1930), pp. 62–63.

83. See Grossman, "Dostoevskii i pravitel'stvennye krugi 1870-kh godov," p. 122. Dolinin suggests two other possible prototypes: G. E. Blagosvetlov (with

The lawyer Fetiukovich is a composite drawing of several liberal lawyers, Vladimir Spasovich (1829–1906) in particular (he is often mentioned in *Diary of a Writer*).[84] The trial itself mirrors the celebrated trial of Vera Zasulich, who had made an attempt on the life of the Petersburg chief of police on 24 January 1878 and was subsequently acquitted by a jury.[85] For some further prototypes see *PSS* 15:416, 456–57.

7. Dostoevsky's Notebooks

Dostoevsky's notebooks not only record the genesis of his works, but also indicate his intentions, reveal his strategy, and help us to interpret obscure or ambiguous passages of the definitive text. Virtually all of the notebooks are important for *The Brothers Karamazov*, as Dostoevsky would often delay the use of an idea, motif, or expression for a long time. For instance, the figure of Elizaveta Smerdiashchaia appears prominently in the notebooks to *A Raw Youth*, but not in the text of that novel. Many motifs which will appear in *The Brothers Karamazov* show up in Dostoevsky's notebooks of 1875–77, before the novel was conceived as a whole. An entry dated 1 August 1875 reads: "Children. Sufferings of children (why didn't you help?)."[86] A note on the excessive specialization of modern physicians appears frequently—it will show up in Ivan Karamazov's nightmare. Kolia Krasotkin's adventure with the goose appears quite early, as do observations connected with the words "not by bread alone," and the "miracle" motif.[87] A note of

---

some justification) and A. A. Kraevsky (with very little evidence). See Dolinin, "K istorii sozdaniia *Brat'ev Karamazovykh,*" p. 59.

84. *Diary of a Writer,* 1873, 1:213–38.

85. See Grossman, "Dostoevskii i pravitel'stvennye krugi 1870-kh godov," pp. 102, 122.

86. *The Unpublished Dostoevsky,* 2:35. This comment is important for the interpretation of *The Brothers Karamazov,* as it gives a response to Ivan Karamazov's rebellion, which is advanced in the novel only by implication.

87. See, for instance, *The Unpublished Dostoevsky,* 2:74 (on physicians), 104 (the goose), 110 (on turning stones into bread).

1875–76 reads: "The Grand Inquisitor and Paul. The Grand Inquisitor with Christ."[88] The commentator of the notebook identifies "Paul" as Tsar Paul I, which does not seem to make sense.[89] Rather it is Saint Paul, and the allusion is to his prophecy of the Antichrist in 2 Thessalonians 2:6–12. Even such notes as "Take the question of deforestation"[90] may be significant. Dostoevsky's preoccupation with this problem suggests that Fiodor Pavlovich's selling his forest for lumber is significant.

The early notes and drafts of *The Brothers Karamazov* are lost. It may be assumed that there were not many, since Dostoevsky wrote this novel book-by-book. For the most part, the extant notes to this novel contain little that could not be found in the definitive text also. Nevertheless, they are of considerable interest. The notes suggest what books Dostoevsky had on his mind as he was working on his novel: historians such as Taine and Carlyle; educators such as Fröbel, Pestalozzi, and Leo Tolstoi; fathers of the Church such as John Damascene, Isaac of Niniveh, Nilus of Sorsk, Tikhon of Zadonsk, and Parfeny, author of *Travels and Pilgrimages* (see 4.b. Sacred Sources); and of course, poets such as Goethe (*Faust,* Pt. II, is mentioned) and Schiller.

In some instances the notebooks make a point of the novel more explicit. For example, some early notes refer to the character who will be Ivan Karamazov as to "the murderer" (*BK Notebooks,* p. 40). Or: "Ivan is the Inquisitor! The Inquisitor!" (p. 75). The following passage states the key issue of "The Grand Inquisitor" more clearly than the definitive text does: "They sing of Thee as Alone without Sin, but I say that Thou alone art guilty" (p. 79). The notebooks suggest that Kolia Krasotkin probably has the real Zhuchka (p. 185), but also that this may not be so (p. 192), with a third passage ambiguous (p. 195). So we are left with an unresolved question. The ambiguity regarding Smerdiakov's father is not resolved by the notebooks

88. Ibid., p. 175.

89. The index of *Neizdannyi Dostoevskii: Zapisnye knizhki i tetradi 1860–1881 gg.,* ed. V. R. Shcherbina (Moscow, 1971), lists "Paul" as "Paul I" (p. 719), suggesting that the commentators took this identification for granted.

90. *The Unpublished Dostoevsky,* 3:36.

either. Other details from the notebooks will come up in various contexts in this Introduction and in the Commentary.

8. Contemporary Critical Reactions

The Brothers Karamazov became the subject of lively discussion even as installments of the novel were appearing in *The Russian Herald*. There was an immediate public reaction to each installment. In 1879 there were about thirty reviews in Moscow and St. Petersburg alone, and there were hundreds of letters written to *The Russian Herald* and to Dostoevsky personally.[91] Strangers would come to see Dostoevsky in person to discuss the novel. Most of these reactions were to the ideological message of the novel, which Dostoevsky's contemporaries could hardly separate from the writer's known political affiliations: the novel was appearing in the conservative *Russian Herald,* and Dostoevsky had made his own conservative political views known through *Diary of a Writer*. Thus, the writing of *The Brothers Karamazov* was quite literally part of an ongoing polemic.

Critical reactions were generally determined by the critic's political stance. Dostoevsky knew this, and expected to be attacked. He also hoped that the public would support his views even against prevailing critical opinion (see a letter to Pobedonostsev, dated 16 August 1880, *Pis'ma* 4:195). Dostoevsky fully expected to continue the polemic after the novel was completed.

Radical and liberal reviewers unanimously attacked Dostoevsky's "mysticism," "religious bigotry," and in particular his message of "humility" and "self-renunciation." The following opinion is typical: "Man does not live by bread alone—this is true, of course, but the fact of the matter is that neither can man

91. See *PSS* 15:487–513. In a letter to V. F. Putsykovich of 3 December 1879 Dostoevsky writes: "*The Brothers Karamazov* are causing a furor here—at the palace and among the public, and at public readings, all of which you may gather from the newspapers (*Golos, Molva,* and others)" (*Pis'ma* 4:48). Dostoevsky answered many of the letters personally. Understandably, these replies tended to go to correspondents or reviewers who had taken a positive view of the novel. See, e.g., the letter to T. I. Filippov, 4 December 1880, *Pis'ma* 4:219.

live without bread [. . .] This is why all preaching of asceticism, of mortification of the flesh, etc., has been the voice of one crying the wilderness and has neither attracted nor excited the masses, while every word that has called for life, for a struggle for happiness, for hope, is greedily snatched up by them."[92] While rejecting Dostoevsky's ideological positions, leftist critics also tended to downgrade his art. At worst, they claimed that *The Brothers Karamazov* was proof of the decline of Dostoevsky's talent (*PSS* 15:501) and that all of its characters "would strike one with their paleness, shallowness, and unnaturalness even if they had appeared in some nameless and talentless melodrama."[93] At best, they gave Dostoevsky credit for "his imagination—powerful, but strange, distorted, degenerate."[94] They also tended to assume that Dostoevsky's views were those of the Grand Inquisitor.[95]

More conservative liberals, in particular the critics of *Novoe vremia* [New time], V. P. Burenin and V. K. Petersen, saw *The Brothers Karamazov* as a powerful and basically correct representation of the crisis in Russian life, but felt that it was overstated, overly negative (Burenin spoke of Dostoevsky's "cruelty"), and subjectively slanted.[96]

Only a few right-wing critics accepted Dostoevsky's message of moral regeneration and considered it realistic.[97] But even among them there were those who were critical of some of Dostoevsky's positions. Konstantin Leontiev's essay "Our New Christians" (which was sent to Dostoevsky by Pobedonostsev and to which Dostoevsky planned to respond some day)[98] found

92. A. Gorshkov in *Russkaia pravda,* no. 51 (22 June 1879), quoted from *PSS* 15:489–90, where other, similar opinions are reported.

93. Evgeny Markov in an essay, "A Novelist-Psychiatrist," *Russkaia rech',* May 1879, pp. 247–75, and June 1879, pp. 151–206. Quoted from *Pis'ma* 4:386.

94. *Novosti,* no. 125 (18 May 1879), quoted from *PSS* 15:489.

95. So M. A. Antonovich in his lengthy essay "A Mystic-Ascetic Novel" (1881).

96. For a detailed account of Burenin's views, see *PSS* 15:493, 498, and for Petersen's *PSS* 15:506–7.

97. For a summary of L. E. Obolensky's review, see *PSS* 15:504–5.

98. See letter to Pobedonostsev, 16 August 1880, *Pis'ma* 4:195. Cf. Linnér, pp. 96–98. For excerpts from Leontiev's essay, see George Ivask, ed., *Against the Current: Selections from the Novels, Essays, Notes, and Letters of Konstantin Leontiev* (New York, 1969), pp. 240–45.

The Brothers Karamazov more acceptable in terms of Orthodox religious thought than Dostoevsky's contemporaneous "Discourse on Pushkin," whose "cult of 'universal man,' 'Europe,' and 'ultimate harmony'" Leontiev resolutely rejected as a return to godless utopian socialist ideas. Leontiev's more positive assessment of *The Brothers Karamazov* centers in his praise for Dostoevsky's acceptance of the tragic essence of life: it is the encounter with the tragic that triggers a higher humanity in Dmitry and Grushen'ka. Leontiev still finds Dostoevsky's Christianity too "rosy," with "love of God" overemphasized at the expense of "fear of God."[99] Also, Leontiev suspects that Dostoevsky's religiousness is too personal, not cognizant enough of the role which the Church must play in a believer's religious life. When Leontiev admonishes Dostoevsky that Christian love should always be love of one's neighbor, not of humanity, he unfairly ascribes Ivan Karamazov's attitude to Dostoevsky (to be sure, mostly on the basis of ideas expressed in "Discourse on Pushkin"). Nevertheless, Leontiev considers Dostoevsky "a remarkable moralist" and his work "useful."

While Leontiev accused Dostoevsky of espousing a "rosy Christianity," the Slavophile I. Pavlov suggested that Dostoevsky was putting too much emphasis on evil and giving too little play to virtue.[100]

Few of these many critical opinions deal with style and structure, and when they do, they do so in a patronizing and condescending manner. Thus, L. Alekseev suggests that if the entire "monastery episode, elder Zosima and Aliosha, and also the story of the boy Iliusha, mechanically inserted into the novel, were thrown out," we would have a good "socio-psychological novel" about Mitia Karamazov. The same critic patronizingly observes that while Dostoevsky tried hard to make himself into an ally of the forces of darkness, he nevertheless remained a bearer of light: "He preached humility and humbled himself,

99. K. Leont'ev, "Nashi novye khristiane," in *Sobranie sochinenii,* 9 vols. (Moscow, 1912), 8:183. Cf. Dolinin, "K istorii sozdaniia *Brat'ev Karamazovykh,*" pp. 75–76, who agrees with Leontiev, suggesting that the conservative and enforcing role of the Church was underplayed by Dostoevsky.

100. *Rus',* no. 3 (29 November 1880). There is some evidence that I. S. Aksakov, a leader of the Slavophiles, agreed with Pavlov's views. See *PSS* 15:499.

but his reason, though trampled underfoot, arose and spoke up louder, more strongly, with fiery words.''[101]

In summary, then, contemporary reviewers sought to find in Dostoevsky's novel no more and no less than a confirmation of their own views. Few of them were satisfied. Dostoevsky found his first genuine apologist in his friend Vladimir Soloviov, whose famous "Three Discourses in Memory of Dostoevsky" (1881–83) were the first statement by an important critic which recognized Dostoevsky as a major historical figure.[102]

9. *The Brothers Karamazov* as a Public Event

The writing of *The Brothers Karamazov* was in a way a public event. In a letter to his old friend Dr. Stepan Ianovsky, dated 17 December 1877 (*Pis'ma* 3:284–86), Dostoevsky writes: "If you knew how much I have learned myself, in the course of these two years of publishing [*Diary of a Writer*], from the hundreds of letters sent to me by Russian men and women!" In particular, Dostoevsky believed to have discovered that there were vastly more people than he had thought turning their backs on the liberal, atheist, and westernizing ideas of the 1860s and returning to the conservative, religious, and nationalist attitudes of the Russian people. Several other letters of the same period say much the same thing. During his work on *The Brothers Karamazov* Dostoevsky received similar reassurance from hundreds of largely encouraging and sympathetic letters.[103] The public's reaction to Dostoevsky's readings from *The Brothers Karamazov* was invariably enthusiastic, regardless of whether the audience was composed of students or of grand dukes and courtiers (see *PSS* 15:518–19). When Dostoevsky scored the triumph of his life with his "Discourse on Pushkin" on 8 June 1880, he felt that his popularity was due in part to the success of *The Brothers Karamazov*. He felt that he was riding a tide of changing public opinion, and that Russia's youth, in particular, were moving

101. L. Alekseev [pseud. of L. A. Panochini], review in *Russkoe bogatstvo*, no. 11 (1881), p. 2, quoted from *PSS* 15:509.

102. In private, even Soloviov allegedly sided with Leontiev. See *PSS* 15:413.

103. See Dostoevsky's letter to Liubimov, 8 December 1879, *Pis'ma* 4:121.

away from materialism and atheism, and toward idealism and Christianity. There is some "feedback" of this feeling to be sensed in *The Brothers Karamazov*.

In a letter to his wife written during the Moscow Pushkin festival (28–29 May 1880, *Pis'ma* 4:157) Dostoevsky says: "The main thing is that I am needed not only by the Society of Lovers of Russian Literature, but by our party as a whole, by our idea as a whole, for which we have been fighting for thirty years." Grossman rightly sees Dostoevsky's "Discourse on Pushkin" as a triumph of his *party*.[104] The evidence is rather consistently in favor of an assumption that by the time Dostoevsky was writing *The Brothers Karamazov* he had reversed his temporary shift away from the extreme right which could be observed in *A Raw Youth*. Dolinin has pointed out that as late as toward the end of 1876 Saltykov-Shchedrin had asked Dostoevsky in a cordial letter to contribute a piece to *Otechestvennye zapiski* [The national annals], the journal of the radicals—a clear indication that the radicals felt, at the time, that they had a great deal in common with Dostoevsky.[105] Their uniformly hostile reaction to *The Brothers Karamazov* and to the "Discourse on Pushkin," as well as Dostoevsky's remarks in his correspondence and in the novel itself, suggest that no trace of this rapprochement was left now.[106] Grossman's analysis of Dostoevsky's relationship with Pobedonostsev suggests that Dostoevsky, while retaining his creative independence, was certainly anxious to have Pobedonostsev's approval and was willing to listen to the latter's advice.[107] Furthermore, if one considers Dostoevsky's explanations of his intentions to his editor, Liubimov, there is no escaping the conclusion that Dostoevsky's intent in writing *The*

104. Grossman, "Dostoevskii i pravitel'stvennye krugi 1870-kh godov," p. 117.

105. See Dolinin, "K istorii sozdaniia *Brat'ev Karamazovykh*," p. 51. Dolinin discusses the question of Dostoevsky's partisanship in considerable detail.

106. References to Saltykov-Shchedrin in *The Brothers Karamazov* are unkind, and Saltykov-Shchedrin's response to the novel was hostile. See *PSS* 15: 435.

107. See especially Dostoevsky's letter to Pobedonostsev, 9/21 August 1879, *Pis'ma* 4:94. Cf. Grossman, "Dostoevskii i pravitel'stvennye krugi 1870-kh godov," pp. 89–90, 138–39, 145.

Brothers Karamazov was both loyally Orthodox and politically conservative. The following passage from a letter dated 10 May 1879 (*Pis'ma* 4:52–54) is characteristic (the subject is Ivan Karamazov):

These convictions present precisely that in which I recognize a *synthesis* of contemporary Russian anarchism. Negation not of God, but of the meaning of His creation. All of socialism issued and started from a negation of the meaning of historical reality and arrived at a program of destruction and anarchism. My hero takes a theme which is *in my opinion* irrefutable—the senselessness of the suffering of children—and develops from it the absurdity of all historical reality. . . . The blasphemy of my hero, however, will be triumphantly refuted in the following (June) book, on which I am now working with fear, trembling, and holy awe, considering my task (the rout of anarchism) a civic deed.

In view of all this, Dostoevsky was visibly annoyed at the unexpected sniping from what he thought was his own side. His draft of a reply to Leontiev's essay "Our New Christians" was unusually sharply worded, suggesting that "besides a disagreement as regards ideas," simple envy had something to do with Leontiev's attack on him.[108]

10. Personal Idiosyncrasies

Certain personal idiosyncrasies may be of some interest to the reader of Dostoevsky's novel. Dostoevsky's letters of the period are revealing of his work habits. In a letter to Ivan Aksakov, dated 28 August 1880 (*Pis'ma* 4:198–99), Dostoevsky writes: "As for myself, I generally work nervously, with pain and care. When I work intensely, I am actually ill physically. . . . I may write a chapter and then discard it, write it anew, and then another time. Only some inspired spots come out at once, in one draught; all the rest is hard work." In several other letters Dostoevsky emphasizes the great care he owes this work, his most important. In a letter to his wife, dated 13/25 August 1879 (*Pis'ma* 4:98) he says that "*The Karamazovs* must be done well,

108. See [N. N. Strakhov, ed.,] *Biografiia, pis'ma i zametki iz zapisnoi knizhki F. M. Dostoevskogo* (St. Petersburg, 1883), p. 369.

given a finish worthy of a jeweller's craft," and in a letter to Liubimov, dated 7/19 August 1879 (*Pis'ma* 4:92), he observes that it is his duty as a craftsman (*khudozhnik*) "fully to express the spirit and the meaning of the novel." This implies that Dostoevsky saw his craft as merely an avenue to knowledge and understanding, and it is not difficult to find explicit statements to this effect: "Recently I heard Vladimir Soloviov say a profound thing: 'Mankind, of this I am deeply convinced, *knows much more* unbeknownst to itself than it has been able to say so far in its science and art.' Well, it is the same thing with me" (letter to E. F. Junge, 11 April 1880, *Pis'ma* 4:136). Dostoevsky was convinced that he had something important to say and felt that he was more right about things in general and Russia's future in particular than any of his contemporaries.[109] He was also convinced that his beliefs were "not so much Slavophile as Orthodox, that is, close to the beliefs of the Russian peasant— Christian beliefs, that is."[110] Certainly, Dostoevsky felt very righteous about the beliefs which he was expressing. He also believed that he had overcome and gone beyond the ideas which his critics advanced against him: "These blockheads have never dreamed of a denial of God which has the power that I put into the 'Inquisitor' and the preceding chapter, to which *the whole novel* is my response. I certainly do not believe in God like some fool (fanatic). And these people wanted to teach me and laughed at my backwardness! Why, their stupid nature never even dreamed of such power of denial as I have passed through. And they want to enlighten me!"[111] This and a number of similar passages make it clear that Dostoevsky was on Christ's side, not the devil's. Any interpretation of *The Brothers Karamazov* which

109. Some notebook entries on Leo Tolstoi are significant: "Count Leo Tolstoi is a candy [*konfetnyi*] talent, and well within everybody's grasp" (*The Unpublished Dostoevsky,* 2:101, with my slightly different translation of the passage from *Neizdannyi Dostoevskii,* p. 402); or, "*Anna Karenina.* Heroes. These people are uninteresting to the point of strangeness. Why, my morbidity is healthier than your health, doctor and patients" (*Neizdannyi Dostoevskii,* p. 420; cf. *The Unpublished Dostoevsky,* 2: 120, where the original is mistranslated).

110. *Neizdannyi Dostoevskii,* p. 400; also in *The Unpublished Dostoevsky,* 2:98.

111. Dostoevsky's notebook of 1880–81, *Neizdannyi Dostoevskii,* p. 671.

reaches the opposite conclusion disregards not only the direct meaning of the novel, but also Dostoevsky's professed intent.[112] The evidence is overwhelming that Dostoevsky at the time he wrote *The Brothers Karamazov* was a Christian, secure in his faith, and anxious to convey his own faith to others.[113] And when Dostoevsky died only a few months after he had completed *The Brothers Karamazov,* he died serenely, a Christian, and at peace with the world.

There are other sides of Dostoevsky's personal experience that are reflected in *The Brothers Karamazov.* As in some other works of his, one important character (Smerdiakov) is an epileptic, like himself. Some readers complained about the excessive cruelty of some passages in *The Brothers Karamazov,* and Nikolai Mikhailovsky, in a famous essay, "A Cruel Talent" (1883), claimed that a penchant for cruelty was a characteristic of Dostoevsky's personality. Turgenev called him a "Marquis de Sade."[114] The accounts of cruelty to children found in the novel, however, are based on authenticated reports and are well motivated by their obvious relevance to the argument of the novel. A case might be made for there having been something "Karamazovian" about Dostoevsky's personality. He once said of himself: "Worst of all is that my nature is base and too passionate: everywhere and in everything I go to the limit, all my life I have been crossing the line."[115] Certainly Dostoevsky could re-create the torments of a passionate and sensual man, such as Dmitry Karamazov, from his own experience.

112. V. V. Rozanov was the first major critic to state affirmatively that Dostoevsky, like Ivan Karamazov, was "with" the devil. See Vasily Rozanov, *Dostoevsky and the Legend of the Grand Inquisitor,* tr. with an afterword by Spencer E. Roberts (Ithaca, 1972), pp. 175–76. The commentators of *PSS* suggest that Dostoevsky was misrepresenting the true meaning of his work to his conservative readers, while revealing it to his more progressive interlocutors. This seems implausible.

113. For a well-documented sketch of Dostoevsky's religious life, see Losskii, *Dostoevskii i ego khristianskoe miroponimanie,* pp. 49–108.

114. I. S. Turgenev to M. E. Saltykov, 6 October/24 September 1882, in I. S. Turgenev, *Pis'ma,* 13 vols. (Leningrad, 1961–68), 13:49.

115. Letter to A. N. Maikov, 16/28 August 1867, *Pis'ma* 2:29.

II

Ideas in
The Brothers Karamazov

DOSTOEVSKY conceived *The Brothers Karamazov* as a novel
with an idea: "In poetry you must have passion, you must have
your idea, you must absolutely have your index finger raised
with passion. An indifferent though realistic representation of
reality is worth exactly nothing."[1] Dostoevsky's correspondence
with Liubimov, Pobedonostsev, and others confirms that this
applies to *The Brothers Karamazov.* Dostoevsky's concern was
not so much whether his ideas were right, but whether he would
succeed in expressing them properly. Hence his great concern
with realistic detail and with finding the proper style (or
"voice") for his ideas. A. Boyce Gibson is quite right when he
suggests that Dostoevsky was writing not about ideas but
"about people who were bitten by ideas."[2]

The Brothers Karamazov is a novel about the basic antinomies
of human life. In a complex, confused, and apparently absurd
world in which death seems to be the only certainty, there live
some men who believe in eternal life and eternal harmony outside time,[3] and other men who rebel against the apparent *status*

1. See *The Unpublished Dostoevsky,* 3:119. Here and elsewhere quotations
are my own translation from *Neizdannyi Dostoevskii,* p. 610.

2. Gibson, *The Religion of Dostoevsky,* p. 39.

3. Soloviov, in his *Ninth Discourse on Godmanhood,* reverses this position,
asserting that religious consciousness, having departed from the Divine, proceeds to find a natural world which does not correspond to the Divine, in that it

quo of the world and dream of establishing their own human harmony in history.[4] Human society pays lip service to justice but tolerates the suffering of innocent children; yet there are men who believe that even the suffering of innocent children has a meaning and that a miscarriage of earthly justice may in fact fulfil a higher law.[5] In the world of *The Brothers Karamazov* even beauty is involved in an antinomy: men who are receptive to the beauty of a Madonna may yet—and at the same time— pursue the beauty of Sodom (Book Three, chap. iii, p. 97).

Such a state of the world is paralleled by an epistemological antinomy. Human reason—called "Euclidean reason" by Ivan Karamazov (Book Five, chap. iv, p. 224; my translation)—perceives the world as absurd, sees no justice but only self-interest effectively protected, and conceives of the beautiful as that which pleases the senses. Yet man also possesses higher, divine reason, which affirms all that his lower reason denies: harmony, justice, beauty.[6] The encounter between intellectual brilliance and simple Christian wisdom is a central theme in *The Brothers Karamazov*.[7] Dostoevsky has no faith in the former. He knows that, if left to its own devices, human reason soon begins to flounder, falling into error, contradiction, and absurdity. Ivan Karamazov is the case in point. Only faith can resolve the "accursed questions" to which human reason succumbs.

While life in the world of *The Brothers Karamazov* is full of suffering and injustice, those who have faith are sustained by their contacts with another, mystic world (Aliosha's vision in "Cana of Galilee," Book Seven, chap. vi, p. 339; Dmitry's hymn, Book Eleven, chap. iv, p. 560–61). Dostoevsky's notebook entries suggest that he was aware that a different logic ap-

---

is imperfect and disharmonious, and therefore incomprehensible to the religious mind. See Vladimir Sergeevich Solov'iov, "Chteniia o Bogochelovechestve" [Discourses on Godmanhood] (1877–81), in *Sobranie sochinenii,* 12 vols. (St. Petersburg, 1901), 3:119.

4. Sandoz suggests that Ivan Karamazov's "new religion" is, in a way, a gloss on Feuerbach—that is, "Jesus atheism" (in modern terms). See Sandoz, *Political Apocalypse,* p. 184.

5. Braun, *Dostojewskij,* p. 244.

6. See Mochulsky, *Dostoevsky,* pp. 591, 630.

7. See Martin Goldstein, "The Debate in *The Brothers Karamazov,*" *Slavic and East European Journal,* 14:326–28.

plies to the material world and to the metaphysical or "other world."[8] Hence his arguments are premised as much on a respect for metaphysical intuition as they are on a lack of confidence in human reason. To a reader not so inclined the novel must suffer from a contradiction between Dostoevsky's realistic view of the world and his unrealistic (metaphysical) way of dealing with that world.[9]

The presence of God in the world (and therefore man's encounters with God—or with "other worlds") is the philosophic leitmotif of the novel.[10] Dostoevsky lets the devil tell Ivan Karamazov that homeopathic doses of faith are perhaps the strongest (Book Eleven, chap. ix, p. 612). The novel is full of subtle little scenes where "homeopathic" doses of metaphysical experience are presented, sometimes with as unlikely a subject as Fiodor Pavlovich Karamazov or the murderer Smerdiakov. The world of *The Brothers Karamazov* is one in which the metaphysical is taken for granted.[11]

1. *The Brothers Karamazov* as an Allegory

Viacheslav Ivanov was the first to read *The Brothers Karamazov* as an allegory. He sees the novel as progressing on three levels: the pragmatic, the psychological, and the metaphysical. Hence there are also three different explanations of the murder. Belknap likewise postulates a "coexistence of two kinds

8. In a notebook entry of 1880–81, Dostoevsky says: "If parallel lines were to meet, this would be the end of the laws of this world. But they meet in infinity, and indubitably there is infinity" (*Neizdannyi Dostoevskii,* p. 699; *The Unpublished Dostoevsky,* 3:178).

9. Cox, "The Grand Inquisitor," p. 192. Cf. Iu. G. Kudriavtsev, *Bunt ili religiia: O mirovozzrenii F. M. Dostoevskogo* (Moscow, 1969), pp. 152–53.

10. See Komarowitsch, *Die Urgestalt der "Brüder Karamasoff,"* p. 33; Losskii, *Dostoevskii i ego Khristianskoe miroponimanie,* pp. 148–49. Leontiev's assertions that "truly mystic feelings are nevertheless expressed but weakly in this novel" ("Nashi novye Khristiane," in *Sobranie sochinenii,* 8:198) and that Dostoevsky leans too much toward "earthly love and earthly peace" (ibid., p. 203) are unfounded.

11. Critics who did not share Dostoevsky's metaphysical beliefs saw in this aspect of the novel a mere allegory, manufactured *ad hoc*. So, for instance, N. K. Mikhailovsky (see *PSS* 15:502–3).

of narrative awareness," one of them allegoric and metaphysical. Thus, Zosima exists "as primarily the instrument of Grace on earth, and only secondarily as a human being."[12]

1.a. CHARACTERS OF THE NOVEL AS ALLEGORIC FIGURES

The Karamazov family is allegorically a microcosm in which the main problems and inner contradictions of humanity are mirrored.[13] Zenkovsky perceives the three brothers as a dialectic structure with Ivan (intellectual man) the antithesis of Dmitry (sensual, aesthetic man), and Aliosha ("the man of God," or spiritual man) the synthesis of both.[14]

Zenkovsky has shown how the Karamazov family may be seen as a symbol of human life, of human vitality, and in particular, of human Eros, or "sexual energy," in all its manifestations.[15] Dostoevsky was a vitalist who consistently hypostatized "living life" (*zhivaia zhizn'*), as against "dead theory."[16] Life is to Dostoevsky an absolute, and man's vitality, just like beauty, extends all the way from Sodom to the Madonna.[17] Fiodor Pavlovich, Ivan, Dmitry, and Aliosha agree on one point: their love of life. Each of the three brothers has his "cosmic" experience (Dmitry's hymn, Book Eleven, chap. iv, pp. 560–61; Ivan's "sticky little leaves," Book Five, chap. iii, p. 211; Aliosha kissing the earth, Book Seven, chap. iv, p. 340). Altogether, *The Brothers Karamazov,* in an allegoric sense, is a hymn to life, life in its entirety.[18] Zenkovsky, Linnér, and others have suggested that the cosmic-vitalist perspective found in *The*

12. Vyacheslav Ivanov, *Freedom and the Tragic Life: A Study in Dostoevsky* (New York, 1971), pp. 16, 38, 142–44; Robert L. Belknap, *The Structure of "The Brothers Karamazov"* (The Hague, 1967), pp. 88, 87.

13. Braun, *Dostojewskij,* pp. 238–39.

14. V. V. Zen'kovskii, "Fiodor Pavlovich Karamazov," in *O Dostoevskom,* ed. A. L. Bem, 3 vols. (Prague, 1929–36), 2:109. Cf. Slochower, "The Pan-Slavic Image of the Earth Mother," pp. 275–76; Mochulsky, pp. 598–99.

15. Zen'kovskii, pp. 111–13.

16. An aphorism from Dostoevsky's notebooks of 1880–81: "Living life has flown away from you, mere formulae and categories are left you, and you people actually seem glad about it. It's more peaceful so (laziness)" (*Neizdannyi Dostoevskii,* p. 678; *The Unpublished Dostoevsky,* 3:153).

17. Linnér, *Starets Zosima,* p. 187; Belknap, *Structure,* pp. 26–34.

18. For details, see Linnér, pp. 144–56 et passim.

Brothers Karamazov is linked with the traditions of Russian Orthodoxy.

Fiodor Pavlovich is "old Adam." He has always timidly avoided, as best he could, any encounters with spiritual life and has clung to the "reality" of physical sexuality and shallow Voltairean "freethinking." Nevertheless, the seeds from which the personalities of his sons could grow are all there. Trubetzkoy has pointed out that the positive traits of each son are grotesquely distorted in their father.[19] Fiodor Pavlovich has an indomitable vitality and in some ways is stronger than any of his sons.

Dmitry has his father's unbridled sensuality. He is also "rebellious, weak, and vile" (the Grand Inquisitor's definition of human nature).[20] Like his father, he is the very image of disorder. But he is himself an example of his own aphorism: "Yes, man is broad, too broad, indeed" (Book Three, chap. iii, p. 97). Dmitry is also capable of divine inspiration, of a noble impulse, of transcending man's petty, utilitarian intelligence. He has a sense of humor, of pathos, of beauty, and of compassion. Dmitry, a poet at heart, expresses Dostoevsky's faith in human intuition and human passion. Dmitry is nearer to God than his brother Ivan.[21] Through suffering—which he has not sought but which he accepts humbly and almost joyously at times—he finds God, and love of humanity as well.

Of Ivan Karamazov, Smerdiakov said that he was more like his father than either Aliosha or Dmitry (Book Eleven, chap. viii, p. 599). In Ivan, sensuality has turned intellectual. Ivan's intellectual passion is more destructive than Dmitry's sensual passion. The devil's remark, "I suffer, but still, I don't live" (Book

19. N. S. Trubetzkoy, *Dostoevskij als Künstler* (The Hague, 1964), p. 171. Volynsky applies the image of the seed (in the epigraph of the novel) to Fiodor Pavlovich and his sons: from the father's petty malice grows Ivan's intellectual misanthropy; from his sentimentality (he is easily moved to tears) grows Aliosha's capacity for love. See A. L. Volynskii, *Tsarstvo Karamazovykh* (St. Petersburg, 1901), p. 47.

20. Jackson, "Dmitrij Karamazov and the 'Legend,' " p. 260.

21. Such allegoric characterization of the Karamazov brothers is suggested even in the text of the novel. The prosecutor says of Dmitry: "In contradistinction to his brother's 'Europeanism' and 'the principles of the people,' he seems to represent Russia directly. . . . Oh, we are spontaneous, we are a marvelous mingling of good and evil" (Book Twelve, chap. vi, p. 663).

Eleven, chap. ix, p. 609), must be applied to Ivan, whose intellectual pride leads him to the sterility of a solipsistic, "theoretical" existence.[22] As Gibson puts it, "The basis of the novel is still the refutation of Ivan Karamazov by his own *praxis*."[23]

In contradistinction to Ivan, dreamer and "theoretical" man, Aliosha is explicitly called a "realist" (Book One, chap. v, p. 19). He is "the man of God" (see I.4.b. Sacred Sources) the "bridegroom" and "savior" (Book Eleven, chap. iii, p. 553).[24] He is often called an "angel," and acts in the capacity of messenger (the original meaning of that word) and confessor throughout the novel.[25] Everything about him conforms with the canon of an Orthodox saint's life.[26] Yet his spirituality manifests itself in real-life situations. Significantly, Aliosha is the youngest brother, and his main feats belong to the future. He concludes the novel with a joyous and confident assertion of immortality (Epilogue, chap. iii, p. 735).

Zosima, Aliosha's spiritual father, counterbalances Fiodor Pavlovich, whose extreme opposite he is: "Much as eternal life shines through elder Zosima, so the life of nature, violent as well as indifferent to good and evil, bursts forth in this old sinner with elemental power."[27]

Smerdiakov's allegoric role depends on whether we take him to be Fiodor Pavlovich's son or not. Mochulsky, who answers the question in the affirmative, sees it as follows: "Every human personality bears in itself a fatal dichotomy: the legitimate Karamazov brothers have an illegitimate brother, Smerdiakov: he is their embodied temptation and personified sin" (p. 598). The strong parallelism between the night of Smerdiakov's birth

22. See Linnér, pp. 167–68.

23. Gibson, p. 199. Or, as Linnér puts it, "The great, theoretical problem of theodicy in the Legend is framed by Ivan's personal question: is his own life worth living?" (p. 161).

24. See L. A. Zander, *Taina dobra: Problema dobra v tvorchestve Dostoevskogo* (Frankfurt am Main, 1960), p. 121. Cf. Vetlovskaia, "Literaturnye i fol'klornye istochniki *Brat'ev Karamazovykh*," p. 334.

25. See Volynskii, p. 147.

26. See Vetlovskaia, pp. 326–30.

27. S. I. Gessen, "Tragediia dobra v *Brat'iakh Karamazovykh* Dostoevskogo," in *O Dostoevskom: Stat'i*, ed. Donald Fanger, Brown University Slavic Reprints, 4 (Providence, 1966), p. 224.

and the night of Fiodor Pavlovich's death certainly supports this allegoric interpretation.[28]

1.b. THE APOCALYPTIC ALLEGORY

The allegoric meaning of *The Brothers Karamazov* has an apocalyptic dimension whose whole content points toward the future.[29] Aliosha is, of course, a symbol of Russia's future as envisaged by Dostoevsky.[30] The fact that Fiodor Pavlovich likens himself to a "Roman patrician of the decadent period" (Book One, chap. iv, p. 17) not only links him to the legend of Saint Alexis, but may also have an allegoric dimension of its own. Dostoevsky's notebooks contain a number of entries which suggest that he saw "The Grand Inquisitor" and the apocalyptic message contained in it in concrete historical terms and that he was inclined to apply this prophecy to the immediate future.[31] Thus, "The Grand Inquisitor" links the biblical Apocalypse with Dostoevsky's own eschatological projections and can be read as a modern political apocalypse.[32] (See also 2.c. The Historical Dimension.)

2. *The Brothers Karamazov* as a Theodicy

The question of whether *The Brothers Karamazov* is a theodicy or its opposite (perhaps a "diabolodicy") has occupied critics ever since the novel first appeared.[33] The author of *The*

28. Edward Wasiolek, *Dostoevsky: The Major Fiction* (Cambridge, Mass., 1964), p. 181.

29. V. E. Vetlovskaia, "Razviazka v *Brat'iakh Karamazovykh*" [Dénouement in *The Brothers Karamazov*], in *Poetika i stilistika russkoi literatury* (Leningrad, 1971), p. 199.

30. Ivanov, pp. 144–57. Cf. Preosviashchennyi [Metropolitan] Antonii, *Slovar'k tvoreniiam Dostoevskogo: Ne dolzhno otchaiavat'sia* (Sofia, 1921), p. 153.

31. See *BK Notebooks*, pp. 77, 106–7; *The Unpublished Dostoevsky*, 3:148.

32. Sandoz has made it quite plausible that "the Legend of the Grand Inquisitor articulates an apocalyptical vision of the present age considered as the penultimate phase of history in the Christian tradition: the reign of Antichrist" (Sandoz, p. 241).

33. See Belknap, *Structure*, pp. 10–11. Rosen suggests that as a theodicy, *The Brothers Karamazov* is modeled after the Book of Job (Rosen, "The *Book of Job* in the Structure of *The Brothers Karamazov*").

Brothers Karamazov has been seen as an apologist of Christianity, and as one of its most powerful critics. There is no question as to Dostoevsky's intent: while he meant to let Ivan Karamazov play the role of devil's advocate well, he also meant the novel as a whole to be a refutation of Ivan's attack on God's world and on the gospel of Christ. But many critics have suggested that Dostoevsky failed in this respect.[34] The success or failure of Dostoevsky's theodicy depends on the reader's acceptance of Dostoevsky's metaphysical anthropology.[35]

Dostoevsky's theodicy and Christianity are anthropological and existential. God, immortality, Christ, and the devil are to Dostoevsky immanent in human nature.[36] His novelistic strategy is to show some men who believe in God and in immortality, and who are willing to accept the teaching of Christ; and some other men who reject God's world, Christ, and immortality, and who would rather create a world based on human reason; and then let the practical consequences of their attitudes speak for themselves. The plot of the novel is as much a destruction of Ivan the

34. The whole question is formulated lucidly by Ronald Hingley, *The Undiscovered Dostoyevsky* (London, 1962), p. 222. Critics with little sympathy for Orthodox Christianity have generally said that Dostoevsky's theodicy is a resounding failure. Some critics, among whom we find Rozanov, have felt that such failure reflects Dostoevsky's own incapacity for true religious feeling, combined, to be sure, with a burning thirst for it (Rozanov, *Dostoevsky and the Legend of the Grand Inquisitor,* pp. 174-75, 189-90). Some critics are in doubt as to whose side Dostoevsky is really on: Berdiaev is one of them, it would seem (see Nikolai Berdiaev, *Mirosozertsanie Dostoevskogo* [Prague, 1923], p. 195). Critics who are in sympathy with Orthodox Christianity generally accept the theodicy in *The Brothers Karamazov.* Among them we find Volynsky, Lossky, and Mochulsky. The devil describes the situation perfectly: "Besides, proofs are no help to believing, especially material proofs. Thomas believed, not because he saw Christ risen, but because he wanted to believe, before he saw" (Book Eleven, chap. ix, p. 603).

35. Wasiolek, p. 169.

36. Dostoevsky's famous dictum that he would stay with Christ even if he were proven "scientifically wrong" suggests no more and no less than a belief in the primacy of moral values over theoretical knowledge. Soloviov, in his *Eighth Discourse on Godmanhood,* had said: "Not God's eternal universe, but rather our own nature, the real world factually given us, presents an enigma to our reason" (Solov'iov, 3:110). And in *The Brothers Karamazov* we read: " 'I think if the devil doesn't exist, but man has created him, he has created him in his own image and likeness.' 'Just as he did God, then?' " (Book Five, chap. iv, p. 220).

human being as it is a refutation of his philosophy. Ivan and Zosima are, however, in essential agreement about the state of the world. Zosima, like Ivan, is painfully aware of the suffering of innocent children. Zosima, believing in God and immortality, feels guilty before all creation and loves all creation, while Ivan, who denies immortality, is reduced to spite and lovelessness. Ivan uses the sufferings of children as a pretext for his revolt, while Dmitry's dream about "the babe" leads him to a recognition of his responsibility to suffering humanity.[37] Rakitin had said that one can love humanity without loving God (Book Two, chap. vii, p. 72). Dmitry demolishes this thesis by a simple *argumentum ad hominem:* "Look at yourself!" (Book Eleven, chap. iv, pp. 556–61).[38]

The three temptations of Christ, which appear in a number of variations throughout the novel, are treated as anthropological questions. As Antanas Maceina has pointed out, Ivan, his Grand Inquisitor, and his devil assume that "the true and real life of mankind lies in everyday life."[39] Lacking faith in an ideal, they attack man's immediate material needs, promising to make bread from stones. Of course, this is an empty promise: the devil cannot and will not deliver on any of his promises. To Father Zosima (and to Christ, of course), the potential for an ideal existence is inherent in being human: besides their physical hunger, men also "hunger and thirst after righteousness" (Matt. 5:6).

The second temptation (Matt. 4:5–7) hinges on one's respect for humanity. As Dostoevsky wrote to Liubimov, "Do you despise humanity, or do you respect it, you, its would-be saviors?" (11 June 1879, *Pis'ma* 4:58).

The third temptation (Matt. 4:8–10) asks whether human life is best organized by force ("for man's own good"). If one assumes, with Ivan, that men are merely weak, vile, and mutinous, the answer can only be in the affirmative. If one believes that man was created in God's image and cherishes freedom above anything else, the contrary is true. In *The Brothers Karamazov* Dostoevsky tries to show that Ivan Karamazov's an-

---

37. Wasiolek, p. 185.

38. The reasoning is that of Matthew 7:16—"Know them by their fruits."

39. Antanas Maceina, *Der Grossinquisitor: Geschichtsphilosophische Deutung der Legende Dostojewskijs* (Heidelberg, 1952), pp. 152–53.

thropology is wrong and that Father Zosima's anthropology is correct.

As Cox (p. 195) has emphasized, Ivan's Grand Inquisitor really rejects miracle, mystery, and authority and proposes instead to meet man's needs by magic, mystification, and tyranny. The Grand Inquisitor assumes that man's faith springs from miracles, while in reality miracles spring from faith, as Dostoevsky's narrator suggests early in the novel (Book One, chap. v, p. 19). The whole drift of *The Brothers Karamazov* is to show that the Grand Inquisitor's scheme will not work, because it is based on a false assumption about human nature.

2.a. THE CHALLENGE TO CHRISTIANITY

The challenge to Christianity, while concentrated in chapters iv–v of Book Five, is present throughout the novel, as is its refutation. The first attack is launched by Fiodor Pavlovich as early as chapter iv of Book One. Dostoevsky's tactic is similar to that employed by Fetiukovich, Dmitry's defender: every attack on religion is ultimately refuted by identifying its perpetrator as a cohort or dupe of the devil, much as Fetiukovich discredits those who testify against his client by exposing their own moral flaws.

Ivan Karamazov, intellectual man, is most exposed to evil, and therefore he serves as the principal instrument of the attack against Christianity.[40] It is he who pronounces the impassioned indictment of a God who allows the suffering of innocent children, and offers to create a better world governed by human reason.

One must not ignore the narrative hierarchy of which "The Grand Inquisitor" is a part: Dostoevsky's narrator presents Ivan, who, as "implied author" (not necessarily in his normal

40. Ivan is not all evil, however. Rather, his fate hangs in the balance: "God, in Whom he disbelieved, and His truth were gaining mastery over his heart, which still refused to submit" (Book Eleven, chap. x, p. 622). Father Zosima observes that Ivan is capable of great good (Book Two, chap. vi, p. 61). Father Paisy may have him in mind when he speaks of "those who have renounced Christianity and attack it" but "in their inmost being still follow the Christian idea" (Book Four, chap. i, p. 156). Cf. Losskii, *Dostoevskii i ego Khristianskoe miroponimanie,* p. 251.

voice), presents the figure of the Grand Inquisitor, whom he believes to have under his conscious control but really does not, as Ivan's interview with the devil (Book Eleven, chap. ix, p. 615) will show. A failure to realize the existence of this hierarchy has led some critics to overestimate the Grand Inquisitor's stature.[41] Thus, Mochulsky says that "the hero of the legend, the Grand Inquisitor, is portrayed with colossal art. . . . The old cardinal is a majestic and tragic figure" (p. 620). Mochulsky ignores the melodramatic, rhetorical, and simply phoney traits which identify the Grand Inquisitor as the self-projection of a much too self-assured, egotistical, emotionally immature, albeit brilliant young man.

Pride is Ivan's cardinal sin. It vitiates his many positive qualities, turning them to sin. On an intellectual level, it leads him to postulate that his human ("Euclidean") reason is sufficient to master life. On a psychological level, it causes him to value his personal independence above all. Smerdiakov, in his character sketch of Ivan, says that his main care is "not to bow to anybody" (*i chtoby nikomu ne klaniat'sia* [*PSS* 15:68]; the Garnett-Matlaw translation has "without having to depend on anyone—that's what you care most about" [Book Eleven, chap. viii, p. 599]). On a metaphysical level, it means that man is not satisfied to receive his divine nature passively, from God: he wants to have it by himself and, hence, establishes himself as separate from God, becoming alienated from Him.[42] Ivan, who as the Grand Inquisitor professes a burning love of mankind, admits that he cannot love his neighbor (Book Five, chap. iv, p. 217) and knocks a drunken peasant into the snow to freeze to death (Book Eleven, chap. viii, p. 588). He cannot conceive of his humanist utopia in terms other than despotic rule by an elite of wise men, which means that he sees mankind at large as weak, vile, and mutinous (Book Five, chap. v, p. 234). Ivan's alienation from God has led to his alienation from his fellow men.

41. See Rozanov, *Dostoevsky and the Legend of the Grand Inquisitor,* p. 174 and passim; Berdiaev, p. 196.

42. Soloviov in his *Tenth Discourse on Godmanhood* (*Sobranie sochinenii,* 3:139). Dostoevsky had expressed this idea in *Diary of a Writer,* 1876, 1:245–49. Cf. Matlaw, *"The Brothers Karamazov,"* pp. 12–13; Sandoz, pp. 195–96.

On the psychological level, Ivan will readily believe that his brother Dmitry is a scoundrel and a murderer—because deep inside he knows that he himself is. Smerdiakov says to his young master: "You've considered me no more than some midge all your life, rather than a man" (Book Eleven, chap. viii, p. 598; my translation). On the metaphysical level, the Grand Inquisitor's notion of "thousands of millions of happy babes, and a hundred thousand sufferers who have taken upon themselves the curse of the knowledge of good and evil" (Book Five, chap. v, p. 240) is a cruel, diabolic joke: as Maceina notes, "In the Grand Inquisitor's domain, man becomes an ontological caricature of himself" (p. 226).[43] Ivan's interview with the devil will reveal that behind his Grand Inquisitor's professed compassion for suffering humanity there is hidden a deep hatred of human freedom and of the image of God in man. Psychologically, Ivan Karamazov's moral and mental deterioration (he is on the verge of a critical illness and insanity) parallels the metaphysical condemnation of his ideas.

In the world of *The Brothers Karamazov* evil is not merely empirical personal or social evil, but also personal transcendental evil. It is not tantamount to the absence of good, but active and conscious of itself. Even Fiodor Pavlovich declares of himself that "an unclean spirit, though of minor caliber" lives in him (Book Two, chap. ii, p. 34; my translation).[44] Ivan Karamazov's devil explicitly presents his world (godless, governed by the laws of nature, "all-too-human") as a distinct alternative to God's transcendental world (Book Eleven, chap. ix, p. 614). The devil's point is that even without God man can build a very decent life here on earth, with human pride, human dignity, and human love (p. 616). This is a ruse: man is persuaded to give up God and human freedom for a utopia which may never work. In practice, this merely leads to the principle "All things are lawful" (p. 616).

43. Sandoz says: "Obsessed with power, the man-god loathes not only God in His transcendence but the image of God in existence. . . . The dehumanization of man is the first task of the humanist" (p. 197).

44. The Garnett-Matlaw translation has "I daresay it's a devil within me. But only a little one." The original has *dukh nechistyi . . . nebol'shogo, vprochem, kalibra* (*PSS* 14:39).

The novelty about Ivan Karamazov's devil, foregrounded by the way he contrasts with the Grand Inquisitor, is that he is "a simple devil and not Satan, with scorched wings, in thunder and lightning. But he is not Satan: that's a lie. He is an impostor" (Book Eleven, chap. ix, p. 619). Dostoevsky thus debunks the glamor of the romantic (Miltonic or Byronic) Satan.[45]

Linnér suggests that it is of secondary importance whether Ivan Karamazov's devil "exists independently of his interlocutor or whether he—as Ivan attempts to maintain in his own defense—is merely a hallucination" (p. 161). Guardini, on the other hand, considers this point important: Ivan so desperately defends himself against the notion that the devil is real, because if the devil is real, he, Ivan, is no "Grand Inquisitor," but simply a poor sinner, trapped by the devil.[46] The evidence in the text is ambiguous.[47] It is significant, however, that Ivan repeatedly uses the devil's name in vain long before he is "visited" by him.

Rakitin, a careerist divinity student, represents a lower form of Ivan's idea. Rakitin seriously believes in mankind without God. Of course, he consistently accepts the lowest possible moral denominator. Therefore, his assertion that mankind will, of its own power, arrive at freedom, equality, and brotherhood is, objectively, nothing but a cruel joke.[48] While proclaiming noble civic goals, Rakitin invariably acts like a perfect cad. A materialist and positivist, he is also the author of a vita of Father Zosima, published by the local diocese (Book Twelve, chap. ii, p. 634). Dmitry says some significant things about Rakitin which also apply to Ivan but are more obvious in the shallow Rakitin:

45. Bem points out that such "demotion of the image of Satan" is part of a Russian literary tradition, started by Gogol (Bem, "*Faust* v tvorchestve Dostoevskogo," p. 118). Ivanov distinguishes between Lucifer as the principle of selfish aloofness and self-detachment from the whole—which is the Grand Inquisitor— and Ahriman, the corrupter of the human will (Ivanov, p. 125).

46. Romano Guardini, *Religiöse Gestalten in Dostojewskijs Werk* (Munich, 1947), p. 156.

47. In a letter to Liubimov, dated 10 August 1880, Dostoevsky points out that Ivan's meeting with the devil has two aspects: the physical (a mental condition where the patient cannot distinguish reality from a phantom) and the metaphysical: "Tormented by unbelief, he (subconsciously) wishes, at the same time, the phantom to be real, and not a figment of his imagination" (*Pis'ma* 4:190).

48. Zander, pp. 28–29.

"And Rakitin does dislike God. Ough! doesn't he dislike Him!" (Book Eleven, chap. iv, p. 557). This is the metaphysical aspect of Rakitin's personality. Its psychological equivalent is this: Rakitin and his kind "can't understand a joke either, that's the worst of such people. They never understand a joke, and their souls are dry, dry and flat" (Book Eleven, chap. iv, p. 556).[49] Atheism means poverty, sterility, lack of originality. Rakitin, like Ivan Karamazov, is a master of rhetoric, but utterly unimaginative.

Smerdiakov, another double of Ivan Karamazov's, is more patently a cohort of the devil. Smerdiakov acts as a tempter and seducer throughout the novel. Ivan, Dmitry, and even that high-minded boy Iliusha Snegiriov are among his victims. Wasiolek suggests that there is some evidence that Smerdiakov and the devil are one: as Smerdiakov takes his own life, the devil appears to Ivan, and during their last meeting he strikes Ivan as a phantom.[50] Smerdiakov is a born atheist who as a boy stumps the pious Grigory with the question: "God created light on the first day, and the sun, moon, and stars on the fourth day. Where then did the light come from on the first day?" (Book Three, chap. vi, p. 112). The boy is also caught performing funeral rites over cats which he has hanged (a version of "black mass"). Significantly, too, Smerdiakov's is a sharp, but purely theoretical mind: when given Gogol's delightful Ukrainian tales, he merely finds that "it's all untrue" (p. 113). Like Ivan Karamazov and Rakitin, the lackey Smerdiakov is the "intellectual type" in his own social set. He, too, subjects the religious, nationalist, and authoritarian principles which Dostoevsky defends to a sharp critical analysis.[51] He concedes defeat before his teacher Ivan does and makes a desperate attempt to change

49. Dostoevsky considered this point important: "As time goes on, 'recti-linearness' develops in an ever-increasing measure: for example, the instinct for adaptation, for metaphor, for allegory, begins to disappear. Noticeably, people cease (generally speaking) to understand jest, humor . . . one of the surest symptoms of the intellectual and moral degradation of an epoch" (*Diary of a Writer,* 1876, 1:536).

50. Wasiolek, p. 176.

51. Grossman, "Dostoevskii i pravitel'stvennye krugi 1870-kh godov," p. 108.

course (Book Eleven, chap. viii, p. 591). Apparently Smerdiakov could not believe in God, but could not go on living in his
condition either—hence, his suicide.[52] Dostoevsky had often asserted that suicide is a logical corollary of materialism and lack
of faith in immortality.[53] As Belknap has pointed out, we lack
the psychological dimension of Smerdiakov's case: we can only
guess what goes on in his mind.[54]

The devil's cohorts are many. Father Ferapont, who can see
devils physically, is an example of the fact that the devil can ape,
parody, and pervert any virtue—and thus, a monk's exemplary
piety and prodigious feats of fasting and mortification of the
flesh. Even children are not safe: little Kolia is Ivan's double,
and Liza Khokhlakov—a sensitive, bright, and charming girl—
has morbid daydreams and a strange affinity to Ivan Karamazov.

2.b. Arguments in Support of Christianity

The positive elements of Dostoevsky's theodicy are likewise
linked to individual characters and individual voices in the
novel. While the devil is positively garrulous, Christ never says a
word in the whole chapter "The Grand Inqusitor." Still,
Aliosha says that the "legend" is in Christ's praise, and does not
blaspheme Him.[55] Dostoevsky's religious feeling and artistic tact
forbid him to make any attempt at creating a "voice" for
Christ: Christ is more than any man could possibly express
(John 20:31). Dostoevsky's silent Christ is the very opposite of
the proud and majestic Inquisitor. More than anything else, He
is the kenotic Christ of Tiutchev's poem, quoted by Ivan, the
Christ who appears to us in every hungry, thirsty, or naked
stranger, in every sick man, and in every prisoner.[56]

52. Zander, p. 25.
53. See Losskii, *Dostoevskii i ego khristianskoe miroponimanie,* pp. 164–66.
54. Belknap, *Structure,* p. 86.
55. See Sandoz, pp. 212–13.
56. See Maceina, pp. 237–44. Berdiaev suggests that the truth about freedom
is inexpressible, while its contrary is readily stated. Hence the truth about human
freedom must prevail through a "negation of the negative" (Berdiaev, p. 196).
Cf. Soloviov's eleventh and twelfth discourses on Godmanhood (*Sobranie
sochinenii,* 3: 156).

While the refutation of Book Five may be seen as implicit even in its text itself,[57] Dostoevsky meant to give a concentrated and explicit statement of his moral and religious ideal in Book Six.[58] His strategy in revealing his ideal is analogous to that used in expressing his conception of evil: he shows men and women in whom the Christian ideal becomes manifest. Dostoevsky believed that the only way for a better life, even in earthly terms, was for more people to become better Christians. He also believed in the beneficial power of even a few righteous believers' spreading God's word by their example.[59] The world of *The Brothers Karamazov* is populated by enough good people (e.g., the police magistrate Mikhail Makarovich Makarov, Dr. Herzenstube, Grigory and his wife, young Kalganov), besides many evil and indifferent ones. And at the monastery Aliosha meets not only Father Zosima but also several other righteous monks who are secure in their faith—Fathers Paisy and Iosif, in particular.

In Father Zosima, Dostoevsky once more attempted to create a truly perfect man. Gessen suggests, not without justification, that in Zosima "the two planes of eternal and human life meet" (pp. 223–24). Yet there is every indication that Dostoevsky also meant Zosima to be a realistic character.[60] Linnér (pp. 49–52) has pointed out the ambiguity of Zosima's saintly traits and powers: they can all be attributed to natural causes, as well as seen as manifestations of divine grace. Many readers will observe that Zosima (as Father Zosima, that is) lacks a psychological dimension (Linnér, p. 37). Also, we know nothing about the last forty or so years of his life, nor does his personality show any visible traces of the inner conflicts he must have endured to become the saint he is. Such lack of a psychological dimension is

57. See Mochulsky, pp. 621–22.

58. See Dostoevsky's letter to Liubimov, 8 July 1879, *Pis'ma* 4:65.

59. See Antonii, pp. 140–41. Cf. this notebook entry from 1876–77: "If [we] were Christians, [we] could solve all problems. But so far it is impossible for all to be Christians; only individual cases are possible. (Perhaps these individual cases guide and *mysteriously* save people.)" *Neizdannyi Dostoevskii*, p. 591; *The Unpublished Dostoevsky*, 3:98.

60. See Linnér, pp. 10–12, 26, 138, et passim.

well motivated, however: Zosima is one of those few men who have found "freedom from self,"[61] so that his actions are guided by his faith and by love, not by personal idiosyncrasies, much less passions.

Some Russian Orthodox critics have charged that Zosima is "too sweet," too "Franciscan."[62] But this is not so: his aphorisms and the things he says in the text of the novel show him reacting fully to the seamy and terrible side of human life.[63] Yet it cannot be denied that the religious *Weltgefühl* represented by Father Zosima is broader than dogmatic Orthodox Christianity. There is in it a strong dose of mystic vitalism and pantheist love of all creation. There is in it an element of "aestheticized" religion, with beauty and beautiful feelings substituted for ascetic discipline, penance, and fear of God. Father Zosima's assertion that through love and faith man can attain paradise even on earth smacks of heresy. His veneration of Mother Earth suggests identification with the pre-Christian mythical religion of the Russian peasant.

Father Zosima as a person is—pointedly, of course—contrasted with Ivan's Grand Inquisitor. He is not at all imposing physically. Though a much younger man, he is neither "tall and erect," nor has he "fiery eyes." Father Zosima is not eloquent. What he has to say are generally moral and religious commonplaces. Still, Father Zosima meets every challenge of Ivan's Inquisitor head-on. He paraphrases the Book of Job, where God seems frivolous and cruel but in effect only reaffirms His approval of His creation: His *is* the best of all possible worlds, so long as man allows it to be so. Ivan Karamazov does not want universal harmony at the price of the sufferings of children. Zosima affirms that "everyone is really responsible to all men for all men and for everything," so that by forgiving the child's tormentor we are only forgiving ourselves (Book Six, chap. ii[a], p. 268). Ivan preaches a humanist utopia. Father Zosima asserts that man cannot live without contact with "mysterious other

61. The ultimate goal of a religious life (see Book One, chap. v, p. 21).
62. See Leont'ev, 8:204–5; Volynskii, pp. 176–77. Cf. Linnér, pp. 100–1.
63. Linnér, p. 182.

worlds.'' Ivan's Grand Inquisitor elevates himself above his fellow men and thus becomes separated from them. Zosima preaches the communion of all men as God's children. Even in death, Father Zosima refutes the second temptation of the devil: his body decays, refusing to produce a material miracle. Yet Aliosha's vision in ''Cana of Galilee'' triumphantly asserts the reality of the ideal miracle. The epigraph of the novel (John 12:24), which recurs in a variety of contexts throughout the novel, tells us that suffering and death are necessary so that there can be resurrection.

The whole figure of Father Zosima is a study in that human freedom which the Grand Inquisitor claims men neither deserve nor want. Zosima was a very ordinary young man, a conformist, and not at all virtuous. Yet one day he asserted his freedom by overcoming the overwhelming social pressure of certain disgrace when he refused to take his shot at a duel he had himself provoked. As we meet Zosima in his old age, he is the image of a free man.

Aliosha, so long as he follows his teacher's example, is also free. Freedom from all social conventions is the least of this. Most of all, Zosima and Aliosha are free of the terrible self-consciousness and pride which consume Ivan Karamazov. Dmitry Karamazov discovers his freedom slowly and painfully. He keeps surprising us by doing the unpredictable thing. His reaction to the terrible injustice which he suffers is not at all the predictable one: ''Rakitin lies! If they drive God from the earth, we shall shelter Him underground. One cannot exist in prison without God; it's even more impossible than out of prison. And then we men underground will sing from the bowels of the earth a tragic hymn to God, with Whom is joy'' (Book Eleven, chap. iv, p. 560). Dmitry has become a free man. When presented with Ivan's escape plan, he does not at all grasp at it, but may very well choose to accept his martyrdom.[64]

While the characters of *The Brothers Karamazov* who are tainted by evil are all isolated, self-centered, and generally alienated from the world, Zosima, Aliosha, and everyone else who partakes of divine Grace participate in the universal com-

64. Goldstein, p. 334.

munity of those who love God—and enjoy all absolute values: beauty, truth, plenitude of life.[65]

2.c. THE HISTORICAL DIMENSION

There is one aspect of Dostoevsky's theodicy which is not explicit in the text of *The Brothers Karamazov:* the time dimension. Ivan Karamazov raises the issue when he says: "I must have retribution . . . not retribution in some remote infinite time and space, but here on earth, and that I could see myself" (Book Five, chap. iv, p. 225). Both the narrator and Father Zosima speak of historical phenomena. They see their own time as crucial and decisive. Aliosha is presented as the man of the future. The chapter "The Grand Inquisitor" imparts an apocalyptic atmosphere to the whole novel.

Dostoevsky's other writings, specifically *Diary of a Writer,* suggest that he was expecting spectacular historic changes in the near future, with Russia playing a decisive role in the further fate of the whole human race. Dmitry Merezhkovsky, in particular, called Dostoevsky a "prophet of the Russian revolution" and claimed that "Dostevsky's true religion, if not in his consciousness as yet, then certainly in his deepest subconscious experience, is not Orthodoxy, not historical Christianity, or even Christianity at large, but that which is beyond Christianity, beyond the New Testament—Apocalypse, the coming Third Testament, the revelation of God's Third Hypostasis, a religion of the Holy Spirit."[66] The text of *The Brothers Karamazov* hardly warrants such interpretation.

3. The Theme of Fathers and Children

The theme of fathers and children was on Dostoevsky's mind all through the 1870s.[67] In both great novels before *The Brothers*

65. Losskii, *Dostoevskii i ego khristianskoe miroponimanie,* pp. 138–39.

66. D. S. Merezhkovskii, *Prorok russkoi revoliutsii* (St. Petersburg, 1906), p. 50.

67. "When Nekrasov eighteen months ago invited me to write a novel for the *National Annals,* I was on the point of beginning my *Fathers and Children,* but I held back, and thank God I did. So for the time being I wrote *A Raw Youth* as the first trial of my idea" (*Diary of a Writer,* 1876, 1:160).

Karamazov, The Possessed and *A Raw Youth,* the theme of the generation gap is important. Several feuilletons of *Diary of a Writer*—for example, "A Colony of Juvenile Delinquents"—deal with children and the problems of their education.[68] Dostoevsky's notebooks and correspondence likewise reflect his concern with children and parent-child relations. Dostoevsky was deeply worried about the apparent disintegration of the Russian family.[69] Only in *The Brothers Karamazov,* however, did the father-son theme and the theme of the suffering, innocent child acquire an allegoric and metaphysical significance.

3.a. THE THEME OF FATHERHOOD

It is conceivable that Dostoevsky's raising of the familiar theme of a father-son conflict from a psychological to a metaphysical level occurred in part under the influence of Nikolai Fiodorov's ideas (see I.4.a. Secular Sources). On the other hand, the mystic-metaphysical conception of fatherhood (and of sonhood, of course) is deeply rooted in religion, and particularly in Russian Orthodoxy (where the father image of the tsar was also a powerful presence). Similar conceptions could also readily be found in contemporary progressive Western thought; Ernest Renan, for example, wrote that Christ's "kingdom of God was, without a doubt, the impending apocalypse that was to take place in the heavens. But it was also, and probably primarily, the kingdom of the soul, created by freedom and by the filial sentiment which a virtuous man feels upon the bosom of his Father."[70]

68. *Diary of a Writer,* 1873, 1:166–82.
69. In an article of *Diary of a Writer,* Dostoevsky wrote: "Never has the Russian family been shaken so loose, more disintegrated, more unsorted, and more uninformed than at present. . . . The contemporary Russian family is becoming more and more *casual*" (1877, 2:753). And here is a passage from Dostoevsky's letter to an anonymous mother, dated 27 March 1876: "Imagine that your child, grown up to the age of 15 or 16, comes to you (influenced by bad friends in school, for example) and asks you or his father: 'Why should I love you and why should this be my duty?' Believe me no knowledge or questions will help you there, nor would there be much sense in answering him. And therefore you must make sure that *he never comes to you with such a question*" (Pis'ma 4:12).
70. *Vie de Jésus* (Paris, 1863), p. 284.

The father-son relationships in *The Brothers Karamazov* appear on a pragmatic, a psychological, and a metaphysical level. As Richard Peace has pointed out, Dmitry has physically attacked three fathers (his natural father, his foster father Grigory, and Snegiriov, whom he humiliates in front of his son), "but his guilt is somehow transcendental—his crime is that of assaulting the very concept of fatherhood itself."[71] Conversely, fatherhood is holy per se, even if it is represented by a Fiodor Pavlovich, the worst father possible.[72] It is significant that there exists a deep parallelism between the physical father, Fiodor Pavlovich, and the spiritual father, Zosima: within less than an hour's time they both order Aliosha to leave the monastery; in his own perverse and clownish way, Fiodor Pavlovich time and again affirms the words of the holy elder; and they die within a day of each other.

Fatherhood being good per se, the attainment of fatherhood in the ideal sense is the mark of moral progress. Aliosha becomes a father figure to a group of schoolboys, Dmitry's rebirth is marked by his dream of "the babe," and even Ivan, shortly before his collapse, saves the life of the drunken peasant whom he had earlier knocked into the snow. Young Iliusha, whose beautiful relationship with his father contrasts with the terrible mess of the Karamazov family, is called "daddy" (*batiushka*) by his father.

On the negative side, all evil forces are enemies of fatherhood. In a notebook entry of 1880–81, Dostoevsky defines the Russian "progressive" movement started by Belinsky as obsessed not only with "a quite unusual drive toward the acceptance of new ideas," but also with an urge "to destroy everything old with hatred, abuse, and disgrace."[73] Ivan, the rebel, whom his father fears even more than Dmitry, explicitly denies the idea of resurrection and eventually states the direct antithesis to Fiodorov's idea of the resurrection of the fathers: "They all desire the death of their fathers!" (Book Twelve, chap. v, p. 651).

71. *Dostoyevsky: An Examination of the Major Novels* (Cambridge, 1971), p. 243.

72. Contrary to the glib arguments of Dmitry's defender, Fetiukovich.

73. *Neizdannyi Dostoevskii,* p. 672; *The Unpublished Dostoevsky,* 3:148.

3.b. "THE NOVEL ABOUT CHILDREN" IN
The Brothers Karamazov

"The novel about children" which is built into *The Brothers Karamazov* (see I.3. Early Versions) is relevant to the focal ideas of the novel in several ways. Ivanov quite appropriately uses the expression "Dostoevsky's metaphysics of childhood" (p. 95). "The novel about children" mirrors the adult world and so makes its meaning clearer: Kolia Krasotkin, a double of Ivan Karamazov's, helps us to understand Ivan. The suffering of innocent children being the pivot of Dostoevsky's theodicy, the stories of the suffering and death of two youngsters, Zosima's brother Markel and Iliusha Snegiriov, are all-imporant: in both instances suffering and early death are shown to be not cruel and meaningless, but meaningful and edifying. Rosen has drawn attention to Father Zosima's question: How could Job, rejoicing in his "new" children, forget his children who died? The answer is that this is a mystery, though psychologically it is, of course, a fact.[74]

Love of children is a test of a man's goodness. In a letter to a lady correspondent of his, Anna Filosofov, dated 11 July 1879, Dostoevsky speaks of how children "humanize" existence (*Pis'ma* 4:67). The devil does not like children (Book Eleven, chap. ix, p. 602). Father Zosima speaks warmly about children, his words being a response to Ivan's charges (Book Six, chap. iii[f], p. 294). The suffering child of Dmitry's dream never leaves him thereafter, giving meaning to his own existence.

The children in *The Brothers Karamazov* are an illustration of Dostoevsky's contention that certain fundamental ideas (God, right and wrong) appear in children very early. Hence the importance of early childhood experience and its beneficial influence in later life—it motivates Zosima's conversion and Aliosha's decision to devote his life to God.[75] On the other hand, Dostoevsky is trying to show that children can be wicked too

74. Nathan Rosen, "Style and Structure in *The Brothers Karamazov:* The Grand Inquisitor and the Russian Monk," *Russian Literature Triquarterly* 1 (1971):357.

75. Linnér, pp. 44–45.

(Liza Khokhlakov's fantasies), while a childlike quality is hidden even in a strong and violent adult (Dmitry Karamazov).

4. *The Brothers Karamazov* as a Social Novel

The Brothers Karamazov may be read as a social novel, that is, with the religious values presented in the novel seen as instruments of sociopolitical conflict. This, of course, was not Dostoevsky's own conception of the novel. But his insistence on psychological and social realism alone created the basis for a sociopolitical interpretation. In fact, an invitation for such a reading of the novel may readily be found in the text itself; for instance: "What after all, is this Karamazov family, which has gained such an unenviable notoriety throughout Russia? . . . Perhaps I am exaggerating too much, but it seems to me that certain fundamental features of our educated class of today are reflected in this family picture"—so the prosecutor in his speech (Book Twelve, chap. vi, p. 660). Dostoevsky certainly believed in the "importance of the literary phenomenon as a social fact" (letter to Aleksei Suvorin, 15 May 1877, *Pis'ma* 3:267).

While the novel is set in the 1860s, the atmosphere is that of the late 1870s (see *PSS* 15:451). Details from *Diary of a Writer* referring to events of the 1870s are used (see I.5.b. *Diary of a Writer*). To discredit a jury trial was in accord with the views of the future Alexander III and his friends, such as Pobedonostsev.[76] Dostoevsky's satirical sorties against political liberalism are as sharp in *The Brothers Karamazov* as they were in *The Possessed*. Rakitin is a stock character who appears in other antiliberal novels of the 1870s (Nikolai Leskov's, for example).[77] The socioeconomic situation described in *The Brothers Karamazov* is that of the late 1870s, when Russia was rapidly becoming a capitalist country. The countryside is impoverished. Local capitalists, such as Fiodor Pavlovich Karamazov, cut

76. Cf. Mochulsky, p. 580; Volynskii, pp. 88–95. Dostoevsky had given a rather vitriolic account of the adversary principle in criminal cases in *Diary of a Writer,* 1877, 2:866–70.

77. See Grossman, "Dostoevskii i pravitel'stvennye krugi 1870-kh godov," pp. 104–7.

down the forests and build nothing except taverns. They not only exploit but also despise the peasant.[78] Small landowners have become ex-landowners, like Maksimov. Large landowners like Mme. Khokhlakov or Miusov are presented very negatively, as are most other members of the "upper middle class." The following notebook entry presents the Russian intellectual essentially as he appears in *The Brothers Karamazov:* "Certainly we [the educated men and women of Russia] are endowed more than the people, for instance, with morbid and hypochondriac self-love, disdain for other people, somber spitefulness, cynicism, a thirst for conformity along with an insatiable thirst for glory, the shallowest vanity, a passion for certain habits, and a sickening timidity in the face of our own conviction that we should drop these habits, etc., etc."[79] Other notebook entries and letters suggest that Dostoevsky considered the Russian educated classes idle, aimless, and lacking in specialized training (or hopelessly uneducated if they had that). All of this is to be found in *The Brothers Karamazov* also. At the same time, the masses of the people are shown to be desperately poor and ignorant, and actually sinking lower through the spreading vice of drunkenness.[80] I. N. Kubikov has suggested that the character of Smerdiakov may be interpreted as typifying the moral corruption of the lower classes, as they, too, begin to become westernized, acquiring all the vices of the bourgeoisie and few of its virtues.[81] Father Zosima's assessment of Russian society is remarkably pessimistic, and remarkably anticapitalist as well (see, e.g., Book Six, chap. iii[f], p. 294).

78. See Dolinin, "K istorii sozdaniia *Brat'ev Karamazovykh*," pp. 61–62. Dostoevsky's account of the wretched condition of Russia's economy in one of his last articles, "Can We Demand European Finances for Russia?" (1881), rather corresponds to what we find in *The Brothers Karamazov.*

79. Notebooks for 1876–77, *Neizdannyi Dostoevskii: Zapisnye knizhki i tetradi 1860–1881 gg.,* Literaturnoe nasledstvo, vol. 83 (Moscow, 1971), p. 525.

80. Dostoevsky's acceptance of the gloomy presentation of village life in Kishensky's play "Drinking to the Last Drop Will Yield No Good Crop" (1873) in an article of *Diary of a Writer* (1873, 1:107–18) coincides with his own depiction of village life in the episode at Mokroe.

81. I. N. Kubikov [pseud. of Ivan Dement'ev], "Obraz Smerdiakova i ego obobshchaiushchii smysl," in *Dostoevskii* (Moscow, 1928), p. 211.

Dostoevsky's message in *The Brothers Karamazov* is that only a moral regeneration, accomplished through a return to the Christian faith of the simple people, can save Russia.[82] Just how this would be brought about is not said. It stands to reason that Father Zosima sends Aliosha out into the world to find a way. Merezhkovsky has suggested that the famous passage in which Aliosha "had fallen on the earth a weak youth, but . . . rose up a resolute champion" (Book Seven, chap. iv, p. 341) refers to Aliosha's future role in "the great religious revolution of Russia and the world" (p. 51).

4.a. THE RUSSIAN NOBLEMAN

Fiodor Pavlovich Karamazov may be seen as a social type. He is proud of his old and genuine nobility, but this does not prevent him from becoming a businessman and actually learning the tricks of the trade from Odessa Jews. Dolinin observes that Fiodor Pavlovich is a humbler version of Stiva Oblonsky in Tolstoi's *Anna Karenina*.[83] A passage early in the novel is significant: when Fiodor Pavlovich ventures the opinion that it might be a good idea to liquidate monasteries and "all that mystic stuff," his son Ivan points out that if it came to liquidating things, Fiodor Pavlovich would himself be among the first to be liquidated. Fiodor Pavlovich immediately concedes that his son is right and quickly changes his mind about monasteries too (Book Three, chap. viii, p. 121).

Yet on the other hand, Father Zosima and Aliosha are of the nobility also. (It may be worth noting that the holy man in Dostoevsky's preceding novel, Makar Ivanovich Dolgoruky of *A Raw Youth,* is a peasant.) There is reason to believe that Dostoevsky to some extent believed in Versilov's proud assertion of the mission of the Russian nobility (*A Raw Youth,* Pt. III,

82. Grossman suggests, however, that the positive clergyman, monk, or nun is a stock character in novels of the "Katkov school" and that Dostoevsky's message is far from unique (Grossman, "Dostoevskii i pravitel'stvennye krugi 1870-kh godov," p. 107). The Katkov school was named after Mikhail Nikiforovich Katkov (1818–87), a reactionary publicist who wielded considerable power as publisher of *The Russian Herald* and *The Moscow News.*

83. Dolinin, "K istorii sozdaniia *Brat'ev Karamazovykh*," p. 60.

chap. vii, 2), which would be accomplished when this "superior type" bowed to the simple truth of the Russian people.[84]

4.b. THE PEOPLE

The argument between Dostoevsky and his radical opponents boils down to a question of the anthropology of the Russian people.[85] Both parties expected great things from the "simple people," but disagreed as to the direction in which the people would lead Russia. The question is focal even in Belinsky's famous correspondence with Gogol back in 1847: Gogol assumed that the Russian people were believers and deeply Christian at heart, while Belinsky claimed that the Russian people were quite indifferent to religion and if anything, hostile to the Church. Ever since his return from Siberia Dostoevsky had maintained that "our people are incomparably purer in heart than our upper classes, and that the people's mind is not bifurcated to such an extent as to cherish, side by side with a noble idea, its dirty little antithesis" (*Diary of a Writer,* 1877, "About Anonymous Abusive Letters," 2:702). There is some evidence that by the time Dostoevsky was working on *The Brothers Karamazov* he was no longer sure that the people would reach the millennium without having to pass, like the educated classes, through a phase of "depravity and lies."[86] Nevertheless, Dostoevsky's populist mystique is fully in force in *The Brothers Karamazov,* as Father Zosima preaches: "One who does not believe in God will not believe in God's people. He who believes in God's people, will see His Holiness, too, even though he had not believed in it till then" (Book Six, chap. ii[b], p. 273).[87]

Ivan Karamazov has lost his faith precisely because he has elevated himself above the people. In this case, "the people" are not necessarily peasants, but are what Ivan, a modern intellectual, is not: human beings who are intellectually and morally

84. In an article, "The Elite," Dostoevsky presents a penetrating study of the historical, social, and moral condition of the Russian élite (*Diary of a Writer,* 1876, 1:480–90). Cf. Berdiaev, p. 173; Komarowitsch, pp. 123–24.

85. Berdiaev speaks of Dostoevsky's "religious populism," as against the socialist populism of his opponents (Berdiaev, pp. 174–75).

86. See *The Unpublished Dostoevsky,* 2:119–20.

87. "God's people" (*bozhii narod*) is here a synonym of "the simple people."

humble enough not to set themselves above the "common crowd."[88] Having separated himself from the people, the intellectual has also separated himself from the faith of the people, and so from God.

Dostoevsky believed that the best among Russia's intellectuals were beginning to find their way back to the faith of the people.[89] This is one of the messages of *The Brothers Karamazov*.[90]

4.c. THE NEW GENERATION

Dostoevsky's correspondence gives evidence of the generation gap he believed existed in the 1870s. He is generally optimistic about the young generation, which, he believed, was "searching for truth with all the courage of a Russian heart and mind, and merely lacking leadership" (letter to Leonid Grigoriev, dated 21 June 1878, *Pis'ma* 4:34). Dostoevsky created his Aliosha in the hope that young men and women with the idealism and energy of the radical youth of the 1860s and 1870s, but with his own Christian and nationalist ideals, would prevail in Russia in the near future. Yet at the same time, Dostoevsky is very much aware of the fact that this will be an uphill fight. Kolia Krasotkin is a young Ivan Karamazov, and it is not at all sure that he will not return to Rakitin's ideas once the novelty of Aliosha's influence has worn off.[91]

4.d. SOCIALISM AND UTOPIANISM, RUSSIA AND THE WEST

Two major questions which otherwise occupied Dostoevsky a great deal—socialism and nationalism—play a relatively marginal role in *The Brothers Karamazov*. Dostoevsky always be-

88. See Gibson, pp. 191-97.

89. In his notebooks for 1876-77, Dostoevsky says: "Our age is that point at which the yearning of the select to be reunited with the people is beginning to appear even among average individuals" (*Neizdannyi Dostoevskii*, p. 557; *The Unpublished Dostoevsky*, 3:59).

90. How good a prophet Dostoevsky really was is a different question. Cf. Berdiaev, p. 193.

91. Grossman points out that the schoolboy-revolutionary (as a negative type) is virtually a stock character in the novels of the Katkov school. Kolia Krasotkin is merely the most famous of them. See Grossman, "Dostoevskii i pravitel'stvennye krugi 1870-kh godov," p. 107.

lieved that atheism (or "humanism," i.e., a belief that human
reason is the only reliable guide to the solution of human problems) and socialism were inseparable.[92] In *The Brothers Karamazov* Dostoevsky looks beyond socialism. Early in the novel
the liberal Miusov tells the story of a French police spy who told
him that his government feared Christians who were also socialists more than ordinary radicals (Book Two, chap. v, p. 58).
Ivan's Grand Inquisitor detaches himself from the socialists, as
he predicts the building of a new tower of Babel and, during it, a
period of persecution of the Church. Only after the collapse of
atheist socialism will people return to the Church in despair.
This is when the Grand Inquisitor will establish his sham theoc-
racy (Book Five, chap. v, p. 237). Socialism, then, is to Ivan Karamazov as much of a mistake as Christianity: it, too, overestimates man. The two believers in socialism in *The Brothers Karamazov* are Kolia, a schoolboy, and Rakitin, a shallow careerist
and a cad.

It is significant that Fiodor Pavlovich and his lackey Smerdiakov both hate Russia. "But Russia's all swinishness. My
dear, if you only knew how I hate Russia," says Fiodor Pavlovich
(Book Three, chap. viii, p. 121). Smerdiakov agrees with his
master. He dreams of leaving Russia for good and becoming a
Frenchman. Ivan Karamazov is indifferent as far as Russia is
concerned— but the West is dear to his heart. On the other side,
Dmitry loves Russia: "I love Russia, Aliosha, I love the Russian
God, though I am a scoundrel myself" (Epilogue, chap. ii, p.
724). Russia as the bearer of Orthodox Christianity is upmost in
Father Zosima's mind (Book Six, chap. iii[f], p. 295).

4.e. THE CHURCH

The question of organized religion is an important side issue
in *The Brothers Karamazov*. It was the key issue in
Pobedonostsev's political program.[93] The ideas of Ivan
Karamazov's article on church and state can be found in

92. See, for example, Dostoevsky's letter to M. P. Pogodin, 26 February
1873, *Pis'ma* 4:298.
93. Grossman, "Dostoevskii i pravitel'stvennye krugi 1870-kh godov," p.
103.

Vladimir Soloviov's second discourse on Godmanhood, and Dostoevsky had often discussed the issue (albeit in connection with the Catholic church) in *Diary of a Writer*.[94] Dostoevsky was certainly opposed to a separation of church and state. But the integration of church and state should under no circumstances take place under the leadership of the state. Dostoevsky believed that religion ought to be absolute and total: nothing is more contemptible than a Sunday religion.[95] He thought that the Orthodox solution of the problem of church and state meant an initial spiritual union from which a sociopolitical union could eventually develop, while the Catholic church, so he thought, proceeded the other way around (Father Paisy's words, Book Two, chap. v, p. 54).[96]

Interestingly, Dostoevsky reduces this question to a question of anthropology also. In a notebook entry of 1880–81 he says: "The state is created for average man. But did the state, in being created, ever say: 'I am being created for average man'? You will say that history did so. No, the leaders were always of the elect. . . . [You will say that] societies were formed as a result of a need to live together. This is not true; rather, it always happened as a result of a great idea."[97] It is on the basis of this idealist anthropology that Dostoevsky lets Fathers Paisy and Zosima develop their Christian utopia.[98] Merezhkovsky has pointed out that their prophecy of the establishment on earth of

94. See, for instance, the March issue of 1876, 1:254–59.

95. Reinhard Lauth, *Die Philosophie Dostojewskis in systematischer Darstellung* (Munich, 1950), p. 396.

96. See L. Karsavin, "Dostoevskii i katolichestvo," in *Dostoevskii: Stat'i i materialy,* ed. A. S. Dolinin (Peterburg, 1922), pp. 43–44.

97. *Neizdannyi Dostoevskii,* p. 676; *The Unpublished Dostoevsky,* 3:152, is badly translated.

98. Soloviov paraphrases Dostoevsky's Christian utopia thus: "This central idea, which Dostoevsky served in all his activities, was the Christian idea of a free ecumenic union of universal brotherhood in the name of Christ. Dostoevsky was preaching this idea when he spoke of the true Church, of ecumenic Orthodoxy; in it he saw the spiritual, as yet unrealized essence of the Russian people, Russia's world historical mission, that new word which Russia was to say to the world" (Solov'iov, *Second Discourse in Memory of Dostoevsky,* in *Sobranie sochinenii,* 3:183). Cf. Dolinin, "K istorii sozdaniia *Brat'ev Karamazovykh,*" p. 32.

an ecumenic church and a just, brotherly, and godly society is in effect based on Revelation 5:10 and 21:4–8. Other Orthodox critics, and Leontiev in particular, rejected this aspect of *The Brothers Karamazov* as another piece of secular utopianism. Leontiev said that according to the Bible, things will *not* be getting better on earth. He suggested that an aesthetic wedding of Christianity and humanist utopia—which he saw in *The Brothers Karamazov*—was impossible because of their incompatibility, humanism being a "simple" and rational idea, and Christianity a "complex" and metaphysical idea.[99]

4.f. PHILOSOPHY OF HISTORY

Linnér has pointed out that though Dostoevsky could think and argue "like a politician"—that is, for limited, practical goals—he was still basically a "visionary and chiliast." Linnér then suggests that Dostoevsky must have been—unconsciously, perhaps—quite desperate about Russia's political future, so that he escaped into apocalyptic visions.[100] Anyway, Dostoevsky believed that cataclysmic historical events were at hand.[101] He believed that a social revolution was imminent in the West.[102] After all, this was the decade which had seen the Paris Commune. Certainly Dostoevsky underestimated the vitality of the West. Indeed, he failed to realize that he was himself a proof of the vitality of European civilization, of which he was willy-nilly a part. When he lets Ivan Karamazov say that Europe is a "graveyard" of past achievements, truths, and struggles (Book Five, chap. iii, p. 212), he expresses his own view.

Dostoevsky shared the Slavophiles' view that Russia was destined to regenerate decaying Western civilization.[103] Soloviov

99. Leont'ev, 8:202–3.

100. Linnér, p. 234.

101. See S. Askol'dov, "Religiozno-eticheskoe znachenie Dostoevskogo," in *Dostoevskii: Stat'i i materialy,* ed. A. S. Dolinin (Peterburg, 1922), p. 7. For a more general discussion of Dostoevsky's apocalyptic visions, see Wladimir Szylkarski, "Messianismus und Apokalyptik bei Dostojewskij und Solowjew," in Maceina, pp. 247–334; and Sandoz, *Political Apocalypse.*

102. See, for instance, *Diary of a Writer,* 1880, 2:1003. Cf. Dolinin, "K istorii sozdaniia *Brat'ev Karamazovykh,*" p. 45.

103. Dostoevsky's theoretical model for this development was a philosphy of history which sees three stages in the development of mankind: primary patriar-

(and many thinkers after him, Oswald Spengler, for example) have likened Russian messianism to Jewish messianism at the time of the Jewish insurrection against Rome.[104] Such regeneration amounted, in Dostoevsky's version, to a substitution of Russian-Orthodox Christian spirituality for Western humanism, "enlightenment," and rationalism. Dostoevsky expressed this notion repeatedly in *Diary of a Writer.*[105] He also believed that the conflict between East and West was rooted in the history of Christendom, East and West: in the West, Christian religion had been incorporated into the state, and only in the East had Christian religion remained detached from the state. The simple Russian people, unaffected by the westernizing and secularizing policies of Peter the Great, were the "Christbearers" who would produce the "God-man," the antithesis to the "man-God" of the West.[106] These ideas are explicitly stated in Father Zosima's words of wisdom.

4.g. MINOR POLITICAL POINTS:
ANTI-CATHOLICISM, CHAUVINISM, ANTI-SEMITISM

Dostoevsky's negative attitude toward Roman Catholicism had been expressed, in rather the same terms as in *The Brothers Karamazov,* not only in *Diary of a Writer* but also in his earlier fiction.[107] The renewed vigor of the Catholic church and the promulgation of the dogma of papal infallibility (1870) made the church controversial in the 1870s, and Dostoevsky energetically sided with those who believed that the Roman church had aspirations to secular power. In an article of 1876, Dostoevsky

---

chal society, civilization (in the plural: Dostoevsky admits the existence of different civilizations, though he is concerned only with modern Western civilization), and Christianity, i.e., the realization of Christian ideas in a universal brotherhood of men. See *The Unpublished Dostoevsky,* 1:95–98. Cf. Linnér, p. 235.

104. Solov'iov, *Third Discourse in Memory of Dostoevsky,* in *Sobranie sochinenii,* 3:192.

105. See, for instance, the article "Confessions of a Slavophile," *Diary of a Writer,* 1877, 2:780. Cf. Mochulsky, pp. 563–64.

106. *Diary of a Writer,* 1880, 2:1005.

107. See, for instance, *Diary of a Writer,* 1877, 2:821, where Dostoevsky speaks of "the Catholic conspiracy"; Prince Myshkin's diatribe, *The Idiot,* Pt. IV, chap. 7; and Shatov's words, *The Possessed,* Pt. II, chap. i(7).

said outright that "Rome had only too recently proclaimed its assent to the third temptation of the devil in the form of a solid dogma" (*Diary of a Writer,* 1876, "Dead Force and Future Forces," 1:255). The notion that the Roman church might ally itself with the socialist movement appears repeatedly in *Diary of a Writer.*[108] Nevertheless, it would be wrong to interpret "The Grand Inquisitor" as primarily an attack against the Roman Catholic church. Rather, its anti-Catholic message is merely coincidental.[109]

The libelous presentation of Polish nationals is a trait which shows up in a number of works by Dostoevsky and is also a virtual cliché of the "Katkov school."[110] Poles were hateful to Dostoevsky because they were Catholics, enemies of the Russian autocracy, and Slavs who had irreversibly chosen to join the West. Perhaps more than anything else, Dostoevsky resented the Polish landowners' contempt for the Russian Orthodox peasantry and their "peasant faith." Dostoevsky's anti-Polish feelings may have had personal roots, too: in *Notes from the House of the Dead,* he speaks of his Polish fellow prisoners with some respect, but never with fondness.

Dostoevsky's anti-Semitism likewise shows up in several of his novels, as well as quite explicitly in *Diary of a Writer.* Anti-Semitic sorties are characteristiic of the Katkov school at large.[111] Dostoevsky shared the view of Russian conservatives, such as K. P. Pobedonostsev, who believed that the international socialist movement already was, or would eventually be, con-

108. See Dolinin, "K istorii sozdaniia *Brat'ev Karamazovykh,*" p. 75. Dolinin calls Dostoevsky's notion "insane." Dostoevsky was wrong as far as the Catholic church was concerned, of course. But he correctly recognized the makings of a secular religion in socialism.

109. A report by V. F. Putsykovich (see *PSS* 15:482) to the effect that the Legend was directed primarily against Roman Catholicism is to be taken very lightly, in view of what we know about the unreliability of this acquaintance of Dostoevsky's.

110. Grossman, "Dostoevskii i pravitel'stvennye krugi 1870-kh godov," pp. 108-9. For an example of Dostoevsky's anti-Polish journalism, see "A Summer Attempt on the Part of Old Poland at Reconciliation," *Diary of a Writer,* 1877, 2:874-76.

111. Grossman, "Dostoevskii i pravitel'stvennye krugi 1870-kh godov," pp. 110-11.

trolled by Jews. Also, Dostoevsky tended to identify modern capitalism, and banking in particular, with a "takeover" by the Jews. These ideas, however, are of only marginal concern in *The Brothers Karamazov*.

5. Moral and Religious Philosophy in *The Brothers Karamazov*

The Brothers Karamazov is Dostoevsky's last and probably his clearest statement of his moral philosophy. It is a novel about good and evil, sin and virtue. The world of *The Brothers Karamazov* is a battlefield: the battle is between God and the devil, for men's souls. Dostoevsky expounds his value system through his narrator and through many of his *dramatis personae* (not only Father Zosima and the other monks but also many other characters in the novel are moralists and theologians of sorts).[112] And he also demonstrates it through the action of his novel. First and foremost he meant to show that the Christian ideal and the traditional Christian virtues of selfless love, charity, and humility were nothing abstract but could be realized in contemporary Russia.[113] Gibson suggests very plausibly that "towards the end Dostoevsky . . . deliberately declared theory to be a constituent of practice" (p. 50). Or, as Linnér puts it, "Theodicy as a theoretical problem is left aside and replaced by an ethical choice: should we live like Ivan or like Zosima?" (p. 184). Ivan Karamazov is shown to be no Grand Inquisitor, much as Raskol'nikov of *Crime and Punishment* had been shown to be no Napoleon; this does not prove that there are no Grand Inquisitors or Napoleons, but the burden of proof is shifted to those who say that there are.[114]

112. For a summary of Father Zosima's religious and moral philosophy, see Pletniov, "Serdtsem mudrye," pp. 91–92.

113. See, for instance, Dostoevsky's letter to Liubimov, 11 June 1879, *Pis'ma* 4:59, or "Seizing upon an Occasion," *Diary of a Writer,* 1880, 2:996–1006, the latter being Dostoevsky's reply to A. P. Gradovsky (1841–89), who had charged that Dostoevsky, in presenting his moral ideals, had neglected to appreciate practical social phenomena.

114. Sandoz suggests that Dostoevsky is simply a better psychologist than his materialist opponents: he sees what they do not see, namely that naked rejection of transcendence leads men to nihilism, anarchy, insanity, and suicide (Sandoz, p. 117).

Dostoevsky's distinction between good and evil is not the comfortable distinction between social right and social wrong.[115] It is based on religious criteria which Dostoevsky believed to be those of Russian Orthodoxy.[116] Good and evil appear on three different levels: the spontaneous (Dmitry's sins and virtues), the intellectual (Ivan's domain), and the spiritual (a synthesis of the other two: Aliosha's love is spiritual, while evil on this level takes the form of acedia or despair).[117]

5.a. Faith and Unbelief

Dostoevsky saw the root of all evil in unbelief.[118] He was convinced that unbelief had to lead, directly or indirectly, to the notion that "all things are lawful," and then to its practical consequences.[119] *The Brothers Karamazov* is a parable of this truth.

The Brothers Karamazov is also a parable of the truth, stated by Father Zosima, that "no one can judge a criminal, until he recognizes that he is just such a criminal as the man standing before him, and that he perhaps is more than all men to blame for that crime" (Book Six, chap. iii [h], p. 300).[120] In particular, the plot of the novel shows how everybody is personally guilty of the murder of Fiodor Pavlovich Karamazov and the unjust conviction of his son Dmitry Fiodorovich—even Aliosha, who at the crucial moment forgot to be his brother's keeper.

With faith in God, a man can accept his guilt and bear suf-

115. Askol'dov, p. 13, Gibson, p. 58.

116. Many Orthodox authorities will agree (e.g., Preosviashchenny [Metropolitan] Antonii in his *Slovar' k tvoreniiam Dostoevskogo*); others will disagree on some points. See N. Gorodetzky, *The Humiliated Christ in Modern Russian Thought* (London, 1938).

117. Gessen, p. 218. Soloviov, in his *Third Discourse in Memory of Dostoevsky,* uses the terms *natural, humanist,* and *mystic* for essentially the same conception (Solov'ov, *Sobranie sochinenii,* 3:196).

118. "You are correct in gathering that I see the cause of evil in unbelief," Dostoevsky wrote to A. F. Blagonravov, 19 December 1880, *Pis'ma* 4:220.

119. Stated very clearly in *Diary of a Writer,* 1877, 2:760–61.

120. For a discussion of this point, see Wasiolek, p. 177; Cox, pp. 209–10. Cf. Dostoevsky's article "Hartung's Suicide and Our Eternal Question: Who Is to Be Blamed?" *Diary of a Writer,* 1877, 2:859–61.

fering. Without faith, guilt will crush a man—which is the danger Ivan Karamazov is in, and to which his disciple Smerdiakov succumbs. A man with guilt and without faith may commit suicide, rejecting life, the gift of God given him once in all eternity. Father Zosima's discourse "Of Hell and Hellfire, A Mystic Reflection" (Book Six, chap. iii[i], pp. 301-2), while not rejecting the notion of a material hell, describes essentially the condition of Ivan Karamazov's soul (Stavrogin of *The Possessed* or Svidrigailov of *Crime and Punishment* also come to mind).[121] Hell is a self-willed condition of lovelessness and spite: "They cannot behold the living God without hatred, and they cry out that the God of Life should be annihilated, that God should destroy Himself and His own creation" (p. 302).

5.b. MYSTICISM, LOVE OF GOD, THE CHRISTIAN IDEAL

Faith is the *conditio sine qua non* of the good life.[122] It is derived from faith in Christ, meaning that every man can overcome guilt, alienation, and death to the extent that he believes in Christ and is willing to follow Him. Faith is difficult to attain and to preserve. Often it comes through suffering.[123]

The Brothers Karamazov, more than any other work of Dostoevsky's, affirms his belief in the reality of mystic experience. The program for it is given in Father Zosima's words: "God took seeds from different worlds and sowed them on this earth, and His garden grew up and everything came up that could come up, but what grows lives and is alive only through the feeling of its contact with other mysterious worlds. If that feeling grows weak or is destroyed in you, the heavenly growth will die away in you. Then you will be indifferent to life and even

121. Pletniov has pointed out that Father Zosima's teaching on hell does not coincide with the teachings of the Orthodox church (Pletniov, p. 89).

122. In the language of the critic Antonovich (who was promptly dubbed "Rakitin" by Dostoevsky's supporters) this means that Dostoevsky "pardons the most terrible outward crimes, but there is no drop of pity in him for the most harmless theological doubt, to say nothing of denial" (quoted from Belknap, *Structure,* p. 12).

123. Father Zosima says to Aliosha: "Life will bring you many misfortunes, but you will find your happiness in them, and will bless life and will make others bless it—which is what matters most." (Book Six, chap i, p. 264).

grow to hate it" (Book Six, chap. iii[g], pp. 299–300).[124]
Vetlovskaia has suggested that the whole novel is a parable to
demonstrate the workings of this principle.[125] Dmitry
Karamazov asserts his faith in a miracle early in the novel (Book
Three, chap. v, p. 110), and his contacts with "other worlds"
are renewed time and again: he does not forget God. Meanwhile,
Ivan Karamazov is one of those whom "God forgets": he
admires "the depth and force" of this expression without
realizing that it applies to him (Book Five, chap. v, p. 228). His
contacts with other worlds are limited to visitations by the devil.
As Guardini has pointed out, Dostoevsky "had the gift to so
translate extrahuman existence into human terms that a real
human being would appear before us, yet so that the image of
that extrahuman element would emerge from it" (p. 100).

As early as in his notebooks to *The Idiot,* Dostoevsky had
distinguished three kinds of love: passionate (immediate) love,
love from vanity, and Christian love.[126] The first is represented
by Dmitry and Grushen'ka, the second by Ivan and Katerina
Ivanovna, and the third by Father Zosima and Aliosha. Father
Zosima's words about love make it clear that true love encompasses all of God's creation, which means not only "every
leaf, every ray of God's light," and "animals, . . . plants, . . .
everything" (Book Six, chap. iii[g], p. 298), but implicitly,
death, decay, and suffering as well.[127] The label of "pantheism"
has been often applied to this attitude. Father Zosima's kind of
love appears in such details as Iliusha's request that some bread
crumbs be spread on his grave for sparrows to eat, in the dying
Markel's words: "Birds of heaven, happy birds, forgive me, for
I have sinned against you too" (Book Six, chap. ii[a], p. 268), or
even in Dmitry's recital of Schiller's "Ode to Joy" (Book Three,
chap. iii, p. 96). Father Zosima calls this "active love" and

124. Sandoz (p. 122) quotes a passage from St. Tychon rather to the same effect.
125. See Vetlovskaia, "Razviazka v *Brat'iakh Karamazovykh,*" pp. 201–3.
Rozanov suggests that by virtue of having committed murder, Smerdiakov has
established contact with "other worlds": like Ivan, he sees ghosts (Rozanov,
Dostoevsky, pp. 70–71).
126. Losskii, *Dostoevskii i ego khristianskoe miroponimanie,* pp. 210–11.
127. Linnér, pp. 172–73.

stresses that it is always directed at somebody or something in particular. Abstract love of humanity is professed by Ivan Karamazov's Grand Inquisitor, by Rakitin, and eventually by Ivan Karamazov's devil. When it comes to meeting a particular individual, Ivan Karamazov, Rakitin, Katerina Ivanovna, Mme. Khokhlakov, and all the others who proclaim themselves to be humanists show themselves incapable of selfless love. Father Zosima teaches that man is made for happiness (Book Two, chap. iv, p. 47) and affirms this with his own example. This opens him (and Dostoevsky) to charges of teaching a "rosy" Christianity and ignoring the message of Good Friday.

Man's sole reliable moral guide is the image of Jesus Christ. Father Zosima says: "On earth, indeed, we are as it were astray, and if it were not for the precious image of Christ before us, we should be undone and altogether lost" (Book Six, chap. iii[g], p. 299). It was Dostoevsky's opinion that the image of Christ had been preserved in its purest form precisely by Russian monkhood (Book Six, chap. iii[e], p. 292). Book Six is, among other things, an apology for Russian monkdom.

5.c. DOSTOEVSKY'S "PRACTICAL" CHRISTIANITY

Dostoevsky's polemic with Tolstoi's pacifist opposition to the war against Turkey (*Diary of a Writer*, 1877, 2:777–812) shows Dostoevsky defending a common-sense, middle-class position featuring patriotism, justification of a "necessary" war, and solidarity with Russia's "Slavic brethren." This contrasts with Father Zosima's mystic teaching of universal love. In a necrologue of 1876 (*Diary of a Writer*, 1:349–50) Dostoevsky had found warm words of praise for George Sand and called her "one of the staunchest confessors of Christ," in spite of her lifelong espousal of socialist and humanist ideas. Dostoevsky's "Discourse on Pushkin" (1880) reaffirms once more Dostoevsky's sympathy and admiration for the traditions of Western culture. Leontiev called Dostoevsky's Christianity "too universal-humanitarian." Linnér and Gibson are quite right in drawing attention to the many ways in which Dostoevsky's religion is determined by the fact that he was thoroughly imbued with Western culture. Dostoevsky's editorials of the 1870s show a man actively interested and well versed in European problems, and this includes religious issues, such as Bismarck's *Kulturkampf* of the 1870s.

All these circumstances, along with Dostoevsky's artistic tact and respect for realism, temper the fervor of his religious message. Zosima is, after all, an educated man who is above all superstition: the incident in which he recommends that a monk who has obsessive dreams take a laxative is significant. Aliosha's firm belief in the "flying coffin" miracle is presented as a youthful trait that will pass (Book One, chap. v, p. 23). Aliosha's speech at the end of the novel could have been delivered by any Boy Scout leader, as a critic has recently suggested. Iliusha wanted to be buried by the huge boulder he so liked, but was buried, properly, in the churchyard. The path which Aliosha envisages for Dmitry after his conviction is one of compromise, and he uses arguments which echo Smerdiakov's "Jesuitic" casuistry.[128] R. L. Jackson points out that the ethic at the base of this decision is "a working ethic for mortals" ("Dmitrij Karamazov," p. 265). And while the two extremists of the novel, Father Zosima and Ivan, may be guilty of ignoring the middle sphere of religious life, and of life at large, as Guardini charges (p. 123),[129] the novel as a whole presents life, including religious life, realistically, giving proper credit to the more pedestrian virtues of order, discipline, tradition, health, and so on.

6. *The Brothers Karamazov* as a Psychological Novel

6.a. PECULIARITIES OF DOSTOEVSKY'S PSYCHOLOGY

The Brothers Karamazov shows Dostoevsky's usual skill at psychological motivation and his usual attention to psychological detail. In fact, Dostoevsky did some psychological research, specifically in connection with Ivan Karamazov's nightmare.[130] Yet in *The Brothers Karamazov* Dostoevsky's

---

128. Jackson, "Dmitrij Karamazov," p. 264; Hingley, p. 213; Volynskii, p. 85.

129. This is one of the central theses of Braun's book.

130. In a letter to Liubimov, dated 10 August 1880, Dostoevsky reports that he has consulted with more than one doctor on this matter (*Pis'ma* 4:190).

antipsychologism, which he had stated many times before,[131] appears in particularly massive doses. This contradiction is explained by the fact that Dostoevsky, while using the conventional psychological tools of the novelist, also had a strong sense of their limitations. While everything that happens in the novel may be accounted for in psychological terms, Dostoevsky also lets it be known that he does not consider psychology an exhaustive explanation of human behavior, or of his characters' behavior within the framework of the novel.

In his harangue on the moral ambivalence of beauty, Dmitry observes that "man is broad, too broad, indeed. I'd have him narrower" (Book Three, chap. iii, p. 97).[132] Following this principle, Dostoevsky's characters are atypical, or perhaps antitypical, as compared to those of a conventional nineteenth-century novel. Rather than confirming any notion which the reader may have developed of them, they keep growing richer and more varied as the novel goes along; they keep surprising us.[133] We are dealing here with what might be called centrifugal psychology, yet developed "from the outside in." As the novel ends, the riddle of each major character's "real self" is far from solved. Such an attitude toward psychology is consistent with Dostoevsky's belief in human free will: no human being is predictable to any other human being, or to himself. Dostoevsky was aware of the criticism leveled at his "weakness for the pathological manifestations of volition" (*Diary of a Writer,* 1877, 2:931–32), as well as of the charges that his characters were "extreme," "exceptional," and "fantastic," rather than "typical." Recently Braun has restated this criticism in cogent terms: "In the depiction of dangerous, truly adventuresome situations, Dostoevsky is unsurpassed to this day; as far as the depiction of normal, healthy phenomena of life, of a life not passing through marginal areas of being, was concerned, he did not do better—if he did try at all—than many other writers"

---

131. For instance, the chapter "Analysis" in *The Eternal Husband* (1870) pointedly leads psychological motivation *ad absurda.*

132. Which is, in fact, what the Grand Inquisitor proposes to do.

133. As Gibson puts it: "In general, unity of character is fixed in his novels by psychological *in*coherence" (p. 62). Cf. Joyce C. Oates, "The Double Vision of *The Brothers Karamazov,*" *Journal of Aesthetics and Art Criticism* 27:213. Oates speaks of Dostoevsky's "splendid unpredictability."

(pp. 274–75). Dostoevsky's answer to this criticism is given in the foreword to *The Brothers Karamazov,* as he lets his narrator say: "Not only is an eccentric 'not always' a particularity and a separate element, but, on the contrary, it happens sometimes that such a person, I dare say, carries within himself the very heart of the whole, and the rest of the men of his epoch have for some reason been temporarily torn from it, as if by a gust of wind" ("From the Author," p. xvii).[134] Elsewhere, Dostoevsky went further. In a famous refutation of conventional "realism" he had said: " 'Reality ought to be represented as it is,' they say, whereas there is no such reality, never has been, because the substance of things is inaccessible to man" (*Diary of a Writer,* 1873, "Apropos of an Exhibition," 1:83). Dostoevsky was convinced that the intuition of a great artist could see things that were inaccessible to ordinary empirical observation. He also believed that there were secrets known only to the saint and the criminal.[135] *The Brothers Karamazov* is meant to be a novel about "real life." That a vision of "real life" should be broken through the prism of the saintly elder and the demonic Karamazovs is for Dostoevsky merely sound realistic procedure.[136]

6.b. PSYCHOLOGICAL MOTIVATION IN *THE BROTHERS KARAMAZOV*

Psychological motivation is not as uniformly strong in *The Brothers Karamazov* as it is in other novels by Dostoevsky, but the actions of the main characters, excepting only Father Zosima, are generally well motivated. Sometimes the mental processes involved are reconstructed by the worldly-wise narrator (for example, Aliosha's decision to become a monk or Fiodor Pavlovich's decision to make a scandal at the Father Superior's). More often these mental processes are revealed directly, as Dostoevsky switches to an omniscient narrator (see III.1.a. The Narrator). Sometimes they are left for the reader to

134. Certainly this is Dostoevsky's own opinion. See, for instance, his letter to E. A. Stakenschneider, dated 15 June 1879, *Pis'ma* 4:62–63.

135. See Rozanov, *Dostoevsky,* pp. 72–74.

136. See Linnér, p. 9.

reconstruct; this is true of the female characters and of Smerdiakov in particular. Father Zosima's mind remains closed to us—but his words and actions are not understood as being psychologically motivated in the conventional sense, for Father Zosima possesses the unrestrained freedom of a man who has overcome the concerns of this world. There is often little or no psychological motivation in the episodes which do not belong to the main body of the narrative.

Psychological motivation is often surprising and even paradoxic, if measured by ordinary standards, but it is careful, serious, and ultimately convincing. Katerina Ivanovna's reaction to Dmitry's betrayals, Dmitry's refusal to be jealous of Musiałowicz, Snegiriov's behavior when offered a gift of two hundred roubles, and many other developments seem unexpected at first sight, but are soon made plausible enough.

In Dostoevsky's psychology, the coexistence of contradictory character traits and conflicting emotions *(coincidentio oppositorum)* is taken for granted and invariably presented without apology or explanation. The consciousness of Dostoevskian characters is often presented in terms of conflicting inner voices.

The principal trait of Dostoevsky's psychology is the realization inherent in it that any judgment based on psychological analysis is necessarily ambiguous. The duel of those two shrewd psychologists, the public prosecutor and the defense counsel, produces a great deal of plausible psychology, but little truth. And thus, the narrator's own psychological statements tend to be equivocal, like the one found at the end of the first chapter of Book One: unable to make up his mind whether Fiodor Pavlovich was really glad to be rid of his wife and putting on an act of lachrymose grief, or whether his grief was sincere, the narrator decides that there was a bit of both in it (Book One, chap. i, p. 4).

6.c. PSYCHOANALYTIC INTERPRETATION OF
THE BROTHERS KARAMAZOV

The Brothers Karamazov has been the subject of a great deal of psychoanalytic interpretation. Freud's famous essay

"Dostoevsky and Parricide" may well be mistaken in its assumptions about Dostoevsky's personal biography, yet it is valuable in suggesting an extra dimension in this novel. More recently, Slochower (p. 268) has proposed a Freudian interpretation of Dmitry's relationship with Ekaterina Ivanovna, according to which the latter is a latent incest-figure, substituted by Dmitry for his mother. Some further points will be brought up in the Commentary.

6.d. DOSTOEVSKY'S PSYCHOLOGICAL WISDOM IN *THE BROTHERS KARAMAZOV*

As in his other novels, Dostoevsky introduces a good deal of psychological wisdom not directly relevant to the central issues of the novel.

Bitsilli points out the "role-playing" which dominates the actions of many of the characters. Fiodor Pavlovich has created an image of himself as a buffoon; Ekaterina Ivanovna, as a martyr to virtue; Dmitry sees himself as an "insect" which pursues "sensual lust" (Book Three, chap. iii, p. 96). Ivan has created his Grand Inquisitor, Rakitin has his future projected by Ivan, and so on.[137] The point is that virtually everybody plays his role badly, failing to live up to his, and the world's, image of himself, and as a result must sooner or later face a crisis in his life.

Such crisis may lead to a "rupture" *(nadryv)*. Book Four, entitled "Ruptures,"[138] introduces several victims of this condition: Liza Khokhlakov, Katerina Ivanovna, Ivan Karamazov, and Captain Snegiriov. The Russian term is a noun derived from the verb *nadryvat'*, "to rupture, to strain (as by lifting too heavy a load)."[139] The psychology of the emotional or mental rupture had interested Dostoevsky for a long time, at

---

137. P. M. Bitsilli, "K voprosu o vnutrennei forme romana Dostoevskogo," in *O Dostoevskom: Stat'i,* Brown University Slavic Reprint, 4 (Providence, 1966), pp. 28–29.

138. In the Garnett-Matlaw text *nadryv* is translated by "laceration."

139. See Swetlana Geier, "Nadryv ili granitsy perevodimosti," *The Third International Dostoevsky Symposium, August 14–20, 1977: Résumés* (Klagenfurt, Austria, 1977), pp. 15–16.

least since the early story "A Faint Heart" (1848). A special case of such a rupture is introduced in the figure of the "wailer," the mother of Ivan and Aliosha.

Dostoevsky's psychological mastery is very largely a function of his stylistic craftsmanship. Some characteristics of Dostoevsky's psychological style are the psychological paradox (see 6.b. Psychological Motivation, above), psychological catachresis (giving a psychological phenomenon a "wrong" term on purpose; see, for example, Book One, note 89), hypostatization of mental states as physical reality (see, for example, Book Five, note 338), insinuation of subconscious implications (by leaving actions and emotions unexplained), and a scattershot method of characterization, where a whole group of more or less synonymous terms will be introduced, each illuminating the phenomenon in question from a slightly different angle (see, for example, Book One, note 103).

III
ℕarrative Technique

The Brothers Karamazov is a dramatic novel, L. P. Grossman has called it a "mystère" or "morality play."[1] The actual plot of the novel presents only the culmination or dénouement of the story: everything else is brought in flashbacks, ingeniously integrated into the main plot.[2] Dostoevsky takes advantage of dramatic license throughout. More action, or conversation, is compressed into short spans of time than is physically possible. The very first day, covered by Books Two and Three, is crammed with more events than could possibly occur between 11:00 A.M. and 9:00 P.M. of any day in real life. All the conversations at the monastery could not have taken place within the hour and a half allotted to them. Likewise, space is turned into a stage, where characters who have to meet just happen to cross each other's paths. Both space and time are treated symbolically (see 5.c. Symbolic Images, below). Dialogue plays a dominant role (as in other novels by Dostoevsky), and the dialogue passages abound in "stage directions" concerning gestures, mimicry, tone of voice, and so on.[3] A distinctive trait is

1. Leonid Grossman, *Put' Dostoevskogo* (Leningrad, 1924), p. 10.
2. D. S. Likhachov, " 'Predislovnyi rasskaz' Dostoevskogo," in *Poetika i stilistika russkoi literatury: Pamiati akademika Viktora Vladimirovicha Vinogradova* (Leningrad, 1971), pp. 190–91. The term *predislovnyi rasskaz,* "introductory story," is taken from the text of *The Brothers Karamazov,* Book One, chap. iii, p. 12 (*PSS* 14:17), where "introduction" translates *predislovnyi rasskaz.*
3. Bitsilli, "K voprosu," p. 11.

the omission of the *verbum dicendi* and its replacement by a
piece of "stage direction."[4]

The drama in *The Brothers Karamazov* features a great deal
of Sophoclean irony: situations where the *dramatis personae* do
not know what the narrator and his reader know. There is a
great deal of "inner dialogue" running parallel to the regular,
audible dialogue, particularly in the case of self-conscious
characters such as Miusov or Kolia Krasotkin. Obviously, this is
a refined equivalent of the dramatic "aside." A very important
detail is the consistent attention which Dostoevsky pays to the
hands of certain characters, whose hands are often as eloquent
as their voices; there are Dmitry's "terrible hands," for example
(see Book Eight, note 193).

The Brothers Karamazov has been called a Christian tragedy.
But as in other novels by Dostoevsky, the element of comedy is
quite strong. Often, perhaps always, important philosophical
and moral issues are presented in a serious and in a comic
version. Fiodor Pavlovich's buffoonery anticipates many of the
points which his son Ivan will raise seriously later, and to which
Father Zosima will respond.

1. The Polyphonic Composition of
The Brothers Karamazov

The Brothers Karamazov shows the world on several levels, or
from several viewpoints, in a style we might call "polyphonic."[5]
Viacheslav Ivanov distinguishes the level of plot, the
psychological, and the metaphysical; Gessen splits the last of
these into the "metaphysical" and the "mystical." Belknap very
aptly says that "it is as if God and Christ and the Devil could
only be approached through a hierarchy of narrators."[6]

4. Ibid., pp. 49–50.

5. The term *polyphony* was first applied to Dostoevsky's narrative style by
M. M. Bakhtin, *Problems of Dostoevsky's Poetics*, tr. R. W. Rotsel (Ann Arbor, 1973). Gibson has found a religious justification for Dostoevsky's
polyphony: the Christian novelist's refusal to "play God" in the world of his
novel, choosing instead to assume the various selves of his characters, is
analogous to Christ's *kenosis* (Gibson, *The Religion of Dostoevsky*, p. 68).

6. Ivanov, *Freedom and the Tragic Life*, pp. 16–17; Gessen, "Tragediia dobra
v Brat'iakh Karamazovykh," pp. 199–200; Belknap, *The Structure of "The
Brothers Karamazov,"* p. 105.

A case can be made for a hierarchy of authority enjoyed by the various voices in the novel. Father Zosima's voice has absolute authority. It is never challenged by the narrator's irony, although it is, of course, involved in a counterpoint with many of the other voices in the novel, not the least of these being that of Fiodor Pavlovich Karamazov. The authority of Aliosha's voice is derived from the elder's, whose voice we often hear through Aliosha's words. The authority—and simple trust-worthiness—of all the other voices in the novel is controlled by various degrees of irony, which makes them ring more or less dissonant, unserious, or simply untrue. Ivan's voice is the principal case in point (see 1.b. Ivan Karamazov, below).

It is obvious that the reader's feeling will have a part in establishing the hierarchy of "voices," all of which together will make up his impression of the novel. Thus, Dolinin, a Marxist critic, likens Dostoevsky's technique in *The Brothers Karamazov* to Liamshin's piece in *The Possessed* (a musical "battle" between the exalted and powerful strains of the "Marseillaise" and a trivial little German waltz, "Ach, du mein lieber Augustin," won by the latter). But of course Dolinin sees the religious motif in the role of the little waltz, while Ivan Karamazov's rebellion corresponds to the "Marseillaise."[7]

The full impact of *The Brothers Karamazov* is achieved only if the text is realized in terms of audible, individualized "voices." (Dostoevsky was himself a magnificent reader of his own work and always held his audiences spellbound.) Each major character has his own voice.[8] In almost every instance this voice is introduced in stages and carefully prepared for his, or her, great scene(s). There are also great duos—such as the clashes between Katerina Ivanovna and Grushen'ka, or Ivan's three interviews with Smerdiakov—and so-called "conclaves" (first used as a literary term by L. P. Grossman), where many characters meet to resolve issues in a kind of "verbal tour-

7. Dolinin, "K istorii sozdaniia *Brat'ev Karamazovykh*," p. 74.

8. Each of my characters speaks his own language and in his own concepts," Dostoevsky says in a letter to A. N. Pleshcheev, 20 August 1872, *Pis'ma* 3:197.

nament" (also Grossman's term).[9] The meeting at the elder's cell in Book Two is a famous example of a conclave.

Dostoevsky stations a considerable number of normal and neutral characters (and their voices) along the edges of his narrative, as points of reference and as reminders that the world of *The Brothers Karamazov* is a model of contemporary Russian reality.[10]

1.a. THE NARRATOR

The polyphony of *The Brothers Karamazov* extends to the narrative voice. Dostoevsky chose a personalized narrative voice. The narrator's manner is that of a "conversation with the reader," and his vocabulary and syntax tend to be those of an improvised oral narrative: sentences and paragraphs are not well-constructed and well-balanced, but appear as " 'chains of sentences' in which thoughts are grasped, as it were, step-by-step, supplemented, and elaborated both in their content and in their verbal expression—as though the author were gradually, and in the course of writing these words, groping his way toward a definitive formulation of his ideas." From the reader's standpoint, this means slower, more difficult reading, but also a greater chance for identification with the narrator's point of view.[11]

There are really two narrators: there is the "personalized" first-person narrator, an anonymous local resident, about whose private views and sympathies we learn a great deal in the course of the novel, and an omniscient "implied narrator" who could be Dostoevsky himself.[12] The local resident is a realist and a skeptic, while his double is an idealist and a believer. The local resident has a penchant for psychological analysis (although he ridicules the same trait in Ippolit Kirillovich, the public

9. Leonid Grossman, "Dostoevskii-Khudozhnik," in *Tvorchestvo Dostoevskogo* (Moscow, 1959), p. 356.

10. Gibson, p. 117.

11. Braun, *Dostojewski,* pp. 271, 272–73.

12. Ibid., p. 270; Matlaw, *"The Brothers Karamazov,"* pp. 40–41; Zundelovich, *Romany Dostoevskogo,* p. 219.

prosecutor), while his *alter ego,* on a deeper level, shows his scorn for psychology. At times the two narrators clash visibly, as for instance when the local resident reports that the presiding judge took a rather indifferent and detached attitude toward the personal character of the case, toward the tragedy of it, which, however, "was perhaps fitting, indeed" (Book Twelve, chap. i. p. 626). Certainly this was not Dostoevsky's idea of justice.[13] The local resident relates background information, provides some foreshadowing by anticipating events, and generally takes care of the material and social setting, while the other narrator moves in and out of the consciousness of different characters.[14] All critics are agreed that Dostoevsky has succeeded in welding his two narrators together very well indeed. The beginning of the novel creates the impression that perhaps Aliosha has told the whole story to the local resident, who has then added some circumstantial detail on his own part.[15] Thus, we get accustomed to the latter's knowing a great deal more than he ought to as a mere local resident. Zundelovich suggests that it is the constant interplay between the different levels of the narrative that camouflages the contradictions between Dostoevsky's two narrators (p. 190). Braun sees a genuine polyphonic effect in the tension between "narrated story" and "ideological action" (p. 268). Then, too, the local resident could very well be Dostoevsky himself, a moderate liberal with humane ideas on social questions and in many ways a sensible man and a realist, but an idealist and almost a fanatic when it came to a discussion of the whole complex of his religious ideas.

A special polyphonic effect is obtained through the tension between chapter headings and the content of a chapter. The effect may be one of mystification (for instance, Book Nine, chap. viii, "The Babe"), ironic contrast between heading and content (for instance, Book Nine, chap. i, "The Beginning of Perkhotin's Official Career"), explanatory commentary (Book

13. Zundelovich, p. 230.
14. For details see Belknap, *Structure,* pp. 82–85.
15. For example, having reported some of Aliosha's naïve utopian dreams, the narrator adds: "That was the dream in Aliosha's heart" (Book One, chap. v, p. 24). This suggests that he heard about these dreams from Aliosha.

Ten, chap. vi, "Precocity"), or ironic commentary (Book Twelve, chap. ix, "Psychology at Full Steam"). Sometimes the chapter heading will establish a leitmotif—for example, Book Five, chap. vii, "It's Always Worthwhile Speaking to a Clever Man."

The stylistic, lexical, and syntactic peculiarities of the narrator's language can be given a common denominator: they are all characteristics of language as a process, rather than as a finished product (*parole* as against *langue*). In fact, many of these traits help give the narrative a quality of what Bakhtin calls "inner dialogue" or "inner polyphony." They are *repetition* (the same word used twice in the same sentence, sometimes for emphasis, sometimes casually), *pleonastic* diction, *hyperbole, slang* expressions, *catachresis* (using what is obviously the wrong word in the context),[16] *awkward* and *prolix* syntax, and the accumulation of *modal* expressions (such as "actually," "even," "seemingly," etc.). A most characteristic stylistic trait is hedging (Russ. *ogovorka*): the narrator will make a statement, then qualify or even withdraw it.[17] Another significant trait is the use of certain key words, some with astounding frequency. The most obvious is the adverb *vdrug* "suddenly," which plays a similar role in *Crime and Punishment.*[18] As Volynsky suggested, it signals the dynamic and altogether indeterminate quality of life in *The Brothers Karamazov,* where the unexpected is the rule, where free human beings "suddenly" make their own decisions.[19] Other such key words are *dazhe,* "even, actually,"

16. Re pleonasm, see Bitsilli, "K voprosu," p. 42. Re catachresis, see D. S. Likhachov, " 'Nebrezhenie slovom' u Dostoevskogo," in *Dostoevskii: Materialy i issledovaniia* (Leningrad, 1976), 2:30–41.

17. Bitsilli sees this trait as a "device to express . . . an awareness of the impossibility to find an exhausting formula for the expression of the entire complexity and contradictoriness of a given situation, but in particular of human nature" (Bitsilli, "K voprosu," p. 7).

18. See V. N. Toporov, "O strukture romana Dostoevskogo v sviazi s arkhaichnymi skhemami mifologicheskogo myshleniia: *Prestuplenie i nakazanie,*" in *Structure of Texts and Semiotics of Culture,* ed. Jan van der Eng and Mojmír Grygar (The Hague and Paris, 1973), pp. 266–71. Cf. Bitsilli, "K voprosu," pp. 9–10; Linnér, *Starets Zosima,* p. 33.

19. Volynskii, *Tsarstvo Karamazovykh,* p. 172.

which, like *vdrug,* carries a connotation of surprise or wonder; *slishkom,* "too (much), exceedingly," indicating emphasis and personal involvement; *pochti,* "almost," suggesting some insecurity or hedging; *kak by,* "as though, as if," likewise indicating a certain diffidence. The extraordinarily frequent use of the indefinite pronoun *kakoi-to,* "some, some kind of, a certain," likewise suggests a certain diffidence.

Another stylistic trait characteristic of *The Brother Karamazov* is the ample use of what the Germans call *erlebte Rede* ("reflected speech"): words, thoughts, and feelings of a personage in the novel, broken through the prism of the narrator's consciousness. It allows the author to inject a subjective evaluation of a character's words or feelings into what appears to be an objective account. Examples will be pointed out in the Commentary.

1.b. IVAN KARAMAZOV

Ivan Karamazov's voice is, next to the narrator's and Zosima's, the most interesting and the most often heard in the novel. The narrator, incidentally, is hostile to Ivan, sometimes in a subtle way and sometimes openly. Several of the characters in the novel also state their dislike for Ivan (Fiodor Pavlovich, Book Four, chap. ii, p. 159; Liza, Book Five, chap. i, p. 202; Smerdiakov, Book Five, chap. ii, p. 207). Father Zosima's words must be seen in direct opposition to Ivan's, as must his whole tone.

Ivan has many voices, none of which is his own, except perhaps for a few brief moments when Aliosha's soothing presence puts him on the right track.[20] We first meet Ivan as the author of an article on ecclesiastic jurisdiction, whose content he summarizes during the meeting at the elder's cell. Here Ivan seems to be articulate in a serious, sincere, and modest way. But the perceptive reader will hear, even here, some false notes, and Father Zosima certainly does. From here on, everything that Ivan says and does will be disrupted, time and again, by shrill

20. Note the passage in which Ivan says that he might, perhaps, like to heal himself through Aliosha (Book Five, chap. iii, p. 217).

dissonances which clash with his general composure and controlled eloquence. On a physical level, we see outbursts of unmotivated violence (Maksimov is his first victim, Book Two, chap. viii, p. 81), and on the verbal, sudden flareups of spite and sarcasm.[21]

Ivan is constantly telling lies, and mostly to himself. His interview with Katerina Ivanovna bodes ill for both, as both are lying, to each other and to themselves (Book Four, chap. v, pp. 172–76). Ivan lies to his father and to Smerdiakov. (There is one moment when he suddenly realizes what an abject role he has been playing at home. Upon arriving in Moscow he whispers to himself: "I am a scoundrel!" [Book Five, chap. vii, p. 260]). After the murder, Ivan's lying to others and to himself becomes criminal. Smerdiakov had told Ivan about his plan to fake an epileptic fit, and Ivan withholds this information from the police (Book Eleven, chap. vii, p. 581). In trying to avoid facing his responsibility for the murder, Ivan goes through a series of mental contortions, lying to the authorities, to Katerina Ivanovna, to Smerdiakov, and to himself. When he finally has to face up to the truth, it is too late: his appearance in court is another lie, involuntary this time.

In the meantime, other versions of Ivan's voice are heard in his "rebellion" against God's world and in his utopian poem "The Grand Inquisitor." Later, still another voice is heard in Ivan's interview with the devil. The voice in "Rebellion" is that of an angry young man who has discovered that there is cruelty, injustice, and suffering in this world. It is the voice of radical Russian journalism in the 1860s and 1870s. Its pathos seems sincere, but there are telltale signs that Ivan does not really care about the children whose sufferings he describes so eloquently. In "The Grand Inquisitor" we hear three voices: the Grand Inquisitor's (a projection of Ivan's ambitious dreams); Ivan's ordinary voice, as he comments upon his "poem"; and Aliosha's voice, which acts as a backdrop and puts things in

21. " 'Am I my brother Dmitry's keeper?' Ivan snapped irritably, but then he suddenly smiled bitterly. 'Cain's answer to God, about his murdered brother, wasn't it?' " (Book Five, chap. iii, p. 213).

perspective. Rozanov has suggested that the images and voices "of the Grand Inquisitor, of the student, of the author himself, and of the Tempting Spirit who stands behind them all" are all fused in the Legend.[22] Anyway, the reader is reminded all along that the Grand Inquisitor's voice is a projection of Ivan's self. That it is also an exercise in self-delusion is suggested by the masquerade and melodrama found in it: a twenty-three-year-old Russian student lets a ninety-year-old Spanish cardinal—"tall and erect" and "fiery-eyed"—express his innermost thoughts.

The ambitious notion that "The Grand Inquisitor" is a "poem"—that is, an inspired product of the imagination—is properly undercut by Ivan himself, as he goes on to call the piece "only a senseless poem of a senseless student, who could never write two lines of verse" (Book Five, chap. v, p. 243). The point, missed by many critics, is that "The Grand Inquisitor" is not a good poem, and when everything is said and done, not very good rhetoric either. The only "poetic" thing about the Legend is the figure of Christ. Dostoevsky makes Ivan stay close to the Gospel and will not allow him to let Christ talk. Aliosha properly observes that his brother's poem praises Christ, rather than blaspheming Him. What detracts from the Legend as a poem is the Grand Inquisitor's voice, which, once the initial melodramatic effect has worn off, begins to falter,[23] is full of "false notes" (which have a ring of the "senseless student"), and generally strikes a tone which is shrill and spiteful, rather than poetic or tragic. Such, of course, was Dostoevsky's intent: the Legend prepares for the eventual destruction of Ivan's humanist atheism, which is to be completed in his interview with the devil. "The Grand Inquisitor" (Dostoevsky's, not Ivan's) is a masterpiece of ambiguity, rich in deep ironies. Time and again Ivan becomes the butt of his own sarcasms. For instance, Rozanov (p. 125) notes the Grand Inquisitor's deadly irony as he recalls Christ's promise, "I will make you free," then adds: "But now Thou hast seen these 'free' men" (Book Five, chap. v,

22. Rozanov, *Dostoevsky and the Legend of the Grand Inquisitor,* p. 200.
23. Rozanov points out one instance in which the Inquisitor concedes that Christ is right: men will abandon even their bread to follow him who has ensnared their conscience (Book Five, chap. v, p. 235). See Rozanov, p. 144.

p. 232). Ivan does not realize that there is one more level to his irony: *he* himself, in his arrogant pride, is the least free of any of the characters who populate the world of *The Brothers Karamazov*.

In his interview with the devil Ivan meets "all his stupid ideas—outgrown, thrashed out long ago, and flung aside like a dead carcass" (Book Eleven, chap. ix, p. 615). Every word the devil says is very much a part of Ivan's own mind, and so the interview with the devil is an "inner dialogue" of Ivan's, much as "The Grand Inquisitor." Only this time Ivan's better self recognizes the true nature of his other self: "You are a lie, you are my illness, you are a phantom" (Book Eleven, chap. ix, p. 604). Ivan's last half-lucid moments with Aliosha give hope that after recovering from his illness, Ivan will finally learn to speak the truth in a voice of his own.

1.c. DMITRY KARAMAZOV

Dmitry Karamazov, unlike his brother Ivan, has a voice that is all his own. Yet his voice, too, is heard in different modes and tonalities.[24] He is the wild young officer, swaggering and brainless, but he is also a man of deep sensitivity and original sensibility, and in the end he is the martyr who through suffering finds God.

Dmitry is a man of the senses and of immediate verbal expression. If Ivan's verbal talent is rhetorical, Dmitry's is poetic. As Volynsky puts it, "His language is full of metaphors, for even the ideal aspect of every object appears to him not in metaphysical abstraction but very much fused with the phenomena of life, in distinct though fantastic images" (p. 62).

Dmitry reacts even to moral phenomena in terms of sense impressions.[25] He can express his emotions in wonderfully

24. "It is typical of Dostoyevsky's methods of characterization in their rich complexity that Dmitry, a figure of immense seriousness with elemental allegorical and symbolical implications, is also treated as a figure of fun" (Hingley, *The Undiscovered Dostoyevsky*, pp. 207–8).

25. "You see, gentlemen, I couldn't bear the look of him, there was something in him ignoble, impudent, trampling on everything sacred, something sneering and irreverent, loathsome, loathsome. But now that he's dead, I feel differently" (Book Nine, chap. iii, p. 436).

precise and pregnant images, such as when he describes his feelings at Katerina Ivanovna's visit to his quarters (Book Three, chap. iv, p. 102). Schiller's verses which Dmitry loves to quote ring true against the backdrop of his own voice.

Quite unlike the humorless, sarcastic Ivan, Dmitry has a sense of humor and can be genuinely funny, such as when he depicts his moral fall and himself singing his hymn falling "headlong with my heels up" (Book Three, chap. iii, p. 96).

Psychologically, Dmitry keeps surprising us, as we keep discovering more new sides of his personality. Stylistically, he keeps surprising us with felicitous expressions of things perceived by his intuition.

1.d. Aliosha as an Echo of Father Zosima

Braun overstates his case somewhat when he calls Aliosha "a mere observer who is only partly involved in the events" and likens his role to that of the narrator in *The Possessed* (p. 236). The difference lies in the fact that Aliosha has his own voice.

Father Zosima's vita and wisdom are presented as a manuscript of Aleksei Karamazov's—hence their different organization.[26] Here, but also elsewhere in the novel, Aliosha's voice is an echo of Father Zosima's authoritative voice, gaining its strength from it. Dostoevsky took the greatest care to give Father Zosima an authentic voice, even at the risk of weakening the impact of his doctrine. If Father Zosima's speech would appear somewhat quaint and remote even to a Russian intellectual of the 1870s, this could not be otherwise if the saintly elder was to be a real person with a living voice. (For details see 2.b. The Religious Content as "Subtext," below.)

Bitsilli has suggested that, since overcoming the separateness of one's "I" is the key issue in developing an ideal Christian, positive characters such as Aliosha are necessarily colorless, pale, and impersonal (p. 40). This is not borne out by the text. The peculiarity of Aliosha's voice is defined early in the novel when the narrator characterizes him as a "realist" (Book One,

---

26. Dostoevsky asked his editor to retain the peculiar structure of this part of Book Six, since "this manuscript was broken down by Aleksei Karamazov after his own fashion" (letter to Liubimov, 7/19 August 1879, *Pis'ma* 4:92).

chap. v, p. 19). Whatever Aliosha says is straightforward and to the point, and hits the very essence of things. Ivan constructs himself a truth which soon turns into a lie. Dmitry grasps the truth metaphorically, in images. Aliosha grasps it directly, which is why he always gets the better of his father and his brothers alike. When Fiodor Pavlovich spins his sly and rather ingenious argument to reassure himself that there is no hell, Aliosha refutes it with a single brief sentence which hits the very heart of the matter: there *is* a hell, even though not of the kind Fiodor Pavlovich had been talking about (Book One, chap. iv, p. 18). Likewise, when Ivan reads his "Grand Inquisitor," Aliosha's few simple words tear through the web of Ivan's self-deception (e.g., Book Five, chap. v, p. 242).

Aliosha, like his teacher Father Zosima, has a faculty for bringing out the true self in the people he meets. He does so through the power of his own truthful words—with Liza Khokhlakov, with the Snegiriovs, with Kolia.

1.e. FIODOR PAVLOVICH

Fiodor Pavlovich's voice is dominated by his buffoonery and role-playing. He will make a travesty of whatever he touches. But Fiodor Pavlovich's voice in a way subsumes the voices of his three sons. He has Dmitry's playful fantasy and Ivan's dialectic skill, and there is some truth to it when he calls himself a "God's fool":[27] like a God's fool, and like his son Aliosha, he can see through people. His truth is that of the jester: it shows people naked, at their lowest, animal level. Paradoxically, Fiodor Pavlovich, a compulsive liar, somehow winds up telling the truth—in a perverse and grotesque way, but the truth.

1.f. OTHER VOICES

There are many other characters in the novel who have their recognizable individual voice: Miusov, Mme. Khokhlakov and

27. *Ia shut korennoi, s rozhdeniia, vsio ravno, vashe prepodobie, chto iurodivyi* (*PSS* 14:39), which Garnett-Matlaw translates as "I am an inveterate buffoon, and have been from my birth up, your reverence, it's as though it were a madness in me" (Book Two, chap. ii, p. 34). Here, as elsewhere, *iurodivyi* has the connotation of "God's fool." It is the word applied to Elizaveta Smerdiashchaia and to Aliosha.

her daughter Liza, Rakitin, Katerina Ivanovna and Grushen'ka, Smerdiakov, Captain Snegiriov, and quite a few others. The peculiarities of their voices are pointed out in the Commentary.

All these many voices interact in a variety of ways. They quote each other (for instance, Rakitin quotes Ivan Karamazov's projection of his, Rakitin's, future career [Book Two, chap. vii, p. 73]); they paraphrase each other's words (for instance, Dmitry reports on Rakitin's "lessons" to him in Book Eleven, chap. iv pp. 558–562); they echo each other's key words (for instance, when Aliosha says "I am not rebelling against my God, I simply 'don't accept His world' " [Book Seven, chap. ii, p. 319], he is echoing Ivan's words of Book Five, chap. iv, p. 226). They discuss the same things, sometimes making a parody of the original argument (Kolia Krasotkin, as a thirteen-year-old Ivan Karamazov, for instance). They report their own versions of the same incident: the beard-pulling scene, for instance, is reported by Fiodor Pavlovich, by Ekaterina Ivanovna, and by the two principals, Dmitry Karamazov and Captain Snegiriov.[28] They express what is their particular version of an idea voiced elsewhere by another character: Miusov, for example, anticipates some ideas of Ivan Karamazov's. And, of course, they respond to one another directly, with irony, mockery, invective, tenderness, respect, and reverence—the whole gamut of emotions that can be expressed in words. Needless to say, Dostoevsky uses some poetic license in that he makes very many of his characters exceptionally articulate.

2. Subtexts

2.a. The Reader's Role in Developing Subtexts: Some Specific Examples

Depending upon the reader, *The Brothers Karamazov* will have more or less of a "subtext" of some kind—a meaning that is not explicitly stated in the text. A great deal depends on the reader's external frame of reference. A well-informed contemporary reader would have read between the lines countless

28. See Belknap, *Structure,* pp. 98–99.

allusions to the contemporary scene, as well as a fairly consistent sociopolitical and ideological message. He would have recognized in the characters and voices of *The Brothers Karamazov* Dostoevsky's attitude toward their equivalents in Russian life. In fact, such a reader would have recognized in the negative images of Rakitin or Miusov, as well as in the positive images of Father Zosima and Aliosha Karamazov, stock characters of the Katkov school.

Of the greatest importance is the reader's attitude toward religion. A reader whose external frame of reference includes a belief in the basic dogmas of Christianity—or perhaps in some other religion which accepts the notions of a transcendental God, immortality of the soul, and human free will—will read the novel quite differently from a reader who lacks these beliefs. Dostoevsky projects this circumstance into the text of the novel, as the atheist Rakitin takes an altogether different view of the drama which unfolds before him from that of the believer Aliosha Karamazov. As Rozanov has pointed out, the real test of one's accepting Christianity is in one's attitude toward monkdom.[29] Monkdom makes sense only if one believes in the spiritual message of the Gospel. Dostoevsky chose to base the positive message of his novel on Book Six, entitled "A Russian Monk," a fact that speaks for itself.

A peculiar subtext which a perceptive reader will be able to pursue throughout the novel is a pattern of the workings of the devil, a pattern which is apparent particularly in those parts of the narrative dealing with Fiodor Pavlovich, Ivan Karamazov, and Smerdiakov. In many instances the devil's invisible presence would seem to account for their words and actions. The devil's personal appearance in Book Eleven, chapter ix, is well-prepared-for and not entirely unexpected. But the devil is present elsewhere, too, even at the monastery, where Father Ferapont and the little monk from Obdorsk are clearly in his clutches and where he triumphs, in the chapter "The Odor of Corruption" (Book Seven, chap. i). The devil is a visitor at the Khokhlakov residence also.

---

29. V. V. Rozanov, *Liudi lunnogo sveta: metafizika khristianstva,* Analecta slavica, 12 (Würzburg, 1977), pp. 100–2 et passim.

Other subtexts depend on the readers's perceptiveness. A recurring pattern developed in a number of versions throughout the novel is the encounter of the wise man and the fool, in which the fool triumphs. The theme is stated explicitly early in the novel, when Aliosha, "the foolish novice," is contrasted to Ivan, the "learned atheist" (Book One, chap. v, p. 25). But the many variations on this theme, culminating in the brilliant Fetiukovich's loss of his case before a jury of peasants, are not identified as parts of a pattern. It is up to the reader to recognize the pattern.

A pattern which an attentive reader may discern in *The Brothers Karamazov* is one which M. M. Bakhtin has labeled the "carnival" side of the Dostoevskian novel. Some of the important positions of the novel have a comic or grotesque mirror image. For example, Fiodor Pavlovich suggests that there ought to be a hell, for "if they won't drag me down what justice is there in the world?" (Book One, chap. iv, p. 19). This is the other side of the theodicy argument raised in Book Five. Mrs. Khokhlakov shows Aliosha a newspaper clipping which presents the whole Karamazov case in "travesty," as it were (Book Eleven, chap. ii, p. 542). While it is a grotesque example of yellow journalism, this account is also undoubtedly true from a certain point of view.

2.b. THE RELIGIOUS CONTENT AS SUBTEXT

The most important subtext in *The Brothers Karamazov* is its implied religious content. The narrator announces at the very outset that his hero's feats will be of a moral and religious nature: Aliosha will carry the message of his revered elder Zosima into the world. Hence, as Vetlovskaia and Perlina have suggested, a traditional saint's life, showing the religious hero fulfilling his predestined mission, may be recognized as a subtext of *The Brothers Karamazov*.[30] Details of the text remind the reader who is familiar with the genre of the saint's life that Aliosha Karamazov, while a normal and healthy young man, is

30. Perlina, "Quotation as an Element of the Poetics of *The Brothers Karamazov*," pp. 89-93. V. E. Vetlovskaia's articles, cited earlier, develop this conception in considerable detail.

also a worthy successor to his sainted teacher. In particular, his identification with Aleksei, man of God, one of the most popular saints of the Russian people, creates a powerful undercurrent of religious-symbolic associations.

"A Russian Monk," quite explicitly a saint's life, or as Rosen puts it, "not a reliable factual biography, but a sort of dramatized sermon,"[31] is thus an emblem of the whole novel. This fact is borne out by the many mirror images and echoes which connect the life and wisdom of Father Zosima with the story of the Karamazov family.

Dostoevsky was well aware that the whole content and presentation of Book Six clashed with the rest of the novel. But he felt that Father Zosima's wisdom had to be presented "as belonging to his person, that is, an artistic representation of his person" (letter to Liubimov, dated 7/19 August 1879, *Pis'ma* 4:91). The language of Russian Orthodox religious literature is traditionally distinct from the Russian vernacular and from the language of secular literature (it is in fact a different language, called Slavonic, or Church Slavonic). Father Zosima's wisdom is written in a somewhat archaic Russian with numerous Slavonicisms, and even his ordinary speech, while it is that of an educated Russian of his generation, is not free of Slavonicisms. The same is true of the speech of the other monks. Besides, the prose of Father Zosima's life and wisdom shows syntactic and stylistic traits which differ from the practices of ordinary literary Russian. Mochulsky suggests they are a reflection of the sentimental religious style of the eighteenth century, as exemplified by the writings of Saint Tikhon.[32] Some of these traits are "rhythmic prose," with repetition, parallelism, and frequent paronomasia; a word order that is partly colloquial (e.g., verb-noun instead of noun-verb) and partly archaic (e.g., noun-adjective instead of adjective-noun); sentences beginning with "and" (as in biblical style); and frequent use of the imperative.[33] The effect of such stylization will depend on how well attuned a reader is to religion. A believer will be deeply moved, for Father

31. Rosen, "Style and Structure in *The Brothers Karamazov*," p. 355.
32. Mochulsky, *Dostoevsky*, pp. 633–34.
33. Rosen, "Style and Structure," p. 359.

Zosima's wisdom is Russian Orthodox religious eloquence at its quintessential best.[34] Rosen suggests that Zosima's style is aimed at the reader's "unconscious memories of childhood" (p. 360). Linnér points out that the reader who is familiar with the Gospels will be constantly reminded of Christ and his words, so that the image and words of Zosima will become fused with the image and words of Jesus Christ (p. 53). But Dolinin says that "here the artist turns preacher and suffers a spectacular defeat . . . as he failed to create a majestic *image,* precisely because the principle of realism had been violated."[35] Dostoevsky had anticipated such reaction too: "Some of the monk's teachings are such that some people will scream that they are absurd, being too rapturous. Of course they are absurd in an everyday sense, but in a different, inner sense they are, so it seems, justified" (letter to K. P. Pobedonostsev, dated 24 August/13 September 1879, *Pis'ma* 4:109).

Cox and Sandoz have pointed out that "The Grand Inquisitor"—and therefore the novel as a whole—can be read in reference to the Book of Revelation. The Grand Inquisitor uses the language of the "false prophet" (Rev. 16:13, 19:20, 20:10).[36] Ivan, so it seems, knowingly identifies with the "false prophet," and so with the Antichrist. Thus, it is not too farfetched to read *The Brothers Karamazov* as a "political apocalypse," as Sandoz does.

3. Narrative Structure

The Brothers Karamazov, like many nineteenth-century novels, is composed of heterogeneous structural elements. There is an inserted novella (Father Zosima's vita), a number of stories and anecdotes told by the narrator and various personages

---

34. Volynskii, p. 196.

35. Dolinin, "K istorii sozdaniia *Brat'ev Karamazovykh,*" p. 78. Dolinin is alluding to Dostoevsky's letter to K. P. Pobedonostsev, dated 24 August/13 September 1879, in which he said that he wanted to create "a modest and majestic image" (*Pis'ma* 4:109).

36. See particularly Cox, "The Grand Inquisitor," pp. 194–95.

("The Onion," told by Grushen'ka, being the most famous),
Father Zosima's wisdom, "The Grand Inquisitor," the story of
little Iliusha and his schoolmates, several confessions, a
digression by the narrator on elderdom, several Platonic
dialogues, the full account of the trial, and so on. Still, it is safe
to assume that all of these elements have an essential function in
the novel. It is, for example, a serious mistake to isolate "The
Grand Inquisitor," or the story of little Iliusha, from the novel
as a whole.

It has been observed that in *The Brothers Karamazov* things
are not presented in their logical (or even in a strictly
chronological) sequence, but that often the effect comes first,
and the causes are unravelled later.[37] There are some chains of
action which follow a causal pattern, while others do not.[38]
Likhachov has observed that the introductory or background
stories belong to the latter type: there is no motivation, staccato
narrative, and no logic in these episodes—all of it enhanced by
stylistic paradoxes, ambiguity, and an acceptance of strange
developments at their face value.[39] The whole story of Adelaida
Ivanovna is a good example of this narrative element. Meanwhile, the main action has all the features of a well-constructed
drama.[40] The chain of events started by Dmitry's *hubris* (when
he tells Katerina Ivanovna's stepsister about his 4,500 roubles)
and leading to his eventual conviction is as logical and as well-
motivated psychologically as anything in nineteenth-century
fiction or drama. As far as the story is concerned, Dmitry is the
main hero and the pivotal figure of the novel.[41] This circumstance makes it clear that the story is not the novel.

All the main theses of the novel, as well as its central tragic
conflict, are introduced early in the novel and built up toward
their climaxes and/or dénouements dialectically: one spin of

37. Marcel Proust, *A la recherche du temps perdu,* vol. 3, ed. Pierre Clarac
and André Ferré (Paris, 1954), p. 378.
38. Belknap, *Structure,* pp. 71–76.
39. Likhachov, " 'Predislovnyi rasskaz' Dostoevskogo," p. 191.
40. Mochulsky, pp. 598–99.
41. Volynskii, p. 57; Mochulsky, p. 599; Braun, *Dostojewski,* p. 236.

fortune's wheel is followed by another spin in the opposite direction, and an argument pro is followed by an argument contra.[42]

Vetlovskaia develops the notion of a "regressive dénouement" in *The Brothers Karamazov*. One of the theses of the novel is a refutation of the theory that environmental factors determine human life. Dostoevsky takes his reader all the way along a story line according to which Dmitry must be the murderer, then forces him to retrace his steps to discover the true story.[43]

In addition to the great religious themes of the novel, several other themes have pattern-building force.[44] Such are "Karamazovism" *(karamazovshchina),* which Zundelovich defines as "abandon" *(bezuderzh,* p. 190), a faculty for going "all the way" in everything; disorder ("I want disorder," exclaims Liza at one point [Book Eleven, chap. iii, p. 549]); unbelief (ranging from Ivan's tortured doubts, through the complacent Rakitin and the smug Fetiukovich, to precocious Kolia);[45] rupture *(nadryv);*[46] *joie de vivre* (stated explicitly by Father Zosima and by all of the Karamazovs); and finally, resurrection, the theme that emerges triumphant at the end of the novel.

3.a. Motifs, Themes, and Variations; Leitmotifs

The narrative structure of *The Brothers Karamazov* is readily broken down into ministructures, or motifs, some of which are dynamic, in the sense that they directly advance the story (e.g., Katerina Ivanovna's visit to Dmitry Fiodorovich to get the 4,500 roubles needed to save her father), while others are static (e.g.,

42. Hingley, p. 210. For instance, the theme of the suffering of innocent children is stated explicitly as early as chapter iii of Book Two (pp. 40–41); the question of freedom and religion is raised explicitly in chapter v of Book One (p. 21); and the basic conflict of the novel is fully stated in chapter vi of Book Two (passim).

43. Vetlovskaia, "Razviazka v *Brat'iakh Karamazovykh,*" pp. 196–200.

44. For a detailed catalogue of themes in *The Brothers Karamazov,* see *PSS* 15:460.

45. Matlaw, *"The Brothers Karamazov,"* p. 25.

46. Belknap, *Structure,* pp. 22–53.

the narrator's discourse on elderdom in Book One). Danow has drawn attention to the inserted anecdote as a special feature of *The Brothers Karamazov:* though describing an event outside the temporal and spatial frame of the novel, it tends to have a discernible metaphoric or metonymic connection with the main plot line; for example, the story of the romantic suicide in the first chapter of Book One is introduced to help illuminate the story of Adelaida Ivanovna.[47]

It is a peculiarity of the narrative structure of *The Brothers Karamazov* that a given motif will appear in a number of variations, and that a given moral or psychological theme will be represented by a number of different motifs. For example, the story of Dmitry's first trip to Mokroe is alluded to frequently in the novel, but we learn the whole truth about it (namely, that it cost Dmitry 1,500 roubles, not "thousands," or three thousand) only in Book Nine; and of course the matter comes up again during the trial in Book Twelve. The two antithetic moral positions of the novel—"all things are lawful" and "everybody is responsible for everyone else"—are stated through specific motifs many times over (such as when Iliusha holds Aliosha responsible for Dmitry's insult to his father, or when Fiodor Pavlovich gets away with the most outrageous things simply because he takes care to avoid any unpleasant material consequences by staying within the law).

Dostoevsky uses a number of leitmotifs, some of which accompany a character through much of the novel, while others dominate a chapter or Book. "All things are lawful" is Ivan's leitmotif, even though the words are first spoken by Miusov. "It is always worthwhile speaking to a clever man" is the leitmotif of chapter vii of Book Five, but it is also a leitmotif shared by those three disciples of the devil Fiodor Pavlovich (see Book Three, chap. viii, p. 121), his son Ivan (Book Five, chap. v, p. 242), and Smerdiakov. The parable of the seed is the leitmotif of Father Zosima and of Aliosha. "Three thousand roubles" is a leitmotif of the mundane plot of the novel. The word "rupture" *(nadryv)* is the leitmotif of Book Four.

47. David K. Danow, "Structural Principles of *The Brothers Karamazov*" (Ph.D. diss., Brown University, 1977), pp. 22–112.

As a result of this technique, the various motifs of the novel are linked by a variety of syntagmatic as well as paradigmatic bonds, much as musical motifs are in a symphonic composition. Belknap cites one passage (Epilogue, chap. i, p. 717) that contains references to no fewer than fourteen different events (or motifs) in the novel (pp. 58–59). Matlaw points out how the many disparate elements of the novel are recapitulated during the trial (p. 43). Belknap also points out that there are actually as many as twelve different accounts of the murder in the novel (p. 100).

3.b. MIRRORING AND DOUBLING

A basic structural device in *The Brothers Karamazov* is "mirroring" (see 1.f. Other Voices, above). A mirror image explains and enhances its counterpart. Thus, the story of Father Zosima's youth is a mirror image of the Karamazov story: Markel is explicitly designated as a double of Aliosha's; Zosima in his youth had many of Dmitry's traits; the murderer tormented by his conscience has traits of Ivan Karamazov.[48]

The story of Iliusha and his friends is a mirror image of, as well as a response to, Ivan's "Rebellion" and "The Grand Inquisitor."[49] Kolia is a mirror image of Ivan: a professed atheist and socialist, he also expresses the Grand Inquisitor's ideas (which he gets from Rakitin, for the most part!) in theory as well as in practice. He has nothing against God, admitting that "He is needed . . . for the order of the universe" (Book Ten, chap. vi, p. 522), and he is a lover of humanity and of "the people," though he believes that they need to be manipulated for their own good (Book Ten, chap. iii, p. 499). In practice, Kolia's goose episode is a mirror image of Ivan and Smerdiakov.[50] And most of all, of course, Kolia manipulates little

48. See Martin Goldstein, "The Debate in *The Brothers Karamazov*," pp. 329–30.

49. Metropolitan Antony suggests that he had pointed this out as early as 1893 (Antonii, *Slovar' k tvoreniiam Dostoevskogo*, p. 132). Cf. Martin Goldstein, p. 332.

50. Matlaw, *"The Brothers Karamazov,"* p. 26.

Iliusha, particularly through the "miracle" of bringing the dog Zhuchka back to life (Book Ten, chap. v, pp. 513-14). On the other side, Iliusha's whole story, and particularly his edifying death, may be read as an answer to Ivan's arguments regarding the sufferings of innocent children. Note that the little boy in Ivan's "Rebellion" dies for having hurt a dog. Iliusha says: "It's because I killed Zhuchka, dad, that I am ill now. God is punishing me for it" (Book Ten, chap. iv, p. 506). The point is, of course, not that Iliusha deserves to die, but that the actual facts are more complex and deeper than Ivan had thought.

"The Grand Inquisitor" is mirrored not only in the novel as a whole, but in several separate passages throughout the novel. After some preliminary skirmishing by Fiodor Pavlovich (Book One, chap. iv, p. 18), the theme of "The Grand Inquisitor" is introduced quite explicitly in the discussion about church and state held at Father Zosima's cell (Book Two, chap. v, pp. 52-57). Some fifty pages later, Dmitry anticipates the Grand Inquisitor's argument regarding the moral inferiority of the human race and responds to it by saying that while man may be "vile and base, he is still a child of God, and can love Him, and feel joy" (Book Three, chap. iii, p. 96). Smerdiakov's harangue on divine justice, the power of faith, and other theological questions resumes the argument (Book Three, chap. vii, pp. 115-20). It is continued by Father Paisy (Book Four, chap. i, pp. 155-56). Once "The Grand Inquisitor" has been read, responses to it can be recognized frequently throughout the rest of the novel. Father Zosima's wisdom contains some responses to it. Dolinin has pointed out how Father Zosima's argumentation coincides with Ivan's to a point (in fact, Father Zosima, too, "simplifies his argument by dealing with children only"), then parts way with him (p. 17). The entire episode of "An Odor of Corruption" is a counterpoint to the theme of the second temptation of Christ. Aliosha's vision in "Cana of Galilee' is the counterpoint to Ivan's later "vision" of the devil, and thus a response to "The Grand Inquisitor" as well. Grushen'ka's folk tale, "The Onion," echoes Ivan's paraphrase of "The Virgin's Descent to Hell." It emphasizes the belief that everybody can be saved—provided he wants to be saved.[51] The coachman Andrei's story reaffirms this notion (Book Eight, chap. vi, p. 389). Finally, the chapter "The Devil: Ivan Fiodorovich's Nightmare" is, as Rozanov put it, "a set of variations on 'The Grand Inquisitor' " (p. 135).

The "landowner" Maksimov acts, in an almost uncanny way, as a double of Fiodor Pavlovich's. A sponger and buffoon like the latter, he is dubbed another "von Sohn" (the victim of an obscene murder) by Fiodor Pavlovich—who thus prophesies his own death. Maksimov reenters the narrative at the death of Fiodor Pavlovich and gives an exhibit of buffoonery and senile lechery at Dmitry's last "orgy." Maksimov then moves in with Grushen'ka—something his double, the late Fiodor Pavlovich, would have dearly wanted to do.

The Khokhlakovs, mother and daughter, are involved in a number of mirroring effects. Mme. Khokhlakov, who quotes Turgenev, the agnostic who considered his lack of faith a personal misfortune, takes rather the same stance as Ivan Karamazov, as she confesses her unbelief to Father Zosima (Book Two, chap. iv, p. 47). This selfish, frivolous, and shallow woman is a lot more like Ivan Karamazov than the latter would like to admit. The detail which suggests this to the reader is the admission of both that, while they love humanity in general, they cannot love their neighbor in particular—especially if that neighbor should happen to be a beggar with festering sores.

Liza Khokhlakov is close to both Ivan and Aliosha for a very special reason: she has sadistic fantasies of a crucified little boy, and of herself eating pineapple compote as she watches him (Book Eleven, chap. iii, p. 552), and she also dreams of devils threatening her. Aliosha admits that he has had the same dream, and Ivan, of course, has the devil for a visitor.

While the rhythm of the patterns in *The Brothers Karamazov* is basically one of thesis-antithesis—that is, binary—there are also a number of instances of what William W. Rowe calls

51. Cf. Grushen'ka's own affirmation of her faith in mankind (paralleling Dmitry's), in Book Seven, chap. iii, p. 331.

"triplicity."[52] The metaphysical-religious idea of triunity was important in Soloviov's discourses on Godmanhood.[53] And it may well be that Dostoevsky consciously created the three Karamazov brothers to correspond to Soloviov's three hypostases of being: spirit, intellect, and soul.[54] Each of the brothers has a vision. The notebooks to *The Brothers Karamazov* suggest that Dostoevsky conceived Dmitry's epiphany at Mokroe as a parallel to "Cana of Galilee" *(Bk Notebooks,* p. 170), and Ivan has his black epiphany in his interview with the devil. Mochulsky (p. 607) draws attention to the parallelism in Books Nine and Eleven: Ivan's three conversations with Smerdiakov parallel Dmitry's three trials. It is not difficult to show that in Book Seven Aliosha is likewise subjected to three trials: by Father Ferapont and his followers, by Rakitin, and by Grushen'ka.

3.c. SUSPENSE

The Brothers Karamazov is, among other things, a novel of suspense. The author received letters from readers asking impatiently who had really killed Fiodor Pavlovich. There are many other instances where information is artfully withheld for suspense, or for the sake of a surprise later in the novel.[55] Grushen'ka's last name and the fact that she is Rakitin's first cousin are revealed only during the trial. Dmitry carries the secret of his shame on his neck well into Book Nine, with the reader getting no more than dark allusions to it. The secret of Smerdiakov's real father is never solved. Neither does it ever become quite clear whether Kolia's dog Perezvon is really Iliusha's Zhuchka.

The Brothers Karamazov also has a good number of scenes

52. William W. Rowe, *"Crime and Punishment* and *The Brothers Karamazov:* Some Comparative Observations," *Russian Literature Triquarterly* 10:331–42; cf. Sandoz, *Political Apocalypse,* p. 136.

53. See Soloviov's *Sixth Discourse on Godmanhood,* in *Sobranie sochinenii* 3:92–94.

54. See Soloviov's *Seventh Discourse on Godmanhood,* ibid., 3:100.

55. See Belknap, *Structure,* pp. 88–95.

and passages which may be viewed as retarding devices, used by Dostoevsky to check the breakneck tempo of his narrative. The description of Kolia's Sunday morning is a good example.

3.d. THE ART OF THE NOVEL AS A THEME

Art and the art of the novel are one of the subjects of *The Brothers Karamazov*. Since Dostoevsky intended his novel to be both a work of art as well as a moral and social statement, the question of the relationship of art to morality and to reality receives some careful attention in the novel.

Dostoevsky was familiar with the concept of the poet as a liar or prostitute[56] and knew that art is morally ambivalent.[57] And so Dmitry's tirade on the ideal of the Madonna and of Sodom (Book Three, chap. iii, p. 97) must be seen in part as a comment directed at the novel itself. Dostoevsky also knew that art could reveal the truth or conceal and distort it. Dmitry's prosecutor and defender both use the analogy of a novelist working on his novel to explain their reconstruction of the truth about the murder. The prosecutor, who works with the solid facts and some pretty plausible psychology, believes to have proven that Dmitry's story is a flawed piece of fiction, which lacks the ring of truth. The prosecutor is wrong, of course: Dmitry's story, through implausible, is true. The defender, while calling his opponent a "novelist," too, comes up with a more imaginative though much less plausible version, which he himself does not believe to be true. It is almost literally true. This is directly relevant to Dostoevsky's belief that human reality can never be explained in terms of the "average man," "rational factors," and "social phenomena," but that "extreme cases," fantastic circumstances, and highly individual facts are the stuff of which reality is made. The very introduction to the novel makes this clear ("From the Author," p. xvii). Moreover, the narrator's

56. See, for instance, *The Unpublished Dostoevsky,* 2:119 and 123. The latter aphorism reads in the original: "Belinsky. A poet, why, that's like a whore" (*Neizdannyi Dostoevskii,* p. 422).

57. Bitsilli ("K voprosu," pp. 36–38) points out that there is a passage on the "beauty of Sodom" in *The Possessed* (Pt. II, chap. i [7]). Cf. Dostoevsky's comments on Shakespeare, *The Unpublished Dostoevsky,* 2:145.

challenging definition of a "realist" (the "realist" is Aliosha) shows that Dostoevsky's notion of realism is utterly unconventional (Book One, chap. v, p. 19).[58] At the same time, those who subscribe to "realism" in the conventional sense (such as Rakitin or Mme. Khokhlakov)[59] are shown to be wretchedly shortsighted and wrong even in their own empirical terms (neither of them doubts for a moment that Dmitry is guilty).

In a way, then, the trial of Dmitry Karamazov is an allegory of Dostoevsky's effort in *The Brothers Karamazov*. Dostoevsky the novelist pleads a difficult case before a jury whose members are likely to be obtuse, inattentive, and careless, and if not so, are more likely to possess Rakitin's intelligence than Dmitry's intuition and appreciation of nuances. The fact that the imaginative "artist" Fetiukovich has a better grasp of the facts than the honest plodder Ippolit Kirillovich is, then, an endorsement of Dostoevsky's belief in the cognitive power of the creative imagination.

3.e. THE BROTHERS KARAMAZOV AS AN EXPOSITORY NOVEL

Maximilian Braun has drawn attention to the fact that *The Brothers Karamazov* is not only ostensibly an "expository" or "introductory" novel (called so by the narrator: *vstupitel'nyi roman* [*PSS* 14:12]), but that elements of this kind are significant for the structure of the novel as well. The narrator points out in his very preface that this is only the first of two parts, with the second to be set thirteen years later. He retains this stance throughout the novel. While answers to the important ideological questions of the novel are suggested at least tentatively (see Braun, p. 229), the fate of the three Karamazov brothers is left hanging in the balance as the novel ends. As Braun points out, however, Dmitry has created the practical premises for further developments, Ivan has stated the ideological issues, and Aliosha is ready to realize both in a "new story." The romance of Ivan (he will live; we know this much

58. See Zundelovich, pp. 197–99.
59. See, for instance, Book Two, chap. vii, p. 72, and Book Eight, chap. iii, p. 361.

from the text [Book Five, chap. vii, p. 255, and Book Eleven, chap. vi, p. 578]) and Katerina Ivanovna is left open, as is that of Aliosha and Liza Khokhlakov. First and foremost, Aliosha is yet to challenge the world with the ideals which have been entrusted to him by Father Zosima. And he is to "see great sorrow, and in that sorrow . . . be happy" (Book Two, chap. vii, p. 67).

Braun points out judiciously that all reconstructions of part 2 (from the text, and from the reminiscences of Mrs. Anna Dostoevsky, Aleksei Suvorin, and others) are of little value, considering the frequent changes Dostoevsky usually made in the plots of his planned works.[60] Dostoevsky would, however, have been bound by the text of part 1. Braun points out that the notion, adhered to by some scholars, that Aliosha would lose his faith and turn revolutionary is based on slender and by no means unequivocal evidence (*Dostojewskij,* p. 260). The actual text contains no indication to this effect, and a great deal to contradict this notion.

Thus, the expository nature of *The Brothers Karamazov* remains primarily an intrinsic feature, making the novel open-ended, and thus connected with the flow of life and the flow of history.

4. Language

Dostoevsky's language had the reputation, in his lifetime as well as later, of being monotonous and lacking in nuance. This opinion contradicts Dostoevsky's well-documented, lifelong interest in language and style, as well as in nuance in particular, and today is recognized to have been entirely in error. Dostoevsky's contemporaries were used to writers "from the notebook," who tried to reproduce social, regional, and occupational dialects with great accuracy, rather than re-creating the speech of their characters in their own creative imaginations. Therefore, they tended to see the minor inaccuracies in

60. See *PSS* 15:485–87. For a comprehensive treatment of this problem, see Maximilian Braun, "*The Brothers Karamazov* as an Expository Novel," *Canadian-American Slavic Studies* 6 (1972):199–208.

Dostoevsky's verbal characterization, ignoring the complete image.

There is ample evidence of Dostoevsky's active concern with the language of *The Brothers Karamazov.* His careful stylization of Father Zosima's life and wisdom is a prime example. Similarly careful stylization of Kolia's schoolboy jargon is another. The legal jargon of the public prosecutor and defender is done no less carefully.[61]

In a letter to Liubimov, dated 16 September 1879 (*Pis'ma* 4:114), Dostoevsky begs his editor to allow the coarse "began to stink" *(provonial)* to stand, instead of a milder "began to smell" *(propakh),* because "the word is said by Father Ferapont, and he couldn't say it otherwise." Other examples of such concern with nuance are plentiful.

4.a. INDIVIDUALIZED LANGUAGE OF DOSTOEVSKY'S CHARACTERS

Interestingly, in the case of *The Brothers Karamazov,* contemporary reviews, which were otherwise anything but complimentary, tended to praise the vivid, individualized language of all the characters, including minor ones.[62] But only M. M. Bakhtin recognized that the same applies to the "voice" of the narrator.[63] Once we are dealing with a personalized narrator, the observation that *The Brothers Karamazov* has its sentimental or even maudlin passages acquires a different meaning.[64] If Bitsilli compares the scene of Aliosha's rebirth under a starry sky with Prince Andrei's similar experience in *War and Peace,* praising Tolstoi's greater restraint, modesty, and discipline,[65] he is, of course, right—but neither Dostoevsky's hero, Aliosha, nor his narrator, who reports Aliosha's feelings, are supposed to feel or

61. See Dostoevsky's comments on this point in his essay, "Mummer," *Diary of a Writer,* 1873, 1:97–98.
62. *PSS* 15:491. It is all the more surprising that Leo Tolstoi once said that all the characters of *The Brothers Karamazov* spoke the same language (L. N. Tolstoi, *Polnoe sobranie sochinenii,* 90 vols. [Moscow, 1928–58], 58:541). Tolstoi had a rather low opinion of the novel as a whole; see, e. g., *Polnoe sobranie sochinenii,* 89:229.
63. See n. 5 and sect. 1.a. The Narrator, above.
64. Linnér, p. 135.
65. Bitsilli, "K voprosu," p. 43.

think like Tolstoi, a great artist; rather, they are presented as ordinary human beings whose speech is more likely to be sentimental and rhetorical than restrained and disciplined.

4.b. SOCIAL STYLIZATION

Social stylization is the least of Dostoevsky's concerns. Virtually all of his characters are extreme types within their social set. Specifically, all four Karamazovs, as well as their servants, are well-read, intellectually alert, and eloquent far beyond what could be expected in real life. Aliosha, in particular, who has not even finished his secondary education, seems to be just as literate as his brother Ivan. Dmitry's knowing his Schiller by heart may not be out of character: in nineteenth-century Russia schoolboys had to memorize a great deal of poetry for their classes. But the way he quotes his poetry, creatively, to give forceful expression to his ideas, is, of course, exceptional.[66] Nevertheless, there is nothing in the text that is socially or historically false about the speech of any of the characters.

The Brothers Karamazov is saturated with concrete detail relating to the place and the period. Also, in addition to the more or less eccentric main characters of the novel, we meet scores of normal people whom we might have met in Tolstoi or Chekhov. *The Brothers Karamazov* has all the trappings of a realistic novel, except for the fact that Dostoevsky believes that it is precisely the eccentric who "carries within himself the very heart of the whole" ("From the Author," p. xvii), meaning that important social trends manifest themselves in exceptional individuals more than in average people.

4.c. PARODY, TRAVESTY, AND DISSONANCE

Parody, travesty, dissonance, and false notes are Dostoevsky's great forte. All of the negative forces in the novel are engaged in a subversion of the living word in one way or another. Fiodor Pavlovich makes a travesty of whatever he touches. For instance, at the monastery he is soon aping the

66. Matlaw, *"The Brothers Karamazov,"* p. 17.

biblical Russian of the monks and turning it into a joke. Mme. Khokhlakov makes a travesty of all the noble feelings by which she fancies herself to be moved. Piotr Aleksandrovich Miusov, in the 1860s still "a man of the forties," is a parody of the Russian liberal. It is in the various "voices" of Ivan Karamazov that Dostoevsky's art of the dissonance and the false note appears at its brightest.

The reader has witnessed Ivan's occasional flare-ups of bad temper and bitter sarcasm even before he takes center stage in Book Five. Ivan's "rebellion' is an example of invective at its sharpest: spite, rage, anger, indignation, outrage, sarcasm, appear in profusion. Yet these feelings are under control, and hence have a tinge of dishonesty. When Ivan suggests that he will limit his discussion to the sufferings of children, even though "that reduces the scope of my argument to a tenth" (Book Five, chap. iv, p. 218), he is cheating: he is merely assuming the most advantageous position. He has his arguments well prepared and his facts well researched, yet he calls his stories of child abuse "certain little facts" *(faktiki)* and "anecdotes of a certain sort" (p. 220). The story of Richard (pp. 220–22) is told with cold sarcasm: it testifies to Ivan's hatred for Richard's tormentors, but not to any love of Richard. (Compare, for contrast, Prince Myshkin's story of Marie in *The Idiot.*) Gradually the reader gets a feeling that Ivan may be enjoying telling his little anecdotes.

Ivan's case histories have been leading up to his main argument: his return of his ticket to God's world "from love for humanity" (p. 226). There is a tinge of dishonesty, a "false note," about this grand passage, too. Ivan says that "it's not God that I don't accept, Aliosha, only I most respectfully return Him the ticket" (p. 226). He neglects to admit that he does not believe in God—except a God created by man. Ivan's paraphrase of the legend of "The Virgin's Descent to Hell" strikes the tone that will persist throughout "The Grand Inquisitor": it is one of romantic irony—that is, the narrator alternately steps in and out of his narrative, once identifying with it and then again treating it ironically as a mere fiction. He finds a certain category of sinners in a fiery lake whom 'even God forgets' "immensely interesting," and the expression itself "of extraordinary depth and force" (Book Five, chap. v, p. 228). There is a false note here: Ivan knows, at least sub-consciously, that he is precisely one of these sinners.

In "The Grand Inquisitor," the gothic melodrama and romantic satanism of the piece are obvious.[67] Some blatant anachronisms enhance this impression. A whole series of false notes is introduced to turn the Inquisitor's argument into a travesty. Thus, the Inquisitor presents his authority, the devil, as "the wise and dread spirit, the spirit of self-destruction and nonexistence" (p. 232)—hardly a trustworthy authority for a philanthropic project. The three temptations prepared by the devil are advertised as ideas of unequalled "depth and force" (p. 233), a transparent bluff, for the ideas (that men need bread to live, are attracted by the miraculous, and respect power) are in themselves trivial: it is Christ's response that makes them profound.

Meanwhile, Ivan's irony keeps falling back upon himself. When the Inquisitor contemptuously calls the masses of mankind a rebellious mob (p. 234), one is reminded that Ivan's own stand was called a "rebellion" only a minute earlier (chap. iv, p. 226). When Ivan speaks of "one martyr oppressed by great sorrow and loving humanity" (p. 241), this is too obviously another self-projection, and somewhat ridiculous, too, con-sidering the facts of Ivan's life so far. And when Ivan goes on to suggest that this "martyr," realizing that Christ has been wrong in his assessment of mankind, will ultimately join "the clever people" (p. 242), the irony becomes deadly, for we are reminded of Fiodor Pavlovich's words when he declared himself a member of that group of "clever people [who] will sit snug and enjoy our brandy" (Book Three, chap. viii, p. 121). And soon Smerdiakov will say to Ivan that "it's always worthwhile speaking to a clever man" (Book Five, chap. vii, p. 259).

67. "After finishing the piece, Lawrence asked Murry, 'Why? It seems to me just rubbish.' He found it to be an irritating 'cynical-satanical' pose" (quoted from Wasiolek, p. 164). What D. H. Lawrence failed to realize, of course, was that Dostoevsky had "set up" Ivan Karamazov in this pose.

Later, in Ivan's interview with the devil (Book Eleven, chap. ix), all these false notes and dissonances will turn into an outright cacophony. And the *qui pro quo* of "The Grand Inquisitor" (which Aliosha notices: we do not really know whose voice we hear or on what level of reality the whole scene is set) turns into hopeless muddle and disorder.

5. Symbolism

Various aspects of the symbolism of *The Brothers Karamazov* have already been discussed in different contexts (see esp. II.1. *The Brothers Karamazov* as an Allegory). The clearest form of symbolism affecting the novel as a whole is connected with the epigraph. The parable of the seed signifies "a deeply organic conception of the world"[68] and the mysterious ways in which God's grace becomes manifest on earth.[69] The parable of the seed may be seen as a symbol of the structure of the novel: God sows his seed, and so does the devil, and the story shows what grows from these seeds. The passage about the "seeds from different worlds" sown by God on this earth (Book Six, chap. iii[g], p. 299) offers a direct explanation of this particular symbol.

That the novel is set in a provincial town with a monastery is no accident: only in such a town could the religious drama of *The Brothers Karamazov* be acted out, and only such a town could be a symbol of all Russia. That there is a father and his three sons, with the youngest, a "God's fool" and "eccentric," projected to become the hero of Russia's future, links the novel with the Russian folk tale (see *PSS* 15:574). So the drama should be symbolic of Russia's fate.

5.a. MIRRORING AND DOUBLING

A great deal of symbolism is connected with the various mirroring and doubling effects, which Bitsilli has called a

68. Komarowitsch, *Die Urgestalt der "Brüder Karamasoff,"* p. 104. Komarowitsch also points out that the parables of the sower and of the seed were favorites of Saint Tychon.
69. Cf. Belknap, *Structure,* p. 74.

"dominant trait" of Dostoevsky's art (p. 32). This phenomenon has been discussed in section 3.b, above.

5.b. Foreshadowing

Symbolic foreshadowing plays a considerable role in *The Brothers Karamazov*. Zosima's low bow before Dmitry is a striking example, but there are many others.[70] When Ivan Karamazov states his conviction that, having lost his faith in God and in immortality, man must necessarily become evil and criminal (Book Two, chap. vi, p. 60), he unwittingly presages his own fate. Early in Book Four, when Aliosha leaves his father, he kisses him spontaneously as he says good-bye. The old man, a little surprised, asks: "What's that for? We will see each other again, or do you think we won't?" (Book Four, chap. ii, p. 160).

5.c. Symbolic Images

The text of *The Brothers Karamazov* contains a large number of images which can be recognized as symbols of some deeper entity. Dostoevsky certainly set up many of them deliberately. For instance, Matlaw draws attention to a notebook entry, "Don't forget the candles," toward the scene of Grushen'ka's (and Aliosha's) moral rebirth (p. 29). The candles are present in the text (Book Seven, chap. iii, p. 324).

Volynsky observes that the description of Karamazov's house (Book Three, chap. i, p. 82) describes the owner himself very well (p. 46). Volynsky also observes that the loud knocking Ivan hears through his daze when Aliosha comes to tell him that Smerdiakov has hanged himself is symbolic of Aliosha's breakthrough into Ivan's life—the actual knocking is not loud at all (p. 146). Many more instances will be pointed out in the Commentary.

The physical presence and movements of many of the characters are suggestive of their personalities. Peace observes Ivan's swaying gait—in contrast to Dmitry's bold, firm strides.[71] Matlaw gives details on several of the leading characters and

70. See ibid., p. 75.
71. Peace, *Dostoyevsky*, p. 227.

suggests that perhaps the most striking descriptive detail concerns Fetiukovich, who bends his back in a peculiar way (Book Twelve, chap. x, p. 689): the bending at unnatural angles symbolizes the man's mind (p. 29). Peace has collected some material details which identify Smerdiakov as a eunuch (p. 262).

5.d. NAME SYMBOLISM

As in other novels by Dostoevsky, in *The Brothers Karamazov* name symbolism appears fairly blatantly. There has been a good deal of speculation on the possible symbolic meaning of the family name, but it is all rather doubtful.[72] The names of the three brothers, however, are clearly symbolic. *Dmitry* (Greek *Demetrios*) is derived from *Demeter* (lit. "Mother Earth"), the goddess in whose honor the Eleusian mysteries were celebrated. Dmitry quotes from Schiller's "Eleusian Festival," and he is close to natural religion, to the earth. Aleksei is "Aleksei, man of God," which the text makes quite explicit.[73] Aleksei is also often called "angel."[74] Other religious symbolism connected with Aliosha will be pointed out in the Commentary. Ivan's name has been connected with both Saint John the Divine and Saint John the Baptist, mostly in view of his apocalyptic visions. The notebooks offer an alternative: Ivan ("John") is the proverbial "average man," and if the notebook entries in question are indeed relevant to *The Brothers Karamazov,* little Iliusha (who appears with "John") is a symbol of the heroic, Il'ia of Murom being the Russian hero of heroes.[75]

Father Zosima's name is derived from the Greek root meaning "alive, living," but then again there was a prototype whose name was also Zosima.[76] That the saintly and suffering mother

72. Peace associates the name with *kara,* "punishment" (pp. 281–82). The text itself points to a Turkish etymology: *kara,* "black," inserted into the Russian adjective *chernomazyi,* "swarthy." *Karamazov* is reminiscent of Karakozov, the name of a revolutionary who attempted to assassinate Tsar Alexander II and was executed (Braun, *Dostojewskij,* p. 260).

73. This is corroborated by notebook passages. See, for example, *The Unpublished* Dostoevsky, 3:93.

74. Guardini, p. 99.

75. See *The Unpublished Dostoevsky,* 3:92–93, 2:154.

76. See Linnér, p. 166.

of Ivan and Aliosha should have been called Sof'ia Ivanovna comes as no surprise. The name *Sof'ia* (lit. "[Divine] Wisdom") is firmly established as a symbol even in earlier works *(Crime and Punishment, A Raw Youth)*.[77] The name *Katerina* had been for a long time, since Princess Katia of *Netochka Nezvanova* (1848–49), Dostoevsky's private code name for a proud and rebellious woman. Some efforts have been made to explain *Grushen'ka* (diminutive of *grusha*, "pear") as a symbolic name parallel to *Dmitry*. The fact that her prototype's name was Agrippina *(PSS* 15:456; cf. I.6.d. Ivan Karamazov and Other Characters), which Grushen'ka's Polish lover actually uses instead of the Russian *Agrafena*, does not exclude name symbolism from consideration.

5.e. BIBLICAL SYMBOLISM

A great deal of biblical symbolism has been pointed out in various connections (see particularly II.5. Moral and Religious Philosophy, and III.1.b. Ivan Karamazov). Perhaps Dr. Herzenstube's story, told in court, of how he taught young Dmitry the German words for *God the Father, God the Son, and God the Holy Ghost* (Book Twelve, chap. iii, p. 641) offers a key to a great deal of biblical symbolism throughout the novel. The characters in the novel do, or do not, recognize the three hypostases of God in specific situations—and this determines their fate. Those who do, soar toward God; those who do not, remain heavy and earthbound. The Grand Inquisitor will not look at that aspect of man which is directed heavenward: he only sees that which drags him down (Book Five, chap. v, p. 234). Father Zosima takes the opposite view (Book Six, chap. ii[b], p. 270, and passim). Father Ferapont, who often sees devils, is in dread that Christ might snatch him up and carry him away (Book Four, chap. i, p. 154). Aliosha has the joyful ascending and expanding vision of "Cana of Galilee" (Book Seven, chap. iv, pp. 339–40).

77. See Zander, *Taina dobra,* pp. 63–98, for an account of various Sofias in Dostoevsky.

5.f. MYTHICAL SYMBOLISM

A good deal of mythical symbolism appears quite explicitly. This is particularly true of the myth of Mother Earth.[78] Zosima's exhortation "Love to throw yourself on the earth and kiss it" (Book Six, chap. iii[h], p. 301) is echoed by both Dmitry (Book Three, chap. iii, p. 96) and Aliosha (Book Seven, chap. iv, p. 340). A religious feeling toward "Mother Earth" was still alive among the Russian peasantry in Dostoevsky's day. It coexisted with Christian mythology and was to some extent fused with the image of the Mother of God. As an element of popular religion, it was dear to Dostoevsky.[79]

Father Vasily Zenkovsky, in a brilliant article entitled "Fiodor Pavlovich Karamazov,"[80] sees sexuality (Russ. *pol*) as the central theme of *The Brothers Karamazov*. Each of the Karamazovs manifests the power of sex in his own way. Zenkovsky's conception, which finds strong support in the text, is based on a Jungian "metaphysics of sex." This symbolism is concealed behind what might be considered a Victorian euphemism: "Karamazovian power" or "strength" (*karamazovskaia sila*). Dmitry's poetic effusions, Ivan's fiery rhetoric, and Aleksei's religious fervor are sublimations of an Eros which appears with cynical frankness in their father. Insect imagery appears as a symbol of sexuality, first in Dmitry's quote from Schiller's "Ode to Joy," and then repeatedly in Dmitry's descriptions of his own powerful sex drive (Book Three, chap. iv, p. 102).[81]

Marcel Proust suggested that *The Brothers Karamazov* can be read as another version of the ancient myth of crime, vengeance,

---

78. For a brilliant exposition of Mother Earth symbolism, see Zander, pp. 31–62. Cf. Ivanov, pp. 70–85; Slochower, "The Pan-Slavic Image of the Earth Mother," pp. 246–48. For an account of Mother Earth in Russian folk beliefs, see F. Fedotov, *The Russian Religious Mind*, 2 vols. (Cambridge, Mass., 1946–66), 2:12–13, 135–36.

79. See Losskii, *Dostoevskii i ego khristianskoe miroponimanie*, pp. 170–71.

80. In *O Dostoevskom*, ed. A. L. Bem, 2: 93–114.

81. Ralph E. Matlaw, "Recurrent Imagery in Dostoevskij," *Harvard Slavic Studies*, 3 (1957): 221.

and expiation, which begins with the rape of Elizaveta Smerdiashchaia (an act of sacrilege, since she is a God's fool and
enjoys the community's protection), leads to the murder of the
offender by his and the victim's son, and ends with expiation
through the innocent suffering of the offender's son Dmitry.
Aliosha, a God's fool himself, is then free of the curse.[82]

82. Proust, 3:380.

COMMENTARY

THE CHARACTERS OF THE NOVEL

Agaf'ia (Agatha), Mme. Krasotkin's maid
Andrei, a driver
Anfim, Father, a monk, Zosima's old friend
Borovikov, a schoolboy
Dardanelov, a schoolteacher
Fenia. *See* Markov
Ferapont, Father, a monk
Fetiukovich, a lawyer
Foma (Thomas), a retired soldier living with Mar'ia Kondratievna
Gorstkin, *alias* Liagavy, a lumber dealer
Grigory. *See* Kutuzov
Grushen'ka. *See* Svetlov
Herzenstube, Dr., a physician
Iosif, Father, a monk, librarian of the hermitage
Ippolit Kirillovich (no last name), assistant prosecutor
Isidor, Father, a monk
Kalganov, Piotr Fomich, a young man of a good family and a relative
    of Miusov's
Karamazov, Fiodor Pavlovich, a landowner
            Adelaida Ivanovna (née Miusov), his first wife
            Sof'ia Ivanovna, his second wife
            Dmitry Fiodorovich (Mitia, Miten'ka), his eldest son
            Ivan Fiodorovich, his second son
            Aleksei Fiodorovich (Aliosha), his youngest son
Kartashov, a schoolboy
Khokhlakov, Katerina Osipovna, a wealthy widow
            Liza (Lise), her daughter
Kolbasnikov, a schoolteacher
Krasotkin, Mme., a young widow
            Nikolai (Kolia), her son
Kutuzov, Grigory Vasilievich, Karamazov's servant
            Marfa (Martha) Ignatievna, his wife

Lizaveta Smerdiashchaia, a holy fool, mother of Smerdiakov
Makarov, Mikhail Makarovich, police captain
Maksimov, a "landowner"
Mar'ia Kondrat'evna (no last name), Karamazov's neighbor
Markov, Fedos'ia Markovna (Fenia), Grushen'ka's maid
Mikhail (no last name or patronymic), the mysterious visitor in Book
    Six, chap. ii(d)
Mikhail, Father, a monk, warden of the hermitage
Miusov, Piotr Aleksandrovich, a wealthy landowner
Musiałowicz, a retired customs official
Neliudov, Nikolai Parfenovich, investigator
Nikolai, Father, abbot
Paisy, Father, a monk
Perkhotin, Piotr Il'ich, a government official
Polionov, Efim Petrovich, a wealthy landowner, benefactor of Ivan
    and Aleksei Karamazov
Porfiry, a novice monk
Rakitin, Mikhail (Misha), a divinity student
Samsonov, Kuzma Kuzmich, a merchant and former mayor of Skoto-
    prigonievsk
Shmertsov, Mavriky Mavrikievich, an officer of the rural police
Smerdiakov, Pavel Fiodorovich, Karamazov's cook
Smurov, a schoolboy
Snegiriov, Nikolai Il'ich, a retired officer
                Arina Petrovna, his wife
                Nina Nikolaevna, his crippled daughter
                Varvara Nikolaevna, his daughter, a student
                Il'ia (Iliusha), his son
Svetlov, Agrafena Aleksandrovna (Grushen'ka), mistress of Samsonov
Thomas. *See* Foma
Trifon Borisych (no last name), an innkeeper at Mokroe
Varvinsky, district physician
Verkhovtsev, Katerina Ivanovna (Katia), a young heiress
                Agaf'ia Ivanovna, her half-sister
Vorokhov, Mme., a rich widow, "benefactress" of Sof'ia Ivanovna
    Karamazov
Wróblewski, a dentist, companion of Musiałowicz
Zosima, Father, a monk (named Zinovy before he took holy vows)

There are many more characters in the novel, some of them with
names.

From the Author

1 xvii$_2$, 14:5$_2$, See Introduction III.3.e. Expository Novel.

2 xvii$_{16}$, 14:5$_{16}$, "protagonist"—translates *deiatel',* "doer, activist, man of action."

3 xvii$_{18}$, 14:5$_{18}$, "One thing, I dare say, is fairly certain"—such "hedging" is characteristic of the narrator's diction throughout. Cf. Introduction III.1.a. The Narrator.

4 xvii$_{27-31}$, 14:5$_{26-30}$, "For not only is an eccentric . . ."—a focal thesis of Dostoevsky's aesthetic theory, applied here to his philosophy of history. Dostoevsky believed that his "extreme" characters and "fantastic" plots were more true to life than those of contemporary "realists." See, for example, Dostoevsky's letter to A. N. Maikov, dated 11/23 December 1868, *Pis'ma* 2:148.

5 xvii$_{35-36}$, 14:6$_4$, "The main novel is the second"—See note 1 above.

6 xviii$_{5-8}$, 14:6$_{17-19}$, Such pleonastic diction is characteristic of the narrator's style. See Introduction III.1.a. The Narrator.

7 xviii$_{12}$, 14:6$_{24}$, " 'with essential unity of the whole' "—the narrator quotes a cliché from the critical jargon of his day.

8 xviii$_{26}$, 14:6$_{37}$, The language and tone of this preface give a condensed preview of Dostoevsky's tricky style. He gives us a narrator who apparently is not a skillful writer. His vocabulary is that of an educated person, but he does not always choose his words well, and his discourse contains a good deal of colloquial speech. Moreover, we are given no semblance of a finished product, but rather a rough draft which mirrors the narrator's thoughts in a nascent state. This is signalled by some awkward syntax, including a few anacolutha. We hear the narrator talking to himself as much as to his prospective reader.

Book One

9   2_2, 14:7_3,   The Russ. *semeika,* diminutive of *sem'ia,* "family," is slightly ironic.

10   2_{11}, 14:7_{13},   Dostoevsky has a penchant for atypical "types." See Introduction II.6.a. Dostoevsky's Psychology.

11   2_{14}, 14:7_{16},   "looking after their worldly affairs"—translates *obdelyvat' svoi imushchestvennye delishki,* where *delishki* is a diminutive of *dela,* "business deals," and the paronymy *obdelyvat' delishki,* "pulling his little deals," is a colloquialism suggesting crooked deals.

12   2_{21-22}, 14:7_{23},   Dostoevsky is very fond of such psychological paradoxes. See Introduction II.6.b. Psychological Motivation.

13   2_{22}, 14:7_{25},   "national"—that is, "Russian."

14   2_{33}, 14:8_4,   " 'romantic' "—gives us a clue as to the narrator's age. The "romantic" generation would be that of the 1830s. It is now 1866 or 1867 as the novel begins, thirteen years after the events related.

15   3_3, 14:8_{12}, "Ophelia"—See Introduction I.4.a. Secular Sources, for echoes of Shakespeare in *The Brothers Karamazov.*

16   3_{9-10}, 14:8_{20},   "the irritation caused by lack of mental freedom"—lit. "the irritation of a captive mind," quoted without quotation marks from M. Iu. Lermontov's poem "Do Not, Do Not Believe Yourself" (1839).

17   3_{14}, 14:8_{23},   "parasitic position"—translates *chin prizhival'shchika,* lit. "the rank of a sponger," which is of course ironic.

18   3_{15}, 14:8_{25},   "progressive epoch"—an ironic jibe at the 1840s, the period of philosophic idealism which laid the groundwork for the social reforms of the 1860s. Cf. Introduction II.4. *The Brothers Karamazov* as a Social Novel.

19   3_{32}, 14:8_{44},   To translate precisely: "Although the family actually accepted the event pretty quickly," where "actually" is

126

dazhe, one of the narrator's key words. The word often appears in contexts where it seems inappropriate and as a result, remains untranslated. See Introduction III.1.a. The Narrator.

20   3_{37}, $14:9_1$, "got hold of all her money"—"got hold of" translates *podtibril,* which is decidedly a slang expression (perhaps: "filched"). There will be many more.

21   3_{44}–4_1, $14:9_9$,   An example of the narrator's hyperbolic style. In the Russian, the effect is enhanced by a combination of sound symbolism, punning, and "loaded" grammar: "extortion and importunity" translates *vymogatel'stvami i vymalivaniiami,* where the extraordinary length of both words is suggestive of Fiodor Pavlovich's harangues, as are the anaphoric and end rhymes (monotonous repetition!). Both words are in the plural, which also suggests frequent repetition.

22   4_2, $14:9_{12}$,   "swindler"—translates *khapuga* (from *khapat',* "to grab, to grasp, to eat greedily"), perhaps: "shark." Another slang expression.

23   4_6, $14:9_{16}$,   Foreshadowing: Adelaida Ivanovna's impulsive character, her "remarkable physical strength," and her wrathful attacks on Fiodor Pavlovich's person will reappear in her son, Dmitry.

24   4_8, $14:9_{17}$,   Divinity students came from the lower classes. Many revolutionaries were former divinity students. The untranslatable syntax of the orginal features an embedded participial clause, lit. "about to perish from poverty" (translated by "utterly destitute"). This phrase may be a reminiscence of the title of a review by D. I. Pisarev, of Dostoevsky's *Notes from the House of the Dead* and N. G. Pomialovsky's *Seminary Sketches,* entitled "Those Who Have Perished and Those Who Are About to Perish" (1866), the latter being divinity students.

25   4_{13}, $14:9_{22}$, "too disgraceful"—*slishkom,* "too, much too, excessively," is another key word of the narrator's. It often appears to be out of place. See Gleb Struve, "Notes on the Language and Style of Dostoevsky" (summary), *Bulletin of the International Dostoevsky Society,* no. 7 (1977), p. 76.

26   4_{15}, $14:9_{24}$,   In the original, lit. "gratify and actually flatter him"; see note 19 above.

27   4_{17}, $14:9_{27}$,   "that you'd got a promotion"—translates *chin poluchili,* where *chin,* "rank," echoes the earlier "rank of a sponger" (see note 17 above).

28   4_{25}, $14:9_{34}$,   "a life of complete emancipation"—a slur by in-

nuendo: the reader may surmise what outrageous things emancipated women will do in Petersburg.

29   4_{29-30}, $14:9_{39}$, The original has a parallelism between this passage (lit. "He threw himself into another bout of reckless drinking") and Adelaida Ivanovna's "throwing herself" into a life of utter emancipation. The verb *pustit'sia,* "to abandon oneself, to let oneself go," labels both parents of Dmitry, who is equally reckless.

30   4_{36}, $14:9_{45}$, The first words of a prayer of the Orthodox liturgy, based on Luke 2:29 ("Nunc dimittis").

31   4_{39-41}, $14:9_{47}$, "It is quite possible that both versions were true"—the first example of Dostoevsky's double-edged psychology. See Introduction II.6.b. Psychological Motivation.

Chapter ii

32   5_{4-5}, $14:10_8$, "His behavior as a father . . ."—the peculiar way in which this leitmotif is introduced is designed to draw attention to the theme of fatherhood and to "foreground" it even at this early stage. See Introduction II.3.a. Fatherhood.

33   5_5, $14:10_9$, "He completely abandoned"—translates *vovse i sovershenno brosil,* lit. "wholly and completely abandoned," an emphatic pleonasm quite characteristic of the narrator's style. These pleonasms are often simplified by the translator.

34   5_{11-12}, $14:10_{16}$, In the original, the word "perhaps" *(mozhet byt')* is inserted before "there would have been." It seems superfluous here, as is often the case throughout the text.

35   5_{28-29}, $14:10_{32}$, The rambling style of this biographic sketch is designed to camouflage a hatchet job. This is the first barb: in the 1860s, Miusov is still a liberal of the forties and fifties, that is, hopelessly behind times. Cf. Introduction II.4. *The Brothers Karamazov* as a Social Novel.

36   5_{30}, $14:10_{34}$, Outright mockery: the word "liberal" is treated as though it meant some high moral or social quality ("great" or "famous"), so that meeting the most liberal men of one's epoch is good for a "career."

37   5_{31}, $14:10_{35}$, Pierre Joseph Proudhon (1809–65), French socialist, and Mikhail Bakunin (1814–76), Russian anarchist.

38   5_{34}, $14:10_{38}$, Another ironic jibe, with the word "almost" carrying the poison.

39 5_{36}, $14:10_{41}$, Before the emancipation of the serfs in 1861, the value of an estate was measured in terms of "souls," i.e., adult male serfs living on it.

40 6_2, $14:11_1$, Miusov is ridiculed for applying a fancy French term ("clericals") to simple Russian affairs. In the original, the irony is enhanced by a stilted hendiadys, lit. "his civic and enlightened duty." The Optina monastery, which Dostoevsky knew well, was engaged in a similar lawsuit. See *PSS* 15:524.

41 6_{11}, $14:11_{11}$, "even as though he was surprised"—translates *dazhe kak by udivilsia,* which contains a combination of two of the narrator's key words: *dazhe,* "even, actually," and *kak by,* "as though." Very common throughout the text.

42 6_{12-17}, $14:11_{12-17}$, An example of Dostoevsky's "dialectic" narrative style. The truth of Miusov's observation is alternately asserted and questioned.

43 6_{18}, $14:11_{18}$, "a very great number of people"—an over-statement quite characteristic of the narrator's style. The narrator likes to produce sententious sayings.

44 6_{23}, $14:11_{23}$, "this cousin's"—translates *dvoiurodnomu diadie,* lit. "uncle once removed." Dmitry's relationship to Miusov is the same as the latter's to the lady in Moscow.

45 6_{24-25}, $14:11_{25}$, Another stab at the Russian liberal: all he is interested in, as far as Russia is concerned, is that his money be consigned to his Paris address regularly.

46 6_{38}, $14:11_{40}$, "on coming of age"—at twenty-one, in nineteenth-century Russia.

47 7_{26}, $14:12_{27}$, "my first introductory novel"—see Introduction II.3.e. Expository Novel.

48 7_{26-27}, $14:12_{27}$, "or rather the external side of it"—one of the first instances of Dostoevsky's "inner commentary." The art of fiction in general as well as the structure of this novel are often discussed in *The Brothers Karamazov.* See Introduction III.3.d. Art of the Novel.

Chapter iii

49 7_{33}, $14:12_{36}$, Regarding the symbolism attached to Sof'ia Ivanovna's name, see Introduction III.5.d. Name Symbolism.

50 7_{35}, $14:12_{38}$, "a Jew"—here as elsewhere, Dostoevsky uses the strongly pejorative *zhid* (actually its diminutive *zhidok*), rather

than the neutral *evrei*. The translator's use of the neutral "Jew" is somewhat justified, because in Dostoevsky's time the pejorative connotation of *zhid* was not as blatant as it is today.

51 7_{39}, $14:12_{42}$, The social status of the lay clergy in Russia was low. As "the daughter of an obscure deacon," Sof'ia Ivanovna was closer to the servant class than to that of her benefactress.

52 7_{41}, $14:12_{44}$, The narrator takes for granted that his audience is familiar with General Vorokhov, suggesting a local audience. Cf. Introduction III.1.a. The Narrator.

53 7_{42}, $14:12_{43}$, "benefactress . . . and tormentor"—a typical Dostoevskian paradox.

54 7_{42}–8_5, $14:12_{45}$–13_5, Note how the narrator refuses to accept responsibility for the accuracy of this story, yet gives a fairly detailed psychological explanation of the event.

55 8_5, $14:13_4$, "tyrant"—translates Russ. *samodurka*, a word whose etymology combines the concepts of "willfullness" (*sam*, "self") and "stupid obstinacy" (*dura*, "fool"). The *samodur(ka)* is a stock character of the Russian scene. Mrs. Vorokhov, meanwhile, is a Dostoevskian stock character whom we meet, for example, in *The Gambler*.

56 8_{8-10}, $14:13_{7-9}$, A striking example of the accumulation of modal expressions in the narrator's speech, *dazhe* and *mozhet byt'* (see notes 19 and 34 above) being among them.

57 8_{13-14}, $14:13_{12}$, The narrator will indulge in an occasional *bon mot*.

58 8_{21-23}, $14:13_{18-21}$, First clash of the leitmotif of Karamazovian sensuality with its opposite, spirituality. At this early stage it is immediately minimized and quickly dropped.

59 8_{31}, $14:13_{29}$, "argumentative servant"—translates *rezonior* (from Fr. *raisonneur*), "wiseacre."

60 9_{13}, $14:14_{10}$, "drunk"—the original has *p'ianen'kii*, diminutive of *p'ianyi*, "drunk." The diminutive gives an undefined emotional connotation to the adjective. Here it may be a sarcasm.

61 9_{22}, $14:14_{19}$, This being before the emancipation of 1861, Grigory is of course Karamazov's house serf. The word *rab*, "slave," was often applied to serfs.

62 9_{28-31}, $14:14_{26}$, "As for the slaps"—slapstick comedy is very much a part of Dostoevsky's repertory. Cf. Introduction III.2.a. The Reader's Role ("carnival" in *The Brothers Karamazov*).

63   9_{37-39}, $14:14_{33}$, "I have not read the will myself . . ."—the
     narrator surfaces for a moment. He will be doing so throughout
     the novel.

64   $9_{39}-10_5$, $14:14_{36-47}$, Such introduction of positive or negative
     minor characters for the details of whose psychology the author
     cannot be held accountable is a hidden lever of Dostoevsky's
     strategy. Cf. Introduction II.6.b. Psychological Motivation.

65   9_{40}, $14:14_{36}$, "Marshal of Nobility"—the highest elective of-
     fice, essentially honorary and ceremonial, in a province of pre-
     reform Russia. It carried social obligations which only a wealthy
     man could afford. Provincial governors and other administrative
     officials were, of course, appointed.

66   10_{15-18}, $14:15_{8-10}$, Ivan's attitude toward charity is significantly
     contrasted with his younger brother's (see the next chapter), a
     trait to be remembered.

67   10_{19}, $14:15_{12}$, In the original, the indefinite pronoun *kakoi-to,*
     "some kind of, a certain," qualifies the assertion of Ivan's early
     brilliance. At this early stage this would seem to be merely
     another detail of the narrator's tentative diction. But it starts a
     pattern of innuendo which undermines Ivan's position and
     stature.

68   10_{22}, $14:15_{15}$, "gymnasium"—a public secondary school, the
     equivalent of a German *Gymnasium* or a French *lycée.*

69   10_{24-25}, $14:15_{18}$, "ardor for good works"—apparently a quo-
     tation from an unidentified poetic work. It carries a tinge of
     irony.

70   10_{26}, $14:15_{19-20}$, By using the word "genius" once too often, the
     narrator pushes the whole episode over the brink, into the
     ridiculous.

71   10_{43}, $14:15_{40-41}$, The key motif of Ivan's alleged "superiority"
     is made explicit for the first time.

72   $10_{44}-11_1$, $14:15_{41-46}$, Dostoevsky drops his mask momentarily:
     here he speaks from his personal experience as a newspaper and
     journal editor.

73   11_5, $14:16_2$, "literary circles"—the narrator uses the diminutive
     kruzhok, which suggests a more narrowly defined body than
     krug, "circle." Therefore, "in certain literary groupings" would
     be a more accurate translation. Together with another *dazhe,*
     "actually, even" (omitted in the translation), this makes for
     another subtle put-down. Cf. note 67 above.

74   11_{5-8}, $14:16_{2-5}$, Another sentence crammed with modal expressions (cf. note 56 above), one of them being *vdrug*, "suddenly."

75   11_{15}, $14:16_{12}$, The Judicial Reform Act of 1864, based on the principle of equality before the Law, necessitated a review of ecclesiastical courts. A legislative committee which dealt with this question found it difficult to "synchronize the demands of contemporary life and the spirit of the age with the inviolability of canonic law" (*Zaria*, no. 5, sect. II [1870], p. 225). The question was hotly debated in the press, and so in *Grazhdanin* [The citizen] while Dostoevsky was its editor-in-chief (1873). See *PSS* 15:524–25.

76   11_{18-19}, $14:16_{16-17}$, *tserkovniki* (from *tserkov'*, "church"), "Church party," and *grazhdanstvenniki* (from *grazhdanin*, "citizen"), "civic, or secular, party."

77   11_{32-38}, $14:16_{31-37}$, "It seemed strange. . . ."—this sentence, while grammatical, is even more involute in the original. The tortuous diction here reflects the narrator's perplexity.

78   11_{43-44}, $14:16_{43}$, The original shows the irony more clearly: *pozhaloval* is close to meaning "graced us with a visit."

79   12_{10-13}, $14:17_{4-8}$, The translation misses the narrator's penchant for qualifying his statements. Literally: "That was the truth: the young man actually had an unmistakable influence over the old man, who, as it were, almost began to obey him sometimes, though he was exceedingly and sometimes even spitefully perverse; he actually began to behave more decently at times." The Russian sentence has *dazhe*, "actually, even," three times.

Chapter iv

80   12_{42-43}, $14:17_{41-42}$, Dostoevsky knew that he was addressing a largely freethinking audience. So he wastes no time anticipating the rejoinders of his critics. *The Brothers Karamazov* was in fact labeled a "mystic-ascetic novel" by one influential critic, M. A. Antonovich.

81   13_2, $14:17_{43}$, "lover of humanity"—translates *rannii chelovekoliubets*, lit. "early lover of mankind." The epithet *chelovekoliubets* will be applied to Christ by Dmitry's defender in Book Twelve, chap. xii, p. 706_{33-34}.

82   13_{4-5}, $14:17_{45-46}$, The change of tone from the worldwise and

mundane of the preceding chapter is striking. The narrator now shows a different face, that of the believer. At this early stage this sentence may strike one as faintly ironic (especially, "the darkness of worldly wickedness"), but as we go on, we see that this is not so.

83   13_8, $14:18_4$,   The word "heart" is a leitmotif for Aliosha.

84   13_{10}, $14:18_5$,   "so indeed from his cradle"—an obvious hyperbole, quite characteristic of the narrator's style.

85   13_{18-20}, $14:18_{14-15}$,   "the slanting rays of the setting sun"— Dostoevsky was fond of this image, which he found beautifully realized in some of Claude Lorrain's (1600–82) landscapes. It also appears in famous passages in "Stavrogin's Confession" and in Versilov's dream in *A Raw Youth*. It is surely connected with Father Zosima's love for "vespertine light." Cf. Book Six, note 26.

86   13_{22}, $14:18_{17-18}$,   "with cries and shrieks"—the Russian *so vzvizgivaniiami i vskrikivaniiami* is more graphic: the length of both words (chosen in lieu of a shorter *s vizgom i krikom*) suggests prolonged wails and screams.

87   13_{25}, $14:18_{21}$,   "protection"—Russ. *pokrov* is a biblical term, the secular equivalent being *pokrovitel'stvo*.

88   13_{39-42}, $14:18_{35-36}$,   Note the emphatic repetition, characteristic of the narrator's style. In the Russian text, "judge," "censure," and "condemn" are all derived from the same root (*sud*), which heightens the effect. Cf. Introduction III.1.a. The Narrator.

89   14_{39}, $14:19_{36-37}$,   "Wild fanatical modesty and chastity"—as so often, Dostoevsky conveys psychological information by using unexpected adjective-noun combinations: *dikaiia, isstuplennaia stydlivost' i tselomudrennost'* is literally "savage, frenzied modesty and chastity."

90   14_{44-45}, $14:19_{42}$,   Dostoevsky's populism shows for the first time in the novel: the simple people are purer in spirit than the educated classes. See Introduction II.4.b. The People.

91   15_{1-4}, $14:19_{45}-20_1$,   This faintly unctuous, moralizing tone reminds one of Dostoevsky's *Diary of a Writer,* where problems of education and child psychology are often discussed. See Introduction I.5.b. *Diary of a Writer,* and II.3.b. "The Novel about Children."

92   15_{20-21}, $14:20_{18-19}$,   "he never cared at whose expense he was living"—a monkish trait!

93   15_{25-26}, $14:20_{23-24}$, This understatement camouflages the narrator's deep sympathy for Aliosha and the religious ideal which he stands for.

94   15_{28}, $14:20_{27}$, "religious eccentric"—Russ. *iurodivyi*, a word whose primary meaning is that of "a mentally deficient or deranged person," is used here in the more positive meaning attached to it by a long tradition of religious awe and fondness for "the poor in spirit" or "God's fools," a tradition which was still alive among the simple people of Russia in the nineteenth century. Its religious meaning, founded on Matt. 5:3, was more pronounced in the Orthodox East than in the Roman Catholic West. Cf. Lev Shestov, *Athens and Jerusalem* (New York, 1966), p. 413.

95   15_{36}, $14:20_{37}$, "sensitive"—translates *shchekotlivyi*, lit. "ticklish." The choice of this adjective is another put-down of Miusov and what he stands for. His "bourgeois honesty" is made out to be of little consequence in the face of Aliosha's saintliness.

96   15_{37-45}, $14:20_{38-45}$, Miusov's pedestrian tirade, ironically called an "aphorism," states the fact of Aliosha's saintliness from the viewpoint of a man who is quite insensitive to the spiritual. The evangelic subtext, of which the reader must be aware, is Matt. 6:25-34. See Introduction III.2.b. Religious Content as Subtext.

97   16_1, $14:20_{47}$, "suddenly" (Russ. *vdrug*), a word which occurs with striking frequency throughout the narrative, has a symbolic significance which is obvious in this instance: in Dostoevsky's world things happen "suddenly." Not causal relationships, accessible to rational analysis, but sudden impulses, generated by deep undercurrents of the soul, or inspired by a higher power, control the action.

98   16_6, $14:21_3$, "liberally"—translates *roskoshno*, "sumptuously, luxuriously." Choosing an adjective a shade too strong ("liberally" would have been appropriate) is characteristic of the narrator's style.

99   16_8, $14:21_6$, Third-class carriages, furnished with wooden benches, were normally used by the lower classes only.

100 16_{25}, $14:21_{23-24}$, " 'a lot of low Jews, Jewesses, and Jewkins' "—in the original, *so mnogimi zhidami, zhidkami, zhidishkami i zhideniatami*, which is difficult to translate. Fiodor Pavlovich comes up with a neat conceit, arranging four versions of the word *zhid* (here, definitely opprobrious) in descending

order, then turns around and uses the neutral term *evrei* (translated by "Jews high and low alike") to produce an antithesis. I suggest: "many Yids, Yiddels, Yidkins, and Yiddelkins" and "reputable Jews."

101   16_{28}, $14:21_{26-27}$, "making and hoarding money"—translates *skolachivat' i vykolachivat' den'gu,* lit. "to knock together and to knock down money." It is slang all the way, so perhaps "rub in and shake down the dough" would be closer, but it fails to render the neat grammatical rhyme of the original.

102   16_{35}, $14:21_{34}$, "he opened a great number of new taverns"—translates *on stal osnovatelem,* "he became the founder," which is mock "high style." The increase in drunkenness and accompanying evils that followed the emancipation of 1861 was a perpetual concern of Dostoevsky's. Making this social evil the main source of Fiodor Pavlovich's wealth is a purposely planted detail.

103   16_{39-42}, $14:21_{38-41}$, Typical of Dostoevsky's scattershot method of characterization. Rather than seeking out one or two well-chosen expressions, he will accumulate a whole group of more or less synonymous terms, each illuminating the condition in question by denotation, metonymy, or metaphor.

104   17_{12}, $14:22_9$, "put it up"—translates *vozdvig,* "erected," an archaism, normally used only in poetry. The narrator uses this pompous word to give Grigory proper credit and also in order to characterize the man: Grigory is righteous, but also pompous. *Vozdvig* may have been the word Grigory used himself.

105   17_{31}, $14:22_{29-30}$, In the original, "testified" is followed by *o kharakteristike i sushchnosti,* lit. "of the characteristics and essence," a hendiadys; read: "of the essential characteristics." The narrator turns moralist for a moment, and so this elegant but pompous figure of speech is in order.

106   17_{34}, $14:22_{33}$, "fat face"—both the adjective and the noun are diminutives in the original. The emotional charge of these diminutives is one of sarcasm.

107   17_{42}, $14:22_{43}$, The allusion to ancient Rome may point to Fiodor Pavlovich's paganism.

108   18_{1-3}, $14:22_{47}-23_2$, This sentence is loaded with Slavonicisms. The language of the monastery has rubbed off on Aliosha, whose words are projected through the narrator's secular diction. We are dealing here with a device called *erlebte Rede* (lit. "reflected speech") in German. It means that the words, thoughts, or

feelings of a given character are projected through someone else's consciousness, the narrator's in this case. See Introduction III.1.a. The Narrator, and III.2.b. Religious Content as Subtext.

109   18_3, $14:23_3$, "living"—in the original, the verb *spasat'sia,* lit. "to save oneself," is used. It means routinely "to live as a monk."

110   18_{14}, $14:23_{13}$, "dowry"—not necessarily a jibe. In Russian, comparing a young man to a maiden (by virtue of his beauty or innocence) is not considered insulting, but the contrary.

111   18_{15}, $14:23_{13}$, "my angel"—the first occurrence of this significant epithet. Addressing someone as "my angel" is more common in Russian than it is in English (often, too, it is ironic), so it will take some time until the epithet's symbolic force is felt by the reader. Cf. Introduction II.1.a. Allegoric Figures.

112   18_{20-21}, $14:23_{19}$, "Thirty women, I believe."—In the original, *shtuk tridtsat' zhon,* lit. "about thirty pieces of wives," almost as gross as the literal translation sounds in English. Russ. *shtuka,* "piece," is used routinely in counting things, but not people, of course.

113   18_{24}, $14:23_{22}$, The silly story about the "the monks' wives" is the first, but not the last absolutely pointless anecdote improvised by Fiodor Pavlovich. The old buffoon knows that if people will not laugh at his joke, they may at least laugh at its stupidity.

114   18_{39}, $14:23_{36}$, A scene depicting devils dragging sinners down to hell with hooks is found on Russian icons. "Spiritual verses" of Russian folk poetry also use this image. It is characteristic of Fiodor Pavlovich to make fun of a folk tradition. See Introduction II.4.b. The People.

115   18_{42}, $14:23_{39}$, Lutheranism had the reputation for being a rational religion, more compatible with a modern, scientific world view than Russian Orthodoxy.

116   19_2, $14:23_{45}$, *Il faudrait les inventer*—"they ought to be invented," ironic adaptation of Voltaire's dictum, *Si Dieu n'existait pas, il faudrait l'inventer.* This is a leitmotif of the novel and will reappear in various forms.

117   19_4, $14:24_2$, First statement of one of the philosophic themes of the novel: the theme of divine justice. Dostoevsky likes to bring up deep metaphysical questions amidst jests, raillery, and irrelevancies. Here, Fiodor Pavlovich backs into the antinomy of justice by "complaining" (actually, he is gloating, of course) that

an unrepenting sinner will go unpunished. This is an example of the "carnival" side of the novel. For a serious statement of this theme, see Book Seven, chap. ii, p. 318.

118   19_{7-8}, $14:24_{6-7}$,   " 'J'ai vu l'ombre . . .,' "—" 'I saw the shadow of a coachman who, with the shadow of a brush, was polishing the shadow of a coach.' " These lines from a parody of the sixth book of the *Aeneid* by the Perrault brothers, Claude, Charles, and Nicolas, and their friend Beaurain were widely known and were spread mostly by word of mouth. For details see *PSS* 15:525-26.

119   19_{10}, $14:24_7$,   "darling"—Fiodor Pavlovich is suddenly turning hostile. Russ. *golubchik,* lit. "my dove," is ironic in this context.

120   19_{22-23}, $14:24_{20-21}$,   "He was wicked and sentimental."—One of Dostoevsky's famous psychological paradoxes.

Chapter v

121   19_{35}, $14:24_{35}$,   "a realist"—a direct repetition of an earlier assertion (p. $xvii_{27-30}$). The narrator—and, one may assume, Dostoevsky—must be anxious to have this point sink in.

122   19_{35-37}, $14:24_{35-37}$,   This provocative statement creates enough suspense to make the reader study the discourse which follows carefully.

123   20_1, $14:24_{40}$,   "Fact" is one of Dostoevsky's favorite words and concepts. He likes to oppose it to the mere intellectual construct, which he calls "theory."

124   20_{3-4}, $14:24_{43}$,   A key position. It flatly contradicts the Grand Inquisitor's argument in Book Five, chap. v. See Roger L. Cox, "The Grand Inquisitor," in *Between Earth and Heaven* (New York, 1969), p. 202.

125   20_{4-5}, $14:24_{43}-25_2$,   A rather strange definition of the word *realist*. It anticipates subsequent discussions of the same topic, and particularly those in the speeches of the prosecutor and the counsel for the defense in Book Twelve. A "realist," according to Dostoevsky, is a person who lives and thinks in terms of an immediately, or intuitively, given reality. The opposite, then, is the "theoretician" *(teoretik),* who seeks to create and to realize a subjective world of his own. It must be understood that in Dostoevsky's Russia *realism* was an emotionally charged term. To be a "realist" meant to be right.

126   20_7, $14:25_{3-4}$,   John 20:28.

127   20_{10}, $14:25_{7-8}$,   Not an exact quote from the Gospel.

128   20_{17}, $14:25_{15}$,   "from darkness to light"—cf. note 82 above.

129   20_{18}, $14:25_{15-16}$,   If Aliosha was twenty in 1867, this would make him a member of that generation which produced the first reaction against the radical materialist wave of the late 1850s and early 1860s.

130   20_{19}, $14:25_{16}$,   Russ. *pravda* is "truth," but also "justice." Hence, "seeking justice" is a reasonable alternative to "desiring the truth." This ambivalence will have to be considered throughout the text.

131   20_{20-21}, $14:25_{18-19}$,   "immediate action"—translates *skorogo podviga,* where *podvig,* "feat (of heroism), deed, exploit," covers almost any area of achievement, including religion. It is readily associated with *podvizhnik,* "hermit, ascetic."

132   20_{35-39}, $14:25_{34-39}$,   Dostoevsky believed that atheism was the focal trait of socialism as he knew it. (Russian socialists, to be sure, tended to be militant atheists.) Dostoevsky saw in the socialists' belief that man could improve the world without taking recourse to religion nothing short of tragic folly. The image of the tower of Babel as a symbol of building a new society without God appears often in Dostoevsky's later works.

133   20_{40-41}, $14:25_{40-41}$,   Slightly inaccurate quote of Matt. 19:21.

134   20_{45-46}, $14:25_{46}$,   The image of the "slanting rays" (p. 13_{19} above) is now hypostatized. Cf. note 85 above.

135   21_9, $14:26_8$,   In the original, the narrator makes a show of being unfamiliar with scholarly terms. He does not say "authorities on the subject," but lit. "special and competent people."

136   21_{17}, $14:26_{18}$,   Russ. *podvizhnik* is less common than Eng. "ascetic," so the narrator adds "as they called him" in parenthesis.

137   21_{18}, $14:26_{19}$,   Paisy Velichkovsky (1722–94). See Sergii Chetverikov, *Starets Paisii Velichkovskii: His Life, Teachings and Influence on Orthodox Monasticism* (Belmont, Mass.: Nordland, 1977).

138   21_{21}, $14:26_{23}$,   "Optina Monastery"—see Introduction I.6.c. Father Zosima and Other Monks.

139   21_{38-39}, $14:26_{42}$,   "a life of obedience, to attain perfect freedom"—a paradox which points to one of the central themes of the novel: the theme of freedom. See Introduction II.2. *The Brothers Karamazov* as a Theodicy.

140   21_{43}, $14:26_{46-47}$,   Here "obedience" is an ecclesiastic term.

141   22_2, $14:27_1$, In the original, lit. "between him who binds and
       him who is bound," an allusion to Matt. 16:19.

142   22_3, $14:27_1$, "The story is told"—this legend is found in the
       Russian Orthodox *Prologue* (Saints Calendar) under October 15.
       It is quoted in full in *Istoricheskoe opisanie Kozel'skoi
       Vvedenskoi Optinoi pustyni* [A historical description of the
       Kozelsk Vvedenskaia Optina Hermitage], 3rd ed. (Moscow,
       1876), pp. 116–17, a book which Dostoevsky apparently used.
       See Introduction I.6.c. Father Zosima and Other Monks.

143   22_{16}, $14:27_{17}$, The Orthodox monasteries of Mount Athos in
       northern Greece have had a Russian section for centuries. The
       monk was Parfeny (his secular name: Piotr Aggeev, 1807–78),
       author of *Travels and Pilgrimages* (see Introduction I.4.b.
       Sacred Sources), one of Dostoevsky's main sources. The
       patriarch's decision remained firm even in face of the fact that
       the elder had died in the meantime. See *PSS* 15:528.

144   22_{33-34}, $14:27_{37-38}$, "that the sacrament of confession was being
       arbitrarily and frivolously degraded"—this detail will come back
       several times later. Cf. pp. 78, 144, 312.

145   22_{43}, $14:27_{48}$, In the original, this paragraph ends in a blatant
       iambic tetrameter. Throughout the novel, the close of a longer
       and more significant paragraph tends to be formally
       "foregrounded," through rhythm, a sententious quality, or
       some surprising revelation.

146   23_{15-16}, $14:28_{21}$, Note how the narrator tries to present a
       rational explanation of the elder's intuition. The holy man's
       clairvoyance is a *topos* of the Russian saint's life. Paisy
       Velichkovsky and Amvrosy of Optina hermitage were credited
       with such clairvoyance.

147   23_{17-19}, $14:28_{21-24}$, Note the massive use of adjectives and
       adverbs meaning "many," "all," "always," etc. Dostoevsky
       often uses them when seeking to convey intense experience.

148   23_{19}, $14:28_{23-24}$, "bright and happy"—Russ. *svetlymi i
       radostnymi*. These two adjectives, but especially *radostnyi*,
       "happy, joyful," are leitmotifs which will accompany Father
       Zosima and Aliosha throughout the text. See Introduction
       III.3.a. Motifs.

149   23_{23-24}, $14:28_{28-29}$, "the greater the sinner the more he loved
       him"—a very Dostoevskian paradox, tempered here by the
       circumstance that it is presented as hearsay.

150   23_{27-28}, $14:28_{33-34}$, "one, for instance, of the older monks"—

this is Father Ferapont, who is to play a significant role in the novel. Dostoevsky likes to introduce a character gradually, the first mention of him being almost off-handed. Then another, longer appearance will make him more familiar to the reader. Only in his final, climactic appearance will Father Ferapont take center stage and, finally, reveal his role in the plan of the novel.

151   23_{29}, $14:28_{34-35}$, "the majority"—in the original, *ogromnoe bol'shinstvo*, "the vast majority," which is a blatant overstatement, as will later develop. In a sense, the translator's correction of Dostoevsky's text is justified. But it is "corrections" like this that destroy the flavor of the narrator's "voice."

152   23_{33-35}, $14:28_{40-41}$,   Miracles that occur soon after a saint's death are a part of the canon of an Orthodox saint's life.

153   23_{35-37}, $14:28_{41-44}$,   Introduces the theme of faith and miracle, highlighted in "The Grand Inquisitor" (Book Five, chap. v). See Introduction II.2. *The Brothers Karamazov* as a Theodicy.

154   24_{13-17}, $14:29_{18-22}$,   "the humble soul of the Russian plebeian . . ."—a sententious statement which reflects Dostoevsky's own version of populism.

155   24_{18-22}, $14:29_{22-26}$,   "Among us there is sin . . ."—a key passage, philosophically and theologically. Dostoevsky is hedging a bit: he will not allow his narrator to make it clear whether or not he shares the people's view. Dostoevsky was attacked, by K. N. Leontiev in particular, for allegedly holding a similar, utopian view, a carry-over, as it were, from the utopian socialism of his early years. See Introduction II.2.c. The Historical Dimension, and II.4.b. The People.

156   24_{19-20}, $14:29_{24}$,   Here Russ. *pravda* means both "truth" and "justice." Cf. note 130 above.

157   24_{38}, $14:29_{42-43}$,   "That was the dream in Aliosha's heart."—The narrator prudently detaches himself from Aliosha's bold, and quite possibly heretical, dreams.

158   25_{13}, $14:30_{16}$,   "that his brother was an atheist"—the basic conflict of the novel is thus brought into the open.

159   25_{43}, $14:31_2$,   In Russia, a man's ideology is often identified by the decade of which it was characteristic. Cf. note 35 above.

160   25_{46}–26_1, $14:31_{6-8}$,   "his lawsuit"—note the repetition of this detail (cf. pp. 5, 28, 74). Such "irrelevant," but highly concrete detail establishes a realistic setting for the action of the novel. Economic, legal, political, and social facts give the novel an external frame of reference in Russian life.

161   26_{10}, $14:31_{19}$,   Luke 12:14, Christ's answer to a man who was asking Him to help him divide his inheritance with his brother.

162   26_{26}, $14:31_{35-36}$,   "half-utterances"—Russ. *nedomolvki,* "words not uttered, but implied."

163   26_{37-38}, $14:31_{45-47}$,   The style of this letter is more distinctive in the original. Thus, Dmitry uses *mankirovat'* (Fr. *manquer*) *uvazheniem,* "to be found lacking in respect," a term which would be appropriate in referring to ordinary social affairs of a nobleman and officer, but seems gauche in this context.

Book Two

Chapter i

1 27_8, $14:32_{8-9}$, "just as it was over"—translates *k shapochnomu razboru,* lit. "in time for the picking-up of hats," a humorous expression which strikes the tone of this "unfortunate gathering."

2 27_{11-23}, $14:32_{16-28}$, This detailed description would seem to suggest that Kalganov will play a significant role in the novel. But this is not so. Careful attention to the stage appearances of his "extras" is a trademark of Dostoevsky's.

3 27_{16-18}, $14:32_{19-21}$, "Like all very absent-minded people . . ."—The narrator likes to impress his reader with minor psychological observations of this kind. They inspire confidence in his judgment and enhance his credibility when it comes to more important matters.

4 27_{26}, $14:32_{31}$, "his son"—translates *synok,* a diminutive of *syn,* "son." Applied to a serious young man of twenty-four, it has a hostile ring. Perhaps: "offspring."

5 28_{9-15}, $14:33_{7-13}$, This whole paragraph is *erlebte Rede,* that is, the narrator reports Miusov's impressions. See Introduction III.1.a. The Narrator.

6 28_{26}, $14:33_{24}$, Dostoevsky likes to use a "honeyed lisp" as a label of genteel but impoverished landowners. The most famous such lisp is Stepan Trofimovich Verkhovensky's in *The Possessed.*

7 28_{44}, $14:33_{41}$, "un chevalier parfait"—this remark is so inappropriate that we recognize Maksimov for the buffoon he is.

8 29_{11}, $14:34_7$, "he added, addressing Maksimov"—in the original: "he turned to Maksimov." Dostoevsky often omits the *verbum dicendi,* replacing it with a bit of "stage direction," a liberty which critics found unwarranted.

142

9   29_{16-17}, $14:34_{12-13}$, This is caricature. Dostoevsky presents this
    liberal intellectual as so alienated from the heritage of his own
    people that he must make a "field trip" to study Russian
    customs.

10 29_{18}, $14:34_{15}$, The original reads literally: "Yes, there is no
    Dmitry Fiodorovich in existence as yet." This is a strange way to
    put it and might be foreshadowing. It fits a pattern of inad-
    vertent clairvoyance on the part of Fiodor Pavlovich: in a
    spiritual way, Dmitry "is not in existence as yet."

11 29_{28}, $14:34_{26}$, In the original, "landowner Maksimov." The
    man has been called a "landowner" once too often. The reader
    begins to suspect that this appellation is ironic.

12 29_{30}, $14:34_{27}$, "von Sohn"—the victim in a notorious Peters-
    burg murder case of 1870 (thus, a slight anachronism). Fiodor
    Pavlovich will report the details of this case later (chap. viii, pp.
    77–78).

13 29_{34-35}, $14:34_{31-32}$, "I can always tell from the physi-
    ognomy."—The depraved Fiodor Pavlovich and the saintly elder
    share this power: *les extrêmes se touchent.* But Fiodor Pavlovich
    does not know how much Maksimov is a double of his.

14 30_7, $14:35_1$, In Russian: "Don't bring your rules when going to
    another monastery," a proverb equivalent to "In Rome do as the
    Romans do." It is not quite to the point here, but this is all a part
    of Fiodor Pavlovich's buffoonery. He is a master at missing his
    mark with a joke or pun.

15 30_{8-9}, $14:35_{2-3}$, "They look at one another and eat cabbage."—
    Another bit of buffoonery, bathos in this case.

16 30_{13}, $14:35_8$, "for ladies of higher rank"—Russ. *dlia vysshikh
    damskikh lits*, lit. "for higher lady-persons." The little monk is
    awkward in his references to the female sex.

17 30_{17}, $14:35_{12}$, "Madame Khokhlakov"—an important per-
    sonage in the novel. She is introduced in stages. Cf. Book One,
    note 150.

Chapter ii

18 31_{16-25}, $14:36_{13-22}$, "a tall young lad . . ."—this is Rakitin, who
    is yet to play a significant role in the novel.

19 31_{19-20}, $14:36_{15}$, "and was wearing ordinary dress"—students
    and civil servants often wore uniform in nineteenth-century
    Russia.

20 31_{28-30}, $14:36_{25-27}$, In the original, the word for "finger" appears in the vernacular form in the first instance, and in the Slavonic (biblical) form in the second. Thus, the elder's superiority is subtly confirmed.

21 31_{38}, $14:36_{36-37}$, A Slavonic word for "kiss(ing)" appears in the original, in lieu of the vernacular expression. Perhaps: "osculation."

22 31_{40}, $14:36_{38}$, "conventional"—Russ. *po-svetskomu* is a pun of sorts, since it means both "secular, worldly" and "conventional, proper to society."

23 32_{14}, $14:37_{10-11}$, "very ancient"—in the original, "(painted) long before the schism," i.e., before the time of Patriarch Nikon (1605–81), whose reforms caused a schism in the Russian Orthodox church.

24 32_{17}, $14:37_{14}$, Father Zosima's Catholic crucifix may be significant as a counterbalance to the negative image of Catholicism in Book Five, chap. v.

25 32_{24}, $14:37_{21}$, " 'conventional' "—translates *kazionshchina*, lit. "official stuff, officialese." The Orthodox church was a state church and was considered by its opponents to be a mere tool of the state. Note that this word is given in quotes, so that the thought belongs to Miusov, not to the narrator.

26 32_{32-33}, $14:37_{31}$, "at least ten years older"—in the context of holiness, this is a positive statement. The unholy Father Ferapont looks much younger than his years.

27 32_{33-39}, $14:37_{31-38}$, As many as ten nouns and adjectives in this description of Father Zosima's face are in a diminutive form. Their cumulative effect creates an impression of smallness, puniness—and intensity.

28 32_{40}, $14:37_{39}$, Miusov's impression of Father Zosima is a "false lead," of course.

29 33_{1-2}, $14:38_3$, "punctuality is the courtesy of kings"—a common phrase in Russian, from the Fr. *L'Exactitude est la politesse des rois,* attributed to Louis XVIII. Fiodor Pavlovich uses it inappropriately to provoke Miusov.

30 33_8, $14:38_9$, "a real buffoon"—translates *shuta voistinu,* "verily a buffoon," where the biblical *voistinu,* "verily," clashes with the context. "Buffoon" is Fiodor Pavlovich's leitmotif.

31 33_{11-13}, $14:38_{12-14}$, In the original, the sentence is full of slang expressions, wholly inappropriate in the present company.

32 33_{17-18}, $14:38_{19-20}$, An *ispravnik* is a police captain. E. F.

Napravnik (1839-1916) was a Russian composer and conductor. It so happens that *napravnik* is derived from *napravit'*, "to direct, to point in the right direction," while *ispravnik* comes from *ispravit'*, "to correct, to straighten out." Hence the pun.

33   33_{30-35}, $14:38_{32-37}$, A silly pun leads up to a face slapping: typical slapstick comedy. There is a lot of it in Dostoevsky. Normally, however, it remains verbal and is not shown "on stage."

34   34_{4-5}, $14:39_3$, "it's as though it were a madness in me"—translates *vsio ravno . . . chto iurodivyi*, "as good as a God's fool." The word *iurodivyi*, "God's fool," has come up in connection with Aliosha. See Book One, note 94. Cf. note 30 above.

35   34_9, $14:39_8$, Here "words" appears in the Slavonic form *sloves* (instead of the vernacular *slov*), Fiodor Pavlovich's mocking echo of his ecclesiastic surroundings, to which he promptly "adapts." The passage presents an example of a figure characteristic of Dostoevsky's style at large: "hedging." A statement is made, immediately followed by a reservation or qualification, which, in turn, gets the same treatment, and so on.

36   34_{10}, $14:39_9$, Fiodor Pavlovich makes a point of pronouncing the name "Diderotte," to parody the diction of a book from which he will presently quote. We already know that Fiodor Pavlovich knows how to pronounce French correctly. Diderot (1713-84) visited Russia in 1773, invited by Catherine the Great (1762-96).

37   34_{12}, $14:39_{10}$, Platon, Metropolitan of Moscow (his secular name: Piotr Egorovich Levshin, 1737-1812), a famous author and preacher. The anecdote about this meeting, reported by Platon's biographer, I. M. Snegiriov, is absurdly distorted by Fiodor Pavlovich. For details, see *PSS* 15:529-30.

38   34_{14-15}, $14:39_{12-13}$, Psalms 14:1 and 53:1.

39   34_{16-17}, $14:39_{14-15}$, E. R. Dashkov (1743-1810), a friend and collaborator of Catherine II, president of the Russian Academy. G. A. Potiomkin (1739-91), general and statesman, the best known of Catherine's lovers.

40   35_{5-6}, $14:40_4$, "or at least some of them"—such superfluous qualification is characteristic of the narrator's colloquial style.

41   35_{17}, $14:40_{16}$, An example of Dostoevsky's technique to create suspense: Rakitin suddenly becomes interesting. See Introduction III.3.c. Suspense.

42 35₃₁, 14:40₃₁, "Great elder, speak!"—The original has a Slavonic expression here: *izrekite!* Perhaps: "make a pronouncement."

43 35₃₉, 14:40₃₉, "To be my natural self?"—Russ. *v natural'nom vide,* bringing to mind *v p'ianom vide,* "drunk," and other such phrases, making *v natural'nom vide* a transparent euphemism.

44 36₁₋₂, 14:40₄₇₋₄₈, Luke 11:27. Fiodor Pavlovich's afterthought, "the paps especially," turns the biblical quote into bathos and a *double entendre.*

45 36₇, 14:41₅₋₆, The very heading of this chapter suggests that its central figure is a buffoon. Buffoonery, only one aspect of Fiodor Pavlovich's character, is foregrounded here. The chapter is also a psychological study of buffoonery as compulsive behavior. See Introduction II.6.d. Psychological Wisdom.

46 36₁₃₋₁₄, 14:41₁₂, Luke 10:25.

47 36₃₂₋₃₃, 14:41₃₀₋₃₁, "You know it is sometimes very pleasant to take offense, isn't it?"—A psychological paradox which jolts the reader into paying closer attention to Father Zosima's exhortations. Up to this point they have seemed rather tame and conventional.

48 36₄₆–37₁, 14:41₄₅, "distinguished" translates *krasivo,* "beautiful." I see no reason why the primary meaning of this word, which is "beautiful," should not be retained, particularly since this ties in with a central theme of the novel, the question of the essence of beauty, introduced here for the first time, again by Fiodor Pavlovich, and again in a jesting manner.

49 37₃₋₄, 14:41₄₆₋₄₇, Slightly distorted quotation of the conclusion of John 8:44: "When he speaketh a lie, he speaketh of his own: for he is a liar, and the father of it." Christ speaks of the devil. The Russian text is ambivalent in that *lozh',* "lie," is used in the singular only, so that "the father of it" may be understood to mean "the father of a lie." In the latter interpretation, the statement here might be seen as a first hint of Ivan's "lie" (see *PSS* 15:530).

50 37₁₅, 14:42₁₁, This miracle belongs to Saint Denis, patron saint of France and first bishop of Paris. It gave Voltaire, Diderot, and others occasion for frequent railleries. Dostoevsky may have been aware of an apocryphal Russian tale about one Merkury of Smolensk, which reports a similar miracle.

51 37₂₂, 14:42₁₉, Fiodor Pavlovich—and Dostoevsky—make sure that the point sinks in: Miusov, the liberal, who resents an

unauthentic story about his champion, Diderot, will not hesitate
to tell tall tales about the Russian church.

52   37_{28}, $14:42_{26-27}$, "more and more shaken ever since"—bathos,
again. Fiodor Pavlovich is now rubbing it in.

53   37_{37}, $14:42_{36}$, A coincidental "dig" of Dostoevsky's: statistics
is a symbol of "dead," "theoretical" pseudoknowledge, as
against a "live" familiarity with the concrete "facts" of life.

Chapter iii

54   38_{21}, $14:43_{19}$, "Peasant Women"—translates *baby,* where *baba*
is "a woman of the people." Not all the women in this chapter
are peasant women; some are from the urban lower classes.

55   39_9, $14:44_5$, "possessed woman"—translates *klikusha,* lit.
"wailer." Aliosha's mother had been one (Book One, chap. iv,
p. 13_{22}). The "wailer" motif is important and will come back in
Book Three, chap. viii.

56   39_{11}, $14:44_7$, "Laying the stole on her forehead"—this detail is
reported by Parfeny. See Introduction I.4.b. Sacred Sources.

57   39_{13}, $14:44_9$, The narrator launches into an apparent digression,
half medical, half sociological. It is, however, a preview of the
central theme of the novel: religion's response to human suffering.

58   39_{31}, $14:44_{27-28}$, "frantic and struggling"—translates
besnuiushcheisia i b'iushcheisia, with alliteration and grammatical end rhyme.

59   39_{34}, $14:44_{30}$, " 'clericals' "—Miusov's language.

60   40_2, $14:44_{45}$, "cried out in singsong voices"—Russ. *prichitali,* a
verb denoting the peculiar style of recitation used by the people
in dirges, incantations, and such.

61   40_{11}, $14:45_6$, Repetition is the prevailing pattern in this scene: it
is symbolic of the nagging grief of a mother who has lost her last
child.

62   40_{17}, $14:45_{11}$, "grief that breaks out"—Russ. *nadorvannoe
gore,* lit. "ruptured grief." First mention of a psychological
phenomenon that will play a focal role in the novel. Russ.
nadorvat'sia/nadryvat'sia (with the noun *nadryv*) is here, as
elsewhere, a metaphor suggesting an emotional trauma similar to
a rupture as a result of heavy lifting or strain. See Introduction
II.6.d. Psychological Wisdom.

63   40_{21-22}, $14:45_{16}$, In the original, lit. "Lamentations are merely a

need to continually irritate the wound." This is harshly ungrammatical—a syntactic metaphor suggesting the untractable quality of grief.

64   40_{23}, $14{:}45_{17}$,   In nineteenth-century Russia, social classes were institutionalized: *meshchanstvo,* "tradesman class," the word used by Father Zosima, designates the lowest urban class. The woman answers that she is of the "peasant class" *(krest'ianstvo)* because this is what it says in her husband's passport.

65   40_{34}, $14{:}45_{26-27}$,   "three years all but three months"—the age of Dostoevsky's son Aleksei when he died in 1878. Mrs. Dostoevsky explicitly calls this episode an echo of the writer's personal experience. See Anna Dostoevsky, *Dostoevsky: Reminiscences,* tr. and ed. Beatrice Stillman (New York, 1975), pp. 291–94.

66   40_{36}, $14{:}45_{28}$,   "Nikita"—in the original, *Nikitushka,* a hypocoristic of *Nikita.* Hypocoristics (forms of endearment) are routinely formed in Russian with suffixes such as *-ok, -ik, -usha, -ushka,* and others. The speaker's social dialect is signaled mostly by the use of many diminutives and hypocoristics where educated speech would have a simple form.

67   41_{7-17}, $14{:}45_{45}$–46_8,   This legend is a very free paraphrase of the "Tale of the Blessed Father Daniel about Andronicus and His Wife," part of the Russian Orthodox *Prologue.* See *PSS* 15:537.

68   41_{44-45}, $14{:}46_{37-38}$,   Matt. 2:18, itself a quotation from Jer. 31:15.

69   42_{5-6}, $14{:}46_{46}$,   Echoes John 16:20 and Jer. 31:13.

70   42_{10}, $14{:}47_1$,   "Aleksei"—on the symbolic function of this name, see Introduction I.4.b. Sacred Sources, and III.5.d. Name Symbolism. Cf. *PSS* 15:474–76.

71   42_{14-15}, $14{:}47_{4-5}$,   Words similar to those Dostoevsky had heard from Father Amvrosy at Optina hermitage. See note 65 above.

72   42_{18}, $14{:}47_8$,   Father Zosima says "beatitude" *(blazhenstvo),* not "happiness." A simple Russian would understand the word and appreciate the difference.

73   42_{28}, $14{:}47_{17}$,   "a very old woman"—Russ. *staren'kaia starushonka* (from *star,* "old"), where both noun and adjective are diminutives. An example of Dostoevsky's colloquial penchant for tautology and pleonasm.

74   43_2, $14{:}47_{33}$,   Brings up the theme of the second temptation of Christ: a rejection of magic and sorcery. Another instance where a focal theme is at first introduced in a trivial form. Cf. Book One, note 117.

75   43_{6-8}, $14:47_{38-39}$,   Cf. Book Four, chap. i, p. 150.
76   43_{39-41}, $14:48_{22-24}$,   Ultimately an echo of Matt. 12:31, often found in the works of the Fathers of the Eastern church.
77    $43_{46}-44_1$, $14:48_{30-31}$,   Inexact quote of Luke 15:7.
78   44_{5-8}, $14:48_{34-38}$,   Here "atone," "redeem," and "expiate" translate three different forms of the Russian verb for "to buy": *pokupat'*, "to buy," *kupit'*, "to buy," and *vykupit'*, "to redeem," in that order. Significantly *iskupit'*, "to expiate," is not used. Father Zosima prefers simpler language.

Chapter iv

79   45_{3-4}, $14:49_{27-28}$,   Dostoevsky satirizes the condescending pseudopopulism of the liberal upper class. Note that Mme. Khokhlakov is concerned solely with her own emotions.
80   45_{25}, $14:50_5$,   Mme. Khokhlakov uses the French form of her daughter's name. Earlier she had said "Liza."
81   46_{12-14}, $14:50_{39-40}$,   Note how Dostoevsky creates suspense. We do not even know who Katerina Ivanovna is, but we know that she is involved in something interesting. Another example of Dostoevsky's habit of introducing his characters step by step. The first reference to the heroine's "suffering" is significant: it comes from a patently unreliable witness and sounds exaggerated. The reader is preconditioned to look at Katerina Ivanovna critically.
82   46_{34}, $14:51_{12}$,   "Obdorsk"—there actually is such a place in northwestern Siberia.
83   46_{38-40}, $14:51_{16-18}$,   This detail, again, is drawn from an episode reported about the elder Leonid by Parfeny. See Introduction I.4.b. Sacred Sources.
84   47_6, $14:51_{30-31}$,   "For men are made for happiness"—a remarkable statement. It contradicts not only the Grand Inquisitor (Book Five, chap. v) and Schiller's "Resignation" (see Introduction I.4.a. Secular Sources), but also, so it would seem, the dogma of the Orthodox church. See Introduction II.5.b. Mysticism.
85   47_{21}, $14:51_{46-47}$,   The theme of Fiodor Pavlovich's diatribe on life beyond the grave (Book One, chap. iv, pp. 18–19) is introduced in a new variation. There will be several more.
86   47_{33-35}, $14:52_{11-13}$,   Mme. Khokhlakov is embarrassed to state the atheists' arguments explicitly, so she comes up with some awkward circumlocutions.

87   47_{37}, $14:52_{14}$,   Turgenev, in the twenty-first chapter of his novel *Fathers and Sons* (1862), lets his atheist hero Bazarov say these words. *The Brothers Karamazov* and other novels by Dostoevsky contain many passages directed against Turgenev and his philosophy, a rather pessimistic, agnostic humanism. See Introduction I.4.a. Secular Sources.

88   48_{11}, $14:52_{32}$,   "This has been tried."—Zosima's theology is existential, even positivist: his proof of the existence of God stems from human experience.

89   48_{19}, $14:52_{40}$,   "I would be ready to kiss such wounds."—Characteristically, this extreme example of "active love" is first brought up by this shallow and frivolous personage. It will come back in Book Five, chap. iv, p. 218.

90   48_{42-45}, $14:53_{18-20}$,   A sententious statement of great importance. Cf. Book Five, chap. iv, p. 218_{31-33}. See Introduction II.2.a. Challenge to Christianity, and II.2.b. Arguments in Support of Christianity.

91   49_{8-9}, $14:53_{31-32}$,   "the more I detest men individually the more ardent becomes my love for humanity"—Dostoevsky makes sure that this paradox will be remembered by his reader. The sententious quality of this concluding statement is enhanced by a rhythmic clausule: *k chèlovéchestvù voobshché* (trochaic tetrameter), "for humanity at large."

92   49_{12-13}, $14:53_{36}$,   Biblical diction (see, for instance, Rom. 4:3).

93   49_{14-15}, $14:53_{38-39}$,   "If you have been talking to me so sincerely, simply to gain approbation for your frankness"—the conversation, as so often in Dostoevsky, suddenly takes a surprising turn.

94   49_{18-19}, $14:53_{42}$,   "slip away like a phantom"—the concept of a godless life that is not life, but "phantom life," "life as a dream," is found even in the Bible (Job 20:8). It was applied by German idealistic philosophy and its followers in Russia to any form of human existence which lacks historical, national, or moral substance. This concept will return as one aspect of the condition in which the devil, Ivan Karamazov's double, finds himself (Book Eleven, chap. ix, pp. 605_{29-30} and 609_{17-18}).

95   49_{30-31}, $14:54_{4-5}$,   "avoid falsehood . . ."—Mme. Khokhlakov is in many ways the female counterpart of Fiodor Pavlovich. Here she receives the admonishment which he had received earlier (chap. ii, p. 36_{22}). See Introduction III.3.b. Mirroring and Doubling.

96   49_{45}–50_3, $14:54_{20-26}$, This seems shallow only at first sight. In effect, Father Zosima suggests that only the person who, after years of tenacious work at self-perfection, discovers in himself the humility to admit that he is as far as ever from true perfection, truly experiences the grace of God.

97   50_{40-41}, $14:55_{15-17}$, An example of Dostoevsky's psychology "from the outside in." Liza's laughter prepares the reader for subsequent revelations of greater depths of her soul. See Introduction II.6.a. Dostoevsky's Psychology.

Chapter v

98   51_2, $14:55_{25}$, "So Be It!"—The Russian word *(búdi)* is an imperative-optative, immediately recognizable as a solemn Slavonic form.

99   51_{3-4}, $14:55_{26-27}$, Obviously there is a gap between narrative time and clock time in this episode. A compression of clock time is one of those aspects of Dostoevsky's novelistic structure which suggests an affinity to the stage drama.

100   51_{16-17}, $14:55_{39-40}$, "the new generation positively ignores us"— Dostoevsky is alluding to the fact that liberal intellectuals of the 1840s, such as Alexander Herzen (1812–70), were often slighted by the radicals of the 1860s—so much so that they sometimes felt obliged to remind the public that they, too, were and had been for a long time "progressives."

101   51_{41}, $14:56_{19}$, "Aliosha watched him intently."—The scene is seen through Aliosha's eyes. This allows the narrator to convey Aliosha's suspense to the reader.

102   51_{42}, $14:56_{20}$, "this gentleman's"—in the original, Father Iosif uses the polite third person plural ("their"), modest monk that he is. A social equal would have simply said "Ivan Fiodorovich's."

103   51_{42}, $14:56_{20}$, We have heard about this article earlier. See Book One, chap. iii, p. 11.

104   52_2, $14:56_{25}$, The "ecclesiastical authority" is M. I. Gorchakov, a professor of Petersburg University, with whose lengthy article "Toward a Scientific Formulation of Ecclesiastic-Judiciary Law" (1875) Dostoevsky was familiar. The text of this chapter fairly reflects the gist of this article. See *PSS* 15:534. Cf. Book One, note 75. Father Iosif's speech reflects his position: it is archaic and bookish, but learned and thoughtful.

105   52_{28}, $14:57_4$, "with fervor and decision"—translates *tviordo i nervno,* "firmly and nervously." Father Paisy is firm in his acceptance of Ivan's words, yet a note of nervousness is heard in his voice, as he suspects that the devil's cloven hoof will soon show in Ivan's argument. The translator has needlessly corrected Dostoevsky.

106   52_{29}, $14:57_6$, The Italian, or "ultramontane," party in the Roman Catholic church of the nineteenth century favored the doctrine of papal supremacy. It is significant that a connection between Ivan's ideas and Roman Catholicism is established at this early stage in the novel. See Introduction II.4.e. The Church, and II.4.g. Minor Political Points.

107   52_{31}, $14:57_8$, A not entirely felicitous pun: "ultramontane," of French coinage, means "transalpine," i.e., "Italian."

108   52_{40}, $14:57_{17-18}$, Christ's response to Pilate, John 18:36.

109   53_{11}, $14:57_{32}$, "divine promise"—Father Paisy is alluding to Rev. 20:4. According to the Book of Revelation, there will be two resurrections, the first of which will affect God's saints only, who will reign with Christ for a thousand years. This provides Christians with a scriptural basis for utopian ("chiliastic") thinking.

110   53_{26}, $14:57_{48}$-58_1, Echoes Matt. 16:18, albeit not very appropriately. Minor lapses like this one add a flavor of authenticity and immediacy.

111   53_{28}, $14:58_3$, "drawing"—translates *obratit',* "to convert." So there is a pun here: "converting the whole world . . . into [a] Church."

112   54_{11-15}, $14:58_{33-37}$, "Russian hopes and conceptions . . ."—the theme of the "Russian way," as against the "European way," was one of Dostoevsky's main preoccupations. The ideas expressed by Fathers Paisy and Zosima were Dostoevsky's own. In the last issue of *Diary of a Writer* (1881) Dostoevsky says much the same under his own name. See *Diary of a Writer* 2:1028-31.

113   54_{23}, $14:58_{45}$, "beating"—translates *rozgi,* "rods." Miusov's words are meant to provoke his opponents. He mentions "rods" (corporal punishment had been largely abolished by the recent judicial reform) as if to suggest that so reactionary a body as the Church would no doubt have them back.

114   54_{26-27}, $14:59_3$, "not all at once of course, but fairly soon"— such hedging is characteristic of the narrator's diction.

115   54_{42-44}, $14:59_{18-20}$, There is a deadly irony in this little dramatic scene: soon enough Ivan will enact it in real life.

116 55_{4-5}, $14:59_{26-27}$, Now Ivan waxes eloquent. But he overdoes it: "regeneration . . . reformation and salvation" is too solemn and, in the present context, has a false ring. See Introduction III.1.b. Ivan Karamazov.

117 55_{16-18}, $14:59_{36-40}$, "the real chastisement . . ."—Dostoevsky had treated this particular problem in his novel *Crime and Punishment* (1866).

118 56_{15}, $14:60_{38-39}$, "the idea that his crime is not a crime"—this notion was widely defended by the radicals of the 1860s. Nikolai Dobroliubov (1836-61), in particular, had expressed it in a famous article, "The Kingdom of Darkness" (1859). Dostoevsky took issue with it in *Crime and Punishment*.

119 56_{18}, $14:60_{41}$, "exclusion"—Russ. *otluchenie* is both "secular exclusion" and "spiritual excommunication," which allows one to state the point more forcefully.

120 56_{24-25}, $14:60_{47}-61_1$, "to pass from the lower form, as Church, into the higher form, as State"—one of the central ideas of "The Grand Inquisitor" (Book Five, chap. v) is stated here summarily. Father Zosima thus anticipates and defuses some of Ivan's arguments in "The Grand Inquisitor."

121 56_{26-27}, $14:61_{1-3}$, "As for Rome"—again, these are Dostoevsky's own views. See Introduction II.4.g. Minor Political Points.

122 56_{30}, $14:61_6$, "cuts him off"—translates *otluchaet*, "cuts off, separates," but also "excommunicates." Cf. note 119 above. The effect of the persistent repetition of this verb is lost in this translation.

123 57_3, $14:61_{25-26}$, "seven righteous men" ("seven men of honest report" in the King James version)—Acts 6:3, on the early days of the Church. Dostoevsky may be responding to a passage in Chernyshevsky's famous novel *What Is to Be Done?* (1863), where a like number of truly reliable followers is claimed for the socialist movement.

124 57_7, $14:61_{29-30}$, "at the end of the ages"—1 Cor. 10:11 τὰ τέλη τῶν αἰώνων, which in Russian translates *v kontse vekov*, "the end of the ages." The King James version has "the ends of the world."

125 57_8, $14:61_{31-32}$, Acts 1:7.

126 57_{12}, $14:61_{36}$, Father Zosima's eschatological utopia is theologically suspect. It smacks of the secular utopian ideas of Fourier and other socialists which had fascinated Dostoevsky in his youth. Cf. Introduction II.2.c. The Historical Dimension.

127 57_{21}, $14:61_{47-48}$,   Pope Gregory VII (1073–85), famous for his feud with Emperor Henry IV, whom he forced to do penance at Canossa (1077). During his struggle with the Catholic church in the 1870s, Bismarck vowed that he would "never make a pilgrimage to Canossa." Hence, the name of Pope Gregory VII was well-known to the general public of that period.

128 57_{24-25}, $14:62_3$, "the third temptation"—Matt. 4:8–9. Once again Ivan's argument in "The Grand Inquisitor" is anticipated. See Introduction II.2.a. Challenge to Christianity.

129 57_{29}, $14:62_8$, Cf. Matt. 2:2.

130 57_{36-38}, $14:62_{15-17}$, Cf. note 41 above.

131 57_{41}, $14:62_{21}$, "the coup d'état of December"—On 2 December, 1851 Louis-Napoleon Bonaparte overthrew the Second Republic. He became Emperor in 1852.

132 58_{22}, $14:62_{46-47}$, "You apply them to us"—this is exactly what was often said of Dostoevsky. Dmitry Merezhkovsky observed that Dostoevsky's "religious revolution," as outlined in this chapter of *The Brothers Karamazov* and elsewhere, was as much, or more, of a threat to the existing state than any political revolution. Cf. Introduction II.1.b. The Apocalyptic Allegory.

Chapter vi

133 58_{29}, $14:63_5$, One of the novel's many provocative chapter headings. Together, the chapter titles form a composition in their own right.

134 58_{31-32}, $14:63_{7-8}$, "much older than his years"—characteristic of the narrator's hyperbolic diction, and not to be taken literally.

135 58_{32-33}, $14:63_9$, "considerable physical strength"—reminiscent of Dmitry's mother, to whom the same expression was applied. See Book One, chap. i, p. 4_6.

136 58_{36-37}, $14:63_{13}$, "firm determination . . . a vague look"—a typical instance of Dostoevsky's "centrifugal" psychology.

137 59_{44}, $14:64_{22}$, Dostoevsky's dialogues lead into many blind alleys, rarely exhaust a question, and in most instances fail to reach a conclusion. See Introduction III.3. Narrative Structure.

138 60_{4-5}, $14:64_{29}$, "liberal dilettantes"—perhaps a dig at the liberal Herzen, author of an article entitled "Dilettantishness in Science" (1843). Cf. Introduction I.4.a. Secular Sources.

139 60_5, $14:64_{30}$, "results"—he means "goals." Such imprecision is surely intentional on Dostoevsky's part. In live discourse one does not always find the right word.

140   60_7, $14:64_{33}$, "dilettantes"—Ivan Fiodorovich makes it quite clear that he means Piotr Aleksandrovich (earlier he had said *diletantizm*, "dilettantishness," translated by "dilettantes"). Hence the acerbity of Miusov's rejoinder.

141   60_{8-9}, $14:64_{34}$, "the police—the foreign police, of course—do the same"—perhaps a very personal barb. Dostoevsky was resentful of the fact that almost until the end of his life he was under secret police supervision because of his early record, despite twenty years of loyal support of the Tsar.

142   60_{17-19}, $14:64_{45-46}$, "because men have believed in immortality"—once more, a major philosophical thesis is brought in through the back door, as it were: it is introduced by a minor character (Miusov is soon to disappear from the pages of the novel), and as an extravagant notion, not to be taken seriously. It is a thought which had been stated clearly by Blaise Pascal. See *PSS* 15:536.

143   60_{24}, $14:65_3$, "cannibalism"—translates *antropofagiia*, "anthropophagy." Russian has a native word for "cannibalism," which Miusov squeamishly avoids.

144   60_{26-30}, $14:65_{6-10}$, "the moral law of nature must immediately be changed . . ."—this is Nietzsche's "transvaluation of all values," and as in Nietzsche, it is a corollary of the "death of God." Dostoevsky was not familiar with Nietzsche, and though Nietzsche knew some of Dostoevsky's works, he arrived at his new morality independently of Dostoevsky.

145   60_{45-46}, $14:65_{27}$, "There is no virtue if there is no immortality."—Cf. Pierre's words in Tolstoi's *War and Peace:* "If there is God and future life, there is Truth and there is Virtue." See L. N. Tolstoi, *Polnoe sobranie sochinenii,* 90 vols. (Moscow, 1928–58), 10:177.

146   61_{22-23}, $14:66_2$, Father Zosima combines two verses from different epistles of Saint Paul: Col. 3:2 and Phil. 3:20. In the original, the text between "of thinking" and "heavens" is given in quotation marks. The King James version has "conversation" for "dwelling."

147   61_{24-25}, $14:66_{3-4}$, The elder's invocation is relevant to the question what will happen to Ivan beyond the events actually described in the novel. See Introduction III.3.e. Expository Novel.

148   61_{37}, $14:66_{15}$, "my flesh"—Fiodor Pavlovich uses the Slavonic form of this biblical expression (Gen. 2:23) to create an impression of solemnity. Of course, he promptly makes a travesty of it.

149 61_{42}, $14:66_{20}$, Schiller's drama *The Robbers* (1781) plays an important role in the novel. Here it foreshadows the novel's plot. Fiodor Pavlovich, like Count von Moor, is mistaken in his assessment of his two sons: it is, in fact, Ivan who in many ways resembles the villain of Schiller's play, Franz von Moor. See Introduction I.4.a. Secular Sources.

150 62_{16-17}, $14:66_{37}$, In the original, Fiodor Pavlovich uses two slang expressions both of which suggest "stealing."

151 62_{32}, $14:67_5$, In the original: *Anna s mechami na shee,* "Anna on-the-neck, with swords." The class of a decoration was signaled by where it was worn (a "star on the breast" would have been higher). The swords merely indicate that the decoration was granted for military service. The decoration about which Fiodor Pavlovich makes so much fuss was not a high one.

152 62_{35}, $14:67_7$, "a certain enchantress"—in the original: "local enchantress." The first, vague version of a story which will be told again more than once in the novel. See Introduction III.3.a. Motifs.

153 62_{42}, $14:67_{14}$, This plural ("thousands," rather than "over a thousand") will play a key role in the plot of the novel.

154 62_{43-44}, $14:67_{16}$, "Shall I say, Mitia?"—More suspense: we shall find out what is behind this many pages later. Fiodor Pavlovich's account, full of lies, half-truths, and blanks, still sketches the situation which generates the plot of the novel.

155 63_{5-6}, $14:67_{23-24}$, The father-son theme is stated here as poignantly as anywhere in the novel. Once again, this early statement of a focal theme is a frivolous one. Cf. Introduction II.3.a. Fatherhood.

156 63_9, $14:67_{28}$, "honorable"—this characterization is immediately "exploded" by the details which follow: characteristic of Fiodor Pavlovich's style.

157 63_{12-16}, $14:67_{31-34}$, The first of several versions of this incident. Dmitry will presently give his. We will also hear about it from Katerina Ivanovna (Book Four, chap. v, p. 176) and from the other principal (Book Four, chap. vii, pp. 186–87), and there will be various allusions to it. Cf. Introduction III.3.a. Motifs.

158 64_{12}, $14:68_{30}$, "creature"—this label, applied here to the heroine of the novel, will reappear often, until its symbolic significance will become clear: "creature" is an opprobrious word, but it also implies the meaning "God's creature."

159   64_{17-19}, $14:68_{35-37}$,   An echo of Schiller's *Cabal and Love* (1784),
Act IV, sc. iii, where the young hero, Ferdinand, challenges his
presumed rival, a cowardly, middle-aged courtier, to a duel
"over a handkerchief" (which belongs to the heroine), with each
adversary holding one edge of the handkerchief with one hand
and a pistol with the other. The courtier flees, of course. The
roles are reversed by Fiodor Pavlovich. Dostoevsky must have
also had in mind Pushkin's *Covetous Knight,* where a father
challenges his son to a duel.

160   64_{24-26}, $14:68_{43-44}$,   "You're acting now . . ."—Dostoevsky was
fascinated by this psychological phenomenon. A notebook entry
suggests that he was delighted at finding an example of this in
Tacitus, *Annals* 1.22, where the story is told of one Vibulenus,
who incites his fellow soldiers to mutiny with an impassioned
account of the cruel death of his brother—who later turns out to
have been a mere figment of his imagination. See *The Unpublished Dostoevsky: Diaries and Notebooks,* ed. Carl R.
Proffer, 3 vols. (Ann Arbor, 1973–76), 2:93.

161   64_{35-37}, $14:69_{5-7}$,   Fiodor Pavlovich is, of course, alluding to his
own first wife, Miusov's cousin, who deserted her husband and
child and went off to live with some student. See Book One,
chap. i, p. 4.

162   65_5, $14:69_{19}$,   This is the moment of Dmitry's fall. He is now
guilty of wishing his father dead, and so of parricide (Matt.
5:22). It is significant that he speaks "evenly and deliberately."

163   65_{9-10}, $14:69_{23-24}$,   "you monks who are seeking salvation!"—
The Russian phrase *(gospoda spasaiushchiesia ieromonakhi)* is
heavily loaded: one does not normally address monks as
"gentlemen" *(gospoda),* "Fathers" being in order; *ieromonakhi,* lit. "holy monks," is the official title of the three
monks, but not normally used in face-to-face address; the
formulaic expression *spasat'sia,* "to live as a monk" (lit. "to
save oneself," i.e., one's soul) is used here with obvious sarcasm.

164   65_{10-11}, $14:69_{24}$,   "ruined   by   her   environment"—Fiodor
Pavlovich uses a popular cliché of the "progressive" ideology of
the 1860s, which held the environment responsible for any sort of
criminal behavior.

165   65_{12}, $14:69_{25}$,   The allusion is to Luke 7:27. This is a
reminiscence of Dostoevsky's article "Mr. Defense Lawyer and
Velikanova," in which he had taken a lawyer to task for having

abused this biblical passage in defending a woman of questionable virtue against a charge of attempted murder. See *Diary of a Writer* (1876), 1:329–30.

166 65_{16}, $14:69_{30}$, Gudgeons are small fish which are easily caught and not very tasty.

167 65_{37}, $14:70_5$, "Was it symbolic or what?"—Translates *eto emblema kakaia-nibud'?* He says "emblem" to avoid the more direct "sign," or even "symbol," trying to appear condescending.

168 66_{21}, $14:70_{36}$, "I'll prove it by the church calendar."— Presumably by pointing out the entry of his marriage to Miusov's cousin.

Chapter vii

169 67_{11}, $14:71_{23}$, Russ. *seminarist*, "seminarian, divinity student," had a pejorative ring. Seminarians, of low social background (at best, from the more or less hereditary lower clergy), were poor, often uncouth, uneducated, and crudely materialistic. Many quit their studies to pursue a secular career. Others became revolutionaries. The word *seminarist* was usually associated with the image of a person exceedingly self-assured and proud of his learning, as well as inclined to literalism and pedantry. Rakitin is a *seminarist* par excellence.

170 67_{21}, $14:71_{34}$, In the original: "Give me your blessing to stay here." With the elder, Aliosha speaks the language of the monastery.

171 67_{24}, $14:71_{37}$, "my son"—in the original: *synok*, diminutive of *syn*, "son," a form which a fond father might use. This explains "the elder liked to call him that."

172 67_{29-30}, $14:71_{42-43}$, "I bless you for great service in the world."—Translates *Blagoslovliaiu tebia na velikoe poslushanie v miru,* which is ecclesiastic diction all the way. There is a near contradiction in terms between *poslushanie*, "task of obedience," and *v miru*, "in the (secular) world." The case form *v miru* suggests that *mir* means "the secular world, the world outside."

173 67_{30-38}, $14:71_{43}$–72_5, Most of Father Zosima's prophecy relates to events beyond the plot of this novel. See Introduction III.3.e. Expository Novel.

174   68_2, $14:72_{12}$, "near both"—it is clear that Dmitry needs all the help he can get. Now, for the first time, we hear that Ivan may be facing a tragedy also. This helps build suspense.

175   68_{31-32}, $14:72_{43}$, "what does that vision mean?"—translates *chto sei son znachit?*, a common phrase in the publicistic prose of the 1860s and 1870s, particularly that of M. E. Saltykov-Shchedrin (1826–89), one of the leaders of the radicals and for twenty years one of Dostoevsky's main adversaries. There will be more echoes of this literary feud later in the novel. At any rate, Rakitin is labeled by this phrase (originally, a misquote from Pushkin's ballad "The Bridegroom").

176   68_{34}, $14:72_{46}$, "your brother"—translates *tvoemu brattsu*. The diminutive *bratets*, lit. "little brother" or "dear brother," is often used ironically, and so here.

177   68_{43}, $14:73_7$, Rakitin's language is pointedly disrespectful. Here "holy mummery" translates *blagogluposti*, a compound consisting of *blago*, "good," and *gluposti*, "foolishness, nonsense." Coined by Saltykov-Shchedrin (see note 175 above), it contrasts ironically with many compounds of the sacred realm, such as *blagoveshchenie*, "Annunciation," *blagogovenie*, "reverence," etc. Cf. S. S. Borshchevskii, *Shchedrin i Dostoevskii: Istoriia ikh ideinoi bor'by* (Moscow, 1956), pp. 313–14.

178   68_{47}, $14:73_{10-11}$, Russ. *ugolovshchina*, "crime," is derived from *golova*, "head" (cf. Eng. "capital offense," "capital punishment," etc.). Hence the word has a more sinister ring than Eng. "crime."

179   69_3, $14:73_{14}$, "family"—translates *semeike*. Cf. Book One, note 9. I would translate: "in your fine family."

180   69_3, $14:73_{15}$, Cf. note 176 above. I would translate: "between your dear brothers."

181   69_{9-10}, $14:73_{17-18}$, Ironic foreshadowing: Dmitry is adjudged guilty even before there has been a crime.

182   69_{10-11}, $14:73_{21-22}$, "Crazy fanatics" translates *iurodivykh;* cf. Book One, note 94. According to a popular legend, a holy man acted as stated here because he could see all the devils gathered in front of the church, awaiting their victims' departure from its protection, while all the guardian angels were at the tavern, anxious to protect their charges.

183   69_{12-13}, $14:73_{22-23}$, Rakitin lets himself be carried away by his own eloquence: the story about the elder and his stick was told

about a different elder, and was also untrue (see chap. i, p. 30_{38-42}). Throughout the novel, Rakitin will express a sober, materialistic view of things—and invariably be wrong.

184   69_{18-19}, $14:73_{28}$, "you're always between two stools"—Saltykov-Shchedrin had used this expression to describe Dostoevsky's position in 1863. See Borshchevskii, pp. 313–14.

185   69_{20}, $14:73_{30}$, "I have"—typical of Dostoevskian dialogue: even Aliosha is unpredictable.

186   69_{27}, $14:73_{37}$, "Mitenka"—a hypocoristic form (Dmitry → Mitia → Mit'ka → Miten'ka) which would ordinarily identify a small boy. Here it is ironic.

187   69_{44}, $14:74_{6-7}$, "sensualist"—one of the leitmotifs of the novel, and a label of the Karamazovs. Russ. *sladostrastnik* is a compound of *sladok,* "sweet," and *strastnyi,* "passionate," hence lit. "he who has a passion for sweetness." Therefore, "voluptuary" may be a better translation in some contexts. But since all four Karamazovs are to be covered by the word, "sensualist" is probably best. Cf. Book Three, note 6.

188   70_3, $14:74_{12}$, "knives"—only a figure of speech. Rakitin dramatizes things a bit.

189   70_{15}, $14:74_{23}$, Pushkin has a number of verses addressed to "little feet." The radicals of the 1860s liked to cite this as evidence of the poet's frivolity and low moral stature. Rakitin will return to the subject of "little feet" later in the novel. Cf. Book Eleven, note 42.

190   70_{25}, $14:74_{34}$, In the original, Rakitin switches here to "Alioshka," less affectionate, but more familiar than "Aliosha."

191   70_{30}, $14:74_{38}$, "birth and selection"—it should be "race and selection." Rakitin is, of course, a Darwinist.

192   70_{32-35}, $14:74_{40-43}$, This foreshadows a scene several hundred pages later, Book Seven, chap. ii, p. 321_{10-14}.

193   71_{16-17}, $14:75_{18}$, "has gone wild about her"—translates *vliubilsia khuzhe koshki,* lit. "fell in love worse than a cat," which is formulaic and also slang.

194   71_{25}, $14:75_{27-28}$, "but he's ready to marry her"—translates *no zato sposoben zhenit'sia,* "but then, he is capable of marrying her." This sounds like catachresis (use of the wrong word). But to Rakitin's thinking, to marry Grushen'ka is an act requiring the kind of heroic madness only a Dmitry Karamazov possesses. Rakitin's vehemently negative attitude toward Grushen'ka is a

detail fraught with a deeper meaning which will be fully revealed only in Book Twelve.

195   71_{28-29}, $14:75_{30-32}$, "mistress of a dissolute old merchant, Samsonov, a coarse, uneducated, provincial mayor"—This translation does not render the flavor of the original. Rakitin has a Russian intellectual's haughty contempt for the uneducated businessman. The word for "merchant" appears in a deprecatory diminutive *(kupchishka)*. He also calls Samsonov a *muzhik*, "peasant, boor." Perhaps: "mistress of Samsonov, that old shopkeeper, lecherous muzhik, and mayor of our town."

196   71_{32}, $14:75_{34}$, "He'll carry off"—translates *priobretiot*, "he'll acquire," another intentional catachresis: Rakitin flaunts his cynicism.

197   71_{38}, $14:75_{40}$, "Katia"—the original has *Katen'ka*. This hypocoristic (Katerina → Katia → Kat'ka → Katen'ka), something like "Cathykin," is disrespectful in this context. It is much too familiar for a young man to use in reference to a lady who stands far above him socially.

198   71_{42-43}, $14:75_{46}$, "He is laughing at you"—Rakitin is projecting his own attitudes upon Ivan, some of whose ideas he shares, though without Ivan's depth. Aliosha promptly calls Rakitin's bluff. See Introduction II.2.a. Challenge to Christianity. This passage is revealing also of Rakitin's background, showing some blatant seminary slang.

199   72_{7}, $14:76_{9}$, The fact that the Karamazovs belong to the nobility, pointed out repeatedly, is significant. See Introduction II.4.a. The Russian Nobleman. Rakitin is the son of a parish priest and thus belongs to the lower middle class.

200   72_{11}, $14:76_{13}$, "That's plagiarism"—a striking phrase which ought to be remembered. It will be used again, by Ivan, helping to link the two scenes in which it occurs. See Book Five, chap. v, p. 244_{21}.

201   72_{17}, $14:76_{19}$, The phrase "everything is lawful" (cf. chap. vi, p. 60_{28-34}) is a leitmotif of the whole novel. It will appear many more times. See Introduction I.4.b. Sacred Sources, and III.3.a. Motifs.

202   72_{20}, $14:76_{21-22}$, "pedantic poseurs"—here "pedantic" translates *shkol'nyi*, which is simply the adjective to *shkola*, "school." Thus, "schoolmasterly" or "schoolboyish" would be in order. I would actually prefer "schoolboyish," since it establishes a first connection between Ivan and the schoolboy

Kolia Krasotkin. See Introduction III.3.b. Mirroring and Doubling.

203 72_{21-23}, $14:76_{22-24}$, " 'Haunted by profound, unsolved doubts' " in the original is meant to be nonsensical. Rakitin turns Aliosha's serious words (l. 9) into an absurdity—something which the translation does not reflect. Perhaps: "unsolvable profundity of thought." Also, " 'on the one hand we cannot but admit' " and " 'on the other it must be confessed!' " is a quote from Saltykov-Shchedrin's *Unfinished Conversations,* Pt. I(1873). See M. E. Saltykov-Shchedrin, *Sobranie sochinenii v dvadtsati tomakh,* 20 vols. (Moscow, 1965-77), 15, pt. 2:159. Dostoevsky is making sure that the "Rakitin" label will stick to his ideological opponents. See Borshchevskii, p. 313.

204 72_{24-26}, $14:76_{26-28}$, Rakitin's ideas are those of the eighteenth-century Enlightenment, popularized by Russian radicals of the 1860s. Rakitin believes (with Immanuel Kant, among others—see L. A. Zander, *Taina dobra* [Frankfurt am Main, 1960], pp. 28-29) that virtue is immanent in human nature. Dostoevsky's refutation of this position is Rakitin himself, a person not only devoid of virtue, but incapable of it. It is significant that Rakitin would be mouthing the slogans of the French Revolution: freedom, equality, fraternity. The Marxist concept of class struggle was still unknown in Russia at the time.

205 72_{33-34}, $14:76_{34-35}$, "I guess from your warmth that you are not indifferent to Katerina Ivanovna yourself"—another surprise, but this one is a dead end, leading to no further complications, at least not in the text of the actual novel.

206 73_4, $14:77_3$, "archimandrite"—an abbot.

207 73_{8-17}, $14:77_{6-19}$, Various prototypes have been suggested for the subject of Ivan's improvisation. There is evidence that Dostoevsky had in mind one G. Z. Eliseev (1821-91). See *PSS* 15:539. Cf. Introduction I.6.d. Ivan Karamazov and Other Characters.

208 73_{13}, $14:77_{14}$, "some Jew"—Russ. *zhidishka.* Again, the opprobrious word, with a condescending diminutive suffix.

209 73_{16}, $14:77_{17}$, The stone bridge was actually built 1875-79, so the chronology is about right.

210 73_{30}, $14:77_{33}$, "I'd forgotten she was a relation of yours"—another little surprise. It will lead to more surprises later in the novel. See Book Twelve, chap. iv, p. 649_{26-28}.

211 73_{36-37}, $14:77_{40}$, "admitted to the kitchen"—this little detail is an exaggeration. Fiodor Pavlovich was a "genteel" sponger.

212 73_{40}, $14:77_{44}$, "a common harlot"—translates *publichnaia devka*, lit. "public wench," i.e. "common prostitute." Aliosha promptly questions the exactness of this adjective: being the mayor's mistress hardly makes one a "common prostitute."

213 73_{41}, $14:77_{44}$, In the original, there is a "sir" added to "I beg you to understand that!" Rakitin is very angry and therefore uses a sarcastic formal form of address. His words are not only coarse, but also ill-chosen. He has no "style."

214 74_{15-16}, $14:78_{14-15}$, "beating the Father Superior"—Dostoevsky will introduce even the zaniest slapstick comedy simply by letting somebody imagine it. This is not the only instance in Dostoevsky where some dignified personage gets thrashed in this way: Karmazinov in *The Possessed* suffers a similar fate.

Chapter viii

215 74_{25}, $14:78_{25}$, "he felt ashamed of having lost his temper"—this statement, which seems rather friendly toward Miusov for a change, is nevertheless ironic. The pointed repetition of the adjective *delikatnyi*, "delicate," in the preceding two lines (translated by the noun "delicacy" and the adjective "inward") is the giveaway: Miusov's thoughts, as reported, are anything but "delicate."

216 74_{34}, $14:78_{34}$, "Aesop"—the fabulist, and hence, as in English, "a liar." "Pierrot"—a clown. Both epithets will also be applied to Fiodor Pavlovich by his sons. See Book Twelve, chap. ii, p. 633_{4-6}.

217 75_{10-19}, $14:79_{1-12}$, This description of a well-set table and many other descriptions found in the novel disprove the opinion, held by some, that Dostoevsky's novels are poor in descriptive detail. Descriptions such as this, having no particular symbolic function, serve the purpose of creating "atmosphere" and a concrete setting.

218 76_{9-13}, $14:80_{1-4}$, This tirade shows that Dostoevsky can write well—i.e., according to all the rules of rhetoric—when this is in character. Miusov's phrases are well turned, and he produces such niceties as *sozhalenie, sokrushenie i pokaianie*, "regret, repentance, and contrition" (I have reversed the word order in

translation so as to reproduce Miusov's elegant play with alliteration; Garnett-Matlaw has "apologies and regrets").

219 76_{14}, $14:80_5$, "tirade"—Dostoevsky gives the reader a bit of a commentary himself, as he identifies the literary style of which he has just availed himself. Such instances of "inner commentary" are frequent throughout the novel.

220 76_{16}, $14:80_8$, "He . . . loved humanity again."—This sarcastic remark points to one of the novel's main theses: the shaky foundation of "love of humanity" without God.

221 76_{22-23}, $14:80_{14-16}$, In the original, Maksimov is once more called a "landowner," and once more, a trivial detail of his behavior is pointed out. Maksimov will remain a minor character, but he will accompany the action to the end and serve up a few surprises.

222 76_{24-25}, $14:80_{17}$, "played his last prank"—in the original: "cut his last caper" (as in a lively dance).

223 76_{33-41}, $14:80_{26-35}$, Another instance of Dostoevsky's pattern of cross-references: Fiodor Pavlovich is quoting himself almost, but not quite exactly (cf. chap. ii, p. 36).

224 76_{40-41}, $14:80_{34-35}$, "I played him a dirty trick, and ever since I have hated him."—Another of Dostoevsky's psychological paradoxes. See Introduction II.6.d. Psychoanalytic Interpretation.

225 77_{40}, $14:81_{32}$, "von Sohn"—cf. note 12 above.

226 78_4, $14:81_{44}$, "harlots"—translates *bludnye pliasavitsy*, "harlot-dancing damsels," a biblical expression which echoes Mark 6:21–28.

227 78_5, $14:81_{45}$, "the piano"—translates *fortopliasy*, a colloquial malapropism derived from "fortepiano." The details here are taken from the actual murder trial, but the outrageous combination of lurid detail and biblical language is Fiodor Pavlovich's contribution.

228 78_{22-23}, $14:82_{15}$, "I am his father . . ."—this is not just plain gall: it leads up to what is almost a *bona fide* argument.

229 78_{24-25}, $14:82_{16-17}$, Fiodor Pavlovich keeps switching his point of view, being alternately spontaneous, well under control, or something in between. Here he suddenly turns objective, observing himself "from the outside," as it were.

230 78_{28}, $14:82_{20}$, "Confession is a great sacrament"—Cf. Book One, chap. v, p. 22_{33-34}, and Book Seven, chap. i, p. 312_{28}. Fiodor Pavlovich comes up with a pun of sorts: he connects

tainstvo, "sacrament, mystery," with *tainyi,* "secret, private," as though confession were a "mystery" because it is "secret." Actually, private confession became the rule only as late as the thirteenth century.

231   78_{36}, $14:82_{28}$, "Flagellants"—Russ. *khlysty,* lit. "whip(per)s." The *khlysty* were a sect who practiced flagellation as one of the rites by which they hoped to achieve purification from evil. Their services were aimed at group ecstasy. Hence, Fiodor Pavlovich has a point—of sorts.

232   78_{37}, $14:82_{29}$, "the Synod"—the highest administrative organ of the Russian Orthodox church, responsible to the Tsar himself.

233   79_{15}, $14:83_6$, "plunged forward blindly"—lit. "plunged down as though from the top of a hill." This is one of Dostoevsky's favorite images: a man flings himself into an abyss, unable to bear standing at its edge.

234   79_{25}, $14:83_{16}$, A quote from Schiller's *The Robbers,* Act I, sc. ii.

235   79_{27}, $14:83_{18}$, "gudgeons" are like a refrain in Fiodor Pavlovich's tirades. Cf. chap. vi, p. 65_{16}.

236   79_{35}, $14:83_{26}$, "Eliseev Brothers"—famous Russian wine merchants.

237   79_{39-40}, $14:83_{30}$, "the tax gatherer"—translates *nuzhd gosudarstvennykh,* "the needs of the state," a cliché of the radicals of the 1860s.

238   80_7, $14:83_{41-42}$, "You cursed me with bell and book"—lit. "you have anathemized me at all seven councils." The Orthodox church recognizes only seven ecumenic councils (all prior to 1054), so that to have been anathemized by seven councils was the maximum reprobation anyone could have incurred.

239   80_{20-22}, $14:84_{4-6}$, Apparently a quotation from a Father of the Eastern church.

240   80_{23}, $14:84_7$, "Bethinking thyself"—Russ. *voznepshchevakhu,* a Slavonic form (3rd pers. pl. of the imperfect), which even in Russian is a grotesque tongue twister.

241   80_{36-37}, $14:84_{17-19}$, "bring your pillow"—a bit of realistic detail, which will not be forgotten. Cf. Book Three, chap. vi, p. 112_5, and chap. ix, p. 145_{25}.

242   81_{13-15}, $14:84_{44}$, The first "dissonance" in Ivan's behavior. It ought to be remembered.

Book Three

Chapter i

1 82_5, $14:85_{22}$, "The Karamazovs' house"—Dostoevsky is describing his own summer home in Staraia Russa (see Introduction I.1. *The Brothers Karamazov* in Dostoevsky's Life). Still, one is tempted to see the house as an extension of its owners, the Karamazovs.

2 82_{10-11}, $14:85_{28-29}$, Rats are, in general, less repulsive to a Russian than to an American. One need not attach any particular significance to this detail.

3 82_{30-31}, $14:86_8$, "after the emancipation of the serfs"—in 1861, that is, about six years before the present events.

4 82_{33-35}, $14:86_{11-13}$, Grigory's quoted statements contain various forms which are definitely substandard, helping to develop a contrast between the man's admirable integrity and his obtuse mind.

5 83_{17-20}, $14:86_{30-33}$, Slapstick comedy: the serf rescues his master from "corporal punishment," then gives him a stern lecture—comic role reversal.

6 83_{26}, $14:86_{39}$, "in his lust"—translates *v sladostrastii svoiom,* where *sladostrastie,* "lust," reminds one of *Sladostrastniki,* "Sensualists," the title of this book and also its leitmotif. Often the paradigmatic effect of such repetition of a word or image is lost through the syntagmatic exigencies of the English translation. Cf. Book Two, note 187.

7 83_{26}, $14:86_{39}$, "like some noxious insect"—a Karamazov leitmotif. Cf. Introduction III.5.f. Mythical Symbolism.

8 83_{29-41}, $14:86_{44}-87_9$, A long passage featuring *erlebte Rede* ("reflected speech"). See Introduction III.1.a. The Narrator.

9 84_{5-8}, $14:87_{17-20}$, A passage to be remembered. It establishes the notion of fatherhood, and respect for fatherhood, as absolutes.

An antithesis to this notion is found in Book Twelve, chap. xiii, p. 706_{37-44}. Cf. Introduction II.3.a. Fatherhood.

10   84_{35-36}, $14:88_{1-2}$,   Wifebeating was almost the rule among the lower classes in Russia and, if moderate, was seldom frowned upon.

11   84_{39}, $14:88_5$,   " 'In the Green Meadows' "—a popular dance tune.

12   84_{43-44}, $14:88_{10-11}$,   Wealthy landowners sometimes had not only private theaters, but even orchestras and ballet and opera ensembles, all recruited from among their serfs, some of whom were trained in Petersburg and Moscow.

13   85_8, $14:88_{22}$,   "a slap in the face"—another "crossreference": see Book One, chap. iii, p. 9_{19}, where it is "a box on the ear." In the original, it is *poshchochina* both times.

14   85_{16}, $14:88_{31}$,   "the clergy"—meaning the parish priest and a deacon.

15   85_{23}, $14:88_{39}$,   In popular superstition, "dragon" and "devil" have a close affinity, and a malformed child could be seen as a vessel of unclean spirits.

16   85_{25}, $14:88_{42}$,   "confusion"—Russ. *smeshenie* is readily associated with *krovosmeshenie,* "incest" (lit. "confusion of blood"), which renders the word more ominous.

17   85_{38}, $14:89_9$,   The story of the Kutuzovs' baby should be remembered in the context of the motif of suffering innocent children, central to the argument of the novel. See Introduction II.3.b. "The Novel about Children." Cf. Father Zosima's words, Book Two, chap. iii, pp. 41_{44}–42_9.

18   85_{43}, $14:89_{13-14}$,   Dostoevsky makes a point of mentioning the Book of Job repeatedly, to make sure the reader will draw it into the context of the novel. See Introduction I.4.b. Sacred Sources.

19   85_{45}, $14:89_{15}$,   "Isaac the Syrian"—a sixth-century hermit (seventh-century, according to other sources) whose sermons were translated into Slavonic by Paisy Velichkovsky. See Introduction I.4.b. This book will reappear later in the novel; see Book Eleven, note 257.

20   86_{1-2}, $14:89_{16-17}$,   "understanding very little of it, but perhaps prizing and loving it the more for that"—another psychological paradox. The character of Grigory and his role in the novel are full of ambiguities. He is a fool, yet sometimes wise; pompous, yet humble; he means well, yet accomplishes little good.

21   86_3, $14:89_{18}$,   "Flagellants"—see Book Two, note 231.

22   86_{9-10}, $14:89_{25-27}$, As often happens, the proper suspense is created, before this new story is told. The following scene ought to be remembered, because its negative mirror image is the murder in Book Eight, chap. iv. See Introduction III.5.f. Mythical Symbolism.

23   86_{26}, $14:89_{43}$, "An idiot girl"—Russ. *iurodivaia,* which has a connotation of "God's fool." Cf. Book One, note 94.

Chapter ii

24   86_{33}, $14:90_2$, "Stinking Lizaveta"—this character and her story appear in the notebooks to *A Raw Youth* of 1874-75, but only as an isolated motif. Dostoevsky would often keep a motif in abeyance until he found a way to incorporate it into the plot of a novel.

25   86_{35}, $14:90_5$, "a very unpleasant and revolting suspicion"— again, suspense!

26   87_{26-27}, $14:90_{41-42}$, "a mischievous lot"—this casual phrase introduces an important subplot: we shall hear a lot about these "mischievous schoolboys" yet.

27   87_{39}, $14:91_{9-10}$, "wattle-fence"—it is this kind of concrete detail, naively reported, that makes the story seem credible.

28   88_{10}, $14:91_{24-25}$, "the long, stinking pool"—some more local color. This topographic information will come in handy later in the novel, though.

29   88_{15}, $14:91_{32}$, "and so forth"—the narrator, a Victorian gentleman, is rather embarrassed as he tries to relate this disgraceful event, so he beats around the bush and gropes for euphemisms: a part of the "impersonation" done by Dostoevsky.

30   88_{16}, $14:91_{32}$, "with lofty repugnance"—note the irony. These "gentlemen" pride themselves on their feelings of disgust, yet are not ashamed of their loose talk. The scene is a social commentary: the "gentlemen," who presumably have received a Western education, are utterly insensitive to what the uneducated merchants and tradesmen of the town hold dear and sacred. To the latter, Lizaveta is a creature of God, "God's fool"; to the "gentlemen" she is an "animal." The narrator has an anti-gentleman bias, as we already know from his treatment of Miusov. See Introduction II.4.b. The Russian Nobleman.

31 89_6, $14:92_{22}$, "Karp"—in the original, *Karp s vintom,* lit. "Karp with the screw." But *vint* is also used for *vintovka,* "rifle," in substandard speech. Perhaps: "Karp the Rifle."

32 89_{19-20}, $14:92_{37}$, In the original: "Some said that 'they lifted her over,' others that 'it had lifted her over,' '' where the impersonal form is decidedly suggestive of something uncanny.

33 89_{30-31}, $14:93_1$, "Our little lost one has sent us this . . ."— Grigory speaks these memorable words with a certain solemnity. Hence one might expect them to foreshadow certain developments in the novel. But this is another false lead.

34 89_{33}, $14:93_3$, In Russia, a fatherless child will normally receive his or her godfather's name for a patronymic.

35 89_{43}, $14:93_{13-14}$, "common menials"—a loaded ambiguity, and more so in Russian than in English. Russ. *obyknovennyi* means "ordinary, routine," as well as "common." Smerdiakov and Kutuzov are common menials, of course, but they are anything but "ordinary" men.

36 89_{45}, $14:93_{16}$, "hoping to say more of Smerdiakov"—he will, only four chapters later. Discussing novelistic strategy with his reader is a trait which appeared in the very Foreword of the novel and will continue to show up occasionally.

Chapter iii

37 90_2, $14:93_{18}$, "Confession"—a literary allusion identifying the genre which this section of the novel will follow. Confessions were a popular literary genre in the romantic period.

38 90_{11-12}, $14:93_{30}$, "to produce an effect"—translates *dlia krasoty,* "for the beauty of it." This chapter climaxes in a discourse on beauty and passion. Note Dostoevsky's "symphonic" technique, by which the leitmotif (beauty) is at first introduced unobtrusively, in a casual, incidental way.

39 90_{16}, $14:93_{35}$, "for the sake of effect"—translates *dlia krasy.* Cf. the preceding note: *krasa* is a synonym of *krasota.*

40 90_{25}–91_5, $14:94_{1-27}$, This rambling passage expresses Aliosha's vague feelings and incoherent thoughts. Note the several double takes and the hedging throughout. It all whets the reader's appetite to hear more about Katerina Ivanovna. Also, the reader is asked to match his own recollections of the details of Rakitin's gossip (Book Two, chap. vii, pp. 71–72) with Aliosha's apprehensions.

41 91_{16}, $14:94_{38}$, "his terrible lady"—ironic, of course. Another instance of Dostoevsky's technique of moving from the outside in. We have heard a great many things about the lady, but so far they have all been vague or misleading, as we shall see.

42 92_{21-22}, $14:96_{3-4}$, Dmitry will repeat these lines in Book Eight, chap. v, p. 383, where we learn that they are his own composition. (In the Russian the text of the two passages is identical.) These lines strike the first chord of the central theme of this chapter: Dmitry's lofty world of romantic poetry and idealist philosophy.

43 92_{38-39}, $14:96_{20-21}$, "von Schmidt"—in the original, "Aleksandr Karlovich von Schmidt," a reminiscence of Aleksandr Karlovich Gribbe, former owner of Dostoevsky's summer house in Staraia Russa. These specific details create a realistic setting for the romantic excursion which follows.

44 93_4, $4:96_{29}$, "Distrust the apparition."—Translates *ne ver' fantomu,* "don't believe in a phantom." This is a jibe at the jargon of idealist philosophy, which asserted that the world of everyday life is a "phantom" world, while only the world of ideas is "real." A bottle of brandy is therefore a mere phantom.

45 93_{5-6}, $14:96_{30-31}$, A quotation from a famous poem by Nikolai Nekrasov, "When from the Darkness of Error" ("Kogda iz mraka zabluzhdeniia," 1865), one of Dostoevsky's favorite poems. See *PSS* 15:541.

46 93_7, $14:96_{32}$, " 'indulging' "—Russ. *lakomstvuiu,* a pedantic derivative of *lakomstvo,* "delicacy, treat." Rakitin had actually used the word ($14:75_{46}$; cf. Book Two, chap. vii, p. 71_{43}, "enjoying himself"). Anyone who would use the verb would have to be a "seminarian" (see Book Two, note 169). It is significant that Dmitry, who is much less educated than Rakitin, intuitively senses Rakitin's inferior style.

47 93_{14}, $14:96_{40}$, " 'jade' "—translates *podlaia,* lit. "low," which is ambiguous: it could mean low birth, or low moral character. By the 1860s the former meaning was an anachronism. Since Dostoevsky has put the word between quotation marks, "lowborn" is suggested.

48 93_{39}, $14:97_{17}$, "even in my ribs"—Dmitry's verbiage sounds just as extravagant in the original: he is a poet. See Introduction III.1.c. Dmitry Karamazov.

49 93_{41}, $14:97_{19}$, "Angel" will gradually become a distinctive epithet (or "label") of Aliosha's. The original meaning of the

word ("messenger") is partly retained here. Aliosha will act as a "messenger" throughout the novel.

50 94_{13}, $14:97_{31}$, "Oh, gods"—the plural is significant. It falls in line with the Hellenizing stanzas from Schiller which are to follow.

51 94_{15}, $14:97_{32-33}$, The allusion is to Pushkin's fairy tale in verse, "Tale about the Fisherman and the Fish" (1833), after a tale from the Grimm brothers' collection.

52 94_{19}, $14:97_{37}$, "someone above me"—translates *vysshii*, "higher, highest." This chapter deals with the fall and resurrection of man. Following an age-old tradition, Dmitry perceives this quite literally as movement along a vertical. Hence, the adjectives "high" and "low" are particularly significant here. As a noun, *vysshii*, "the Highest," means God—as it does in Dmitry's little poem (p. 92_{21-22}).

53 94_{25}, $14:97_{43}$, Dmitry's logic is not very good, nor is his syntax: he has been drinking.

54 94_{32-33}, $14:98_3$, A quotation from Goethe's poem "The Divine" ("Das Göttliche," 1783), in A. Strugovshchikov's translation (1845).

55 94_{39}, $14:98_{10-11}$, Schiller's ode "An die Freude" (1785) cele- brates Joy, which unites humans in brotherly love and leads them to God. The celebration of Joy is one of the leitmotifs of *The Brothers Karamazov*. See Introduction II.5.b. Mysticism.

56 95_{1-2}, $14:98_{14-15}$, A quotation from the poem "Bas-relief" (1842) by Dostoevsky's friend Apollon Maikov (1821–97).

57 95_4, $14:98_{16}$, Here the original has a pun: *Silen*, "Silenus," and *silion* (spelled *silen*), "strong."

58 $95_{10ff.}$, $14:98_{22ff.}$, Second, third, and fourth stanzas of Schiller's poem "The Eleusinian Festival" ("Das Eleusische Fest," 1798) in Vasily Zhukovsky's translation. The Eleusinian mysteries were celebrated every spring in honor of Demeter (Lat. *Ceres*) and her daughter Persephone (Lat. *Proserpina*). They symbolized the annual death and resurrection of nature. Schiller's poem celebrates the triumph of civilized ways, order, and human brotherhood over crude barbarism. It falls in line with Schiller's idea of an "aesthetic education of mankind." Cf. Introduction II.1.a. Allegoric Figures.

59 96_{1-4}, $14:99_{8-11}$, Stanza 7 of "The Eleusinian Festival." Here, for the first time in the novel, the symbolism of Mother Earth makes its appearance. See Introduction III.5.f. Mythical Symbolism.

60   96_6, $14:99_{13}$, "cleave her bosom"—this image is probably taken from a well-known poem by Afanasy Foeth, "Spring Has Come" (1866). See *PSS* 15:542.

61   96_{15}, $14:99_{23}$, "I begin a hymn of praise"—a leitmotif which is yet to play a major role. Cf. Book Eleven, chap. iv ("A Hymn and a Secret").

62   96_{16-17}, $14:99_{24}$, "the hem of the veil in which my God is shrouded"—the image is taken from the first stanza of Goethe's poem "The Limits of Mankind" ("Grenzen der Menschheit," 1789) in A. A. Foeth's translation (1878).

63   96_{19}, $14:99_{27}$, "without which the world cannot stand"—a realization of the affinity of the religious experience to the aesthetic, and of the disparity between both of these and morality: Dmitry senses that he has been wrong all his life, but also that he is not therefore evil. See Introduction II.5. Moral and Religious Philosophy.

64   96_{20-36}, $14:99_{28-43}$, Stanzas 4 and 3 from Schiller's ode "To Joy" in Fiodor Tiutchev's translation.

65   96_{40-41}, $14:99_{46-48}$, "insects"—the German original has *Wurm*, which is any "creeping thing" (as at least one English translator has actually translated the word). Hence, "reptile" is also in order, as well as "insect," the word used by Tiutchev. As for "sensual lust," it is *sladostrast'e* all the way, Tiutchev's translation of Schiller's *Wollust*. Cf. note 6 above.

66   97_4, $14:100_{6-7}$, "Here the boundaries meet"—translates *Tut berega skhodiatsia*, "Here's where two banks of a river meet." This metaphor (used by Descartes, among others) expresses Dmitry's acceptance of the paradox in human life: his statement pointedly ignores the law of "no contradiction," foreshadowing Ivan's refusal to admit the notion of two parallel lines ("two banks of a river"!) which meet in infinity (Book Five, chap. iii, p. 216_{22-24}). The Garnett translation misses the point.

67   97_5, $14:100_{7-8}$, "I am not a cultivated man"—a modern reader may not believe that this is an ingenuous statement: after all, Dmitry has just quoted all kinds of lofty poetry. The point is that progressive journalists of the 1860s called everybody who was not abreast of recent scientific discoveries and social ideas "uneducated" (Pushkin was so called by Dobroliubov). In Rakitin's terms, Dmitry is in fact hopelessly "uneducated."

68   97_{9-10}, $14:100_{11-12}$, "the ideal of the Madonna" and "the ideal of Sodom"—the former being Beauty linked to the Good and the True, the latter Beauty (or better, sensual pleasure) seen as

inherently amoral. This takes up the argument started by Fiodor
Pavlovich in Book Two, chap. ii, p. 36$_{44ff.}$. Cf. Book Two, note
48.

69   97$_{14-15}$, 14:100$_{15-16}$, "I'd have him narrower."—Announces the
theme of human freedom—and the desirability of its cur-
tailment, which will dominate Book Five, chap. v ("The Grand
Inquisitor").

70   97$_{19-20}$, 14:100$_{20-21}$, "God and the devil . . ."—with this sententious remark, Dmitry has concluded that Beauty is morally
ambivalent: the devil uses it to his ends, and God to His. Dmitry
has arrived at a rejection of Schiller's optimistic faith in the
"aesthetic education of man."

Chapter iv

71   97$_{24}$, 14:100$_{24}$, See Introduction III.3.a. Motifs for the use of
anecdote as an element of plot structure.

72   97$_{26-27}$, 14:100$_{26}$, "That's a swinish invention"—translates *Eto
svinskii fantom,* "that's a swinish phantom," which does not
sound like *le mot juste,* and is not. But such things happen in live
discourse. Garnett's translation, as so often, "improves" on the
original.

73   98$_8$, 14:101$_3$, "gentle indignation"—this apparent oxymoron is
characteristic of Dostoevsky's psychology of "counterpoint,"
rather than "variation on a theme."

74   98$_{12-13}$, 14:101$_9$, "I'm not dishonorable"—pregnant with an
irony of which Dmitry is not yet aware. After all, telling all these
things to his young brother is not exactly honorable. Dmitry will
soon be seen guilty of indiscretions a lot worse than this one.

75   98$_{15}$, 14:101$_{11}$, Paul de Kock (1794–1871) was a popular French
writer of entertainments, some of which were considered immoral.

76   98$_{23-25}$, 14:101$_{18-20}$, This little psychological surprise follows a
pattern: Aliosha admits, time and again, that he too is a
Karamazov. Cf. Book Two, chap. vii, p. 69$_{23-25}$.

77   98$_{39-40}$, 14:101$_{35-37}$, "From this field . . ."—a mistranslation.
Russ. *pole* here means "margin." Hence, one might translate:
"Let's pass on from all these abominations, from mere margins
fouled by flies, to my tragedy proper, that is, also a mere margin
fouled by flies, that is, by all sorts of vileness." Dmitry sees his
personal experiences as a series of scrawls and blots on the
margins of the book of life.

78   99_{1-2}, $14:101_{42}$,   Bitter irony, of which Dmitry is not aware: Ivan is the last person who should have known. And, as we shall see, this is not the end of it yet.

79   99_3, $14:101_{44}$,   This laconic way of saying "Ivan is as secret as the grave" makes for a bit of symbolic foreshadowing. Aliosha's redundant response suggests this much. The phrase is repeated, later in this chapter, and in Book Five, chap. iii, p. 211_{4-5}.

80   99_8, $14:101_{48}$,   "convict"—translates *ssyl'nyi*, "exile." Dmitry had been reduced to the ranks earlier, for duelling (see Book One, chap. ii, p. 6_{41-42}). Hence his low rank was socially excusable. Dostoevsky had had a similar experience, with the difference that he *was* an exile.

81   99_{18}, $14:102_{10}$,   "was of a humble family"—translates *byla iz kakikh-to prostykh*, lit. "was of some sort of plain folks," an example of Dostoevsky's use of the indefinite pronoun (*kakikh-to*, "some sort of") to suggest a reality more complex than can readily be expressed in precise terms. See Introduction III.1.a. The Narrator.

82   99_{21-22}, $14:102_{13-14}$,   The characterization of these two women has the elegance of a *bon mot* in the original. Perhaps: "That aunt was simple in a humble way, and her niece, the colonel's older daughter, simple in a lively way."

83   99_{31-32}, $14:102_{25}$,   "which made it very amusing"—best explained by a parallel from another novel of Dostoevsky's, where the hero is greatly amused by a young lady who discusses serious human problems with great frankness, yet is "definitely quite unaware of the whole secret of relations between man and woman" (*The Insulted and Injured,* Pt. III, chap. ix).

84   99_{33}, $14:102_{26}$,   "a young lady"—Russ. *baryshnia*, "young lady, miss." Dostoevsky takes a great deal of interest in verbal nuances, testing them against the facts of life. Here, it is established that the virtuous twenty-four-year-old daughter of a colonel is definitely not "a young lady."

85   99_{43}, $14:102_{35}$,   "a great beauty"—Russ. *raskrasavitsa iz krasavits,* where *ras-* is an emphatic prefix meaning "super-" or "arch-." The Russian expression is less slangy than "super beauty," though.

86   100_4, $14:102_{43}$,   "the young lady"—Russ. *institutka*, from *institut dlia blagorodnykh devits,* "institute for well-born young girls."

87   100_6, $14:102_{45}$,   "Excellency" was the official title of address of military and civil service officers of general's rank.

88   100_{19}, 14:103_9, "high-principled"—Russ. *dobrodetel'naia*, "virtuous," Katerina Ivanovna's leitmotif: it will return often, in different variations.

89   101_{11}, 14:103_{42}, "Scoundrel" is a sticky label which Dmitry will vainly struggle to get rid of.

90   101_{14}, 14:103_{45}, "the secret would be kept sacred"—deep irony: the secret will become known to more and more people as the story goes on and will become public in the end.

91   102_{23}, 14:105_{1-2}, "Aliosha, are you listening . . ."—Dmitry is deeply moved, so he overcompensates by inserting a brash apostrophe. In the original, there is a nonchalant, condescending "Alioshka," instead of an affectionate "Aliosha."

92   102_{28-35}, 14:105_{8-15}, On the massive insect imagery found here, see Introduction III.5.f. Mythical Symbolism. Cf. note 7 above.

93   102_{42}, 14:105_{23}, "I'm honest"—not only ambiguous, but also fraught with irony. Foreshadows Dmitry's long struggle for his self-respect.

94   102_{43}, 14:105_{23-24}, "some voice seemed to whisper in my ear"— the whole scene is an example of Dostoevsky's polyphonic technique. Dmitry's account is a counterpoint of conflicting voices, all of them generated by Dmitry's consciousness.

95   103_{24}, 14:106_{1-2}, "in a French dictionary"—note the concrete detail.

96   103_{26}, 14:106_{3-4}, This "deep bow" is a leitmotif which will be reintroduced in many different contexts throughout the novel. For Book Three, see pp. 106_{35}, 108_{14}, 110_{25}, and 128_9.

97   103_{31-32}, 14:106_{9-10}, Dmitry was about to go out when Katerina Ivanovna came, and an officer would normally carry his sword when wearing his dress uniform.

98   103_{39-40}, 14:106_{17}, "to hell with all who pry into the human heart"—a certain hostility against psychologists is a recurring theme in *The Brothers Karamazov*. See Introduction II.6.a. Dostoevsky's Psychology.

99   103_{41-42}, 14:106_{19}, Still the same irony (cf. notes 78 and 90 above). Dostoevsky makes sure Dmitry repeats this assertion often enough so that the reader will notice and remember it.

Chapter v

100   104_{4-5}, 14:106_{29-30}, Some more internal commentary. Dmitry correctly assesses the literary genre of the piece whose hero he is: in Russian, a drama is a serious play, but less exalted than

tragedy, a "high" genre of poetry. At this stage, Dmitry says it half-facetiously.

101 105_{14}, $14:107_{38}$, "in my vulgar tone"—the irony of it is that Dmitry, sensitive as he is to words and their nuances, has captured the gist, as well as the tone, of Katerina Ivanovna's letter very well, and that he knows it, too, with another part of his consciousness.

102 105_{32}, $14:108_{8}$, "She loves her own virtue, not me."—A sententious statement which is also true. Cf. note 88 above.

103 105_{42}, $14:108_{18}$, "show off"—"declaiming" is the word used in the original. Another detail of internal commentary.

104 105_{45}, $14:108_{22}$, "monster"—Russ. *izverg,* which originally meant "outcast" and still bears the connotation of "somebody who (through his cruelty, crimes against God and nature, etc.) has lost his right to be considered a member of the human race." The word will become a label of Dmitry's, so we have here some ironic foreshadowing. At this stage Dmitry hardly deserves so harsh an epithet.

105 106_{7}, $14:108_{30}$, "his filthy back alley"—established as a symbol in the preceding chapter (p. 97_{35-36}).

106 106_{10}, $14:108_{33}$, "I've no words left."—In the original: "I've got a feeling that I've worn out all my words," another apt and penetrating observation. Dmitry's "other voice" is that of his deep aesthetic sense, which discerns beauty and ugliness alike. See Introduction III.1.c. Dmitry Karamazov.

107 106_{11}, $14:108_{34}$, "I shall drown in the back alley"—a mixed metaphor, quite fitting for a speaker who has "worn out all his words."

108 106_{25-26}, $14:108_{47-48}$, The source of these lines is not known. They could be Dostoevsky's own. Dostoevsky was not a good lyric poet, but he was a master of verse parody and nonsense verse.

109 106_{34-35}, $14:109_{8-9}$, The Russian verb *klaniat'sia* routinely means as much as "send greetings," but its literal meaning is "to bow," and here there is a definite allusion to the scene in the preceding chapter which featured an exchange of deep bows between Dmitry and Katerina Ivanovna. Cf. note 96 above.

110 106_{42}, $14:109_{16}$, A cross-reference to Book Two, chap. vii, p. 71_{37-39}.

111 107_{4-5}, $14:109_{22}$, "I went . . . to beat her."—Another instance

of an outrageous comedy scene ("hero beats up heroine"), which remains in the mind, however. Cf. Book Two, note 214.

112 107_{14}, $14:109_{31}$, "it struck me down like the plague"—sounds less strange in Russian than in English, as falling in love is routinely likened to falling ill.

113 107_{18}, $14:109_{34-35}$, The sum of three thousand roubles is a significant item in the plot of the novel and seems to have a life of its own. This passage is of key importance because it is subtly misleading as to the amount spent by Dmitry. See Introduction III.3.a. Motifs.

114 107_{22-23}, $14:109_{37-38}$, "I was stripped bare . . ."—An untranslatable pun in the original. First, Dmitry changes the saying *gol kak sokol,* "poor as a church mouse" (lit. "bare as a falcon"), to *gol, no sokol,* lit. "bare, but a falcon," i.e., "broke, but a hero"; then he "realizes" the metaphor, saying: "Do you think that the falcon got anywhere?"

115 107_{23}, $14:109_{38-39}$, "Not a sign of it from her."—In the original, lit. "She didn't show it to me, not even at a distance," which sounds more obscene in Russian than in my translation.

116 108_{11}, $14:110_{25}$, "He isn't a thief though."—This line is to be remembered. It is fraught with a hidden ambiguity. Cf. Book Nine, chap. vii, p. 464_{43}.

117 108_{22-24}, $14:110_{35-37}$, Dmitry is a great raconteur. With a few well-chosen words he paints a vivid picture of a semi-cuckold, semi-pimp husband of a beautiful and loose woman. Needless to say, it is wholly imaginary. Grushen'ka is not like this at all.

118 108_{26}, $14:110_{39-40}$, Aliosha tactfully calls Dmitry's condition "trouble." In the original, he also says "will become reconciled," rather than "forgive." Tact is a paramount trait of Aliosha's.

119 109_{6-7}, $14:111_{16}$, "and he'll draw my soul out of hell"—the Russian text, *i dushu moiu is ada izvlechiot,* is a direct quotation from Jonah 2:6. The King James version has "corruption" instead of "hell." Cf. *PSS* 15:543.

120 109_{10-11}, $14:111_{19-20}$ "Tell him God Himself sends him this chance."—A deep ambiguity. On a mundane psychological level these are the flimsy words of a man clutching at a straw. But on a metaphysical level Dmitry is a good prophet. Fiodor Pavlovich comes very close to taking advantage of this chance. See Book Four, chap. ii, p. 159_{32-35}.

121   109_{44}, $14:112_5$,   Chermashnia was the name of a village bought
       by Dostoevsky's father in 1832.

122   110_{25}, $14:112_{31}$,   Dostoevsky makes quite sure that the deep bow
       of the original scene be remembered. The bow has become a
       symbol in a drama of pride and humiliation. Cf. notes 96 and
       109 above.

Chapter vi

123   112_1, $14:113_{45}$,   "Smerdiakov's an artist"—a significant detail.
       In a sense, Smerdiakov, like the Karamazovs, loves beauty. See
       p. 114_{17-21}.

124   112_{10}, $14:114_{6-7}$,   "It makes me laugh all over."—The Russian
       expression is a bit stronger, lit. "My whole insides begin to laugh
       as I look at him." Fiodor Pavlovich's sensuality is morally
       ambiguous: here, it is positive.

125   112_{11}, $14:114_{7-8}$,   A significant reminder. Cf. Book Two, chap.
       vi, p. 63_5.

126   112_{16}, $14:114_{12}$,   An allusion to Num. 22:21–33.

127   112_{28}, $14:114_{22-26}$,   A detail to be remembered. It reveals
       Smerdiakov's necrophilic personality.

128   112_{34-35}, $14:114_{30-31}$,   "You grew from the mildew in the
       bathhouse."—A proverbial expression which Dostoevsky had
       heard from his fellow prisoners in Siberia. It means "you came
       from nowhere," but in this instance the metaphor is partly
       realized, as Smerdiakov was born in Fiodor Pavlovich's
       bathhouse.

129   112_{42-44}, $14:114_{39-41}$,   An allusion to Gen. 1:3–5, 14–19. The
       question turns up in apocryphic literature, in Russia and
       elsewhere.

130   113_{12-14}, $14:115_{5-7}$,   One of the many ambiguities of the novel,
       and an example of Dostoevsky's thesis that psychology "cuts
       both ways" (see Introduction II.6.a. Dostoevsky's Psychology).
       Does this solicitude prove that Fiodor Pavlovich is the boy's
       father? But then he never cared for his other sons. So it may
       actually prove that he does *not* consider the boy to be his son. If
       his conscience were not clear on this score, perhaps he might have
       been afraid to show such solicitude. The argument can be
       continued *ad infinitum*.

131   113_{16-17}, $14:115_{8-9}$,   "The fits varied, too, in violence"—the
       same as Dostoevsky's own condition. See *The Notebooks for*

"The Possessed," ed. Edward Wasiolek, tr. Victor Terras (Chicago, 1967), pp. 3–4, 11, 24, 28–33, 415, where Dostoevsky registers his epileptic fits.

132 113_{27}, $14:115_{19}$, *Evenings on a Farm near Dikanka*—a famous collection of romantic tales in which Nikolai Gogol (1809–52) tried to re-create the atmosphere of the Ukrainian folk tale and folk humor. Fiodor Pavlovich assumes that its folksy quality will appeal to Smerdiakov.

133 113_{34}, $14:115_{27}$, Fiodor Pavlovich quickly realizes what is wrong with Smerdiakov: he is intelligent enough, but has no imagination. He can see only the material and utilitarian side of things.

134 113_{35}, $14:115_{29}$, "Smaragdov's *Universal History*"—a well-known high school text.

135 114_{43-44}, $14:116_{33}$, "had . . . a liking for him"—Russ. *liubil ego.* In Russian, there is only one verb for "to like" and "to love." Therefore it is a matter of interpretation to let the English text suggest that Fiodor Pavlovich "loved" Aliosha, but "liked" Smerdiakov.

136 115_7, $14:116_{42}$, I. N. Kramskoi (1837–87) was a well-known Russian painter whom Dostoevsky knew personally. The painting referred to here was first exhibited in 1878. See *PSS* 15:544. In the original the painting is called *The Contemplator.* Dostoevsky took an interest in painting and reviewed art exhibitions on occasion. He often describes paintings in his works, using them as a visual aid to illustrate a point. *The Deposition of Christ* (1521) by Hans Holbein (the Younger) in *The Idiot* is a more famous example than the present one.

Chapter vii

137 115_{30-35}, $14:117_{16-22}$, A real event. The soldier, Sgt. Foma Danilov, perished on 21 November 1875. Dostoevsky had previously written about this incident in *Diary of a Writer* (1877), 2:569–74, under the title "Foma Danilov: The Russian Hero Tortured to Death."

138 115_{34-35}, $14:117_{20}$, "was tortured"—Russ. *prinial muki,* lit. "accepted torments," the stock expression used in lives of saints and martyrs.

139 116_{4-5}, $14:117_{33-35}$, A foreshadowing detail: Ivan and Smerdiakov are linked for the first time.

140   116_{11}, 14:117_{41}, "on such an emergency"—Smerdiakov speaks almost the same language as his masters, but here and there he will use a word incorrectly. Here, he uses *sluchainost'*, "fortuity, accident, chance," instead of *sluchai*, "instance." His frequent use of "sir" is another telltale sign of his origins.

141   116_{12-14}, 14:117_{42-44}, To be kept in mind: we shall hear the same argument from Aliosha, of all people. See Epilogue, chap. ii, p. 723.

142   116_{16}, 14:118_2, "and be roasted there like mutton"—note the bathos. Fiodor Pavlovich continues where he left off earlier (see Book One, chap. iv, p. 18).

143   116_{42}, 14:118_{28}, Smerdiakov runs afoul of some difficult words, but his meaning is clear.

144   116_{43}, 14:118_{29}, "a heathen"—in the original, Smerdiakov comes up with a neat folk etymology, as he conflates *iazychnik*, "heathen," and *inoiazychnyi*, "in a foreign language," producing the noun *inoiazychnik*, "a foreign heathen."

145   117_7, 14:118_{40}, "Praise him."—It must be understood that this is said in a whisper. It establishes the fateful relationship between Ivan and Smerdiakov, also defining its nature.

146   117_{33}, 14:119_{20}, "discharged"—Russ. *razzhalovan* is more clearly a military term than Eng. *discharged;* hence, the irony is stronger.

147   117_{39}, 14:119_{26}, Russ. *poganyi*, "heathen," has the connotation "foul, vile, abominable" (which today is the only meaning of the word). In popular usage *poganyi* includes Mohammedans and Christian heretics.

148   117_{45}, 14:119_{33}, "come into the world"—translates *proizoshol*, "originated." Again, Smerdiakov uses a fancy expression somewhat incorrectly and ungrammatically.

149   118_6, 14:119_{41}, "he caught something in his rigmarole"—relevant to the main argument of the novel. Grigory is, of course, unable to handle the intricacies of Zeno's paradox (which Smerdiakov is manhandling), but his common sense tells him that there is a catch somewhere and that the whole argument is false. See Introduction II. Ideas. Also, Martin Goldstein, "The Debate in *The Brothers Karamazov*," *Slavic and East European Journal* 14:326–40.

150   118_{12}, 14:119_{45}, "stinking Jesuit"—*iezuit smerdiashchii*, a pun on Smerdiakov's name. The mention of Jesuits and Ivan all in

one breath is significant. Smerdiakov is a disciple of the Jesuits, but he is also a disciple of Ivan's.

151 118_{28-30}, $14:120_{13-16}$, Matt. 17:20 and 21:21. Smerdiakov is making a travesty of the biblical text, of course.

152 118_{38}, $14:120_{24}$, "taking into consideration"—here, Smerdiakov uses the form *vziamshi,* instead of *vziav,* which is at least as bad grammar as "having took" would be in English.

153 118_{44}, $14:120_{30}$, The theme of the divine miracle is thus also introduced in a distorted and scurrilous manner. Note that Smerdiakov insists on a link between faith and miracle. Cf. Book Five, chap. v, p. 236, and Book One, note 124.

154 118_{45}, $14:120_{32-33}$, "except a couple of hermits"—anticipates another main theme of "The Grand Inquisitor" (Book Five, chap. v): that of the arrogance of the chosen few.

155 119_3, $14:120_{36}$, "in a transport"—*v apofeoze,* "in an apotheosis." The narrator means "transport," of course, but such mistakes will occur in spontaneous discourse. The translator has once again "corrected" Dostoevsky.

156 119_{33}, $14:121_{18}$, "like a cockroach"—bathos. Smerdiakov is rubbing it in, as he produces yet another travesty of the biblical passage.

Chapter viii

157 120_7, $14:121_{38}$, "Brandy" is a leitmotif of sorts. It will come back in Book Four, chap. ii, and in Book Twelve, chap. xiii, p. 705_{44}.

158 120_{21}, $14:122_5$, "A prime candidate"—translates *peredovoe miaso,* lit. "progressive flesh." Suddenly we see an entirely different side of Ivan: the nihilist and revolutionary. Dostoevsky's characters keep surprising us (see Introduction II.6.a. Dostoevsky's Psychology). The Russian expression is apparently an echo of Herzen's article "Miaso osvobozhdeniia" [Cannonfodder of the emancipation] (1862). Hence: "cannonfodder of progress."

159 120_{29}, $14:122_{12-13}$, "a Balaam's ass like that thinks and thinks"—foreshadowing. "The Contemplator" of chapter vi (p. 115) becomes a self-fulfilling prophecy.

160 120_{39-40}, $14:122_{22-23}$, It is significant that Fiodor Pavlovich should have a low opinion of the Russian people (he shares it

with Smerdiakov: see Book Five, chap. ii, p. 207$_{10-11}$), for he stands for what is rotten about the Russian gentry and hence is unaware of the regenerative powers which Father Zosima believes are latent in the Russian people. See Introduction II.4. *The Brothers Karamazov* as a Social Novel, and II.4.a. The Russian Nobleman.

161   120$_{43}$, 14:122$_{26}$, There was much talk about the perils of deforestation at the time. Fiodor Pavlovich invents another reason why it ought to be stopped.

162   121$_2$, 14:122$_{27-28}$, After the emancipation of 1861, corporal punishment was generally abolished. Nevertheless, rural courts, now elected by the peasants themselves, were left with the authority to mete out mild corporal punishment in minor criminal cases.

163   121$_{3-4}$, 14:122$_{28-29}$, Fiodor Pavlovich gives his own version of Luke 6:38.

164   121$_7$, 14:122$_{31}$, *Tout cela c'est de la cochonnerie.*—"That's all swinishness." Fiodor Pavlovich speaks like a true Westernizer, while himself guilty of all the "Russian" vices.

165   121$_{7-8}$, 14:122$_{33}$, "Do you know what I like? I like wit."— Fiodor Pavlovich now begins to ramble. The brandy is taking its effect.

166   121$_{16}$, 14:122$_{40}$, Count Donatien de Sade (1740–1814). Dostoevsky was familiar with some of the writings of this advocate of uncompromising sensualism. See *PSS* 15:546.

167   121$_{19-20}$, 14:122$_{43}$, "the girls at Mokroe"—Russ. *pro Mokrykh devok,* a pun. *Mokroe* means lit. "wet (place)." So literally: "about those wet girls."

168   121$_{22-24}$, 14:122$_{46}$–123$_1$, An inversion of Pascal's famous "bet." Instead of worrying about what might be if there *is* a God, and therefore, retribution, Fiodor Pavlovich intimates that a belief in a nonexisting God may deprive people of many pleasures in which they might otherwise indulge. The last lines of Schiller's "Resignation" express the same idea: *Was man von der Minute ausgeschlagen, / Gibt keine Ewigkeit zurück.* ("No eternity will give you back what you failed to accept from the minute.") Of course, Fiodor Pavlovich is not interested in "progress." His position is that of his son Ivan, grotesquely overstated, and therefore readily recognized for what it is: sensualism, pure and simple.

169   121$_{24}$, 14:123$_2$, "they keep back progress"—a cliché of the

1860s. When at his worst, Fiodor Pavlovich will follow the "progressive" line.

170   121_{34-35}, $14:123_{12}$,   Now Fiodor Pavlovich is preaching the revolution! "Reason" was the god of the Russian progressives, and nationalization of church property one of their principal objectives.

171   121_{38-39}, $14:123_{16}$,   "you'd be the first to be robbed and then ... suppressed"—it was not at all extraordinary for Russian intellectuals of the 1860s to speak of the revolution as something imminent.

172   121_{42-43}, $14:123_{19-20}$,   "And we clever people"—a phrase to be remembered. Fiodor Pavlovich is only the first of several characters in the novel who, explicitly or implicitly, count themselves among the "clever people" who have discovered that God is dead and who use this knowledge to their advantage.

173   121_{44}, $14:123_{21-22}$,   Fiodor Pavlovich makes a travesty of the argument for the existence of God from design. This must indeed be the best of all possible worlds, and God its creator, so long as I sit snug, enjoying my brandy.

174   122_{35}, $14:124_{8}$,   "It must be the devil"—a leitmotif. For the first time, Ivan uses the devil's name in vain. From here on there will be other hints of Ivan's commerce with the devil, culminating in chapter ix of Book Eleven.

175   122_{37}, $14:124_{10}$,   The preceding dialogue resembles somewhat an allegoric dialogue between Life and the Young Generation in one of the "Letters of a Pretty Woman," which had appeared in *The Citizen,* then under Dostoevsky's editorship, on 18 February 1874. (no. 7, p. 209). See *PSS* 15:546.

176   122_{39}, $14:124_{12}$,   Legend has it that Judas hanged himself on an aspen tree.

177   122_{41-42}, $14:124_{13-14}$,   "if they hadn't invented God"—Ivan echoes an idea of Ludwig Feuerbach (1804–72) which by the 1860s had become a cliché very much current among the Russian intelligentsia.

178   123_{13}, $14:124_{30}$,   *Il y a du Piron là dedans.*—"There's something of Piron in him." Alexis Piron (1689–1773) authored some risqué pieces early in his career and was eventually denied admission to the Academy on that score. He had the reputation of being a great wit. Toward the end of his life he turned to religion. Nevertheless, Fiodor Pavlovich's analogy is patently absurd.

179   123_{15-16}, $14:124_{31-33}$, "there's a hidden indignation boiling
within him"—now Fiodor Pavlovich actually anticipates the
Grand Inquisitor of Book Five.

180   123_{19}, $14:124_{36}$, "all the clever people"—see note 172 above.

181   123_{23-24}, $14:124_{39-40}$, The Faust theme is to play a major role in
the novel (see Introduction I.4.a. Secular Sources). Faust's devil
(and alter ego), Mephistopheles, is introduced through the back
door, as it were, in this display of buffoonery.

182   123_{25}, $14:124_{40}$, Fiodor Pavlovich purposely names Arbenin,
hero of Lermontov's play *Masked Ball,* instead of Pechorin,
hero of the famous novel *A Hero of Our Time* (1840) by the same
author. Absurd as it might seem at the moment, there is a grain
of truth in Fiodor Pavlovich's fanciful assertion: as a young
man, Father Zosima had been a little like Pechorin. See Book
Six, chap. ii(c).

183   123_{29}, $14:124_{45}$, "the ladies send him liqueur"—this is gossip,
rather than pure invention. See Book Seven, chap. i, p. 312_{24}.

184   123_{32-33}, $14:125_3$, "I've pulled off plenty of tricks"—translates
naafonil, a neologism, formed from *Afon,* "Mount Athos" (cf.
Book One, chap. v, pp. 21–22). Fiodor Pavlovich gives the word
a negative connotation, as though something shameful were
routinely performed on Mount Athos. Perhaps: "I've done the
Mount Athos bit."

185   124_{17-18}, $14:125_{28-29}$, The Russian phrase has a neat rhymed
paronymy: *podozritel'nye tvoi glaza, prezritel'nye tvoi glaza,*
where *podozritel'nye,* "mistrustful," seems to generate
prezritel'nye, "contemptuous."

186   124_{42}, $14:126_4$, "ugly women"—Russ. *moveshka,* a slang
expression, formed from French *mauvaise,* analogically to Russ.
durnushka, "ugly girl," from *durnaia,* "bad, ugly."

187   124_{44}, $14:126_{5-6}$, In the original, *v'el'fil'ka,* a Russianized
vieille fille, "old maid." Another slang word.

188   125_{15-16}, $14:126_{22}$, "shrieking hysterically"—Russ. *klikushei
vyklikat',* "wail like a wailer," a paronymic folk expression.
Fiodor Pavlovich keeps calling his second wife "the wailer"
(klikusha), a detail which gets lost in this translation. Cf. Book
Two, note 55.

189   125_{33}, $14:126_{40}$, "I'll spit on it"—the motif of willful sacrilege
is a recurring one in Dostoevsky. It occurs in *Diary of a Writer*
(see Introduction I.5.b), in *The Possessed,* and in *A Raw Youth.*

190   126_9, $14:127_{14}$, A significant detail: while Aliosha's reaction is

sympathetic (he relives his mother's shock), Ivan's is purely negative. He finds time to feel contempt, while his brother needs immediate attention.

191   126_{12-13}, $14:127_{17-18}$,   Once again Fiodor Pavlovich's devious mind stumbles upon a deep truth: in a certain sense Sof'ia Ivanovna is not Ivan's mother.

Chapter ix

192   126_{43}, $14:127_{44-45}$,   "The old man fell like a log"—this episode, seemingly of little consequence, will come back as a *déjà vu* later in the novel (Book Eight, chap. iv, p. 371_{35-36}).

193   127_{21}, $14:128_{20}$,   "Vanechka" and "Lioshechka" are tender hypocoristic forms of "Ivan" and "Aleksei."

194    $127_{29ff.}$, $14:128_{29ff.}$,   All the details of this scene are important beyond their immediate context. They help set the stage for the climactic scene in Book Eight, chap. iv, of which this scene is a "dress rehearsal."

195   127_{44}, $14:128_{44}$,   "You've killed him!"—A significant detail on several levels: it shows wishful thinking on Ivan's part, and it is yet another instance of foreshadowing.

196   127_{46}, $14:128_{46}$,   "I'll come again and kill him"—these words will come back to haunt Dmitry.

197   128_{37}, $14:129_{36}$,   "He's insulted me!"—Russ. *on menia derznul,* where Grigory uses a book word incorrectly (the verb is normally intransitive). Ivan promptly comes up with a mocking echo.

198   129_{1}, $14:129_{47}$,   "viper"—Russ. *gad* and *gadina,* lit. "reptile." Ivan's use of a reptilian metaphor falls in line with his preoccupation with the devil. His words are a significant clue to the further development of the plot.

199   129_{19-20}, $14:130_{17}$,   "I'm afraid of Ivan"—Again Fiodor Pavlovich says something that seems absurd, but later turns out to be prescient.

200   131_{1}, $14:131_{42-43}$,   Ivan scoffs at moral criteria. A naturalist, he assumes that the struggle for survival which goes on in the animal kingdom (he had alluded to it when he spoke of "one viper devouring another") also reigns in human affairs.

201   131_{6}, $14:131_{47-48}$,   " 'two vipers will devour each other' "—the first echo of these words, but not the last. Cf. Book Four, chap. v, p. 171_{1-2}, and Book Twelve, chap. v, p. 651_{45} (where *gad* is translated by "reptile").

202   131_{12}, $14:132_7$,   "I reserve myself full latitude"—a key phrase which determines Ivan's part in the plot of the novel. It entails a deep irony: Ivan's reserving himself full latitude marks the beginning of his compulsive behavior.

203   131_{15-17}, $14:132_{11}$,   The conclusion of this chapter breaks the ground for the meeting of Ivan and Aliosha in Book Five.

Chapter x

204    $131_{26ff.}$, $14:132_{20ff.}$,   The whole passage is an example of *erlebte Rede*. We have Aliosha's confused thoughts as perceived by the narrator, whose detachment borders on irony. For instance, "this terrible woman" (line 28) carries some irony, for we shall soon meet her—and smile, remembering Aliosha's fear of her.

205   132_{24-37}, $14:133_{15-28}$,   This fairly long descriptive passage sets the stage for a dramatic scene. The descriptive detail is hardly significant in itself here. Its function may be one of retardation or building suspense.

206   134_{22}, $14:135_{14}$,   In the original, the effect of this game with a single word is more subtle. The verb used all along is *klaniat'sia*, whose original meaning, "to bow," has all but disappeared behind the routine meaning "to greet, to send greetings." The noun which appears here is *poklon*, "bow," not immediately recognizable as going with *klaniat'sia* and hence italicized. Cf. note 109 above.

207   134_{32-33}, $14:135_{26-27}$,   In the original: "sensing with all his heart that hope was returning to his heart." Dostoevsky does not avoid repetition, and in the case of certain key words ("heart" is one of Aliosha's leitmotifs) actually seeks it.

208   134_{43-46}, $14:135_{38-40}$,   The repetition of the word "ashamed" is loaded with psychological significance. Subconsciously, Katerina Ivanovna is obsessed with her shame. This obsession drives her to humiliate Dmitry, the cause of her shame. Dostoevsky does a masterful job of suggesting this between the lines of Ekaterina Ivanovna's noble pronouncements.

209   135_{20}, $14:136_{15}$,   "That girl is an angel."—The first in a series of surprises.

210   135_{23}, $14:136_{18}$,   Russian has several words for "creature." One of them—*tvar'*, opprobrious when applied to a human being—was applied to Grushen'ka earlier, and will be again. Here another word—*sozdanie*, often used with the epithets "divine"

or "heavenly"—appears. A Russian reader will notice the 180-degree shift.

211 135_{23}, $14{:}136_{18}$, "bewitching"—echoes an epithet ("enchantress") applied to Grushen'ka by Fiodor Pavlovich (Book Two, chap. vi, p. 62_{35}). In Russian: *obol'stitel'na* and *obol'stitel'nitsa*.

212 135_{29}, $14{:}136_{24}$, "Show yourself to him."—Another surprise. Note how the scene is staged: by Katerina Ivanovna from the inside, and by Dostoevsky from the outside. It is pure theater. See Introduction III. Narrative Technique.

213 $135_{32\text{-}33}$, $14{:}136_{27}$, "smiling and beaming"—Russ. *smeias' i raduias'*, lit. "laughing and rejoicing." It is Grushen'ka's leitmotif in this scene.

214 136_2, $14{:}136_{45}$, The shawl is a recurring "attribute" of Grushen'ka's. Cf. Book Nine, chap. viii, p. 476_{23}; Book Twelve, chap. iv, p. 648_1.

215 136_9, $14{:}137_4$, Sable eyebrows are a proverbial trait in a Russian beauty. For a pictorial representation of a Russian beauty, B. Kustodiev's painting *Kupchikha za chaem* [A merchant's wife having tea] (1918) may be suggested. The woman in that picture might very well be Grushen'ka.

216 136_{13}, $14{:}137_9$, "childlike good nature"—note that this is Aliosha's impression, and not necessarily an objective psychological fact.

217 $136_{32\text{-}33}$, $14{:}137_{29}$, "with an unpleasant sensation"—Aliosha, a member of the educated class, would not mind a peasant woman's dialectal speech. What he finds offensive are a semiliterate's affected speech habits.

218 137_3, $14{:}137_{48}$, "and I was not mistaken"—the reader senses the deadly Sophoclean irony of this: Katerina Ivanovna is *too* sure of herself.

219 137_7, $14{:}138_3$, "excellent"—Russ. *dostoinaia*. Grushen'ka uses an adjective which no educated person would have used in this context. Perhaps: "honorable."

220 $137_{11\text{-}13}$, $14{:}138_{8\text{-}9}$, Dostoevsky is one of the first Russian writers to describe female homoeroticism in physical terms. In his early novel *Netochka Nezvanova* (1848-49) there is an episode of torrid lovemaking by two young girls. One of the two girls is named Katia and is obviously the first version of the character of which Katerina Ivanovna is the last. A homoerotic tendency fits well into the general picture of Katerina Ivanovna's personality.

221   137_{35}, $14:138_{31}$,   Katerina Ivanovna's condescending manner
       (note the first person plural which she uses consistently) soon
       turns ridiculous: she is Grushen'ka's social superior, but she is
       younger and less worldly-wise. She is asking for a comeuppance.

222   137_{40}, $14:138_{28}$,   Russ. *ruchka,* "little hand," is a feminine
       diminutive, which enhances the embarrassing eroticism of this
       scene.

223   138_2, $14:138_{45-46}$,   "He felt a peculiar uneasiness"—raises the
       suspense.

224   138_{31}, $14:139_{28}$,   "I feel sorry for him"—Russ. *zhalet',* "to take
       pity," has in substandard speech a definite connotation of
       "giving one's affection" or even "granting sexual favors."
       Katerina Ivanovna senses the *double entendre.*

225   138_{35}, $14:139_{32}$,   "character"—Russ. *kharakter,* here in the
       colloquial meaning "bad temper, stubborn nature."

226   138_{44-45}, $14:139_{42}$,   "you incredible beauty"—Grushen'ka's
       speech is more substandard now, and of course quite insolent.

227   139_{26}, $14:140_{23}$,   "creature"—Russ. *tvar',* the word Miusov had
       used.

228   139_{28}, $14:140_{26}$,   "used to visit"—Russ. *khazhivali,* an iterative
       verb, indicating repeated action. This and the plural "gen-
       tlemen" *(kavaleram)* need not be taken literally. Rather, both are
       emphatic.

229   139_{29}, $14:140_{27}$,   "You see, I know."—The final bombshell!
       Who told her?

230   140_4, $14:141_1$,   In the original, it is *tigr,* "tiger," not *tigritsa,*
       "tigress." Obviously it is the wrong word. Hence, the effect is
       one of bathos—Katerina Ivanovna is made to look quite
       ridiculous.

231   140_5, $14:141_2$,   Another scene of slapstick comedy is conjured
       up: two beautiful young women having a catfight ("tiger"
       virtually suggests that).

232   140_8, $14:141_5$,   The times when public floggings were performed
       were still remembered in the 1860s, but Katerina Ivanovna must
       have gotten this bloodthirsty fantasy from a gothic novel. It
       sounds ridiculous.

Chapter xi

233   140_{36}, $14:141_{33}$,   "Your money or your life!"—The Russian
       phrase is a calque from Fr. *la bourse ou la vie!* It may be yet

another quotation from Schiller's *Robbers* (Act I, sc. i), where it is in French.

234 140_{43}, 14:141_{40}, "Crush me like a cockroach."—A recurring image, and part of the pattern of insect imagery in the novel.

235 141_{16}, 14:142_{11}, "that man"—Russ. *chelovechek,* lit. "little man." Here the diminutive suggests fondness. See Introduction I.4.b, note 51.

236 141_{33-36}, 14:142_{27-30}, In a way, Dostoevsky is describing his own narrative technique here: such "laying bare of the device" *(obnazhenie priioma),* as the Russian Formalists called it, occurs quite often in Dostoevsky.

237 141_{38-39}, 14:142_{34}, "his face became . . . menacing"—suspense followed by anticlimax. Characteristic of Dmitry, whose emotions are uncoordinated and unpredictable. Cf. Book Two, chap. vi, p. 58_{41-43}.

238 141_{41-45}, 14:142_{36-39}, Note the accumulation of modal expressions (it is even more striking in the original). Dostoevsky uses such accumulation to emphasize a certain impression. Here it is one of suddenness.

239 142_3, 14:142_{46}, The translation misses a nuance here. Dmitry does not say "flogged." Katerina Ivanovna had said that. Reckless though he is, Dmitry will not repeat Katerina Ivanovna's embarrassing words in full. But "scaffold" *(eshafot,* from the French) must have struck his imagination.

240 142_7, 14:143_1, "infernal woman"—Russ. *infernal'nitsa,* a neologism.

241 142_{13}, 14:143_8, Dmitry is getting directions (East, South, West, North) mixed up with continents. Even his slips are entertaining.

242 142_{38-40}, 14:143_{31-32}, "What worried Aliosha"—what follows is *erlebte Rede.*

243 143_2, 14:143_{40}, "image"—Russ. *obraz* is ambiguous, meaning "image, picture" as well as "saint's image, icon." The Russian expression is a cliché which Dmitry uses in what is close to its literal sense.

244 143_4, 14:143_{42}, "she cried herself"—We discover a new trait of Grushen'ka's, along the way, as it were.

245 143_6, 14:143_{43}, "women"—Russ. *u bab,* where *baba* is deprecatory.

246 143_{13}, 14:144_{1-2}, "as a last resource"—in the original, lit. "until perhaps the very last moment," a dark and ominous statement which is also prophetic. Aliosha will be absent at "the very last moment."

247   143$_{13}$, 14:144$_2$, "Good-bye"—Russ. *proshchai,* a leave-taking
which means that one does not expect to see the other for some
time.

248   143$_{18-35}$, 14:144$_{6-25}$, This passage is all-important for the plot of
the novel. See Book Twelve, chap. iv, pp. 643–44.

249   143$_{36}$, 14:144$_{25}$, "The filthy back alley"—alludes to chapters iv
and v of this book (pp. 97 and 106).

250   143$_{43}$, 14:144$_{31}$, "I shall look him up."—An ironic false lead.
Aliosha will not realize his good intention.

251   144$_{15-17}$, 14:145$_{2-4}$, "a profanation of the sacrament of confession"—cf. Book One, chap. v, p. 22$_{33-34}$, and Book Two,
chap. viii, p. 78$_{28}$.

252   144$_{20-41}$, 14:145$_{7-29}$, This passage is typical of Dostoevsky's
contrapuntal (or "dialectical") style. The situation at the
monastery is described in a series of statements, each being an
antithesis of the preceding.

253   145$_{3-4}$, 14:145$_{36}$, "Those were his words about you."—Russ.
izrek, a biblical form ("spake" or "quoth"). It foregrounds
Zosima's words as important and prophetic.

254   145$_{25}$, 14:146$_{11}$, "The mattress"—note how Dostoevsky will
bring back seemingly trivial details: cf. Book Two, chap. viii, p.
80, and chap. vi, p. 112.

255   145$_{32}$, 14:146$_{18}$, "Joy" *(radost')* is established as a key word of
this scene. It is also one of Aliosha's leitmotifs.

256   145$_{39ff.}$, 14:146$_{26ff.}$, Liza's letter is clearly derived from
Tatiana's letter in Pushkin's *Eugene Onegin* (1825–30). Indeed,
several passages are so close that Dostoevsky may be trying to
suggest that Liza has been "cribbing."

257   146$_{35-38}$, 14:147$_{20-23}$, The words of Aliosha's prayer are a
mixture of Russian and Slavonic, as might be expected in a
person of his description. To some extent, every Russian prays in
Slavonic. In a literal sense Aliosha's prayer remains unanswered:
things will go from bad to worse. Yet in the end God's ways will
appear in their wisdom and wonder.

Book Four

Chapter i

1 148₂, 14:148₃, "Lacerations"—Russ. *nadryvy,* lit. "ruptures." This is the leitmotif of this book. See Introduction II.6.d. Psychological Wisdom.

2 148₄, 14:148₄, See Introduction I.6.c. Father Zosima and Other Monks.

3 148₁₀, 14:148₁₁, "he desired"—Russ. *vozzhelal* is biblical language, setting a solemn tone.

4 148₂₆₋₃₃, 14:148₂₅₋₃₂, Internal commentary. The observation that Father Zosima's "speech was somewhat disconnected" (line 28) helps to prepare the reader for Book Six.

5 148₃₁₋₃₂, 14:148₃₁, "all men and all creation"—*vse i vsia,* lit. "all men and all things," a formulaic expression characteristic of religious discourse. It will recur often, signifying Father Zosima's all-encompassing love.

6 148₁₈₋₃₃, 14:148₁₉₋₃₂, This passage is dominated by the verbs *uchit',* "to teach, to preach," and *govorit'/skazat',* "to speak, to talk, to say." This suggests that Zosima's power lies in the Word. It is through words that he seeks to express his mystic joy. It is also significant that his speech is far from elegant and in fact "somewhat disconnected."

7 148₃₅, 14:149₂, "God's people"—Russ. *Bozhii narod,* with a strong connotation of "the Russian people" and "the simple people." See Introduction II.4. *The Brothers Karamazov* as a Social Novel.

8 148₃₇, 14:149₅, "those that are outside"—Russ. *mirskie,* "laymen," lit. "worldly, in the world."

9 149₇₋₁₁, 14:149₁₁₋₁₅, The key position of Father Zosima's teaching. It is Dostoevsky's response to Ivan Karamazov's attack on divine justice in Book Five, chap. iv. See Introduction II.2.b. Arguments in Support of Christianity.

10 149_{39}, $14:149_{42}$, Father Zosima's teaching of universal guilt and universal love would indeed sound strange to an Orthodox monk. The Orthodox church does not teach that original sin led to the loss of sanctifying Grace, but rather that, while it caused man to lose his divine identity ($\delta\mu o\acute{\iota}\omega\sigma\iota s$), man has still retained his divine likeness ($\epsilon\acute{\iota}\varkappa\omega\nu$). Some of Dostoevsky's Orthodox critics were quick to point out that Zosima overemphasizes love of mankind at the expense of fear of God.

11 149_{45}, $14:149_{47}$, "death"—Russ. *uspenie* is a religious term, signifying the metaphysical and ritual aspect of death. One would expect it to be applied to a sainted individual after his or her death. The expression is loaded, setting the stage for some important developments in Book Seven.

12 150_{18}, $14:150_{19}$, Mme. Khokhlakov, an eyewitness, reports the scene accurately. See Book Two, chap. iii, p. 43.

13 150_{23}, $14:150_{24}$, "Ekaterinburg"—now Sverdlovsk, in western Siberia.

14 150_{44}, $14:150_{45}$, "We shall see greater things!"—The Russian phrase is an idiom, and difficult to translate; perhaps: "We have seen nothing yet." In the original, the difference between Father Paisy's cautious tone and the confident tone of the other monks is signaled by the use of a question mark in the first case, vs. an exclamation mark in the second.

15 151_{13-14}, $14:151_{11-12}$, Cf. p. 46_{38}.

16 151_{41}, $14:151_{42}$, In the original, an "as it were" *(kak by)* is inserted after "had been appointed," telling us by way of innuendo that Father Ferapont was a nuisance and that his "appointment" was a pretext to get him out of the way.

17 152_1, $14:152_1$, "him"—translates *blazhennomu,* a word whose meaning is ambiguous: "blessed, holy, beatific," but also "imbecile, fool."

18 152_8, $14:152_{8-9}$, "some one strange saying"—we shall soon be given an example of this.

19 152_{25}, $14:152_{26}$, Though Father Ferapont is uneducated, his speech is laced with solemn Slavonic expressions, here *vosstani,* "arise," instead of *vstan',* "get up."

20 152_{27-28}, $14:152_{28-29}$, "Where have you come from?"—Russ. *otkuleva zaneslo* is definitely substandard usage. Only an uneducated man would say *otkuleva.* I would translate: "Where you from?"

21 152_{36-37}, $14:152_{39-40}$, "He spoke with a broad accent."—The

most characteristic feature of the North Russian dialects is their retention of an unstressed *o,* while the Central and Southern dialects pronounce unstressed *o* and *a* identically.

22   152_{38}, 14:152_{42},   Not only monks but peasants, too, girded themselves with rope.

23   152_{41-42}, 14:152_{44-45},   "he wore irons . . ."—a not uncommon ascetic practice. We shall hear more about these chains (p. 313_{44}).

24   153_{21}, 14:153_{23},   Up to this point the little monk has been quoting from his monastery rules, in rather correct Russo-Slavonic. Now he is on his own and immediately lapses into the vernacular of the uneducated.

25   153_{26}, 14:153_{28-29},   "mushrooms"—Russ. *gruzd',* "milk agaric," a common edible mushroom. In the original we read: " 'What about milk agarics?' Father Ferapont suddenly asked, pronouncing the letter *g* as a spirant, almost like a *kh.* 'Milk agarics?' repeated the little monk, taken aback." The pronunciation of *g* as a spirant is common in various Russian dialects, but not in educated speech. It enhances the comic bathos of this exchange.

26   153_{30-31}, 14:153_{33},   "in bondage to the devil"—doubly loaded! Father Ferapont's obsession with the devil will soon become his label. The connection between "bread" and "bondage to the devil" will be a focal point in "The Grand Inquisitor" (Book Five, chap. v).

27   154_4, 14:154_{4-5}, Insect imagery once more.

28   154_{36}, 14:154_{36},   "It's terrible, terrible!"—A revealing conversation. Father Ferapont has not the slightest fear of devils. But, like these devils, he fears Christ and the sign of the cross.

29   154_{40}, 14:154_{40}, Luke 1:17.

30   155_5, 14:155_3,   As so often, a serious point (here, the reality of metaphysical evil) is at first presented in an unserious context.

31   155_8, 14:155_6,   Cf. pp. 21_{20}, 78_{43}–79_2.

32   155_{17-18}, 14:155_{16-17},   This is a false lead: the little monk from Obdorsk will not play a significant role in the novel.

33   155_{36}, 14:155_{36},   "Rapture" *(vostorg)* is one of Aliosha's leitmotifs.

34   156_{2-3}, 14:155_{48}–156_1,   Quotes Matt. 16:18.

35   156_{6-10}, 14:156_{5-9},   Ivan Karamazov and his creation, the Grand Inquisitor, serve as examples of this thesis. See N. Losskii *(Dostoevskii i ego Khristianskoe miroponimanie* (New York, 1953), p. 257.

36   156_{10-11}, $14:156_{9-10}$, A favorite thought of Dostoevsky's; cf. *Diary of a Writer,* 1:151. The language of the passage, however, is stylized, having an archaic, biblical, and ecclesiastic flavor which is not found in Dostoevsky's publicistic writings. I would translate *urodlivosti* by "abominations" rather than "grotesque."

37   156_{16}, $14:156_{15}$, "my orphan"—Father Paisy alludes to Aliosha's imminent loss of his spiritual father.

38   156_{17-27}, $14:156_{16-27}$, Typical Dostoevsky. Father Paisy's words seem unmotivated, and the reader may think that he is dealing with a rather clumsy ploy on Dostoevsky's part to insert some of his own pet ideas into the text. But very quickly we are given a profound and compelling motivation for Father Paisy's words: a withdrawn and bookish man *would* express his love by sharing his most cherished beliefs with the one his heart went out to.

Chapter ii

39   156_{31-32}, $14:156_{31-32}$, Not quite what we read on p. 130.

40   157_{5-8}, $14:157_{5-8}$, The barrage of modal expressions in this sentence   invites the reader to stop and imagine Fiodor Pavlovich' face. The translator has left out *reshitel'no,* "decidedly," before "giving."

41   157_{33}, $14:157_{31}$, Ironic foreshadowing.

42   157_{38}, $14:157_{36-37}$, Sophoclean irony! The reader has been told as early as in the introductory paragraph of Book One, chap. i (p. 2), that Fiodor Pavlovich's days are numbered.

43   157_{39}, $14:157_{36}$, "my dear Aleksei Fiodorovich"—ironic.

44   158_{2-10}, $14:158_{1-7}$, The philosophy of a frank sensualist.

45   158_{11-13}, $14:158_{8-10}$, "Ivan is a conceited coxcomb . . ."—a big surprise. But as always, Fiodor Pavlovich's words carry more weight than might appear at first glance. His judgment is but another step in Dostoevsky's argument *ad personam,* meant to undermine Ivan and his atheist philosophy.

46   158_{17}, $14:158_{14}$, "Grushka"—a disrespectful version of "Grusha," "Grushen'ka" being the affectionate version. "Grushka" has a connotation of "that wench."

47   158_{36-37}, $14:158_{35}$, "your old father"—in the original, "father" is in the plural, which allows the motif of "the fathers" to emerge as a more universal and abstract entity. Cf. Introduction II.3.a. Fatherhood.

48   158₄₆–159₁, 14:158₄₄₋₄₅,   Fiodor Pavlovich is almost never wrong in his assessment of people.

49   159₂₋₃, 14:158₄₆₋₄₇,   "and come to me"—*da ko mne pridiot navestit'*, "and will come to visit me." We already know that Grushen'ka's "visit" has a very special meaning for Fiodor Pavlovich. Here *navestit'*, "to pay a visit," is definitely lubricious.

50   159₁₈, 14:159₁₅,   "Vanka" is the disrespectful version, such as was used by a master addressing a servant boy. Something like "Johnny boy."

51   159₂₃₋₂₅, 14:159₁₉₋₂₀,   More insect imagery.

52   159₂₉₋₃₀, 14:159₂₆,   Fiodor Pavlovich unwittingly quotes from Psalm 1:4: "The ungodly are not so: but are like the chaff which the wind driveth away." (The translator has missed this nuance.) Once again Fiodor Pavlovich displays an uncanny gift of prophecy, of which he is not himself aware.

53   159₃₉₋₄₀, 14:159₃₆,   "I won't give him anything, not a penny" —*Nichego ne dam, nichegoshen'ki,* where *nichegoshen'ki* is an emphatic double diminutive of *nichego,* "nothing," an inverted "big, fat nothing," as it were. Rhythmically, the phrase makes a perfect folk verse. Such nuances are important in creating a character's voice. See Introduction III.1.e. Fiodor Pavlovich.

54   160₁₅, 14:160₈,   Foreshadowing: this is indeed the last time Aliosha will see his father alive.

Chapter iii

55   161₂₈₋₃₂, 14:161₁₈₋₂₂,   Dostoevsky's own strategy. See *PSS* 15:548.

56   162₆, 14:161₄₆,   "gentlemen"—*gospoda.* Today it sounds odd to address a group of ten-year-olds that way, but it is perfectly in character in the setting given here. Aliosha makes a point of treating the boys as equals.

57   162₁₂, 14:162₆,   "Krasotkin"—another major character is introduced indirectly. Here "tell tales" translates *fiskalit'*, "to snitch" (schoolboy jargon).

58   162₂₁, 14:162₁₅,   "Wisp of tow"—Russ. *mochalka,* "wisp of tow, washrag, loofah (the fibrous substance of the pod of a tropical gourd, used as a sponge)." We shall learn later why the boy is called by this name: see p. 186₁₂. At this stage the nickname merely arouses the reader's curiosity.

59   162_{29-30}, $14:162_{22-23}$,   An example of Dostoevsky's technique to
      introduce dramatic action through the dialogue, or other indirect
      means.

60   163_{23}, $14:163_{18}$,   "Monk in silk trousers!"—*Monakh, v
      garniturovykh shtanakh,* a children's rhyme. To be mocked and
      abused by children in the street is a cliché of the Orthodox saint's
      life. I suggest: "Friar, friar, pants on fire!"

61   164_{13}, $14:164_3$,   Note that Aliosha treats a nine-year-old as
      though he were a responsible adult. This, as well as the details of
      the scene (rock-throwing, a hurt hand) link it to another scene
      (Book Five, chap. iv, p. 223_{36-38}), both of crucial importance to
      Dostoevsky's argument. Cf. Introduction II.3.b. "The Novel
      about Children."

Chapter iv

62   164_{31-35}, $14:164_{22-26}$,   Cf. chap. i, pp. 150–51.

63   165_2, $14:164_{37}$,   "creature"—*tvar'* again. This word has be-
      come Grushen'ka's label.

64   165_2, $14:164_{38}$,   *C'est tragique*—it was more comic than tragic,
      as Dmitry's reaction showed very well.

65   165_8, $14:164_{42-43}$,   "a serious conversation"—*torzhestvennyi* is
      "solemn." In her excitement, Mme. Khokhlakov keeps choosing
      the wrong word ("serious" would seem correct here). Her syntax
      is also off balance. The translator has chosen to "correct" her,
      destroying another nuance of Dostoevsky's.

66   165_{10}, $14:165_1$,   "lacerating"—see note 1 above.

67   165_{12-13}, $14:165_4$,   "I've been watching for you! I've been
      thirsting for you!"—In the original: *Ia vas zhdala! Ia vas
      zhazhdala!,* a pun of sorts, which makes the whole phrase sound
      more natural, though not less *outré.*

68   165_{20}, $14:165_{11}$,   "strained"—*nadryvchatyi,* lit. "rupturous,"
      i.e., "breaking, ready to break." Dostoevsky is preparing the
      word *nadryv* for its role as a leitmotif. See note 1 above.

69   165_{27-29}, $14:165_{19-21}$,   This is *erlebte Rede.* The doctor is German
      and speaks a somewhat primitive Russian. "I can make nothing
      of it" is his label.

70   165_{38}, $14:165_{30-31}$,   "our honored visitor"—obviously ironic,
      since Aliosha is a former playmate and almost in her own age
      group.

71   166_7, $14:165_{45}$,   "A comedy, perhaps, not a tragedy."—Mme.

Khokhlakov, like Fiodor Pavlovich, silly though she may sound, often hits the nail on the head when it comes to recognizing the negative side of life and of people. Her remark is another instance of internal commentary. The scene in the drawing room is Chekhovian comedy.

72 166_{9-10}, $14:165_{47-48}$, "it's all nonsense, all nonsense"—Mme. Khokhlakov projects the state of her own mind on the world at large. This circumstance, easily recognizable in her case (or Fiodor Pavlovich's), is really true of every character in the novel. Mme. Khokhlakov is important as a foil.

73 166_{34-35}, $14:166_{25-26}$, "frightened at this alarm"—Russ. *ispugavshis' ikh ispuga,* "frightened by their fright," which, in addition to the paronymy (a more popular figure of speech in Russian than in English), is also a perfect trochaic tetrameter—with alliteration, yet. Such intrusions of highly organized, outright "poetic" language occur quite frequently in the text. Of course, they are all lost in translation.

74 167_{5-7}, $14:166_{41-43}$, Obviously narrative and clock time are at odds here. Dostoevsky will use a little trick to cover this rather glaring gap, as we shall soon see. Cf. note 77.

75 167_{20}, $14:167_{9-10}$, "will you give me . . ."—in the original, this is preceded by: "This very moment, my dear Aleksei Fiodorovich . . ." The word *migom,* "this very moment, in a jiffy," is then repeated later in the sentence. Both inversion and repetition underscore Liza's impatience.

76 167_{28}, $14:167_{18-19}$, "as a child, a little girl"—*za devochku, za malen'kuiu-malen'kuiu devochku,* lit. "as a little girl, a teeny, teeny little girl." The effect of this emphatic repetition gets lost in the translation.

77 168_{14-15}, $14:168_5$, Her mother does not even notice the irony, nor does she realize that Liza had simply sent her to the wrong place to look for the cotton. This little ruse allows Liza (and the author) to insert her *tête-à-tête* with Aliosha.

78 168_{26}, $14:168_{15}$, "isn't he a child, a child himself?"—in the original: "isn't he himself little, a little man," another allusion to Aleksei, "man of God." Cf. Book Three, chap. xi, p. 141_{15-16}, and note 235 to Book Three. Russ. *malen'kii* is used colloquially in the meaning "childish."

79 168_{33}, $14:168_{22}$, "and perhaps the boy was rabid"—Mme. Khokhlakov is a comic figure. Here she comes up with a harebrained *non sequitur* which earns her Liza's sarcasms.

80 168_{41}, $14:168_{30}$, Liza is pulling her mother's leg. She wonders whether Aliosha is developing symptoms of hydrophobia.

81 169_{21-22}, $14:169_{10}$, "and how fortunate it is"—Mme. Khokhlakov is talking nonsense again, but here it is excusable: we hear a worried mother.

82 169_{29}, $14:169_{17}$, The original says "comedy," not "farce." Some more internal commentary. As so often, a literary term is used to describe a situation. Cf. Book Three, note 100.

Chapter v

83 169_{34}, $14:169_{23}$, Liza has already given us a preview of what "laceration" may imply. Cf. notes 1, 66, and 68 above.

84 170_{15-18}, $14:170_{1-4}$, This allusion to Aliosha's dream seems to be in conflict with the last paragraph of Book Three (p. 146). At any rate, Dostoevsky makes sure that *nadryv*, "rupture" (translated by "laceration"), becomes firmly established as a symbol of a certain human type, represented by Katerina Ivanovna, Ivan Karamazov, and their assorted doubles. The integrity and happiness of these men and women is "ruptured" by the strain of their self-conscious pride.

85 170_{33}, $14:170_{19}$, The preceding is *erlebte Rede*. By using this narrative mode, Dostoevsky disguises his allowing so young and innocent a person as Aliosha to engage in subtle psychological analysis.

86 170_{42-44}, $14:170_{30-32}$, The word *slishkom*, "too (much)," occurs twice in this sentence, translated by "immense" and "a great deal." The use of *slishkom* not only gives the text a more colloquial flavor, but it also gives it an emotional charge. Cf. Gleb Struve, "Notes on the Language and Style of Dostoevsky," p. 76.

87 170_{45}, $14:170_{32}$, "reptile"—cf. Book Three, chap. ix, pp. 129, 131, where Russian *gad* was translated, perhaps more appropriately, by "viper."

88 171_{1-2}, $14:170_{34-35}$, In the original, the word *gad*, "viper," is repeated for greater emphasis; "had long done so" is a stylistic "correction" of Dostoevsky's text.

89 171_{11-12}, $14:170_{43-44}$, Cf. Father Zosima's words about "active love," Book Two, chap. iv, p. 49_{43-45}.

90 171_{20}, $14:171_{3}$, Again, *erlebte Rede*. In this passage, Aliosha's

and the narrator's voices blend in a way that is in fact somewhat dissonant.

91   171_{35}, $14:171_{21}$, "the same actions"—Russ. *dvizheniia,* "movements," a rather gauche euphemism: she remembers how she could barely be restrained from starting a catfight with Grushen'ka.

92   171_{35-36}, $14:171_{21-23}$, ". . . you checked me in one of them"—these awkward circumlocutions reflect Katerina Ivanovna's embarrassment.

93   172_{1-7}, $14:171_{33-40}$, Katerina Ivanovna's language is that of the finishing school and "genteel" novels. It is quite ludicrous. In particular, Katerina Ivanovna's image of Ivan Fiodorovich is grotesquely askew.

94   172_{27}, $14:172_{13}$, "creature"—cf. p. 139_{26}. Note the irony. Here she is, talking of "something higher . . . perhaps even than duty," and a second later she cannot help lapsing into the bathos of name-calling.

95   172_{29-30}, $14:172_{16-17}$, "with an outburst of a sort of pale, tormented ecstasy"—*s kakim-to nadryvom kakogo-to blednogo vymuchennogo vostorga.* The translation omits another occurrence of *nadryv,* "rupture." Russ. *vymuchennyi,* lit. "extorted, squeezed out by force," suggests that her ecstasy is self-induced. The repetition of the indefinite pronoun (*kakim-to* and *kakogo-to,* "some sort of") is characteristic of the narrator's style. I suggest: "in the ruptured voice of a pale, tortured ecstasy which she had somehow managed to squeeze from her soul."

96   172_{33}–173_1, $14:172_{19-34}$, The persistent repetition of the word "life" clashes with the dead, cerebral nature of Katerina's passion.

97   172_{40}, $14:172_{26-27}$, "I will be a god"—a loaded statement. The motif of the "man-god" emerges nakedly—and in a grotesquely underplayed version. See Introduction II.2.a. Challenge to Christianity.

98   173_{4-5}, $14:172_{38}$, "too hurried and crude"—*slishkom pospeshno i slishkom obnazhenno,* lit. "too hurried and too bald": internal commentary provided by the narrator. He leaves it up to the reader to perceive the ludicrous aspect of Katerina Ivanovna's harangue.

99   173_8, $14:172_{41}$, "Unpleasant" is a little too weak to translate *nekhorosho,* while "evil" would be too strong; perhaps "ugly."

100   173_{15}, $14:172_{48}$,   Ivan has started on a false note and will insist
      on playing his dissonant piece to the end. See Introduction
      III.4.c. Parody, Travesty, and Dissonance.

101   173_{29}, $14:173_{14}$,   "heroism"—translates *podvig,* "feat of
      heroism, heroic deed," often with a moral connotation (it may
      also mean "ascetic feat"). The travesty which Ivan makes of this
      lofty word is symptomatic.

102   173_{19-33}, $14:173_{6-20}$,   This moral lecture, bitterly ironic of
      course, may be seen as a parody of Father Zosima's words of
      consolation (Book Two, chap. iii, p. 42_{6-8}). Ivan does not realize
      that, while making fun of Katerina Ivanovna very cruelly, he is
      actually projecting upon her some of his own attitudes.

103   173_{36}, $14:173_{23}$,   The point of the narrator's comments is that a
      man is hardly ever sure of the overtones of what he—or anyone
      else—says and that he may not always have control over them,
      not to speak of his listener.

104   174_{8-9}, $14:173_{41}$,   "laceration"—*nadryv,* once more.

105   175_5, $14:174_{39}$,   "I seemed to see in a flash"—Russ. *ozarenie,*
      "illumination," seems too solemn for the context, and the
      translator has "corrected" Dostoevsky accordingly. But
      Aliosha, in his excitement, does not find a more suitable expres-
      sion. Besides, it helps to build his image.

106   175_{12}, $14:174_{46}$,   "nobody here will tell the truth"—Aliosha's
      words are significant not only for the matter at hand, but also for
      the novel at large: Ivan and Katerina Ivanovna are caught in a
      web of lies. See Introduction III.4.c. Parody, Travesty, and
      Dissonance.

107   175_{15-16}, $14:175_{1-2}$,   A different version of an image which has
      occurred several times before. Cf. Book Two, note 233, and note
      278.

108   175_{23}, $14:175_9$,   "you are a little religious idiot"—another
      surprise. The original reads *vy malen'kii iurodivyi.* The word
      iurodivyi, "God's fool," has been applied to Aliosha before
      (Book One, chap. iv, p. 15_{28}, where it was translated by
      "religious eccentric"). Cf. Book One, note 94; Book Two, note
      34; and Book Three, note 23. The word links characters so
      different as Aliosha, Lizaveta Smerdiashchaia, and Fiodor
      Pavlovich—an effect which is lost in this translation. Here,
      Katerina Ivanovna means to hurt Aliosha: from her viewpoint—
      that of an educated woman of the upper class—what she says is
      an insult.

109   175_{28-29}, $14:175_{15-16}$,   One of Ivan's better moments, important as a seed of his possible redemption.

110   175_{38}, $14:175_{25-26}$,   "She has talked to me of nothing but her love for him."—This phrase is very awkward in the original: "I've been doing nothing but hearing about her love for him." Ivan, normally eloquent, is very excited. Hence this momentary awkwardness.

111   175_{41}–176_5, $14:175_{29-38}$,   The word "laceration" appears in quotation marks in the translation, *nadryv* without quotation marks in the original.

112   175_{46}, $14:175_{33}$,   Ivan is one of several characters in the novel who try their hand at psychological analysis. He is very good at it—but he fails to see that psychological truth has many levels and many facets. Mme. Khokhlakov has seen more than Ivan.

113   176_{11}, $14:175_{44}$,   Note the drama involving the hands of the protagonists. In Dostoevsky, it is always a good idea to watch the protagonist's hands.

114   176_{11-12}, $14:175_{45}$,   *"Den Dank, Dame, begehr ich nicht."*—"Madam, I do not want your gratitude." A quotation from Schiller's ballad "Der Handschuh." The title is untranslatable since *Handschuh* is both "glove" and "gauntlet." In the ballad, a frivolous damsel flings her glove into a lions' den, challenging a knight, her admirer, to pick it up. He does, flings the glove in her face, and speaks the words quoted here.

115   176_{15}, $14:176_3$,   Schiller's idealist philosophy and lofty humanism, which inspired generations of young Russians, would not seem to match Ivan's intellectual profile, that of a young naturalist of the 1860s, a materialist and "practical man." See Introduction I.4.a. Secular Sources.

116   176_{24}, $14:176_{13}$,   "angel"—by now the word has become Aliosha's label.

117   176_{27}, $14:176_{16}$,   "Her face beamed with delight"—to a gossipy and sentimental woman, witnessing a "drama" such as this *must be* sheer delight, the narrator reasons.

118   $176_{36ff.}$, $14:176_{27ff.}$,   At this point the reader ought to recollect Book Two, chap. vi, p. 63. See Introduction III.3.a. Motifs.

119   176_{36}, $14:176_{27}$,   "somehow"—translates *pochemu-to*, "for some reason." A subtle nuance: Katerina Ivanovna will not mention that reason, because the reason was, albeit indirectly, Grushen'ka.

120   176_{37}, $14:176_{28}$, "dragged"—translates *vyvel*, "led (out)."
Another subtle nuance: Katerina Ivanovna would not use so
graphic an expression as "dragged" (Russ. *vytashchil*). The
language of her narrative is stylized all the way, as she very
gingerly comes up with one euphemism after another. She does
not say, "There is a low tavern here" (line 34), but rather,
"There is a bad place here in town, a tavern": it costs her an
effort to bring the word "tavern" *(traktir)* to her lips.

121   176_{43}, $14:176_{34}$, *His* is italicized to suggest that Katerina
Ivanovna emphasizes that, though the other man was disgraced,
it was Dmitry whose role in this scene was disgraceful.

122   177_1, $14:176_{36}$, "his anger . . . and in his passions!"—high
sounding words for what was clearly a tavern brawl.

123   177_4, $14:176_{40}$, "discharged"—translates *vykliuchili*, another
subtlety: it is the word that would apply to a pupil "dismissed"
from school, not an officer "discharged" from the service.

124   177_{13}, $14:177_2$, "assistance"—Russ. *vspomozhenie*, a rather
stilted expression.

125   177_{16-18}, $14:177_{4-6}$, By mentioning the possibility of a lawsuit,
Katerina Ivanovna neutralizes her "sympathy." What might her
real motive be? To embarrass Dmitry?

126   177_{21}, $14:177_{10}$, Addresses in mid-nineteenth-century Russia
were identified by the owner's name, rather than by house
numbers.

127   177_{45-46}, $14:177_{33-34}$, In the original: "I'm always against
women in such cases; I'm for men." The plural sounds a little
odd, but perhaps Mme. Khokhlakov is "for men," period.

128   178_6, $14:177_{40}$, See note 116 above.

129   178_{14}, $14:177_{48}$, "I ask you and you don't answer."—Liza's
concerns and remarks run against the grain of the main line of
action throughout this chapter. Here, this circumstance is
reflected in a Chekhovian "nondialogue." A subtle detail of
Dostoevsky's dramatic technique. See Introduction III.
Narrative Technique.

130   178_{16-17}, $14:178_{2-3}$, In the original, the maid's language is
established by her referring to Katerina Ivanovna in the plural
("they"), generally used by social inferiors when referring to
their betters.

131   178_{35}, $14:178_{20}$, Mme. Khokhlakov has a weakness for young
men—much as Fiodor Pavlovich has a weakness for young
women.

Chapter vi

132   179_7, 14:178_{37}, "grieved"—in the original, the noun "grief" *(gore)* appears. This creates a particularly striking example of the way in which Dostoevsky will create a transition from one chapter to the next: "grief" was the leitmotif of the concluding scene of chapter v.

133   179_{15-16}, 14:178_{45}, Cf. the preceding chapter, p. 175_{18}.

134   179_{36}, 14:179_{22}, *Erlebte Rede.*

135   179_{38-39}, 14:179_{25}, "taking out of his pocket . . ."—another cross-reference. Cf. p. 159_{8-9}.

136   179_{41}, 14:179_{26}, "Dmitry was not at home"—Aliosha's presentiment (line 22) thus turns out to have been correct. The fact that he tried to contact Dmitry, but failed, is significant. Dostoevsky "foregrounds" it by introducing Aliosha's presentiment.

137   180_{15}, 14:179_{42}, "a simple hut"—mistranslation of *v chistuiu izbu,* "to the living room." The whole house consisted of a living room, a smaller room, and the hall.

138    $180_{27ff.}$, 14:$180_{5ff.}$, The Russian stove, the wooden bench, and the square table are standard for a Russian peasant hut *(izba).*

139   180_{41}, 14:180_{24-25}, "a few drops of vodka remaining"— translates *so slabymi ostatkami zemnykh blag,* lit. "with faint remnants of earthly blessings," ironically euphemistic for "vodka." Note the careful detail of this description. This is one of Dostoevsky's many studies of poverty, and its material roots are shown fully. From the economics of poverty Dostoevsky immediately proceeds to its psychology.

140   181_{1-2}, 14:180_{29-31}, The description of this woman is a grotesque false lead. We shall soon enough learn the truth about Mrs. Snegiriov. Note that we perceive everything through the eyes of Aliosha as he enters the room.

141   181_{15}, 14:180_{47}, "A wisp of tow" was pretty well established as a leitmotif earlier. Cf. p. $162_{21,38}$. It will stay around: cf. p. 186_{12}.

142   181_{28}, 14:181_{12}, "retreat"—translates Russ. *nedra,* lit. "the bowels (of the earth)," also used metaphorically in such expressions as *v nedrakh naroda,* "amidst the masses of the (common) people." Here the sentence may mean: "What prompted you to go slumming?"

143   181_{31-32}, 14:181_{15}, "Though he had obviously been drinking, he

was not drunk."—The kind of ambiguity Dostoevsky relishes. It starts a series of psychological paradoxes. See Introduction II.6.b. Psychological Motivation.

144 181_{38}, 14:181_{23}, "crazy"—translates *iurodlivyi* (not *iurodivyi;* cf. note 108 above), suggesting craziness without the saving virtue of godliness. Perhaps: "cracked."

145 181_{44}, 14:181_{29}, "checked trousers"—that makes him a figure out of the early Dickens, perhaps an effect Dostoevsky was pursuing. Snegiriov is a very Dickensian figure. Dickens was immensely popular in nineteenth-century Russia.

146 181_{46}, 14:181_{31}, "like a boy"—translates *kak malen'kii mal'chik,* "like a little boy, like a small boy." The adjective is significant, since we will have a role reversal, where a "little boy" becomes "father," and vice versa. See Introduction II.3.a. Fatherhood.

147 182_{3-5}, 14:181_{35-36}, The Russian text reads literally: "Staff I'm Captain, Sir, Snegiriov, Sir," which is ungrammatical, but not as impossible as it would be in English. The staff captain's speech is strongly stylized throughout: overelaborate, full of inversions and verbal double takes.

148 182_{17}, 14:182_{1-2}, "Yessirov"—Russ. *Slovoersov,* where *slovoers* is a humorous term for the obsequious *s* (short for *sudar',* "Sir") and *-ov,* a suffix equivalent to Eng. *-s.* So: "Yessirs." *Snegiriov* means "bullfinch's." Bird symbolism will play a role in Snegiriov's story.

149 182_{30}, 14:182_{14}, "meeting"—an awkward euphemism which makes things worse.

150 182_{31}, 14:182_{15}, "blurted out"—translates *otrezal,* "snapped," one of the few instances where the translator's "correction" of the text seems in order.

151 182_{41}, 14:182_{25}, "under the icons"—there may be, but need not be, a symbolic meaning to this detail.

152 183_{11}, 14:182_{42}, "Iliushechka"—a tender diminutive.

153 183_{13-14}, 14:182_{46}, "I am sorry about your finger"—Russ. *pal'chik* (diminutive of *palets,* "finger") is ironic. Perhaps: "I am sorry about your precious little finger."

154 183_{34}, 14:183_{18}, "his highness"—Russ. *ego svetlost',* a title used in reference to princes and princesses (or strictly speaking, dukes and duchesses; not royalty). It is, of course ironic, but there is the fact of Dmitry's noble birth and inherited fortune—while Snegiriov is a penniless commoner.

155 183_{46}, $14:183_{30}$, "playing the fool"—Russ. *paiasnichat'*, "clowning." This word, and the whole sentence, smack of the young, "progressive" generation (represented also by Rakitin).

156 184_5, $14:183_{36}$, In the original Snegiriov says "our character," patronizing for "her character."

157 184_{7-8}, $14:183_{37-38}$, A quotation from Pushkin's poem "The Demon" (1823).

158 184_{23}, $14:184_7$, "Mr. Chernomazov"—an inadvertent pun: the first half of the name means nothing to Arina Petrovna, so she changes it to something that has a meaning: *chernomazyi*, "swarthy," where *cherno-* means "black" and *maz-* "smear." She does not know, of course, that Turkish *kara* also means "black."

159 184_{36}, $14:184_{20}$, "Buffoon!"—This label links Snegiriov to Fiodor Pavlovich: they are both fathers, as well as "buffoons" before their own children.

160 184_{37}–185_{17}, $14:184_{21-46}$, Arina Petrovna's speech is incoherent and makes little sense. The translation actually gives it more direct meaning than it has in the original. It has a flavor of lower-class diction, mixed with the staff captain's more "genteel" speech.

161 184_{40}, $14:184_{24}$, In the original, *batiushka* is inserted after "many such guests." This is probably to be translated "Father" (Aliosha is wearing a monk's cassock), adding to the comedy of the situation. But it may be simply "my good man."

162 185_1, $14:184_{28-29}$, "you are a little spitfire"—translates *ty i mala kucha, da voniucha,* a rhymed formulaic saying, obviously scatological ("you're a small pile, but you're sure smelly").

163 185_{11}, $14:184_{40}$, "The dead smell worse still!"—the first occurrence of one of the key motifs of the novel. Cf. Book Seven, chap. i, "The Odor of Corruption."

164 185_{17}, $14:184_{46}$, This is Dostoevskian psychopathology. The air in the Snegiriovs' abode is bad, literally and figuratively, as Snegiriov will observe at the beginning of the next chapter. The deranged woman has heard someone say that, and she now projects her own misery and guilt on the air which she breathes.

Chapter vii

165 186_{13}, $14:185_{44}$, "beard"—Russ. *boroden'ka,* diminutive of *boroda,* "beard."

166   186_{14-25}, $14:185_{46}-186_9$,   This is the definitive version of a scene
      about which we have heard several times before. Cf. pp. 63, 176.
167   186_{21}, $14:186_5$,   "it's my dad"—this phrase is of great symbolic
      significance: the fact that Snegiriov is a father is reason enough
      not to hurt his dignity. In the original, *papa,* "dad," is repeated
      for greater emphasis. See Introduction II.3.a. Fatherhood.
168   186_{22-23}, $14:186_7$,   "that hand, that very hand"—meaning the
      hand that inflicted this terrible indignity on his father. It must be
      understood that touching a man's face is a mortal insult. Pulling
      a man's beard is an insult to his dignity as a father in the image of
      the Heavenly Father, so that "that hand" is worse than the hand
      of a murderer.
169   186_{30}, $14:186_{14}$,   "a draft project"—Russ. *v. prozhekte,* where
      the French pronunciation (*v proekte* would be normal) is ironic.
170   186_{39}, $14:186_{22}$,   "retired"—ironic, instead of "slunk away."
171   186_{39}, $14:186_{23}$,   "a family record"—lit. "this genealogical
      family picture," logically the wrong word, but it delivers the
      irony better. Only chivalrous and soldierly families have a
      genealogy. Iliusha's genealogy will contain nothing but a dis-
      graced and cowardly father. The harsh catachresis in its expres-
      sion enhances the grotesque ugliness of the fact.
172   186_{40-41}, $14:186_{24-25}$,   "the privileges of noblemen"—by virtue
      of his officer's rank, Snegiriov is technically still a "nobleman."
      Morally, he still had his honor—until it was taken from him by
      Dmitry's insult.
173   187_1, $14:186_{28}$,   "student"—Russ. *kursistka,* from *kurs,*
      "course." At the time, women were not admitted to universities
      as regular students, but could enroll in university courses.
174   187_{2-3}, $14:186_{29}$,   "the emancipation of the Russian woman on
      the banks of the Neva"—women's rights were among the top
      priorities of the Russian radical movement. Cf. Book One, chap.
      i, p. 4_{25}. Varvara Nikolaevna is the "Ivan" of the Snegiriov
      family. See Introduction III.3.b. Mirroring and Doubling.
175   187_{4-5}, $14:186_3$,   "all of them"—translates *so vsemi etimi
      nedrami.* Cf. note 142 above. Perhaps: "all these depths of
      misery." The word *nedra* will appear again ($14:187_{12}$, translated
      by "retreat," p. 187_{30}). It becomes a label of Snegiriov's. This ef-
      fect is lost in the translation.
176   187_{17}, $14:186_{45-46}$,   "Agrafena Aleksandrovna"—Grushen'ka.
      To the poor staff captain she is "the boss." He dares not refer to

her with the familiarity of everyone else we have heard speaking of her.

177   187_{18-25}, $14:186_{45}-187_7$,   We meet Grushen'ka from yet another side, the only side known to Snegiriov. We have here another instance of *erlebte Rede*, as we hear Grushen'ka's voice through Snegiriov's. The language in the original is a great deal more colloquial: "crooked deals" rather than "dishonesty," "shopkeeper" rather "merchant," "get rid of you" rather than "dismiss you."

178   187_{43-44}, $14:187_{26}$,   We will find out later that Mr. Krasotkin has been dead for some time.

179   188_{4-5}, $14:187_{31-32}$,   An important point: Iliusha is not a passive victim but, moved by his own strong passions, a full-fledged actor in this drama. See Introduction II.3.b. "The Novel about Children."

180   188_{7-9}, $14:187_{35-36}$,   Dostoevsky projects upon Snegiriov some of his own insights into child psychology.

181   188_{10-13}, $14:187_{38-40}$,   The outlines of the ethical implications of the father-son motif are emerging now. See Introduction II.3.a. Fatherhood.

182   188_{16}, $14:187_{43}$,   To Snegiriov, Aliosha is the son of Fiodor Pavlovich Karamazov, a wealthy nobleman.

183   188_{21}, $14:187_{47-48}$,   "had grasped all that justice means"—translates *vsiu istinu proizoshel*, lit. "passed through the whole truth," where *proizoshel* is an etymologism. Snegiriov uses the verb in its etymological meaning, "went all the way through." Normally, the verb means (1) "to happen, to transpire," and (2) "to originate." Because the form is, in this meaning, a neologism, it has tremendous impact.

184   188_{33}, $14:188_{11-12}$,   "in Russia men who drink are the best"—not to be taken as a particularly original aphorism. The kindly, even saintly, drunkard is a cliché of nineteenth-century literature. Dostoevsky had created several himself, starting with the hero of his first novel, *Poor Folk* (1846).

185   189_{1-3}, $14:188_{28-29}$,   The big stone is a landmark even in the plot of the novel. Cf. the title of chapter iii of the Epilogue.

186   189_{4-6}, $14:188_{31-32}$,   In Russian, this sentence is loaded with tender diminutives (both nouns and adjectives, eight in all), which cannot be rendered in English. They convey a father's tenderness for his child.

187   189_{46}–190_1, $14:189_{26}$, A personal echo. Mrs. Dostoevsky reports that her husband had made this observation watching his own son, Fiodor. See *PSS* 15:549.

188   190_{26}, $14:190_{1-2}$, "insulted"—translates *unizil*, "humiliated." The use of so sophisticated a concept by a nine-year-old may be questioned. But Dostoevsky was a firm believer in the ability of very young children to grasp the facts of life.

189   190_{29-30}, $14:190_5$, "service record"—translates *formuliar*, strictly an official term. This dissonance enhances the pathos of the scene: an example of Dostoevsky's art of tear-jerking.

190   190_{32}, $14:190_{8-9}$, Note the internal commentary, given here in the form of "stage directions." See Introduction III. Narrative Technique.

191   191_1, $14:190_{23}$, "help"—Russ. *vspomozhenie*. Aliosha repeats the stilted term which he had heard from Katerina Ivanovna (cf. note 124 above). He is embarrassed and, quite surprisingly for him, falls into some awkward verbiage.

192   191_4, $14:190_{26}$, "entreats"—obviously the wrong word: "urges" would have been in order, but Aliosha is embarrassed and his speech is off-key.

193   191_{13}, $14:190_{36}$, Aliosha's diatribe is incoherent, his words are not well-chosen, and the notion of Katerina Ivanovna as Snegiriov's "sister" is rather funny. An example of the comic strain found in many of Dostoevsky's most pathetic scenes.

194   191_{36}, $14:191_{13}$, A subtle psychological detail: Aliosha's scrupulous honesty interferes with his diplomatic mission. Note the comical implications: how safe will a secret be with Mme. Khokhlakov?

195   191_{39}, $14:191_{17}$, "The poor fellow"—the narrator shows his face for a moment. This is done on purpose.

196   192_1, $14:191_{25}$, "I can make nothing of it"—Herzenstube's label. Cf. note 69 above.

197   192_9, $14:191_{34}$, "without servants"—this is the nineteenth century: it never occurs to Snegiriov, an ex-officer and a "gentleman," that *he* might carry the water, etc.

198   193_9, $14:192_{37}$, This is one time when Aliosha looks fairly ridiculous. He sounds like Mme. Khokhlakov.

199   193_{35}, $14:193_{20}$, "Look there!"—Translates *nu tak vot zhe-s!*, lit. "well, so there, then, Sir!" (*zhe* is an emphatic particle). Russian is rich in modal and emphatic particles and interjections,

whose combinations often suggest intricate emotional attitudes. Here we have four such words, all quite untranslatable.

200   194_{1-2}, $14:193_{33-34}$,   In the original there is an anacoluthon in this sentence: "He turned for the last time, this time without the former contorted smile on his face, but on the contrary, it was all quivering with tears." The break in the syntax of the sentence is symbolic of its content. Dostoevsky will do this kind of thing quite often.

201   194_2, $14:193_{34-35}$,   One of the many sentences in the novel which read like stage directions. One word has remained untranslated: *skorogovorkoi,* "talking very fast." Snegiriov is torn between his more immediate natural impulses and a desire to live up to a certain image. Whenever the latter prevails, he begins to playact and performs like an actor on stage, with wild gestures, grimaces, and a shrill voice: he is not a very good actor.

202   194_9, $14:193_{42}$,   "he knew why"—anticipates the psychological analysis of the whole scene in the next chapter (pp. 197–98).

203   194_{15}, $14:193_{48}$,   "the success of her commission"—this outright irony renders the implicit irony of the scene quite explicit, the point being that Snegiriov had not *torn up* the bank notes.

Book Five

Chapter i

1 195_{13}, $14:194_{10}$, "brain fever"—Dostoevsky's medicine is that of the mid-nineteenth century. "Brain fever" *(goriachka)* is a frequent element in his plots. It requires more suspension of disbelief today to see it as a realistic motif than was the case in Dostoevsky's lifetime. See L. Galich, "Realizm Dostoevskogo," *Novyi zhurnal* 13:188–98.

2 196_{3-4}, $14:194_{39-40}$, "this pine tree and pine for it"—translates a pun: *sosnu, kak so sna,* lit. "a pine, like in a dream."

3 197_1, $14:195_{40}$, Prepared by Book Four, chap. viii, p. 194_9. Cf. Book Four, note 203.

4 197_{43}, $14:196_{31-32}$, "Father Zosima told me so"—Aliosha's subtle psychological analysis is thus partly motivated. This is one of many indications, direct or indirect, that Aliosha's consciousness is very largely a carbon copy of the elder's. Aliosha's wisdom is Father Zosima's.

5 197_{45}–198_1, $14:196_{33-35}$, Typically Dostoevskian double-edged psychology: he did not know, but yet in a way he did.

6 198_{3-4}, $14:196_{38}$, Aliosha is having one of his intuitions.

7 198_{23}, $14:197_9$, It might seem that this monologue does not show Aliosha at his best: isn't he smug, condescending, even cynical? The point is that he is a *realist,* like his elder. His sober assessment of human nature (including his own) is one aspect of his humility.

8 198_{40}, $14:197_{25}$, "on a higher footing"—Liza has picked up Aliosha's infelicitous expression and treats it as though it were perfectly good usage. Their love story has barely begun, yet they are already developing their own private language.

9 198_{42-46}, $14:197_{28-32}$, Liza expresses what the reader has felt all along. Cf. note 7 above.

10 199_{9-11}, $14:197_{41-43}$, Cf. note 4 above. This may be an echo of Mark 2:17.

11   199_{12-13}, $14:197_{44-45}$,   A deep irony: Liza is herself sick, and not just physically.

12   199_{15-16}, $14:197_{46-48}$,   "I am sometimes very impatient and at other times I don't see things. It's different with you." Aliosha is sincere, as always, and he is also right, as almost always.

13   199_{19-21}, $14:198_{3-4}$,   "Formal"—translates *pedant;* "a little pedantic . . . not pedantic at all" would be just as good. This is another example of Dostoevsky's dialectic psychology. As in Hegel's dialectic, negation of a thesis leads to sublation *(Aufhebung)* in a dual sense: it is established that Aliosha is not pedantic, and also that "not being pedantic" is with him on a higher level than with other people.

14   199_{23-24}, $14:198_{8-9}$,   "no one was listening"—loaded! Mme. Khokhlakov is an invisible third actor in this scene, as we shall soon discover.

15   199_{32}, $14:198_{17}$,   "joyfully"—the three leitmotifs of this love scene are joy, laughter, and blushing, each appearing repeatedly and in a number of variations.

16   200_{3-4}, $14:198_{34-35}$,   "on her lips"—translates *v samye gubki,* lit. "right on her little lips" (*gubka* is a diminutive of *guba,* "lip").

17   200_9, $14:198_{42}$,   "And in that dress!"—Aliosha is wearing a monk's cassock.

18   200_{23}, $14:199_8$,   "You are more innocent than I am"—loaded: Liza has her secrets, too.

19   200_{24-25}, $14:199_{9-10}$,   "I, too, am a Karamazov"—a recurring motif.

20   200_{42-43}, $14:199_{27-28}$,   These things must be visualized: the fancy outfit of a young society lion contrasts wildly with the cassock Aliosha is now wearing. This draws attention to the bizarre trappings of this love scene.

21   202_{3-4}, $14:200_{36-37}$,   In the original this sentence is not nearly this smooth, but rather: "That's how it ought to be. So let me tell you that I, too, shall on the contrary be ready to give in to you not only in the most important matters, but in everything, and I solemnly swear right now that this will be in everything and for all my life."

22   202_{10}, $14:200_{44}$,   "conscience"—Liza actually says "providence" *(providenie).* In her excitement she does not find the right word, but it is pretty clear what she means.

23   202_{23}, $14:201_{10}$,   "I don't like . . . Ivan"—a surprising and important development: the relationship between Ivan and Liza is one that is to be kept in mind.

24　　202_{28-30}, $14:201_{15-17}$, "primitive"—translates *zemlianaia,* "earthy" (from *zemlia,* "earth, soil"), important in view of the earth symbolism in the novel. See Introduction III.5.f. Mythical Symbolism.

25　　202_{30-31}, $14:201_{17}$, Echoes Gen. 1:2. There is a strong presence of myth in these words. Cf. Introduction II.1.a. Allegoric Figures, and III.5.f. Mythical Symbolism.

26　　202_{35}, $14:201_{21}$, "And perhaps I don't even believe in God." A typical Dostoevskian surprise.

27　　202_{37-38}, $14:201_{23-26}$, *slishkom,* "too (much), exceedingly," one of the narrator's key words, occurs three times in this short sentence. Cf. Book One, note 25.

28　　203_{1-2}, $14:201_{34-35}$, Sudden drama.

29　　203_{11-13}, $14:201_{44-46}$, Another surprise, perhaps Sophoclean irony in reverse: Aliosha may have known all along that Mme. Khokhlakov was listening.

30　　203_{24-25}, $14:202_{10-11}$, ". . . another year and a half"—that is, until Aliosha comes of age and receives legal title to whatever his inheritance would be.

31　　203_{29-32}, $14:202_{15-18}$, The allusion is to the last scene of Aleksandr Griboedov's comedy *Woe from Wit* (1824), where Famusov eavesdrops on a tête-à-tête between his daughter Sof'ia, and Chatsky, a slightly crazy young man. Like Mme. Khokhlakov, Famusov rather misunderstands the scene which he has witnessed. Cf. A. L. Bem, "*Gore ot uma* v tvorchestve Dostoevskogo," *O Dostoevskom,* 3 (Prague, 1936): 13–33.

32　　204_{1-2}, $14:202_{30-31}$, Note the grotesque incongruity between Mme. Khokhlakov's frivolous request and her pathetic verbiage. This is comedy!

33　　204_{2-3}, $14:202_{32-33}$, Some more comic "action," conveyed verbally only. Suggesting a slapstick situation without actually realizing it is one of Dostoevsky's specialties. Cf., for example, Book Two, note 256.

Chapter ii

34　　204_{15-16}, $14:203_{1-2}$, "a great inevitable catastrophe was about to happen"—this detail serves a dual purpose: it is yet another example of Aliosha's clairvoyance, and it heightens the suspense.

35　　204_{20-23}, $14:203_{4-8}$, A key passage: Aliosha will go on to do exactly what he so smugly believes to have avoided. His guilt is thus foreshadowed.

36 205_{18-23}, $14:203_{43-48}$,   See Introduction I.4.a. Secular Sources, and n. 37. See also *PSS* 15:447–48.

37 205_{24}, $14:204_{1-2}$,   A "lackey's song" would be a hybrid between a drawing room romance and a Russian folk song. The vocabulary is mixed, and so is the imagery. As a result, it appears styleless, maudlin, and vulgar. "Lackeydom" is Smerdiakov's label.

38 206_{1-3}, $14:204_{22-24}$,   Typical of Dostoevsky's centrifugal psychology (see Introduction II.6.a. Dostoevsky's Psychology). We discover Smerdiakov the Romeo—something we would never have suspected.

39 206_6, $14:204_{27}$,   Smerdiakov tends to misuse, often ever so slightly, book words such as "essential."

40 206_{6-10}, $14:204_{27-31}$,   Cf. Book Three, chap. vi, p. 113_{28-34}. Smerdiakov is made to come forth with the arguments advanced against poetry by Dostoevsky's opponents in the radical camp. By implication their ideas are turned into a lackey's notion of poetry. Thoughts such as Smerdiakov's are found in N. G. Chernyshevsky's *Aesthetic Relations of Art to Reality* (1855).

41 206_{11}, $14:204_{32}$,   "you've gone so deep"—translates *proizoshli,* lit. "you've gone all the way through." In literary usage the verb does not have this meaning, but means (1) "to happen, to transpire," and (2) "to originate, to be descended" (cf. Book Four, note 183). Mar'ia Kondrat'evna's slip leads Smerdiakov on to his tirade on his origins.

42 206_{13-15}, $14:204_{34-35}$,   "if it had not been for my destiny from my childhood up"—the Russian phrase is ungrammatical by literary standards, clashing with the book word "destiny" *(zhrebii).*

43 206_{15}, $14:204_{36}$,   "called me names"—translates *proiznios, chto ia podlets,* "told me to my face that I'm a villain." Russ. *podlets,* though it originally meant "lowborn" (much as Eng. "villain"), was used only in a moral sense by the 1860s. Such confusion of values is characteristic of Smerdiakov and his social class.

44 206_{19}, $14:204_{39}$,   "birth"—Smerdiakov uses the word *rozhdestvo,* in literary usage only "the Nativity," instead of *rozhdenie,* "birth."

45 206_{19-20}, $14:204_{40}$,   " 'You rent her womb' "—Russ. *lozhesna otverz,* "opened her matrix," a biblical term (Exodus 13:12) which makes no sense in ordinary discourse.

46 206_{23-24}, $14:204_{44}$,   "like a mat on her head"—translates *s koltunom,* "with a plica; with a Polish plait."

47 206_{24}, $14:204_{45}$,   "a wee bit"—translates Russ. *s malyim,* in lieu

of *s malym*. *S malyim* is an archaic form found in Russian folk poetry; by using it, the old lady tried to express her affection for the "holy fool." Smerdiakov's analysis is quite correct—another instance of internal commentary.

48 206_{29-30}, $14:205_2$, "From my childhood up"—translates *s samogo syzdetstva,* very much substandard speech.

49 206_{31}, $14:205_4$, "I hate all Russia"—signals the drift of this important scene. The semiliterate lackey Smerdiakov is in his own social set the equivalent of Fiodor Pavlovich, most of whose views he shares, as we shall presently see. The point is that "the people," too, are subject to the corruption and decay caused by atheism, materialism, and rationalism. See Introduction II.4.b. The People, and d. Socialism and Utopianism.

50 206_{38-43}, $14:205_{11-15}$, An idea which in itself is not absurd at all. Many Russian liberals felt likewise. But Smerdiakov's idea is rendered ridiculous by his ignorance of history. Napoleon I was the uncle, not the father, of Napoleon III. Dostoevsky is not above using such tricks to discredit opinions which are hateful to him.

51 $206_{44}-207_1$, $14:205_{16-17}$, There are some comic punch lines in this scene: Smerdiakov, whom one imagines as a real "creep," is *so* attractive to the ex-chambermaid!

52 207_{10-11}, $14:205_{26-27}$, Cf. Book Three, chap. viii, pp. 120–21, and Introduction II.4.d. Socialism and Utopianism. A disrespect for the Russian people is a common trait of Dostoevsky's negative types.

53 207_{14}, $14:205_{30}$, In the original, Smerdiakov uses a deferential plural ("they") in his references to Ivan Karamazov, while referring to Dmitry (and earlier to Fiodor Pavlovich) in the ordinary singular.

54 207_{18-19}, $14:205_{34-35}$, Smerdiakov's evaluation of Dmitry's character is not unfounded: his contacts with Dmitry have been unpleasant. Nevertheless, he is wrong. Dmitry is respected and in fact liked by many people for a quality which is beyond Smerdiakov's comprehension. Another case of Dostoevsky's multilevel psychology.

55 207_{19}, $14:205_{35}$, "soup maker"—echoes an earlier scene (Book Three, chap. vii, p. 116_{37}).

56 207_{21-22}, $14:205_{36-37}$, In the original, Smerdiakov uses the word "special" in a specific sense: professional jargon, no doubt (something like *à la mode* in English).

57 207_{23}, $14:205_{38}$, "beggar"—translates *goloshtannik* (*gol,* "bare," and *shtany,* "pants"), a slang word.

58 207_{31-32}, $14:205_{46-47}$, "for the sake of some lady"—translates *za kotoruiu-nibud',* "for someone" (where the ending suggests that this "someone" is a female), which sounds very vulgar. Perhaps: "for some female."

59 207_{34-36}, $14:206_{1-3}$, Some more low comedy. Smerdiakov quickly deflates the ex-chambermaid's romantic conceit.

60 208_{12-13}, $14:206_{28}$, Cain's words, of course (Gen. 4:9). Very soon we shall hear the same words from Ivan (in the next chapter, p. 213_{8-9}). Another link is thus formed between Ivan and the lackey.

61 208_{35}, $14:207_5$, "the master"—translates *barin,* a word which poses a problem. In direct address it would be "Sir," but in the third person "master" is really an anachronism (besides, Smerdiakov never was Fiodor Pavlovich's serf). Perhaps: "the boss."

62 208_{33-38}, $14:207_{3-7}$, Speaking to Aliosha, who is after all the boss's son, Smerdiakov now refers to Dmitry in the deferential third person plural, and the free-and-easy diction which he employed with Mar'ia Kondrat'evna gives way to attempts at "high style" ("merciless," "threatened me with death").

63 208_{40}, $14:207_9$, "Do you suppose he'd think much of that"—translates a sentence in which Smerdiakov mixes bookish and colloquial language, something like: "That wouldn't constitute a big deal for him."

64 208_{44-45}, $14:207_{13}$, "the police"—translates *gorodskoe nachal'stvo,* "municipal authorities," which is of course a euphemism for "police."

65 208_{45}, $14:207_{14}$, "God only knows what he might not do, sir!"—In the original Smerdiakov comes up with yet another misshapen phrase, using a book word inappropriately. Something like: "He is capable even of producing God only knows what, sir!"

66 $208_{47}-209_1$, $14:207_{15}$, Might be foreshadowing. A pestle will be the murder weapon later in the novel.

Chapter iii

67 210_{3-11}, $14:208_{15-23}$, Note how carefully Dostoevsky draws the setting of this scene. See Introduction III.4.b. Social Stylization.

68   210_{41}, $14:209_{7-8}$, "the little man"—another allusion to "Aleksei, man of God." Cf. Book Three, note 235.

69   211_3, $14:209_{13}$, In this paragraph the Russian verb *liubit'* is translated by "to love," "to like," and "to be fond of." Understandably, the total impression is different, but this is unavoidable in this case.

70   211_{4-5}, $14:209_{14-15}$, Cf. Book Three, chap. iv, p. 99_{3-4}.

71   211_{12}, $14:209_{23}$, "green"—translates *zheltorotyi,* lit. "yellow-beaked," even more graphic than the English expression. In his response, Ivan will create a noun, *zheltorotost',* lit. "yellow-beakedness." The passage foreshadows Ivan's mirror image in the schoolboy Kolia Krasotkin. See Introduction III.3.b. Mirroring and Doubling.

72   211_{18-24}, $14:209_{30-35}$, A significant passage. Note especially the words "damnable" ("damned" would be a more literal translation) and "devil-ridden," which have a far-reaching foreshadowing effect.

73   211_{24}, $14:209_{35}$, In the original Ivan mixes metaphors: "I shan't let go of it before I have mastered it all." Ivan's image of the cup of life is itself somewhat gauche, since in Russian this image is normally associated with suffering and death (Matt. 26:39). One should not overlook the subtle way in which Dostoevsky undercuts Ivan by perverting his style. See Introduction III.1.b. Ivan Karamazov.

74   211_{25}, $14:209_{36}$, "leave the cup"—a mistranslation of *broshu kubok;* "fling down the cup" is correct. The commentators of *PSS* (15:550) quote a poem by A. I. Polezhaev, "Consumption" (1837), suggesting that Ivan's image is taken from it. Still, flinging down one's cup to announce the end of the feast of life is also found in other poems which Dostoevsky must have known, such as in Gretchen's song, *Faust,* Pt. I, ll. 2759–82.

75   211_{29-30}, $14:209_{40}$, "Unseemly" is perhaps too weak for *neprilichyni* here; "obscene" seems better in this context. An "obscene thirst for life" as a "Karamazovian" trait is a recurring motif in the novel. Cf., for instance, Book Eleven, chap. x, p. 619_{37} (where the translator has translated *zhazhda,* "thirst," by "love"). See also Introduction III.5.f. Mythical Symbolism.

76   211_{35-36}, $14:209_{46-47}$, Here, for once, Ivan's scientific background shows. Russian materialists of the 1860s, like their prede-

cessors, the eighteenth-century *philosophes,* saw a "scientific" approach to human affairs in terms of simple Newtonian physics.

77   211_{36-37}, $14:209_{48}$,   "Logic," meaning "reason," tells one that life is mostly senseless suffering, followed by death, which is nothingness.

78   211_{38}, $14:210_{1-2}$,   A reminiscence from Pushkin's poem "Chill Winds Still Blow"(1828), whence the expression "sticky leafbuds" *(kleikie listochki)* is taken.

79   212_{1-2}, $14:210_{8-9}$,   "I am only going to a graveyard"—according to Nina M. Perlina ("Quotation as an Element of the Poetics of *The Brothers Karamazov*" [Ph.D. diss., Brown University, 1977], p. 134), a reminiscence from chapter iv of Herzen's *From the Other Shore* (1847–50). The chapter bears the title "Vixerunt" (Lat. "They were once alive"). The notion that Western civilization had given its best and was now in decay was held not only by Russian Slavophiles.

80   212_3, $14:210_9$,   "Precious are the dead that lie there"—conceivably a quotation from A. A. Foeth's poem "It's Not the First Year . . ." ("Ne pervyi god u etikh mest," 1864), which otherwise has nothing to do with the subject at hand. See *PSS* 15:550.

81   212_{16-17}, $14:210_{23-24}$,   An explicit statement of vitalism. See Introduction II.2.b. Arguments in Support of Christianity. Ivan immediately sees the theological implication.

82   212_{21-22}, $14:210_{29-30}$,   "I have thought so a long time. . . .—A surprise, to which Ivan immediately reacts.

83   212_{26}, $14:210_{33}$,   "Why, one has to raise up your dead"—this may be an allusion to the ideas of Nikolai Fiodorov. See Introduction I.4.a. Secular Sources.

84   212_{26-27}, $14:210_{34}$,   A denial of death—that is, a belief in resurrection—is Aliosha's (and Father Zosima's) leitmotif. Cf. Sven Linnér, *Starets Zosima in "The Brothers Karamazov"* (Stockholm, 1975), pp. 197–207.

85   212_{28-29}, $14:210_{37}$,   *professions de foi*—"professions of faith."

86   212_{32}, $14:210_{40}$,   "in the world"—here in the sense "outside monastery walls."

87   212_{39-40}, $14:210_{45}$,   Perhaps a reminiscence from *Faust,* Pt. II, ll. 6787–88, where the Baccalaureus expresses the same idea, much to the Devil's satisfaction.

88 212_{39}, $14:211_1$, " 'a shadow of nobility' "—an inexact quotation from Pushkin's epigram "A King Was Told" ("Skazali raz tsariu," 1825).

89 213_1, $14:211_{10}$, Foreshadowing. Smerdiakov is Ivan's evil spirit.

90 213_2, $14:211_{11}$, "Damn him"—in the original: "to the devil." The translator faces a dilemma. The Russian expression is not a very strong one—"to hell with him" would seem correct. But then the devil is being established as an important symbol.

91 213_{12}, $14:211_{22}$, See note 60 above.

92 213_{15}, $14:211_{25}$, "Oh, hell"—translates *E, chort,* "what the devil." Ivan's frequent mention of the devil is an important symbolic trait. It creates a subtext. See Introduction III.2.a. The Reader's Role.

93 214_{3-5}, $14:212_{7-9}$, "Laceration" (*nadryv,* "rupture") has occurred so often that it may now be used as a kind of shorthand notation for what is really an involved psychological complex.

94 214_{7-8}, $14:212_{12-13}$, Very Dostoevskian: a psychological paradox is reported as though it were the most natural thing in the world.

95 214_{9-10}, $14:212_{14}$, "I can simply go away for good."—Ivan will soon have to eat his words.

96 214_{17}, $14:212_{21-22}$, "as a relief"—a mistranslation of *liubia,* lit. "lovingly," so perhaps: "as a blessing." Ivan makes a show of cynicism.

97 214_{31-32}, $14:212_{36}$, In the original: "A whole eternity of time, immortality!" A kind of Freudian slip: it reveals that Ivan has been thinking a lot about eternity and immortality.

98 214_{42-44}, $14:212_{45-47}$, Lays bare the plan of the novel: we are told that the real subject of the novel are "the eternal questions."

99 214_{45-46}, $14:212_{48}-213_1$, "the young in Russia talk of nothing but the eternal questions now."—An anachronism: this statement would have been historically correct in 1879, but not in 1866. In the 1860s the young generation went for science, economics, and practical questions of social and economic life. In the 1870s there was a resurgence of interest in the humanities and in philosophy. Cf. Introduction II.4. *The Brothers Karamazov* as a Social Novel.

100 $214_{47}-215_1$, $14:213_3$, The translation misses a nuance here: Ivan uses the formulaic question addressed to a bishop of the Orthodox church at his investiture, to which he responds by reciting the credo.

101   215_{16}, $14:213_{19-20}$, "it all comes to the same"—translates *odin zhe chort vyidet,* "the same devil will come of it." The Russian phrase is not really formulaic, so there is again a suggestion of a subconscious preoccupation with the devil.

102   215_{45}, $14:214_1$, Voltaire, *Epistles,* CXI, "To the Author of a New Book on the Three Impostors" (1769).

103   215_{45}–216_1, $14:214_{1-2}$, "And man has actually invented God."—This notion was first made popular by Ludwig Feuerbach (1804–72), whose philosophy had considerable influence on Dostoevsky's generation.

104   216_8, $14:214_{10}$, "all derived from European hypotheses"—the irony is that this is also true of Ivan's own "axioms."

105   216_{8-11}, $14:214_{10-14}$, In his *Diary of a Writer* of 1876 Dostoevsky had said: "In the West, Darwin's theory is an ingenious hypothesis, while in Russia it has long been an axiom" (*Diary of a Writer,* 1:316). In speaking of "Russian professors" who are "just the same boys themselves" Dostoevsky may have had in mind his young friend Vladimir Solov'iov (1853–1900). See Introduction I.6.d. Ivan Karamazov and Other Characters.

106   216_{15}, $14:214_{18}$, "I accept God simply"—translates a more emphatic *prinimaiu Boga priamo i prosto,* "I accept God outright and simply." This is the first stage of Ivan's argumentation. In traditional metaphysics the assertion of God's existence was the last step. By making it his point of departure Ivan follows the romantic philosophers, Schelling in particular. He plans to conduct an *argumentum e contrario,* demonstrating that accepting God leads to absurd conclusions.

107   216_{17-19}, $14:214_{19-21}$, Ivan's acceptance of "Euclid's geometry" is the key to his error—or the devil's swindle. God is denied any mystic extension on the grounds that human reason (more exactly, Ivan's reason, or the devil's) cannot grasp it.

108   216_{24}, $14:214_{28}$, The principles of non-Euclidean geometry were developed by the Russian mathematician N. I. Lobachevsky (1792–1856). Dostoevsky may have become familiar with these principles in engineering school.

109   216_{28}, $14:214_{32}$, "not of this world"—the quotation from John 18:36 is ironic, as is the whole phrase. Ivan implies that there is no other world.

110   216_{36-38}, $14:214_{39-41}$, An allusion to John 1:1. "The Word" (Russ. *Slovo*) translates Greek λόγος, which means "word" as well as "rational order," "reason," something which Ivan knows very well, of course.

111 216_{38}, $14:214_{41}$, "and so on, to infinity"—the impatient conclusion of this phrase means that Ivan is willing to concede all these metaphysical points to his opponent, because they are irrelevant to his argument. It is characteristic of Dostoevsky's debaters to be most generous in their concessions to their opponents—only to turn around and attack on a different level.

112 216_{41}, $14:214_{44}$, "I don't accept it at all"—sounds like a paradox, but is not, as we shall immediately see. Both Ivan's "acceptance" of God and his "rejection" of God's world must be understood as formal steps in the dialectic of his argument.

113 217_3, $14:215_{2-3}$, "Euclidean mind of man"—this repetition establishes this metaphor as a symbol. It will return in this chapter as well as later (see Book Eleven, chap. ix, p. 605). The equation

$$\frac{\text{Euclidean geometry}}{\text{Non-Euclidean geometry}} = \frac{\text{rational (human) world}}{\text{mystical (God's) world}}$$

works against Ivan, because there *is* such thing as non-Euclidean geometry.

114 217_{11}, $14:215_{11}$, "but still I won't accept it."—Ivan has been truly eloquent in this passage and has succeeded in creating a great deal of suspense. Yet there is no substance to his eloquent words. He cannot understand non-Euclicean geometry, and therefore he excludes it from his argument. Since he rejects divine order out of hand, the question of its nature, or even of its existence, is *eo ipso* excluded from his argument. So what is left?—Ivan's personal nihilism.

115 217_{21}, $14:215_{20}$, "for the sake of being Russian"—translates *dlia rusizma,* lit. "for Russism." Cf. Book One, chap. iv, p. 18_{23}, where the same expression appears in the original.

116 217_{23}, $14:215_{22}$, Another paradox which promptly turns out to be quite plausible psychologically.

117 217_{30-34}, $14:215_{28-32}$, A key passage. it contains the seed of Ivan's salvation.

Chapter iv

118 217_{36}, $14:215_{34}$, Note the surprise involved in this chapter title after the concluding lines of the preceding chapter. Dostoevsky's chapter titles are very much an active ingredient of his story.

119   217_{38-40}, $14:215_{37-38}$,   The original has an untranslatable pun: *blizhnii*, "neighbor" (lit. "nearby") and *dal'nii*, "far away."

120   217_{40}, $14:215_{38}$,   "John the Merciful" is John the Almsgiver, Patriarch of Alexandria (611-19). Dostoevsky's source, though, is Flaubert's "La légende de Saint Julien l'Hospitalier" (1876), translated into Russian by Turgenev in 1877. See *PSS* 15:551.

121   218_6, $14:215_{43-44}$,   St. Julian in Flaubert's legend is a parricide who spends a lifetime to atone for his crime.

122   218_{8-12}, $14:216_{1-5}$,   See Book Two, chap. iv, p. 49. One of many instances in which Ivan and Father Zosima are shown to depart from a similar basis of fact, yet differ in their conclusions.

123   218_{30}, $14:216_{24}$,   Ivan introduces the theme of suffering, focal to his argument, in a backhanded way—much as other important motifs were first brought up earlier. Cf., for example, Book One, note 117.

124   218_{36}, $14:216_{31}$,   "But even then we would not love them."— Ivan's bilious—but *theoretical*— observations bring to mind Aliosha's *practical* experiences with the Snegiriov family which prove the contrary.

125   218_{39-40}, $14:216_{34-36}$,   Ivan is cheating: by limiting his argument to the sufferings of children he actually presents the strongest part of his case.

126   218_{46}, $14:216_{41}$,   "they have retribution"—a kind of shorthand notation for "they are subject to retribution."

127   219_1, $14:216_{42}$,   Gen. 3:5.

128   219_{2-3}, $14:216_{43-44}$,   This will not sound as heretical to an Orthodox Christian as it might to a Christian of the Western church. Orthodox theology is less categorical about the effects of original sin.

129   219_{4-8}, $14:216_{45}-217_2$,   Much of the novel is devoted to a discussion of this position. We have already met Iliusha and his father, who exemplify it.

130   219_{10}, $14:217_{2-3}$,   "I am awfully fond of children"—a statement the truthfulness of which is in question. Ivan, unlike his brothers, will do nothing to show that it is true.

131   219_{20}, $14:217_{13}$,   The motif of a dangerous criminal's friendship with a boy shows up often in Dostoevsky's notebooks, e.g., in *The Notebooks to "The Possessed,"* pp. 59, 65. It is hardly autobiographic, since there were no children playing in the prison yard at Omsk, where Dostoevsky served his term. Ivan's acquaintance with a convicted killer comes as a bit of a surprise,

but we remember that he used to work as a journalist, and he may well report hearsay as direct experience.

132   219$_{26-27}$, 14:217$_{19-20}$, "crimes committed by Turks and Circassians"—Turkish atrocities and the liberation of the Balkan Slavs from Turkish rule were frequent topics in Dostoevsky's *Diary of a Writer.* He had strongly supported the Russian war effort against Turkey in 1877–78.

133   219$_{33-34}$, 14:217$_{26-27}$, "so artistically cruel"—translates *tak artisticheski, tak khudozhestvenno zhestok,* "so artfully, so artistically cruel," where *khudozhestvenno* definitely implies creative imagination. We are reminded of Dmitry's "ideal of Sodom" (Book Three, chap. iii, p. 97).

134   220$_4$, 14:217$_{42}$, It was through passages like this that Dostoevsky earned his reputation of a "cruel talent." The effect of moral outrage produced by this scene depends largely on the narrator's refusal to comment on it: he leaves this to the reader.

135   220$_{7-8}$, 14:217$_{44-45}$, A double perversion of Gen 1:27. Aliosha promptly restores at least one-half of the biblical truth.

136   220$_{10-11}$, 14:218$_{44}$, Alludes to *Hamlet,* Act I, sc. iii, lines 134–38. The Russian translation by A. Kroneberg (1866) suits Ivan's reading better than the original. See *PSS* 15:552. Cf. Ralph E. Matlaw, *"The Brothers Karamazov": Novelistic Technique* (The Hague, 1957), pp. 7–8.

137   220$_{12-13}$, 14:218$_{1-2}$, The positions of both brothers have now been stated. The difference between them is that Ivan has a low opinion of humanity, and Aliosha a high one.

138   220$_{15-16}$, 14:218$_5$, "I even copy anecdotes . . ."—lays bare not only Ivan's "device," but even Dostoevsky's: the "anecdote" is a basic nucleus of the structure of this novel. See Introduction III.3.a. Motifs.

139   220$_{25-28}$, 14:218$_{16-17}$, Dostoevsky lets Ivan utter a partly self-fulfilling prophecy. Dostoevsky himself and like-minded intellectual leaders, such as his friend Vladimir Solov'iov, were to some extent responsible for the growing interest in religion among educated Russians. But this actually happened in the 1870s, not in the 1860s. Naturally, Dostoevsky did not view his own influence as a part of the general revival of interest in theosophy, religious sects, spiritualism, etc., which was well under way by the end of the 1870s. On the contrary, in his *Diary of a Writer* Dostoevsky often combated these tendencies.

140   220_{28-29}, $14:218_{18-19}$, "a charming pamphlet . . ."—no such brochure has ever been discovered. Hence Richard may be a purely fictional character.

141   221_3, $14:218_{39-40}$, There had been no official death penalty in Russia, except for high treason, since Empress Elizabeth abolished it in 1753–54.

142   221_{8-14}, $14:218_{45}$–219_1, This passage contains some gallicisms and is generally stylized to re-create the atmosphere of French-speaking, Calvinist Geneva.

143   221_{18}, $14:219_6$, "die in the Lord"—Here Ivan begins to lose control over his indignation. His account now turns into a satirical grotesque. Note the mocking repetition of "die in the Lord." Ivan wants to make sure that Aliosha notices the bitter irony of the situation as he, Ivan, sees it. The author's irony is that Ivan does not see that the poor Richard does indeed die a Christian and in the Lord.

144   221_{18-21}, $14:219_{7-10}$, Here Ivan's sarcasm turns grotesque. He puts his own outburst of outrage into the mouths of the good burghers of Geneva, ascribing to them (or to the pious brochure which is his source) a quite monstrous and incredible hypocrisy.

145   221_{30}, $14:219_{19}$, "chopped off"—translates Russ. *ottiapali*, a slang expression ("zapped off") which stands in grotesque contrast with the descent of God's grace.

146   221_{35-37}, $14:219_{25-27}$, Typical of Dostoevsky's paradoxic style: he lets Ivan grossly distort the logic of his hateful adversary.

147   221_{39-40}, $14:219_{28-29}$, The poem in question is "Before Dawn" from N. A. Nekrasov's cycle "About the Weather" (1859). Dostoevsky alludes to the poem in *Diary of a Writer,* 1:183, where he discusses the Russian Society for the Protection of Animals and comes to a conclusion quite similar to Ivan's: with so much cruelty to humans, a concern for cruelty to animals seems trivial. There is a mistake in the punctuation of the translation here. There should be a period after " 'on its meek eyes,' " followed by: "Everyone must have seen that; it's peculiarly Russian" (p. 221_{40-41}).

148   222_{6-7}, $14:219_{39-40}$, "But that's only a horse"—sarcasm, of course.

149   222_{7-8}, $14:219_{40-41}$, An allusion to the "Tartar yoke," which lasted for over two hundred years after the conquest of Russia by the Tartars in the 1230s. It was customary in Russia to blame the Tartars for some of the worst traits of Russian life.

150 222_{19}, $14:220_{5-6}$, "a lawyer"—Dostoevsky uses the form *ablakat,* a popular distortion of *advokat,* "lawyer."

151 222_{25}, $14:220_{11-12}$, Ivan's account is close to the case of S. L. Kroneberg, which Dostoevsky had discussed at considerable length in *Diary of a Writer* (1876), 1:210–38. Dostoevsky's journalistic reaction was almost as emotional as Ivan's. The lawyer for the defense was V. D. Spasovich (1829–1906), a possible prototype of Dmitry's lawyer Fetiukovich in Book Twelve.

152 222_{42}, $14:220_{28}$, Note the rhetorical quality of Ivan's discourse: multiple repetition, accumulation of synonyms, hyperbole, metaphor, personification—all of a fairly banal, readily accessible variety, yet apt to arouse strong emotions.

153 223_{6}, $14:220_{37}$, Dostoevsky took these details from the account of a trial in the daily *Golos* [The voice], nos. 79, 80, and 82 (20–23 March 1879). He refers to this trial in a letter to N. A. Liubimov, dated 10 May 1879 (*Pis'ma,* 4:54). See *PSS* 15:554.

154 223_{10}, $14:220_{41}$, "aching heart"—translates *nadorvannuiu grudku,* lit. "ruptured little breast"—another variation on the theme of *nadryv,* "rupture." Cf. Book Four, note 1.

155 223_{11-12}, $14:220_{42-43}$, "dear, kind God"—translates *bozhen'ka,* diminutive of *Bog,* "God." *Bozhen'ka* is a form used mostly by children and by adults when addressing children.

156 223_{12-14}, $14:220_{43-45}$, Very powerful rhetorical questions, which Ivan answers himself. He has now put his cards on the table: he is challenging God using the argument from design. Russ. *akhineia,* "absurdity, nonsense, rigmarole," is translated first by "infamy" and then by "rigmarole." This weakens the point, which is in the *absurdity* of God's world.

157 223_{20}, $14:221_{2}$, Note, once more, Ivan's frequent invocation of the devil.

158 223_{25}, $14:221_{9}$, The periodicals in question are the *Russian Archive* (1863–1917) and *Russian Antiquities* (1870–1918). Dostoevsky's actual source, however, was the *Russian Herald,* the very same journal in which the novel was appearing. The incident was reported in a piece entitled "Memoirs of a Serf," *Russian Herald,* 1877, no. 9, pp. 43–44. See *PSS* 15:554. Note that Dostoevsky partly discredits the reliability of the story by letting the "scholarly" Ivan forget his exact source.

159 223_{27}, $14:221_{11}$, "the Liberator"—Tsar Alexander II (1855–81), who emancipated the Russian serfs.

160 223_{33}, $14:221_{16-17}$, "Two thousand souls" meant "two thousand male heads of household and their families."

161 223_{28-36}, $14:221_{9-19}$, The whole description is reminiscent of Pushkin's story "Dubrovsky" (1832–33).

162 224_{7-8}, $14:221_{36}$, "the general was afterwards declared incapable of administering his estates"—translates *Generala . . . v opeku vziali,* a specific legal term. A serf-owner could be declared legally incompetent to manage his estate, and a trustee would be appointed by the court to manage it. Ivan's comment is ironic, of course: the general was never tried for his crime.

163 224_{14}, $14:221_{42}$, "You're a pretty monk!"—Translates *Ai da skhimnik!* Russ. *skhimnik* refers to a monk who has vowed to follow the most severe set of monastic rules. Of course Aliosha is not an ascetic, nor is he even a monk.

164 224_{18-20}, $14:221_{46-47}$, "The world stands on absurdities . . ."—a key sentence. We shall hear the same from the devil himself. See Book Eleven, chap. ix, p. 609_{12-13}.

165 224_{27-28}, $14:222_6$, "with a bitter outburst"—translates *s nadryvom gorestno,* lit. "with ruptured bitterness."

166 224_{30-31}, $14:222_9$, Very important: Ivan and Zosima are now identified as antagonists.

167 224_{34}, $14:222_{11-12}$, Ivan lays bare his own strategy. Cf. note 125 above.

168 224_{35-36}, $14:222_{12-13}$, "Of the other tears . . ."—A rather grotesque rhetorical overstatement. These little details give a certain shrillness to Ivan's discourse—the effect pursued by Dostoevsky. See Introduction III.1.b. Ivan Karamazov.

169 224_{37}, $14:222_{14}$, "bug"—translates *klop,* "bedbug." The use of insect imagery links Ivan to his brother Dmitry.

170 224_{37}, $14:222_{15}$, "I recognize in all humility"—Ivan's "humility" is only a rhetorical posture. He goes on to assume the task of correcting this unsatisfactory state of affairs.

171 224_{40}, $14:222_{16-17}$, "stole fire from heaven"—an allusion to the myth of Prometheus, a Titan, who rebelled against the Olympic gods and sought to make man independent of the gods. Prometheus is a symbolic figure often found in romantic literature.

172 224_{43}, $14:222_{23}$, "there are none guilty"—although there are no quotation marks in the original, it is quite likely that the phrase is meant as a quotation from *King Lear,* Act IV, sc. vi, line 166: "none does offend."

173   224_{45}, $14:222_{21}$,   Gives a new twist to the term "Euclidean" (cf. chap. iii, p. 216): life in a Euclidean universe (where there is no law beyond the laws of nature) is senseless.

174   225_{8-9}, $14:222_{31}$,   Inexact quotation of Isaiah 11:6.

175   225_{11-12}, $14:222_{33-34}$,   "But then there are the children"—Ivan makes it suddenly clear that the preceding was delivered from his hypothetical opponent's point of view, and will now be refuted.

176   225_{16-17}, $14:222_{38-39}$,   The verb *stradat'*, "to suffer," has become a leitmotif of Ivan's discourse. Here, it contrasts ironically with its counterpoint, "harmony."

177   225_{22-25}, $14:222_{44-47}$,   The theme of theodicy is now linked with the theme of fathers and children.

178   225_{25-27}, $14:222_{47}-223_1$,   "Some jester will say . . ."—This bit of bathos is almost a relief from the strain of the preceding invective.

179   225_{29}, $14:223_3$,   "in heaven and earth"—translates *na nebe i pod zemlioiu*, "in heaven as well as underground," definitely ironic bathos.

180   225_{31}, $14:223_{4-5}$,   A free variation in the style of Ps. 117, Rev. 15:3–4, etc.

181   225_{34-35}, $14:223_{7-8}$,   "and all will be made clear"—the triumphant climax of Ivan's paradox: he has taken his (hypothetical) opponent's argument *ad absurdum*.

182   225_{35}, $14:223_8$,   "But what pulls me up here"—lit. "But this is where I put a comma," an idiomatic expression whose meaning is well rendered by the translation.

183   225_{39-40}, $14:223_{12-13}$,   Cf. Book Five, chap. v, p. 228, where the Virgin does just that!

184   225_{40}, $14:223_{13}$,   "but I don't want to cry aloud"—this passage is to be kept in mind, for it will be echoed by the devil. See Book Eleven, chap. ix, p. 614.

185   226_{18-20}, $14:223_{39}$,   ". . . *even if I were wrong*"—another echo of Pascal's bet. Cf. Book Three, note 168. This is the climax of Ivan's rebellion. To metaphysical (non-Euclidean) religion, he opposes his own humanist (Euclidean) faith. He rejects God's order, replacing it by his own self-will. Cf. Ellis Sandoz, *Political Apocalypse* (Baton Rouge, 1971), p. 109.

186   226_{21-22}, $14:223_{40-41}$,   "And so I hasten to give back my entrance ticket"—an echo from Schiller's poem "Resignation" (1784) in V. A. Zhukovsky's translation. See Introduction I.4.a. Secular Sources. Cf. also V. G. Belinsky's letter to V. P. Botkin, dated 1 March 1841 (V. G. Belinskii, *Polnoe sobranie sochinenii,* 13 vols.

[Moscow, 1953–59], 12:22–23), where Belinsky rejects Hegel's optimistic philosophy of history in much the same terms—probably likewise under the influence of Schiller's poem.

187   226_{25}, 14:223$_{44}$,   Ivan's declaration says, in an oblique way, that he wishes to eliminate all metaphysics from his discussion of the human condition. See Introduction II.2.a. Challenge to Christianity.

188   226_{34-35}, 14:224$_6$,   "to bet the architect"—a (Freudian?) misprint for "to be the architect."

189   226_{39}, 14:224$_{10-11}$,   "unexpiated"—translates *neopravdannyi,* "unjustified, unwarranted," where the focus is once more not so much moral or legal as rational: not so much "it is wrong" as "it does not make sense."

190   226_{44}, 14:224$_{16}$,   "He"—Russ. *ono,* "it," since *sushchestvo,* "being," is neuter. In the original the neuter gender is maintained throughout the sentence.

191   226_{44}–227$_1$, 14:224$_{16}$,   "all *and for all*"—first occurrence of a key phrase. Cf. Book Six, chap. ii (a), p. 268.

192   227_{3-4}, 14:224$_{19}$,   Aliosha's invocation of Christ puts suffering and retribution into an entirely different context. Suffering was assumed voluntarily by Christ and was accepted as a privilege by His martyrs, while retribution was superseded by grace. Ivan now faces the much more formidable task of refuting Christ's Gospel.

193   227_9, 14:224$_{23}$,   "a poem"—Russ. *poema* is normally a narrative poem of some length. But ever since Gogol called his prose epic *Dead Souls* a *poema,* the term has been applied to various kinds of works. Dostoevsky himself gave his novel *The Double* (1846) the subtitle *A Petersburg Poem.*

194   227_{18}, 14:224$_{33}$,   "ridiculous"—translates *nelepaia,* "preposterous, monstrous." This characterization must be viewed on two levels: psychologically, it is an expression of a rather vain author's false modesty; as Dostoevsky's internal commentary to the novel, it accurately signals the incongruous and dissonant quality of Ivan's composition: "The Grand Inquisitor" is a travesty of a poem and of a legend.

Chapter v

195   227_{33-34}, 14:225$_{4-5}$,   The French reads "The merciful judgment of the most holy and gracious Virgin Mary." Victor Hugo's novel *Notre Dame de Paris* (1831) had appeared in Dostoevsky's

journal *Vremia* [Time] in 1862. The details of this episode are not rendered quite exactly.

196   227_{35-37}, $14:225_{6-8}$, "Similar plays . . ."—Ivan's statement is historically correct. The most popular by far of these spectacles was an enactment of the miraculous escape of Shadrach, Meshach, and Abednego from the fiery furnace (Dan. 3:11–30).

197   228_1, $14:225_{13}$, The period of the "Tartar yoke" (cf. note 149 above) was considered to have been a time of cultural decline.

198   228_1, $14:225_{13}$, "one such poem"—translates *odna monastyrskaia poemka*. Ivan labels the medieval legend with a deprecatory diminutive *(poemka)*, while calling his own work a *poema*, and with an equally deprecatory adjective ("monastic, monkish"). This invites comparison—which will not be in Ivan's favor.

199   228_{2-3}, $14:225_{14}$, Dostoevsky was familiar with some recent editions of Russian medieval literature and knew this legend in its medieval version. See *PSS* 15:556 for details.

200   228_6, $14:225_{17-18}$, "noteworthy"—a mistranslation of *prezanimatel'nyi;* "most entertaining" is correct. Ivan's flippancy leads up to a deep irony.

201   228_{7-8}, $14:225_{19-20}$, The irony: as we shall soon enough discover, Ivan is precisely one of those sinners.

202   228_{11-12}, $14:225_{23}$, "immensely interesting"—more condescending flippancy on Ivan's part.

203   228_{14-16}, $14:225_{26-27}$, The response to Ivan's angry "no!" by the mother who would forgive the tormentors of her son (cf. chap. iv, p. 226).

204   228_{19-20}, $14:225_{31-32}$, "Well, my poem would have been of that kind if it had appeared at that time."—Ivan's shallow irony points to a very deep irony of which he is not aware: his "poem" expresses the despair of the godless much as the medieval legend had expressed the faith of a believing soul.

205   228_{23-24}, $14:225_{35}$, Rev. 3:11.

206   228_{24-25}, $14:225_{36-37}$, Inexact quotation of Mark 13:32.

207   228_{29-30}, $14:225_{41-42}$, A quotation from Schiller's poem "Sehnsucht" ("Yearning," 1801). The original: *Du musst glauben, du musst wagen, / Denn die Götter leihn kein Pfand* ("You must believe, you must dare, / For the gods will not give you a pledge"). It fits Ivan's thought even better than the Russian version. Dostoevsky mentions this poem in his *Diary of a Writer* (1873), 1:66.

208   228₃₂₋₃₅, 14:225₄₃₋₄₄,   "Miracle" now becomes a leitmotif. We
      have met it earlier, in Book One, chap. v, pp. 19–20; Book Two,
      chap. vii, p. 68; etc.

209   228₃₅, 14:226₂,   "did not slumber"—a mistranslation; it should
      be "does not slumber."

210   228₃₇, 14:226₄,   "a terrible new heresy"—Lutheranism.

211   228₃₇₋₃₉, 14:226₅₋₆,   Inexact quotation of Rev. 8:10–11.

212   229₂₋₃, 14:226₁₁,   Misquotation of Ps. 118:27, which is part of
      the Orthodox liturgy. Ivan has misunderstood a Church Slavonic
      aorist for an imperative. The correct text is "God is the Lord,
      which hath shewed us light." Dostoevsky's notebooks suggests
      that he may well have caused Ivan to bungle his biblical
      quotations as a part of his strategy to discredit the atheist. See
      The Notebooks for "The Brothers Karamazov," ed. and tr.
      Edward Wasiolek (Chicago, 1971), p. 36.

213   229₃₋₆, 14:226₁₂₋₁₅,   Again, that flippant irony of the atheist.

214   229₈₋₁₁, 14:226₁₇₋₂₀,   The last stanza of F. I. Tiutchev's poem
      "These Poor Villages . . ." (1855). Dostoevsky also quoted these
      lines in his "Discourse on Pushkin" (*Diary of a Writer*, 2:980).
      Tiutchev's conservative and strongly Orthodox views were close
      to Dostoevsky's. The kenotic Christ who appears in this poem is
      a more common figure in the Eastern than in the Western church.
      Incidentally, the mention of a living poet's name destroys the
      illusion of Ivan's story.

215   229₁₆, 14:226₂₅₋₂₆,   "every   day"—obviously   a   rhetorical
      overstatement.

216   229₁₇₋₁₈,   14:226₂₇₋₂₈,   Inexact   quotation   from   a   poem,
      "Coriolanus" (1834), by A. I. Polezhaev.

217   229₂₁₋₂₂, 14:226₃₁,   Inexact quotation of Matt. 24:27.

218   229₂₆,₂₉, 14:226₃₆,₃₇,   "'hot pavement'" and "magnificent
      auto da fé" (both in quotation marks in the original) are from
      the poem mentioned in note 216 above.

219   229₂₇₋₂₈, 14:226₄₁,   *ad majorem gloriam Dei*—should be *Dei
      gloriam*—"To God's greater glory," motto of the Society of
      Jesus.

220   229₃₁, 14:226₄₁,   The setting established here is that of Gothic
      melodrama and romantic glamor.

221   229₃₃₋₃₄, 14:226₄₂₋₄₄,   Ivan does not bother to try to answer his
      own question ("I mean, why they recognized Him"). Note how
      he keeps interrupting his "poem" to comment on it, thus shifting
      the drama from the fiction of his story to the reality of his own
      soul.

222   229_{37-38}, $14:227_2$,   "Enlightenment" does not seem to be the
right word, sounding rather prosaic between "Light" and
"power" (all three words are capitalized in the original), but
Dostoevsky lets Ivan make these lapses.

223   230_{1-2}, $14:227_7$,   After Mark 8:22-25.

224   230_{11}, $14:227_{16}$,   "priest"—Ivan uses *pater,* a foreign word,
which at once places the priest in a bad light.

225   230_{16}, $14:227_{22}$,   Mark 5:41-42.

226   230_{18}, $14:227_{24-25}$,   "holding a bunch of white roses"—this is
Ivan's addition to the biblical text. Obviously it is corny—and
meant to be so by Dostoevsky.

227   230_{21-23}, $14:227_{27-29}$,   Note the conventional Gothic quality of
this description of the Grand Inquisitor. The glamorous exterior
of Ivan's imaginary hero is in stark contrast with Aliosha's
unprepossessive real hero, Father Zosima.

228   230_{32}, $14:227_{38}$,   The clash between Christ returned to earth and
a representative of the Church is a theme treated by many writers
and poets ever since the Middle Ages, including some with whose
works Dostoevsky may well have been familiar: Voltaire,
Goethe, Balzac, Hugo, F. M. Klinger (1752-1831), and others.
See *PSS* 15:462-65, 559. A direct Russian source may have been
A. N. Maikov's epic poem "The Queen's Confession: A Legend
about the Spanish Inquisition," which had appeared in
Dostoevsky's journal *Time* (1861, No. 1). Maikov's fanatical
apologist of the Inquisition, the monk Juan di San-Martino, is,
however, very different from and certainly shallower than Ivan
Karamazov's Grand Inquisitor. See V. S. Nechaeva, *Zhurnal
M. M. i F. M. Dostoevskikh "Vremia," 1861-1863* (Moscow,
1972), pp. 219-20.

229   230_{40-41}, $14:227_{46-47}$,   Quoted from Pushkin's play *The Stone
Guest* (1836, publ. 1840), a treatment of the Don Juan theme.

230   231_4, $14:228_5$,   In Russian there is no special pronominal form
used in addressing God and Jesus Christ. Hence the "Thou" of
this translation creates a tone somewhat different from that of
the original.

231   231_{20}, $14:228_{21}$,   *qui pro quo*—"a case of mistaken identity."
Aliosha asks the right questions all along. If the Cardinal is who
we have reason to assume he is, the miracle which he has just
witnessed should have affected him quite differently. Ivan
promptly dismisses the whole preceding story as irrelevant to his
argument.

232 231_{24-25}, $14:228_{26}$, "he might well be crazy over his set idea"—unwitting self-irony, for the Grand Inquisitor's idea is, of course, Ivan's.

233 231_{28}, $14:228_{31}$, "But does it matter"—what this really means is that the person of the Grand Inquisitor is irrelevant, as is the whole "poem." What matters are Ivan's ideas.

234 231_{34-36}, $14:228_{37-38}$, Follows Matt. 5:17–18.

235 231_{37}, $14:228_{39}$, "in my opinion at least"—Ivan now begins to give up on his "poem" and more and more continues to develop his argument in his own voice.

236 231_{41-42}, $14:228_{44}$, While this is not directly relevant to the text, it may be pointed out that Dostoevsky knew Catholic theology mostly from the works of Slavophile writers such as F. I. Tiutchev and A. S. Khomiakov. See Introduction I.4.a. Secular Sources.

237 232_2, $14:229_2$, "freedom"—a new leitmotif.

238 232_7, $14:229_6$, Cf. John 8:32: "And ye shall know the truth, and the truth shall make you free."

239 232_{19-20}, $14:229_{18-19}$, Again, Aliosha's question is most appropriate. From his viewpoint, that of a true lover of humanity, the preceding cannot have been said seriously.

240 232_{25}, $14:229_{24}$, "Man was created a rebel"—a mistranslation of *Chelovek byl ustroen buntovshchikom,* "Man was made a rebel," where *ustroen,* moreover, has a connotation of "arrangement" or "mechanical construction"; "created" is *sozdan.* Russ. *buntovshchik* is more negative than "rebel," since it implies unsuccessful, senseless, and chaotic resistance to authority; perhaps "mutineer" would be closer.

241 232_{28-29}, $14:229_{28-29}$, "Thou didst reject the only way by which men might be made happy."—An intriguing proposition is taken up, but not immediately spelled out. This creates suspense.

242 232_{31}, $14:229_{30}$, "the right to bind and to unbind"—an allusion to Matt. 16:18–19.

243 232_{36}, $14:229_{35}$, "the chief part"—Ivan has expected Aliosha's question and believes that it will lead him to a triumphant conclusion of his argument. But it is exactly from here on that he loses control over it. The careful reader will notice how Ivan now begins to flounder.

244 232_{37-38}, $14:229_{36}$, The first deep irony: what is so "wise" and "great" about "self-destruction and nonexistence"?

245 232_{40}, $14:229_{38}$, Matt. 4:1–11 and Luke 4:1–13.

246   232_{43}, $14:229_{42}$,   "stupendous"—translates *gromovoe,* lit. "thunderous."

247   232_{44}, $14:229_{43}$,   This enthusiasm is only too clearly Ivan's, not that of a ninety-year-old Spanish cardinal. By making Ivan overstate his point, Dostoevsky undermines the atheist's position. Here Dostoevsky parodies the naive enthusiasm with which Russian radicals would proclaim their simplistic positivism as a social panacea.

248   233_{13}, $14:230_{11}$,   "the absolute and eternal"—a brazen perversion of the truth: the devil's offer is a ruse whose attractiveness lies precisely in the fact that it appeals to a limited, all-too-human intelligence; there is no "power" or "wisdom" behind it. The "absolute and eternal" is in Christ's answers to the devil. Again Dostoevsky parodies those of his contemporaries who would parade their woefully limited scientific knowledge as the absolute truth.

249   233_{23-24}, $14:230_{21}$,   "Remember the first question . . ."—here, and in many other instances, Ivan's diction becomes modern and colloquial, abandoning all pretense to re-creating the voice of a Grand Inquisitor.

250   233_{27-28}, $14:230_{25-26}$,   "for nothing has ever been more insupportable for a man and a human society than freedom"—the cornerstone of Ivan's anthropology. Its refutation is one of the main objects of *The Brothers Karamazov.*

251   233_{36}, $14:230_{34}$,   "the spirit of the earth"—translates *dukh zemli,* which more clearly than the English translation expresses the simple notion that men will abandon their spiritual selves for the sake of earthly material concerns.

252   233_{38-39}, $14:230_{35-36}$,   Combines parts of Rev. 13:4 and 13 with an apparent reminiscence of the Prometheus theme.

253   233_{40-41}, $14:230_{39}$,   "there is no crime"—an obvious anachronism so far as the Grand Inquisitor is concerned: this is one of the central ideas of the 1850s and 1860s. Dostoevsky may be paraphrasing Herzen, *My Past and Thoughts,* Pt. VI, chap. ix (devoted to Robert Owen).

254   233_{45}, $14:230_{42-43}$,   Gen. 11:1–9. The tower of Babel is used as a symbol of a godless and materialist society. In some other works, Dostoevsky uses the Crystal Palace of London in the same meaning.

255   234_{7}, $14:231_{2}$,   It was one of Dostoevsky's pet ideas that Catholicism would eventually merge with atheist socialism. Cf. Book Two, chap. v, p. 58.

256   234_{19-23}, $14:231_{14-18}$,   A key juncture: Ivan simply takes this division of humanity for granted.

257   234_{40}, $14:231_{34}$,   "worship"—translates Russ. *preklonit'sia,* lit. "to bow down," which has a connotation of submission.

258   234_{40-41}, $14:231_{34-36}$,   One of Dostoevsky's psychological paradoxes. Dostoevsky's spokesman Zosima will agree with Ivan, but give "worship" and "freedom" a different, more positive content.

259   $234_{46}-235_1$, $14:231_{42}$,   *"community"*—translates Russ. *obshchnost'.* Dostoevsky puts into Ivan's mouth an idea which, albeit with a different "accent," was very much his own. Community of worship was one of the central positions of the Slavophile conception of the Russian Orthodox way of life. Dostoevsky's friend K. P. Pobedonostsev had expressed similar ideas. See *PSS* 15:560.

260   235_{9-10}, $14:232_3$,   "Infallible banner" does not seem to be quite the right expression—but neither does Russ. *absoliutnoe znamia.*

261   235_{18}, $14:232_{10-11}$,   "invincible banner"—again, not the right phrase, but Russ. *besspornoe znamia,* "unchallenged banner," is not either. Ivan is carried away by his own rhetoric.

262   235_{19-21}, $14:232_{12-14}$,   A patent flaw in the Grand Inquisitor's argument: if man will so easily follow one who will "ensnare" his conscience, why will he not also follow a righteous teacher?

263   235_{39-40}, $14:232_{31}$,   The Grand Inquisitor projects his own vanity and arrogant contempt for man on Jesus.

264   235_{44}, $14:232_{36-37}$,   "the fearful burden of free choice"— another paradox: man's greatest good is denounced as an unbearable burden.

265   236_{3-4}, $14:232_{40}$,   "the foundation for the destruction"—an awkward way to put it, but well in line with the general shrillness of Ivan's rhetoric.

266   236_8, $14:232_{45}$,   "Thou hast rejected all three"—this is a brazen lie: what Christ rejected were sorcery, mystification, and tyranny. See Introduction II.2. *The Brothers Karamazov* as a Theodicy, and Roger L. Cox, "The Grand Inquisitor," in *Between Earth and Heaven* (New York, 1969), p. 195.

267   236_{10-14}, $14:232_{46}-233_2$,   Ivan quotes Matt. 4:6 inaccurately—on purpose, it would seem. The motif of testing Christ's sonhood and faith is absent in the biblical text.

268   236_{20}, $14:233_8$,   "and wouldst have been dashed to pieces"— Dostoevsky's (not Ivan's!) point is that the devil was offering his

"miracles" knowing very well that he could not deliver them. See Introduction II.2.

269   236_{32}, $14:233_{19-20}$, "for man seeks not so much God as the miraculous"—this aphorism is to be remembered. Its truth will be demonstrated in Book Seven, chaps. i–ii. Cf. Book One, chap. v, p. 20, and note 140. The commentator of *PSS* suggests that Augustine may be the source of the aphorism. See *PSS* 15:561.

270   236_{38}, $14:233_{24-25}$,   Inexact quotation of Matt. 27:42.

271   236_{43-44}, $14:233_{29-30}$,   "Rebellious" and "slave" does not imply any contradiction in terms. The Russian word *bunt* means a rebellion which is not guided by noble principles or a quest for freedom, but rather by a sullen and spiteful resentment of authority. The positive term is *vosstanie*, "uprising."

272   237_{6}, $14:233_{38}$,   The steady flow of abuse directed at the human race suggests that the speaker is not exactly a lover of mankind— one of the ways in which Dostoevsky undermines Ivan's argument.

273   237_{6-8}, $14:233_{38-39}$,   The word *bunt*, "rebellion" and its derivatives, *buntovat'*, "to rebel," and *buntovshchik*, "rebel," are repeated so often the reader must eventually hit upon the irony of the situation: Ivan keeps denouncing "rebels," yet only minutes earlier (in the preceding chapter) he was himself identified as a "rebel" by Aliosha.

274   237_{18-19}, $14:234_{2-4}$,   "unrest, confusion and unhappiness"—not necessarily an anachronism: this describes Ivan's own age as well as the Inquisitor's.

275   237_{22}, $14:234_{6-7}$,   A reference to Rev. 7:4–8.

276   237_{25-26}, $14:234_{9-10}$,   An allusion to Matt. 3:4.

277   237_{28-29}, $14:234_{12-13}$,   "and gods at that"—the motif of the "godhead" of the elect, or of the "man-god," emerges explicitly now.

278   237_{39}, $14:234_{22}$,   See note 266 above.

279   238_{9}, $14:234_{36}$,   "eight centuries"—In 756 King Pepin the Short of the Franks granted Ravenna to Pope Stephen III. Since this scene is set in the mid-sixteenth century, we may assume that Dostoevsky dates the Church's betrayal of Christ's legacy by that event. Also, after the second Nicaean Council (in 787), the last ecumenic council recognized by the Eastern church, the Eastern and the Western church drifted apart.

280   238_{23-24}, $14:234_{48}$,   Ivan gives his argument an unexpected turn. The anthill is Dostoevsky's symbol for a socialist society. Once

more Catholicism is shown to be headed ·toward godless socialism.

281   238_{38}, 14:235$_{15-16}$, "science and cannibalism"—"science and anthropophagy" in the original, where the scientific ring of "anthropophagy" enhances the sarcasm of this hendiadys (read: "science that leads to anthropophagy"). The notion that science, if unchecked by moral judgment, would lead mankind to inhuman practices, such as infanticide, was one of Dostoevsky's main preoccupations.

282   239_{40-41}, 14:235$_{17-19}$, A conflation of the beast in Rev. 13 and 17 with a scene in Pushkin's *Covetous Knight,* sc. ii: "Submissive, timid, blood-bespattered crime / Comes crawling to my feet, licking my hand, / looking me in the eye . . ."

283   238_{41-43}, 14:235$_{19-20}$, "And we shall sit . . ."—an echo of Rev. 17:3-7, where it is the Great Harlot who sits upon the beast. The Great Harlot of the Apocalypse has often been identified with the Roman church.

284   239_{2-6}, 14:235$_{23-27}$, This sounds very much like Ivan, a young intellectual of the 1860s, and very much unlike a ninety-year-old prince of the Church.

285   239_{10-11}, 14:235$_{31}$, They will be lying, of course. The leitmotif of the "lie" joins those of "freedom," "rebellion," and "love of mankind."

286   239_{18}, 14:235$_{38}$, The speaker's contempt for the masses of humanity emerges as the dominant emotion of his diatribe.

287   239_{22-25}, 14:235$_{40-44}$, "They will see . . ."—this complements the Grand Inquisitor's earlier admission that the devil would not deliver the miracle he had promised (p. 236$_{20}$).

288   239_{28}, 14:235$_{48}$, "Too, too well"—in the original a very colloquial *slishkom,* "too much," is repeated here. Cf. Book One, note 29.

289   239_{35-36}, 14:236$_{7}$, "Thou didst lift them up and thereby taught them to be proud"—he is right in that Christ had told men that they were God's children and immortal. This paradox suggests that the real, satanic pride is that of the Grand Inquisitor, who exalts only himself, while Christ exalted mankind.

290   239_{44-45}, 14:236$_{14-15}$, "they will be quick to shed tears"—a parody of the "gift of tears" *(slioznyi dar)* of holy men in the Orthodox church.

291   239_{46}–240$_{3}$, 14:236$_{17-19}$, The familiar picture of utopia; the Inquisitor's is not unlike Plato's in *The Republic.* Dostoevsky's

direct source is to be found in works of French utopian socialism, such as Etienne Cabet's *Voyage en Icarie* (1840), which had fascinated him as a young man.

292   240_{8-9}, $14:236_{23-25}$,   Christ's real sacrifice is parodied by the sham sacrifice of the elect, who know that there is no retribution. In the original the mockery is enhanced by a distinctly colloquial tone.

293   240_{22-23}, $14:236_{37}$,   "the curse of the knowledge of good and evil"—another irony: the secret is that there is no good or evil—or so the elect believe.

294   240_{24}, $14:236_{39}$,   "and beyond the grave they will find nothing but death"—this may echo a passage in Jean Paul's *Ehestand, Tod und Hochzeit des Armenadvokaten F. St. Siebenkäs* (1796–97) entitled "Oration of a Dead Christ, delivered from the Edifice of the Universe, on how there is no God." See Walter Rehm, *Jean Paul—Dostojewski: Eine Studie zur dichterischen Gestaltung des Unglaubens* (Göttingen, 1962).

295   240_{26}, $14:236_{40}$,   This would seem to be the conclusion of the argument: there is no God, no afterlife, no retribution—but for the good of mankind they are "re-invented" by Ivan's "wise men." But now the argument is given another, surprising twist.

296   240_{30-34}, $14:236_{44-47}$,   Rev. 17:3–5, 16. The "harlot" in Rev. 17 is obviously the Rome of the emperors, as verses 9 and 18 make clear.

297   240_{34}, $4:236_{47}$,   The first person singular reminds us that the Grand Inquisitor is really Ivan Karamazov, speaking mainly for himself.

298   240_{38-39}, $14:237_{3-4}$,   Echoes Matt. 3:4. This has a faintly ironic ring, as it also projects Ivan's own studious and frugal youth.

299   240_{41-42}, $14:237_{6-7}$,   Rev. 6:11.

300   240_{44}, $14:237_{8}$,   *"work"*—translates Russ. *podvig*, "feat, great deed, act of heroism," a key word throughout the novel and in Dostoevsky in general. Cf. Book One. note 131.

301   241_{6}, $14:237_{15}$,   *Dixi*—"I have spoken."

302   241_{14}, $14:237_{23}$,   "And who will believe you about freedom?"— Aliosha challenges Ivan's argument very capably. Here he correctly grasps the focal importance of freedom, as well as its perversion, in Ivan's argument.

303   241_{17}, $14:237_{25}$,   In the nineteenth century the sinister image of the Jesuits, proverbial in the eighteenth, still lingered. The Jesuits had been expelled from Germany in 1872.

304 241_{17-18}, $14:237_{25-26}$, Aliosha intuitively senses the psychological and historical falseness of Ivan's creation, another instance of internal commentary.

305 241_{18-19}, $14:237_{27}$, "What are these sins . . ."—Aliosha calls the Inquisitor's bluff. Cf. notes 292 and 293 above.

306 241_{23-25}, $14:237_{30-32}$, "They are not that . . ."—Here Aliosha is clearly repeating what he had heard from Father Paisy—as is actually suggested a moment later.

307 241_{28}, $14:237_{34-35}$, "serfdom"—translates *krepostnoe pravo*, the Russian legal term for serfage as an institution. We must keep in mind that Aliosha is talking only six years after the abolition of serfage.

308 241_{29-30}, $14:237_{36-37}$, "Your suffering inquisitor is a mere fantasy."—This touches Ivan to the quick, and he tries to put up a defense.

309 242_3, $14:238_5$, "all his life he loved humanity"—the point is that he loves "humanity" in the abstract. Cf. the beginning of the preceding chapter (pp. 217–18).

310 242_{3-10}, $14:238_{6-18}$, This long sentence (in the original it is almost twice as long) contains some stylistic lapses and pell-mell thinking. Likening men to geese and calling Christ "the great idealist" is very bad style. Ivan is slipping noticeably.

311 242_{10-11}, $14:238_{18-19}$, "the clever people"—the first echo of Fiodor Pavlovich's aphorism on "clever people" (Book Three, chap. viii, p. 121_{42-43}), where "clever people" are those who have discovered that there is no God and go on to use this discovery to their advantage.

312 242_{21}, $14:238_{31}$, "any tolerable sort of life"—a concession: earlier Ivan had spoken of a utopian existence of mankind under the Inquisitor's leadership.

313 242_{22}, $14:238_{32}$, " 'incomplete, specimen creatures created in jest' "—in quotation marks in the original also. If there is a literary source, it is unknown.

314 242_{24}, $14:238_{34}$, "the dread spirit of death and destruction"—a bit stronger and more explicit than the earlier "spirit of self-destruction and nonexistence" (p. 232).

315 242_{32-33}, $14:238_{42-43}$, "enough to make a tragedy"—internal commentary. Ivan claims for his own predicament the lofty status of a tragedy. It will be at best an ugly tragedy, at worst a tragicomedy.

316 242_{44}–243_2, $14:239_{8-12}$, Ivan is voicing some popular prejudices,

commonly heard in the 1870s. The whole argument seems to be falling apart now.

317   243$_{3-4}$, 14:239$_{12-13}$,   Some more internal commentary, and once again it draws the reader's attention to some serious weaknesses in Ivan's argument.

318   243$_5$, 14:239$_{15}$,   Cf. Book Eleven, chap. iv, p. 561$_{38}$. It must be understood that to a Russian Orthodox Christian a Mason is a very dangerous heretic.

319   243$_{8-9}$, 14:239$_{19}$,   After the anticlimax of the last passage there comes now yet another surge of surprising developments.

320   243$_{10}$, 14:239$_{20}$,   "I meant to end it like this."—Once more draws attention to the fact that the legend is Ivan's conscious creation and a vehicle of his ideas.

321   243$_{20}$, 14:239$_{30}$,   "into the dark squares of the town" (in quotation marks in the original)—an inexact quotation from Pushkin's poem "Reminiscence" (1828).

322   243$_{27-28}$, 14:239$_{36-38}$,   "a senseless poem of a senseless student"—an important bit of internal commentary. Psychologically, it only signals Ivan's hurt vanity (he would like to see his self-disparagement contradicted). On a deeper level, it is a judgment (Dostoevsky's, not the narrator's) of the legend— one of the many ways in which Ivan's argument is undermined and eventually exploded.

323   243$_{32-33}$, 14:239$_{42}$,   "dash the cup to the ground"—cf. chap. iii, p. 211, and note 74 above.

324   243$_{34-35}$, 14:239$_{43-44}$,   Cf. chap. iii, p. 211. See also Linnér, pp. 160–61.

325   243$_{37-38}$, 14:239$_{46-47}$,   "that's just what you are going away for, to join them"—These are strangely prophetic words. Vladimir Solov'iov, most probably the prototype of Ivan Karamazov, eventually traveled to the West, where he published some essays which, to a Russian Orthodox Christian, would appear "more papist than the Pope" (K. Mochul'skii, *Vladimir Solov'ev: Zhizn' i uchenie* [Paris, 1951], p. 184). The text referred to by Mochulsky is Solov'iov's essay "Saint-Vladimir et l'Etat chrétien," *L'Univers*, 1888, nos. 4, 11, 19. Dostoevsky knew of some instances where Russian intellectuals had converted to Catholicism and actually joined the Society of Jesus. One such case was that of Vladimir Sergeevich Pecherin (1807–85), about whom Herzen speaks in some detail in *My Past and Thoughts*, Pt. VII, chap. vi. Cf. *A Writer's Diary*, 1:357.

326   243$_{45-46}$, 14:240$_{5-6}$,   "To sink into debauchery . . ."—it is

significant that the saintly Aliosha should foresee precisely this solution. Cf. V. V. Zen'kovskii, "Fiodor Pavlovich Karamazov," in *O Dostoevskom,* ed. A. L. Bem, 2 (Prague, 1933): 107.

327   244_6, $14:240_{12}$, " 'Everything is lawful' "—in quotation marks in the original and therefore certainly a quote from 1 Cor. 6:12: "All things are lawful unto me" (King James Version; Gk. $\pi\acute{\alpha}\nu\tau\alpha$ $\mu o\iota$ $\overset{\prime}{\epsilon}\xi\epsilon\sigma\tau\iota\nu$). Aliosha is recalling Ivan's ideas, expressed in Book Two, chap. vi, pp. 60–61.

328   244_{21}, $14:240_{27}$, "That's plagiarism"—cf. Book Two, chap. vii, p. 72_{11}. The reader's attention is drawn to the interaction between the empirical-psychological plot of the novel and its metaphysical content.

329   244_{30-31}, $14:240_{35-36}$, Inexact quotation of Gen. 13:9. The left is of course the side of the devil.

330   244_{32-33}, $14:240_{37}$, "I think I certainly shall go"—in the original the oxymoron ("I think"—"certainly") is more pronounced. Such psychological oxymora are characteristic of Dostoevsky's style.

331   244_{43-44}, $14:241_1$, *Pater Seraphicus*—An explicit echo from Act V of *Faust,* Pt. II, where a *Pater seraphicus* leads a chorus of blessed boys to even higher awareness of God's presence and eternal love (lines 11918–25).

332   245_{5-7}, $14:241_{7-9}$, In the original: "This strange little observation flashed, like an arrow, through Aliosha's saddened mind, sorrowful and saddened at this moment." An example of emphatic repetition, often used by Dostoevsky.

333   245_{8-9}, $14:241_{10-12}$, "Ivan swayed . . ."—a very strong metonymic symbol: Ivan is "out of joint"; there is something wrong with him.

Chapter vi

334   245_{32}, $14:241_{35}$, For the first time the narrator identifies with Ivan Karamazov, and we begin to become acquainted with his inner life.

335   245_{39}, $14:241_{42}$, This whole passage is *erlebte Rede.* See Introduction III.1.a. The Narrator.

336   245_{40}, $14:241_{42}$, "apprehension"—Russ. *toska* and its derivative *toskovat',* "to be depressed," appear throughout this passage. The translation has "depression" and "apprehension."

337   246_5, $14:242_4$, "a rigmarole like that"—more internal criticism of "The Grand Inquisitor."

338   246_{14-21}, $14:242_{15-22}$,   This hypostatized presentation of a mental
state is characteristic of Dostoevsky's psychology. See Introduction II.6.d. Psychological Wisdom.

339   246_{24}, $14:242_{25}$,   All this beating about the bush does more than
build suspense. It gives Ivan's involvement with Smerdiakov an
ominous character and suggests deep subconscious implications.

340   246_{25-28}, $14:242_{26-28}$,   In the original, we have a pun, almost as
gauche in Russian as it is in English: "On a bench in the gateway
the lackey Smerdiakov was sitting . . . and at the first glance Ivan
Fiodorovich realized that the lackey Smerdiakov was sitting in
his soul, too." Dostoevsky likes to hypostatize mental states.

341   246_{41}, $14:242_{42}$,   "this hatred"—translates *protsess nenavisti,*
"the process of hatred." Dostoevsky is not afraid of unusual
word combinations when describing psychological phenomena.
See Introduction II.6.d. Psychological Wisdom.

342   246_{43-45}, $14:242_{44-46}$,   In the original we have something like:
"Then Ivan Fiodorovich had suddenly begun to take a kind of
very special interest in Smerdiakov, even finding him very
original." The sentence is saturated with modal phrases, which
signal that the narrator has trouble grasping this important
development and indirectly urges the reader to pay attention to
it.

343   247_2, $14:243_1$,   An allusion to Book Three, chap. vi, p. 115.

344   247_{3-5}, $14:243_{3-5}$,   An allusion to Book Three, chap. vi, pp.
112–13.

345   247_{23-24}, $14:243_{24}$,   "revolting familiarity"—a detail of tone of
voice which will dominate the whole relationship between Ivan
and Smerdiakov. It has various symbolic implications, as we
shall see.

346   247_{27-32}, $14:243_{29-33}$,   Note the many modal phrases and indefinite pronouns and adverbs ("some sort of," "some kind
of," "at some time"); together, they give the whole thing an
enigmatic, mysterious air.

347   247_{32-35}, $14:243_{34-36}$,   "But for a long while . . ."—the reader is
still in the dark as to the relationship between Ivan and Smerdiakov. But his curiosity has been aroused.

348   247_{42}, $14:243_{44}$,   "emasculate"—translates *skopcheskuiu,*
"eunuch-like" (from *skopets,* "eunuch"). The fact that
Smerdiakov is a "eunuch" (we have heard him sing in a falsetto
voice, and we know that he has no interest in women) is sym-

bolic: in spite of his various and not inconsiderable talents, Smerdiakov is sterile not only physically, but spiritually as well.

349   247_{43}, $14:243_{45-46}$, "eye"—in the original, *glazok* (diminutive of *glaz*, "eye"), "little eye," throughout this scene.

350   247_{44-45}, $14:243_{47-48}$, "we two clever people"—see note 311 above.

351   248_{1-2}, $14:244_3$, "but to his profound astonishment he heard himself say"—the start of a pattern: this will keep happening to Ivan often from here on. He is no longer in control of himself, but driven by a mysterious, evil force.

352   248_{4-6}, $14:244_{6-7}$, This scene creates the impression, to be corroborated later, that Smerdiakov is Ivan's evil demon, perhaps the devil himself.

353   248_{12}, $14:244_{12}$, "foot"—translates *nozhku* (diminutive of *noga*, "foot"), "little foot."

354   248_{14-17}, $14:244_{14-17}$, Ivan's split personality is beginning to show: he feels something with one side of his self, observes his own feelings with the other.

355   248_{26-27}, $14:244_{26-27}$, "I put you off . . ."—the original has the first person, but without quotations marks, a kind of hypothetical direct speech which Dostoevsky's narrator uses on occasion.

356   248_{28}, 244_{28}, "Damn you!"—Translates *E, chort,* "Eh, the devil!" Since Russian has no article, only the context can determine whether Ivan invokes "the devil" or addresses Smerdiakov "you devil." Ivan's recurring mention of the devil, particularly in Smerdiakov's presence, is symbolically significant. The translator uses "damn," "hell," and "devil," neutralizing the effect.

357   248_{38}, $14:244_{39}$, "he moved"—translates *kachnulsia,* "rocked (forward)"—reminding us of Ivan's "rocking" gait at the end of the preceding chapter.

358   249_7, $14:245_8$, "gun" translates *oruzhie,* "weapon." Smerdiakov has seen no particular weapon of any kind, so he uses this general term.

359   249_{8-9}, $14:245_{10}$, ". . . before anyone"—hinting that other murders will follow. Note the complex game of innuendo in this harangue. Here the thought of murder is introduced in this roundabout way. (Smerdiakov knows very well that Dmitry will not murder *him*.)

360   249_{10}, $14:245_{11}$, "worrying me to death"—translates Russ. *muchitel'ski muchit'*, "torturing me like a torturer," definitely substandard speech.

361   249_{13}, $14:245_{15-16}$, "I shall kill myself"—deep irony: Smerdiakov does not suspect at all that he is predicting his own end.

362   249_{20}, $14:245_{22}$, "Licharda" (from "Richard")—a devoted servant in the popular folk tale "Prince Bova." Licharda serves his master, King Gvidon, faithfully—but also the king's wicked wife, Militrisa (from Lat. *meretrix*, "prostitute), when she plots to murder him. Cf. Book Eleven, chap. viii, p. 590.

363   249_{21-22}, $14:245_{23}$, "I feel certain"—translates *Naverno polagaiu*, lit. "I suppose for certain." The contradiction in terms is significant: if an event which at best can be *supposed* to happen is predicted with *certainty,* something is not right about the whole thing.

364   250_{1-6}, $14:246_{1-7}$, Smerdiakov's speech is essentially literate, but there are some grammatical slips, non sequiturs, and pleonasms which betray the uneducated person.

365   250_{9-10}, $14:246_{11}$, Most significant: Smerdiakov's come-on releases Ivan's subconscious wish. Cf. Book Three, chap. ix, p. 129_{1-2}.

366   250_{15-16}, $14:246_{16-17}$, There is a pun in the original: *soobshchnik*, "accomplice," and *soobshchit'*, "to let know." It reflects Smerdiakov's muddled thinking, probably feigned.

367   251_{12}, $14:247_{12}$, "hesitation"—translates Russ. *sumlenie,* "doubt, suspicion," a word characteristic of substandard diction.

368   251_{17}, $14:247_{16}$, "It was through fright I did"—Smerdiakov is lying, of course: this detail is the key to his plan.

369   251_{21}, $14:247_{20}$, "slavish devotion"—translates Russ. *rabolepie*, "servility." Smerdiakov does not quite mean what this book word really implies, but he gets his meaning across.

370   251_{21-22}, $14:247_{21}$, "and might be satisfied that I was not deceiving him"—deep irony: in fact, Dmitry is being lured into a deadly trap.

371   251_{28}, $14:247_{32}$, "Hang it!"—"The devil take it!" in the original. We are once more reminded of him who is the silent interlocutor in this dialogue.

372   252_{2}, $14:248_{1}$, All these details are significant and will reappear later in the novel. See Book Twelve, chap. ii, pp. 631–32.

373   252_{15-16}, $14:248_{14}$, "If he means to do anything, he'll do it"—here, "to do" translates Russ. *uchinit'*, "to commit," a verb

which requires an object such as "a crime, an act of violence, murder." Though the word "murder" has not fallen, this gets very close to it.

374   252_{22-23}, $14:248_{22}$,   "I want to know what you are thinking!"— Note how Ivan has talked himself into a situation where he finds himself on equal terms with the lackey.

375   253_{19}, $14:249_{20}$,   "you see what will happen here"—still only innuendo, but positions are well set now.

376   253_{26}, $14:249_{26}$,   "because I felt sorry for you"—Russ. *vas zhaleiuchi*, a substandard expression, intolerably condescending in the context.

377   253_{35}, $14:249_{35}$,   "would have flung himself on Smerdiakov"— note the wordless drama. The word "murder" has not fallen, but it is now clear that Ivan and Smerdiakov have understood one another.

378   253_{42-43}, $14:249_{42-43}$,   "and wondered himself afterwards . . ." —another suggestion that an invisible, evil power is guiding Ivan. Cf. note 351 above.

379   254_{7-9}, $14:250_{6-8}$,   Note throughout this scene the contrast between Ivan's nervous energy and the pitiful words and gestures which it produces.

380   254_{13-15}, $14:250_{13-14}$,   Smerdiakov finally gets what he wanted: an admission from Ivan that he does anticipate an event which will call him back from Moscow or Chermashnia. There can be little doubt as to what this event will be.

Chapter vii

381   254_{25}, $14:250_{25}$,   "It's Always Worthwhile Speaking to a Clever Man"—a leitmotif. Cf. note 350 above.

382   254_{26}, $14:250_{26}$,   Dostoevsky likes to produce smooth transitions from one chapter to the next, but usually the transition is unmarked. Here it is marked.

383   254_{35}, $14:250_{35}$,   "his son"—Russ. *synok*, diminutive of *syn*, "son." Ironic, of course.

384   255_2, $14:250_{45}$,   "and these questions we will omit"—for a moment, the narrator surfaces. The next sentence also suggests his presence quite strongly.

385   255_{7-13}, $14:251_{4-11}$,   This passage features a peculiar point of view: we have an omniscient narrator who can look into Ivan's soul, but finds it difficult to read. In effect, the point of view is close to being Ivan's own in retrospect. Note also the "dialectic"

style, with each consecutive statement a qualification of the preceding.

386 255_{13-17}, $14:251_{13-15}$, Ivan's occasional penchant for physical violence is becoming a leitmotif which signals the unbearable tension under which he lives. There will be more such instances. Cf. Book Two, note 242.

387 255_{18-20}, $14:251_{17-19}$, "as one who had insulted him"—a surprising statement which makes the reader wonder what has been going on in Ivan's mind.

388 $255_{33ff.}$, $14:251_{30ff.}$, A significant passage. It suggests quite unequivocally that Ivan will survive. In effect, the reader may gather from this passage that the narrator has this information from Ivan himself. See Introduction III.3.e. Expository Novel.

389 $255_{45}-256_2$, $14:251_{43-47}$, This description is a preview of the scene in Book Eight, chap. iv, p. 369.

390 256_{17-18}, $14:252_{15-16}$, "had not dreamed that his first act . . ."—a passage characteristic of Dostoevsky's psychological indeterminism. Dostoevsky's heroes often surprise not only the reader, but themselves, too.

391 256_{32}, $14:252_{30}$, "my dear boy"—translates *otets ty moi rodnoi*, "father-of-mine," a colloquial phrase used in addressing someone who is in a position to do one a favor. It is unexpected, but not unnatural, coming from a father addressing his own son. Similarly, Captain Snegiriov calls his son Iliusha *batiushka*, "daddy," to express his fondness and respect for him. It is almost certain that we are dealing with outright symbolism in both instances. Fiodor Pavlovich calls Ivan his "father" at a moment when Ivan has become involved in a plot to take his life—a deadly irony. See Introduction II.3.a. Fatherhood.

392 257_{17-24}, $14:253_{12-17}$, Gorstkin is a double of Fiodor Pavlovich's: disorganized, an inveterate liar, a drunkard, but surprisingly, a successful businessman. See Introduction III.3.b. Mirroring and Doubling.

393 257_{36-38}, $14:253_{29-31}$, The Russian text reads lit. "He is Gorstkin, only he isn't Gorstkin, but Liagavy, so don't tell him he's Liagavy, or he'll be miffed." Gorstkin (from *gorst'*, "handful") is the man's real surname, but he is known by his nickname, Liagavy ("bird dog"). This detail will come back. See Book Eight, chap. ii, p. 353.

394 257_{41-42}, $14:253_{34}$, In the original: "eight or eleven—that's a difference of three thousand," an important detail because

"three thousand roubles" has already been established as a leitmotif and magic number. See Introduction III.3.a. Motifs.

395   257_{43-44}, $14:253_{36}$, "I'm in desperate need"—translates *do zarezu*, lit. "to the point of cutting (somebody's) throat." This brings back the image of Dmitry and his plight.

396   258_7, $14:253_{42-43}$, "Venice"—reminds one of Ivan's plans to visit that "precious graveyard" which is Europe (chap. iii, p. 212_2).

397   258_{9-10}, $14:253_{44-45}$, "a clever man"—the phrase has become a leitmotif. Cf. notes 350 and 381 above. Here it is deeply ironic: little does Fiodor Pavlovich realize *how* "clever" his son is.

398   258_{14-15}, $14:254_1$, Sophoclean irony: the reader gets the point (that Fiodor Pavlovich is precipitating his own doom), but of course Fiodor Pavlovich does not.

399   258_{36-41}, $14:254_{23-27}$, Another instance of Sophoclean irony. The godless detractor of Christ, now plotting his father's murder, is committed to God and Christ by his unsuspecting father: "Good luck" translates *s Bogom*, lit. "with God". In his last contact with Ivan, Fiodor Pavlovich is very much a father.

400   259_{2-3}, $14:254_{33-34}$, "the words seemed to drop of themselves"—again the implication that Ivan is under an evil spell. Cf. notes 351 and 378 above.

401   259_{5-6}, $14:254_{36-37}$, The leitmotif again. We know all too well by now what a "clever man" means: a man who knows that "all things are lawful" and acts accordingly.

402   259_6, $14:254_{37}$, "significantly"—translates *proniknovenno*, "heartfelt, sincere, moving." Since the literal meaning of the word is "penetrated," "with a penetrating look" is also a possibility. Perhaps: "with a deep look," or best, "gratefully."

403   259_{45}, $14:255_{29}$, "and no looking back!"—more Sophoclean irony: we know that Ivan is deceiving himself.

404   260_{22}, $14:256_3$, "God had preserved him"—more Sophoclean irony: the reader knows better.

405   260_{34}, $14:256_{17}$, "a most estimable old man"—in the original we have a pleonastic—"a most estimable elderly gentleman of advanced age,"—quite characteristic of the narrator's colloquial diction. While the narrator is very fond of Dr. Herzenstube, he also likes to make fun of him.

406   260_{38}, $14:256_{19}$, "did not fully understand it"—Herzenstube's label again. Cf. Book Four, chap. iv, p. 165_{29}.

Book Six

Chapter i

1   262_{22-25}, $14:257_{22-24}$, Father Zosima's speech is strongly stylized. In addition to biblical language and Slavonicisms, it features unmistakable elements of the rhetorical diction of eighteenth-century sentimentalism. See Introduction III.1.d. Aliosha as an Echo of Father Zosima. In this sentence, "dear faces" translates *milye liki,* where *lik* is the biblical equivalent of *litso,* "face, visage, aspect." The difference is that *lik* carries the connotation of an awareness that the human face was made in the image of God; *lik,* then, is the human face in its spiritual aspect. This very powerful nuance is necessarily lost in translation. Furthermore, "without the delight" translates *chem eshche raz ne up′ius′,* lit. "without having once more drunk in" (from *upit′sia,* "to drink in, to become intoxicated with")—a very strong term when the object is a spiritual conversation.

2   263_{2-4}, $14:257_{39-42}$, "though perhaps there was no one . . ."—this is as awkward in Russian. Dostoevsky's narrator will sometimes give up on formulating a thought exactly, trusting that the reader will catch the correct meaning anyway. Naturally, Dostoevsky does this intentionally.

3   263_6, $14:257_{46}-258_1$, Kostroma is in northern Russia.

4   263_{8-14}, $14:258_{1-7}$, Note the detail. Dostoevsky wants to create maximum credibility for what follows this description and so he dwells on some credible, though inconsequential, details.

5   263_{28-29}, $14:258_{20-21}$, "the sixty kopeks . . ."—see Book Two, chap. iii, p. 44_{24-27}.

6   264_{1-4}, $14:258_{40-42}$, The one clear instance where Father Zosima shows a clairvoyance which is very nearly supernatural—yet there is an immediate retreat, reducing it to great psychological perspicacity.

7   264_{17}, $14:259_7$, "brotherly face"—*bratskii lik,* cf. note 1 above.

8   264_{18-20}, $14:259_{8-10}$,   The epigraph of the novel. Its meaning is
still obscure here, but it is the first explicit counterpoint to
chapters iv and v of Book Five, as it suggests that death and
suffering have their meaning.

9   264_{22-27}, $14:259_{12-17}$,   "This is what I think of you . . ."—this is
as close as we get to hearing about Aliosha's future.

10 264_{38-43}, $14:259_{29-35}$,   One of the many instances of mirroring in
the novel is pointed out here. We shall meet several more
correspondences between the story of the Karamazovs and the
story of Father Zosima.

11 265_{15}, $14:260_7$,   "story"—translates *povest'*, in Russian literary
terminology a piece of fiction longer than a short story *(rasskaz)*,
but shorter than a novel *(roman)*.

12 265_{28}, $14:260_{21}$,   "effort of love"—translates *umilenie*, one of
the few genuinely untranslatable words in the text, and a key
concept in this Book. It suggests a movement of the heart and
soul toward love, tenderness, and worship.

Chapter ii

13 266_{2-4}, $14:260_{30-32}$,   The whole title is in Church Slavonic.
"Life," in particular, is *zhitie*, normally a "saint's life." The
relationship between *zhitie* and the ordinary *zhizn'* is the same as
that between *lik* and *litso* (see note 1 above): *zhitie* is the human
life from a spiritual aspect.

CHAPTER II (A)

14 266_{21-22}, $14:261_{7-8}$,   "who had gained distinction in
philosophy"—translates *znatnyi filosof*, "an eminent
philosopher." The time is approximately 1810, so that the exile
would belong to the generation of Aleksandr Radishchev
(1749–1802), a freethinking *philosophe* of the Enlightenment.

15 266_{32-34}, $14:261_{18-21}$,   "I remember my mother selling . . ."—
starts a pattern of parallels between the discourses of Father
Zosima and Ivan Karamazov. Both mention some of the worst
abuses of serfage. The point is that from the very same facts
Father Zosima develops an entirely different philosophy.

16 266_{33-34}, $14:261_{20}$,   In the first half of the nineteenth century a
"silver rouble" was worth roughly twice as much as a "paper
rouble."

17 266_{37}, $14:261_{24}$,   "of very pleasing countenance"—translates

ves'ma blagoobrazen. The words *blagoobrazie* (also *blagolepie*) and *bezobrazie,* compounds of *blago,* "good," and *bez,* "without," with *obraz,* "form, image," play a central role in Dostoevsky's religiously oriented aesthetics. They point to spiritual beauty or ugliness. See Robert L. Jackson, *Dostoevsky's Quest for Form: A Study of His Philosophy of Art* (New Haven, 1966), p. 68.

18   267_{22}, $14:261_{45}$,   "Face" is once more *lik;* see note 1 above.

19   267_{22}, $14:261_{45}$,   "bright and joyous"—*vesiolyi, radostnyi:* key words throughout Book Six.

20   268_{3}, $14:262_{19-20}$,   "wait on"—translates *sluzhit',* "to serve," a verb with a much more general meaning. This is the first statement of a theme which will be treated in detail later in this chapter.

21   268_{8-9}, $14:262_{24-25}$,   "every one of us has sinned against all men"—one of the key positions of Father Zosima's teaching and a central thesis of the novel. See Introduction II.2.b. Arguments in Support of Christianity.

22   268_{14}, $14:262_{28}$,   "little heart of mine"—translates Russ. *krovinushka,* lit. "droplet of (my) blood," not a very common expression.

23   268_{29-30}, $14:262_{42-44}$,   ". . . and glorify life."—Father Zosima's version of utopia—not so different from the Grand Inquisitor's (Book Five, chap. v, pp. 239_{46}–240_{3}).

24   268_{32}, $14:262_{46-47}$,   "The disease is affecting his brain."—A Dostoevskian ambivalence: every mystical detail has a "natural" explanation also.

25   268_{40-42}, $14:263_{5-8}$,   One of the pantheist and Franciscan passages in *The Brothers Karamazov.*

26   269_{6-7}, $14:263_{16-17}$,   One of Dostoevsky's favorite images. Cf. Book One, chap. iv, p. 13_{12-20}, and note 85. Durylin interprets the image of the setting sun—in this passage, in particular—as a symbol of faith in immortality, for the setting sun is also the rising sun. See S. N. Durylin, "Ob odnom simvole u Dostoevskogo," in *Dostoevskii* (Moscow, 1928), p. 194. Florensky points out the connection between the ancient hymn *Svete tikhii* ("Gentle Light") and the Dostoevskian passages, especially the present one. Zosima's praise of vespertine light is shown to come from Saint Basil the Great's equal affection for a φῶς ἑσπερινός. See Pavel Florenskii, *Stolp i utverzhdenie istiny: Opyt pravoslavnoi teoditsei v dvenadtsati pis'makh* (Moscow, 1914), p. 659.

27 269_{10}, $14:263_{20}$, "enjoy life for me, too"—translates *zhivi za menia*, "live for me," where the verb *zhit'*, "to live," appears in the pregnant meaning "to enjoy life."

CHAPTER II (B)

28 269_{36}, $14:263_{44}$, "mourning and grieving"—translates *grustila i trepetala*, "grieved and trembled," meaning that she was grieving for Markel (and for Zinovy, too, since he was away) and trembling for the safety of Zinovy. Such "sloppy" diction is only too often needlessly "corrected" by the translator. Obviously Dostoevsky had taken great pains to introduce it into the text.

29 270_{1-2}, $14:264_{8-9}$, An autobiographic trait. The book in question is a translation of Johannes Hübner's *Hundert und vier heilige Geschichten aus dem Alten und Neuen Testament* (1714). See Andrei M. Dostoevskii, *Vospominaniia* (Leningrad, 1930), p. 63. Hübner was a Protestant theologian and decidedly an "enlightened" pietist. See Konrad Onasch, *Der verschwiegene Christus: Versuch über die Poetisierung des Christentums in der Dichtung F. M. Dostojewskis* (Berlin, 1976), p. 20.

30 270_{5-11}, $14:264_{15-19}$, One of the few passages in Dostoevsky in which the ritual of the Orthodox church is thus honored.

31 270_{17-34}, $14:264_{25-39}$, This paraphrase of the Book of Job is introduced as a counterpoint to Ivan Karamazov's "Grand Inquisitor." See Introduction I.4.b. Sacred Sources.

32 270_{38-39}, $14:264_{43-44}$, "The camels at that time caught my imagination"—such concrete psychological detail is typical of Dostoevsky's manner.

33 270_{45-46}, $14:265_{1-3}$, "And how much that is great, mysterious and unfathomable there is in it!"—Father Zosima does not disdain such rhetorical phrases, clearly from the arsenal of eighteenth-century pietism.

34 271_{6-9}, $14:265_{8-11}$, Father Zosima's response to Ivan's "rebellion." This is Father Zosima's theodicy. See Introduction II.2.b. Arguments in Support of Christianity.

35 271_{10-12}, $14:265_{12-13}$, An explicit assertion, in the face of innocent human suffering, of God's being the best of all possible worlds.

36 271_{24-25}, $14:265_{26-28}$, Zosima shifts the focus of the miracle from the Grand Inquisitor's "magic" plane to a psychological plane, as is pointed out by Nathan Rosen, "The Book of Job in the Structure of *The Brothers Karamazov*."

37 271_{28}, $14:265_{30-31}$, See note 26 above.

38 271_{31}, $14:265_{34}$, "My life is ending . . ."—note that Father Zosima speaks of childhood and old age only, leaving out energetic, active, and rebellious youth and middle age.

39 271_{32-33}, $14:265_{35-36}$, Prepares us for Zosima's great mystic passage (pp. 299–300). Cf. S. I. Gessen, "Tragediia dobra v *Brat'iakh Karamazovykh* Dostoevskogo," in *O Dostoevskom* (Providence, 1966), p. 223.

40 271_{34-35}, $14:265_{37-38}$, Zosima, true to eighteenth-century thought, sees three human faculties: the spirit, the intellect, and the heart. The whole passage seems to be derived from Saint Tychon of Zadonsk. See R. V. Pletniov, "Serdtsem mudrye: O Startsakh u Dostoevskogo," in *O Dostoevskom,* ed. A. L. Bem, 2 (Prague, 1933): 82.

41 271_{39-43}, $14:265_{40-45}$, "They plainly state . . ."—a carry-over from Dostoevsky's publicism. See *Diary of a Writer* (1876), 1:180.

42 272_1, $14:266_2$, "work"—rural priests often worked their own farms.

43 272_{17}, $14:266_{16}$, "This place is holy"—Gen. 28:17. The King James version reads: "How dreadful is this place." Actually, the wrestling with the Lord comes later (Gen. 32:24).

44 272_{40}, $14:266_{38}$, The biblical passage alluded to here is Gen. 49:10. Father Zosima's account deviates from Genesis. If anything, it is closer to the version of *A Hundred and Four Biblical Tales* (see note 29 above).

45 272_{46}, $14:266_{43-44}$, "Only a little tiny seed . . ."—another echo of the epigraph. Cf. note 8 above.

46 273_3, $14:266_{46}$, "foulness"—translates *smrad,* "stench, malodorous foulness," another echo from "The Grand Inquisitor": Ivan, too, speaks of the people as "malodorously sinful" *(smradno greshnye)* in Book Five, chap. v, p. 229_{14}. This translation has "sunk in iniquity" for *smradno greshnye.*

47 273_{12}, $14:267_7$, "Aleksei, the man of God"—see Introduction I.4.b. Sacred Sources.

48 273_{13}, $14:267_8$, Mary of Egypt, a calendar saint whose memory is celebrated by the Orthodox church on 1 April, was a harlot in her youth, became a famous hermit, and spent forty-seven years in the desert in penance and prayer. Dostoevsky mentions her repeatedly in his various works.

49 273_{25-27}, $14:267_{19-21}$, "Only the people . . ."—The nucleus of Dostoevsky's mystic populism, which he shared with the

Slavophiles. See Introduction II.4. *The Brothers Karamazov* as a
Social Novel.

50   273_{29-30}, $14:267_{21-23}$, "For the Word and for all that is good"
translates *Slova i vsiakogo prekrasnogo vospriiatiia,* lit. "the
Word and every beautiful percept." This is one of several spots
where Father Zosima comes close to a Neoplatonic, quasi-
aesthetic conception of religious feeling. See Introduction II.2.b.
Arguments in Support of Christianity.

51   274_{4-5}, $14:267_{41-42}$, A pantheistic trait. Cf. Introduction II.2.b.

52   274_{18}, $14:268_9$, The saint is Sergius of Radonezh (Sergii
Radonezhskii, 1314–92), whose vita contains this episode.

CHAPTER II (C)

53   274_{33-35}, $14:268_{23-25}$, "I picked up . . ."—Very much in the
manner of the later Tolstoi. Zosima, like Tolstoi, sees the world
from an "estranged" point of view.

54   274_{39-40}, $14:268_{28-29}$, "I was so much more impressionable
. . ."—An important psychological detail. The first indication
that there is something special about this seemingly very ordinary
boy.

55   275_9, $14:268_{42}$, Rev. 10:15.

56   275_{11-16}, $14:268_{42-46}$, The situation described parallels Dmitry's
in Book Two, chap. iv.

57   275_{16-17}, $14:269_{1-2}$, Even Father Zosima inserts phrases which
serve to create suspense.

58   275_{40}, $14:269_{25-26}$, "blinded by my conceit"—a mistranslation;
the text should read "blinded by my own sterling qualities"—
ironic, of course. Father Zosima keeps building up the contrast
between the very ordinary, shallow, not-too-bright young man
before his spiritual illumination and the depth of the same man
after that experience.

59   276_4, $14:269_{34}$, "all eagerness for revenge"—a feeble translation of *zapylal otomshcheniem,* "inflamed with vengefulness"
(biblical diction).

60   276_{12-13}, $14:269_{42}$, This event must have been the Decembrist
rebellion of 14 December 1825.

61   276_{14}, $14:269_{44}$, "Explanation" is here a formulaic expression:
it is the next-to-last stage in a scene that leads to a challenge to a
duel.

62   277_8, $14:270_{30}$, "a sharp dagger"—it is "a sharp needle" in the
original. Dostoevsky does not mind using fairly simple and trite

metaphors when describing a mental state at a key juncture. This
is the turning point in Zosima's life.

63   278_{4-5}, $14:271_{18-19}$,   There was always a great deal of tension
between officers and civilians, and to show fear before a civilian
would have been particularly disgraceful.

64   278_{37-42}, $14:271_{47}-272_6$,   Tolstoian technique of "making it
strange." The "normal" view of things is discredited by an
observer who takes an "estranged" moral view of the situation
and perceives the "normal" view as "monstrous" (*bezobrazno*,
translated by "grotesque"; cf. note 17 above).

65   $278_{45}-279_5$, $14:272_{8-13}$,   Father Zosima's present point of view is
projected back into the words he spoke when he was a young
man. They are, however, well motivated by his recollection, only
the night before, of his brother Markel's words.

66   279_{8-9}, $14:272_{17}$,   This may be read as a bit of internal commentary. The whole scene presents, in microcosm, the reader's
reaction to the message of *The Brothers Karamazov*.

67   280_{14-19}, $14:273_{14-19}$,   The notion of a world "made strange" is
now stated conceptually. Cf. notes 53 and 64 above.

68   280_{32-33}, $14:273_{31-32}$,   A smooth transition to the next episode,
which also creates some suspense.

CHAPTER II (D)

69   281_{36-37}, $14:274_{34}$,   "some strange secret in his soul"—Father
Zosima (or his mouthpiece, Aleksei Karamazov) is not above
using routine narrative retardation to create suspense. There is
no stylish simplicity or artlessness here. In fact, Zosima tells the
story as any moderately gifted amateur storyteller would, that is,
not very well.

70   282_{25}, $14:275_{15-16}$,   "we are all responsible to all for all"—cf. p.
268_{8-9}. In the original the same expression (*vinovat*, "guilty") is
used in both instances. Hence, this passage should read: "And
that every one of us has sinned against all men and in every way,
apart from our own sins." See note 21 above.

71   282_{28-29}, $14:275_{18-19}$,   Here the mysterious stranger, Zosima,
and Ðostoevsky tread on dangerous grounds theologically.
Any form of paradise on earth smacks of heresy and utopian
socialism.

72   282_{39-43}, $14:275_{28-31}$,   This image of man is essentially that of
the Grand Inquisitor in Book Five, chap. v. Cf. Linnér, p.
227.

73 282_{45}, $14:275_{33}$, "isolation"—Russ. *uedinenie,* derived from *edin,* "one." Here Dostoevsky expresses one of his own favorite ideas. The word is the leitmotif of this passage.

74 283_{5-6}, $14:275_{39}$, "self-destruction"—translates *samoubiistvo,* "suicide."

75 283_{17-20}, $14:276_{2-5}$, A difficult and somewhat obscure sentence. I suggest this translation: "Everywhere now human reason is beginning ironically to ignore that a person's true security lies not in his isolated individual effort, but in the common solidarity of people." This smacks very much of Nikolai Fiodorov's philosophy of the common cause. See Introduction I.4.a. Secular Sources.

76 283_{24-25}, $14:276_9$, Matt. 24:30.

77 283_{33}, $14:276_{16-17}$, "Besides, my vogue was somewhat over."— This aside shows Father Zosima as the man of the world he once was.

78 283_{46}, $14:276_{30}$, More suspense!

79 284_{18-19}, $14:276_{48}$, Echoes Zosima's words on p. 281_{45} above. In the Russian we read *stal na dorogu,* "I have started on my road," in both instances. These little nuances are important.

80 284_{25}, $14:277_8$, The story which follows is told in a somewhat awkward, clearly old-fashioned style.

81 284_{30}, $14:277_{11}$, "Away at the front"—the time is approximately 1812, the year of Napoleon's invasion of Russia.

82 285_1, $14:277_{30}$, "with devilish and criminal cunning"—these are Father Zosima's words, not the stranger's.

83 285_{8-9}, $14:277_{37-38}$, In the original, this sentence is stylized to reflect Zosima's language.

84 285_{19}, $14:277_{47-48}$, Landowners prior to the emancipation of 1861 acted as agents for the draft, each landowner being required to meet a quota. The draft was sometimes an expedient way to get rid of undesirables.

85 285_{35}, $14:278_{15}$, This whole episode foreshadows Dmitry's fate. See Introduction III.3.b. Mirroring and Doubling.

86 285_{36}, $14:278_{15-16}$, "And after that the punishment began."— Another surprise. Note the staccato rhythm of the mysterious stranger's narrative.

87 285_{43-46}, $14:278_{23-25}$, This attitude has a parallel in Dmitry Karamazov's insane jealousy.

88 286_{14}, $14:278_{40-41}$, "almost forgot the past"—translates Russ. *pochti zabyval,* where the imperfective aspect of the verb makes

it clear that the struggle never ceased. The perfective form *pochti zabyl,* which one would have expected in the context, would have meant "almost forgot."

89   286_{34-36}, $14:279_{10-12}$, "At last he began to be bitterly . . . haunted . . ."—This passage, as well as several other passages in this chapter, are not well written. Father Zosima and Aliosha are incapable of fathoming the depths of a murderer's soul. It would be out of character if they could.

90   286_{46-47}, $14:279_{21-22}$, In the original an expression suggesting that this thought stuck to his heart like a leech is used.

91   287_{21}, $14:279_{41}$, A nobleman would lose his privileges if convicted of a serious crime, one of these privileges being the right to own land.

92   287_{43}, $14:280_{13}$, "what my punishment has cost me"—translates *chego stoilo mne stradanie moio,* "what my suffering cost me," a shorthand notation for "what it cost me to accept my suffering." Such careless style is characteristic of Dostoevsky's narrators.

93   287_{45}, $14:280_{15}$, "great deed"—translates Russ. *podvig,* one of Dostoevsky's key words. Cf. Book Five, note 300. Often the "feat" contemplated is the confession of a particularly heinous crime, as in "Stavrogin's Confession," a chapter excluded from the novel *The Possessed.*

94   288_{13-14}, $14:280_{29}$, *The Children's Magazine—Detskoe chtenie,* lit. "Readings for Children." Several magazines of that title existed in Russia, although not at the time in question. See *PSS* 15:567.

95   288_{14-15}, $14:280_{30}$, "No one is wise from another man's woe."—*Chuzhaia beda ne daiot uma,* a rhymed proverb.

96   288_{26}, $14:280_{41}$, "What is right in this case?"—*Gde tut pravda?* Once more, the ambiguity of Russ. *pravda,* which means "truth" as well as "justice," poses a problem for the translator.

97   288_{26-27}, $14:280_{41-42}$, The mysterious stranger now develops arguments in favor of living a lie, which we have heard from the Grand Inquisitor earlier. But here, their wretched, self-serving nature is revealed nakedly.

98   288_{38-40}, $14:281_{4-6}$, The epigraph and central theme of the novel. See Introduction II.2.b. Arguments in Support of Christianity.

99   289_{1}, $14:281_{12}$, It now becomes clear that the root of the evil lies in the fact that the mysterious stranger does not believe in God.

100   289_{5}, $14:281_{14-15}$, The passage in Paul's epistle deals with those who, having heard the Gospel, refuse to live by it.

101 289_{10}, $14:281_{19}$, "heaven"—Russ. *rai* is translated by "paradise" and by "heaven" in this chapter. The murderer and Zosima have developed a special, private meaning for this word. Cf. p. 287_{38}.

102 289_{31-32}, $14:281_{40}$, In Russian the familiar singular *ty*, "thou," is used between family members and intimate friends only. The age difference between the two men is ample reason for their having kept to the polite *vy*, "you."

103 289_{41}, $14:282_{2-3}$, "I cast myself out from men as a monster."— Russ. *Kak izverga sebia izvergaiu*. Russ. *izverg*, "monster," originally meant "outcast," and the connection with the verb *izvergat'*, "to cast out," is still felt. This gives the sentence a pithiness which the translation lacks.

104 290_{19}, $14:282_{26}$, We thus get an inverted mirror image of Dmitry Karamazov's case: the evidence is meaningless, as the verdict is based on a preconceived notion of guilt or innocence.

105 291_{34}, $14:283_{36}$, Irony! The deceased is eulogized for all the wrong reasons.

106 291_{41-45}, $14:283_{43-47}$, Paradise through suffering has been the leitmotif of this story. Fittingly, the edifying clausule speaks of Mikhail's suffering, not of his crime. Note that his name is revealed only now. The conclusion, starting with "and five months later," is written in solemn rhythmic prose, much as the conclusion of a sermon.

Chapter iii

CHAPTER III (E)

107 292_{13-15}, $14:284_{12-15}$, A position which makes explicit why Father Zosima, a monk, is the positive hero of this novel. It suggests a resolute acceptance of Christian otherworldliness and the monastic ideal which goes along with it. See Introduction II.2. *The Brothers Karamazov* as a Theodicy.

108 292_{16-17}, $14:284_{16}$, Rev. 10:15.

109 292_{18}, $14:284_{17-18}$, "fair and undefiled"—*blagolepno i neiskazhenno*. Cf. note 17 above.

110 292_{20-21}, $14:284_{19-20}$, "to the tottering creeds of the world"— translates *pokolebavsheisia pravde mira*, lit. "to the wavering truth of the world," a hypallage for "to a world whose truth is wavering." Such rhetorical figures appear quite often in Father Zosima's exhortations.

111   292₂₁₋₂₂, 14:284₂₀, An echo of Matt. 2:2. W. Komarowitsch,
      Die Urgestalt der "Brüder Karamasoff" (Munich, 1928), p. 134,
      sees this in counterpoint with Father Ferapont's addressing the
      setting sun (Book Seven, chap. i, p. 315₂₁, where the sentence is
      mistranslated).

112   292₂₄₋₂₅, 14:284₂₂₋₂₃, "the people of God"—meaning "the
      simple people of Russia."

113   292₂₉₋₃₁, 14:284₂₇₋₂₉, The polemic with the Grand Inquisitor has
      begun in earnest, and human freedom is a key issue.

114   292₃₆, 14:284₃₄, *"isolation"*—Russ. *uedinenie,* the same word
      that was applied earlier to express the "solitude" of a monk (line
      17). Cf. note 73 above.

115   292₄₁ff., 14:284₃₈ff., Here Father Zosima's thoughts are
      Dostoevsky's own, often stated in *Diary of a Writer.*

116   293₉₋₁₀, 14:285₂₋₃, Again there is a direct parallel between
      Father Zosima's prophecy and the Grand Inquisitor's (Book
      Five, chap. v, p. 318). Father Zosima openly predicts a social
      revolution.

117   293₁₁₋₁₄, 14:285₄₋₈, "Champion of freedom" is a very loose
      translation of *bortsa za ideiu,* "champion of an idea." In the
      original we then read: "and betrayed his 'idea.' " Like other
      personages in the novel, Father Zosima is not above telling an
      occasional anecdote to make his point.

118   293₂₃, 14:285₁₄, "dying out"—translates *ugasaet,* a verb which
      refers to a flame.

119   293₂₈₋₂₉, 14:285₁₉₋₂₀, "They have succeeded . . ."—One of the
      many sententious statements made by Father Zosima, always
      expressing Dostoevsky's own ideas.

120   293₃₆₋₄₂, 14:285₂₇₋₃₂, *Uedinenie* and the verb *uedinit'sia* are used
      to express both the solitude of a monk and the isolation of
      modern man. This makes the argument even more poignant. The
      difference is that the monk is alone with God, while modern man
      is alone without God. Zosima's defense of monastic solitude
      would seem to come from Saint Isaac of Niniveh, who puts great
      stock in it. See Introduction I.4.b. Sacred Sources.

121   293₄₅₋₄₆, 14:285₃₅, "The salvation of Russia comes from the
      people."—See Introduction II.4.b. The People.

122   294₁, 14:285₃₆₋₃₇, Isolation from the values of modern civiliza-
      tion is meant.

123   294₇, 14:285₄₂, "for the peasant has God in his heart"—in the
      original we have a solemn *ibo sei narod—bogonosets,* "for this is

a godbearing people." The word *bogonosets,* lit. "godbearer," is formed by analogy from *khristonosets,* "christophoros," echoing the legend of Saint Christopher.

CHAPTER III (F)

124   294_{11-12}, $14:285_{46}$, "from above downwards"—from the educated classes, that is.

125   294_{13}, $14:285_{47}$, "Moneylenders and devourers of the commune"—Russ. *kulaki i miroedy.* A *kulak,* lit. "fist," is a peasant to whom other peasants are in debt and who makes them pay usurious interest, often in labor; a *miroed,* lit. "commune eater," is a *kulak* who takes over the land of a peasant commune *(mir).* The peasant communes were rapidly disintegrating after the emancipation of 1861, and private ownership of land was becoming the rule.

126   294_{14-17}, $14:285_{47}-286_3$, The Russian merchant class was a bulwark of native Russian ways.

127   294_{20}, $14:286_6$, "drunkenness"—one of the main concerns of Dostoevsky the publicist. Cf. *Diary of a Writer,* 1:100–107.

128   294_{25-27}, $14:286_{11-13}$, Father Zosima's answer to Ivan's treatment of the theme of suffering children. Father Zosima's words seem to echo Nikolai Nekrasov's poem "Children Crying" ("Plach detei"). See *Diary of a Writer* (1876), 1:416–20.

129   294_{28}, $14:286_{15}$, "filthy sin"—translates *smradnyi grekh.* Ivan had used the same adjective in the same context (Book Five, chap. v, p. 229_{14}). See note 46 above.

130   294_{33}, $14:286_{19}$, "but not with Christ, as before"—there are many such instances of shorthand notation throughout Aliosha's notes of Father Zosima's wisdom, certainly intentional on Dostoevsky's part.

131   294_{34-35}, $14:286_{20}$, "there is no crime . . ."—Father Zosima takes up Ivan's thesis "All things are lawful unto me" (Book Two, chap. vi, p. 60).

132   294_{39}, $14:286_{23-24}$, Slightly modified quotation of Gen. 49:7.

133   294_{44}, $14:286_{28}$, "their true and seemly dignity"—*dostoinstvo blagolepnoe i istinnoe.* Cf. note 17 above.

134   295_3, $14:286_{30}$, "servile"—translates *rabolepnyi,* a counterpoint to *blagolepnyi* in the preceding sentence.

135   295_3, $14:286_{30-31}$, Dostoevsky takes the position that serfage became institutionalized only under the Romanovs in the seventeenth century.

136 295_{12}, $14:286_{38}$, "serene goodness"—translates *blagolepnoi pravdy*. Perhaps: "godly righteousness." Cf. note 17 above.

137 295_{12-13}, $14:286_{39}$, "for the rich among them are for the most part corrupted already"—see note 125 above.

138 295_{15}, $14:286_{41-42}$, "for Russia is great in her humility"—a sententious statement of focal importance.

139 295_{16-20}, $14:286_{42-46}$, Father Zosima deliberately treats the problems of a modern world, such as class struggle, in spiritual terms. Here he makes it explicit why: he believes in an imminent spiritual revolution. See Introduction II.1.b. The Apocalyptic Allegory.

140 295_{35}, $14:287_{11}$, "bright and clean"—translates *chisten'kaia, radostnaia,* lit. "neat and happy," not a normal context for the adjective "happy."

141 296_{27-29}, $14:287_{43-45}$, Cf. p. 268_{1-2}.

142 296_{33-34}, $14:288_1$, Cf. *Diary of a Writer* (1880), 2:998, where Dostoevsky brings up the example of Saint Paul's relationship with his disciple and attendant Timothy.

143 296_{38-41}, $14:288_{7-10}$, Matt. 20:26.

144 297_{7-8}, $14:288_{21-22}$, Ps. 118:22.

145 297_{15-16}, $14:288_{29-30}$, "they will end by flooding the earth with blood"—Father Zosima—and Dostoevsky—consider this to be as much of a possibility as the coming of a religious utopia. The retraction of this gloomy prophecy which follows immediately is somewhat diffident.

146 297_{16-17}, $14:288_{30}$, Matt. 26:52.

147 297_{17-21}, $14:288_{30-34}$, This apocalyptic image may well be an echo of Byron's poem "Darkness" (1816). See *PSS* 15:568.

148 297_{22-23}, $14:288_{35-36}$, Matt. 24:22 has "the elect," not "the humble and meek," but Father Zosima's words are certainly in the spirit of the Gospel.

149 297_{24-30}, $14:288_{36-42}$, The awkwardness and understatement of this contrast with the inspired prophecies preceding it. This is the "real" serving as a backdrop for the "ideal."

CHAPTER III (G)

150 298_{16-20}, $14:289_{27-30}$, "Man, do not pride yourself . . ."—This is the pantheist, Franciscan aspect of Father Zosima's (and Dostoevsky's) teaching, which caused some raised eyebrows among Orthodox clerics.

151   298_{20-26}, $14:289_{30-36}$, Father Zosima's answer to Ivan's argument in Book Five, chap. iv.

152   298_{30-32}, $14:289_{40-42}$, "Loving humility is marvelously strong . . ."—One of Dostoevsky's favorite thoughts. It echoes Matt. 5:5.

153   298_{34}, $14:289_{43}$, "seemly"—*blagolepnyi* again. Cf. note 17 above.

154   298_{38-39}, $14:289_{48}$, The other side of the seed metaphor. Cf. p. 264_{18-20} and note 8 above.

155   298_{46}, $14:290_7$, See chap. ii(a), p. 268.

156   299_{1-5}, $14:290_{10-13}$, Another version of the leitmotif, according to which "every one of us has sinned against all men." See note 21 above.

157   299_5, $14:290_{12}$, "nobler"—in the original it is again *blagolepnee*. Cf. note 17 above.

158   299_{6-9}, $14:290_{13-16}$, Here Father Zosima (and with him Dostoevsky) certainly falls into pantheist heresy.

159   299_{21-23}, $14:290_{27-29}$, "you will end by sharing the pride of Satan"—this and what follows to the end of this chapter applies to Ivan Karamazov in particular, and especially to his "rebellion."

160   299_{36}, $14:290_{41}$, "Much on earth is hidden from us"—from here to the end of the chapter we have what is probably the master key to the philosophic interpretation, as well as to the structure, of *The Brothers Karamazov*.

161   299_{42-44}, $14:290_{45-47}$, Cf. notes 8 and 154 above. The biblical reference is the parable of the sower, Matt. 13:1–8.

162   300_1, $14:291_2$, Zosima means acedia, a mortal sin, when he speaks of indifference to life.

CHAPTER III (H)

163   300_4, $14:291_6$, Echoes Matt. 7:1–5. Dostoevsky expressed similar thoughts in *Diary of a Writer* (1873), 1:9–22.

164   300_{18-20}, $14:291_{21-24}$, "then another . . ."—foreshadows Dmitry Karamazov's fate.

165   300_{29-30}, $14:291_{32-33}$, *Zemlia*, "earth," is feminine in Russian. "Mother Earth" symbolism is very common in Russian folklore. This passage is only one of several in *The Brothers Karamazov* where Mother Earth appears with a religious connotation. Cf. Book Three, chap. iii, p. 96_{5-6}, and Book Seven, chap. iv, p.

340_{30-36}. See Introduction III.5.f. Mythical Symbolism. See also R. Pletniov, "Zemlia" [Earth], in *O Dostoevskom,* ed. A. L. Bem, 1 (Prague, 1929): 153–62.

166   300_{34-37}, $14:291_{37-40}$, Ironically, this echoes Smerdiakov's hypothesis of only two righteous men in the whole world (Book Three, chap. vii, p. 118_{41}). Father Zosima's vision of the trials of the faithful grants the enemies of the Faith every point, and then some—typical of Dostoevsky's debating style.

167   300_{36}, $14:291_{39}$, "tenderly"—translates *v umilenii.* Cf. note 12 above.

168   300_{38}, $14:291_{41}$, "grieve even unto death"—Matt. 26:38. The King James version has "sorrowful, even unto death."

169   300_{38-41}, $14:291_{41-44}$, A striking example of Father Zosima's rhetoric: triadic arrangement, repetition, antithesis, and rondo— all in one brief paragraph. The leitmotif is "rejoice."

170   300_{44}, $14:291_{46}$, "shun above all things that feeling"—directly relevant to Ivan Karamazov's "rebellion." Cf. Linnér, pp. 230–31.

171   301_{5-9}, $14:292_{4-7}$, A variation on John 1:5.

172   301_{19}, $14:292_{19}$, "serene"—*blagolepnyi* again. See note 17 above.

CHAPTER III (I)

173   301_{28-32}, $14:292_{27-31}$, Father Zosima's concept of hell is a key position, derived from Saint Isaac of Niniveh (the passage in question is quoted in *PSS* 15:570). Father Zosima's speculations appear more Neoplatonic than biblical, but so do the reflections of some Fathers of the Church.

174   301_{37}, $14:292_{37}$, "the parable of the rich man and Lazarus"— Luke 16:19–31.

175   301_{44}, $14:292_{43-44}$, Here Zosima goes beyond the biblical text, inserting his own allegory of the "living water," which is, however, well documented in other passages of the New Testament, e.g., John 4:10.

176   302_{8-9}, $14:293_{5-6}$, ". . . they would be glad of it"—a typically Dostoevskian paradox.

177   302_{25}, $14:293_{21-22}$, "I cannot express this clearly"—the speculation which Father Zosima concludes with these diffident words smacks of eighteenth-century "enlightened" pietism. From the viewpoint of the Orthodox church this is just another Protestant heresy. The unctuous yet awkward rhetoric of the

passage is very much in character, being reminiscent of Saint Tikhon of Zadonsk. See Introduction III.1.d. Aliosha as an Echo of Father Zosima, and Pletniov, "Serdtsem mudrye," pp. 88–89.

178   302_{29-33}, $14:293_{25-28}$, "but in my secret heart . . ."—a heretical position which echoes some analogous pronouncements of Saint Tikhon's. See ibid., p. 80.

179   302_{36-37}, $14:293_{31}$, "who have given themselves over to Satan"—translates *priobshchivshiesia satane,* where the verb *priobshchat'* is a religious term meaning "to administer (the sacraments)." So perhaps: "communion with Satan."

180   302_{38-39}, $14:293_{33-34}$, "For they have cursed themselves, cursing God and life."—A direct counterpoint to "The Grand Inquisitor." Ivan's hero, a projection of Ivan's own condition, is in this state.

181   302_{39-41}, $14:293_{34-36}$, This ghoulish image is taken from Saint Isaac of Niniveh. See *PSS* 15:570.

182   302_{42-47}, $14:293_{36-40}$, The concluding passage of the document is written in solemn rhythmic prose, with alliteration, assonance, and a rhythmic clausule.

183   303_{1-2}, $14:293_{42}$, "I repeat, it is incomplete and fragmentary."—This (and the whole passage) is significant as an internal commentary.

184   303_{19-23}, $14:294_{15-19}$, "But though suffering . . ."—This sentence, too, reads like rhythmic prose in the original. Three key words (*zemlia,* "earth," *tikho,* "quietly," and *radostno,* "joyously") appear twice—an effect not rendered by the translation. The concluding phrase is a cliché of the Orthodox saint's life. The physical details of Father Zosima's death seem to have been taken from the life of Zosima Verkhovsky. See Introduction I.6.c. Father Zosima and Other Monks.

185   303_{21-22}, $14:294_{17-18}$, Here *zemlia* should have been translated by "earth" rather than "ground" in view of the symbolic significance of this passage. Cf. note 165 above. The detail of a holy man expiring on his knees is reported about the Blessed Serafim of Sarov (1759–1833), among others.

186   303_{31-35}, $14:294_{26-32}$, "I will only add . . ."—the book ends in a very simple ploy to create suspense.

Book Seven

Chapter i

1 306_8, $14:295_9$, "designated"—translates Russ. *uchinennyi,* a religious term which is explained in parenthesis.

2 306_{10}, $14:295_{11}$, "sponge"—translates Russ. *guba,* another religious term whose secular equivalent ("a Greek sponge") is given in parenthesis.

3 306_{18}, $14:295_{18}$, These details of the preparation for burial, provided by K. P. Pobedonostsev (see Introduction I.1), create an air of authenticity. Dostoevsky's Russian readers were almost as unfamiliar with them as a Western reader might be.

4 307_2, $14:296_6$, The remains of a saint were traditionally believed to have the power to effect miraculous cures. This whole scene is reminiscent of some passages in the Gospel, e.g., Matt. 4:24.

5 307_{5-9}, $14:296_{10-14}$, The translator has split Dostoevsky's very long and convoluted sentence in two, thus destroying its flavor. Its syntax reflects Father Paisy's somewhat cumbersome but well-schooled thinking: ". . . Father Paisy considered a blatant temptation, foreseen by him a long time before, yet in fact exceeding his expectations."

6 307_{27-30}, $14:296_{31-34}$, The word "everywhere" (or its synonyms) are repeated so often in this passage that one begins to suspect something uncanny: the little monk from Obdorsk is turning into a petty demon.

7 308_{27-40}, $14:297_{28-41}$, "something took place . . ."—see Introduction III.3.e. Expository Novel. Note the somewhat naive relish with which the narrator (here obviously the "local citizen") builds suspense here.

8 $308_{45}-309_3$, $14:297_{47}-298_3$, The narrator is obviously beating about the bush: an ambiguous maneuver, as it may project either

262

sincere reluctance to report an embarrassing truth, or gloating at reporting a sensational event.

9 309_{17-19}, $14:298_{17-20}$, The incorruptibility of a holy man's remains was traditionally considered to be a sign of his true sainthood and a step toward eventual canonization. Dostoevsky was aware of at least two instances where a scandal similar to the one related here had happened. One of them is related by Parfeny. See Introduction I.4.b. Sacred Sources, and *PSS* 15:571.

10 309_{34}, $14:298_{37}$, "blessed"—translates *blagolepnyi*. Cf. Book Six, note 17.

11 309_{35-36}, $14:298_{37-39}$, "as a promise . . . of still greater glory from their tombs"—Miracles, especially miraculous cures, effected by the remains of a monk could lead to his canonization and increase the fame—and the revenues—of his monastery.

12 310_5, $14:299_7$, "a sweet fragrance"—another cliché of Orthodox hagiology.

13 310_9, $14:299_{11}$, Here the narrator's presence becomes explicit—and once again we see him wholly unaware of the deeper meaning of a key event in his narrative. We are dealing here, of course, with a variation, and eventual solution, of the theme of the second temptation of Christ, as developed in "The Grand Inquisitor" (Book Five, chap. v). See Introduction II.2. Theodicy.

14 310_{34-35}, $14:299_{38-39}$, "the delight which gleamed unmistakably in their malignant eyes"—one of the psychological oxymora so characteristic of Dostoevsky.

15 310_{41-42}, $14:299_{45-46}$, "peasantry"—translates *prostogo narodu,* "simple people." The implication is that the "simple people" have more tact, compassion, and good sense than the educated.

16 311_3, $14:300_{4-5}$, Counterpoint: the firm and righteous voice of Father Paisy is contrasted to the ugly dissonance of the unholy hubbub around him.

17 311_{19-26}, $14:300_{21-27}$, This whole passage is laced with ecclesiastic jargon difficult to duplicate in English.

18 311_{27-41}, $14:300_{28-41}$, These details, again taken from Parfeny's *Pilgrimage* (see Introduction I.4.b. Sacred Sources), accurately reflect the world of the Russian monastery. A deep spirituality would often go hand in hand with what to many modern readers must appear to be crude superstition.

19 312_3, $14:300_{48}$, "and they have no bells even"—another detail

reported by Parfeny, about some churches in Orthodox lands under Turkish rule.

20   312_{21-22}, $14:301_{17-18}$,   Cf. Book Six, chap. ii(i), pp. 301–2.

21   312_{23-24}, $14:301_{20}$,   "ate cherry jam with his tea"—this little detail links Father Zosima with Aliosha; see Book Five, chap. iii, p. 210.

22   312_{24}, $14:301_{20}$,   "ladies used to send it to him"—cf. Book Three, chap. viii, p. 123_{29}.

23   312_{28}, $14:301_{24-25}$,   Cf. Book One, chap. v, p. 22_{33-34}, and Book Two, chap. viii, p. 78_{28-30}.

24   312_{36-39}, $14:301_{32-34}$,   Note the skillful transition from the general commotion to the intervention of Father Ferapont, with the monk from Obdorsk acting as a connecting link.

25   312_{41}, $14:301_{37}$,   "He was seldom even seen at church"—a loaded detail, to be kept in mind.

26   312_{42}, $14:301_{38}$,   "on the ground of his craziness"—translates *iakoby iurodivomu,* better "on the ground of his being a God's fool." Cf. Book One, note 94. The Russian expression shows respect for Father Ferapont, but beginning to turn to irony.

27   313_{14}, $14:302_{6-7}$,   "reading the Gospel over the coffin"—again, the counterpoint to the general hubbub.

28   313_{21-22}, $14:302_{14}$,   "The door was flung open and Father Ferapont appeared in the doorway."—Note the dramatic staging of the whole scene. Cf. Introduction III. Narrative Technique.

29   313_{28-29}, $14:302_{22-23}$,   "and under his right arm . . ."—the diabolic comedy featuring the little monk from Obdorsk continues.

30   313_{33}, $14:302_{27-28}$,   Throughout this scene, vocables clearly perceived as biblical or ecclesiastic usage remind the reader of the setting of this scene, adding to its grotesquery. Thus, "aloft" translates Russ. *gore,* a Slavonicism used only in ecclesiastic language, or as a poetic archaism. Perhaps "heavenward" would be a more appropriate translation.

31   313_{34}, $14:302_{29}$,   "Casting out I cast out!"—A formulaic expression used in casting out evil spirits. Deep irony: if there is anybody in need of exorcism it is Father Ferapont himself.

32   313_{44-45}, $14:302_{40}$,   Ascetics sometimes wore heavy chains under their clothes as a form of penance. Cf. Book Four, chap. i, p. 152_{41-42}.

33   314_{4-5}, $14:302_{46-47}$,   Father Ferapont says this in Church

Slavonic. The translation "crazily" for *iurodstvuia* is inaccurate. Perhaps: "putting on his God's fool's act." See note 26 above.

34   314_{9-10}, $14:303_3$, "perhaps you are serving him yourself"—the point of the whole scene.

35   314_{16}, $14:303_9$, "did not believe in devils"—rather, Father Zosima had doubted the existence of a material hell. See Book Six, chap. ii(i).

36   314_{18}, $14:303_{11}$, "has begun to stink"—translates *provonial,* a coarse vulgarism which clashes with the pompous Slavonic Father Ferapont had used a moment earlier. In a letter to N.A. Liubimov (16 September 1879), Dostoevsky urged his editor not to substitute a more genteel *propakh* "because it is Father Ferapont who says it, and he cannot say anything else, and even if he could say *propakh,* he won't say it, but will say *provonial*" (*Pis'ma* 4:114).

37   314_{20-29}, $14:303_{13-22}$, The flow of the narrative is interrupted by one of the many anecdotes found in the novel. See Introduction III.3.a. Motifs. The incident confirms Father Zosima's realism. Cf. Linnér, p. 182.

38   314_{31-32}, $14:303_{24-25}$, The incident will become a decisive "sign" in the life of Aliosha Karamazov, for one.

39   314_{35-37}, $14:303_{28-29}$, "Fanatic" translates *izuver,* "zealot," a noun derived from *vera,* "faith," and thus limited to the religious sphere. The narrator now clearly shows that he is siding with Father Paisy against Father Ferapont.

40   314_{42-43}, $14:303_{35-36}$, "like some frivolous youth"—this may be foreshadowing, aimed at Aliosha.

41   314_{45}–315_3, $14:303_{38-42}$, The psychological background of Father Ferapont's long and lonely stand is now revealed. In the broad context of the novel it is significant that Father Ferapont, who is "of the people" (as is the little monk from Obdorsk), is a negative character. See Introduction II.4.a. The Russian Nobleman and b. The People.

42   315_{21}, $14:304_{12}$, "Christ has conquered the setting sun!"—A mistranslation. The correct translation is "Christ has conquered as the sun goes down!" Here *zakhodiashchu solntsu* is a Slavonic dative absolute, lit. "(with) the sun going down." Cf. Durylin, p. 195.

43   316_{10}, $14:305_4$, The full impact of the "odor of corruption" now becomes clear. Aliosha is caught in the web of the second

temptation of Christ (Matt. 4:5-7), as he allows his faith to depend on a miracle.

Chapter ii

44 316_{37-38}, $14:305_{33}$, "I could of course confidently answer for Aliosha no, he is not with those of little faith."—A significant passage so far as Dostoevsky's narrator is concerned. It shows a strong sense of solidarity, almost identification, with Aliosha, and specifically with Aliosha the believer.

45 317_5, $14:305_{44-45}$, "young hero"—in Russian simply *iunosha,* "youth." The word will occur eight times before the end of this paragraph; together with a couple of other derivatives of the root *iun-,* "young," this creates the effect of a prose poem on youth and how youth ought to be unreasonable.

46 $317_{5ff.}$, $14:305_{45ff.}$, The word "heart," a label of Aliosha's, shows up repeatedly in this passage.

47 317_{11}, $14:306_9$, "of little value"—translates *deshovyi,* "cheap," definitely not the word one might expect in the context. The translator has made an "improvement" on Dostoevsky's text.

48 317_{21}, $14:306_{19}$, This passage sounds most "unliterary" in the original. It smacks of oral discourse, hurried because an opponent is getting ready to make his objections, and therefore circuitous and clumsy. The narrator seems to be taking the defense of his young hero all too seriously, but he is apparently not a very skillful advocate. The whole thing is a tease on Dostoevsky's part. Aliosha does not need the narrator's clumsy excuses, but will have triumphantly regained his faith before this Book is over.

49 317_{31-32}, $14:306_{32}$, "'everyone and everything'"—translates *'vsem i vsia',* hearkening back to Father Zosima's exhortations in Book Six, where this formulaic expression occurs repeatedly.

50 317_{42}, $14:306_{44}$, It seems a long time since we last saw either Dmitry or Iliusha, and this insertion, while hinting at a sin of omission on Aliosha's part, also introduces a bit of suspense: what is Dmitry doing in the meantime?

51 317_{42-45}, $14:306_{44-47}$, ". . . 'the higher justice' . . ."—brings up another aspect of Dostoevsky's theodicy: divine justice has been challenged and will have to be vindicated.

52 318_{24}, $14:307_{25}$, "(so Aliosha thought it)"—laying bare the

device: the narrator reminds his reader that we are dealing with *erlebte Rede.* See Introduction III.1.a. The Narrator.

53   318_{25}, $14:307_{25-26}$, "submitting to the blind, dumb, pitiless laws of nature"—a motif whose most famous version in Dostoevsky is the interpretation of Holbein's "Deposition of Christ" in *The Idiot,* Part Three, chap. vi. The context there is the same as here: if Nature would show no mercy even to *Him,* what hope is there for ordinary mortals?

54   318_{30-31}, $14:307_{31-32}$, The narrator rarely appeals to the reader in person. Hence, he hopes that this urgent apostrophe will carry some weight. Meanwhile Dostoevsky uses the confidence which the reader must have acquired in the narrator's homespun common sense to advance one of his own pet ideas, the primacy of the human heart over human reason.

55   318_{43-45}, $14:307_{39-46}$, The connection between Ivan's rebellion and Aliosha's own version of the same is made explicit.

56   319_{12}, $14:308_{15}$, "foolery"—translates Russ. *blagogluposti;* perhaps: "holy nonsense" or "holy foolery." Cf. Book Two, note 177.

57   319_{24}, $14:308_{26}$, "from the angels"—even at this low point, Aliosha's label appears. See Introduction II.1.a. Allegoric Figures.

58   319_{26-27}, $14:308_{28}$, "I always took you for an educated man . . ."—In Rakitin's private language—which is that of the "progressive" Russian intelligentsia—"educated" means "embracing a progressive world view based entirely on science."

59   319_{30-31}, $14:308_{31}$, "has begun to stink"—translates *provonial* (see note 36 above). Rakitin is quoting Father Ferapont.

60   319_{31-32}, $14:308_{32-33}$, "that he was going to work miracles" —translates *chudesa otmachivat' nachniot,* which is definitely slang. Perhaps: "that he was going to start pulling off all kinds of miracles."

61   319_{36-37}, $14:308_{37-38}$, "no schoolboy of thirteen . . ."—an allusion to Kolia Krasotkin, who has been mentioned briefly in the episode of Aliosha's encounter with the schoolboys (Book Four, chap. iii, p. 162) and who is to play a major role in Book Ten. We shall learn that Kolia has been a disciple of Rakitin's. Another example of the tightness of Dostoevsky's novelistic texture. Cf. Introduction III.3.a. Motifs.

62   319_{36-38}, $14:308_{37-39}$, The word "rebelling" (Russ. *vzbuntovalsia*) and the repeated mention of the devil (translated by

"damn it" and then left out in the English text) establishes a connection with Ivan and his rebellion in Book Five, chap. iv.

63   319₃₈₋₃₉, 14:308₃₉₋₄₀,   Rakitin uses the common anticlerical line of charging that religion is nothing but a bureaucracy. But yet he unwittingly puts Aliosha's thinking back on the right track.

64   319₄₅₋₄₆, 14:308₄₄₋₄₅,   Aliosha quotes Ivan (Book Five, chap. iv, p. 226)—and like Ivan he *is* rebelling.

65   320₂₇₋₂₈, 14:309₂₂₋₂₃,   "suddenly the image of his brother Dmitry rose"—cf. note 50 above. It is by the insertion of such little details that Dostoevsky keeps the novel together.

66   320₃₁₋₃₂, 14:309₂₇,   The primacy of the heart over the mind! Cf. note 54 above.

67   320₃₄₋₃₅, 14:309₂₉₋₃₀,   Here Rakitin voices his spite by mixing pompous ecclesiastic diction with seminary jargon: "declared" translates *izrek,* a Slavonicism, while the conclusion of the sentence might be rendered by "pedestrian liberal windbag."

68   320₃₇₋₃₈, 14:309₃₂₋₃₃,   Here Dostoevsky uses an aside, a form of dramatic license. See Introduction III. Narrative Technique.

69   320₄₃₋₄₄, 14:309₃₉,   Ostensibly the joke is on the scatterbrained Mme. Khokhlakov. But it makes Rakitin look even worse: it shows the baseness and coarseness of his nature.

70   321₃, 14:309₄₄,   "Dawned" misses a nuance, as it translates *osiiavshei,* "illuminated," which, considering the nature of the "idea," is of course sarcastic.

71   321₁₂, 14:310₆,   One of Dostoevsky's patented surprises, but this development is not unprepared for. Cf. Book Two, chap. vii, p. 70₃₂₋₃₅.

72   321₂₇, 14:310₂₂,   "of which more will be said later"—the narrator arbitrarily withholds information to create suspense. The reader also relishes the narrator's rather innocent pleasure of setting up the obnoxious Rakitin for a well-deserved comeuppance.

Chapter iii

73   322₁₈₋₂₃, 14:311₁₄₋₁₉,   Note the accumulation of adjectives in the description of the old and the new Grushen'ka. It is typical of Dostoevsky's style. See Introduction II.6.d. Psychological Wisdom.

74   322_{33}, $14:311_{30}$, " 'speculation' "—translates Russ. *'gesheft'* (from Yiddish), "business deal" (esp. a shady or irregular one). Perhaps "wheeling and dealing."

75   322_{35}, $14:311_{32}$, "a Jew"—translates Russ. *zhidovka,* "Jewess," but the context suggests that the word is used with no ethnic connotation. Perhaps: "any usurer," or "a regular Shylock."

76   322_{44-45}, $14:311_{41}$, These lines feature three Russian idioms. The first means literally "to hold someone with spiked gloves," the second "to keep someone's body dirty" (cf. Eng. "to keep her barefoot and pregnant"), and only the third is translatable ("on Lenten fare"). One of the instances where the narrator displays an amateur writer's fondness for a catchy phrase.

77   323_{32}, $14:312_7$, "profligate"—translates *slastoliubets,* lit. "lover of sweetness." Cf. Book Two, note 187. Perhaps "voluptuary" or "lecher."

78   324_{28-31}, $14:313_{23-26}$, See Matlaw, *"The Brothers Karamazov,"* p. 29, for comments on the candle symbolism here. The repetition of the word "candle" draws the reader's attention to this symbol. Dostoevsky stages his scenes, and the candles are an important symbolic ingredient of this scene: the champagne party celebrating Aliosha's fall turns into a moment of moral rebirth for Grushen'ka. The symbol is also a link with the following scene, "Cana of Galilee."

79   325_{38-43}, $14:314_{27-31}$, A significant detail of social stylization. Grushen'ka and Rakitin are separated by a gulf from the genteel life of the Westernized ruling class. Balls are for the gentry. But the merchant class is beginning to catch up, as Grushen'ka's repartee suggests.

80   325_{44}, $14:314_{32}$, "a prince"—Grushen'ka uses some expressions that mirror the atmosphere of the Russian folk tale. The "prince" is the prince of the fairy tale. There are several more expressions in this passage that strike this tone. The prosaic "I never thought" translates a poetic *ne zhdala ne gadala,* lit. "I expected not, I guessed not," with the formulaic tautology (rhymed, in this case) so characteristic of Russian folk poetry.

81   326_4, $14:314_{37}$, "my bright young moon"—another expression from the sphere of Russian folk poetry. A rare and welcome guest is likened to the new moon.

82   326_{22}, $14:315_6$, "simple and good-natured"—translates *prosto,*

prostodushno, "simple, simplehearted." Dostoevsky is never afraid of such repetition—and here it enhances the impression that Grushen'ka is "of the people." Cf. note 80 above.

83   326_{23}, $14:315_7$, An example of Dostoevsky's centrifugal psychology. We keep discovering new traits of Grushen'ka's character. See Introduction II.6.a. Dostoevsky's Psychology.

84   326_{42}, $14:315_{25}$, "stinks"—translates *propakh,* which is not as coarse as *provonial* (see notes 36 and 59 above), but even more insulting in its feigned "propriety." Probably: "smells." These little nuances are important.

85   327_{12}, $14:315_{42}$, "Yet in spite"—Dostoevsky would not be Dostoevsky if the seemingly categoric statement in the preceding sentence were not immediately put in question, if not reversed.

86   327_{14}, $14:315_{45}$, "This woman"—"woman" is the leitmotif of this passage. Aliosha has discovered woman.

87   327_{31-32}, $14:316_{14-15}$, "I long for some dissipation"—Translates *deboshirovat' khochetsia,* which is very colloquial. Perhaps: "I feel like having a fling."

88   327_{40}, $14:316_{23}$, "My officer is coming"—one of the many complete surprises in the plot of the novel.

89   328_{15-16}, $14:316_{42-44}$, "a little cruel line showed in her smile"—and this after "dreamily." Dostoevskian psychology! See Introduction II.6.b. Psychological Motivation.

90   329_{12}, $14:317_{35}$, "to the gates of paradise"—inadvertently Rakitin introduces the leitmotif of the following chapter: as so often, a central theme enters through a back door, as it were.

91   329_{22-23}, $14:317_{47-48}$, "and ready to eat sausage"—translates *kolbasu sobiralsia zhrat',* where *zhrat'* is a coarse vulgarism; perhaps: "getting ready to stuff his face with sausage." Rakitin's sarcastic bathos does strike home, but not the way he meant it. The point is that Aliosha's rebellion suddenly looks very childish.

92   330_{15-16}, $14:318_{40}$, There is no mention of a "spiritual crisis" in the original, but the translator's psychological jargon does render what Dostoevsky's narrator says in an awkwardly powerful, very "private" phrase.

93   330_{23}, $14:319_1$, "a story"—Grushen'ka calls her story *basnia,* "fable." She may not, however, be aware of the literary meaning of the word and uses it in its vernacular meaning—so "story" is perhaps correct. Grushen'ka story is a folktale which Dostoevsky had written down himself, having heard it from a

peasant woman (see letter to N. A. Liubimov of 16 September 1879, *Pis'ma* 4:114). Dostoevsky was unaware that some variants of the story had been printed. See *PSS* 15:572.

94 330_{26}, $14:319_3$, "peasant woman"—translates *baba,* here simply "woman."

95 330_{26-27}, $14:319_{3-4}$, "and a very wicked woman she was"—the original has *zliushchaia-prezliushchaia,* with the emphatic repetition characteristic of the Russian folk tale.

96 330_{28}, $14:319_5$, "the lake of fire"—cf. Book Five, chap. v, p. 228_6. A preoccupation with hell ("hellfire in the material sense," as Father Zosima calls it) emerges as a recurrent motif in *The Brothers Karamazov.* Cf. Book One, chap. iv, p. 18; Book Three, chap. vii, p. 116; Book Six, chap. ii(i); Book Eight, chap. vi, p. 389. All these passages together create a notion of the reality of hell as a condition willed by man himself.

97 331_3, $14:319_{25}$, "I am bad, I'm a wicked woman"—translates *zlaia ia, zliushchaia-prezliushchaia,* lit. "wicked, very wicked, most wicked." This gradation, again very much in the style of the Russian folk tale, cannot be duplicated in translation.

98 331_{14}, $14:319_{38-39}$, "fools are made for wise men's profit"— Rakitin's words of wisdom are of his own coinage. In fact, the seminarian shows even here, for Rakitin uses the barbarism *profit* instead of a Russian *prok, pribyl',* or such. The translation misses an important nuance; "wise men's" translates *umnomu cheloveku,* "clever men's," where "clever man" puts Rakitin in the company of Smerdiakov and Fiodor Pavlovich. Cf. Book Three, chap. viii, p. 121_{43} and note 172; Book Five, chap. v, p. 242_{10-11}, and note 311; Book Five, chap. vii, p. 259_{5-6}, and note 401.

99 331_{19}, $14:319_{44}$, The twenty-five rouble bill will come back to haunt Rakitin. See Book Twelve, chap. ii, p. 634.

100 331_{33-34}, $14:320_{9-10}$, In the original Grushen'ka tells Rakitin not to address her in the familiar second person singular.

101 331_{37}, $14:320_{13}$, "wretch"—translates Russ. *tvar',* "creature," which has a strong pejorative meaning if applied to a human being. The word has clearly become a label of Grushen'ka's— and now she uses it herself! Cf. Book Two, note 158.

102 332_2, $14:320_{24}$, "coming to Agrafena Aleksandrovna with any evil purpose"—Russ. *za khudym etim delom priiti,* lit. "come to her for this bad thing," is a rather crude euphemism which shows

Grushen'ka's lower-middle-class background. A lady could not have possibly used this expression. Perhaps: "obtaining any illicit favors from Agrafena Aleksandrovna."

103   332_{22}, $14:320_{42}$, "shaking"—translates Russ. *triasus'-triasus'*, a reduplication characteristic of colloquial and folk speech.

104   332_{24}, $14:320_{43-44}$, "saving money"—translates *kapital kopit'*, "saving capital," as Grushen'ka's folk etymology creates a paronymy here. The use of *kapital* in the meaning "money" is substandard.

105   332_{33}, $14:321_4$, "dog"—translates *sobachonka,* diminutive of *sobaka,* "dog." Perhaps: "doggie."

106   332_{46}, $14:321_{18}$, " 'tragic' "—translates *zhalkoe,* which means "tragic," but only as applied to a tearjerker.

107   333_{10-11}, $14:321_{29-30}$,   In a literal translation: "What happened is that they loaded you with your elder yesterday, and now you've fired off your elder at me." The metaphor sounds just as awkward in Russian as it does in English. Rakitin has no sense of style and consistently abuses the Russian language, for which he has no respect. A significant trait.

108   333_{11}, $14:321_{30}$, "man of God"—really "little man of God." See Introduction I.4.b. Sacred Sources, and note 51. Note the ambiguity: Rakitin wants to hurt Aliosha by likening him to the well-known saint, yet he repeats the very words which Dmitry had spoken with love and reverence (see Book Three, chap. ix, p. 141_{16}, and note 235).

109   333_{33}, $14:323_3$, "such a tirade"—this is internal commentary: Aliosha's words, while heartfelt, are rhetorical and not really well-chosen. They are, rather, what one might expect from an enthusiastic twenty-year-old: overstated, naive, incoherent.

110   333_{44}, $14:322_{14}$, "Joy" and "happiness" are beginning to emerge as the leitmotifs of this Book.

111   334_6, $14:322_{23}$, "Abject" sounds too bookish for Grushen'ka. Russ. *podlyi* initially meant "lowborn" (still so used by Smerdiakov; see Book Five, note 43), then began to be used in a moral sense. Perhaps: "low-down."

112   334_{33-34}, $14:323_{2-3}$, "I'll tear off my finery . . ."— Grushen'ka's hysterical words echo the Lives of various saints and martyrs who had started their lives as sinners and harlots. See *PSS* 15:572.

113   334_{40-41}, $14:323_8$, "I'll snap my fingers in his face"—in the original lit. "I'll show him a fig," a coarse expression.

114   335_{17}, $14:323_{32}$, "not only with a shameful love"—in the original lit. "not only for my shame," i.e., for sexual gratification. Grushen'ka vacillates between sexual levity and outright rejection of erotic love as shameful. This reflects the attitude of the Russian people, as against that of the Westernized upper class, in which romantic love prevailed.

115   335_{19-21}, $14:323_{35-36}$, The onion of Grushen'ka's story has become a symbol—a technique used often throughout the novel (cf. for example Katerina Ivanovna's bow; see Book Three, note 96).

116   335_{28}, $14:323_{43}$, "with three horses"—translates *na troike*. The *troika* is somewhat of a symbol of a Russian and Russia on their way to destiny (cf. Book Twelve, chap. ix, "The Galloping Troika"). This symbolism originates with the famous *troika* passage in Gogol's *Dead Souls* (at the conclusion of chap. xii).

117   336_{9-10}, $14:324_{22-23}$, Grushen'ka's sudden tenderness for Dmitry is a foreshadowing. See Book Eight, chap. i, p. 342_{5-7}, chap. v, p. 374_{6-7}, chap. viii, p. 414_{23}.

118   336_{29}, $14:324_{40}$, "puny little beggar of a Pole"—see Introduction II.4.g. Minor Political Points.

119   336_{29-31}, $14:324_{40-42}$, "He's heard now that Grushen'ka's saved a little money"—bathos: Grushen'ka's high-strung romantic reaction to her "officer's" return is countered by a bit of prose.

120   336_{34-36}, $14:324_{44-45}$, "The Magdalene" translates *Bludnitsu*, "the harlot," but it is a good translation, since Rakitin is clearly alluding to Luke 8:1–2 and Mark 16:9.

121   336_{46}–337_2, $14:325_9$, In the original, Rakitin invokes the devil twice. His frequent use of the word *chort*, "devil," aligns him with Ivan Karamazov. The phrase "there's your road" prepares for a key image in the next chapter (p. 338_{14-15}).

Chapter iv

122   337_{27}, $14:325_{32-33}$, "Joy" is the leitmotif of this chapter, prepared for in the preceding chapter.

123   337_{34-38}, $14:325_{39-42}$, "Fragments of thought . . ."—cosmic imagery signals the beginning of Aliosha's illumination. "A sense of the wholeness of things" is a paraphrase (correct as such) rather than a translation of the original, which reads: "But instead something whole, firm, and comforting was reigning in his soul." The "whole" *(tseloe)* is, of course, the key concept here.

124   338₃, 14:326₃,   One of two famous instances in Dostoevsky where
a passage from the New Testament is used much as a symphonic
composer would use a familiar theme in a new symphony. The
other is, of course, the reading of John 11:1-45 in *Crime and
Punishment*. The text here is John 2:1-10. The symbolism here is
derived from "the marriage supper of the Lamb" (Rev. 19:9).
Nuptial symbolism was widespread in eighteenth-century pietism
and is prominent in Tikhon of Zadonsk. See Pletniov, p. 83.
Note that throughout the whole scene Aliosha's stream of
consciousness is accompanied by the "soft, solemn, distinct
reading of the Gospel" (p. 340₆₋₇).

125   338₉, 14:326₈,   "tragic"—cf. chap. iii, p. 332₄₆, and note 106.

126   338₁₁₋₁₅, 14:326₁₁₋₁₃,   Aliosha is now beginning to dream.
"Rakitin has gone off to the back alley" is a metaphor (cf. Book
Three, chap. iv, p. 97₃₅₋₃₆) which is promptly "realized" by
dream logic. Rakitin had shown Aliosha "the road"—and this
metaphor, too, is now "realized."

127   338₂₁₋₂₄, 14:326₁₈₋₂₁,   The word *radost'*, "joy," appears three
times here. It is the leitmotif of this scene, of this Book, and
perhaps of the whole novel. *Radost'* is variously translated by
"gladness," "happiness," "joy," etc. This destroys some of the
effect.

128   338₂₄, 14:326₂₂,   The allusion is to Dmitry's recital of Schiller's
"Ode to Joy," Book Three, chap. iii, p. 96. But it is also yet
another subconscious reminder. Cf. chap. ii, p. 317, and note 50.

129   338₃₄₋₃₅, 14:326₂₈₋₃₀,   "the people living about the Lake of
Gennesaret . . ."—this particular detail was probably taken
from Ernest Renan's *Vie de Jésus* (1863). See *PSS* 15:572.

130   338₃₇, 14:326₃₂₋₃₃,   "His great terrible sacrifice"—translates
velikogo strashnogo podviga, "His great terrible feat."

131   339₃₀₋₃₉, 14:327₁₈₋₂₆,   "We are rejoicing . . ."—the lyrical
composition of this passage is motivated by the fact that it
mirrors a dream. The biblical passage, the recent experience with
Grushen'ka, the memory of Father Zosima, the leitmotifs of joy
and resurrection (with the Sun of Jesus its ultimate symbol), are
all fused into a piece of rhythmic lyrical prose.

132   340₅, 14:327₃₅,   Note that this mystic scene is put into a realistic
frame.

133   340₃₅₋₃₆, 14:328₁₄₋₁₅,   "Water the earth with the tears of your
joy"—echoes Book Six, chap. ii(h), p. 300₂₉₋₃₀. The image will be

repeated in Book Eight, chap. vi, p. 386_{39-40}. See Introduction III.5.f. Mythical Symbolism.

134 340_{38-39}, $14:328_{17}$, The image of the "abyss of space" elicits, in the Russian reader, Lomonosov's famous ode "Nocturnal Reflection on the Majesty of God," and was probably taken from it.

135 340_{41-42}, $14:328_{20}$, "'in contact with other worlds'"—echoes Book Six, chap. ii(g), p. 299_{45}.

136 340_{43-44}, $14:328_{21-22}$, Once again, an echo of Book Six, chap. ii(a), p. 268_{8-9} (see note 21). A Russian reader will recognize the phrase *za vsio i za vsia,* "for all and for everything," on account of its biblical ring.

137 340_{46}–341_1, $14:328_{25-26}$, "that vault of heaven had entered into his soul"—this is an experience of which mystics of all nations and religions have spoken. The "inner heaven" is virtually a cliché of romantic poetry.

138 341_9, $14:328_{33-34}$, Cf. Book Six, chap. i, p. 264_{22-23}.

Book Eight

Chapter i

1 342_4, $14:328_{37}$, Dostoevsky's chapter titles are both provocative and structurally active. "Kuzma Samsonov" is a link to chapter iii of the preceding Book, and since Samsonov is Dmitry's rival and Book Eight is entitled "Mitia," it promises a conflict.

2 342_{5-6}, $14:328_{38-39}$, "flying away to a new life"—note Dostoevsky's skill at creating transitions: here he repeats Grushen'ka's words from Book Seven, chap. iii, pp. 335_{40} and 336_{10-12}.

3 342_{12-13}, $14:328_{44}-329_2$, Dostoevsky is covering up some all-too-patent seams of his plot. Aliosha's meeting with Ivan in Book Five was contrived, first, by Aliosha's being told by Smerdiakov that Ivan and Dmitry were to meet at the local inn (Book Five, chap. ii, p. 209) and, second, by Dmitry's not showing up.

4 342_{24}, $14:329_{13}$, "an hour"—translates *chasochek*, double diminutive of *chas*, "hour;" earlier (line 7) it was *chasok*, the simple diminutive. Perhaps: "a short hour" and "the shortest (little) hour."

5 342_{32-33}, $14:329_{21}$, "that she was making up her mind to something, and unable to determine upon it"—translates a pregnant *na chto-to reshaetsia i vsio reshit'sia ne mozhet*, where the imperfective present *reshaetsia* describes her indecision and the negation of the perfective *(reshit'sia ne mozhet)* confirms this notion. The power of the Russian phrase is enhanced by the circumstance that the word for "indecision," *nereshitel'nost'*, is derived from the same verb, *reshit'*, "to decide."

6 343_4, $14:329_{30}$, "voluptuary"—translates *slastoliubets*, the word that was applied to Samsonov earlier (Book Seven, chap. iii, p. 323_{32}).

7 343_{4-5}, $14:329_{31}$, The three thousand roubles are first brought

up in Book Three, chap. v, p. 109. Cf. Book Three, note 113, and Introduction III.3.a. Motifs.

8   343_{15-16}, $14:329_{41}$, "from her seducer"—translates *ot etogo byvshego eio obol'stitelia,* lit. "from that former seducer of hers," a significant nuance: the narrator discusses the peripeties of Grushen'ka's love life with a certain condescension.

9   343_{27}, $14:330_5$, "indefinite, high-flown, and full of sentimentality"—the original is even more ironic, perhaps "very nebulous, very high-flown, and full of nothing but sentimentality": another example of Dostoevsky's technique of predisposing his reader for or against a character even before his or her actual appearance.

10 343_{31-32}, $14:330_{10}$, "this missive from Siberia"—the commentators of *PSS* see here an echo (in parody, of course) of Pushkin's famous missive to his Decembrist friends languishing in their Siberian exile, "In the Depth of Siberian Mines" ("Vo glubine sibirskikh rud," 1827), and the Decembrist A. I. Odoevsky's response, "The Fiery Sounds of Prophetic Strings" ("Strun veshchikh plamennye zvuki," 1828 or 1829). This sidethrust of Dostoevsky's may be aimed at a familiar target: the Polish patriots, many of whom were exiled to Siberia after the uprising of 1863. Here is a Polish "patriot" who went to Siberia voluntarily, as an "officer" of the Tsar's, and whose "missive" is anything but an assertion of unbroken pride and noble resolve. See Introduction II.4.g. Minor Political Points.

11 343_{36}, $14:330_{15}$, "final conflict"—translates *okonchatel'naia sshibka,* perhaps "decisive clash," where *sshibka* is a martial term meaning "joust, encounter."

12 343_{44}, $14:330_{23}$, *incognito*—sounds funny in the context and tells us that we see Dmitry's daydreams through the eyes of the worldlywise narrator, who is mildly amused by them.

13 343_{46}, $14:330_{24-25}$, "a new life would begin at once!"—the important motif of "a new life" is introduced in Dostoevsky's usual backhanded way. Its serious version will appear in Book Eleven, chap. iv, and in the Epilogue.

14 344_{1-2}, $14:330_{26-27}$, " 'virtuous' "—accurately translates *dobrodetel'nyi,* but the Russian word, a compound of *dobro,* "good," and *deiat',* "to do," has a somewhat broader meaning, suggesting moral quality as well as good works.

15 344_{17}, $14:330_{40-41}$, "had planned no crime"—the Russian

phrase is more ominous, so much so that "never planned his crime" might be closer. This subtlety depends entirely on a point of grammar: the use of the nominative or genitive case, and of the perfective or imperfective aspect of the verb.

16   344_{32-33}, $14:331_{9-10}$,   Characteristic of the narrator's dialectic style. Here he has just said that he will not "enlarge on this fact or analyze it here," and yet he proceeds to do just that, even down to its roots in the subconscious.

17   344_{38}, $14:331_{13}$,   "knows"—a mistranslation for "learns" or "will find out."

18   344_{42}–345_1, $14:331_{17-23}$,   A bit of playful romantic irony. Dostoevsky lets his narrator say naively that there is no need to tell the reader more "as it will all become [be is a mistranslation] clear later," knowing of course that most readers will respond: "Of course, but we know that you are only trying to create suspense." It must be kept in mind, however, that Dostoevsky is addressing a reader who is reading a serialized novel and knows that the fate of a hero may still quite literally hang in the balance.

19   345_{1-2}, $14:331_{23}$,   "common pickpocket"—correctly translates *karmannyi vor;* however, *vor* means "thief," a word which has already appeared a moment earlier ("dishonestly," p. 344_{35}, translates *vorovski,* "like a thief"). The repetition of the word *vor,* "thief," is part of a significant pattern started in Book Three, chap. v, p. 108_{11}, and to be continued in Book Nine, chap. vii, p. 464_{43}, and Book Twelve, chap. vi, p. 665_{39}. The translation obscures this pattern.

20   345_{6-11}, $14:331_{28-33}$,   Recalls the events of Book Three, chap. xi—important because it contains a clue to the mystery just hinted at (see note 18 above).

21   345_{13-15}, $14:331_{35-37}$,   A literal translation would read: "Let me rather stand before him, whom I murdered and robbed, a murderer and a thief, and so before all people, and go to Siberia, than that Katia would have the right to say. . . ." Dmitry's language is awkward and incoherent, reflecting his inner torments. Nevertheless, this anticipation of a confrontation with his victim is significant. Dmitry *is* committing the crime in his mind.

22   345_{21-29}, $14:331_{42}$–332_3,   We have followed Dmitry's stream-of-consciousness in the narrator's rendition *(erlebte Rede).* Now the narrator takes over for a moment and comes up with some bitter but true observations on Dmitry's character. They characterize the narrator almost as much as they do Dmitry. The text of this

Book is turning into a counterpoint, as it were, of Dmitry's confused thoughts and the narrator's worldly-wise and mildly ironic comments.

23   345_{34-35}, $14:332_{7-9}$, "the most impossible ... seem most practical"—in the original, the narrator produces a rather elegant sentence with an antithesis of *nevozmozhnyi*, "impossible," and *vozmozhnyi*, "possible," each in a different form of the superlative grade.

24   345_{44}–346_2, $14:332_{16-20}$, This sentence is an example of the counterpoint mentioned in note 22 above. Of the many modal expressions in it, some belong to Dmitry, and some to the narrator. A more literal translation will show this more clearly: "But for some unknown reason he had developed a conviction, and this actually quite long ago, that the old debauchee, now lying at death's door, would perhaps not at all object at the present moment, if Grushen'ka were to arrange her life in some honest way and if she were to marry a 'trustworthy' man." Here "trustworthy" translates *blagonadezhnyi*, an official term used in service records. Dmitry, who holds an honorable discharge from the army, is "trustworthy" in this sense.

25   346_{10}, $14:332_{27-28}$, "great coarseness and want of delicacy"—translates *slishkom uzh grubym i nebrezglivym*, where the point is not the coarseness of Dmitry's character, but the lack of conventional propriety in his winning his ladylove. Hence perhaps: "excessive bluntness and disregard of proprieties."

26   346_{11-12}, $14:332_{29-30}$, "Mitia looked upon Grushen'ka's past as something completely over"—the translation misses a delicate nuance: in the Russian sentence, *proshloe*, "the past" (lit. "bygone"), is seemingly a tautology of *proshedshee*, "gone by" (both from the verb *proiti*, "to go by"). But *proshloe* also has a special meaning, as in Eng. "a woman with a past," so that Dmitry says in effect that Grushen'ka's "past is past" (cf. Eng. "let bygones be bygones"), drawing a wry smile from the narrator.

27   346_{19}, $14:332_{37-38}$, "in that remote past"—translates *v etom prezhnem provalivshemsia proshlom*, lit. "in that former, vanished past." The game with *proshloe*, "the past" (see note 26 above), has just begun: Grushen'ka, formerly a woman with a past, has now lost it.

28   346_{20-21}, $14:332_{40}$, "and who was now himself 'a thing of the past' "—the game continues (see notes 26 and 27 above). In

Russian, *kotoryi . . . uzhe tozhe 'proshol'*, lit. "who himself had 'gone by' now." Since Samsonov was the man responsible for Grushen'ka's past, with that past gone, Samsonov must be gone, too. We are dealing with *erlebte Rede* throughout this passage: Dmitry's confused and naive rationalizations, broken through the prism of the narrator's rather good-natured irony.

29   346_{22}, $14:332_{41}$, "hardly looked upon him as a man at all"—misleading, since the original has *chelovek*, "man" (in the sense of "human"), and not *muzhchina*, "man" (in the sense of "male"). We are dealing with a "realized" metaphor: Samsonov has just been called *chelovek rokovoi*, "a fateful man" (lines 18–19); now he is no longer a "man," but only "a shattered wreck." The Russian word for "wreck" is *razvalina*, a feminine noun, so that the next reference to Samsonov is then in the feminine gender—but then that feminine "wreck" has "paternal" relations with Grushen'ka. The fact that in Russian grammatical gender takes precedence over natural sex is exploited for language games.

30   346_{25-26}, $14:332_{44-45}$, "and that this had been so for a long time"—in the original: "and not at all on the previous basis, and indeed so for a long time, in fact for almost a year now," with an implied snicker which shows up the narrator's philistine mind.

31   346_{31}, $14:333_2$, "past relations"—translates *proshloe*: now Samsonov has a "past." Cf. notes 26–28 above.

32   347_3, $14:333_{21}$, "chandeliers under shades"—the chandeliers are perpetually wrapped in covers, meaning that they are never lit.

33   347_6, $14:333_{25}$, "with a kerchief on her head"—in a more westernized household she would be wearing a lace cap.

34   347_{11}, $14:330_{30}$, This glimpse of an old-fashioned merchant household is quite negative. The merchant class was a strong conservative and anti-Western force in nineteenth-century Russia. Dostoevsky's strategy is to bring out its strength, while making sure not to idealize it. Old Samsonov is drawn after a wealthy Petersburg merchant who was Dostoevsky's landlord in 1866. See *PSS* 15:573.

35   347_{16}, $14:333_{33}$, "sober"—translates *tverez*, a solecism for *trezv*, which immediately puts the image of the speaker in focus. The blunt question whether Dmitry is drunk or sober introduces a note of comic bathos into this painful scene.

36   347_{25-26}, $14:333_{42}$, "of exceptional physical strength"—misses a

nuance, as *nepomernoi* is "immense, vast." The point is that the young man is as awe-inspiring physically as his father is morally. The family name Samsonov becomes functional now.

37   347_{32}, $14:333_{48}$, "waddled"—a mistranslation of *vplyl,* lit. "came sailing in," suggesting slow, majestic movement. The old man is awesome even in his infirmity. Perhaps: "emerged."

38   347_{38}, $14:334_5$, Note the way this scene is staged. The setting is symbolic of its mood: it "lays a weight of depression on the heart" (line 35). Mitia on his ridiculous little chair (Russ. *stul'chik,* "little chair," sounds positively ludicrous) is not only forlorn but also grotesquely out of place in this room—which is symbolic of the whole situation. A Kafkaesque scene.

39   347_{41}, $14:334_8$, Dmitry's "long, military stride" is a label of his. Compare it with Ivan's swaying gait (Book Five, chap. v, p. 245_8).

40   347_{45}, $14:334_{12-13}$, "dignified and unbending"—translates *vazhno i strogo,* lit. "grave and severe." I believe the literal translation to be more proper.

41   348_1, $14:334_{14}$, "Greatly impressed" seems odd in the context. Rather: "Mitia was struck, also, by Kuzma Kuzmich's face, extraordinarily swollen of late."

42   348_{18-24}, $14:334_{32-38}$, Dmitry's little speech is an exhibit of Dostoevsky's psychological ambiguity. Thus, "most honored" translates *blagorodneishii,* "most noble, most honorable, most generous," which would seem unctuous and insincere (we know that Samsonov is neither noble nor generous). But then, Dmitry's wishful thinking endows Samsonov with nobility and generosity, for without these qualities, how could he possibly give a sympathetic ear to Dmitry's request? So Dmitry is sincere after all—or is he?

43   348_{34-36}, $14:334_{47-48}$, "But these breaks . . ."—in the original the narrator comes up with an elegant punning conceit. The word *obryv,* "break, gap, precipice," is a derivative of the verb *obryvat'sia,* "to break, to halt." The "break" in Dmitry's speech is made into a "gap," or "precipice," over which he must leap—an image which is symbolic of Dmitry's present condition.

44   349_{3-6}, $14:335_{13-15}$, The whole passage is an intricate web of direct speech, indirect speech, *erlebte Rede,* and narrator's comments. Here all four come up in a matter of three lines. Literally: "So there, says I, Mitia, I let go of that business then, because I don't know how to, with the law," where the inserted

"Mitia" suggests that Mitia's words are filtered through the
narrator's consciousness.

45   349_{7-8}, $14:335_{16-17}$, "Excellent and honored" again translates
blagorodneishii (see note 42 above), while "unnatural monster"
renders *izverg,* a word which is otherwise Dmitry's own label (cf.
Book Three, note 104).

46   349_{19-21}, $14:335_{28-29}$, "for a good, I might say an honorable
action"—here "honorable" is again *blagorodneishii,* which is
repeated in the next line. Together with two earlier occurences
(see notes 42 and 45 above), the word has been put in the
foreground enough for the reader to recall that Grushen'ka had
called Dmitry *blagorodnyi,* "noble" (Book Seven, chap. iii, p.
336_{10}, where the adjective is translated by "noble heart").
Dmitry unwittingly returns the compliment.

47   349_{23}, $14:335_{31-32}$, "it's a struggle of three in this business"—in
the original we have a more graphic "it's where three men are
banging their heads together."

48   349_{25}, $14:335_{33}$, "real life"—translates *realizm,* a modish word
of the 1860s, meaning in progressive jargon something like "the
facts of life."

49   349_{26-28}, $14:335_{34-36}$, In the original the metaphor pointed out in
note 47 is taken up again: "only two heads are left" and then
"one head is mine and the other is that monster's."

50   349_{34}, $14:335_{41}$, "clumsy"—translates *nelepyi,* which is worse
than "clumsy." Perhaps "preposterous" or "absurd."

51   349_{36-37}, $14:335_{42-44}$, Dostoevsky's centrifugal psychology:
Dmitry, an utter fool a moment earlier, suddenly is again the
intelligent and perceptive young man we know. Something
similar has happened a couple of times before; see Book Three,
chaps. iii and xi.

52   350_{6-7}, $14:336_{11}$, A slight mistranslation. It should be:
"There'll be litigation, lawyers, nothing but trouble!"

53   350_{9}, $14:336_{14}$, "faltered"—translates *vdrug zalepetal,*
"suddenly stammered." This is the fifth time after the conclusion of Mitia's speech that the word *vdrug,* "suddenly,"
occurs. Here as elsewhere it is a sign of the discontinuity and
indeterminacy of mental processes as Dostoevsky perceives them.
It is one of the key words of the novel and of Dostoevsky in
general. See Introduction III.1.a. The Narrator.

54   350_{10-11}, $14:336_{16}$, "He is a peasant"—more accurately: "He is
of the peasantry." Samsonov's remark is condescending:

Liagavy is a newcomer to the business world. We know Liagavy from Book Five, chap. vii, p. 257.

55 350_{33-34}, $14:336_{38-39}$, Dmitry's "Russianness" is made explicit for the first time. As so often, this important motif is introduced in a backhanded way. Cf. Epilogue, chap. ii, p. 724_{30}.

56 350_{41}, $14:336_{46}$, "cried"—translates *riavknul,* "roared, bawled, bellowed"; any of these verbs brings out the comedy of the situation better.

57 351_{3-4}, $14:337_5$, "Could the old man have been laughing at me?"—Once again Dmitry finds himself at the crossroads. The sensible alternative presents itself to him even with each new folly. Dmitry's consciousness, like that of so many Dostoevskian characters, is made up of conflicting voices. See Introduction II.6.b. Psychological Motivation.

58 351_7, $14:337_9$, "Lyagavy"—the reader remembers that Fiodor Pavlovich had warned Ivan not to call the man by that name (meaning "bird dog"). See Book Five, chap. vii, p. 257_{37}.

Chapter ii

59 351_{36}, $14:337_{47}$, "And I didn't expect that"—a mistranslation; it should be "I didn't expect even this much!"

60 352_4, $14:338_2$, "almost one of *themselves*"—translates *kak na svoego cheloveka,* an idiomatic expression, perhaps: "almost one of the family, and not at all a proud 'gentleman.' " A significant trait.

61 352_{7-10}, $14:338_{4-8}$, Note the quotation marks: embedded into the narrator's voice, there appears here the voice of public opinion with which the narrator has been carrying on a running dialogue ever since the introduction. Until this point he has had only minor disagreements with that voice (such as regarding Aliosha's "realism," in Book One, chap. v, p. 19). This is the first time that the narrator hypostatizes "the other voice" in order to detach himself from it.

62 352_{16-18}, $14:338_{15-17}$, *Post factum* motivation—and quite plausible.

63 352_{38}, $14:338_{40}$, "man"—in the original, *chelovechek,* "little man."

64 353_{1-5}, $14:339_{1-5}$, This passage has been smoothed out in the translation. In the original we read "that though the man was indeed Liagavy, he wasn't Liagavy either, because he took

grievous offense at that name." An example of Dostoevsky's keen sense of the nominalist aspect of language. He practices Gorstkin-Liagavy's principle all the time, arbitrarily calling things and people by spurious and self-invented names.

65 354_1, $14:339_{46}$, "real life"—again translates *realizm* (see note 48 above). This sentence is loaded with ambiguities. Dmitry observes that, unlike in fiction, little accidents—not great events—destroy men in real life. The contemporary theory of Realism taught that the typical, rather than the fortuitous, should reign in fiction. Dostoevsky not only subscribed to this notion, but also believed that it was ultimately true of real life as well. So Dmitry is wrong when he sees himself as a victim of trivial circumstances. He will come to realize his error later in the novel. The relationship between fact and fiction is a major side issue in the novel. It will briefly take center stage in Book Twelve, chap. ix, p. 685, and chap. xi, p. 695. See Introduction III.3.d. Art of the Novel.

66 354_{32}, $14:340_{29}$, "flaxen"—is a mistranslation of *rusyi*, "light brown, dark blond."

67 354_{43}, $14:340_{39}$, "Tipsy peasant" misses a nuance: *p´ianogo* is "drunken," and *muzhika*, "peasant," is pejorative, reflecting Dmitry's anger.

68 355_2, $14:340_{43-44}$, "something made him add"—a plausible interpretation of the text, though not an accurate translation. The original reads: "he added, for some reason."

69 355_{38}, $14:341_{29}$, "coat"—translates *poddiovka*, a long-waisted coat worn by men of the lower classes. We know it to be blue (Book Five, chap. vii, p. 257_{18}, where *poddiovka* is translated by "caftan").

70 356_3, $14:341_{40}$, "That's a lie!"—Translates *Eto ty vriosh´*, where the familiar *ty* (second person singular, instead of the polite plural) immediately shows that Gorstkin is so drunk he cannot even see that the man before him is a well-dressed gentleman.

71 356_{13}, $14:342_{1-2}$, "You're drunk, perhaps."—Misses a nuance: actually Dmitry uses a tactful *khmel´noi*, "tipsy," not *p´ianyi*, "drunk," which would have been, of course, more appropriate.

72 356_{16}, $14:342_4$, "painter"—actually, "dyer." This may be a pun on "Karamazov" (from *kara*, "black," and *maz-*, "smear, daub, paint"; cf *bogomaz*, "icon painter"). Cf. Book Four, chap. vi, p. 184_{23}, and note 158.

73   356_{20}, $14:342_8$, "The peasant stroked his beard importantly."—We know what this means: Fiodor Pavlovich had warned Ivan to watch out for this as a sign of Liagavy's telling yet another of his cock-and-bull stories. See Book Five, chap. vii, p. 257.

74   357_{14}, $14:342_{46}$, "got into the trap"—perhaps better: "After some discussion they agreed to give Dmitry a lift."

75   357_{30}, $14:343_{13}$, This whole chapter seems to be a digression as well as a diversion: the plot required Dmitry to be out of town temporarily. Yet it is firmly woven into the texture of the novel. Fiodor Pavlovich and Samsonov had introduced Liagavy and Father Il'insky, and Ivan very nearly might have had Dmitry's experience with Liagavy.

Chapter iii

76   357_{32}, $14:343_{15}$, "Gold Mines"—a surprising chapter heading, announcing a chapter of comic relief before the tragic climax. The chapter features veritable fireworks of apparent surprises which all fizzle quickly.

77   357_{40}, $14:343_{22}$, "'to settle his accounts,'"—more accurately: "to help him with his accounting" (lit. "counting money").

78   358_{19}, $14:343_4$, An inexact quotation from Pushkin's "Table Talk." Dostoevsky's works and notebooks contain many references to Shakespeare. See Introduction I.4.a. Secular Sources.

79   358_{25-26}, $14:343_{14}$, "The truly jealous man is not like that."—Here Dostoevsky allows his narrator to insert a little excursus, a psychological essay "On Jealousy." It is functional in that it elucidates one aspect of Dmitry's character. It is also a masterpiece in its own right.

80   359_{15}, $14:344_{41}$, "'curve of her body'"—the reference is to Book Three, chap. v, p. 107_{24}. Dmitry's passion for the curve of Grushen'ka's body, while sensual, is not so much carnal as aesthetic.

81   359_{40-44}, $14:345_{17-22}$, Cf. notes 20 and 61 above. The reader begins to realize that, parallel to the narrated plot, another plot (or pseudoplot) is beginning to develop: the plot which will be summarized by the prosecutor in Book Twelve, chaps. vi–ix.

82   $359_{45}-360_3$, $14:345_{22-29}$, This little summary of what has happened at Fiodor Pavlovich's house in the meantime helps not

only Dmitry, but the reader, too. See Introduction III.3.a. Motifs.

83 360_{35-37}, $14:346_{10-11}$, To call Ivan "chivalrously educated" (he holds a degree in the natural sciences) is another absurdity of Mme. Khokhlakov's. If anyone deserves the attribute "chivalrous," it is Dmitry.

84 360_{39}, $14:346_{13-14}$, "at her ease"—translates *razviazna,* which has a definitely negative connotation in this context: "pert, forward."

85 361_{10-14}, $14:346_{32-37}$, This is Dostoevsky's specialty: the hero has reached a "limiting situation," and now something will have to give. The idea of a murder which has hovered over the Karamazovs since the beginning of the novel has now become a distinct possibility.

86 361_{30-35}, $14:347_{4-8}$, Mme. Khokhlakov produces some progressive clichés. Since the late Father Zosima disappointed her with *"such conduct"* of his (Book Seven, chap. ii, p. 320_{43-44}), she no longer believes in miracles. Dmitry obliges by producing a progressive inanity of his own: "the realism of actual life."

87 361_{45-46}, $14:347_{18-19}$, "Triviality" is the wrong word (Dmitry is not too good at using foreign words correctly): Dmitry is apologizing for a colloquialism, *vsio provalitsia,* lit. "everything will fall through," which might be understood as "everything will go to the devil."

88 362_{4-5}, $14:347_{23-24}$, "I'm an experienced doctor of the soul"— she is right, so long as the lowest functions of the soul are concerned. She shares this quality with Fiodor Pavlovich Karamazov.

89 362_{14}, $14:347_{33}$, "Madame Bel'mesov"—the name enhances the absurdity of the scene: *ni bel'mesa* (from the Tartar) is a colloquial expression meaning "not a word, not a fig."

90 362_{15}, $14:347_{34}$, "characteristically" (Russ. *kharakterno*)—a subtle hint of Mme. Khokhlakov's displeasure at Dmitry's rather free language (see note 87 above).

91 363_{2-3}, $14:348_{21-22}$, "I will save you as I did Bel'mesov,"—In the Russian this sounds like open mockery (see note 89 above).

92 363_{16-17}, $14:348_{35-36}$, "After all this business with Father Zosima"—again she brings up the late Zosima's "conduct" (cf. note 86 above).

93 363_{19}, $14:348_{38}$, "Enough!"—the title and leitmotif of a prose

piece by Turgenev, written as a farewell to literature (1862). Turgenev went on writing for twenty more years, until his death in 1883. "Enough" is a piece of pretentious rhetoric, showing Turgenev at his egotistic worst. It was especially hateful to Dostoevsky because it also contains a strong statement of Turgenev's godless and pessimistic world view. Dostoevsky parodied it brilliantly in *The Possessed,* where the "great writer" Karmazinov's "Merci" is an obvious take-off on "Enough." By placing Turgenev in the company of the frivolous Mme. Khokhlakov, Dostoevsky downgrades Turgenev.

94   363_{26}, $14:348_{45}$, "leader"—translates *deiatel'*, lit. "man of action, activist," another cliché of progressive jargon. Cf. "From the Author," p. xvii$_{16}$.

95   363_{30-32}, $14:349_{1-4}$, The uncontrollable depreciation of the paper rouble, which, unlike West European currencies, was not fully backed by gold and/or silver holdings, was a perennial editorial topic in the Russian press of the 1860s and 1870s. Dostoevsky himself brought it up repeatedly in *Diary of a Writer.*

96   363_{43-44}, $14:349_{15}$, "Answer mathematically."—More absurd progressive jargon.

97   364_{24}, $14:349_{38}$, "triumphantly"—a mistranslation of *torzhestvenno,* "solemnly."

98   364_{32-39}, $14:350_{3-9}$, This brings the comic clash to a head. Dmitry has been talking about his predicament. Mme. Khokhlakov has been talking about her own fanciful ideas. Neither is listening to the other. Now, by pure accident their spheres collide: Mme. Khokhlakov would like to send Dmitry to the gold mines of Siberia (foreshadowing?), Dmitry would like to marry Grushen'ka—but there is no place for women among gold prospectors!

99   365_{1-15}, $14:350_{12-26}$, This passage is a side-thrust at M. E. Saltykov-Shchedrin (1826–89), leading radical publicist, satirist, and novelist, with whom Dostoevsky had an off-and-on literary feud for nearly twenty years. The Russian radicals were strong feminists. Mme. Khokhlakov's letter, though, is patterned after an anonymous letter Dostoevsky had himself received in 1876 in response to his articles on a case of child abuse in *Diary of a Writer. The Contemporary* was the organ of the Russian radical movement until closed by the authorities in 1866, understandably a heavy blow to their cause. Saltykov reacted to this passage with

two angry attacks on Dostoevsky, published in the *National Annals* ("October First" and "November First–December First," 1879). See *PSS* 15:574 and Borshchevskii, pp. 315–23.

100   365_{23}, $14:350_{34}$, "Siberia"—one of the deep ironies of the novel: Mme. Khokhlakov will in fact help to send Dmitry to Siberia.

101   365_{40}, $14:351_3$, "stupidly"—translates *nelepo*, "absurdly, senselessly." The narrator's "stage directions" are important in these dramatic scenes. Here he is trying to convey not so much the objective quality of Dmitry's repartee as its tone, which is one of a mad desperation which would make one shudder.

102   366_8, $14:351_{14}$, "roared"—again, the "stage directions" are not quite accurate; in the original we have *vzrevel vdrug Mitia*, "Mitia suddenly gave out a roar."

103   366_{10}, $14:351_{16}$, "alarmed"—*v ispuge* is "frightened."

104   366_{13}, $14:351_{19}$, "into the darkness"—introduces the title and leitmotif of the following chapter.

105   366_{14-25}, $14:351_{20-30}$, Alludes to Book Three, chap. ix, p. 143_{21-24}. Cf. notes 20 and 22 above.

106   366_{25-26}, $14:351_{31-32}$, "so strong in appearance"—translates *stol' sil'nyi fizicheski*, "so strong physically," which is the point: Dmitry is physically a strong man, but emotionally he is a child. His "crying like a little child" has a symbolic function. It foreshadows Dmitry's epiphany in Book Nine, chap. viii ("The Babe"). "Crying like a little child" suddenly puts Dmitry right with the suffering children of the novel.

107   366_{35}, $14:351_{40-41}$, One of the more obvious contrivances in the plot of the novel. The chain of events that seal Dmitry's fate is long and intricate. Running into this old woman is but one of its many links. Dostoevsky was convinced, however, that his "contrived" and "fantastic" plots were a better likeness of real life than the circumstantially and psychologically plausible plots of contemporary realists. See Introduction III.3.d. Art of the Novel.

108   367_9, $14:352_{9-10}$, "not more than a quarter of an hour"—another link in the chain of fateful accidents.

109   367_{14-15}, $14:352_{14-15}$, "he fell all of a heap at her feet"—sudden drama. Dmitry's action was not as bizarre in nineteenth-century Russia as it would be in this country today. Flinging oneself at someone's feet as a gesture of supplication was certainly practiced by the lower classes, or had been in recent memory. In-

cidentally, the adverb *vdrug,* "suddenly," has, as so often, remained untranslated. On its role in the text, see Introduction III.1.a. The Narrator.

110   367_{21-22}, $14:352_{22-23}$, Dostoevsky has succeeded in making it quite plausible that Dmitry jumps to the conclusion that Grushen'ka went to see his father.

111   367_{28}, $14:352_{28}$, "a brass mortar, with a pestle in it"—a common household utensil in the nineteenth century.

Chapter iv

112   368_{7-13}, $14:353_{4-10}$, The reference is to Book Three, chap. i, p. 86. It may be understood as a hint that the tragedy which is now to reach its climax is retribution for the wrong that led to Elizaveta's death a generation before. See Introduction III.5.f. Mythical Symbolism.

113   368_{21}, $14:353_{18}$, " 'And nought but the whispering silence' "— an inexact quotation from Pushkin's mock-heroic epic "Ruslan and Liudmila" (1820). The quotation is an appropriate one, since the passage in question also describes fearful anticipation in silent darkness.

114   368_{28}, $14:353_{25}$, "white hazel"—translates *kalina,* "snowball tree, guelderrose," a tree remarkable for its large round heads of white flowers and red berries, celebrated in Russian folk songs.

115   368_{38-39}, $14:353_{34-35}$, " 'How red the white hazel berries are!' "—The quotation has not been identified, but cf. note 114.

116   369_{28}, $14:354_{14}$, "disappointed"—a slightly misleading translation of *prigoriunivshis'.* Perhaps: "dejected."

117   369_{32-35}, $14:354_{17-21}$, "a queer, irrational vexation . . ."—A psychological ambiguity, typical of Dostoevsky (see Introduction II.6.d. Psychological Wisdom). As so often, it is expressed in terms of an inner dialogue, here between what might be called the id and the ego.

118   369_{41-43}, $14:354_{27-29}$, The "signal" is described in Book Four, chap. vi, p. 250_{39-40}.

119   370_{4}, $14:354_{34}$, "my angel"—translates *matochka, angelochek* (diminutives of *mat',* "mother," and *angel,* "angel"), each of them stronger endearments than "my angel."

120   370_{19}, $14:354_{47}$, "greedy"—inexact translation of *sladostnyi,* "sweet, delightful." The point is that the old man is, in his own carnal and lecherous way, deeply in love with Grushen'ka.

121   370_{27-32}, $14:355_{7-10}$, "I don't know . . ."—Cf. Book Three, chap. v, p. 110_{35-40}. In the original, the exact words of the earlier passage are repeated here. In the translation, a correct "shameless snigger" (p. 110_{38}) is replaced by "shameless grin."

122   370_{36}, $14:355_{15}$, "God was watching over me then"—makes it quite clear that Dmitry did not kill his father. Dostoevsky foregoes this sort of suspense, shifting his suspense to a different level. Dmitry's words are significant: but for the grace of God, he would have become a murderer. Note the repeated switch of point of view: from immediate experience, to recollected experience, to *erlebte Rede*.

123   370_{38}, $14:355_{18}$, "the treatment"—a seemingly trivial detail, this is one of the links in a chain of accidents that leads to Dmitry's ruin. The reference here is to Book Five, chap. vi, pp. 251–52. It will come up again in Book Twelve, chap. ii, pp. 631–32.

124   371_3, $14:355_{25}$, "back"—"lower back" or "small of his back," to be exact (Russ. *poiasnitsa*).

125   371_{33}, $14:356_6$, " 'monster' "—Russ. *izverg*. See note 45 above.

126   371_{37}, $14:356_{10}$, "a brass pestle"—it should be "the brass pestle": it was mentioned at the conclusion of the preceding chapter.

127   371_{39-40}, $14:356_{12}$, "in a most conspicuous place"—clearly a detail relevant to future developments (why else would it be mentioned?): see Book Twelve, chap. x, p. 691_{34-42}.

128   372_{16}, $14:356_{30}$, "running"—the original has *neistovo begushchego*, "running frenziedly." Note the sudden shift of perspective. It follows a pattern established earlier (cf. note 61 above): a whole chain of witnesses is summoned to report on these fateful hours of Dmitry's life.

Chapter v

129   372_{41-42}, $14:357_5$, "seized her by the throat"—translates *krepko skhvatil eio za gorlo*, "seized her firmly by the throat." The pattern of Dmitry's violence continues.

130   373_{8-9}, $14:357_{14}$, "Who threw her over five years ago" correctly gives the gist of what Fenia says, but fails to reproduce her frightened, rapid-fire speech. Literally: "five years back who was, threw over, and left."

131 373_{11-27}, $14:357_{15-32}$, A silent scene. Note the staging. In this scene, as in some others, hand gestures are particularly important. See Introduction III. Narrative Technique.

132 373_{36-38}, $14:357_{41-43}$, An interesting bit of psychology: "monstrous thing" is a single noun in Russian *(chudishche)*, more concrete than the translation; perhaps: "monster." Thus an emotional state is hypostatized, given a material presence. Dostoevsky does this on occasion.

133 374_{6-7}, $14:358_{10-11}$, See Book Seven, chap. iii, p. 336_{10-12}.

134 374_{21}, $14:358_{25}$, "That's blood, Fenia"—"blood" has become a leitmotif of this chapter, and it will cast its shadow over later chapters.

135 374_{25}, $14:358_{29}$, "when the sun rises"—the phrase is given in quotation marks in the original. The Russian *vzletit,* lit. "flies high," is poetic, the standard expression being *vzoidiot.* Cf. p. 378_{25-26}, where the same applies.

136 374_{25-26}, $14:358_{29-30}$, "Mitia will leap over that fence"—Dmitry is always the poet: the terrible moment astride the fence is still in his mind, so he uses this image to express his suicide plan—on the other side of the fence there is the man he believes to have killed, and his own death.

137 374_{29}, $14:358_{33}$, "You loved me for an hour"—cf. note 133 above. "Miten'ka" is a tender hypocoristic of "Dmitry." Normally only a child would be called Miten'ka. Cf. note 106 above.

138 375_{3-4}, $14:359_{5-7}$, Another change of perspective. By now it is clear that all these comments will be made by witnesses at Dmitry's trial.

139 375_{10-11}, $14:359_{9-10}$, "two thousand, or perhaps three"—the sum of three thousand has been mentioned so often by now that one expects it to be the answer. This passage introduces a development in the plot to be resolved later (see Book Nine, chap. vii, pp. 462–63).

140 375_{16-17}, $14:359_{17-18}$, "not at all dejected but quite cheerful"—a "Dostoevskian" psychological paradox. See Introduction II.6.d. Psychological Novel.

141 376_8, $14:360_8$, "Plotnikov's"—the details regarding this store, and even the owner's name, are those of Dostoevsky's own favorite delicatessen in Staraia Russa. See *PSS* 15:574.

142 376_{23}, $14:360_{25}$, "everything I took to Mokroe before"—see Book Three, chap. v, p. 107_{18-21}.

143   377_{28-29}, $14:361_{28-29}$,   We have not heard of Snegiriov for some
       time. Here we get yet another angle on the scene which was
       earlier described, or mentioned, by Fiodor Pavlovich, Katerina
       Ivanovna, as well as the two principals. See Introduction III.3.a.
       Motifs.

144   377_{33-34}, $14:361_{33-34}$,   See chap. iii, p. 366_{30-31}.

145   377_{42-45}, $14:361_{40-43}$,   "if he had got up . . ."—This is said in
       despair, as Dmitry assumes Grigory to be dead.

146   378_{12-14}, $14:362_{8-10}$,   "Three, you bet"—Dmitry's answer (note
       that he laughs as he gives it) is loaded with irony, as the reader
       will discover in Book Nine (cf. note 139 above).

147   378_{16}, $14:362_{11}$,   Perkhotin's question triggers some gallows
       humor on Dmitry's part. Dmitry never loses his sense of humor,
       a significant trait (cf. Book Eleven, chap. iv, p. 556_{8-11}).

148   378_{25-26}, $14:362_{19-20}$,   "The sun rises" translates *solntse vzletit,*
       "the sun flies high," a poetic phrase which appeared in
       quotation marks earlier (see note 135 above). Dmitry has in mind
       some line in which "Phoebus, ever young, flies high" (it might
       be Schiller, but Phoebus occurs often even in the poetry of
       Pushkin and his Russian contemporaries; the exact source, if
       there is one, has not been found). Dmitry promptly proceeds to
       mix his metaphor by adding a biblical "glorifying and praising
       God" (Luke 2:20)—intentionally, it would seem, since he is
       being facetious.

149   378_{30-31}, $14:362_{24-25}$,   Once more, an ominous note is struck by
       the mention of Siberia. Cf. chap. iii, p. 365_{23}.

150   378_{35}, $14:362_{28}$,   "Once the lad had all, now the lad has
       nought"—A quotation from a folk ballad whose hero, Mastriuk,
       is robbed of all his clothes as he lies unconscious. See *PSS*
       15:575.

151   378_{40-42}, $14:362_{33-35}$,   A quotation from Schiller's poem "Das
       Siegesfest" (1803) in F. I. Tiutchev's translation. The words, an
       allusion to Clytemnestra's betrayal and murder of Agamemnon,
       are spoken by Ulysses. Dmitry is thinking of Grushen'ka, of
       course.

152   379_{33-35}, $14:363_{20-21}$,   "golden-haired Phoebus and his warm
       light"—"golden-haired" is a Homeric epithet ($\chi\rho\upsilon\sigma\sigma\kappa\acute{o}\mu\eta\varsigma$); the
       original has *goriachii,* "hot," rather than "warm" (this nuance
       may be significant). Dmitry asserts his love of life in the very face
       of despair, much as his brother Ivan did earlier (Book Five, chap.
       iii, p. 211_{27-30}).

153 380_2, $14:363_{32}$, "shut up"—too strong for *shabash,* "enough of it," which is colloquial and curt, but not rude.

154 380_{5-6}, $14:363_{35-36}$, This may hark back to Dmitry's recital of Schiller's verses in Book Three, chap. iii, p. 95, where the adjective *dikii,* "savage," occurs repeatedly.

155 380_{13-18}, $14:363_{43-47}$, Perkhotin's words are a sudden intrusion of the prose of everyday life into Dmitry's fantastic condition. Good for enhancing the contrast between two entirely different points of view.

156 380_{30}, $14:364_{12}$, Here the translation misses a nuance. In the original the line, "I punish myself for my whole life, my whole life I punish!" *("Kazniu sebia za vsiu zhizn', vsiu zhizn' moiu nakazuiu!")* is distinctly poetry, not prose, with two metrically identical lines linked by a chiastic pattern of repetition: *kazniu . . . vsiu zhizn'/ vsiu zhizn' . . . nakazuiu.* We have, then, a poetic improvisation serving as a suicide note. Cf. chap. vi, p. 387_{25-26}.

157 380_{38}, $14:364_{20}$, "the brothers Eliseev"—see Book Two, note 236.

158 380_{40-44}, $14:364_{22-25}$, Refers to the general decline of the Russian countryside after the Emancipation of 1861. See Introduction II.4. Social Novel.

159 380_{45}–381_{20}, $14:364_{25-45}$, We have heard the story of Dmitry's escapade to Mokroe before (Book Three, chap. v, p. 107). This passage refreshes our memory and acts as a dress rehearsal, as it were, to the chapters to follow. The "dress rehearsal" is a device often used by Dostoevsky. For instance, Dmitry's first attack on Grigory (Book Three, chap. ix) had been a dress rehearsal of the almost fatal blow struck by him in chapter iv of this Book.

160 381_{22}, $14:364_{47}$, "a cart with three horses"—a *troika,* then. Cf. Book Seven, note 116.

161 381_{31-32}, $14:365_{7-8}$, "a certain enchantress"—this brings to mind Fiodor Pavlovich's references to Grushen'ka as "a certain enchantress" (Book Two, chap. vi, p. 62_{35}), but only because of a lack of attention to nuance in the translation. Actually Fiodor Pavlovich uses *obol'stitel'nitsa,* "seductress," and Dmitry, *volshebnitsa,* "enchantress."

162 381_{37}, $14:365_{14}$, "Middle-aged driver" misses a nuance; in the original he is called a "lad" *(paren')* and "rather young" *(eshcho ne staryi,* lit. "not yet old"), which makes him thirty-five or so, at most—that is, young enough to risk his neck, and his horses, on a fast ride.

163   382_{23-24}, $14:365_{44-45}$, "on second thought"—translates *kak by vdrug odumavshis'*, lit. "as though suddenly having thought better of it." As so often, two key words of the original, *vdrug,* "suddenly," and *kak by,* "as though," have remained untranslated.

164   382_{26}, $14:365_{47}$, "economist"—translates *ekonom,* "steward, manager," which is readily associated with *ekonomit',* "to economize." The meaning, then, is something like "my thrifty manager."

165   382_{35}, $14:366_9$, "cried"—should be "snapped."

166   382_{41-42}, $14:366_{15-16}$, "There's no order in me"—the theme of disorder is now stated explicitly. See Introduction I.3. Early Versions, and II.4. Social Novel.

167   383_{1-2}, $14:366_{19-20}$, Cf. Book Three, chap. iii, p. 92_{21-22}, and note 42.

168   383_{4-5}, $14:366_{22-23}$, Once more, Captain Snegiriov. It is significant that the beard-pulling incident should weigh so heavily on Dmitry. See Introduction II.3.a. Fatherhood.

169   383_{10-19}, $14:366_{28-37}$, A direct counterpoint to Ivan's rebellion in Book Five, chap. iv, In desperate straits, on the verge of suicide, Dmitry does not blame God or His creation, but only himself.

170   383_{16-17}, $14:366_{33-35}$, Once again, the insect imagery so characteristic of Dostoevsky.

171   383_{21-23}, $14:366_{40-41}$, Reminds the reader of what has happened at the Karamazov residence.

172   383_{33-34}, $14:367_{4-5}$, Better: "I am so sad, I am so sad, Horatio. . . . 'Alas, poor Yorick.' " *Hamlet,* Act V, scene i, reads simply: "Alas, poor Yorick! I knew him, Horatio." Note how Dmitry makes a quotation his own. Hamlet's character sketch of Yorick ("a fellow of infinite jest, of most excellent fancy") fits Dmitry quite well.

173   384_{8-9}, $14:367_{22}$, Dmitry's dark hints allude to Katerina Ivanovna's money which he squandered at Mokroe. But there is a hint of something deeper which will surface in Book Nine, chap. vii, p. 462.

174   384_{26-27}, $14:367_{36-37}$, "A few more last words" misses a nuance: Russ. *Eshcho poslednee skazan'e* is obviously a quotation from Pushkin's drama *Boris Godunov* (1824–25). The words are spoken by the monk-chronicler Pimen, a character admired by Dostoevsky. See *Diary of a Writer* 2:942, 960.

175   384_{29}, $14:367_{39}$, "think kindly of me"—translates *ne pominai*

likhom, a formulaic expression which suggests a long separation, or even death.

176   384_{38}, $14:367_{48}$, "Andrei, coughing from the brandy"—misses a nuance: Russ. *kriaknul,* "cleared his throat," suggests a sound which, in this context, expresses appreciation for a free drink.

177   384_{45}, $14:368_{6}$, "he came first, he's hers!"—translates *prezhnii ved' on, ikhnii,* lit. "he's her former one, you know." This is significant because the word *prezhnii,* "former," will then appear in the title of chapter vii.

178   384_{46}, $14:368_{8}$, "he's come back from Siberia"—another ominous reference to Siberia. Grushen'ka's former lover has come back from Siberia; this does not bode well for her present lover.

179   385_{11-12}, $14:368_{19}$, "scoundrel"—Dmitry's humble acceptance of this label (when it last came up in Book Three, chap. xi, p. 143_8, he was not quite so meek) is another hint of some hidden trauma. Cf. note 173 above.

180   385_{15}, $14:368_{23}$, "My last tear is for you!"—Russ. *Tebe posledniaia sleza* is a perfect iambic tetrameter, but there are no quotation marks in the original. While this sounds like a quotation, I am not aware of the source.

181   385_{20}, $14:368_{28}$, "He turned away with a curse" is a little awkward for *pliunul,* lit. "he spat" (but meaning as much as "he said: 'to hell with it!' ").

182   385_{26}, $14:368_{33}$, The translator must have misread "bawler" as "brawler" in her dictionary; Russ. *gorlan* is "loudmouth." Also, "drink" should be "get drunk," and "They are not men who do anything real" should be "They never mean business."

183   385_{31}, $14:368_{37}$, "the villains"—it should be "the scoundrels" (cf. note 179 above). Incidentally, Perkhotin's remark is another instance of inner commentary, and it is also quite correct.

184   385_{39}, $14:368_{44}$, "three thousand roubles"—note the round figure again. It is beginning to haunt Dmitry. See Introduction III.3.a. Motifs.

185   385_{41-42}, $14:368_{45-48}$, An example of what difference Dostoevsky's modal expressions can make. The translator has left untranslated *pochti,* "almost," *kak-to,* "somehow," and *dazhe,* "even." Here is the same passage in a literal translation: "This news was received with almost unexpected curiosity by his listeners. And they all began to talk about it, not laughing, but somehow with a strange gravity. They even stopped playing."

186 385₄₆, 14:369₄, In the original "old man," not "old father."

187 386₁₆, 14:369₁₈, "is it my business to look after them?"—translates *diad'ka ia im, chto li?* "Am I their nurse, or what?" (*diad'ka,* "governor"). Dostoevsky likes to provide even minor characters with a verbal label. "Am I his nurse, or what?" has become Perkhotin's label (cf. p. 358₃₁).

188 386₁₇₋₃₁, 14:369₁₉₋₃₂, A good example of Dostoevskian psychology: Perkhotin keeps thinking one thing and doing another. See Introduction II.6.d. Psychological Wisdom.

189 386₃₁, 14:369₃₂, The chapter ends, and this particular line of action will not be taken up again until Book Nine: clearly an artificial device to create suspense.

Chapter vi

190 386₃₇, 14:369₃₇₋₃₈, "The swift motion revived Mitia."—Again, the narrator's key words, *kak by,* "as though," and *vdrug,* "suddenly," have been left untranslated. Literally: "It was as though the swift ride had suddenly refreshed Mitia."

191 386₃₉–387₁₆, 14:369₄₁–370₁₃, Note the changes in point of view in this passage: from objective impersonal narrator (who wonders if this was "perhaps the very hour, in which Aliosha fell on the earth," meaning that he cannot be sure—yet who can look straight into Dmitry's soul), to *erlebte Rede,* to Dmitry's stream of consciousness.

192 386₄₀, 14:369₄₀₋₄₁, In the original the quotation marks stand before "rapturously," establishing a concordance with Book Seven, chap. iv, p. 340₃₄₋₃₅. Also, in the original there is a perfect coincidence of the wording of this phrase in both passages. Obviously this enhances the effect.

193 387₇, 14:370₅, "his fierce hands"—misses a nuance. Russ. *strashnye ruki* is "terrible hands," with a suggestion of mystic horror, for these hands have thrice smitten a father: Snegiriov, Grigory, and Fiodor Pavlovich. See Introduction III. Narrative Technique.

194 387₁₉, 14:370₁₆, "plan of action"—translates *reshimost',* "resolution, resolve." Dmitry has no "plan of action," but only an intuited resolution.

195 387₂₅₋₂₆, 14:370₂₃, " 'I punish myself.' "—Cf. chap. iii, p. 380₃₀, and note 156 above. Here the Russian words, while different from the line on p. 380, again form a perfect iambic tetrameter.

196   387_{37}, $14:370_{35}$, "images"—it should be "phantoms" or "specters."

197   387_{44}, $14:370_{41}$, "devoutness"—a mistranslation of *molenie.* Perhaps: "adoration."

198   388_{34}, $14:371_{28}$, "Fenia" is "Fedos'ia Markovna" in the original. To the driver she is a person of some standing, so he refers to her by her full name and patronymic.

199   389_{3-7}, $14:371_{35-39}$, Andrei's speech features several expressions, as well as a syntax, characteristic of the idiom of the uneducated. The English translation does not duplicate these features. The last sentence might read: "There's no holding him, he just keeps going, he just keeps going straight." This makes Dmitry's repartee more natural.

200   389_{8-20}, $14:371_{47}-372_{11}$, This little digression brings up one of the recurrent themes of the novel, hell, presenting it from yet another angle. Cf. Book I, chap. iv, pp. 18–19; Book Three, chap. vii, p. 116; Book Five, chap. v, p. 228; and Book Six, chap. iii(i). Andrei's prose version goes back to a popular verse legend *(dukhovnyi stikh).* See *PSS* 15:375–76.

201   389_{15}, $14:372_{6}$, "the devil groaned"—in the original: "hell groaned." Russian *ad,* "hell" (from Gr. *Hades*), is a masculine noun.

202   389_{23-25}, $14:372_{14-16}$, "but you're like a little child . . ."— another detail which leads up to Dmitry's vision of "the babe" in Book Nine, chap. viii. Cf. note 106 above.

203   389_{29}, $14:372_{19}$, "for everyone"—a contrapuntal echo of one of the leitmotifs of Father Zosima's biography; see Book Six, chap. ii, p. 268_{8-9}, and passim.

204   389_{34-44}, $14:372_{26-35}$, This prayer is in fact a poem in which Dmitry's leitmotifs are woven into a lyric composition. The rhythmic cadence of the passage, the numerous repetitions and parallelisms, and its whole logic are so intensely poetic that it could easily pass for poetry if printed as a poem. The striking line, "If Thou sendest me to hell, I shall love Thee there, and from there I shall cry out that I love Thee forever and ever. . . .", originally appeared in Dostoevsky's notebooks to *A Raw Youth,* where they are spoken by Elizaveta Smerdiashchaia. See *Notebooks to "A Raw Youth,"* ed. Edward Wasiolek, tr. Victor Terras (Chicago and London, 1969), pp. 173, 176, 177.

205   390_{11}, $14:372_{48}$, "I'm coming, too!"—This is the chapter heading. The Russian phrase means literally "I'm coming myself," but Russ. *sam,* "myself," is used here for emphasis.

The translator has omitted the phrase "Mitia kept shouting in a frenzy," which follows.

206   390_{21}–391_3, $14:373_{10-38}$,   The inserted character sketch of Trifon Borisych acts as a moment of respite before the start of a new whirl of events. The sketch also shows Dostoevsky's negative assessment of the new social order emerging in the Russian countryside after the disintegration of the peasant commune. See Introduction II.4. Social Novel.

207   391_{20-21}, $14:374_7$,   "a gentleman called Maksimov"—in the original we read "Maksimov, a landowner," and remember that "landowner" is Maksimov's ironic label.

208   391_{30}, $14:374_{17}$,   Combing a lover's hair was a sign of affection, a part of the courtship ritual among the uneducated classes. Hence Dmitry jumps to the conclusion that Grushen'ka's former lover is the recipient of this favor.

209   391_{42-45}, $14:374_{29-32}$,   Trifon Borisych's speech is stylized all the way: he tries to speak in a more genteel way than the driver Andrei, for example, but his coarse peasant background comes through all the time. This is not conveyed by the translation. Also, instead of "village," we have the name of a village, *Rozhdestvenskaia,* "Nativity," perhaps with an ironic effect intended: Jewish musicians coming from a place called Nativity. Russian villages were often named after their church, here the church of the Holy Nativity. Professional musicians were often Gypsies or, in the Western provinces, Jews.

210   392_{4-11}, $14:374_{37-44}$,   Trifon Borisych's disrespect for the peasants of Mokroe is symptomatic. It shows him to be of the same ilk as Fiodor Pavlovich (Book Three, chap. viii, p. 120, and note 160).

211   392_{14-15}, $14:374_{47-48}$,   Literally: "he picked it up and squeezed it in his fist. And so it remained in his fist." Russ. *kulak,* "fist," also means "a rich peasant who has other peasants in his clutches" (cf. Book Six, note 125). Since Trifon Borisych answers this description, such pointed use of the word *kulak* may be meant to be suggestive.

212   392_{19}, $14:375_3$,   "three thousand"—again. Dmitry continues to build the case against himself.

213   392_{30-31}, $14:375_{17}$,   "Remember Karamazov"—translates *Pomni barina Karamazova,* where *barin* is "gentleman, squire." Said with bitter self-irony.

214 393_{14-15}, $14:375_{46}$, "with a throbbing heart . . . feeling cold all
over"—translates *kholodeia i zamiraia,* adverbial participles of
kholodet', "to grow cold," and *zamirat',* "to grow numb, to
sink (of the heart)." Dmitry's heart, which was throbbing
violently a moment earlier (line 1), is now sinking and about to
stand still. Dostoevsky is very particular about the physical
manifestations of mental states. See Introduction II.6.d.
Psychological Wisdom.

Chapter vii

215 393_{19}, $14:376_3$, Dmitry's "long, rapid strides" have become a
label of his. Cf. chap. i, p. 347_{41}, and note 39 above.

216 393_{22-23}, $14:376_{6-7}$, "I'm all right!"—Translates *Ja nichego!*
which is repeated twice in the following line. Russ. *nichego*
means literally "nothing," but it might have been better to repeat
the soothing "I'm all right!" instead of "I—there's nothing the
matter."

217 393_{31}, $14:376_{15}$, *"Panie"*—"Sir" in Polish (it is the vocative
case of *pan;* the feminine is *pani,* the plural *panowie*).
Musiałowicz and his friend speak Russian mixed with Polish
throughout, though this is not reflected in the translation. There
are a few Polish words and forms not necessarily intelligible to a
Russian reader; many expressions which, while Polish, are close
enough to Russian to be understood; some Russian phrases
pronounced with a Polish accent; and some sentences simply in
Polish, to some of which the narrator's own translation is added
in parenthesis. All in all, the speech of the two Poles is a
caricature of a Pole trying to speak Russian. Musiałowicz and
Wróblewski are stereotypes which appear in other novels by
Dostoevsky *(The Gambler, Crime and Punishment)* as well as in
a number of Russian "antinihilist" novels by other authors. See
Introduction II.4.g. Minor Political Points, and *PSS* 15:576.

218 393_{37-39}, $14:376_{21-23}$, "How tight you squeeze! . . ."—A
significant detail: Dmitry's extraordinary physical strength
causes him to hurt people even when he means well.

219 394_1, $14:376_{27}$, "she was impressed"—better: "she was struck."

220 394_{14-15}, $14:376_{38-39}$, "(Something made him pull out his bundle
of bills.)"—This translation is in effect an interpretation, albeit a
correct one. The text reads: "For some reason he suddenly pulled
out his bundle of bills."

221 394_{16}, $14:376_{40}$, "as we had before"—he is referring to the first "orgy" at Mokroe.

222 394_{16-17}, $14:376_{41}$, "But the worm, the unnecessary worm"—once more Dmitry waxes poetic. The Russian phrase sounds very much like poetry. Perhaps: "The worm, that useless worm, will end his crawl on earth, and be no more." The earth symbolism is important as ever. See Introduction III.5.f. Mythical Symbolism.

223 394_{23-24}, $14:376_{41}$, "and my last night"—translates *v posledniuiu noch' moiu,* "on my last night."

224 394_{23-24}, $14:376_{47}$–377_1, " 'suverin' "—a not too felicitous attempt to duplicate Musiałowicz's Polish. He says *królewa,* "queen," the Russian equivalent being *koroleva,* so that Grushen'ka has little trouble understanding.

225 394_{32}, $14:377_8$, "bursting into tears"—once more this childlike trait in Dmitry. Cf. note 106 above.

226 394_{39}, $14:377_{14-15}$, *"As though you had anything to cry for!"*—Grushen'ka is, of course, thinking of the rivalry between Dmitry and her former lover and cannot know how much there is for Dmitry to cry about. There is an undercurrent of fear and doom present throughout this scene, as Dmitry—and the reader—are continually reminded of what has happened a few hours earlier. For example, when Dmitry says, "Me, me frighten you?" (line 29), one is reminded that he may have just killed an innocent old man.

227 395_{21}, $14:377_{43}$, "In confusion"—translates *konfuzlivo,* which means "embarrassed."

228 395_{31-32}, $14:378_6$, "a look of something childlike came into his face"—cf. notes 106 and 225 above.

229 395_{34-35}, $14:378_{8-9}$, "a dog . . ."—the Russian version is kinder—*sobachonka* means "little dog, doggy"—and more graphic—"who has been petted and let in again."

230 395_{43}–396_2, $14:378_{15-21}$, In the original, the caricature of the Pole is enhanced by a string of diminutives ("nose," "moustache," and "wig" are all in diminutive forms, as are the adjectives that go with them) and superlatives. The phrase about the moustaches, in particular, reads like a satirical epigram: the moustaches seem alive.

231 396_{9-10}, $14:378_{29-30}$, Here the translation should read: ". . . the tall Pole must be the friend and associate of the other, 'his bodyguard,' as it were, and that the little Pole with the pipe was of course giving orders to the tall Pole." Note the "cute" chiastic

syntax of the sentence, with the "little Pole" flanked by the "tall Pole." As so often, Dostoevsky carries his comedy into his grammar.

232 396_{33-35}, $14:379_{7-9}$, "Interest" translates Russ. *zanimal(o)* which, in this context, means "entertain." Hence: ". . . if there was anything that he found entertaining it was Maksimov."

233 $396_{40}-397_{6}$, $14:379_{14-25}$, Once more we are treated to a rather lengthy description of Kalganov's character, and again it is a dead end (cf. Book Two, chap. i, p. 27, and note 2). Kalganov will remain a marginal character.

234 397_{9-11}, $14:379_{29-30}$, See Book Two, chap. viii, p. 81_{13-15}. Recalling this instance of Ivan Fiodorovich's uncharitable and violent behavior is a part of Dostoevsky's strategy.

235 397_{16-18}, $14:379_{32-33}$, "He spoke Russian fairly well . . ."—this remark becomes understandable if one is aware of the fact that the preceding phrase is 90 percent Polish.

236 397_{28}, $14:380_{1}$, "like a kitten"—possibly another reminiscence from Pushkin, in whose ballad "Budrys and his Sons" (1833, from Mickiewicz) Polish girls are likened to kittens.

237 397_{29}, $14:380_{2}$, Maksimov, the buffoon, is aping Musiałowicz's macaronic style: "pan-father and pan-mother" is said in Polish.

238 397_{33}, $14:380_{5}$, "The *pan* is a *lajdak!*"—In Polish a person is normally addressed in the third person, with *pan (pani)* replacing the personal pronoun. Hence the phrase means: "You are a scoundrel!"

239 397_{39}, $14:380_{11}$, "*Pani* Agrippina"—Musiałowicz has converted a Russian Agrafena into a Polish Agrippina. Curiously, the name of a possible prototype of Grushen'ka was actually Agrippina. See Introduction I.6.d. Ivan Karamazov and Other Characters.

240 $398_{8ff.}$, $14:380_{24ff.}$, Maksimov is now beginning to play his role as a genteel buffoon. Telling of his various misfortunes, true or imaginary, is a part of his routine. Fiodor Pavlovich went through a similar routine in Book Two, chap. ii, p. 33.

241 398_{17-18}, $14:380_{34}$, "I thought it was for fun."—Better: "I thought it was her high spirits," which makes Kalganov's repartee understandable.

242 398_{24-25}, $14:380_{40-41}$, The translation misses a nuance of Maksimov's buffoonery. He purposely uses absurd phrasing (catachresis). Here he makes his wife say: "I once jumped over a puddle," she said, "in the years of my youth and thereby injured my footsie."

243   398_{42-46}, $14:381_{10-15}$, Kalganov produces a nutshell analysis of
the voluntary buffoon, a stock character not only in Dostoevsky,
but in nineteenth-century Russian literature at large. He stands
for a social type, created by a society in which a déclassé member
of the gentry had few alternatives to that of becoming a parasite
to some more fortunate member of his class.

244   399_{1-10}, $14:381_{16-24}$, The episode alluded to is found at the end
of chapter iv of Gogol's *Dead Souls* (1842). In a way, Dostoevsky
lays bare his own devices here. A great deal of literature has
entered the world of *The Brothers Karamazov* much in the same
way as *Dead Souls* has entered Maksimov's biography. (See
Introduction I.4.a. Secular Sources.)

245   399_7, $14:381_{21}$, "that he was beaten"—it should be: "that it
was he who got thrashed." We are offered another bit of
slapstick comedy, a *Prügelszene*. In Dostoevsky, as in Gogol, the
fun of seeing a "landowner" flogged like a peasant is purely
imaginary. Cf. Book Two, chap. vii, p. 74_{15-16}, and note 215.

246   399_{31-40}, $14:381_{44}-382_4$, "Besides, all that's by way of allegory
in Gogol . . ."—This passage is relevant to the running
discussion on the relationship between fact and fiction which
culminates in Book Twelve. Maksimov, a storyteller himself,
claims that the names in Gogol's *Dead Souls* are disguised
("allegoric") names of real personages: Nozdriov, "Nostril,"
for Nosov, "Nose"; Kuvshinnikov, "Jug," for Shkvorniov,
"Pintle." Fenardi, a historical personage, is alleged to have
entered *Dead Souls* under a pseudonym, and only Maksimov is
depicted under his real name. (Miss Fenardi is Maksimov's own
creation.) The whole passage is a brilliant example of romantic
irony and shows up the complexity of the relationship between
different frames of reference in a novel. See Introduction III.3.d.
Art of the Novel.

247    $399_{41}-400_{21}$, $14:382_{6-29}$, Maksimov still pretends that he was at
that very same country fair at which Nozdriov met Lieutenant
Kuvshinnikov in chapter iv of *Dead Souls*. He alludes to some
"sophisticated" witticisms which were lost on Nozdriov—and
are lost on his present audience, for that matter. In the first,
Krylov, the famous fabulist, makes fun of an exceedingly
homespun translation of Boileau's *L'Art poétique* by presenting
it as Boileau in travesty (the original meaning of "travesty"
being "disguise, masquerade"). In the second, Batiushkov's
"Madrigal to a New Sappho" (1809) is quoted. It is an epigram
on an unsuccessful woman poet, and its unkind point implies

regret that the new Sappho, unlike the Sappho of old, will not fling herself into the sea. The epigram by Piron reads: "Here lies Piron who was nothing, / Not even a member of the Academy." It is a sarcastic jibe at the French Academy, which had refused to elect the brilliant Piron a member. The epigram is quoted by N. M. Karamzin in his *Letters of a Russian Traveller* (1791–92). Note that Fiodor Pavlovich, too, had mentioned Piron (Book Three, chap. viii, p. 123, and note 178). This, along with his buffoonery, pushes the reader toward a realization that Maksimov is in some uncanny way Fiodor Pavlovich's double. See Introduction III.3.b. Mirroring and Doubling.

248   400_{36}, $14:382_{42-43}$, "I drink to your Poland!"—With the action set around 1866—that is, only a few years after the Polish uprising of 1863—drinking to Poland was a gesture of great good will on the part of a Russian officer. Dmitry is in an exuberantly conciliatory mood.

249   401_{10}, $14:383_{17}$, "to Russia, the old grandmother!"—An allusion to the concluding lines of Ivan Goncharov's novel *The Precipice* (1869), and hence an anachronism. See *PSS* 15:577. That Dostoevsky would put this "credit" into the mouth of a Maksimov suggests a low opinion of Goncharov's novel, stated elsewhere; see Dostoevsky's letter to N. N. Strakhov, 26 February/10 March 1869 (*Pis'ma* 2:447).

250   401_{21}, $14:383_{28}$, "To Russia as she was before 1772."—That is, before the initial partition of Poland between Russia, Prussia, and Austria.

251   401_{24}, $14:383_{31}$, "You're fools"—Russ. *durach'io* sounds more good-natured than the English version.

252   402_{1-6}, $14:384_{7-11}$, "lite"—Again, an attempt to duplicate in translation the mispronunciation of Russian (cf. note 224 above), this time the mispronunciation of Russ. *pozdno* as Pol. *późno*. (The spelling makes the words look closer than they are in actual pronunciation.) The joke is, from a Russian viewpoint, that Polish sounds like broken Russian pronounced with a lisp. In the following exchange in the original the narrator introduces several Polish phrases with a Russian translation in parenthesis.

253   402_{46}, $14:385_3$, "plices"—an attempt to duplicate the use of Pol. *miejsca* for Russ. *mesta*.

254   403_5, $14:385_8$, "To cover?"—Translates *otvetnyi*, a technical term meaning that the bank will cover unlimited stakes. The term is then used by Musiałowicz as he describes the bank in Warsaw (line 11 below).

255   403_{11-21}, $14:385_{14-23}$,   In a letter to Liubimov of 16 November
      1879 (*Pis'ma* 4:119) Dostoevsky calls this "a legendary anecdote
      of all petty Polish gamblers-cardsharps." He adds that he had
      heard it three times from different Poles. As for the name
      Podwysocki, Dostoevsky may have seen this book: A. Pod-
      vysotsky, *Memoirs of an Eyewitness of the Events in Warsaw in
      1861 and 1862* (St. Petersburg, 1869).

256   403_{12-13}, $14:385_{15}$,   "stakes against the bank"—does not make
      the point quite clear. In the original, Podwysocki says: *va
      banque,* thinking that there are a thousand gold pieces in the
      bank.

257   403_{22-24}, $14:385_{24-26}$,   "That's not true . . ."—The naive
      Kalganov takes the story seriously, as do the Poles—on a dif-
      ferent level of thinking: they do not believe that the story is true,
      but demand that everybody act as if it were so. Dostoevsky often
      attacked the hollowness of "good manners," in *The Gambler,*
      for instance, where it is a central theme.

258   403_{28}, $14:385_{30}$,   "You see how I talk Polish"—Dmitry actually
      uses the Polish word *honor,* "honor," instead of Russian *chest'.*

259   403_{31}, $14:385_{33}$,   *Panienochka* is Pol. *panienka,* "miss," with a
      Russian diminutive suffix.

260   404_{14}, $14:386_{12}$,   "with a curious [better: "strange"] note in her
      voice"—cf. pp. 394_{39-40}, 396_{13-14}. These little hints build up
      toward a climax.

261   404_{21-23}, $14:386_{21-23}$,   "something in Grushen'ka's face . . ."—
      cf. the preceding note.

262   404_{25-26}, $14:386_{25-26}$,   Dmitry has finally "read" the situation
      and suddenly strikes a grossly familiar tone with his rival.

263   404_{27}, $14:386_{27}$,   "Most   illustrious   one"—translates
      iasnevel'mozhnyj, an ironic Polonism.

264   404_{34-35}, $14:386_{34-35}$,   "The bodyguard"—shows that Dmitry
      has now fully grasped the quality of these two gentlemen (cf. p.
      396_9): Musiałowicz is the brains and Wróblewski the muscle of a
      duo of small-time adventurers. He marches them to a back room
      quite unceremoniously.

265   405_5, $14:386_6$,   The three thousand again! But Dmitry no longer
      has three thousand.

266   405_{39}, $14:387_{35}$,   "You're a couple of capons"—the Poles have
      been acting like a couple of roosters (see p. 401_{26}, and p. 404_{20}).
      Now Dmitry calls their bluff.

267   406_9, $14:388_5$, "the Pole gasped with offended dignity"—
misses a couple of nuances in *Pan zapykhtel ot gonora,* lit. "the
pan was now huffing and puffing with honor." The verb is comic
per se, and *gonor* is "Polish honor," in Russian usage a
superficial sense of "status" or "face."

268   406_{25-28}, $14:388_{23-26}$, There is some intriguing play with the
"poetry of grammar" in the Russian text here. Grushen'ka asks:
"Are you saying that he actually did not take the money?" (with
the perfective past tense *vzial,* "took"). Dmitry answers: "Oh
yes, he was taking it all the way, only he wanted to get the whole
three thousand at once, and I was only giving him seven hundred" (with the complementary imperfective past tense *bral,*
"was taking"). This play of aspects creates an ambiguity in
which he "didn't take it" in the perfective aspect, yet "took it"
in the imperfective aspect.

269   406_{36}, $14:388_{36}$, "anger"—it should be "spite."

270   406_{38}, $14:388_{38}$, "He was a falcon, but this is a gander."—
Literally, "falcon" and "drake," both common symbols of a
lover or bridegroom in Russian folk songs.

271   406_{44}, $14:388_{44}$, In the original, "Sodom" bears a stress mark:
Sódom. This is the Polish pronunciation, the Russian being
Sodóm. This little detail may be meaningful, as one remembers
Dmitry's significant use of that word in Book Three, chap. iii, p.
$97_{10ff.}$

272   407_{15}, $14:389_{13}$, "change a card"—translates *perediornul,* a
slang expression meaning "to skip a card" and "to cheat at
cards" in general.

273   407_{20}, $14:389_{19}$, "confused"—a mistranslation of *skon-
fuzhennyi,* "embarrassed."

274   407_{22}, $14:389_{21}$, "You low harlot!"—Pan Wróblewski's
Publichna shel'ma is a grotesque combination of Russ.
publichnaia devka, "prostitute" (lit. "public wench")—cf. Book
Two, chap. vii, p. 73_{40}, and note 212—and *shel'ma,* "rascal,
rogue." It sounds ridiculous as well as insulting.

275   407_{27}, $14:389_{26}$, "He's struggling"—better: "he fights back."
Note this further display of Dmitry's extraordinary physical
strength.

276   407_{31}, $14:389_{29}$, In the original, Dmitry concludes his sarcastic
invitation with a Polish *przepraszam,* "excuse me."

277   408_{1-2}, $14:389_{47}$, "that she would marry him"—a mistrans-

lation of *chto pani poidiot za nim,* "that she would follow him" ("marry him" would have *za nego* instead of *za nim*).

Chapter viii

278 408_{9-10}, $14:390_7$, "a feast to which all were welcome"—translates *pir na ves' mir,* a formulaic expression meaning as much as a "sumptuous feast" (Russian style).

279 408_{13}, $14:390_{11}$, "His happiness" is in quotation marks in the original, making it clear what Dmitry is hoping for.

280 408_{16}, $14:390_{13}$, " 'let the stove and cottage dance' "—part of the refrain of a popular dancing song. See *PSS* 15:577.

281 408_{39}, $14:390_{35-36}$, "an absurd chaotic confusion followed"—translates *nachalos' nechto besporiadochnoe i nelepoe,* lit. "there began something disorderly and absurd." Disorder is one of the themes of the novel (see Introduction I.3. Early Versions). Significantly, Dmitry is in his natural element here. He has reached the turning point of his life: order will begin to emerge from this disorder in the next Book.

282 409_{9-10}, $14:391_{4-6}$, The original is a little more graphic: "I'd give them a kick with my knee, every one of them, and order them to consider it an honor—that's all they're worth." The rural capitalist's contempt for the peasantry is a significant trait. Cf. note 210 above.

283 409_{43-44}, $14:391_{36-38}$, "Nothing . . . I left a man ill . . ."—The irony of Dmitry's situation comes to a head: he has a presentiment of happiness, yet also a foreboding of doom, as he must keep thinking of Grigory lying there in a pool of blood.

284 409_{45-46}, $14:391_{39-40}$, "So you meant to shoot yourself tomorrow!"—Some more Sophoclean irony, one of the indications of the dramatic quality of the novel. See Introduction III. Narrative Technique.

285 410_{12}, $14:392_5$, "he's drunk"—Grushen'ka says *okhmelel,* which is more tactful than "he's drunk." Perhaps: "he's had too much."

286 410_{17}, $14:392_{10-11}$, "coarse"—translates *skoromnoe,* lit. "fleshly" (specifically of food not to be eaten during Lent). The choice of this term characterizes the narrator as much as it describes the dance.

287 410_{24}, $14:392_{17}$, "ecstatic"—translates *blazhennyi,* which might be better translated as "blissful."

288 410_{28}, $14:392_{20}$, "this peasant foolery"—translates *eta vsia narodnost'*, lit. "all these national roots," where *narodnost'*, "national roots," is a slogan used by the Left and Right alike. In this particular context, Kalganov voices a westernizing liberal's disapproval of the earthiness of Russian peasant folklore, praised extravagantly by Slavophile folklorists. Cf. Potugin's observations in chapter xiv of Turgenev's novel *Smoke* (1867).

289 410_{29}, $14:392_{21-22}$, "it's the games they play when it's light all night in summer"—inexact translation; it should be: "These are their spring rites, when they guard the sun all through the summer night." This is an allusion to the rites of the summer solstice, when fires were lit on mountain tops and people waited all night for the sun to rise. Mummery and a certain licentiousness were a part of these rites. The mere fact that here both are transferred to late summer suggests that the old peasant culture is disintegrating. See *PSS* 15:577.

290 410_{30}–411_{14}, $14:392_{25}$–393_8, In a letter to N. A. Liubimov, dated 16 November 1879 (*Pis'ma* 4:119), Dostoevsky says that "the song sung by the chorus was written down by me from nature and is indeed an example of the more recent [*noveishii*] peasant folklore." The "new" songs differed from the traditional songs both in form and in content. Unlike traditional songs, the "new" *chastushki* feature regular rhyme and stanzaic patterns (couplets and quatrains of trochaic tetrameters). Their content tends to be aggressively satirical and even cynical, often featuring a witty and surprising point (which is sometimes obscene). Kalganov's reaction here is that of many Slavophiles, to whom these "new" songs were decidedly unwelcome, because they were looking for quite different qualities in peasant culture.

291 411_{36-37}, $14:393_{28-30}$, The joke is that the *sabotière* (from *sabot*, "wooden shoe") is of course a peasant dance, too.

292 412_1, $14:393_{35-36}$, "Maksimov danced his dance."—Having to dance for the amusement of his patron is the ultimate humiliation of an old "hanger-on." Cf., for example, the story "My Neighbor Radilov" in Turgenev's *Sportsman's Sketches* (1847). Maksimov actually does it *con amore*, and the naive Dmitry fails to see the whole abjectness of the scene, which Kalganov senses. Scenes of human abjectness are Dostoevsky's forte.

293 412_{15-17}, $14:394_{6-8}$, Dostoevsky will always find a way to give the screw another turn. All of a sudden we remember that

Maksimov is also "von Sohn," the elderly gentleman whose lechery led to his disgraceful death (in a brothel). See Book Two, chap. i, p. 29$_{30-35}$, and chap. viii, pp. 77–78. Cf. note 247 above.

294   412$_{28-30}$, 14:394$_{20-21}$, "and suddenly clutched . . . a sudden light"—the occurrence of the key word *vdrug*, "suddenly," twice within little more than one line emphasizes another turning point. Changes come "suddenly" in Dostoevsky. Dmitry is once more at the crossroads and will have to make a decision.

295   412$_{46}$–413$_1$, 14:394$_{38-39}$,   In the original the triple occurrence of a word for "life" or "live" is even more striking. "Life" ushers in God: Dmitry starts praying.

296   413$_{2-3}$, 14:394$_{39-40}$, "Let this fearful cup pass from me!"—Dmitry echoes Matt. 26:39.

297   413$_6$, 14:394$_{43}$, "I'd get it somehow. . . ."—In the original: "I'll get it from under the ground. . . ," a foreshadowing of the "underground" passage in Book Eleven, chap. iv, p. 560.

298   413$_9$, 14:394$_{46-47}$, "Yet a ray of bright hope shone to him in his darkness."—The Russian phrase differs from the English by the presence of several qualifying modal expressions, literally: "But still a ray, as it were, of some kind of bright hope flashed to him in the darkness." The tension between a strong positive statement ("bright hope flashed") and equally massive modal expressions which qualify that statement ("But still . . . as it were . . . some kind of . . .") is characteristic of the narrator's style. It creates a flavor of immediacy and suspense, reflecting the speaker's struggle for adequate expression.

299   413$_{17}$, 14:395$_6$, "he looked gloomy and worried"—we shall soon find out why. This little scene is a preview of the dénouement at the end of this chapter.

300   413$_{39-40}$, 14:395$_{25-26}$,   "anger"—"spite" is correct. Cf. note 269 above.

301   413$_{41}$, 14:395$_{28-29}$, "kind"—"tender" is better here for *laskovyi*. "Merry" translates *razvesiolyi*, which is "merry" with an emphatic prefix, so perhaps "gay and merry."

302   414$_{15-16}$, 14:395$_{48}$–396$_2$, "A smile lighted up her face . . ."—In the original, this sentence ends in an iambic tetrameter and obviously is euphonically "orchestrated." In emotionally charged passages Dostoevsky (like Dickens, for example) will sometimes veer into poetry.

303   414$_{17-19}$, 14:396$_{2-4}$,   The falcon is Dmitry, of course. Cf. note 270 above. In the original it is even clearer that Grushen'ka

likens her beloved to the Sun, another common metaphor in popular love songs. Note, too, how the word "love" dominates everything Grushen'ka says: it acts as a refrain of sorts.

304   414_{22-24}, $14:396_{7-9}$, Cf. Book Seven, chap. iii, p. 336_{9-13}, and Book Eight, chap. v, p. 374_{5-7}.

305   414_{31}, $14:396_{14}$, "passionately"—the original reads simply "began to kiss her"; however, Russ. *brosilsia,* "began," suggests a quick and sudden impulse.

306   414_{35}, $14:396_{17}$, Flinging one's glass to the ground is a gesture of abandon.

307   414_{39-41}, $14:396_{21-22}$, No particular meaning should be attached to Grushen'ka's desire to be a "slave" and to be "beaten." These are more or less formulaic phrases of Russian folk poetry. "And I do deserve to suffer" is a misinterpretation. It should be: "Kiss me! Beat me up, treat me rough, do something to me. . . . Oh, oughtn't I to be treated rough."

308   415_{5-6}, $14:396_{32-33}$, Better: "Her eyes, which had been flashing, were turning bleary; there was a lure of passion in her eyes."

309   415_{20}, $14:396_{46}$, "like a red-hot coal in his heart"—this may be the paraphrase of a line from Pushkin's famous poem "The Prophet" (1828), a poem Dostoevsky was particularly fond of.

310   415_{30-36}, $14:397_{8-14}$, There are several Russian folk songs with this refrain. See *PSS* 15:578.

311   415_{37}–416_{15}, $14:397_{15-36}$, Grushen'ka is tipsy and begins to ramble. Dostoevsky uses this as motivation for a lyric passage in which Grushen'ka's leitmotifs are woven into a prose poem. In particular we recognize the phrase "I gave a little onion," leitmotif of Book Seven, chap. iii.

312   416_{4-6}, $14:397_{25-26}$, "Everyone in the world is good . . ."—Here Grushen'ka definitely joins the roster of positive characters in the novel led by Father Zosima, as she affirms the goodness of God's world and the good that is inherent in man. A passage of great importance.

313   416_{22-23}, $14:397_{44-45}$, These lines are also from a folk song. See *PSS* 15:578. Maksimov is making a pig of himself.

314   416_{35-36}, $14:398_9$, In the original Dmitry, always the poet, comes up with a neat pun: *a ty pódlaidak! Melkii ty podlechonochek,* "and you are a sub-*lajdak* [Russ. *pod-,* "sub-"]," punning this with Russ. *podlets,* "scoundrel"; *podlechonochek* is a triple diminutive of *podlets.*

315   416_{37-38}, $14:398_{11}$, "He too was drunk."—this translation

simplifies the remark found in the original. Perhaps: "He, too, had gotten tipsy beyond his capacity."

316   416_{44}, $14:398_{17}$, " 'Ah, my hall, my hall!' "—A popular dance tune whose lyrics fit the present situation: a young girl offers to make love to the young man of her choice, overcoming her shame and even her fear of her stern father. Dostoevsky mentions this song in one of his notebooks of 1880–1881. See *The Unpublished Dostoevsky*, 3:146, where the entry is mistranslated. It should be: "Ah, you hall, my hall. Analysis of the song. She is full of passion. She has just granted her favors once . . . Her father is stern. But she still intends to grant more favors. His father's only son, as a pretext. The poet [who made this song] is not beneath Pushkin."

317   417_{17-18}, $14:398_{36}$, "Kissed her on the lips" is an understatement: *vpilsia v eio guby potseluem* is lit. "glued his lips to hers in a kiss," where *vpilsia* describes a powerful sucking action (as of a leech). The scene is more heavily sensuous in the original.

318   417_{33}, $14:399_3$, "That blood" keeps reappearing as a discordant note in this love scene.

319   417_{35-37}, $14:399_{5-6}$, The names of the two rivals appear in significant contrast here: "Grusha" is the affectionately intimate form that a husband or lover will use ("Grushen'ka" is slightly condescending). "Kat'ka" (which the translator has rendered by "Katia") is disrespectful and cutting. Fiodor Pavlovich, in an ugly mood, had used "Grushka" (Book Four, chap. ii, p. 158_{17}).

320   417_{40-41}, $14:399_{9-10}$, "We shall waste it anyway."—Translates *My ikh i bez togo prokutim,* where *prokutim* implies a spree of some kind, normally the kind of spree Grushen'ka and Dmitry are on at the moment.

321   417_{41-42}, $14:399_{10-11}$, In the original both "the land" and "the earth" are *zemlia*. Grushen'ka thus joins Dmitry, Aliosha, and Father Zosima in their worship of the earth. Dmitry considered working the land as early as Book Three, chap. iii, p. 96_{5-7}.

322   418_5, $14:399_{18}$, "in Siberia"—the motif of Siberia becomes positively persistent now. Cf. notes 98, 149, and 178 above.

323   418_{7-10}, $14:399_{20-23}$, Note the skilful transition from Siberia, to snow, to sleighbells, and on to a heart-stopping silent scene. The effect is enhanced by the circumstance that Dmitry and Grushen'ka are unaware of the drama.

324   418_{26}–419_6, $14:399_{39}$–400_{14},   "And suddenly he had a strange fancy . . ."—Note how Dostoevsky lets the whole horror of this scene filter through Dmitry's consciousness.

325   419_1, $14:400_{11}$,   "Jurisprudence"—short for "Imperial School of Jurisprudence."

326   419_{16-17}, $14:400_{25-26}$,   "The old man! . . ."—Sophoclean irony doubled! Both Dmitry and his accusers are under a delusion, while the reader can guess the truth.

327   419_{20-27}, $14:400_{29-36}$,   This brief incident has considerable symbolic importance. The young jurist from an elite institution thinks of due process of law. The old police captain, a good man, acts naturally and straightforwardly. Both are mistaken. Thus begins Dmitry's (and Dostoevsky's) battle with the reformed and westernized legal system of post-Emancipation Russia.

328   419_{28}, $14:400_{37}$,   "This is delirium"—the title of this chapter is "Delirium." This passage gives it an ironic twist, for in a way the police captain sees madness where there is none.

329   419_{28-31}, $14:400_{37-39}$,   The tragic conflict between reality and appearances. At a moment when she least deserves it, Grushen'ka is called a "disreputable wench" (Russ. *devka* is "wench," not "woman"). The blood on Dmitry's hands is not his father's. This conflict will dominate the remainder of the novel. The second chapter of the Epilogue bears the title "For a Moment the Lie Becomes Truth." In the last chapter temporal truth fades into insignificance before faith in immortality.

Book Nine

Chapter i

1 420₄, 14:401₇, The chapter title is a bit of a mystification. We never learn anything specific about Perkhotin's "career." The narrator, as a local resident, presumes that other local residents, who are his immediate audience, know all about it. The reader at large can guess, for the time being, that the publicity Perkhotin got in connection with the Karamazov case helped to launch his career. Later we realize that it caused him to meet the wealthy Mme. Khokhlakov. As with some other chapter titles, this one stands in marked ironic contrast to the narrative covered by it. See Introduction III.1.a. The Narrator.

2 420₅₋₆, 14:401₈₋₉, The reference is to Book Eight, chap. v, p. 386₃₀₋₃₁.

3 420₂₄₋₂₅, 14:401₂₅₋₂₆, In the original, the verb *kapat'*, "to drip," is used three times in a row; "flowing" is a needless "improvement" on Dostoevsky's text. Note also the repetition of the words "blood," "hands," and "kill" in this scene. We have followed Dmitry's every move until his arrest. We shall now retrace the various moves which will later make up the case against him. The very first detail suggests that we ought to watch out for discrepancies.

4 421₂₅₋₂₉, 14:402₂₀₋₂₄, "It would make a scandal . . ."—Note the meticulous attention paid by the narrator to the psychology of this minor character (cf. the similar treatment of Kalganov in the preceding two chapters). Dostoevsky, the dramatic novelist, treats his "extras" as though they had star billing—somewhat like Stanislavsky at the Moscow Art Theater some decades later.

5 421₂₈₋₂₉, 14:402₂₄, A pattern is started: the "investigation" follows the path least likely to lead to the truth. Ironically, the sober and sensible Perkhotin makes the first mistake.

6   422_{32-36}, $14:403_{22-26}$,   In the original: "parenthetically and in passing," with obvious irony. These details are setting up Mme. Khokhlakov for some further developments in Book Eleven, chap. ii.

7   $423_{5ff.}$, $14:403_{40ff.}$,   Once more, the words "kill" (Russ. *ubit'* is diluted somewhat by its being translated by "kill" or "murder"), "blood," and "hands" dominate the text.

8   423_{17}, $14:404_5$,   "two or three thousand roubles"—in the original we find a more prudent "two or even three thousand." Still, there is that "three thousand" again. Dmitry's joke (Book Eight, chap. v, p. $378_{19-20, 27-28}$) comes back to haunt him.

9   423_{33}, $14:404_{21-22}$,   "he positively spat at me"—here "positively" translates *dazhe,* "even, actually," which makes for more comic bathos. Clever misuse of *dazhe* is one of Dostoevsky's trademarks. See Introduction III.1.a. The Narrator. Of course Dmitry did not spit "at her" (cf. Book Eight, chap. iii, p. 366_{12}).

10   423_{44}, $14:404_{32}$,   "the pestle"—once more, the "murder weapon." Dostoevsky reviews every detail surrounding the crime repeatedly, and from various angles.

11   $424_{1ff.}$, $14:404_{35ff.}$,   At this tense juncture of the plot, we are treated to a leisurely comedy routine by Mme. Khokhlakov.

12   424_{11-14}, $14:404_{46}-405_1$,   "I don't believe in miracles . . ."— Mme. Khokhlakov has changed her mind about miracles before (cf. Book Two, chap. iv, p. 45; Book Four, chap. i, p. 150; Book Seven, chap. ii, p. 320, Book Eight, chap. iii, p. 363_{16-19}). She belongs to that part of humanity which needs miracles in order to have faith. Accordingly, she stumbles from one absurdity to another.

13   424_{15-16}, $14:405_3$,   Mme. Khokhlakov has great talent for comic bathos. Here, they are talking about parricide, and she is indignant about having been spat at.

14   424_{32-33}, $14:405_{16-17}$,   "how they'll try him . . ."—there is no doubt in her mind: Dmitry is already convicted. More and more, Mme. Khokhlakov turns into a caricature of the Russian liberal. She takes it to be quite natural that Dmitry should have killed his father, and in the same breath she reassures herself that his punishment will not be too severe.

15   425_{2-3}, $14:405_{35}$,   Now "three thousand roubles" have become part of a document.

16   425_{34-40}, $14:406_{23-31}$,   "I would not, however . . ."—This and

similar passages keep the novel "open" in more ways than one.
The dark tragedy of the Karamazovs is not only part of a broad
panorama of life in which ordinary and not at all unpleasant
characters, such as Perkhotin, predominate. The novel, as it
were, merges with the life outside of it. The boundary between
external and internal frames of reference becomes fluid. And
once more, a sequel to the novel is promised.

Chapter ii

17   426_{3-4}, $14:406_{35}$, In the original: "a retired lieutenant colonel,
redesignated a court councilor" (the latter being the civil service
rank equivalent to that of a lieutenant colonel in the military).
The character sketch of this man mixes cautious political satire
with a rather gentle, human irony. Along with other such passages, it helps to create a realistic, everyday setting for the tragic
plot of the novel. See Introduction II.4. Social Novel.

18   426_{30-39}, $14:407_{16-25}$, The reforms of the early 1860s affected
every aspect of Russian life. They not only emancipated the serfs,
but also established, at least theoretically, equality before the
law, universal military conscription (thus doing away with class
privileges), and the foundations for local self-government.

19   426_{33-34}, $14:407_{20-21}$, "but from carelessness . . ."—better:
"but from a happy-go-lucky strain in his character, because he
never got around to looking into these matters."

20   426_{43}–427_2, $14:407_{30-32}$, The contemporary reader must have
chuckled at the old-fashioned police captain, an obvious retrograde, playing cards with the young "district doctor" *(zemskii
vrach),* recently graduated from what was known as a hotbed of
radicalism and employed by the *zemstvo,* an organ of local self-
government instituted a mere two or three years earlier (1864).
We shall meet Varvinsky again (Book Twelve, chap. iii, p. 639).

21   427_{3-4}, $14:407_{32-33}$, "he was really the deputy prosecutor"—one
of the many details by which Dostoevsky creates the proper provincial atmosphere and a narrator who is a part of it.

22   427_{10-12}, $14:407_{41-44}$, "Knowledge" translates *dar poznavaniia,*
lit. "a gift of cognition," a pompous expression which pushes
the whole sentence over the brink, into pointed irony. Ippolit
Kirillovich's "psychology" will become the target of bitter sarcasm in Book Twelve, chap. ix, "Psychology at Full Steam." See
Introduction II.6.a. Dostoevsky's Psychology.

23   427_{19}, $14:408_{2-3}$, "But I am anticipating."—Once more Dostoevsky feigns the inexperienced amateur narrator who cannot keep the sequence of events straight.

24   427_{25-26}, $14:408_{9-10}$, "Yet it was perfectly simple . . ."—An example of Dostoevsky's mirroring technique. Here, several quite ordinary events make up an odd coincidence: the same is true of the circumstances that cause Dmitry to be accused of the murder of his father.

25    $427_{29ff.}$, $14:408_{13ff.}$, The character sketch of Nikolai Parfenovich Neliudov is important, since it is he who will interrogate Dmitry. The condescending irony with which he is introduced reflects on the whole travesty of justice (legal justice, that is) which will be presented in the following chapters.

26    $428_{14ff.}$, $14:408_{43ff.}$, Note the neatness with which the action now unfolds in reverse order: it is like peeling an onion.

27   428_{17-18}, $14:408_{46}$, "a fearful epileptic scream from Smerdiakov"—the attentive reader will see this as a clue to the identity of the real murderer. Cf. Book Eleven, chap. viii, p. 596_{34}.

28   428_{32}, $14:409_{14}$, "Good Lord! Just as it was with Lizaveta Smerdiashchaia!"—An important hint: what has just happened may well have been retribution for the wrong done to the holy fool. See Introduction III.5.f. Mythical Symbolism.

29   428_{36-37}, $14:409_{18-19}$, "in a weak, moaning, dreadful voice"—in the original: *slabym, steniashchim, strashnym golosom,* with alliteration and a rhythmic cadence.

30   428_{45-46}, $14:409_{26}$, "he has murdered . . . his father"—the last word Grigory had shouted before being hit by Dmitry's pestle was "parricide" *(ottseubivets);* his first word now is "murdered . . . his father" *(ubil . . . ottsa).* A notion conceived earlier (see Book Three, chap. ix) and fixed in a moment of intense excitement has now become a "fact." Note how the phrase "killed his father" dominates the text long before there is any direct evidence that he did.

31   429_{15}, $14:409_{41}$, We have heard of Thomas (Russ. Foma) in Book Three, chap. v, p. 109_{34}.

33   429_{24-26}, $14:410_{3-4}$, Cf. note 27 above.

34   429_{30-31}, $14:410_{8}$, The open door will play a key role from here on.

35   429_{44}, $14:410_{23}$, "witnesses"—translates a Russian legal term designating a person deputized to assist in a criminal investigation.

36   429₄₅₋₄₆, 14:410₂₄, "according to the regular forms"—"for-
      malities," that is. Dostoevsky is now well along in his effort to
      discredit "modern" and of course thoroughly "civilized" legal
      procedures imported from the West.

37   430₉₋₁₀, 14:410₃₆, "no signs of disturbance"—another signifi-
      cant clue: we remember what the place looked like when Dmitry
      broke into the house two days earlier (Book Three, chap. ix, pp.
      126–28).

38   430₁₂₋₁₅, 14:410₃₉₋₄₅, We know the envelope well from Smer-
      diakov's report to Ivan Fiodorovich (Book Five, chap. vi, p.
      252₃₁₋₃₃). Again the legend is slightly mistranslated. It should
      read: "and my little chick." The legend and the pink ribbon re-
      mind us that the old man was shamelessly and mushily in love
      with Grushen'ka. The addition of "and my little chick" adds a
      whole new dimension to Fiodor Pavlovich. It is in this kind of de-
      tail that Dostoevsky excels.

39   430₂₆, 14:411₅, See Book Eight, chap. v, p. 380₃₃. The trans-
      lator has neglected to observe this significant concordance (in the
      original it is an identical *ne uspeesh,* "you won't make it"). The
      passage is an example of Dostoevsky's masterful use of *erlebte
      Rede:* Piotr Il'ich's account is presented as perceived by Ippolit
      Kirillovich.

40   430₃₃₋₃₇, 14:411₁₂₋₁₅, "the fellow that murdered a merchant
      . . ."—the prototype of this anonymous criminal was a certain
      Zaitsev, whose case was reported by the Petersburg papers in
      January 1879. The same case will reappear in the defender's
      speech (Book Twelve, chap. xi, p. 694).

41   431₂₋₅, 14:411₂₆₋₂₉, Alludes to Book Eight, chap. viii, p.
      413₁₆₋₁₈.

42   431₁₃₋₁₅, 14:411₃₇₋₄₀, "recurring continually for two days"—we
      now remember Smerdiakov's hints to Ivan Fiodorovich (Book
      Five, chap. vi, p. 251₂₅₋₃₂).

Chapter iii

43   431₂₂, 14:412₂₋₃, "The Torments of a Soul. The First Tor-
      ment."—Echoes Orthodox eschatology. After death, as it as-
      cends heavenward from earth, the human soul is intercepted by
      evil spirits who subject it to various trials, twenty in all. These
      trials are called *mytarstva,* translated here by "torments of the
      soul." In a notebook entry of 24 December 1877, Dostoevsky
      had suggested that he was planning "to write a poem, *Soro-*

koviny.'' It was to be in the form of a "Book of Pilgrimage," describing "trials 1 (2, 3, 4, 5, 6, etc.)" (see *PSS* 15:409). *Sorokoviny* (from *sorok,* "forty") is a memorial service held on the fortieth day after a person's death. This chapter title (two more "trials" are to follow) is apparently borrowed from this particular plan. Here Dmitry's soul undergoes a series of trials at the conclusion of which he emerges a new man.

44   431_{26-28}, $14:412_{7-8}$,   According to the commentators of *PSS,* this passage, as well as the whole situation, may have been influenced by Balzac's short story "L'Auberge rouge" (1821). See *PSS* 15:579–80. But Dostoevsky had essentially the same episode in the real-life Il'insky case. See Introduction I.1.a. *The Brothers Karamazov* in Dostoevsky's Life, and I.6.b. Il'insky and Dmitry Karamazov.

45   431_{31-36}, $14:412_{12-16}$,   "It was my fault . . ."—The seed of Father Zosima's teaching is beginning to come up: Grushen'ka is willing to share another human being's guilt. See Introduction II.5.a. Faith and Unbelief.

46   431_{34}, $14:412_{15}$,   "I tortured that poor old man that's dead"—an entirely new angle on Fiodor Pavlovich.

47   432_{20-26}, $14:412_{41-47}$,   The detail involving the district attorney's rings has been prepared for earlier (chap. ii, p. 427_{43-44}). It is yet another illustration of Dmitry's inability to concentrate—a child-like trait. Cf. Book Two, chap. vi, p. $58_{35ff.}$.

48   432_{38-39}, $14:413_{13-14}$,   "Punish me" translates *kaznite,* which suggests capital punishment, while "wide-open" is not quite accurate for *vypuchivshimsia,* "bulging, goggle-eyed." We know from Book Two, chap. vi, p. $58_{35ff.}$, that Dmitry has somewhat prominent eyes.

49   432_{46}, $14:413_{20}$,   The translator translates two further occurrences of the word *krov',* "blood," by "murder." Since Dmitry's speech tends to be poetic, such repetition (it is like a refrain or leitmotif) is certainly in character. The translation destroys this effect.

50   433_{1-3}, $14:413_{21-24}$,   Dmitry is beginning to show his mettle. Here he is genuinely eloquent: we have a nice rhetorical gradation concluding a triadic construction built around the phrase "who killed?"

51   433_{13-17}, $14:413_{34-38}$,   Note the contrast between the prosecutor's dry "officialese" (lines 8–12) and Dmitry's heartfelt, marvelously appropriate response. Also, note that Dmitry crosses himself, ceremoniously and properly, three times.

52   433₃₅, 14:414₇, "he was like a father to me"—translates *byl
      ottsom rodnym,* lit. "he was my own father," symbolically im-
      portant for the "sons and fathers" theme. See Introduction
      II.3.a. Fatherhood.

53   433₄₁, 14:414₁₂, "drum"—the original has "drum skin."

54   433₄₄₋₄₅, 14:414₁₇₋₁₈, "His whole bearing was changed"—
      "bearing" translates *ton,* lit. "tone, tone of voice." What
      Dmitry just said—"A man is not a drum skin, gentlemen!"—is
      suggestive of this change, a change to the tone a man uses with
      equals.

55   434₈₋₁₀, 14:414₂₇₋₃₁, Note Dostoevsky's careful attention to
      "off-stage" characters. This is the third time the prosecutor's
      wife has been mentioned (previously: p. 427₆, ₂₆₋₂₇), and each time
      we hear something quite specific and unexpected.

56   434₁₄, 14:414₃₄₋₃₅, "lawyer"—translates *sledovatel',* "in-
      vestigator," which is also Nikolai Parfenovich's official title.

57   434₁₅₋₁₆, 14:414₃₆, "I feel like a new man"—translates *ia
      voskreshen,* lit. "I am risen from the dead." The translation is
      correct insofar as the meaning of Dmitry's words is concerned,
      but it fails to bring out the implied Christian symbolism.

58   434₂₈₋₂₉, 14:415₁₋₃, Note Dostoevsky's careful "stage direc-
      tions" concerning Dmitry's behavior before his interrogators.
      Dostoevsky is working on a psychological side thesis: it is dif-
      ficult, if not outright impossible, to judge a man's inner life by
      his behavior.

59   434₃₆₋₄₂, 14:415₁₀₋₁₅, The motif of guilt is now foregrounded.
      Dmitry sees himself as personally guilty of certain misdeeds (the
      reader knows several of them), but he still sees things from a con-
      ventional legalistic viewpoint. He will have to grow a great deal
      before he will embrace Father Zosima's teaching of universal
      guilt. Cf. note 45 above.

60   435₃₁, 14:416₁₋₂, "I'm shocked to the core"—translates *Ia ved'
      i sam porazhon do epidermy,* "You see, I am myself shocked to
      my epidermis." Dmitry is naturally eloquent, but poorly edu-
      cated: he does not know the exact meaning of "epidermis" (the
      outermost layer of the skin) and really says the exact opposite of
      what he means—but the impact of the word is exactly what he
      wants it to be.

61   435₃₉₋₄₀, 14:416₁₀₋₁₁, "That's horrible! . . ."—This is impor-
      tant: Dmitry's reaction is not one of impious exultation at his
      hated father's death, but one of sincere horror and shock.

62   436_1, 14:416_{18},   The three thousand roubles are now becoming a matter of record. See Introduction III.3.a. Motifs.

63   436_{10-11}, 14:416_{28-29},   What Dmitry has just said seems to be incriminating evidence, inadvertently blurted out by the criminal himself—something like what occurs in Schiller's famous "Cranes of Ibycus." But then, an innocent man could very well have said what we have just heard—or a crafty criminal, trying to play the role of an innocent man. We are back with the inherent ambiguity of all psychological analysis. See Introduction II.6.b. Psychological Motivation.

64   436_{15-17}, 14:416_{34-36},   "Fact" translates *ulika*, "evidence (in a criminal case)." What is evidence against Dmitry in the eyes of his accusers is to him evidence that exonerates him. Cf. note 63 above.

65   436_{19-22}, 14:416_{38-42},   "You have to deal with a man of honor . . ."—one of those psychological paradoxes so characteristic of Dostoevsky. See Introduction II.6.d. Psychological Wisdom.

66   436_{24-28}, 14:416_{43-47},   Dmitry senses the awkwardness of his own words and tries to turn them into something less than serious, by an overstatement ("a martyr to a sense of honor"), a wholly inappropriate simile (Diogenes, the cynic philosopher, was seen wandering about with a lantern, in broad daylight, "looking for man"), and finally, a bit of bathos ("that is like me alone"). As always, Dmitry is witty and, willy-nilly, entertaining.

67   436_{29-32}, 14:416_{48}–417_3,   "I couldn't bear the look of him . . ."—Yet another view of Fiodor Pavlovich. The translator's "irreverent" stands for *bezverie*, "unbelief," which is—so far as the plan of the novel is concerned—the key word here. The enmity between father and son is suddenly raised to a higher plane: Dmitry the believer could not stand his father's cynical unbelief. Of course, to one who believes in Dmitry's guilt this is merely a desperate man's ploy to gain the sympathy of his accusers.

68   436_{37}, 14:417_{8-9},   "I'm not very beautiful"—Dmitry never says anything trite. Here he comes up with a striking synthesis of the moral and aesthetic planes of being, whose relationship has always occupied him. Cf. Book Three, notes 63, 68, and 70.

69   437_{27-29}, 14:417_{47}–418_1,   Important for the plan of the novel. Mikhail Makarovich, an uneducated military man and a retrograde, is the man who had so angrily denounced Dmitry and Grushen'ka only a short time earlier (Book Eight, chap. viii, p. 419). Now the "monster and parricide" has become a

neschastnyi (translated by "luckless prisoner"), the affectionate
vernacular term used by the people for a prisoner. Perhaps:
"poor man." Dostoevsky attached great significance to the fact
that the Russian people would call a convicted criminal a "poor
man." This human reaction of a simple Russian soul is contrasted
to the cold legalism of the educated and westernized lawyers.

70   437₃₇, 14:418₈₋₉, "she would have kissed my old hands"—the
expression in the original is a good deal more colloquial, as is the
whole tirade. The detail is a significant one. Grushen'ka's
reaction is straightforwardly Russian: a good woman will
humble herself for the sake of the man she loves and will do so
sincerely, without affectation. (Katerina Ivanovna's "Russian-
style" low bow before Dmitry comes to mind.) And Mikhail
Makarovich, himself a good man and a Russian, understands
Grushen'ka perfectly.

71   437₄₁₋₄₂, 14:418₁₃₋₁₄, "she is a Christian soul . . . a gentle
soul"—another instance of Dostoevsky's centrifugal psychology: we discover a completely different Grushen'ka.

72   437₄₅₋₄₆, 14:418₁₆, "said a great deal that was irregular"—
translates *nagovoril mnogo lishnego,* which means simply "said
too much, said more than was necessary."

73   438₃₋₂₃, 14:418₁₉₋₃₈, Dmitry's tirade is still eloquent, but now
definitely hysterical. Repetition *(vesel(o),* cheerful, gay," appears four times) and blatant overstatement are telltale signs.

74   438₂₄₋₂₅, 14:418₃₉₋₄₀, Again we see Dmitry crying. Cf. Book
Eight, notes 106, 225.

75   438₃₅₋₃₆, 14:418₄₈₋₄₁₉₁, "and don't rummage in my soul"—an
expression of antipsychologism, shared by Dostoevsky with his
hero. See Introduction II.6.a. Dostoevsky's Psychology. Interestingly, some of Dostoevsky's critics (Turgenev, for instance)
felt that precisely this "rummaging in the souls" of his heroes
was a discreditable trait of his novelistic style.

Chapter iv

76   438₄₂₋₄₃₉₉, 14:419₇₋₁₈, The investigator's language is also
eloquent, yet very much unlike Dmitry's spontaneous and
imaginative speech. Note the long sentences, with adroitly
embedded subordinate clauses, well-chosen but bookish words,
and smooth, grammatical syntax. Where Dmitry says *doverie,*
"trust" (translated by "confidence," p. 438₃₄), the investigator

says *doverennost'*, "confidentiality." Where Dmitry speaks as man to man, Nikolai Parfenovich uses legal jargon ("the suspected party").

77   439_{13-25}, $14:419_{22-36}$, This detailed information on the prosecutor and his young colleague is relevant to the subsequent course of events. The "unappreciated" prosecutor's unrequited thirst for recognition and excessive trust in his own psychological acumen are factors in Dmitry's downfall. Incidentally, the translation "the sharp-witted junior" misses a nuance: in the original, "Nikolai Parfenovich's sharp little mind" (*vostren'kii um*, where the diminutive suffix goes with the adjective) suggests that the investigator's mind, efficient in a petty and shallow way, will perform ancillary duties well, but is hopelessly below the task of understanding the generous Dmitry.

78   439_{30-31}, $14:419_{42}$, "Little fact" *(faktik)* is ironic and shows that the investigator is not keeping his side of the bargain: he keeps pursuing his own preconceived notion of Dmitry's guilt.

79   440_{5-9}, $14:420_{16-20}$, Those three thousand roubles are now beginning to haunt Dmitry. See Introduction III.3.a. Motifs.

80   440_{12-13}, $14:420_{23}$, Introduces a new leitmotif: that of fact and fiction. The irony of the encounter between Dmitry and the prosecutor is that the latter assumes that Dmitry is creating a fiction, while his own version of the events is true to fact. The exact contrary is, of course, the case. See Introduction III.3.d. Art of the Novel.

81   440_{14-16}, $14:420_{24-26}$, Note once more Dostoevsky's careful attention to "intonation." See Introduction III.

82   440_{37}, $14:420_{46}$, "And on what did you step?"—In Russian, this sounds more disrespectful than in English, as there is only one thing that the preposition used *(vo)* allows one to have "stepped on."

83   440_{38}, $14:420_{47}$, "and you will put it all down against me"—in the original, Dmitry's remark is even more penetrating. It is the reversal of a saying to the effect that not every mistake is counted against one (lit. "not every string of bast is woven true to pattern"). Dmitry says that they will take advantage of each and every mistake he makes and weave it into a pattern of guilt.

84   440_{42}, $14:421_4$, "conventional method"—translates *kazion-shchina*, "red tape" (from *kazionnyi*, "official"); the word is translated by "regulation method" in line 46, which seems to be a better translation.

85   441_{10-11}, $14:421_{18-20}$, In the original, the adjective *maleishii,* "slightest, smallest," appears four times in this sentence, and in addition, two of the nouns appear in a diminutive form. This foregrounds the prosecutor's attention to detail.

86   441_{17-24}, $14:421_{25-32}$, "I understand . . ."—The general impression of this tirade is the same in the original: Dmitry is certainly overdoing it. In the original, however, a pattern of repetition ("understand," "appreciate," "noble," "honor," and "offense" are all repeated) gives it a certain unaffected quality.

87   441_{29}, $14:421_{36}$, "tricky"—translates *kriuchkotvornye,* a humorous compound equivalent to Eng. "pettifogging."

88   442_{17-20}, $14:422_{25-28}$, "we will not reproduce . . ."—in other instances the narrator will not hesitate to report the same incident for a second or third time. The scene in question just is not relevant to any important aspect of the novel as a whole.

89   442_{28-29}, $14:422_{25-26}$, The original has: "He was now beginning to realize fully that he had been fooled then," where the imperfective aspect (*dogadyvalsia,* "was beginning to realize"), in typically Dostoevskian fashion, clashes with the adverb "fully" *(vpolne).*

90   442_{34}, $14:422_{43}$, "Surly" does not seem quite correct for *ugriumyi;* perhaps: "gloomy." The Russian adjective suggests a state of mind which is directed inward.

91   442_{36}, $14:422_{44}$, "stifling"—translates *ugarnyi,* adjective to *ugar,* "carbon monoxide gas, charcoal fumes," alluding to Book Eight, chap. ii, p. 355.

92   442_{41}, $14:422_{48}-423_1$, "a place of ambush"—translates *nabliudatel'nyi punkt,* "observation post," a military term which, unlike "ambush," does not imply an impending attack.

93   $442_{45}-443_8$, $14:423_{3-14}$, An interesting passage as regards narrative technique. The point of view shifts from that of an omniscient observer, to that of an outsider present at the scene, to direct identification with Dmitry's stream of consciousness. The quotation (inaccurate) from Tiutchev's poem "Silentium" (1833), which many contemporary readers knew by heart, introduces an added extratextual frame of reference. A famous line from that poem, "A thought once uttered is a lie," would inevitably have come to the reader's mind and made him reflect, with Dmitry, on the futility of the latter's attempts to share with his accusers what he knows to be the truth.

94   443_{10-11}, $14:423_{15-16}$, "When he came . . ."—In the original,

dazhe, "even," occurs twice in this sentence, signaling a strong shift of mood.

95   443_{19}, $14:423_{23}$,   "when he learned"—the original has "when he suddenly learned." As so often, the translator omits one of Dostoevsky's key words as apparently redundant. Here, "suddenly" is altogether essential to the mood of the scene.

96   443_{24}, $14:423_{28}$,   "That, too, was carefully written down."—And so, Dmitry's steps, well known to us from Book Eight, are retraced one by one, yet with important shifts of emphasis. The "facts" are the same, yet there is a new story. See Introduction III.3.a. Motifs.

97   443_{34-35}, $14:423_{37-38}$,   "Do you suppose I could have managed without it?"—Ironic, on Dmitry's part: he would have gotten to the brass pestle anyway when telling about his encounter with Grigory, so Nikolai Parfenovich's "surprise" is no triumph at all. The commentator of *PSS* sees here a pun made by Dmitry, who had said: "Never mind, what the devil!" and who then relates the district attorney's question to "the devil" rather than to "the pestle." Both words are masculine in Russian. If this interpretation is correct, "it" should be replaced by "him" in this exchange, and "Damn it" by "the devil."

98   444_1, $14:423_{47}$,   "Mitia's wrath flared up."—A mistranslation of *V Mite kipela dosada,* lit. "Mitia was seething with vexation," where *dosada* is a feeling of vexation or annoyance, and *kipela* an imperfective verb suggesting a state of mind, rather than a reaction.

99   444_2, $14:423_{48}$,   "Malignantly" may be too strong for *zlobno;* perhaps: "angrily."

100   444_4, $14:424_2$,   "spontaneously"—in the original: "with such effusions," suggesting self-irony on Dmitry's part.

101   444_{27}, $14:424_{24}$,   *passons*—"enough of that."

102   444_{29-30}, $14:424_{27-28}$,   "a feeling of nausea"—it should be "a bad feeling" or "an ugly feeling."

103   444_{33-42}, $14:424_{30-40}$,   This dream does not seem to have any particular symbolic meaning. But it adds another dimension to Dmitry's psychological *Gestalt,* and it is most apropos as a simile in the present context. Dmitry's predicament is indeed like a bad dream.

104   445_{3-5}, $14:424_{45-46}$,   Once more, Dmitry produces a marvelously apt image: the two lawyers are engaged in their favorite sport, while their victim is fighting for his life.

105   445_{11-13}, $14:425_{7-9}$,   Highly relevant to the running argument

about the theory of fiction which continues throughout the
novel. Dmitry cannot admit the notion that a feeling sincerely
and spontaneously expressed might be taken for a fiction—while
a fiction will be taken for the truth. See Introduction III.3.d. Art
of the Novel.

Chapter v

106   445_{30-35}, $14:425_{27-31}$, "Mitya could gather nothing . . ."—
Dmitry does not realize that his interrogators have already
created a different version of the events in their minds—nor does
the reader, at this stage. This is not the first time that the reader is
made to share Dmitry's unawareness of current developments
(cf. Book Eight, chap. viii, p. 413_{15-28}).

107   446_5, $14:425_{44}$, This dramatic pause shows Dostoevsky's stage
sense. After Dmitry's violent flare-up and the district attorney's
dry repartee, apt to pour more oil onto the fire, the moment has
come for the suspense of a great silent scene which enhances the
pathos of the following lines.

108   446_6, $14:425_{45}$, "softly"—the key to the dramatic effect of this
scene.

109   446_7, $14:425_{46}$, "or my mother prayed to God"—in Russian,
umolila is the perfective aspect of the verb, suggesting a prayer
which was answered. So perhaps: "or God answered my
mother's prayers," though this does not duplicate the amazing
tautness of the Russian form.

110   446_{8-9}, $14:426_{1-2}$, "But the devil was conquered."—Dmitry has
used the devil's name in vain repeatedly during this interrogation
(it is translated by "damn it," "hell," etc.). Now he uses the
word literally, in its canonic sense.

111   446_{24-26}, $14:426_{16-17}$, "A poem! . . ."—Cf. note 105 above.

112   446_{41}–447_2, $14:426_{32-38}$, Now we see the reason for the interrogators' skeptical reception of Dmitry's account (see note 106
above). The open door, seemingly a minor detail, is the crux of
the case.

113   447_{10}, $14:426_{46}$, "signals"—cf. Book Five, chap. vi, pp.
250–51, and Book Eight, chap. iv, p. 369_{41-44}.

114   447_{13-18}, $14:427_{1-6}$, An example of Dostoevsky's "expanding"
psychology (see Introduction II.6.a. Dostoevsky's Psychology).
Suddenly we discover an entirely new aspect of Ippolit
Kirillogich's personality. Note, too, the apparent overstatement

and paradox of "cringing timidity" in a prosecutor addressing an accused murderer—yet it describes the phenomenon perfectly.

115   447_{29}, $14:427_{16}$, "The prosecutor swallowed this without a murmur."—The original is somewhat more graphic, lit. "The prosecutor ate up all these pills," where "without a murmur" is implied in the connotation of the verb form *skushal,* "ate up."

116   447_{40}, $14:427_{27}$, "dead father"—it is "late parent" *(pokoinyi roditel')* in the original.

117   447_{44-45}, $14:427_{37}$, "Besides, you will need God yourselves."— These apparently pointless words acquire a meaning when we learn, at the beginning of chapter vi of Book Twelve that Ippolit Kirillovich is to die only nine months after Dmitry's trial. We do know that he is "inclined to be consumptive" (chap. ii, p. 427_5).

118   448_{7-9}, $14:427_{39-41}$, This paragraph, while accurately translated, is much more compact than in the original, where it seems purposely drawn out to enhance an impression of painful suspense.

119   448_{11}, $14:427_{43}$, "beast"—the original has "rascal" *(merzavka)*.

120   448_{27-29}, $14:428_{10}$, "I can't get Smerdiakov out of my head."— This reminds the reader of Smerdiakov's irritating, tormenting presence in Ivan's mind (Book Five, chap. vi, pp. 245–46). Note, too, the *crescendo* in which Smerdiakov's name appears in this scene, until it is foregrounded in this paragraph, then allowed to recede into the background.

121   448_{42}, $14:428_{23}$, "He has the heart of a chicken."—In the original: "He was born of a chicken," yet another version of Smerdiakov's origins. Cf. Grigory's words: "You grew from the mildew in the bathhouse" (Book Three, chap. vi, p. 112_{34-35}) and "this, who has come from the devil's son and a holy innocent" (Book Three, chap. ii, p. 89_{30-31}). A moment later, Dmitry "realizes" the metaphor as he calls Smerdiakov a "puling chicken" (p. 449_1).

122   449_{5-9}, $14:428_{31-34}$, "he's very likely his son . . ."—Russ. *mozhet byt'* is "maybe" or "perhaps," not "very likely." In this instance it makes a difference. This is the only instance in which one of the Karamazovs alludes to the rumors which were heard in town a quarter of a century earlier. (The counsel for the defense will bring up the matter in Book Twelve, chap. xii, p. 701.) The exchange is significant: Dmitry and his interrogators think on different levels—he senses the whole monstrosity of the crime of

parricide, while they do not. Also, Dmitry, whose mind and soul are deeper and broader than theirs, can understand them, while they cannot follow him.

123   449_{10}, $14:428_{35}$, In the original, Dmitry once more shows some imaginative diction. His words mean literally: "A rock into my kitchen garden, and a mean, a nasty, rock at that!" Russ. *kameshek v ogorod,* "a pebble into one's kitchen garden," means a "dig, thrust, taunt." Dmitry converts *kameshek,* "pebble," into *kamen',* "rock," then "realizes" the metaphor.

124   449_{30}, $14:429_{8}$, "the devil must have killed my father"—after the play given to the devil earlier in the novel and with much more to come in Book Eleven, these words are more than a figure of speech. See Introduction III.2.a. The Reader's Role.

125   450_{14-17}, $14:429_{37-40}$, At this point it becomes clear that the prosecutor sees the evidence entirely from the viewpoint of someone convinced of Dmitry's guilt. For one who has more or less accidentally felled a man, Dmitry's is the only natural reaction; not so, however, for a man who has just murdered his father. This will be pointed out by the counsel for the defense (Book Twelve, chap. x, pp. 691–92).

126   450_{36}–451_{2}, $14:430_{10-20}$, A strange passage so far as point of view is concerned: it switches from the narrator's consciousness ("Alas!" belongs to him), to Dmitry's, and then to the prosecutor's. The gulf between the prosecutor's "fiction" and Dmitry's "truth" is widening. Cf. note 125 above.

127   451_{1-2}, $14:430_{19-20}$, "and he has said more than he meant to"— translates a short idiomatic phrase *on i progovorilsia,* "so he blabbed it out."

128   451_{5}, $14:430_{23-24}$, "Fenia"—in the original it is an "official" Fedos'ia Markov.

129   451_{13}, $14:430_{32}$, In the original "make way for their happiness" (lit. "make way for the happy ones") is between quotation marks also. The reference is to Book Eight, chap. v, p. 379_{35-38}.

130   451_{43-46}, $14:431_{10-12}$, Again, "the devil" is more than a mere figure of speech. Dostoevsky used to say that his "fantastic" plots ("dream" in line 46 translates *fantazija*) were in fact more "real" than those of his "realist" competitors. The point is that God's ways—or even the devil's—are "marvelous" indeed, and that Dmitry's "marvelous" story is true.

131   452_{44}–453_{3}, $14:432_{8-12}$, The translation is not quite accurate here. Dmitry expresses himself in a highly pregnant manner, lit.

"all this was in a fog of things to come" *(v dal'neishem tumane);* "simple" *(prost)* means "naive, simpleminded" here; "supposition" is a mistranslation of *predlozhenie,* "suggestion"; "in my case" is needlessly added; "barrier" translates *zabor,* "fence," the same word that has just played such a role in a literal meaning (p. 449$_{40ff.}$, where *zabor* is translated by "wall").

132   453$_{24}$, 14:432$_{32}$, "you pounce upon it"—translates *lyko v stroku,* lit. "each string of bast true to pattern," Dmitry's peculiar use of a Russian saying (see note 83 above).

133   454$_{13-14}$, 14:433$_{18-19}$, "which will, of course, take place in your presence"—Nikolai Parfenovich, a modern and progressive lawman, continually emphasizes the fairness of the proceedings. The deadly irony of it is by now apparent.

134   454$_{34-35}$, 14:433$_{39-40}$, The key fact of the case. The point pursued by Dostoevsky is that, with a fact staring them in the face, the prosecutor and his colleague will overlook it and go on to pursue their preconceived fiction of Dmitry's guilt.

135   455$_6$, 14:434$_8$, "It will be necessary to take off your clothes, too."—A natural step of the examination, yet it is also symbolic: Dmitry is gradually stripped naked even morally and spiritually.

Chapter vi

136   455$_{17}$, 14:434$_{17}$, Note the ironic tension between the chapter heading and the narrative to which it refers. The chapter heading (and those of the following chapters) assumes a detached, even estranged stance, while the narrative presents things essentially from Dmitry's point of view. See Introduction III.1.a. The Narrator.

137   455$_{18-22}$, 14:434$_{18-22}$, The convoluted diction of this passage (it is more awkward in the original) is symbolic of Dmitry's acute embarrassment.

138   455$_{24-25}$, 14:434$_{25}$, "From pride and contempt he submitted without a word."—Typically Dostoevskian paradoxic psychology. See Introduction II.6.b. Psychological Motivation.

139   456$_{35}$, 14:435$_1$, "answered"—translates *otpariroval,* "countered." Dostoevsky's "stage directions" which suggest the tone of an utterance must be kept in sight.

140   456$_{38}$, 14:435$_{34}$, "awkward"—translates *konfuzno,* "embarrassing, distressing, awkward," where a feeling of shame is the key component.

141 456_{45-46}, $14:435_{40-41}$, "It's like a dream . . ."—this nightmare of shame and degradation stands in counterpoint to Dmitry's good dream in chap. viii.

142 457_{1-2}, $14:435_{42-43}$, "They were very dirty, and so were his underclothes"—another perfectly natural detail—yet the symbolism is inescapable.

143 457_3, $14:435_{43-44}$, "he disliked his feet"—perhaps a counterpoint to Grushen'ka's lovely little feet, which Dmitry adores. See Book Three, chap. v, p. 107_{24-25}.

144 457_8, $14:435_1$, "Would you like to look anywhere else . . ."— This coarse phrase is even more blunt in Russian: "somewhere else" would be a closer translation. Sometimes a nuance will depend on such trifles as "somewhere" vs. "anywhere."

145 457_{22-23}, $14:436_{14}$, "a puppy"—Russ. *shchenok* is used opprobriously. Perhaps: "whelp."

146 457_{35}, $14:436_{26}$, "I won't have other people's clothes!"—In nineteenth-century Russia, wearing other people's clothes (a servant's lot) was considered degrading.

147 458_{46}, $14:437_{37}$, "like a peevish child"—once more, a childlike quality is shown in Dmitry. Cf. Book Eight, notes 106, 202, and 225.

148 459_{10}, $14:437_{48}$, "killed myself"—in the original, a more emphatic *istrebil*, "destroyed," the term used for vermin, or human scum.

149 459_{20-21}, $14:438_{9-10}$, ". . . blind moles and scoffers"—to the born poet Dmitry, the prosecutor and his aide appear lacking in vision and imagination. Here *nasmeshnik*, "scoffer," implies a shallow irreverence.

150 459_{45-46}, $14:438_{35}$, "the door, standing wide open"—cf. chap. v, p. 446_{30ff}. The whole case hinges on this detail. Morally, it is only fitting that Dmitry should suffer because of the evidence, inadvertently false, given by his "second father," whom he twice struck brutally, though inadvertently.

151 460_{14}, $14:439_1$, "warmly"—translates *s zharom*, perhaps: "with ardor." Both Nikolai Parfenovich and the prosecutor are carried away by a piece of false evidence which they have accepted for a fact.

152 460_{15-18}, $14:439_{3-7}$, "It's false . . ."—Dmitry's arguments are inconsistent and carry little weight. (The counsel for the defense will make the same point much more persuasively in his cross-

examination, in Book Twelve, chap. ii, p. 632.) The irony of it is that Dmitry is right: it *was* a hallucination.

153 460_{44-45}, $14:439_{31-32}$, "But you, too, knew . . ."—Dmitry's vivid imagination has done him in. He actually said (chap. iii, p. 436_{6-7}) he knew that the old man kept the bundle under his pillow—but not because he knew this for a fact.

154 461_{4-6}, $14:439_{37-39}$, This brings to mind Porfiry Petrovich's "trap" in *Crime and Punishment*. He asks Raskol'nikov, a murderer, for a detail which he could know only if he was at the scene of the murder on the day in question. Raskol'nikov does not fall into the trap—and thereby only confirms the detective's suspicions. An innocent man might have blundered and said the wrong thing. This is precisely what happens to Dmitry. A brilliant detective like Porfiry Petrovich would have long since recognized his innocence, but Ippolit Kirillovich has "caught" the wrong man (see the chapter title).

155 461_{26-30}, $14:440_{8-11}$, "But you're again forgetting . . ."—This passage has an ironic counterpoint in Book Eleven, chap. viii, p. 595_{40-42}: the taps were made, even though there was "no need," strictly speaking.

156 462_8, $14:440_{33-34}$, "in a voice of almost pathetic delight"—in the original, "voice" is in the diminutive: *goloskom,* "in a little voice." Nikolai Parfenovich is so excited his voice cracks. He expects a confession any moment now.

Chapter vii

157 462_{18}, $14:440_{44}$, "The attorneys' faces lengthened."—In the original, this observation is enhanced by *dazhe,* "even, actually, in fact," one of Dostoevsky's key words.

158 463_2, $14:441_{26}$, "she has hated me ever so long"—this comes as a bit of a surprise, although it is probably true.

159 463_{8-21}, $14:441_{32-45}$, "that evening at my lodging"—he alludes to the events related in Book Three, chap. iv, pp. 102-3. We thus hear yet another, corrected, account of Dmitry's first trip to Mokroe.

160 463_{18}, $14:441_{43}$, "Locket" (and later, "amulet") translates *ladonka* (or *ladanka*), a little cloth bag containing incense *(ladan)* or some other sacred substance and worn around the neck as protection against evil.

161   463_{22-24}, $14:441_{46-47}$, Dmitry's lie has now become the prosecutor's truth. The three thousand roubles continue to play their fateful role. See Introduction III.3.a. Motifs. ˙

162   463_{43}, $14:442_{18}$, " 'disgraceful' "—the quotation marks which foreground this word are significant. This section of the interrogation is dominated by the word *pozor,* "shame, disgrace" (lit. "spectacle," the noun being derived from the verb *zret',* "to see"), and several semantically related words.

163   464_{20-21}, $14:442_{42}$, "disconnectedly and incoherently"—in the original: "almost incoherently"; *pochti,* "almost," is another key word often left out by the translator. This passage is another example of Dostoevsky's internal commentary: the prosecutor's words are commented upon not only from a psychological, but even from an aesthetic, angle.

164   464_{24-30}, $14:442_{46}$-443_4, "What is there disgraceful . . ."—No wonder the prosecutor is irritated. His modern, thoroughly bourgeois concept of *honesty* clashes with Dmitry's antiquated notion of *honor.* Once more, Dmitry can understand Ippolit Kirillovich's pedestrian casuistry, while the latter lacks the ability to think like the honorable, chivalrous Dmitry.

165   464_{35}, $14:443_8$, "It's incomprehensible." Cf. the preceding note. Dmitry proceeds to make his point: the distinction between a scoundrel and a thief makes sense only in a context of chivalry— a nobleman turned scoundrel may perhaps redeem himself by some feat of great heroics or generosity. But once a thief, he cannot possibly ever regain his honor. In bourgeois morality, on the other hand, there is little difference between a thief and a scoundrel.

166   466_{7-10}, $14:444_{19-22}$, The attorneys' laughter and Nikolai Parfenovich's response show that they have understood nothing.

167   466_{17-18}, $14:444_{28-29}$, "I didn't dare even to tell Aliosha . . ."— in fact, he almost did: see Book Three, chap. xi, p. 143_{18-38}.

168   466_{25-26}, $14:444_{36}$, "a downright thief"—translates *okonchatel'nyi i besspornyi vor,* lit. "a definitive and unquestionable thief," where the poignancy of the expression is enhanced by its ungrammatical syntax.

169   466_{42-45}, $14:445_{3-6}$, "I tell you again . . ."—A significant statement: Dmitry realizes that he has reached the end of his old life. He has sunk so deep that there is only one way left to go— up.

170   467_1, $14:445_9$, "I am beginning to understand you"—another irony, for his words will show that he understands nothing.

171   467_{44-45}, $14:466_{3-4}$, "That would have been filthy beyond everything!"—The original has it even stronger: *eto tak by vonialo*, "this would have raised such a stench." Dmitry is really beside himself.

172   467_{46-47}, $14:446_6$, Note the paradoxic psychology in "she'd have given it to me to satisfy her vengeance"; Dmitry (and Dostoevsky, of course) take it as a matter of course. See Introduction II.6.b. Psychological Motivation.

173   468_{1-3}, $14:446_{7-9}$, It may be noted that "infernal" here (as earlier, on p. 467_{27}) translates Russ. *infernal'nyi*, not a very common word in nineteenth-century Russian (it does not appear in the 1881 edition of Vladimir Dal's *Tolkovyi slovar'*). Dmitry uses quite a few other foreign words, too—not always correctly. Dmitry's words square with Katerina Ivanovna's own promise, of which he is not aware. See Book Four, chap. v, pp. 172-73.

174   468_{18-19}, $14:446_{24}$, "looking at him in surprise"—the prosecutor and his aide still fail to understand Dmitry.

175   468_{25-27}, $14:446_{31-33}$, This strong metaphor is even more graphic in the original: "Look, I have, so to speak, torn my soul asunder before you, and you seize the opportunity to rummage with your fingers in both halves of the torn spot." Dmitry is somewhat embarrassed by his own outburst and inserts an apologetic "so to speak"; such details are important.

176   468_{38-46}, $14:446_{45}-447_5$, "we have perhaps a dozen witnesses . . ."—The reader knows all this very well: to him, as to the prosecutor, the figure three thousand has acquired a solid, palpable quality. Dmitry's—and Dostoevsky's—point is that this seemingly "solid" quality is based entirely on hearsay.

177   $469_{12ff.}$, $14:447_{16ff.}$, The counterpoint to the nonexistent three thousand roubles in whose existence the prosecutor firmly believes is the little cloth bag, in whose existence the prosecutor does not believe for a moment. Hence his impressive "That's very difficult to decide, Dmitry Fiodorovich, what makes a man tell lies."

178   470_{42-46}, $14:448_{39-43}$, "He bent his head . . ."—A silent scene of great power, which succeeds in topping even the preceding outburst.

179   471_{12-18}, $14:449_{6-11}$, This descriptive passage is not only sym-

bolic of Dmitry's mood, but it also helps to create a transition to Dmitry's dream in the next chapter as well as opening a window into the world at large. Dmitry's "golden-haired Phoebus" suddenly becomes very unreal opposite the depressing misery of a Russian village.

180 471_{39}–472_1, $14:449_{33-42}$,   Contrary to the opinion of some critics, Dostoevsky is well aware that men eat and drink. This passage helps build the reader's sense of witnessing real events.

Chapter viii

181 472_9, $14:450_2$,   "The Babe" translates *Ditio,* a form heard in uneducated speech only (educated speech has *ditia*), which makes this chapter title even more of a mystery.

182 $472_{10ff.}$, $14:450_{3ff.}$,   The beginning of this new chapter coincides with a change of pace and of point of view. In the preceding chapters Dmitry's perceptions were foregrounded, and there was a great deal of nervous tension. Now the narrator takes over, at a more relaxed pace and with a good deal of irony.

183 472_{26-28}, $14:450_{20-23}$,   "He had, on the contrary . . ."—The narrator starts the job of deflating the credibility of the witnesses against Dmitry, a job which will be completed by the counsel for the defense in Book Twelve, chap. ii. The irony is even stronger in the original: "which undeniably gave him an appearance of extraordinary truthfulness and personal dignity."

184 473_{1-8}, $14:450_{34-41}$,   Trifon Borisych's speech is the *koine* of the uneducated. His faulty grammar (from an educated Russian's viewpoint, that is) enhances the impression that what he says is unreliable.

185 473_{21-24}, $14:451_{7-10}$,   "the 'sixth' thousand . . ."—more irony. The investigators are taking wild hearsay for a positive fact. "Sixth," however, is set off by quotation marks in the translation only.

186 473_{31-32}, $14:451_{17}$,   " 'psychologist' "—the quotation marks are Dostoevsky's, who is well on his way toward demolishing the "psychologist" and his psychology. The irony is quite open. See Introduction II.6.a. Dostoevsky's Psychology.

187 474_6, $14:451_{36}$,   " 'romance' "—in Russian, *roman* means "romance" as well as "novel." This is relevant to the theme of fact and fiction (real life and novel) in Dmitry's evidence, as well as in the novel at large. See Introduction III.3.d. Art of the Novel.

188 $474_{9ff.}$, $14:451_{39ff.}$, The baiting of the two Poles continues. Musiałowicz turns out to have been, not an officer, but a low-ranking clerk in the civil service. Wróblewski is, in the original, a "free-lancing dentist." The phrase "though not without some fear" suggests that these two gentlemen may have reason to fear the police. The assertion that "they could speak Russian quite correctly" insinuates that these Poles, when not awed by authority, actually abuse the Russian language on purpose, from contempt for everything Russian.

189 474_{29-30}, $14:452_{12}$, "and begged that it should be put down in the deposition"—a bit of farce: Musiałowicz asks to be officially certified a "scoundrel." His request is promptly met. Dostoevsky is not above low comedy, as we know by now.

190 474_{36-37}, $14:452_{19}$, "romantic"—translates *romanicheskii*. See note 187 above.

191 474_{39-44}, $14:452_{22-27}$, "Mitya had tried to buy off . . ."—As each and every step of Book Eight is retraced, it takes on a totally different aspect. Dmitry's version, which we know to be true, now seems false; and the investigator's version, which we know to be false, becomes "the truth."

192 475_{11}, $14:452_{37}$, "baffling"—translates *shchekotlivoe*, "ticklish." The point is that the prosecution refused to be "baffled," but simply dismissed the fact.

193 475_{22-23}, $14:452_{48}$, "at the 'innocence of this subterfuge' "—the quotation marks are also found in the original. For the first time, the narrator enters the prosecutor's mind and makes it unequivocally clear that the latter is fully convinced of Dmitry's guilt.

194 475_{28}, $14:453_6$, "Poles and Jews"—in the original: *poliachkov da zhidkov*, "little Polacks and Yiddels."

195 475_{43}, $14:453_{20}$, "blue check handkerchief"—this is the power of Dostoevsky's concrete details: the scene would not have been half as pathetic if the color of the handkerchief had not been mentioned. Incidentally, a blue check handkerchief plays a central role in what is perhaps Dostoevsky's greatest tear-jerking scene: *A Raw Youth*, Part Two, chap. 9, sect. ii.

196 476_{7-13}, $14:453_{30-35}$, This miniature farce is of course a distorted mirror image of the investigators' own procedures, an internal parody, as it were.

197 476_{22-23}, $14:453_{45}$, "her magnificent black shawl"—we already know this shawl; see Book Three, chap. x, p. 136_2. It will be mentioned again in Book Twelve, chap. iv, pp. 647–48.

198   476_{26-34}, $14:454_{2-9}$,   Nikolai Parfenovich is made the butt of the narrator's sarcasms. The dandified Petersburg lawyer completely misjudges Grushen'ka, a Russian woman of the people. The provincial ladies, of course, resent her promotion to "the best society."

199   476_{45}, $14:454_{22}$,   "but had won his heart as well as his old father's 'in my nasty spite' "—more accurately: "but had enticed him 'in my vile wickedness,' just as I had that 'little old man.' " We see Fiodor Pavlovich from a wholly different point of view: to Grushen'ka he was a rather pitiable "little old man" *(starichok)*.

200   477_{43-44}, $14:455_{15-16}$,   "I had faith in his noble heart."— Grushen'ka has called Dmitry "noble" before (Book Seven, chap. iii, p. 336_{10}), and Dmitry has himself asserted a belief in his own "noble heart" (chap. iv, p. 445_{11-12}, above). Note that Katerina Ivanovna called Dmitry a "scoundrel" (Book Three, chap. x, p. 140_{13-14}), a label which he has also accepted, having called himself a "scoundrel" repeatedly. We have, then, a prime example of Dostoevskian *coincidentio oppositorum.* See Introduction II.6.b. Psychological Motivation.

201   $477_{45}-478_{12}$, $14:455_{17-31}$,   A great dramatic scene whose religious overtones are significant. Both Dmitry and Grushen'ka publicly declare that their faith in each other is linked with their faith in God.

202   478_{29}, $14:455_{48}$,   "this old gentleman"—in the original: "this little old man, the landowner," which reminds us of Maksimov's label in Book Two, chap. i, p. 28_{27}. The reader knows, of course, that Maksimov is only a former landowner.

203   $478_{39ff.}$, $14:456_{9ff.}$,   Dmitry's dream is one of the highlights of the novel. It parallels Aliosha's vision in "Cana of Galilee," at the conclusion of Book Seven. The dream is told in the present tense in the original, making it more vivid.

204   479_{4-11}, $14:456_{19-26}$,   Dostoevsky may have wanted his readers to visualize this mother and her child as resembling certain representations of the Holy Virgin and Her Child found in old Russian icons. A brownish, elongated, wan face is found in many of them.

205   479_{13}, $14:456_{27}$,   "gaily"—a mistranslation of *likho,* "briskly."

206   479_{15-16}, $14:456_{29-30}$,   See note 181 above.

207   479_{29-37}, $14:456_{45}-457_5$,   "And he felt . . ."—The counterpoint to Ivan Karamazov's bitter words about the suffering of innocent

children (Book Five, chap. iv). It also serves as a transition to Book Ten. See Introduction II.3.b. "The Novel about Children."

208   479_{40-43}, $14:457_{8-11}$, "his whole heart glowed . . ."—the epiphany. Cf. Aliosha's epiphany, Book Seven, chap. iv, p. 340_{3-5}. Dmitry has come all the way from the terrible "darkness" of Book Eight, chap. iv, to this "light."

209   480_{14-15}, $14:457_{28-29}$, The surprising and edifying conclusion to Dmitry's "torments."

Chapter ix

210    $480_{18ff.}$, $14:457_{32ff.}$, This time the transition from the preceding chapter is effected through contrast: "joy" and "light" are overtaken by the dry legal jargon of a deposition.

211   481_{8-9}, $14:458_{18}$, "But the thunderbolt has fallen."—An allusion to the Russian proverb "A man won't cross himself unless he hears thunder." In a letter to N. A. Liubimov, dated 16 November 1879, explaining Dmitry's character to his correspondent, Dostoevsky quotes this proverb in full (*Pis'ma* 4:118).

212   481_{9-11}, $14:458_{18-20}$, States the allegoric meaning of the plot of this novel quite explicitly (see Introduction II.1.a. Allegoric Figures). Dostoevsky's heroes are often presented as quite conscious of the motives of their actions. This is in accord with Dostoevsky's belief in the individual's personal responsibility for his actions.

213   481_{12-14}, $14:458_{22-23}$, Once more the verb "to kill" is pronounced three times. Dmitry, innocent of the actual killing, realizes his deep guilt. Cf. Introduction II.5.a. Faith and Unbelief.

214   481_{21-25}, $14:458_{30-34}$, "he stretched out his hand . . ."—another powerful silent scene.

215   481_{31-34}, $14:458_{41-43}$, "All of us here . . ."—States the leitmotif of Dmitry's trial: virtually everybody believes that Dmitry killed his father, and almost everybody also thinks that it was not such a terrible thing to do, but rather excusable. Note, too, that Nikolai Parfenovich calls Dmitry, his senior by a few years, a "young man." One is reminded of the scene in Gogol's *Overcoat,* where a fortyish "important person" calls the hero, who is over fifty but a mere clerk, a "young man."

216   482_{3-8}, $14:460_{9-16}$,   Note the solemnity of this scene: as so often
       in Dostoevsky, what started out as a lowly scandal has grown
       into a high tragedy.

217   482_{21-24}, $14:460_{29-32}$,   "Forgive me at parting . . ."—Here a
       nuance is lost in translation. Dmitry says: *Proshchaite, bozh'i
       liudi!* where *proshchaite* is ambiguous, meaning "good-bye,"
       but also "forgive me." The answer is: *I nas prosti,* where the
       perfective form of the verb suggests quite unequivocally:
       "Forgive us, too." Dmitry then responds with another *Prosh-
       chai i ty,* "Good-bye to you, too," addressed to Trifon Borisych.
       This exchange reintroduces the motif of shared guilt. See In-
       troduction II.5.a. Faith and Unbelief.

218   482_{36-37}, $14:460_{43-45}$,   ". . . low peasants"—introduced for
       ironic contrast: these same "low peasants" have just shown their
       high moral stature (see the preceding note).

219   482_{40-44}, $14:460_{48}$–461_2,   "old fellow"—in the original, it is a
       question of addressing the police officer in the familiar second
       person singular (*ty*), as a former drinking companion, or switch-
       ing to an official plural (*vy*).

220    $483_{9ff.}$, $14:461_{13ff.}$,   Another study in contrast: Trifon Borisych,
       a man of the people, is set off against Kalganov, a young
       aristocrat. It is Kalganov who shows generosity and good nature.
       Cf. Introduction II.4.a. The Russian Nobleman.

221   483_{20-21}, $14:461_{23-24}$,   "But the cart moved . . ."—In the
       original these two lines are highly organized euphonically and
       rhythmically: *No telega tronulas', i ruki ikh raznialis'. Zazvenel
       kolokol'chik—uvezli Mitiu.* There is plain alliteration *(t—t, r—r)*
       and consonance (ra*zn*ia*l*is'—*z*a*zv*enel—u*vez*/i). The rhythm of
       this section is also close to regular verse. Dostoevsky will do this
       kind of thing in crucial passages. Here, *uvezli Mitiu,* "Mitia was
       driven off," is also the chapter heading. The translator has failed
       to observe this.

Book Ten

Chapter i

1 486₂, 14:462₃, "The Boys"—"Boys" would be as correct, since Russian has neither a definite nor an indefinite article. Book Ten as a whole is a master stroke of novelistic "retardation," serving as a smooth transition to the climactic conclusion of the novel. At the same time it establishes, fixes, or reinforces some important motifs. Furthermore, Aliosha, the declared hero of the novel, once more moves into the focus of attention. See Introduction I.3. Early Versions, for Dostoevsky's plans to write a novel about children.

2 486₄, 14:462₅, Kolia Krasotkin has been mentioned before (Book Four, chap. iii, p. 162₁₁₋₁₃, and chap. vii, p. 187₄₁₋₄₄). The name Krasotkin (from *krasotka,* "pretty girl, sweetheart") might be symbolic (Kolia is a very vain boy). Kolia is a double of Ivan Karamazov's. See Introduction III.3.b. Mirroring and Doubling.

3 486₈, 14:462₈, " 'dry and sharp' "—a quotation from N. A. Nekrasov's poem "Before the Rain" (1846). See *PSS* 15:580.

4 486₁₁, 14:462₁₁, "Plotnikov's shop"—the familiarity topos: the narrator treats the reader as someone familiar by now with his town. We know the shop from Book Eight, chap. v. The original has this whole descriptive passage in the present tense, making it more lively and homey. The passage also features some colloquialisms and regionalisms.

5 486₁₃, 14:462₁₃, "provincial secretary"—a low civil service rank of the twelfth class. The "table of ranks" had fourteen classes.

6 486₁₄₋₁₅, 14:462₁₄₋₁₅, "a lively still attractive woman of thirty"—in the original: "a still very comely little lady" *(ves'ma smazlivaia soboiu damochka),* which strikes a familiar, somewhat condescending tone. As for her age, *tridtsatiletniaia,*

337

lit. "thirty-year-old," may also mean "in her thirties" or "about thirty." Hence there really is no contradiction between her age and that of her son. Dostoevsky's editor had suggested making Kolia fourteen instead of thirteen. Dostoevsky agreed under the condition that he be "almost fourteen, that is, fourteen in two weeks." See letter to N. A. Liubimov, 13 April 1880 (*Pis'ma* 4:137–38).

7   486_{33-35}, $14:463_{1-3}$, "Mamma's boy" and "tremendously strong" are schoolboy jargon. There will be a good deal of it in this chapter. The narrator will often switch to young Kolia's point of view, or even "quote" him.

8   487_3, $14:463_6$, "beat"—better: "put out" or "rattle."

9   487_{10}, $14:463_{13}$, "disorder, rebellion, and lawlessness"— translates *besporiadok, bunt i bezzakonie* (note the alliteration), where *bunt,* "rebellion," is the key word of Ivan's "rebellion" and also the title of chapter iv of Book Five. Thus, we are instantly reminded of the "schoolboy rebellion" in "The Grand Inquisitor" (Book Five, chap. v, p. 237_{8-9}), and the link between Ivan and Kolia is established.

10 487_{12-14}, $14:463_{16-17}$, "as for creating a sensation, inventing something, doing something effective, flashy, and conspicuous"—in the Russian every word here is schoolboy—or schoolmaster—jargon. Thus, "doing something effective" translates *zadat' 'ekstrafeferu',* lit. "to let them have some extra pepper" (Ger. *Extrapfeffer*), i.e., "give it to them extra hot."

11 487_{14-16}, $14:463_{19-20}$, "Give way" translates *podchinit'sia,* "to submit." Hence: "And she had submitted to him, oh, she had submitted to him long ago."

12 487_{17-18}, $14:463_{21}$, "that her boy had no great love for her"—in the original, *malo liubit,* "does not love her enough," is in quotation marks, so it is the expression Mme. Krasotkin uses. The expression itself is a formulaic one.

13 487_{30-31}, $14:463_{34-35}$, "And in that way Kolia read some things unsuitable for his age."—The conservative narrator surfaces.

14 487_{39-41}, $14:463_{42-44}$, Once again Dostoevsky finds a way to remind his reader of Ivan Karamazov. Cf. note 9 above.

15 488_{44}, $14:464_{45}$, "a middle-aged bachelor"—creates the wrong impression, as Russ. *nestaryi,* lit. "not old," stresses the fact that he is still a relatively young man. Perhaps: "a youngish bachelor."

16 $488_{44ff.}$, $14:464_{45ff.}$, The episode featuring the romance of

Dardanelov and Mme. Krasotkin is told in a tone of gentle irony, as a bit of town gossip. Dostoevsky likes to introduce some perfectly ordinary good people on the fringes and in the interstices of his plots.

17   489_{3-6}, $14:465_{2-5}$, In the Russian, an accumulation of modal expressions mockingly underscores Dardanelov's timidity. Perhaps: "though Dardanelov might have, perhaps, actually had, to judge from certain mysterious symptoms, a certain reason for dreaming that he was not entirely an object of aversion to the charming, but indeed too chaste and tenderhearted, widow."

18   489_{16}, $14:465_{14}$, " 'beat' "—see note 8 above.

19   489_{25}, $14:465_{22}$, S. N. Smaragdov (1805–71) was the author of several widely used history texts.

20   489_{27-28}, $14:465_{25}$, "Krasotkin would not tell his secret, and his reputation for knowledge remained unshaken."—The parody of Ivan and his "Grand Inquisitor" is underway. Kolia's reputation is based on a "secret."

21   489_{32-39}, $14:465_{30-38}$, "She had such terrible attacks of hysterics . . ."—A scene from a *comédie larmoyante*—turned into a parody, in that it features a mother and her thirteen-year-old son instead of a pair of young lovers.

22   490_{13-14}, $14:466_{11-12}$, "or would investigate the state of his boots"—translates a formulaic *ili razgliadyval, ne prosiat li u nego sapogi kashi,* lit. "or would investigate if his boots were asking for porridge" (that is, if they were yawning at the toes)—very much in the humorous vein in which this whole chapter is told.

23   490_{15-17}, $14:466_{12-15}$, In the original, the tone of mystery surrounding this dog is a bit stronger. The dog's name, *Perezvon,* lit. "Chimes," is of the masculine gender; however, the narrator refers to it as "she," since *sobaka,* "dog," is of the feminine gender. Later, when the reference is to the dog's name, it is "he." Eventually, the dog' name turns out to be *Zhuchka* (feminine), and it becomes a "she" again.

24   490_{17-23}, $14:466_{15-22}$, "He bullied him . . ."—This passage, so much in a good-natured and humorous vein, does not look as if it were leading up to anything serious. But in Dostoevsky one expects that such simplehearted good cheer is but a prelude to something deep and tragic. And so it is.

25   490_{24-28}, $14:466_{23-27}$, See note 2 above.

Chapter ii

26 490_{41}, $14:466_{42-43}$, Orenburg is in the Urals, Tashkent in Central Asia.

27 491_{15}, $14:467_{17}$, " 'kids' "—translates *'puzyri'*, lit. "bubbles," a colloquial expression for "youngsters, kids."

28 491_{37}, $14:467_{40}$, " 'these days' "—translates *'v nash vek'*, "in this day and age," an expression characteristic of progressive jargon.

29 492_{9}, $14:468_{9}$, "catskin"—Russ. *kotik* is "sealskin" (genuine or imitation).

30 492_{13-20}, $14:468_{13-20}$, Note how carefully Dostoevsky describes the details of a mere dog's behavior.

31 492_{31-32}, $14:468_{32}$, "old women"—translates *povival'nye babushki*, "midwives."

32 $492_{39ff.}$, $14:468_{40ff.}$, The narrator, who is obviously very fond of children, shows them to be as intelligent and even as rational in their arguments as most adults—only their premises are wrong.

33 $493_{7ff.}$, $14:469_{8ff.}$, Kolia's speech is a mixture of stilted "adult" expressions, highfalutin book words, and schoolboy jargon. What is most important, he maintains a constant edge of "cool" and swagger. The translation misses much of this. For example, "You're terrible people" (lines 7–8) translates *opasnyi vy . . . narod*, "you're dangerous people," obviously the language of "cops and robbers."

34 494_{10}, $14:470_{10}$, "I know, I only said it for stylistic reasons."— Lit. "for beauty of style." A case of laying bare the device: Kolia says, and does, most things "for beauty of style."

35 494_{11-17}, $14:470_{12-15}$, This exchange shows the delightful comedy of this scene at its brightest. Note Dostoevsky's careful attention to the tone in which Kostia and Nastia make their repartees.

36 494_{18}, $14:470_{16}$, "Oh, children, children, how fraught with peril are your years!"—Kolia quotes from a fable by I. I. Dmitriev (1760–1837), "The Rooster, the Cat, and the Young Mouse." The commentators of *PSS* suggest that the quote ironically fits Kolia himself (*PSS* 15:581).

37 494_{40}, $14:470_{39}$, "you brat"—the Russ. *pupyr'* rhymes with *puzyr'*, applied by Kolia to the smaller children, and means about the same: lit. "blister, pimple." The first of the comeuppances suffered by Kolia.

38 495_{20-21}, $14:471_{15-16}$, Kolia is the enlightener all the way. He has

just heard the children speak of cabbage leaves and is naturally opposed to such misinformation.

Chapter iii

39   496₁₀, 14:472₂,   Zhuchka is a common name, originally for a black mongrel dog, lit. "Beetles" or "Bugs." Here the plot thickens.

40   496₁₇₋₁₉, 14:472₉₋₁₁,   "Boy, shun a lie . . ."—Kolia keeps using the rhetoric of his teachers. This admonition to Smurov introduces another counterpoint to "The Grand Inquisitor." Ironically, Kolia is himself a violator of his maxim.

41   496₃₃₋₃₄, 14:472₂₄₋₂₅,   Aliosha's prediction has come true: the captain has accepted Katerina Ivanovna's money (cf. Book Five, chap. i, p. 197₆₋₇).

42   496₃₇₋₃₈, 14:472₂₈₋₂₉,   Kolia's opinion is not necessarily Dostoevsky's, although in this instance Kolia will soon have confirmation of his low opinion of the medical profession (see chap. vii, pp. 529–30). This passage is a barb directed at some Russian radicals who would make categoric pronouncements and "study the matter later" (which is what Kolia says, although the translation does not make it quite clear).

43   496₄₃₋₄₆, 14:472₃₅₋₃₇,   "Aleksei Karamazov"—note how Dostoevsky will find a way to get in yet another "cross reference" to another plot line.

44   497₈₋₁₂, 14:472₄₅₋₄₈,   Kolia is the youngest of Dostoevsky's many self-willed heroes. Being independent is more important to him than doing the right thing, another trait that links him to Ivan Karamazov.

45   497₂₂, 14:473₁₀,   "murderer"—in the original it is *ottseubiitsa,* "parricide." A significant phrase. Young Smurov is wrong in a literal sense, but he also points to Dmitry's deep guilt: beating a father before his son's eyes is a great sin. See Introduction II.3.a. Fatherhood.

46   497₄₁, 14:473₂₉,   "I like to watch such realistic scenes"—in the original: "I like to observe realism," a bit of progressive jargon we have already heard from Dmitry (see Book Eight, note 48).

47   497₄₄–498₅, 14:473₃₃₋₄₀,   Dostoevsky is mocking the Russian progressives who would make momentous social conclusions from simplistic scientific (or pseudoscientific) observations. Rakitin, who has played a significant role in Aliosha's and Grushen'ka's story, now enters the plot from a new side.

48   498_{8-10}, $14:473_{42-43}$, Kolia's definition of what socialism stands
      for is fairly accurate: the Russian radicals of the 1860s were
      opposed to all existing social institutions—state, judiciary,
      church, and family. The commentators of *PSS* suggest that the
      phrase *kak komu ugodno,* "whatever each likes best," is a dig at
      M. E. Saltykov-Shchedrin, who published a cycle of essays under
      that title in 1863. See Borshchevskii, pp. 76–77.

49   498_{13-18}, $14:473_{47}$–474_5, The travesty of progressive thought
      continues. Kolia's smug pronouncements, based on trivial
      evidence, are very much in the style of radical journalists such as
      Nikolai Dobroliubov (1836–61) or Dmitry Pisarev (1840–68).

50   498_{46-47}, $14:474_{30-31}$, "That was a nice peasant"—a parody of
      the condescending populism of the Russian intelligentsia.

51   499_{7-11}, $14:474_{37-40}$, An obvious counterpoint to "The Grand
      Inquisitor."

52   499_{12-13}, $14:474_{41-42}$, "another scrape . . . about that goose"—
      an incident referred to earlier (chap. i, p. 489_{42-43}) and to be
      foregrounded later (chap. v, p. 518). Dostoevsky will take care to
      prepare for even minor episodes.

53    $500_{11ff.}$, $14:475_{44ff.}$, The following lighthearted episode has a
      moral of sorts: it is perfectly possible to create "something" out
      of "nothing," if one has a receptive audience. The comedy
      staged by Kolia has a venerable tradition: it is the "graded" joke
      which keeps promising a point that never comes.

54   501_{22-26}, $14:477_{3-8}$, "There's another blockhead . . ."—Kolia
      now goes too far in his hubris and gets his comeuppance. The
      following little episode is an allegory of one of the central themes
      of the novel: the natural intelligence of the simple people will
      defeat the clever dialectics of "educated" reason. See In-
      troduction II. Ideas, note 7.

                              Chapter iv

55   502_{21}, $14:478_2$, "The Lost Dog"—in the original it is
      "Zhuchka" (see note 39 above). The chapter title, as so often,
      creates suspense.

56    $502_{22ff.}$, $14:478_{3ff.}$, Kolia's encounter with Aliosha is in some
      ways a mirror image of, and a commentary on, Aliosha's
      meeting with Ivan in Book Five. The reader will remember how
      Ivan had spoken about "Russian boys" concerned with nothing
      short of solving "eternal questions" and how he had admitted

that he was himself "such a little boy" (Book Five, chap. iii, p. 215$_7$).

57   503$_{12-16}$, 14:478$_{35-39}$, Note the narrator's firm control over Kolia's presence in the text. He will allow the reader to identify with Kolia for a while, then step back, as it were, and take a detached, objective view of the boy. The reader may be tempted to see in young Kolia a self-portrait of Dostoevsky (the face described might be his own); however, Dostoevsky is describing a typical Russian face.

58   503$_{18}$, 14:478$_{41-42}$, "He looked delighted" is a correct translation of *kakoe-to sovsem radostnoe litso,* lit. "a kind of altogether happy (joyful) face." But it fails to bring out Aliosha's leitmotif, "joy," which is contained in the adjective *radostnyi,* "joyful." Cf. Book Seven, notes 110, 122, and 127.

59   503$_{24}$, 14:478$_{46-47}$, "quite handsome"—an understatement of the translator's. It should be: "very handsome indeed."

60   504$_{14-16}$, 14:479$_{32-34}$, "holes in his boots . . . gave it to them hot"—Kolia keeps mixing schoolboy jargon into his otherwise precociously literate diction. Here two slang expressions met earlier in this book show up: "his boots were asking for porridge" (see note 22 above) and "I let them have some extra pepper" (see note 10 above).

61   504$_{22}$, 14:479$_{41}$, "obeyed me as though I were God"—the little "Grand Inquisitor" shows his face!

62   504$_{40}$, 14:480$_{10}$, "that he was simply rebelling *(buntuet)* against me"—now even the least attentive reader will notice that we are in the middle of a parody of Ivan's "Grand Inquisitor."

63   504$_{44}$, 14:480$_{14}$, "to make a man of him"—translates *sozdat' cheloveka,* which is exactly the biblical phrase in "God created man" (Gen. 1:27).

64   505$_3$, 14:480$_{19}$, Rakitin was introduced into the "novel about children" earlier (see note 47 above). Now Dostoevsky finds a way to bring in Smerdiakov too.

65   505$_{19-29}$, 14:480$_{33-44}$, More of the "Grand Inquisitor": Kolia uses Iliusha's remorse to establish his own authority over the child.

66   505$_{32}$, 14:480$_{47}$, "the silent treatment"—translates *na ferbante,* schoolboy jargon from Ger. *verbannt,* "banished, exiled." The translation is excellent anyway.

67   505$_{37}$, 14:482$_{4-5}$, "So he's going in for a little temper."—In the original: "So he's developed a little free spirit of his own," where

vol'nyi dukh, "free spirit," is presented in the travesty of a diminutive form: *vol'nyi dushok.*

68   505_{41}, $14:482_8$, Snegiriov's beard ("the 'wisp of tow' ") is another leitmotif which links the novel about children with the main story line.

69   506_{28-29}, $14:482_{40-41}$, "God is punishing me for it."—A significant line: it reflects Dostoevsky's belief that even young children have a sense of guilt and responsibility. The fact that Iliusha is guilty of hurting a dog links him with the boy about whose horrible death Ivan told Aliosha (Book Five, chap. iv, p. 223).

70   506_{31}, $14:482_{43-44}$, "the joy would cure him"—translates *on by voskres ot radosti,* lit. "he would be resurrected by joy." Iliusha's illness is of course incurable, barring a miracle, but his spiritual anguish could be alleviated and in fact turned to joy.

71   506_{46}–507_5, $14:483_{11-15}$, The psychology of the "self-styled buffoon" (*dobrovol'nyi shut*) is one of Dostoevsky's recurring concerns. In Book Two, Fiodor Pavlovich had been the case in point; in Book Eight, Maksimov.

72   507_{17}, $14:483_{29}$, "we are all egoists"—a dig at Chernyshevsky's doctrine of "rational egoism," propounded in the latter's famous novel *What Is to Be Done?* (1863).

73   507_{43}–508_7, $14:484_{7-16}$, Here Dostoevsky lets Aliosha express one of his own favorite ideas. Dostoevsky followed Schiller in believing that art is a natural human need, the product of a "play drive" *(Spieltrieb).*

74   508_{13}, $14:484_{23}$, Aliosha treats children as equals because he believes that they are just that. See Introduction II.3.b. "The Novel about Children."

75   508_{17-18}, $14:484_{27}$, In the original: "Right now I'm going to show you a trick, Karamazov, also a kind of theatrical performance." The word for "trick" (*fortel',* a colloquialism from Pol. *fortel,* "trick") is significantly foregrounded, for it also appears as the concluding word of the chapter: "you'll see some trick" (the translation has: "you'll see something"). Clearly this is an allusion to the theme of "magic" vs. "mystery" in "The Grand Inquisitor."

Chapter v

76   509_{28}, $14:485_{38}$, "Sheepish sentimentality" (in Russian, it is "a calf's sentimentality") has become a label of Kolia's.

77 509_{36-46}, $14:485_{48}-486_9$, "And often . . ."—We see a pointed reversal of father-son roles. It is the father who displays typically childish behavior, while Iliusha reacts like a responsible adult. Significant for one of the central themes of the novel. See Introduction II.3.a. Fatherhood.

78 510_{3-4}, $14:486_{12}$, Another echo of the beard-pulling scene. It reminds the reader of Dmitry Karamazov, perpetrator of an impious assault on a father.

79 510_{7-10}, $14:486_{15-18}$, Mrs. Snegiriov is reverting to childhood. This adds emphasis to the ambivalence of the parent-child relationship. Cf. note 77 above.

80 510_{41-42}, $14:487_{2-3}$, "forgot his pride . . ."—here the translation misses a nuance: "pride" translates *gonor*, which carries a negative connotation (it is a loan from Pol. *honor*, "honor," which appears in the speech of the two Poles in Book Eight), and "assistance" stands for *podaianie*, which is "handout, alms."

81 $510_{45}-511_4$, $14:487_{6-14}$, "a new doctor . . ."—Yet another detail linking Iliusha's story with the main plot.

82 511_{15-16}, $14:487_{25-26}$, Once more the child-adult roles in the family are reversed. Dostoevsky makes sure that no reader will miss this point.

83 511_{18-19}, $14:487_{28-29}$, "the thought of the unhappy dog he had killed"—the translation misses what may be a key cross-reference: "killed" translates *zamuchennoi*, which means "tortured to death" and is precisely the expression applied to the little five-year-old girl who is abused by her parents (Book Five, chap. iv, p. 223_{16} in the Russian text, translated by "tortured" in the English text, p. 225_{43}).

84 511_{31-32}, $14:487_{42-43}$, ". . . the manners of good society."—The tone of irony is even stronger in the original. Nevertheless, the irony directed at the precocious Kolia is good-natured throughout.

85 512_{6-12}, $14:488_{15-23}$, The frightening change in Iliusha's appearance is brought out by presenting it through the eyes of Kolia, who has not seen his friend for two months. Typical of Dostoevsky's attention to detail. Also, a switch of point of view from the narrator to Kolia, the captain, and Iliusha himself defuses the risk of making this scene too sentimental.

86 512_{38-39}, $14:490_{2-3}$, "You are welcome . . ."—The translation misses the obsequious tone in which the captain addresses his thirteen-year-old guest: "Be welcome, dear guest, our guest whom we have been awaiting so long."

87 $512_{43ff.}$, $14:490_{7ff.}$. Kolia does everything for show. Much as the Grand Inquisitor makes a show of giving people the bread which they have produced with their own hands (Book Five, chap. v, p. 239_{20-21}), Kolia makes a show of bringing back a lost dog. He stages a "miracle," where the simplest possible action was indicated. Kolia's teaching the dog all these tricks now becomes symbolic of his attitude toward the world.

88 514_{22-24}, $14:491_{32-34}$, "Krasotkin's great! . . ."—The translator overinterprets the texts somewhat. Russ. *molodets* means "fine fellow," or "well done, that's a boy." But the point is that Krasotkin gets the applause for which he thirsts.

89 515_{18-22}, $14:492_{27-29}$, In the original, *neuzheli,* "really," is repeated for emphasis—and to suggest that Aliosha is speaking from pain, not anger. Aliosha's remark is an example of Dostoevsky's skilful use of the discordant note.

90 515_{44-45}, $14:493_{6-9}$, *A Kinsman of Mahomet or Salutary Folly*— the book, a translation from the French, appeared in Moscow in 1785. Significantly, Kolia has nothing but contempt (Russ. *zabubionnaia,* "scandalous, dissolute," is substandard diction) for the lubricity of this entertainment. The Russian radicals of the 1860s were puritanic in their attitude toward sex. See *PSS* 15:584.

91 516_{25-38}, $14:493_{33-48}$, Once more the parent-child relationship is reversed. First, the captain is more delighted with the toy than his son. Now it is the boy's mother who gets the toy, gladly ceded to her by her son.

92 517_{5-7}, $14:494_{15-17}$, Borovikov's formula is quite correct. But the technique of preparation is primitive and dangerous. It is significant that Kolia, the young "radical," should be playing with explosives. At any rate, note Dostoevsky's careful attention to detail.

93 517_{33}, $14:494_{43}$, "The captain was abject in his flattery of Kolia."—In the original we have a more graphic "The captain was fawning on Kolia something terrible," where *lisil,* "was fawning" (from *lisa,* "fox"), is the same colloquialism that described Mme. Krasotkin's efforts on behalf of Kolia (chap. i, p. 486_{30}).

94 517_{37-38}, $14:494_{47-48}$, ". . . and was continually missing the note he tried to keep up"—observe Dostoevsky's concern with tone of voice. See Introduction III.1. Polyphonic Composition.

95 518_{3-4}, $14:495_{11-12}$, "Peasantry" and "peasants" translate *narod,* also rendered by "the people" further down. Dostoevsky

satirizes the radicals' cult of "the people," which he felt was coupled with a profound contempt for the beliefs and traditions of the people. See Introduction II.4.b. The People.

96 518_{9-12}, $14:495_{17-19}$, Aimed at the Grand Inquisitor. Even the Latin smacks of him.

97 518_{43-44}, $14:496_3$, "I simply stated the general proposition, had spoken hypothetically"—establishes a perfect analogy with Ivan's role in the murder of his father: he had stated the general proposition (that "all things are lawful") and had tacitly approved Smerdiakov's project (the original has *v proekte,* "in project," for "hypothetically"). But on a different level, the scene with the goose is yet another bit of "genre painting" which helps create a broad basis of popular life in the novel.

98 $519_{6ff.}$, $14:496_{9ff.}$, Here Kolia's performance trails off into outright schoolboy clowning. Some details of his "routine" are funny enough: *klassik Kolbasnikov,* with its cute alliteration and rhyme *(klassik : kolbasnik),* is funny because *kolbasnik* means "sausage maker." The unpopularity of the classics teacher is a cliché of nineteenth-century Russian literature (Chekhov's "Man in a Shell" being the most famous example). The classics teacher stood for reaction and the authorities, as whose spy he was often seen. Hence the "realized" metaphor of the "long ears" (line 6) of the "green ass" (line 9). Incidentally, Dostoevsky was in favor of a classical education. See note 108 below.

99 519_{9-10}, $14:496_{12-13}$, In the original: "got a dowry of a thousand roubles from the Mikhailovs"—the familiarity topos: everybody must know the Mikhailovs. Cf. note 4 above.

100 519_{10}, $14:496_{13}$, "a regular fright of the first rank and the last degree"—more of Kolia's schoolboy wit: "a regular fright" translates *rylovorot,* lit. "mug-turner" (meaning she is so ugly everybody looks the other way).

101 519_{13-14}, $14:496_{16-17}$, In the original the rhyme is *tret'eklassnikov* ("third graders") : *Kolbasnikov.*

102 519_{18}, $14:496_{26}$, "the founders of Troy"—the question of who founded Troy is one of the recurring motifs (cf. chap. i, p. 489_{20-21}) which help create atmosphere and continuity in the novel about children. It will come back in the epilogue (chap. iii, p. 731_{45}).

103 519_{30}, $14:496_{33-34}$, "He had by now completely recovered his dignity"—translates *On uzhe uspel vpolne voiti v ton,* lit. "He was by now completely in tune," taking up an earlier comment on Kolia's struggle to hit the right note (see note 94 above).

104   520₁, 14:497₄,   "Smaragdov"—see note 19 above.

105   520₁₃, 14:497₁₆,   "a discordant note"—translates *dissonans*.
       Note, once more, Dostoevsky's attention to "tone."

106   520₂₈₋₃₀, 14:497₃₂₋₃₄,   "these old wives' tales"—the founding of
       the Russian state by Riurik, a legendary Varangian (Viking)
       prince, reported by the Nestor Chronicle, was often attacked by
       Russian nationalists, and in precisely these terms. A rejection of
       "universal history" as irrelevant to Russia and her problems was
       also quite common. See *PSS* 15:581.

107   520₃₄₋₃₆, 14:497₃₈₋₃₉,   Kolia echoes the views of such leading
       radicals as D. I. Pisarev. Note that Ivan Karamazov, too, has
       studied the natural sciences. The statement that universal history
       is "the study of the successive follies of mankind and nothing
       more" is taken from Voltaire's "Essay on the Manners and
       Spirit of Nations," where we find these obervations: "All his-
       tory, then, in short, is little else than a long succession of useless
       cruelties," and, "It must once again be acknowledged that
       history in general is a collection of crimes, follies, and misfor-
       tunes." This coincides with the ideas of Ivan Karamazov's Grand
       Inquisitor and Ivan's other double, the devil (Book Eleven, chap.
       ix). Nineteenth-century thought, on the other hand, is generally
       characterized by a teleological view of history and a belief in
       human progress.

108   521₁₋₉, 14:498₁₋₇,   Kolia's harangue against the classics is a
       rather accurate statement of the progressive position on this
       matter in the public debate which raged in the 1860s and 1870s.
       The official policy of the government was to support the
       humanities, and the classics in particular, at the expense of the
       natural sciences. Only graduates of so-called classical secondary
       schools *(klassicheskaia gimnaziia)* were admitted to universities,
       while graduates of schools that taught modern languages and
       natural sciences *(real'naia gimnaziia)* were limited to a higher
       technical education. Dostoevsky, who had himself received a
       technical education, was a staunch supporter of the classics. He
       wrote: "Exactly five years ago we inaugurated the so-called
       classical reform of education. Mathematics and the two ancient
       languages—Latin and Greek—were recognized as the most
       effective means of mental, and even spiritual, development. It
       was not we who recognized and invented this: this is a fact, an
       undeniable fact, empirically ascertained by the whole of Europe

in the course of centuries" (*Diary of a Writer*, 1876, 1:401). Cf.
PSS 15:582.

109   521_{23-26}, $14:498_{22-25}$, "all the classical authors have been
translated . . ."—Here Dostoevsky apparently lets Kolia echo
the views of one V. I. Modestov, who had suggested that the
teaching of the classical languages be replaced by the teaching of
classical authors in translation (*Golos* [The voice], 10 October
1879, no. 280). See *PSS* 15:582-83.

110   $521_{46ff.}$, $14:498_{46ff.}$, This scene must be visualized. It is a study in
contrast between the large, imposing figure of the doctor (a
bearskin coat alone fills up a lot of space) and the poverty-stricken
room and its thin and sickly occupants.

Chapter vi

111   522_{20}, $14:499_{17}$, "Precocity"—here the chapter title serves as an
internal commentary, drawing the reader's attention to a fact
which is essential to an understanding of the text.

112   522_{22-23}, $14:499_{20}$, "I can't endure medicine!"—It should be:
"I can't stand medicine!" or "I hate medicine!" Kolia's dislike
of the medical profession has become another of his labels.

113   522_{24}, $14:499_{21-22}$, "Iliusha will die. I think that's certain."—
Note the frequent strategically placed details which establish
Aliosha as a realist who takes a sober view of things.

114   522_{33-36}, $14:499_{30-33}$, "I have heard you are a mystic . . ."—A
key passage, in which Father Zosima's exhortation about man's
need for "contact with other, mysterious worlds" (Book Six,
chap. iii, p. 299_{45}) is reversed. Georgy Chulkov has suggested
that this passage parodies certain lines from Belinsky's famous
"Letter to Gogol" (1847), in which Belinsky urges Gogol to turn
his back on mysticism and to embrace "the progress of
civilization, enlightenment, and humanism" (Belinskii, 10:213).
See Georgii Chulkov, "Poslednee slovo Dostoevskogo o
Belinskom," in *Dostoevskii* (Moscow, 1928), pp. 68-69.

115   522_{41}–523_{2}, $14:499_{38-41}$, A key cross-reference to Book Five,
chap. iii, p. 215_{45} (English text), pp. 213_{48}–214_{1} (Russian text),
where Ivan quotes Voltaire's dictum in the original French.

116   523_{2-6}, $14:499_{41-45}$, Note the counterpoint between Kolia's
progressive ideas, which quite accurately reflect the "advanced"
thought of his day, and the petty private thoughts of a vain boy

of thirteen: an example of Dostoevsky's technique of inner dialogue conducted simultaneously with the regular dialogue. Dostoevsky always maintained that a great deal of petty vanity was hidden behind the "enlightened" rhetoric of his progressive opponents.

117 523_{8-10}, $14:500_{2-3}$, This is the phraseology of Rakitin, Kolia's mentor (cf. Book Two, chap. vii, p. 72_{23-26}), but the thesis is Ivan's, or more precisely, the Grand Inquisitor's. Dostoevsky makes a point of identifying the "advanced" views of the Russian radicals with the "old-fashioned" ideas of the eighteenth-century Enlightenment. Chulkov suggests that this, too, is the paraphrase of a passage from Belinsky's "Letter to Gogol," in which Belinsky had said that "Voltaire, who by his mockery put out the fires of fanaticism and ignorance in Europe, was more a son of Christ, flesh of His flesh, and bone of His bones, than all your priests, bishops, Metropolitans, and Patriarchs" (Belinsky, 10:214–15). Belinsky adds that "this is not new to most schoolboys." See Chulkov, "Poslednee slovo," p. 68.

118 523_{19}, $14:500_{13}$, *Candide* (1759), Voltaire's philosophical satire, accompanied Dostoevsky through his whole life. A notebook entry dated 24 December 1877 suggests that he actually planned to write a "Russian Candide." See *PSS* 15:409.

119 523_{27}, $14:500_{20-21}$, "I am a socialist, . . . I am an incurable socialist"—apparently a quotation from Herzen's "Letter to Emperor Alexander the Second" (1855). See *PSS* 15:583. Dostoevsky keeps up the pattern of discrediting the leaders of the progressive movement by putting their words into the mouth of a precocious schoolboy.

120 523_{37-38}, $14:500_{29-30}$, "When you are older . . ."—this does not sound like a twenty-year-old. But one must keep in mind that the wisdom of Father Zosima also speaks through Aliosha.

121 523_{41-44}, $14:500_{33-36}$, Kolia mouths the antireligious clichés of the Russian radicals. Belinsky had written: "The Church . . . has supported inequality, fawned on those in power, has combated and persecuted the brotherhood of men—and still does to this day" (Belinskii, "Letter to Gogol," *Polnoe sobranie sochinenii,* 10:214).

122 524_{4-8}, $14:500_{40-43}$, In his *Diary of a Writer* of 1873, Dostoevsky relates that Belinsky had actually said that if Christ

were to appear in our day, "he would join the socialists and
follow them" (*Diary of a Writer* 1:8). Cf. Chulkov, "Poslednee
slovo," p. 69.

123   524_{12-13}, $14:500_{48}$,   Belinsky was venerated almost like a saint by
the first generation of Russian radicals. But to the younger
generation (D. I. Pisarev, for example), he became "old
Belinsky," a somewhat old-fashioned, naive idealist.

124   524_{14-16}, $14:501_{1-3}$,   This exchange implies that Aliosha is well
familiar with Belinsky's works—a bit of poetic license on
Dostoevsky's, or Aliosha's, part. It also contains an
anachronism: the report which informed the Russian public that
Belinsky had said this (Dostoevsky's own; see note 122 above)
only appeared in 1873, six years after the action of *The Brothers
Karamazov*.

125   524_{18-19}, $14:501_{5-6}$,   Tatiana, heroine of Pushkin's novel *Eugene
Onegin* (1830), married to an older and presumably unloved
man, refuses to have an affair with Onegin, the man she loved as
a girl and admittedly still loves. In his "Ninth Essay on Pushkin"
(1844-45), Belinsky had reproached Pushkin's heroine for her
decision to remain faithful to her marriage vows, "a relationship
which is a profanation of feminine feeling and chastity, because a
relationship which is not sanctified by love is immoral to the
highest degree" (Belinskii, 7:501). In his own "Discourse on
Pushkin" (1880), Dostoevsky, on the contrary, set up Tatiana as
an example of pure Russian womanhood, highly praising her
decision. See *Diary of a Writer*, 2:971-74.

126   524_{25}, $14:501_{12-13}$,   Most Russian radicals were strong propo-
nents of the emancipation of women.

127   524_{26-27}, $14:501_{14}$,   *Les femmes tricottent*—"a woman's job is
knitting."

128   524_{29-31}, $14:501_{17-20}$,   "I think, too, that to leave one's own
country and fly to America is mean, worse than mean—silly."—
An allusion, perhaps, to Chernyshevsky's novel *What Is to Be
Done?* (1863), whose hero, Lopukhov, emigrates to America,
land of opportunity. In an article of *Diary of a Writer* (1873),
Dostoevsky had discussed the story of three Russian schoolboys
"who were charged with some crime connected with their
contemplated flight to America" (*Diary of a Writer*, 1:153). In
The Possessed (1871), Dostoevsky had drawn a bleak picture of
the American experience of Russian immigrants who went there

in the footsteps of Chernyshevsky's hero. See *PSS* 15:584–85.
Cf. Dieter Boden, *Das Amerikabild im russischen Schrifttum bis zum Ende des 19. Jahrhunderts* (Hamburg, 1968), pp. 165–72.

129   524_{38-40}, $14:501_{24-28}$,   The translator has properly changed the text to make it immediately understandable: "secret police" translates *Tret'ego otdeleniia*, lit. "the Third department" (of His Imperial Majesty's Own Chancellery), which was the secret police. Its headquarters was located near the Chain Bridge in St. Petersburg. The name of that bridge, an ironic accident, was changed to Pestel Bridge after the Revolution of 1917, in memory of Pavel Pestel', one of the leaders of the Decembrist revolt of 1825.

130   525_{1-2}, $14:501_{28-29}$,   These two lines are from a widely known antigovernment satire, repeatedly printed in various émigré periodicals and almanacs, first in *The North Star* 6 (1861): 214. Though it did not appear in *The Bell,* best known of these publications, *The Bell* did print a sequel to this poem (no. 221 [1 June 1866], p. 1812). For details see *PSS* 15:585–86. At any rate, Dostoevsky commits another anachronism, since Kolia's father had died many years before the appearance of any of these publications. *The Bell* was published from 1857 to 1867, which means that it began to appear after Mr. Krasotkin's death.

131   525_{9-11}, $14:501_{37-39}$,   A neglect of or even outright hostility to Pushkin was characteristic of the Russian radicals of the 1860s, who saw him as a poet of the dying aristocracy and its antiquated ideals at best, and as a frivolous bard of "wine, women, and song" at worst. It is, then, symptomatic that Kolia has read Belinsky's comments on Pushkin's *Eugene Onegin,* but not Pushkin. Dostoevsky was a lifelong enthusiastic admirer of Pushkin. See Introduction I.4.a. Secular Sources.

132   525_{15}, $14:501_{43}$,   "Tell me, Karamazov, have you an awful contempt for me?"—As so often in Dostoevsky's dialogues, the conversation takes a surprise turn. Kolia's inner voice, which up to this point has played the role of "the other voice" (see note 116 above), surfaces and becomes the dominant.

133   525_{28-33}, $14:502_{12-18}$,   "the criticism made by a German . . ."—this little anecdote amplifies Ivan Karamazov's remarks on Russian schoolboys (Book Five, chap. iii, p. 216_{6-9}).

134   525_{34}, $14:502_{20}$,   "truthissimo"—a rather infelicitous attempt to render Russ. *vernissimo,* schoolboy slang from *verno,* "true," a cognate of Lat. *verus,* It. *vero,* "true."

135   525_{38-40}, $14:502_{23-25}$,   "there is an independent spirit almost

from childhood, boldness of thought and conviction"—deep irony: Kolia has been mouthing the clichés of the shallow Rakitin. One of Dostoevsky's political theses was that the ideas of the Russian radicals were but slavish copies of poorly digested Western ideas.

136   525_{39}, $14:502_{25}$, "sausage makers"—a common ethnic slur.

137   526_{7-12}, $14:502_{32-37}$, Dostoevsky skilfully combines several narrative concerns: he accounts for the length of the conversation between Aliosha and Kolia; he builds up a motif only hinted at earlier (Kolia's frivolous delay in coming to Iliusha's bedside); he brings to life yet another character (Nina); and he launches the transition from the old to the new Kolia.

138   526_{22}, $14:502_{48}$, "You make it worse!"—Translates *Vy menia rastravliaete,* "you're rubbing salt into my wounds" or "don't rub it in."

139   526_{25-26}, $14:503_{3-4}$, "I am a scoundrel in lots of ways"—Ivan Karamazov, too, had said at one point: "I am a scoundrel!" (Book Five, chap. vii, p. 260_5). The turning point in Kolia's life presages a similar dénouement in the life of Ivan Karamazov, his double.

140   526_{29}, $14:503_{6-7}$, "this generous, morbidly sensitive boy"— "generous" translates *blagorodnyi,* which is "noble, high-minded" as well as "generous." The point is that a quality ordinarily reserved for truly outstanding men and women is seen in a ten-year-old boy.

141   526_{45-47}, $14:503_{25-28}$, "because I was so pleased"—translates *ot radosti,* lit. "from joy." The word *radost',* "joy," repeated three times here, is a leitmotif associated particularly with Aliosha (cf. Book Seven, notes 122 and 127). Its appearance suggests that Aliosha is about to gain ascendancy in Kolia's life.

142   527_{1-4}, $14:503_{30-32}$, This confession of a "revolutionary" is a recurrent motif in Dostoevsky. A fear of appearing ridiculous dominates the most demonic of his characters, Stavrogin (*The Possessed*). The murderer Raskol'nikov (*Crime and Punishment*) must drain the bitter cup of ridicule on his road to salvation. The concept expressed here by Kolia is the focal theme of "Dream of a Ridiculous Man" (1877).

143   527_{15-16}, $14:503_{43-44}$, An important passage. Aliosha quite unequivocally expresses a belief in personal metaphysical evil: he believes in the devil "canonically." This passage, then, prepares the reader for the appearance of the devil in Book Eleven.

144   527_{22-27}, $14:504_{1-7}$, "even if everyone is like that . . ."—

Aliosha is not at all afraid to produce sententious moral statements, entirely of the kind we have heard from Father Zosima. The authority of the latter's voice has passed on to him. See Introduction III.1.d. Aliosha as an Echo of Father Zosima.

145   528_{3-4}, $14:504_{33-34}$, "something made Aliosha say suddenly"— this translation includes an interpretation, as the text actually reads: "Aliosha suddenly said, for some reason." Along with everything else, Aliosha has inherited Father Zosima's gift of prophecy. Note, too, the sudden drama.

146   528_7, $14:504_{37}$, "But you will bless life on the whole, all the same."—Another echo of Ivan Karamazov (see, for instance, Book Five, chap. iii, p. 211_{36-42}).

147   528_{22-23}, $14:505_{4-5}$, "His face . . ."—An example of Dostoevsky's play with mimicry. The scene following is staged, with all of the participants except Aliosha playacting in a grotesque skit.

148   528_{26-29}, $14:505_{8-11}$, The captain, still the buffoon, joins the cast.

149   529_{4-5}, $14:505_{30}$, "with an almost wrathful sternness that made the captain start"—the comedy is on.

150   529_5, $14:505_{31}$, "to Sy-ra-cuse"—this bit of medical advice to a Russian pauper is to be understood as a piece of social satire directed at a society doctor's unfeeling attitude toward suffering humanity. See *PSS* 15:586.

151   529_{24}, $14:506_7$, "apothecary"—translates *lekar'* (a cognate of Eng. *leech*), which meant "doctor" (it is now an archaism), but with a connotation of homegrown, old-fashioned, or crude medical skill. Cf. Book Twelve, chap. iii, p. 639_{44}.

152   529_{35-36}, $14:506_{17-19}$, In the original, we have a pun. The doctor hears *zvon*, "peal," for *Perezvon*, "Chimes," and Kolia jumps in with a proverb: *Slyshal zvon, da ne znaet, gde on*, lit. "He's heard the bell, but where it is he can't tell," that is, "He doesn't know what he is talking about."

153   529_{45}, $14:506_{29-30}$, All of a sudden we have another bit of slapstick comedy: the dignified, elegant doctor chased by a shaggy mongrel dog. Of course the comedy remains in the mind. Cf. Book Two, chap. vii, p. 74_{15-16} (the Father Superior getting a thrashing) or Book Three, chap. x, p. 140_{4-5} (Katerina Ivanovna and Grushen'ka having a catfight).

154   530_{5-7}, $14:506_{34-37}$, Kolia ends the comic scene with a pathetic flourish.

155   530$_{22-23}$, 14:507$_{4-5}$,   Once more it is the child who feels sorry for his father.

156   530$_{35-36}$, 14:507$_{18-19}$,   "bury me by our big stone, where we used to go for our walk"—see Book Four, chap. vii, p. 189$_{1-2}$. The stone will reappear prominently in the final scene of the novel ("The Speech at the Stone," p. 727). The commentators of *PSS* suggest that the stone "has a symbolic meaning as the first building stone of the future harmony which Aliosha and his disciples, the schoolboys, have already begun to erect" (*PSS* 15:586).

157   531$_9$, 14:507$_{38}$,   "crying, and no longer ashamed of it"—Aliosha's first great triumph: Kolia is reformed.

158   531$_{14-15}$, 14:507$_{44-45}$,   A free quotation of Psalm 137:5-6: "If I forget thee, O Jerusalem, let my right hand forget her cunning. If I do not remember thee, let my tongue cleave to the roof of my mouth; if I prefer not Jerusalem above my chief joy."

159   531$_{17-18}$, 14:507$_{48}$,   "with absurd whimpering cries"—note once more Dostoevsky's attention to inarticulate expression. Snegiriov cries as adults seldom cry.

160   531$_{23-25}$, 14:508$_{6-9}$,   "Jerusalem"—the repetition of the word "Jerusalem" establishes it as a symbol. Aliosha may be thinking of the "new Jerusalem" (Rev. 21:2) in his own heart. Dostoevsky had used Jerusalem as a symbol before, in the last chapter of *Crime and Punishment,* for example.

Book Eleven

Chapter i

1   532_2, $15:5_3$, "Brother Ivan Fiodorovich"—The title of the Book featuring Ivan gives his name in this formal manner, while the Books devoted to the other brothers were entitled "Aliosha" and "Mitia."

2   532_{19-21}, $15:5_{19-21}$, Literally: "A certain spiritual transformation was apparent about her, and a certain steadfast, humble, yet good and unshakeable resolve could be discerned in her." Here "good" is *blagoi,* which has a connotation of "godly." Grushen'ka has by no means turned into a saint, as we shall see soon enough. But this detail establishes one particular and important trait of her current condition. Her character has "expanded." See Introduction II.6.a. Dostoevsky's Psychology.

3   533_9, $15:6_{17}$, There is something uncanny about Maksimov's appearance at Grushen'ka's. A double of Fiodor Pavlovich's (cf. Book Eight, note 247), he showed up at Mokroe at the time of Fiodor Pavlovich's death. Now he substitutes for him as an importunate suitor.

4   533_{31}, $15:6_{38-39}$, "the destitute wanderer"—translates *skitaiushchiisia prizhival'shchik,* "wandering sponger," which is ironic rather than sentimental.

5   533_{44-45}, $15:7_4$, "feeling the end approaching"—translates *pochuvstvovav blizkii final,* "sensing the impending *finale,*" with a touch of flippancy. The narrator, a member of the local gentry, treats the businessman and ex-mayor with ironic condescension.

6   534_{2-3}, $15:7_{8-9}$, "The master wishes you long life and happiness and tells you to forget him."—In the original, these words have a strong flavor of the merchant class.

7   534_{32}, $15:7_{37}$, The mention of Rakitin prepares the reader for that character's significant appearance in chapter iv.

356

8   534_{34}, $15:7_{39}$, "carelessly"—it should be "absentmindedly."

9   535_3, $15:8_{5-6}$, "vodka"—translates *bal'zamchik,* "balsam, cordial." Maksimov would not dare to ask for vodka outright, so it is "balsam," strictly for medicinal purposes, of course.

10   535_{15-16}, $15:8_{15}$, "characteristically eloquent"—more accurately: "flowery after his usual fashion." The grotesque comedy involving the men around Grushen'ka is in each case connected with genuine suffering (even the two Poles are stranded in a Russian provincial town "without food or fuel"): it is this kind of "fun" that earned Dostoevsky the reputation of a "cruel talent."

11   536_{24}, $15:9_{26}$, "Katka"—Grushen'ka is using the disrespectful diminutive form of her rival's name quite unceremoniously.

12   537_{10}, $15:10_9$, "Three thousand" again; the money which Dmitry so desperately needed is suddenly there. See Introduction III.3.a. Motifs.

13   537_{13}, $15:10_{11}$, "Fetiukovich"—the lawyer's name is derived from *fetiuk,* "jerk, drip, sourpuss," a slang expression Dostoevsky may have learned from Gogol's *Dead Souls,* chap. iv, where Gogol's footnote defines it thus: "*Fetiuk,* a word insulting to a man, comes from the letter Θ [theta], considered by some to be an obscene letter." (The letter theta resembles a "fica.") The commentators of *PSS* suggest that the name rhymes with the name of V. D. Spasovich (1829–1906), a lawyer with whom Dostoevsky had polemicized in the Kroneberg case in 1876 (*Diary of a Writer,* 2:218–38) and whom he held to be an unscrupulous manipulator of the law. L. P. Grossman has pointed out that the defender of Vera Zasulich in 1878, P. A. Aleksandrov (1836–93), is also part of the composite image of Fetiukovich. See *PSS* 15:586–87.

14   537_{37-41}, $15:10_{34-38}$, "the door was open"—The one piece of really false evidence in the case. Dostoevsky takes pains to repeat it often enough and to underscore its importance. At no time is it intimated that it is anything but an honest mistake on Grigory's part.

15   538_{3-10}, $15:10_{46}-11_5$, The motif of the "babe" in Dmitry's dream (Book Nine, chap. viii, pp. 478–79) is brought back. Significantly, Grushen'ka is deeply moved by Dmitry's words and finds them "good" ("nicely" translates *khorosho,* "good"), even though she does not understand them: the primacy of intuition over reason is asserted once more.

16 538_{11}, $15:11_6$, "It must be Rakitin"—answers "what do you suppose he's always talking about?" (p. 537_{46}). Dmitry is fighting off Rakitin's attempts to convert him to atheist materialism.

17 539_{1-2}, $15:11_{42}$, "though he were a baby himself"—a very clear statement of Dmitry's "childhood." Cf. Book Eight, notes 106 and 202, and note 15 above.

18 539_{7-10}, $15:11_{46}$–12_2, This passage, rather flat in translation, is heavily charged in the original: "besought him with sudden eagerness" translates *vskinulas' i vzmolilas' vdrug,* lit. "started up and took to imploring him suddenly," with alliteration and parallel prefixes *vs-/vz-,* where the prefix suggests upward vertical motion. Grushen'ka's words are close to the language and style of the popular lament (a genre of folk poetry, along with wedding songs, harvest songs, etc.). One must imagine the words "Set my mind at rest that I may know the worst that's in store for poor me" as delivered in almost a chant or singsong (cf. Book Two, chap. iii, p. 40_{13}).

19 539_{14}, $15:12_6$, "There is a secret"—prepares the reader for chapter iv of this book ("A Hymn and a Secret") and chapter i of the Epilogue ("Plans to Save Mitia").

20 539_{27-28}, $15:12_{17-18}$, "Ivan is not in love with Katerina Ivanovna, I think"—Aliosha has not seen Ivan since their meeting right after Ivan had broken with Katerina Ivanovna, and on that occasion Ivan certainly did not act as if he were in love (Book Five, chap. iii, p. 214). Things are more complicated than this, as we shall soon see.

21 539_{36}, $15:12_{25}$, "I'll tell everything then!"—Grushen'ka knows the secret of Katerina Ivanovna's visit to Dmitry (Book Three, chap. x, p. 139_{28-29}).

Chapter ii

22 540_9, $15:12_{43}$, "The Injured Foot"—an inadequate translation of *Bol'naia nozhka,* lit. "An Ailing Little Foot," where *nozhka* is a diminutive of *noga,* "foot," implying that the subject is a child or an attractive woman. Dostoevsky's preoccupation with ladies' feet (often ailing) may be a personal idiosyncrasy (it occurs in several of his works), literary borrowing (from Pushkin), or a mixture of both. Cf. Book Three, chap. v, p. 107_{24-26}. The chapter heading signals the tone of the whole

chapter: its absurd comedy of frivolous fantasies is a complement of the tragic reality which we have just met in chapter i.

23   540_{21}, $15:13_9$,   We now begin to understand the heading of Book Nine, chap. i: "The Beginning of Perkhotin's Official Career."

24   540_{42}–541_1, $15:13_{28-31}$, "Since the death of Father Zosima . . ."—Mme. Khokhlakov will not separate the serious or even the holy from the trivial and frivolous. Her flippancy is reminiscent of the late Fiodor Pavlovich.

25   541_{11-12}, $15:13_{40-41}$, "thank God, she can walk now"—a mild surprise and, in a way, another Dostoevskian false lead. We think that everything is well with Liza, only to learn in the following chapter that this is not so.

26   541_{20-21}, $15:13_{48}$–14_1, "Everything seems mixed up in a sort of tangle."—Reminds one of Fiodor Pavlovich. He, too, had suffered from an inability to concentrate and had shown signs of neurotic confusion. See Book One, chap. iv, p. 16_{38-42}.

27   541_{43}–542_3, $15:14_{23-27}$, "This Katya . . ."—Like Fiodor Pavlovich, Mme. Khokhlakov mixes absurd prattle with cynical good sense and sound psychological judgment. Her prediction seems to be a plausible one. Note that she never for a moment doubts Dmitry's guilt—nor finds anything very terrible about it.

28   542_{10}, $15:14_{33}$, *Gossip*—translates *Slukhi*, "rumors, hearsay" ("Gossip" would be *Spletni*). The name of this scandal sheet is patterned after the newspaper *Molva* ("Rumor" or "Common Talk"), which appeared in Petersburg from 1879 to 1881 and certainly answered the description given here. *Molva*, incidentally, had printed an unfavorable reaction to Dostoevsky's "Discourse on Pushkin." See *PSS* 15:587.

29   542_{17-21}, $15:14_{42-45}$,   See note 26 above.

30   $542_{25ff.}$, $15:15_{4ff.}$,   This spirited takeoff on progressive exposé journalism which flourished in the 1860s and 1870s is one of Dostoevsky's own excursions into a journalistic manner of which he was a master. Other works of his feature similar pieces. See, for instance, *The Idiot*, Part II, chap. viii.

31   542_{31}, $15:15_9$, *Skotoprigonievsk* is derived from *skotoprigonka*, "stockyard." "Cattle Run" would be a good equivalent. The provincial town described in *The Brothers Karamazov* is essentially Staraia Russa, Dostoevsky's summer residence in the 1870s.

32   543_{1-4}, $15:15_{24-26}$,   Dostoevsky's sarcasm is directed at the crude

vulgarity (the pasquil is "playful," if a bull in a china shop is) and shallow truisms (the evils of parricide and of serfage) of the progressive scandal sheets.

33   543_8, $15:15_{29-30}$, "middle-aged charms"—the insult is much worse in the original, where it reads "forty-year-old charms": Mme. Khokhlakov is nowhere near forty, but an exceptionally attractive lady "of no more than thirty-three" (Book Two, chap. iii, p. 38_{30}).

34   543_{11}, $15:15_{32}$, "It's your friend Rakitin."—Rakitin is now involved in every plot line in the novel, even that involving the Khokhlakovs.

35   543_{27-29}, $15:16_{1-2}$, Another instance of inversion of generations, here in travesty, of course. And once more, Aliosha assumes the role of his teacher, the late Zosima.

36   543_{45}–544_1, $15:16_{20-23}$, "I shall certainly, certainly try and get promotion for him."—The original is not quite that blunt: "I shall certainly, certainly intercede in his behalf," where *prosit'*, "intercede," has the simple basic meaning of "beg, ask." The premise of Perkhotin's having "the mind of a statesman" and "future diplomat" is to please Mme. Khokhlakov: an absurd *non sequitur* in the style of Gogol. In *Dead Souls,* chap. ii, a diplomatic career is predicted for young Femistoklius, sitting in a high chair, by his proud father, Manilov, on the strength of the youngster's knowledge of the fact that the capital of France is Paris.

37   544_{1-4}, $15:16_{22-24}$, Here the translation misses yet another Gogolian effect. In the original, the sentence about Perkhotin's having saved Mme. Khokhlakov's life (absurd in itself) is connected to the one about Rakitin's dirty boots by *Nu, a,* "Well, meanwhile" or "On the other hand," which puts these wholly incommensurable facts on the same level.

38   544_{15-16}, $15:16_{35-36}$, Mme. Khokhlakov remembers the lines wrong. The correct text will appear on p. 559.

39   544_{18-20}, $15:16_{38-40}$, Mme. Khokhlakov's praise of Rakitin's poem and its "charming idea" is a time fuse which prepares for its eventual explosion.

40   $544_{30ff.}$, $15:17_{1ff.}$, "Piotr Ilyich began to laugh . . ."—The comedy of this scene is enhanced by the clever "staging" given it by Mme. Khokhlakov. Much as Fiodor Pavlovich, she makes herself look sillier than she is, as she pretends that she cannot see through the vulgar antics of her youthful admirers. We have seen

her in her better moments and know that she is only playing naive.

41   544$_{31-32}$, 15:17$_3$, "some divinity student must have written them"—"divinity student" translates *seminarist,* which is decidedly deprecatory in connection with poetry. See Book Two, note 169.

42   544$_{36-38}$, 15:17$_8$, A campaign to erect a monument to honor Pushkin was started in the Russian press as early as 1862, but the subscription for it began only in 1871. The monument was unveiled in Moscow on 6 June 1880, and on 8 June 1880 Dostoevsky delivered his celebrated "Discourse on Pushkin." Rakitin's characterization of Pushkin as a frivolous poet of "women's feet" is fully in character with the disparaging attitude toward the great poet found in the writings of the radicals of the 1860s, D. I. Pisarev in particular. A similar view of Pushkin is found in Tolstoi's *What Is Art?* (1897–98). The motif of "pretty little feet" is a recurrent one in Pushkin, the most famous instance being stanzas xxx–xxxiv of the first chapter of *Eugene Onegin.*

43   545$_{13-14}$, 15:17$_{25-26}$, "One voice seemed to be telling me, 'speak,' and the other 'no, don't speak.' "—Dostoevsky lays bare his favorite device, that of "the other voice" or inner dialogue, the basis of his polyphonic technique (see Introduction III.1. Polyphonic Composition). As a rule, the "other voice" is not identified as such, but is, on the contrary, well disguised. Here it appears in a blatant parody.

44   545$_{18-21}$, 15:17$_{30-32}$, Exactly like Fiodor Pavlovich! Mme. Khokhlakov dearly loves making a scene—quite literally so. But also like Fiodor Pavlovich, she gets so involved in her own playacting that she loses control of herself and of her "scene."

45   545$_{35ff.}$, 15:17$_{45ff.}$, "Aberration" translates *affekt,* "a fit of passion," and, as a legal term, the Russian equivalent of "temporary insanity." Dostoevsky lets Mme. Khokhlakov make a travesty of the practice of acquitting criminals on grounds of "temporary insanity," a practice which had become common in the 1870s. Dostoevsky, though generally opposed to this practice, was himself instrumental in the eventual acquittal, on grounds of temporary insanity, of one Ekaterina Kornilov, who had been initially sentenced to a term of two years and eight months in prison for having thrown her stepdaughter, a child of six, from a fourth-floor window. Dostoevsky took up the case in

Diary of a Writer (1876), 1:459–65 and 527–34, caused it to be reopened, and could report to his readers in April of the following year that Mrs. Kornilov had been retried and found innocent (*Diary of a Writer,* 2:690–92 and 910–35).

46 546_{28-29}, $15:18_{32-33}$, "it'll be better, ever so much better, if Dmitry Fiodorovich murdered him"—Mme. Khokhlakov, like Fiodor Pavlovich, has lost all sense of the moral aspect of things: a perverted aesthetic sense has all but superseded it.

47 546_{45-46}, $15:18_{46-47}$, "And then he might be made a justice of the peace or something in another town"—Mme. Khokhlakov's thinking, perverse though it seems, represents only a slight exaggeration of some "liberal" ideas current in Russia at the time.

48 $547_{1ff.}$, $15:18_{48ff.}$, "Aberration" is still *affekt*. See note 45 above. Mme. Khokhlakov's tirade now culminates in a comedy of the absurd.

49 547_{21-22}, $15:19_{18-19}$, "he's been to see Lise and I knew nothing about it!"—another surprise development which weaves yet another strand into the pattern of the main plot.

50 547_{31-32}, $15:19_{29}$, *vous comprenez* . . .—"you understand, that business and the terrible death of your papa." Mme. Khokhlakov's speech features Gallicisms and unnecessary loanwords from the French all along. This effect is lost in the translation. French phrases, such as this one, draw attention to this trait.

51 548_{11-12}, $15:20_{7-8}$, "I am always polite to my servants"—in the original she points out that she uses the polite plural *vy* (Fr. *vous*), rather than the condescending or familiar singular *ty* (Fr. *tu*).

52 548_{12-13}, $15:20_{8}$, "And an hour later she was hugging Julia's feet and kissing them."—The incident mirrors an episode in Father Zosima's story. See Book Six, chap. ii(c), p. 277_{40}.

Chapter iii

53 548_{38}, $15:20_{33}$, The title of this chapter is a gesture of literary collegiality addressed to Vsevolod Krestovsky (1840–95), who had dedicated his long short-story "A Little Demon" ("Besionok," 1860) to Dostoevsky. The heroine of Krestovsky's story is Liza's age and has somewhat similar problems. See *PSS* 5:362, 15:583 and 588.

54 549_{20}, $15:21_{12-13}$, "There is something spiteful and yet open-

hearted about you"—the Russian adjectives *zlobnyi* and *prostodushnyi* form an even stronger *coincidentio oppositorum*. See Introduction II.6.b. Psychological Motivation.

55 549_{38}, $15:21_{31}$, "disorder"—one of the leitmotifs of the novel. Dostoevsky had devoted his preceding novel, *A Raw Youth* (1875), to the theme of social and personal disintegration and disorder in the Russia of the 1870s, and particularly among the young generation.

56 549_{39}, $15:21_{32}$, "I keep wanting to set fire to the house."— Liza will now come up with one startling revelation after another, as a pattern begins to develop in her ramblings.

57 550_9, $15:21_{46}$, "I should like to reap, cut the rye"—cutting rye with a sickle was woman's work and considered the hardest of all the work a peasant woman had to do (it was called *strada*, "torture").

58 550_{11}, $15:21_{48}$, "Kalganov"—this character, like Maksimov, keeps turning up on the fringes of the novel. By now we know the patterns well enough to guess that Liza will not marry Kalganov.

59 550_{24-25}, $15:22_{12-13}$, "What will they do to me in the next world for the greatest sin?"—Matt. 12:31-32 is the biblical text relevant here. "The greatest sin" is blasphemy against the Holy Ghost, and Liza is flirting with it.

60 550_{26}, $15:22_{14}$, "God will censure you."—The bookish "censure" is not a good translation of *osudit*. Perhaps simply: "judge."

61 550_{31-33}, $15:22_{18-19}$, "There are children of twelve who have a longing to set fire to something"—the case of a child arsonist, Olga Umetsky, occupied Dostoevsky during his work on *The Idiot*. See *Notebooks for "The Idiot,"* ed. Edward Wasiolek, tr. Katharine Strelsky (Chicago, 1967), pp. 5-12 ff. passim.

62 550_{36}, $15:22_{22}$, "You take evil for good"—Liza has joined the company of her mother, Fiodor Pavlovich Karamazov, and all those who substitute aesthetic criteria ("pleasure," "thrill," "fascination") for moral criteria and pursue "the ideal of Sodom" (cf. Book Three, note 68).

63 550_{45}-551_2, $15:22_{30-31}$, One of Dostoevsky's favorite images. Stavrogin (in "Stavrogin's Confession") and the hero of "Dream of a Ridiculous Man" are among those who imagine having this experience. Placing Liza, a mere child, in the company of the archfiend Stavrogin may be a part of Dostoevsky's strategy to neutralize Ivan's argument regarding the suffering of innocent children.

64   551_{3-4}, $15:22_{33-34}$,   "It's a craving to destroy something good or, as you say, to set fire to something."—In the Russian, "destroy" is a more graphic *razdavit'*, "crush, squash." Aliosha's sententious statement expresses one of Dostoevsky's favorite thoughts: that the demonic principle is as inherent as the godly in human nature. Aliosha, as Father Zosima's disciple, shows no surprise at a flare-up of the demonic in a sweet young girl.

65   551_{18}, $15:22_{47}$,   "There are moments when people love crime"— in Russian, the same verb (*liubit'*) signifies a moral feeling (as in "to love God"), an erotic feeling (as in "to love a woman"), and a pleasurable sensation (normally translated by "to like"). This makes the confusion of moral, emotional, and aesthetic values much easier.

66   551_{32}, $15:23_{11}$,   "everyone loves his having killed his father"— the description of Dmitry's trial in Book Twelve will amply bear this out.

67   551_{40}–552_5, $15:23_{19-29}$,   This allegoric dream establishes a direct link between Liza and Ivan Karamazov (see chap. ix of this book).

68   552_6, $15:23_{30}$,   "I've had the same dream, too"—another surprise. But it is consistent with Aliosha's image as a saint and "angel" that he should suffer such visitations. Temptations by evil spirits are a recurrent motif of Eastern hagiography.

69   552_{20}, $15:23_{44}$,   "I'll always come to see you, all my life"—this might be relevant to the [putative] sequel to this novel. See Introduction III.3.e. Expository Novel.

70   552_{26-28}, $15:24_{1-3}$,   "is it true that at Easter the Jews steal a child and kill it?"—"Easter" should be "Passover"; Russ. *paskha* has both meanings. The fact that Dostoevsky lets the saintly Aliosha answer "I don't know" to this question is indicative of Dostoevsky's anti-Semitic attitude. There were occasional reports, never substantiated, in the Russian press of the 1870s of alleged ritual murders of Christian children by Jews. See Leonid Grossman, "Dostoevskii i pravitel'stvennye krugi 1870-kh godov," *Literaturnoe nasledstvo* 15:110–14. Similar reports were circulated in the press of Central Europe. Of course, anti-Semitism is a side issue here.

71   552_{29-35}, $15:24_{5-9}$,   Another counterpoint to Ivan's stories of tortured children (Book Five, chap. iv).

72   552_{37-40}, $15:24_{11-13}$,   Pineapple compote was a rare delicacy in nineteenth-century Russia, the *non plus ultra* of sybaritic

pleasure. It is the concrete detail of pineapple compote that drives home the horror of Liza's daydream.

73 553_{3-4}, $15:24_{22-23}$, "He laughed and said it really was nice."—"He" is Ivan. Suddenly, Ivan's penchant for gathering material about torture inflicted on children appears in a quite different light.

74 553_{16}, $15:24_{36}$, "That person behaved honorably"—there will be an explanation of this statement later (chap. v, p. 568_{23-24}).

75 553_{18}, $15:24_{39-40}$, "he believes in the pineapple compote himself"—in his characteristic fashion, Dostoevsky has hypostatized "pineapple compote" as a symbol of "the ideal of Sodom."

76 553_{26-28}, $15:24_{47}-25_2$, Here what seemed to be a minor difficulty catches up with the translator: "nice" has been the translation of Russ. *khorosho* throughout this exchange; *khorosho* can mean "nice" in a given context, but its basic meaning is "good," including "morally good" (as in *khoroshii chelovek,* "a good man"). In this passage, *khorosho* is translated first by "good," and then again by "nice." Clearly the Russian text brings out Liza's confusion of values better than the English version does. We have here a clear objection to Ivan's argument in Book Five, chap. iv: Unlike Ivan's Turkish soldiers, to whom killing babes seems to be pure pleasure, Liza is tormented by the wickedness of her thoughts. Evil is not the absence of God's care, but the *willed* evil (called "good" by them) of those who are against God.

77 553_{30-31}, $15:25_{5-6}$, "Aliosha, save me!"—Another surprise. Note how unpredictable each turn taken by the plot of this scene is.

78 553_{44}, $15:25_{20}$, "trample me under foot"—the Russ. *razdaviat nogoi* is more graphic, suggesting the crushing of an insect or a reptile. Cf. note 64 above. It also falls in line with the last surprise of the scene, Liza's crushing *(pridavila)* of her finger. (The translation has "pinching.")

79 554_{8-9}, $15:25_{31-32}$, "to Ivan Fiodorovich Karamazov"—the next-to-last surprise of this scene.

Chapter iv

80 554_{26}, $15:26_2$, "A Hymn and a Secret"—We remember Dmitry's "hymn" from Book Three, chap. iii, p. 96_{15}. The "secret" has been hinted at in chap. i, p. 538_{34-35}.

81　554₃₉, 15:26₁₆,　The translator has the patronymic wrong: it is Mikhail Makarovich (see Book Eight, chap. viii, p. 419).

82　555₃, 15:26₂₁₋₂₂,　"like a Swede"—part of the Russian saying "to come to grief like a Swede at Poltava" (the Swedes were defeated by the Russians at Poltava in 1709); hence there is no reflection here on the Swedish national character ("drinking and dissipation"), as the translation might suggest.

83　555₁₅, 15:26₃₃₋₃₄,　" 'self-taught' "—the narrator uses the good man's own words (hence the quotation marks) to put him down. The two expressions quoted, although they comprise only four words (*premudrosti,* "wisdom," translated by "sacred subjects," and *svoim umom doidia,* lit. "having advanced there by the effort of his own mind," translated by "self-taught"), paint a perfect picture of the man.

84　555₁₇, 15:26₃₅₋₃₆,　"Apocryphal Gospels," such as the Gospel of St. James or that of Nicodemus, were often translated, and sometimes were used by the Orthodox church, which, unlike the Western church, never developed a definite biblical canon. See George P. Fedotov, *The Russian Religious Mind,* 2 vols. (Belmont, Mass., 1975), 1:43.

85　555₄₀₋₄₁, 15:27₁₁,　"to your own family, who've always been a slave-driving lot"—translates *krepostnich'e vashe otrod'e,* lit. "your serf-owning brood," where *krepostnik* is a "modern" word, meaning "a serf-owner, a supporter of serfage"—something like "racist" in today's America. Cf. Book Two, chap. vii, p. 73₃₄.

86　556₂, 15:27₁₈₋₁₉,　"I've not been simply waiting, but thirsting for you"—in the original, there is a pun here: *ne to chto zhdal, a zhazhdal.* We are immediately met by Dmitry's vigorous, creative speech.

87　556₈₋₁₂, 15:27₁₄₋₁₇,　"They can't understand a joke either"—an observation to which Dostoevsky attributed great significance. He felt that a decline in a society's ability to appreciate irony, parody, and humor was a sure sign of the general decline of that society.

88　556₁₂₋₁₃, 15:27₂₈,　"it's all over with me now"—although this is a false lead, as we shall presently see, this provocative statement is a proper beginning for one of the great Socratic dialogues of the novel. Set against a background of assorted comic trivia and irrelevancies, there emerges Dmitry's "I am sorry about God" and the outline of Dostoevsky's *argumentum ad hominem* for the existence of God.

89   556_{25}, $15:27_{39}$, "ethics"—Dmitry says *efika,* the archaic Byzantine form, instead of the modern Latinate *etika.*

90   556_{30}, $15:27_{44}$, "damn him!"—in the original: "the devil take him!" (which may be relevant in view of the subsequent diabolic imagery associated with Rakitin).

91   556_{32}, $15:27_{46}$, "of an elevating tendency"—translates *s blagorodstvom napravleniia,* "of a noble tendency," meaning that it promotes humanitarian and libertarian ideas. In the original, the grammatical form of the phrase makes sure that it will sound ludicrous. Incidentally, Ivan Karamazov's prediction about Rakitin's career (Book Two, chap. vii, p. 73_{6-17}) is already coming true.

92   556_{32}, $15:27_{47}$, "he may be of use"—in the original, a cliché which means "to serve humanity."

93   556_{35}, $15:27_{48}$, "you man of God!"—See Introduction I.4.b. Sacred Sources, and II.1.a. Allegoric Figures.

94   556_{36-38}, $15:28_{2-4}$, Claude Bernard (1813–78), French naturalist, physiologist, and pathologist, philosophically a positivist. His works were widely known in Russia. His famous *Leçons de physiologie experimentale appliquée à la médicine* (1865) was translated into Russian by Dostoevsky's friend and collaborator Nikolai Strakhov (1866).

95   557_{1-3}, $15:28_{10-12}$, Dmitry quickly hypostatizes "Bernard" as a symbol of the positivism which he finds so repulsive in Rakitin.

96   557_{2}, $15:28_{11}$, "Rakitin will get on anywhere"—in the original, lit. "Rakitin will crawl through a crack in the wall."

97   557_{3}, $15:28_{12}$, Again, "They are all over the place" is not as suggestive as *Mnogo ikh rasplodilos',* lit. "they have bred in large numbers," something one would say of insects, or of devils! Cf. the preceding note.

98   557_{7-9}, $15:28_{16-17}$, " 'he couldn't help murdering his father, he was corrupted by his environment' "—Rakitin is an adherent of social determinism and social Darwinism. Compare his impersonal "scientific" view of a human life with Mikhail Makarovich's compassionate personal view (p. 555_{2-3}) which, however, in no way relieves Dmitry of his responsibility.

99   557_{16}, $15:28_{23}$, "low fellow"—translates *smerd,* "knave, peasant," somewhat of an archaism even then. It brings to mind

Smerdiakov and thus builds an association between Rakitin and
that character.

100   557_{17-18}, $15:28_{24}$, " 'de ideabus non est disputandum' "—
misses a nuance: Dmitry says de myslibus non est disputandum,
where myslibus is the Russian word mysl', "thought, idea," with
the Latin plural ablative ending, substituted for gustibus,
"tastes." A naive schoolboyish joke, which Eng. de thoughtibus
would have made clearer.

101   557_{23}, $15:28_{30}$, "I am sorry to lose God"—translates Boga
zhalko, which may mean "I am sorry for God" or "I am sorry
about God." It is a phrase someone might utter upon hearing of
a friend's death. The point is that Dmitry, who has loved God all
his life (cf. Book Three, chap. iii, p. 96_{18}), is sorry to hear that
God is dead (to borrow Nietzsche's aphorism).

102   557_{27}, $15:28_{33}$, "the little tails of these nerves"—more diabolic
imagery. The devil himself appears twice in this passage, once
translated by "damn."

103   557_{38}, $15:28_{45}$, See note 101 above. Dostoevsky makes sure that
the words "I am sorry about God" will not pass unnoticed.

104   557_{43}, $15:29_{2-3}$, "And Rakitin does dislike God."—The
polarity is established. Dmitry loves God, while Rakitin dislikes
Him, a very personal feeling in both instances. Dmitry is God's
child (cf. Book Three, chap. iii, p. 96_{18}), Rakitin the devil's.

105   558_{4}, $15:29_{8}$, "All things are lawful"—we are back to the
leitmotif first heard in Book Two, chap. vi, p. 60_{24}.

106   558_{6-7}, $15:29_{9}$, Another leitmotif, that of the "clever man" who
has discovered that there is no God and takes advantage of this
situation. See Introduction III.3.a. Motifs.

107   558_{15-17}, $15:29_{17-19}$, An example of Hegelian dialectic
reasoning. Rakitin, a Left-Hegelian, assumes that "reality"
determines "personality."

108   558_{37-39}, $15:29_{36-38}$, "and his mouth was simply watering
. . ."—Rakitin makes a travesty even of sensuality ("sensual"
here is sladostrastnaia, the leitmotif of the Karamazovs which
appears in the title of Book Three). Fiodor Pavlovich, whose
mouth waters for Grushen'ka, is much the better man.

109   558_{46}–559_{2}, $15:29_{43-46}$, Here Dostoevsky mocks the utilitarian
aesthetics of his radical opponents.

110   559_{5-6}, $15:29_{48}$–30_{1}, Cf. note 42 above.

111   559_{10-21}, $15:30_{5-16}$, The translation rather successfully renders
the spirit of the original. The translator's art of versification is

quite up to its model. Lines 16–17 might have been translated more accurately; they say, literally: "I'm grieving for her little head / Because it does not understand ideas." As always, Rakitin is insufferably pedantic and condescending, a typical *seminarist*. Cf. Book Two, note 169. The poem is an antiparody of D. D. Minaev's parody of Pushkin's poem "City of luxury, city of poverty" (1828). Pushkin's eight-line gem starts on a "civic" note, then playfully shifts to yet another apotheosis of "that little foot." Minaev, a "civic" poet, found it flippant, hence his parody. Dostoevsky's antiparody makes fun of Minaev's obtuse vulgarity. See *PSS* 15:589.

112   559_{34-35}, $15:30_{30-31}$, "the judgment of God will be accomplished"—prophetic. Aliosha is not speaking of human justice, of course. Rather, the verdict of human justice will be an instrument of divine justice.

113   559_{39-40}, $15:30_{35-36}$, "the stinking son of Stinking Lizaveta!"— according to the commentators of *PSS*, this may be a free quotation of a line from a folk legend (in verse) on the theme of the rich man and poor Lazarus.

114   559_{43-44}, $15:30_{39-40}$, "in a sort of exaltation"—the tone of the following lyric effusion and Dmitry's attitude as he delivers it ("His eyes glowed") are important. This is one of the highlights of the novel.

115   560_{6-8}, $15:30_{45-46}$, "He was hidden in me, but would never have come to the surface, if it hadn't been for this blow from heaven."—One of Dostoevsky's favorite ideas, his belief in the salutary effect of suffering, is stated explicitly.

116   560_{18}, $15:31_9$, "we are all responsible for them"—echoes the leitmotif of Book Six: "everyone is really responsible to all men for all men and for everything" (Book Six, chap. ii(a), p. 268_{16-17}).

117   560_{19}, $15:31_{10}$, "the babe"—the full impact of Dmitry's "epiphany" in Book Nine, chap. viii, becomes apparent only now.

118   560_{28}, $15:31_{18-19}$, "we shall rise again to joy"—Dmitry's variation on the theme of "Cana of Galilee" (Book Seven, chap. iv).

119   560_{30-31}, $15:31_{21}$, "What would I be underground there without God?"—Another favorite idea of Dostoevsky's: God is, because man needs Him.

120   560_{35}, $15:31_{25}$, "a tragic hymn to God, with Whom is joy."—A

counterpoint to Dmitry's recitation of Schiller's "Ode to Joy" in Book Three, chap. iii. Dmitry had spoken of his own secret "hymn" even then (p. 96_{15}).

121 560_{37-39}, $15:31_{27-28}$, Cf. note 114 above. The language of Dmitry's effusion is indeed "wild." He uses a great deal of solemn biblical and poetic language, yet some pedestrian diction as well: in line 29, for example, "God gives joy: it's His privilege," where *privilegiia,* a stiff official term, sounds even more grotesque than its equivalent in English.

122 560_{42-43}, $15:31_{31-32}$, "within these peeling walls"—Dmitry repeats this phrase several times. Dostoevsky uses it as a kind of refrain to give shape to Dmitry's rambling effusion.

123 560_{45-46}, $15:31_{34}$, "even if it were beyond reckoning"—a characteristic catachresis which appears even more clearly in the original (*beschislenno,* "countless"): suffering may be "immeasurable," but not "countless." But Dostoevsky knows that a "wrong" word, properly placed, will only add emphasis and pathos.

124 561_4, $15:31_{38}$, "I exist" translates *ja esm',* "I am," an archaic form, which gives a solemn air to Dmitry's assertion. Dmitry is saying in effect that he not only exists, but that he *is,* much as God *is.* Only in the sentence "Though I sit alone on a post—I exist!" does the original have *sushchestvuiu,* "exist." Incidentally, "on a post" is a mistranslation, albeit a felicitous one (it evokes the image of a stelite, Russ. *stolpnik*). The original has *v stolpe,* "in a tower." Hence: "I sit in a tower, but even there do I exist, and see the sun, and if I do not see the sun, I still know that it is."

125 561_{7-8}, $15:31_{40-41}$, "And there's a whole life in that, in knowing that the sun is there."—Here Dmitry veers into a pantheism which we know well from Father Zosima's exhortations.

126 561_8, $15:31_{41}$, "my cherub"—Aliosha's label.

127 561_{17}, $15:32_1$, "Ivan is a sphinx"—another exhibit of Dostoevsky's symphonic technique. This is Ivan's Book. His voice will become dominant later in the Book. For the time being, he is announced, his leitmotifs are introduced, and interest in him is created.

128 561_{17-18}, $15:32_2$, "It's God that torments me."—By "God," Dmitry means "the question of whether there is a God."

129 561_{19-26}, $15:32_{3-10}$, Dmitry in his usual vigorous manner rephrases Ivan's argument, paraphrased by Miusov in Book

Two, chap. vi, p. 60_{16-30}. The brothers are in substantial agreement, and both have nothing but scorn for Rakitin's optimistic humanism. For Rakitin's version see Book Two, chap. vii, p. 72_{11-26}.

130 561_{30-31}, $15:32_{14-15}$, "you, without God, are more likely to raise the price of meat"—apparently Dostoevsky's reply to an article in *Molva* (see note 28 above) in which his "Discourse on Pushkin" was taken to task for wasting time on lofty philosophical ideas while "even the middle class could hardly afford meat and the price of wheat had risen to 17 roubles a *chetvert'*." See *PSS* 15:589.

131 561_{33-35}, $15:32_{17-19}$, "Goodness is one thing with me and another with a Chinese, so it's a relative thing."—"Goodness" translates *dobrodetel'*, "virtue," which makes it clear that Dmitry speaks of cultural relativism ("virtue" may be defined differently in Russia and in China). Rakitin uses cultural relativism to support his moral nihilism.

132 561_{38}, $15:32_{23}$, "I believe he is a freemason."—Cf. Book Five, chap. v, p. 243_5, where Aliosha makes the same observation.

133 561_{38-39}, $15:32_{23-24}$, "I wanted to drink from the springs of his soul"—such flowery language, often amidst colloquialisms and even slang, is characteristic of Dmitry's diction.

134 561_{42}, $15:32_{27}$, "everything is lawful"—this has become Ivan's leitmotif. Cf. notes 105 and 127 above.

135 561_{43}, $15:32_{28-29}$, "pig"—in the original it is a somewhat milder *porosionok*, "suckling pig."

136 562_{10}, $15:32_{41}$, "a Bernard"—see note 94 above.

137 562_{16-17}, $15:32_{48}$, "a woman of 'great wrath' "—see Book Nine, chap. vii, p. 468_1. "They repeated it" should be "They told her."

138 562_{22-24}, $15:33_{6-7}$, "how she bowed to the ground . . ."—a leitmotif from Book Three (see Book Three, notes 96, 109, and 206) is reintroduced. Here, "to the last cent" misses a nuance, as the Russ. *poslednii kodrant* is "the uttermost farthing" of Matt. 5:26. This allusion underscores the theme of judgment and retribution.

139 562_{38}, $15:33_{21}$, "Suddenly Mitia laughed almost mirthfully."— Sudden changes in mood are a psychological label of Dmitry's. Cf. Book Two, chap. vi, p. 58_{41-43}.

140 562_{39ff}, $15:33_{22ff.}$, This psychological excursus is very much in character. Correct or incorrect, it is—like everything Dmitry

says—provocative and original. A Karamazov, whose life is dominated by Eros, Dmitry is a male chauvinist. He loves women, and is loved by them, precisely because, like his father, he looks for "the woman in woman."

141   563_{15-18}, $15:33_{44-46}$, We know Grushen'ka's "supple curve" (Book Three, chap. v, p. 107_{24}) as an object of Dmitry's desire. Sensual desire is now transformed into spiritual love. Very Schilleresque: even as announced in Book Three, chap. iii, sensual beauty has become the steppingstone to a higher ideal.

142   563_{24}, $15:34_4$, " 'I've a fierce heart myself!' "—Cf. chap. i, p. 536_{20-21}.

143   563_{29}, $15:34_{9-10}$, "It was almost dark."—Note the synchronization between setting and drama.

144   563_{36-40}, $15:34_{16-20}$, "He looked round . . ."—Note Dostoevsky's careful "stage directions."

145   563_{43-46}, $15:34_{23-26}$, A pivotal passage: "superior" is *vysshii* in the first instance, but in the second it translates *vysshii chelovek*, "superior man," and "higher conscience" is *vysshei sovesti*, "superior conscience." The question thus boils down to whether "superior man" is a man-god (Ivan) or a God-man (Aliosha).

146   564_{18-19}, $15:34_{42}$, "I have a way of salvation and I turn my back on it."—In the original, lit. "I have a way of purification—and I take a left-hand turn the other way." Dostoevsky has projected on Dmitry his own rare ability to "sense" and to hypostatize ideas. Dmitry expresses his moral dilemma in surprisingly graphic terms.

147   564_{20-21}, $15:34_{44-45}$, "But what becomes of our hymn from underground?"—In the original: "But where, then, will our underground hymn take place?" The question "where?" exposes the absurdity of a "Russian" plot of purification through suffering to be enacted in the United States. Cf. Book Ten, note 128.

148   564_{28-29}, $15:35_3$, "He doesn't believe in the hymn."—Another example of Dostoevsky's technique of setting up a special, or private, meaning for a word, "hymn" in this case. Dmitry had spoken of his "hymn of praise" in Book Three, chap. iii, p. 96_{14-15}. Dmitry's hymn, a silent prayer, really, is in praise of God.

149   564_{46}, $15:35_{20}$, "He's rabidly set on it."—Translates *Do isteriki khochet*, lit. "He wants it to the point of hysterics," which describes Ivan's condition better than "rabidly."

150 565$_{12-13}$, 15:35$_{35}$, "Bernard"—see note 94 above, and cf. note 148 above.

151 565$_{20-21}$, 15:35$_{41}$, The original features a more pregnant paronymy: *perekresti na zavtrashnii krest,* lit. "cross me for tomorrow's cross."

152 565$_{29-30}$, 15:36$_{1ff.}$, "Aliosha was just going . . ."—The very moment the reader thinks that this scene is over, the real drama starts.

153 565$_{44-45}$, 15:35$_{16-17}$, "and he raised his right hand in the air"—as so often in dramatic scenes, hands play a decisive role. See Introduction III. Narrative Technique.

154 566$_5$, 15:36$_{23}$, " 'Love Ivan!' was Mitia's last word."—Another surprise. It creates suspense and makes for a smooth transition to the next chapter.

Chapter v

155 566$_{16}$, 15:36$_{35}$, "Not You, Not You!"—This chapter heading, like some earlier ones (for example, "It's Always Worthwhile Speaking to a Clever Man"), is a leitmotif which will continue beyond this chapter. It also carries a deep irony.

156 566$_{28}$, 15:37$_2$, "she's 'upset' "—we shall find out why only 150 pages later. See Epilogue, chap. i, p. 718$_{3-4}$.

157 567$_{11}$, 15:37$_{26}$, "that I bowed down to the ground"—another bit of private language. Cf. note 148 above.

158 567$_{24}$, 15:37$_{39}$, "monster"—Russ. *izverg,* now Dmitry's label. Unfortunately, the English word lacks the connotation of *izverg.* See Book Three, note 104.

159 567$_{31}$, 15:37$_{46}$, "It was you, you"—in Russian, the familiar second person singular of *Eto ty, ty* is a giveaway, suggesting an intimacy which can be explained only by the fact that they are lovers. Aliosha's reaction is based not so much on the *tone* of Katerina Ivanovna's voice, as on this "thou" *(ty).*

160 567$_{41}$, 15:38$_8$, "He's mad!"—This surprising revelation prepares the reader for chapter ix of this Book.

161 568$_{20}$, 15:38$_{34}$, "that little demon"—harks back to the title of chapter iii.

162 568$_{23}$, 15:38$_{37}$, "She's not sixteen yet, I believe, and already offering herself"—explains Liza's dark allusions in chap. iii, p. 553.

163 568$_{28}$, 15:38$_{42}$, "you are insulting a child"—suddenly brings

back the leitmotif of Ivan's rebellion in Book Five, chap. iv: Ivan, who blamed God for the suffering of innocent children, is now himself "insulting" a child, instead of helping her. Aliosha's response is foregrounded by a strong alliteration: *gorestno i goriacho zastupilsia Aliosha,* lit. "sorrowfully and fervently Aliosha rose to her defense."

164   568_{36}, $15:39_2$,   "She will be praying all night now to the Mother of God"—said ironically. This remark opens up a totally new aspect of the proud Katerina Ivanovna's character: she is religious in a conventional way. Another example of Dostoevsky's centrifugal psychology.

165   569_{5-6}, $15:39_{18-19}$,   "I must wait till sentence is passed on the murderer."—Deep Sophoclean irony: sentence will be passed even before the day is over and before Dmitry's trial has started.

166   569_{10}, $15:39_{23}$,   "monster"—see note 158 above.

167   569_{16}, $15:39_{30}$,   "document"—Ivan overstates his point. We shall see the document in chap. vii, pp. 585–86, and its contents will hardly warrant the term "document."

168   569_{25-26}, $15:39_{39-41}$,   "he asked, with apparent coldness . . ."—at the climax of a tense dramatic scene, intonation becomes all-important, more important than the actual words spoken.

169   569_{29-30}, $15:39_{44-45}$,   "You mean the myth about that crazy idiot, the epileptic Smerdiakov?"—Again, Ivan hysterically overstates his point.

170   569_{37}, $15:40_4$,   The italics are found in the original, too. They convey the peculiar undertone of Aliosha's whispered words, suggesting implicitly what will be made explicit a moment later: that Ivan is accusing himself of his father's murder.

171   569_{44-45}, $15:40_{10}$,   "They were standing again under a lamp post."—More stage directions.

172   570_{7-12}, $15:40_{16-20}$,   One of the passages in which Aliosha reaches the stature of a holy man. This passage creates deep ambiguities, because the following chapters will show that Ivan has ample reason to accuse himself.

173   570_{17-19}, $15:40_{15}$,   "when he came"—the identity of "he" will remain a mystery until chapter ix.

174   570_{36-41}, $15:40_{46}-41_3$,   Note the stiffly formal "Aleksei Fiodorovich." In the original, Ivan also uses the formal second person plural, which symbolizes the break of their brotherly relations.

175 570_{37}, $15:40_{47}$, "epileptics"—Ivan has some reason to hint that Aliosha is an epileptic: he had witnessed Aliosha's hysterical crying fit (Book Three, chap. viii, pp. 125–26).

176 $571_{1ff.}$, $15:41_{10ff.}$, From here to the last line of the chapter, the narrator inserts a "breather," as it were, to allow his reader to recover from the tension of the preceding dramatic scene.

177 571_{24-25}, $15:41_{35-36}$, "drawn by a sudden and irresistible prompting"—the reader remembers the "irresistible command" that made Aliosha tell Ivan that the latter was accusing himself of their father's murder (p. 570_{8-9}). In the original, the two passages appear less similar: different words are used for "irresistible," and while it is decidedly "command" *(velenie)* in the first instance, it is "consideration" *(soobrazhenie)* rather than "prompting" in the second.

178 571_{27}, $15:41_{38}$, Ivan's three interviews with Smerdiakov correspond to the three torments of Dmitry in Book Nine. In both instances a tortuous dialectic agon leads to a painful dénouement, followed by an epiphany: Dmitry's "Babe" and Ivan's "Devil."

Chapter vi

179 571_{28}, $15:41_{39}$, "This was the third time"—the preceding chapter had ended in a surprise; now this chapter starts by going one better.

180 572_{13}, $15:42_{22-23}$, "unattractive"—translates *nesimpatichen,* which has no real equivalent in English. It expresses a more intense dislike than "unattractive."

181 572_{30}, $15:42_{39}$, "it was 'the devil that opened it' "—another deep irony: Dmitry's absurd statement is almost literally true.

182 572_{34}, $15:42_{42}$, " 'everything was lawful' "—Dmitry has correctly caught Ivan's leitmotif (cf. notes 105 and 134 above).

183 572_{41-43}, $15:43_{1-2}$, "for the time"—this starts a pattern: by temporizing, Ivan makes a first concession to the devil. We now remember the strange paralysis which overcame Ivan when Smerdiakov made him privy to his designs (Book Five, chap. vi).

184 573_2, $15:43_{7-8}$, "whether he might not have been shamming"—in the original, this question is given as direct speech, in quotation marks, no doubt in order to make it clear that Ivan is asking a leading question.

185 573_{12-13}, $15:43_{17-18}$, "abnormalities"—in this passage, as elsewhere, Dostoevsky makes fun of the doctors' hiding their ignorance behind medical jargon.

186 573_{27}, $15:43_{33}$, "emasculate"—translates *skopcheskoe,* an adjective derived from *skopec,* "eunuch." A symbolically significant trait.

187 573_{31}, $15:43_{37}$, " 'It's always worthwhile speaking to a clever man.' "—Ivan's first leitmotif, "all things are lawful," has already come back to haunt him (p. 572_{34}). Now it is joined by this other diabolic phrase (see Book Five, note 401).

188 574_4, $15:44_9$, "Have you said so at the examination yet?"—Suddenly shows who is in charge: Ivan is already hopelessly trapped in his own lies.

189 574_{11}, $15:44_{16}$, "as in God Almighty"—abysmal irony: Ivan the man-god has his comeuppance, as a petty demon like Smerdiakov mocks him with impunity.

190 574_{22-23}, $15:44_{28-29}$, "but you can always have a presentiment of it"—open mockery.

191 575_{19-22}, $15:45_{23-25}$, Smerdiakov's casuistry shows up the whole hollowness of Ivan's position. Smerdiakov's point is well taken: a normal son, upon hearing what Ivan had heard from Smerdiakov in their conversation at the gate (Book Five, chap. vi), would have understood it as a warning and would have stayed to make sure that nothing happened to his father.

192 576_{10}, $15:46_{10}$, "You are being cunning with me"—better: "You are dodging me." Ivan is flattering himself: it is a game of cat and mouse, with Smerdiakov firmly in control.

193 576_{31-33}, $15:46_{32-33}$, "Only when I said these words to you, it was not by way of praise, but of reproach."—Shows Smerdiakov's easy command of ambiguity. To be called a "clever man" for deserting one's own father in an hour of danger is hardly a compliment. It is either an ironic euphemism for cowardice, or an accusation of complicity in a plot against one's father.

194 577_{3-4}, $15:47_{1-2}$, "I liked you so much then, and was openhearted with you."—Another ambiguity. Smerdiakov had in fact been sincere with Ivan, but hardly because he "had grown fond of him" (the Russian has *poliubil,* which is stronger than "I liked"). Rather, he had sized him up as a reliable accomplice. Or had Smerdiakov really become Ivan's "disciple," the way Fiodor Pavlovich had seen it (Book Three, chap. vii, p. 117_{5-7})?

195   577_8, $15:47_6$, "Grigory Vasilievich saw the door open"—cf. Book Nine, chap. vi, pp. 459-60. We get our first inkling of what really happened.

196   577_{16-18}, $15:47_{13-16}$, "If I had been planning such a murder could I have been such a fool as to give evidence against myself beforehand? And to his own son, too!"—Smerdiakov is a master of double-edged psychology (see Introduction II.6.b. Psychological Motivation). Obviously he is right—unless the son wishes his father dead.

197   577_{20}, $15:47_{18}$, "Providence"—apparently used flippantly, with a touch of blasphemy. Yet it prepares for a key passage in chap. viii, p. 591_8.

198   577_{25-30}, $15:47_{23-27}$, Ivan does not see the ambiguity (cf. note 196 above) because he does not want to see it. His desire not to see his guilt is so strong that he is developing a split consciousness, one side of which is blind to what the other side sees only too well.

199   577_{35-36}, $15:47_{31-33}$, "something made Ivan say suddenly"—this translation adds an interpretation. The Russian text has: "Ivan suddenly said, for some reason." This continues the pattern of Ivan's seemingly unintended utterances and actions, started in Book Five, chap. vi, p. 254_{8-9} and passim. It is another symptom of Ivan's split personality (see note 198 above).

200   577_{37-38}, $15:47_{34-35}$, "And if you don't speak of that . . ."—A surprising development. Ivan has sealed his pact with the devil. He is now not only morally but even legally guilty.

201   577_{40-44}, $15:47_{37-41}$, Another indication of Ivan's split consciousness. What Dostoevsky describes here is a drastic case of repression.

202   578_{2-3}, $15:47_{45-46}$, "He felt as though he wanted to make haste to forget something."—Describes the phenomenon of repression quite explicitly. Ivan actually succeeds in "forgetting" the damning evidence—but only with the conscious half of his mind.

203   578_{12}, $15:48_6$, Once more, the "open door."

204   578_{18-24}, $15:48_{11-17}$, A significant detail is repeated: Smerdiakov hates Russia and would rather be a Frenchman. Cf. Book Five, chap. ii, p. 206_{38-43}.

205   578_{25-27}, $15:48_{18-21}$, Note Dostoevsky's dialectic style. The positive statement, "Ivan Fiodorovich ended by dismissing all doubts," almost inevitably is followed by an antithesis: "Only one thing was strange, however."

206   578_{37-40}, 15:48_{29-32}, "This is not the time . . ."—Suggests that
      Ivan will survive and that he and Katerina Ivanovna will ex-
      perience further peripeties of fate. See Introduction III.3.e.
      Expository Novel.

207   578_{42-43}, 15:48_{35},   Refers to chap. v, p. 568_{45}.

208   579_{4-10}, 15:48_{43-48},   With great tact, Dostoevsky (we must not
      forget that he is a "Victorian" writer) manages to say all that is
      necessary about the erotic side of the relationship between Ivan
      and Katerina Ivanovna, without producing any details: enough
      has happened for her to feel that she has "betrayed" ("deserted"
      is inexact for *izmenila*) Dmitry.

209   579_6, 15:48_{44},   "Karamazov recklessness"—one of the few
      instances where we are shown that Ivan is indeed a chip off the
      old block.

210   579_{16-22}, 15:49_{7-12},   "It's enough to say . . ."—Refers to events
      described in Book Five, chap. vii, serving a dual end: it describes
      what goes on in Ivan's consciousness, and it synthesizes im-
      portant elements of the psychological plot for the reader.

211   $579_{28ff.}$, 15:$49_{17ff.}$,   "Do you remember when Dmitry burst in
      . . ."—Refers to Book Three, chap. ix. Cf. note 210 above.

212   579_{43}, 15:49_{31},   "Forgive me . . ."—Aliosha's admission
      follows a pattern: none of the thoughts or feelings of his two
      brothers are alien to him.

Chapter vii

213   580_{16}, 15:50_4,   "greatly superior"—in the original, lit. "as a
      superior man," establishing yet another link between Ivan and
      Smerdiakov. Cf. note 145 above.

214   580_{22-23}, 15:50_{9-10},   "cockroaches   swarmed   in   amazing
      numbers"—creates a proper setting for another dramatic scene.
      See Introduction III.5.c. Symbolic Images.

215   580_{42}–581_1, 15:50_{29-32},   "he slowly took them off . . ."—note
      the subtlety of this description. Ivan is simply rude. Smerdiakov
      is rude and condescending.

216   581_{1-5}, 15:50_{32-36},   The dialogue of this scene unfolds on two
      levels: spoken and silent ("What do you want to intrude for?" is
      the equivalent of an aside in conventional drama). See Introduc-
      tion III. Narrative Technique.

217   581_{26-28}, 15:51_{8-9},   "You want to have everything . . ."
      —Another aside.

218   581_{34-38}, $15:51_{16-20}$, "Controlling himself" should be "in control of himself." Much of the drama depends on gesture, facial expression, and tone of voice. The spoken dialogue is only the tip of an iceberg, as it were.

219   581_{46}, $15:51_{28}$, "stinking rogue"—Russ. *smerdiashchaia shel'ma,* an ugly insult which takes advantage of Smerdiakov's name and the memory of his mother, Elizaveta Smerdiashchaia.

220   582_3, $15:51_{32-33}$, Such violent behavior does not come unexpectedly. As early as in Book Two, we saw Ivan strike Maksimov, a feeble old man. See Book Two, chap. viii, p. 81_{13-15}.

221   $582_{26-27, 37}$, $15:52_{9, 20}$, "Clever man" has now definitely acquired a private meaning for Smerdiakov and for Ivan. See note 187 above.

222   583_{29-31}, $15:53_{9-12}$, "For if you had a foreboding . . ."—Finally the cat is out of the bag. The dialogue seems to have reached its logical conclusion. But Doestoevsky finds a way to introduce new ambiguities.

223   583_{42}, $15:53_{23-24}$, "a punch in the face"—translates *po mordasam otkolotit',* where *po mordasam* is a vile slang expression (from *morda,* "snout, muzzle, mug"). Ivan readily picks up the expression from Smerdiakov.

224   584_{6-7}, $15:53_{34-35}$, "I should have pounded your ugly face to a jelly."—Ivan's impotent rage finds an outlet in coarse invective: "face" translates *kharia,* "mug," an ugly slang word.

225   584_{9-17}, $15:53_{37-46}$, Smerdiakov continues his grotesque discourse on the universal human need for an occasional punch in the face (still *mordasy;* see note 223 above) in a mixture of lackey's slang and unctuous "journalese." It may be a counterpoint to some similar discourses found in progressive literature, for instance, in Part I, chap. v, of N. A. Nekrasov's *Who Has a Good Life in Russia?* (1878), where a reactionary landowner expatiates on the virtues of a good punch in the face. Dostoevsky is trying to insinuate that the reactionary landowner and the rebellious lackey really believe in the same things. Cf. Book Five, chap. ii, p. 207_{10-11}.

226   584_{20-22}, $15:54_{1-3}$, Deeply ironic. Smerdiakov is a westernizer! Had not Ivan himself dreamed of going to Europe?

227   584_{35-37}, $15:54_{16-18}$, The phrase about the "clever man" plays a role similar to Mark Antony's "And Brutus is an honorable man" in Shakespeare's *Julius Caesar* (Act III, sc. ii).

228   584_{37}, $15:54_{18}$, "And you will be clever, sir."—This is the climax of Smerdiakov's drama, the moment when he feels that he has triumphed.

229     $584_{41ff.}$, $15:54_{22ff.}$, Ivan is paralyzed by conflicting feelings: his deeper and better self tells him to go to the police; his conscious reason clings to the notion that Smerdiakov is innocent. Cf. notes 183 and 199 above.

230   585_{5-6}, $15:54_{32-33}$, Perhaps the expression of a subconscious urge to rid himself of the Smerdiakov (the devil, that is) in himself.

231   585_{20-22}, $15:54_{47-48}$, "Conclusive" ("mathematical" in the original, as also in chap. v, p. 569_{16-17}) and "document" are ironic. A person as clever as Ivan would never have considered this "document" to be anything approaching "conclusive" but for his strong wish that it be so.

232   585_{22-26}, $15:55_{1-4}$, Another cross-reference which helps the reader to reconstruct the sequence of earlier events. The reference is to Book Three, chaps. x and xi.

233   585_{31}, $15:55_9$, "a drunken letter in fact"—in the original, "drunken" is given in quotation marks, making a "drunken letter" a generic term. The narrator goes to great pains to demonstrate that the document which will ultimately convict Dmitry is a farce.

234     $585_{43ff.}$, $15:55_{21ff.}$, Dmitry's letter is another lyric "poem" (cf. his prayer in Book Eight, chap. vi, p. 389). Several motifs well known to the reader are recapitulated. We have already heard "woman of great wrath," "scoundrel," "I am not a thief," and —most important—"I bow down to the ground before you." But the most significant item is a new motif: "And he doesn't love you." This "drunken" letter is yet another exhibit of what may be called Dostoevsky's histrionic talent.

235   586_{45-46}, $15:56_{16-17}$, "They were like two enemies in love with one another."—Though this sounds trite, it accurately describes the relationship and explains a lot of what will follow.

236   587_8, $15:56_{26}$, "but just *because he was the murderer of his father!*"—a head-on clash between Ivan's conscious and unconscious self. His hatred for the murderer of his father is a subconscious hatred of himself, something his conscious self refuses to see.

237   587_{35}, $15:56_{47-48}$, "I've been at Smerdiakov's myself!"— Another surprise, the last in this chapter.

Chapter viii

238 588₁₆₋₁₇, 15:57₂₇₋₂₈, "Van'ka" is a hypocoristic of "Ivan"; hence Ivan must, subconsciously at least, recognize himself in the peasant's song: he went away (to Moscow, rather than to Petersburg), and Smerdiakov did not wait for him to return. The song becomes a leitmotif. Cf. Matlaw, *"The Brothers Karamazov,"* p. 17.

239 588₂₇₋₂₈, 15:57₃₉₋₄₀, This is the nadir of Ivan's life: he is about to become a murderer once more. We are long familiar with his reckless and violent temper. Cf. note 220 above.

240 589₅₋₇, 15:58₁₅₋₁₆, The deterioration of Smerdiakov's condition matches Ivan's. The scene is between two very sick men.

241 589₃₀₋₃₁, 15:58₃₈₋₃₉, "But why are your eyes so jaundiced? . . ."—In the original, this develops a link between Ivan and Smerdiakov. The latter is said to have grown "yellow" (*pozheltel,* line 6 above, translated by "sallower"). Now Ivan's eyes are "jaundiced" (*pozhelteli*).

242 589₃₇, 15:58₄₅, "Damn it!"—translated *E, chiort,* lit. "Oh, the devil," which may be significant. Cf. Book Five, note 356.

243 590₂₋₃, 15:59₇₋₈, Ivan's subconscious fear, long suppressed, suddenly invades his consciousness.

244 590₆, 15:59₁₀, "a clever man"—see note 227 above.

245 590₇₋₁₀, 15:59₁₁₋₁₄, This quiet observation sets the stage for the dramatic climax of the scene.

246 590₁₃₋₁₄, 15:59₁₇, *"you* did not murder him"—in the original, the whole sentence is italicized, thus establishing a fateful ambiguity with the same phrase as uttered by Aliosha in chap. v, p. 569₃₇, where it is also italicized.

247 590₂₄, 15:59₂₆, "as though pondering something"—more correctly: "as though having caught on to something."

248 590₃₀₋₃₄, 15:59₃₂, "Aren't you tired of it? . . ."—For the first time Smerdiakov's words have a ring of sincerity, emphasized by several solecisms (which get lost in the translation). Ivan has heard the expression "servant Licharda" before (Book Five, chap. vi, p. 249₂₀). It alone should have told him then what Smerdiakov was up to, since Licharda is a willing tool in the murder of his master. See Book Five, note 362.

249 590₄₂₋₄₃, 15:59₄₅₋₄₆, See note 238 above. There is a man freezing to death in a ditch outside.

250 591₁₋₂, 15:60₁₋₂, Anticipates the following chapter: could Smerdiakov be a double of the devil's?

251   591$_5$, 15:60$_6$, "Who is that third person?"—Harks back to chap. v, p. 570$_{18-24}$, and again points to the following chapter.

252   591$_{8-9}$, 15:60$_{9-10}$, "That Third is God Himself, sir, Providence, sir . . ."—The greatest surprise of all. Smerdiakov, long before Ivan, has realized that the game is up: it just is not true that "all things are lawful."

253   591$_{14-15}$, 15:60$_{17}$, " 'throw it all on him to his face' "—echoes p. 590$_{32}$.

254   591$_{45}$, 15:60$_{45}$, "You frightened me . . . with your stocking"—the stocking has been foregrounded as the object of Ivan's horror. Did Ivan expect the devil's cloven hoof to emerge from under it? Dostoevsky had introduced a hint of the cloven hoof in a diabolic personage (Piotr Verkhovensky) in an earlier novel, *The Possessed*.

255   592$_5$, 15:61$_3$, "With my brother's help or without my brother?"—Ivan clutches at a straw.

256   592$_{10-11}$, 15:61$_8$, "You said 'everything was lawful,' and how frightened you are now"—Ivan is finished as "man-god." In the context of "The Grand Inquisitor," he is not one of "the proud and strong" (Book Five, chap. v, p. 240$_{29}$).

257   592$_{20-21}$, 15:61$_{18-19}$, Isaac the Syrian, known as Isaacus Ninivita in the West, anchorite and bishop towards the end of the sixth century, was popular in Muscovite Russia. Inasmuch as Isaac treats of the ways in which every rational soul can approach God (these ways are love, fear, and divine discipline) in his sermons, he would seem to be an appropriate guide to a lost soul such as Smerdiakov. See Introduction I.4.b. Sacred Sources.

258   592$_{24}$, 15:61$_{23}$, "take off your greatcoat"—note this attention to detail: it is infernally hot at Smerdiakov's.

259   592$_{36-37}$, 15:61$_{34-35}$, "The details, above everything, the details, I beg you."—Mrs. Dostoevsky reported that "these were her husband's own favorite words, whenever he was interested in something" (L. P. Grossman, *Seminarii po Dostoevskomu: Materialy, bibliografiia i kommentarii* [Moscow and Petrograd, 1922], p. 69). What follows is yet another version of the events with which we are already familiar. In contrast with what we find in most detective novels, the murderer's confession does not, however, conclude the novel, but rather, creates new complications.

260   593$_{20}$, 15:62$_{15}$, "for I had prepared him for it"—if there is

anybody in this novel who succeeds in manipulating his fellow men, it is Smerdiakov.

261   593_{28-43}, $15:62_{22-38}$, "he would never have found the money . . ."—the game of "fact" and "fiction," started in Book Nine (cf. Introduction III.3.d. Art of the Novel) continues. The "fact" of yesterday turns out to be a clumsy fiction.

262   594_{5-6}, $15:62_{45-46}$, For one last time Ivan clutches at a straw.

263   594_{30-31}, $15:63_{21-22}$, "you wouldn't have had a cent"—in the original, a coarse "you'd have gotten a fig." The reader of the English translation should remember that in the original Smerdiakov's speech is quite different from Ivan's. For all his big words ("Providence," for example), Smerdiakov is still very much the lackey. And, as an extra dimension, Smerdiakov speaks like a lackey who is rude to his master—as in this instance.

264   595_{9-10}, $15:63_{46-48}$, ". . . He evidently had some design."—We shall learn the reason for Smerdiakov's resolute candor only in the next chapter.

265   595_{31}, $15:64_{20-21}$, "longing"—translates *zhazhda*, "thirst."

266   595_{34-35}, $15:64_{23}$, "like a baby"—the Russ. *mladenets* is the biblical expression for "child" (as in Matt. 2:8-18). It may be significant that even the wicked Fiodor Pavlovich should become a "child," at least in the hour of his death.

267   595_{38-42}, $15:64_{26-30}$, "I thought of knocking . . ."—Cf. note 260 above. Smerdiakov plays on Fiodor Pavlovich's conditioned reflex: truly diabolic.

268   596_{14}, $15:64_{45-46}$, "he was awfully crazy about her"—in the original it is *vliubleny,* "in love," which may be significant. Fiodor Pavlovich dies with a feeling of love (carnal, sensual—but still love) in his heart.

269   597_{6-11}, $15:65_{37-43}$, The mystery of the open door has now been solved. Cf. Book Nine, chap. vi, pp. 459-61.

270   597_{40-45}, $15:66_{25-29}$, Even the authorities are manipulated by Smerdiakov.

271   598_5, $15:66_5$, "it was the devil who helped you!"—this metaphor is in fact a "realized" metaphor, as the next chapter will show.

272   598_{8-11}, $15:66_{38-41}$, This futile movement is symbolic of Ivan's situation.

273   598_{14-26}, $15:66_{44}-67_7$, Note the tone of hollow rhetoric here. Significantly, in line 14 Ivan says "man" (*chelovek*), not

"creature." The very choice of this word gives a hollow ring to his tirade (cf. note 276 below). Another detail: "a secret desire for my father's . . . death" (in the original, "a secret wish that my father . . . die") is a blatant euphemism—"death" for "murder."

274   598_{27-28}, $15:67_{8-9}$, ". . . it would be so."—An ironic false lead: of course nothing of the kind will happen.

275   598_{39-45}, $15:67_{20-26}$, "it will be no use at all, for I shall say straight out that I never said anything of the sort to you . . ."—another reminder of the theme of "fact" and "fiction" (cf. note 261 above).

276   598_{43-44}, $15:67_{25}$, "for you've always thought no more of me than if I'd been a fly"—in the original, he adds: "rather than a man," harking back to line 14 above (see note 273 above).

277   599_2, $15:67_{30}$, "Take the money away with you"—another surprise.

278   599_8, $15:67_{36-37}$, "or, better still, abroad"—now we know why Smerdiakov has been learning French.

279   599_{9-13}, $15:67_{37-40}$, Again, Ivan's leitmotif. Smerdiakov says almost literally what we first heard from Miusov over five hundred pages earlier (Book Two, chap. vi, p. 60_{24}). See Introduction III.3.a. Motifs.

280   599_{28-30}, $15:68_{8-9}$, ". . . without having to depend on anyone"—translates *chtoby nikomu ne klaniat´sia,* lit. "so you won't have to bow to anyone." This part of Smerdiakov's characterization is borne out by many details, starting with Ivan's youth (Book One, chap. iii, p. 10_{15-17}). Pride is Ivan's cardinal sin. See Introduction II.2.a. Challenge to Christianity.

281   599_{39}, $15:68_{17}$, "It was your pride made you think I was a fool."—Matt. 5:22 applies here: "But whosoever shall say, Thou fool, shall be in danger of hell fire."

282   599_{44-46}, $15:68_{21-22}$, "Nobody will believe you . . ."—Smerdiakov's prediction is correct. See Book Twelve, chap. viii, p. 677.

283   600_{12-15}, $15:68_{34-37}$, The Russian equivalent of "good-bye," *proshchaite,* is more cordial, and its original meaning is "forgive me." Smerdiakov wishes to part friends with the last human being he will see in his life. There are other details suggesting that Smerdiakov has decided to commit suicide. He asks to take one final look at the money which he had hoped would make him free. And he gives Ivan a strange look as he says: "Well, kill me."

284 600_{20-24}, $15:68_{41-45}$, "Something like joy . . ."—The translation underplays the almost solemn and exalted tone of the original. This is the turning point of Ivan's story. It is promptly signalled by an action, the rescue of the half-frozen peasant.

285 600_{35}, $16:69_{9-10}$, "this business took a whole hour"—this is important for the plot. Cf. chap. x, p. 617_{31}.

286 600_{38-43}, $15:69_{11-17}$, Ivan's own observation shows that his personality split is as bad as before: his subconscious self has made him undo his crime, his conscious self congratulates him on this, but in a chillingly heartless manner.

287 600_{41-43}, $15:69_{14-17}$, "I am quite capable . . . although they have decided that I am going out of my mind!"—Sophoclean irony: the reader knows better.

288 600_{44}–601_{3}, $15:69_{17-21}$, The last and decisive of the many duels which Ivan's better, subconscious self loses to his evil, rational self. Cf. note 183 above.

289 601_{4-7}, $15:69_{21-25}$, Climaxes the buildup of suspense which will be resolved in the next chapter. There have been several hints of the impending catastrophe throughout chapters v–viii.

Chapter ix

290 601_{23}, $15:69_{42}$, "The Devil"—Finally! Of all the personages in the novel the devil gets by far the most detailed description. A phantom, he is yet more "material" than ordinary human beings.

291 601_{24}, $15:69_{43}$, "I am not a doctor"—according to Dostoevsky's letter to Liubimov, dated 10 August 1880, Dostoevsky took care to make inquiries of several physicians regarding the symptoms of Ivan's disease (*Pis′ma,* 4:190). This is one of the passages in which the narrator steps forward for more than a moment, almost always to lend authority to a crucial episode of the novel.

292 601_{39}, $15:70_{11-12}$, "a fantastic notion of Katerina Ivanovna's" —cf. chap. iv, p. 562_{13}. Dostoevsky, like Katerina Ivanovna, uses the Moscow doctor to several different ends. We met him at Snegiriov's house; we shall see him at the trial, of course; and here he adds verisimilitude to a key chapter.

293 602_{9}, $15:70_{22}$, "almost conscious himself of his delirium"—still the split consciousness. It will remain this way through the whole hallucination.

294   602_{15}, $15:70_{27-28}$, "a Russian gentleman of a particular kind"—the following character sketch is a satirical gem in its own right. Dostoevsky describes a Russian gentleman and liberal of the 1840s in his post-Emancipation decline. This type had been a target before: Stepan Trofimovich Verkhovensky in *The Possessed* and Versilov in *A Raw Youth* are examples. Alexander Herzen (1812–70), Timofei Granovsky (1813–55), and Ivan Turgenev (1818–83) had served as subjects of Dostoevsky's caricature before. It is likely that he had the same men in mind as he drew this figure of the Russian devil." See Victor Terras, "Turgenev and Ivan Karamazov's Devil," *Canadian Slavic Studies* 6 (1972): 265–71. Incidentally, "gentleman" translates *dzhentl'men,* which often has an ironic ring, especially when applied to a Russian.

295   602_{15-16}, $15:70_{28-29}$, It should be *qui frisait la cinquantaine,* "pushing fifty."

296   603_{16-17}, $15:71_{30-31}$, "I only mention it to remind you"—In Russian, both Ivan and his visitor use the familiar second person singular, suggestive of a close relationship. Cf. note 301 below.

297   603_{24-26}, $15:71_{38-39}$, "Why do you interfere . . ."—The first suggestion that Ivan feels his visitor is a projection of his own self, or tries to convince himself that this is so.

298   603_{28-39}, $15:71_{41}-72_3$, Among the many aphorisms that we shall hear from Ivan's visitor, there will be some which we have heard before, not necessarily from Ivan. Like Goethe's Mephistopheles, Dostoevsky's Russian devil expresses some of the author's own opinions. The one on the apostle Thomas has an almost exact equivalent in the narrator's own remarks in Book One, chap. v, p. 20_{5-10}. The devil says that he is a "realist, but not a materialist," but this also describes Aliosha, as characterized at the beginning of Book One, chap. v. Dostoevsky had discussed spiritualism in some articles of 1876. See *Diary of a Writer,* 1:190–96, 301–8, where some of the things said by the devil here are said by Dostoevsky in his own name (for instance: "among those people who do not believe in God there are very many who, with pleasure and readiness, believe in the devil" [1:191]).

299   603_{42-43}, $15:72_{6-7}$, "as you did last time"—only now does the meaning of Ivan's dark allusions to Aliosha (chap. v, p. 570_{18}) become clear: the devil has been there before.

300   603_{45-46}, $15:72_{9-10}$, "for it's I, *I myself speaking, not you.*"—A deep ambiguity. Is this Ivan's rational, conscious self trying to

ward off an intrusion of the subconscious, or is it a desperate attempt to deny the existence of the devil?

301   604_6, $15:72_{16-17}$,   "I am glad you treat me so familiarly."—This refers to Ivan's addressing his visitor in the familiar second person singular. Cf. note 296 above.

302   604_{11}, $15:72_{22}$,   "you   are   a   sponger"—the   word prizhival'shchik, "sponger, parasite, hanger-on," has been applied to the devil several times and becomes a label of his. This epithet, borne out by the physical description (p. 602), is symbolic of all that Ivan and his creator, Dostoevsky, find hateful about the modern liberal: the devil is unoriginal, dependent upon ideas imported from the West; he is a has-been (his ideas and his jokes are equally stale); he lacks spirit and is ready to do anything for the sake of mere physical comfort. The psychological motivation of Ivan's preoccupation with a "hanger-on" complex is a deep-seated childhood trauma: as a youngster, Ivan had been a "hanger-on" and had hated it (Book One, chap. iii, p. 10_{15-18}). Regarding literary implications, see Terras, "Turgenev and Ivan Karamazov's Devil," p. 269.

303   604_{16}, $15:72_{26}$,   "For what am I on earth but a sponger?"—A pun: Russ. prizhival'shchik, "sponger," is derived from the verb zhit', "to live," and means literally "he who lives with somebody."

304   604_{20-27}, $15:72_{30-37}$,   See note 300 above.

305   604_{28-32}, $15:72_{38-43}$,   See note 299 above.

306   604_{38}, $15:73_2$,   "I've   treated   him   badly   over   Father Zosima"—he alludes to his having tempted Aliosha through "the odor of corruption" (Book Seven, chap. i). This helps to establish a diabolic subtext for the whole novel. See Introduction III.2.a. The Reader's Role.

307   604_{39}, $15:73_3$,   "you lackey!"—brings to mind Smerdiakov, who had appeared as almost as much of a phantom as the devil does now (cf. chap. viii, p. 591_{1-2}).

308   605_{1-3}, $15:73_{9-11}$,   The French—"that's noble, that's delightful" and "that's chivalrous"—enhances the irony. It is also in character for a person of the visitor's description to lace his speech with some French phrases.

309   605_4, $15:73_{12}$,   Ivan continues in his violent ways which he just displayed at Smerdiakov's.

310   605_{10-11}, $15:73_{18-19}$,   "You are myself"—Ivan has said this so often that it begins to sound as if he protests too much.

311   605_{23}, $15:73_{30}$, "that I am a fallen angel"—the first indication
      that there may be a link between the prosaic sponger and the
      Grand Inquisitor and his "wise and dread spirit," a version of
      the glamorous Miltonic Satan. See Introduction II.2.a. Chal-
      lenge to Christianity.

312   605_{29}, $15:73_{36-37}$, "my life gains a kind of reality"—harks back
      to Father Zosima's words, addressed to Mme. Khokhlakov: "it
      will all get no further than dreams, and your whole life will slip
      away like a phantom" (Book Two, chap. iv, p. 49_{17-19}). It was
      one of Dostoevsky's favorite ideas that the westernized Russian
      intelligentsia, having lost its native soil from under its feet, was
      leading an entirely abstract, theoretical, and phantom-like exis-
      tence. The devil's professed attempts at living a "real life" are
      not too different from Mme. Khokhlakov's.

313   605_{32}, $15:73_{39}$, "here all is formulated and geometrical"—a jibe
      at Ivan's professed "Euclidean understanding" (Book Five,
      chap. iv, p. 224_{42}), which is suddenly revealed as something that
      is good for superstitious two-hundred-and-fifty-pound mer-
      chant's wives.

314   606_2, $15:74_7$, "the cause of the Slavs"—that is, toward the
      liberation of the Balkan Slavs still under the Turkish yoke.

315   606_{15-16}, $15:74_{20-21}$, "Satan *sum et nihil humanum a me alienum
      puto.*"—An adaptation of the line *Homo sum, humani nihil a
      me alienum puto,* "I am a man, and believe that nothing human
      is alien to me," from Terence's *Heauton Timorumenos,* Act. I,
      sc. i, line 25. The devil's solidarity with "human nature" implies
      a denial of man's divine nature—a denial in which he agrees with
      the Grand Inquisitor. The parody of "The Grand Inquisitor"
      has begun.

316   606_{22}, $15:74_{28}$, *C'est du nouveau, n'est ce pas?*—"That's
      something new, isn't it?" Ivan has slipped into recognizing the
      devil as an entity separate from himself, a notion which the devil
      acknowledges and proceeds to "rationalize" for him.

317   606_{24}, $15:74_{30}$, "from indigestion or anything"—an allusion to
      Father Zosima's advice to a monk who suffered from evil dreams
      (Book Six, chap. i, p. 314_{16-17}).

318   606_{28}, $15:74_{35}$, "Leo Tolstoi"—Dostoevsky was an admirer of
      Tolstoi's genius. He had hailed *Anna Karenina* as "a fact
      capable of giving Europe an answer on our behalf" and a "per-
      fect" work "as an artistic production." See *Diary of a Writer*
      (1877), 2:784–85. Dostoevsky seems to suggest (with Schopen-

hauer, among others) that the creative imagination is akin to the workings of our dream consciousness.

319   607_{8-16}, $15:75_{17-24}$,   The devil's flight through space is a motif found in folklore and even in Old Russian literature. It features prominently in Gogol's story "The Night before Christmas." Dostoevsky himself had used the motif of flight to a distant star in his "Dream of a Ridiculous Man" (*Diary of a Writer*, 2: 672–89). Space travel was a common theme in nineteenth-century fiction and science fiction. Dostoevsky provides a touch of "scientific" realism by pointing out what will happen to an ax left in space. The motif of space travel will reappear in a different context a little later (p. 610_{28-30}).

320   607_{14-15}, $15:75_{22}$,   "in the water that is above the firmament"— in the original, an accurate quotation from Gen. 1:7, in Slavonic and with obvious mockery.

321   607_{33}, $15:75_{39}$,   A. A. Gattsuk (1832–91) was a newspaper and almanac publisher in Moscow in the 1870s and 1880s. See *PSS* 15:591.

322   607_{36-38}, $15:75_{42-43}$,   "You want to get the better of me by realism, to convince me that you exist . . ."—Ivan is still fighting back. Cf. notes 297, 300, 310, and 316 above.

323   607_{39-40}, $15:75_{45-46}$,   "the truth is unhappily hardly ever amusing"—here, "hardly ever amusing" translates *pochti vsegda neostroumna,* lit. "almost always banal," reminiscent of Turgenev's words: "What is terrible is that there is nothing terrible, that the very essence of life is petty and uninteresting, and shallow in a beggarly way." The words are from Turgenev's piece "Enough!" (1865), mentioned by Mme. Khokhlakov (Book Eight, chap. iii, p. 363_{19}). Cf. Terras, "Turgenev and Ivan Karamazov's Devil," p. 269.

324   607_{40-41}, $15:75_{46}-76_{1}$,   "something big of me, and perhaps something fine"—this phrase is in cross-reference with p. 614_{11-12} ("'everything great and noble'"), where the quotation marks suggest that the phrase is from Schiller, *The Robbers,* Act I, sc. i ("Grösse und Schönheit"). Hence the translation ought to be: "something great of me, and perhaps something beautiful." The exposé of the Grand Inquisitor continues: the devil cannot perform miracles.

325   $607_{44ff.}$, $15:76_{4ff.}$,   The devil's medical problems emphasize his all-too-human nature. The rather flat joke about the doctor who treats the right nostril only is a variation on an episode in

Voltaire's *Zadig,* where it is the right eye (see *PSS* 15: 591). But the overspecialization of modern doctors seems to have been a personal concern of Dostoevsky's, as his notebooks suggest. See *The Unpublished Dostoevsky,* 2:74 and passim.

326   608$_{20}$, 15:76$_{23-24}$, "Hoff's malt extract"—a popular commercial brand.

327   608$_{26-30}$, 15:76$_{29-32}$, *Le diable n'existe point.*—"The devil doesn't exist at all." Cf. note 298 above.

328   608$_{42}$, 15:76$_{44}$, "'I also write vaudevilles of all sorts.'"—a quotation from Gogol's comedy *The Inspector-General* (1836), Act III, sc. vi. The words are spoken by the harebrained impostor Khlestakov, whose name comes up in the next line.

329   608$_{44}$–609$_{1}$, 15:77$_{2}$, "I was predestined 'to deny'"—an allusion to Mephistopheles' words in Goethe's *Faust:* "I am the spirit that always denies!" (*Faust,* Pt. I, line 1338). Ivan's devil in some ways resembles Mephistopheles, who is a jovial and witty fellow, with a touch of bonhomie. A few lines earlier, Mephistopheles had said that he is "a part of that power which always wants Evil and always creates Good" (lines 1335–36). This line will come up on p. 614$_{27-28}$. Dostoevsky's devil, likewise, produces his own, rather elaborate justification of his own existence, a "diabolodicy," as it were.

330   609$_{5-6}$, 15:77$_{5}$, "the hosannah must be tried in the crucible of doubt and so on, in the same style"—the ironic "and so on, in the same style" is important, for here Dostoevsky has expressed a private thought very dear to him—so the devil must make fun of it. In his notebooks of 1880–81, which contain drafts for a reply to his critic K. D. Kavelin, Dostoevsky wrote: "Accordingly, it is not like a child that I believe in Christ and profess faith in Him, but rather, my *hosanna* has come through the *great crucible of doubt,* as the devil says in that same novel of mine" (*The Unpublished Dostoevsky,* 3:175).

331   609$_{10}$, 15:77$_{10}$, "that comedy"—the notion of life as a farce or comedy is a cliché of pessimistic romanticism.

332   609$_{10-11}$, 15:77$_{11}$, "I, for instance, simply and directly demand that I be annihilated."—the devil's rejection of God's world, with suicide as its logical corollary, coincides with Smerdiakov's suicide, of which we shall hear a few pages later. Cf. Linnér, p. 161.

333   609$_{12-13}$, 15:77$_{12-13}$, "If everything in the universe were sensible, nothing would happen."—Ivan had said much the same: "The world stands on absurdities, and perhaps nothing would have

come to pass in it without them" (Book Five, chap. iv, p. 224_{18-20}).

334 609_{17-18}, $15:77_{18}$, "They suffer, of course . . . but then they live, they live a real life, not a fantastic one, for suffering is life."— The devil once more expresses one of Dostoevsky's own ideas. Cf. Introduction II.2.B. Arguments in Support of Christianity.

335 609_{22-23}, $15:77_{23}$, "I am a sort of phantom of life who has lost all beginning and end"—the last phrase translates *kontsy i nachala*, lit. "ends and beginnings," which is important because this is the title of a work by A. I. Herzen (see Perlina, p. 134). Herzen is one of the figures from whom the composite picture of the Russian devil is drawn. Cf. note 312 above.

336 609_{35-36}, $15:77_{35}$, "upon my word I don't know"—the devil has no supernatural knowledge or power: his only distinction is that he does not believe in God. Unlike the Grand Inquisitor (Book Five, chap. v, p. 242_{15}), he is not proud of it. His unbelief is a mark of weakness, not strength.

337 609_{41-44}, $15:77_{40-43}$, *Je pense, donc je suis*—"I think, therefore I am." From Descartes's famous aphorism, the devil immediately drifts into the subjective idealism of J. G. Fichte (1762–1814), which makes the world "a logical development of my ego." Fichte's ideas were popular in Russia in Dostoevsky's youth. For the philosophical background of this, see *PSS* 15:443–44.

338 610_4, $15:78_3$, "or rather a legend"—identifies it as a direct antithesis to "The Grand Inquisitor."

339 610_{12}, $15:78_9$, "we had to tuck in our tails"—a *double entendre,* the subjects being devils.

340 610_{15}, $15:78_{12}$, "a certain department"—the secret police. Cf. Book Ten, note 129.

341 610_{17}, $15:78_{13-14}$, "our middle ages—not yours"—we are facing a mirror image of "The Grand Inquisitor"!

342 610_{22-23}, $15:78_{19}$, "a thinker and philosopher . . ."—Ivan himself: it is he who is getting ready for his quadrillion-kilometer march. In the original, the quotation marks are positioned differently: " 'He rejected everything, law, conscience, faith.' " The quotation is from A. S. Griboedov's famous comedy *Woe from Wit* (1825), Act IV, sc. iv. Repetilov, who utters these words (in the first person singular), is a comic character; using his words thus gives a touch of levity to the "legend."

343 $610_{32ff.}$, $15:78_{28ff.}$, Once more, the motif of hell. See Book Eight, note 200, for other occurrences of this motif.

344 610_{37}, $15:78_{32-33}$, " 'mellowing of your manners' "—a cliché

from the eighteenth-century debate between Rousseau and Voltaire on the progress of civilization. See *PSS* 15:592. In this paragraph, Dostoevsky ironically paraphrases Saltykov-Shchedrin's *Unfinished Conversations,* iii (1875), where the point is made that modern "psychological" persecution and torture are even more vicious than the physical violence of old. See M. E. Saltykov-Shchedrin, *Sobranie sochinenii,* 20 vol. (Moscow, 1965–77), 15, pt. ii:172–85.

345   611_7, $15:78_{44}$, "What did he lie on there?"—Ivan is a chip off the old block: Fiodor Pavlovich had wondered if hell had a ceiling to hang hooks from (Book One, chap. iv, p. 18).

346   611_{24-30}, $15:79_{10-16}$, The idea of eternal cosmic palingenesis seems to have been one of Dostoevsky's preoccupations. The image of the Earth become a deserted, ice-covered globe whirling through space, in particular, seems to have haunted him. See *Notebooks for "A Raw Youth,"* pp. 38, 39, 48, 57, 108, 112, 152–53, 219, 224, 367. Even in this chapter, a "geological cataclysm" will be alluded to (p. 615_{34-35}). The point here is that time, historical as well as cosmic, may be relative. The "miracle" becomes natural.

347   611_{27}, $15:79_{13}$, "again 'the water above the firmament' "—i.e., creation. See note 320 above.

348   $611_{43ff.}$, $15:79_{30ff.}$, The struggle regarding the devil's identity continues. The name of Ivan's schoolmate, Korovkin (from *korovka,* "little cow"), is a particularly prosaic one.

349   612_{5-6}, $15:79_{38}$, "even when people are taken to be executed"—a personal reminiscence of Dostoevsky's, no doubt. On 22 December 1849 he, along with other members of the Petrashevsky circle, was taken to Petersburg's Semionovsky Square in closed carriages, believing that they were to be executed.

350   612_{26}, $15:80_8$, "it's better to hang oneself at once"—Smerdiakov may be hanging himself at this very moment.

351   612_{32-33}, $15:80_{15}$, ". . . a tiny grain of faith"—a counterpoint to the epigraph of the novel and its various echoes throughout the text. See Introduction III.3.a. Motifs.

352   612_{35}, $15:80_{16-17}$, " 'the hermit monks and chaste women' "—the first line of a poem by Pushkin (1836), which is a paraphrase of a Lenten prayer by Ephraim Syrus.

353   612_{36-37}, $15:80_{18-19}$, "You'll dine on locusts . . ."—points back to "The Grand Inquisitor" (Book Five, chap. v, p. 240_{38-39}).

354 613_8, $15:80_{34}$, I. F. Gorbunov (1831–96) was an actor, raconteur, and writer with whom Dostoevsky was on friendly terms. See Anna Dostoevsky, *Dostoevsky: Reminiscences,* p. 311.

355 613_{13-28}, $15:81_{1-13}$, The source of this anecdote ought to be an epigram (1821) by Pushkin:

> Get treated—or you'll be like Pangloss,
> a victim of pernicious beauty—
> And, watch it, friend, don't end up led by the nose
> while without a nose.

Pleasantries about noses and their loss (a common symptom of second-stage syphilis) were popular in the eighteenth and early nineteenth century. Episodes featuring such pleasantries are found in Sterne's *Tristram Shandy* and Voltaire's *Candide* and *Zadig.* Gogol's grotesque "The Nose" (1836) is the best-known Russian example. By telling this joke, the devil shows once more how dated he is.

356 613_{42-44}, $15:81_{21-23}$, *Ah, mon père* . . .—"Ah, Father, it gives him so much pleasure and me so little trouble!" Inexact quotation of the last two lines of an anonymous epigram on the celebrated French actress Jeanne-Catherine Gaussain (1711–67). The whole anecdote resembles an episode of the mock epic *La guerre des dieux anciens et modernes* (1799) by Evariste Parny (1753–1814). See *PSS* 15:593–94. Again, the devil shows himself as sadly behind times.

357 614_{11-12}, $15:81_{35-37}$, "don't demand of me 'everything great and noble' and you'll see how well we shall get on"—the quotation is very properly from Schiller (see note 324 above), and the point is clear: abandon all idealist pretense and embrace a simple positivism, even without any humanist aspirations.

358 614_{13-16}, $15:81_{37-40}$, In the original, "with thunder and lightning" *(gremia i blistaia)* is in quotation marks and has been identified as possibly a quotation from an Old Russian apocryphic text (*PSS* 15:594). This makes sense as a counterpoint to the beginning of "The Grand Inquisitor," which also looks back at Old Russian apocrypha. Cf. Book Five, notes 198 and 199. The image of the glamorous devil "with scorched wings" was familiar to every Russian reader from Lermontov's verse epic *The Demon* (1839). Its ultimate source is Milton's Satan.

359 614_{19}, $15:81_{43}$, The critic V. G. Belinsky (1811–48) devoted a

great deal of energy to the deflation of popular romantic epigoni like A. A. Bestuzhev-Marlinsky (1797–1837) and V. G. Benediktov (1807–73).

360   614_{22-25}, $15:82_{2-5}$, "a star of the Lion . . ."—here Dostoevsky makes some puns. The "star of the Lion and the Sun" was an Iranian decoration that was sometimes received by high Russian officials serving in the Caucasus. The "Polar Star" is a Swedish decoration. But it was also the title of almanacs published by the Decembrists (1823–25) and by the émigrés Herzen and Ogariov (1855–62, 1869). As for "Sirius," the hero of Voltaire's *Micromegas* (1752) is an "inhabitant of the world of the star Sirius." See *PSS* 15:594. The devil is slippery: all along he had played the "progressive" and "liberal"; now suddenly he will have no part even of the moderate Herzen, but would rather identify with some despotic Shah of Persia.

361   614_{27-28}, $15:82_{7-8}$, "Mephistopheles declared . . ."—See note 329 above. Now Dostoevsky challenges Goethe's conception head-on. To Goethe, the devil's negativism was indeed a necessary component of human striving and of human progress. Dostoevsky's all-too-human devil, through his affirmation of human frailties and concerns, betrays the divine. In a notebook of Dostoevsky's (1876–77), we read: "What is the difference between demon and man? In Goethe, Mephistopheles says in answer to Faust's question: who are you: I am part of that part of the whole which wishes evil but does good. Alas! man could answer, speaking conversely of himself: 'I am part of that part of the whole which eternally desires, thirsts, hungers for good, but as a result of his actions there is only evil' " (*The Unpublished Dostoevsky*, 3:129).

362   614_{32-33}, $15:82_{13}$, "the joyful shrieks"—translates *radostnye vzvizgi,* where *vzvizg* is decidedly deprecatory, meaning "squeal, yelp." The devil is making fun of the great mystery.

363   614_{37-39}, $15:82_{17-20}$, A key passage. Like Ernest Renan, author of the famous *Vie de Jésus,* or Turgenev, author of the moving story "A Living Relic," the devil is "susceptible and aesthetically impressionable." He appreciates the sentimental appeal of religion. But he lacks the inner strength to sustain his religious feeling when it is challenged by reason. He is an unbeliever from weakness, not strength.

364   615_3, $15:82_{31}$, "I know, of course, there's a secret in it"—the counterpoint to the second temptation of Christ in "The Grand

Inquisitor." There had been no secret nor mystery there, only a pretense of it. Now the devil suggests that there exists a secret after all. Of course he turns it all into yet another grotesque joke.

365   615_{13-16}, 15:82$_{39-41}$, A counterpoint to Father Zosima's warm appreciation of the Book of Job. Cf. Book Six, chap. ii(b), p. 270.

366   615_{16-19}, 15:82$_{42-44}$, "there are two sorts of truth"—a direct echo of Ivan's own words about "Euclidean understanding" and a "higher harmony" of which he knows nothing (Book Five, chap. iv, pp. 224–26).

367   615_{25}, 15:83$_{3-4}$, "that ironical tone à la Heine"—Heinrich Heine (1797–1856) was well known in Russia and is referred to repeatedly in Dostoevsky's works. According to Komarovich, Dostoevsky had in mind Heine's poem "Peace" ("Der Frieden") from the cycle "The North Sea" (1826), where Heine, known for his irreverence toward all traditional values, poses as a Christian visionary. Komarovich's supposition is made plausible by the fact that Heine's cycle is explicitly mentioned in a passage of *A Raw Youth* which deals with the same ideas. Cf. note 370 below. See V. Komarovich, "Dostoevskii i Geine," *Sovremennyi mir*, no. 10, pt. ii (1916), p. 104.

368   615_{26}, 15:83$_5$, "I never was such a lackey"—reminds us of Smerdiakov.

369   615_{34}, 15:83$_{13}$, " 'Geological Cataclysm' "—cf. note 346 above. Here "cataclysm" translates *perevorot*, lit. "revolution." The latter translation seems necessitated by the apparent source of this title, pointed out by the commentators of *PSS* (see *PSS* 15:595). In chapter vii of Ernest Renan's *Vie de Jésus*, which deals with Christ's idea of the Kingdom of God, we read: "We know the history of our Earth; cosmic revolutions of the kind Jesus expected do not take place for reasons other than geological or astronomical, which have never been found in any way connected with things moral" (8th ed. [Paris, 1863], pp. 123–24). Renan goes on to point out that the idea of a moral revolution of cosmic proportions is nonetheless an admirable and a noble one, and meaningful even to this day.

370   615_{37}–616$_{18}$, 15:83$_{18-42}$, "The Geological Cataclysm" is apparently a cruder earlier version of "The Grand Inquisitor." It sounds embarrassingly like Rakitin. Dostoevsky had developed a similar conception in *A Raw Youth*, Part Three, chap. 7, sects. ii–iii, where a universal community of men without God, united

by their love of mortal humanity, is celebrated as "the Russian idea." Versilov, who advances this idea, was drawn after Herzen, at least in part. He is, like Ivan Karamazov, a failure. An even earlier version of this conception is found in "Stavrogin's Confession," written as a chapter of *The Possessed.*

371 616_{21-27}, $15:83_{45}-84_3$, "The question now is . . ."—Finally, the point! The grandiose edifice of the Grand Inquisitor is reduced to Smerdiakov's interpretation of the sentence that "all things are lawful"—lawful to the "clever man" who "recognizes the truth," the nonexistence of God, that is.

372 616_{35-38}, $15:84_{11-14}$, "but if you want to swindle . . ."—one more turn of the screw: the whole philosophy of atheist humanism, godmanhood and all, is reduced to a hypocritic ploy which gives the "clever man" an advantage over those who in their "inveterate stupidity" are plagued by moral scruples. It must be understood how these lines outraged the Russian radicals, who saw themselves as unselfish, high-principled idealists.

373 617_1, $15:84_{21}$, "Luther's inkstand"—alludes to an apocryphal anecdote according to which Martin Luther, while working on his Bible translation at the Wartburg, was tempted by the devil and flung his inkstand at him. By throwing his glass at the devil, Ivan has joined Luther—who was a firm believer in the physical existence of the devil.

374 617_{13-14}, $15:84_{33-34}$, "Sir, do you know what kind of weather it is? You wouldn't put a dog out in it."—In Dostoevsky's notebooks of 1876-77 this phrase appears as part of an often-told joke. The repartee is of course: "But, look, you aren't a dog, are you?" (*The Unpublished Dostoevsky,* 3:133).

375 617_{16}, $15:84_{36}$, "something seemed to fetter his arms and legs"—this detail, as well as the "loud, persistent knocking" (which was in fact "quite subdued") which "grew louder and louder" (hardly so, objectively) and, of course, the fact that the glass is still on the table suggest that Ivan's hallucination was experienced in a dreamlike state.

376 617_{31}, $15:85_7$, "An hour ago . . ."—We were just reassured that there was nothing supernatural about Ivan's hallucinatory dream. But now we realize that the "dream" may have started at the exact moment of Smerdiakov's death.

Chapter x

377   618_{6-7}, $15:85_{22-23}$,   Smerdiakov's suicide note, like everything he says, has a touch of the semiliterate about it and is not quite grammatical.

378   618_{23}, $15:85_{39}$,   " 'Who is *he?*' asked Aliosha"—Aliosha has spoken the same words once before (chap. v, p. 570_{23}).

379   618_{26}, $15:85_{42}$,   "a dove like you"—"dove" translates *golub'* (a masculine noun), the symbol of the Holy Ghost, but in Russian also used as an affectionate form of address.

380   618_{26-27}, $15:85_{42}$,   "You are a 'pure cherub' "—"pure cherub" is most likely a quotation from Lermontov's *Demon* (cf. note 358 above), but, as the commentators of *PSS* point out, it is also found in a Russian version of Schiller's "Ode to Joy," several stanzas of which were quoted in Book Three, chap. iii.

381   618_{27-28}, $15:85_{44-45}$,   "the thunderous howl of the seraphim"— Ivan drifts into snatches of the devil's monologue (see chap. ix, p. 614_{33}). More of the same is to follow.

382   618_{29}, $15:85_{45}-86_{1}$,   "But perhaps that constellation is only a chemical molecule."—We must remember that Ivan studied the natural sciences at the university. Accordingly, his consciousness contains some pretty good science—also a forte of Dostoevsky's, who had studied to be an engineer.

383   618_{30}, $15:86_{1}$,   "a constellation of the Lion and the Sun"—Ivan drifts from one association to another. The devil had mentioned the Iranian order of the Lion and the Sun (chap. ix, p. 614_{22}), which now generates the constellation of the Lion.

384   619_{15}, $15:86_{28}$,   "The devil!"—The word is finally out. Aliosha understands immediately and takes Ivan's story quite seriously.

385   619_{21}, $15:86_{33}$,   "like a dachshund's"—it should be "like a Great Dane's" *(datskaia sobaka)*.

386   619_{28}, $15:86_{39}$,   "What were you telling me just now about Liza?"—The correct translation is "earlier today" *(davecha)*. The conversation took place at least six hours earlier (chap. v, p. 568).

387   619_{37}, $15:86_{47}$,   "Is it from love of life?"—Brings back Ivan's earlier confession to his brother (Book Five, chap. iii, p. 211_{36}).

388   $619_{43}-620_{8}$, $15:87_{5-14}$,   The ambiguity about the devil's identity is never lifted.

389   619_{45}, $15:87_{6-7}$,   "Yes, I am a romantic."—Important for our

understanding of Ivan's personality and philosophy. His proud individualism, his dream of mangodhood, and his cosmic fantasies are indeed romantic. Moreover, the very style of his two poems, "The Grand Inquisitor" and "The Geological Cataclysm," is arch-romantic.

391   620_{11}, $15:87_{17-18}$, "What is conscience?"—Now Ivan drifts into some thoughts which were not brought up by the devil, but might have been. The suggestion that conscience is but a "universal habit of mankind" that should be given up is as diabolic as anything the devil said.

392   620_{16-19}, $15:87_{21-24}$, Aliosha has realized that his brother is delirious and tries to humor him.

393   620_{29}, $15:87_{33}$, "and you don't believe in virtue"—actually it was Smerdiakov who had brought this up (chap. viii, p. 599_{11}). The last interview with Smerdiakov and that with the devil are beginning to merge in Ivan's mind.

394   621_{13-14}, $15:88_{12-14}$, "how could he have told you of Smerdiakov's death before I came"—he actually did not, at least not explicitly so (see chap. ix, p. 617_7).

395   621_{19-20}, $15:88_{18}$, "But you are a little pig like Fiodor Pavlovich"—cf. chap. iv, p. 561_{43}. In both instances Ivan says porosionok, "suckling pig," not svin'ia, "pig." Fiodor Pavlovich was, after all, his father.

396   621_{31}, $15:88_{28-29}$, " 'It is not for such eagles to soar above the earth.' "—In Russian, oriol, "eagle," is used routinely as a metaphor for "hero, great man." Here we have a formulaic phrase meaning "he is no hero." Smerdiakov said just that (chap. viii, p. 600_{5-7}). It was also Smerdiakov who said that Ivan Fiodorovich was like Fiodor Pavlovich (p. 599_{32}).

397   621_{36-37}, $15:88_{33-34}$, "The monster" (izverg) has become Ivan's label for Dmitry. Cf. chap. v, p. 569_{10}.

398   622_{12-14}, $15:89_{5-7}$, God comes to Ivan through his conscience, conquering the resistance of his proud reason. The devil, true to the maxim that "he desired evil, but did only good" (chap. ix, p. 614_{27-28}, and note 329), has cleansed Ivan of much of his unholy pride and cured him of what might be called his "Grand Inquisitor complex." But Ivan has a long way to go.

399   622_{18-20}, $15:89_{11-12}$, The Book ends on a final note of ambiguity.

Book Twelve

Chapter i

1 623_2, $15:89_{15}$, "A Miscarriage of Justice"—translates *sudebnaia oshibka,* lit. "a judicial error," which is not as drastic as the English expression.

2 623_{8-18}, $15:89_{21-31}$, The narrator's *captatio benevolentiae* is hardly necessary, for what follows is a brilliant piece of trial reportage. Dostoevsky was well acquainted with the lawcourts. He had reported on several trials in his *Diary of a Writer.* It is in this Book that the narrator's voice becomes the dominant. He is in full control.

3 $623_{19ff.}$, $15:89_{32ff.}$, According to Leonid Grossman's plausible observation, Dostoevsky is in fact describing the atmosphere that reigned at the celebrated trial of Vera Zasulich on 31 March 1878, which he attended. On 24 January 1878, Vera Zasulich (1849–1919) had shot at the Petersburg chief of police, Trepov. She was acquitted by a jury. Dostoevsky's correspondence indicates that he disapproved of the carnival atmosphere at that trial, as well as of its outcome (Grossman, "Dostoevskii i pravitel'stvennye krugi 1870-kh godov," pp. 102, 122).

4 $623_{21ff.}$, $15:89_{34ff.}$, "everyone was surprised"—in the eight lines starting with this line, the Russian word *vsio* (or its plural *vse*), "all, every," occurs eight times, not to speak of its synonyms *tselyi,* "all," and *kazhdyi,* "each," as well as other words apt to create a similar impression (*dazhe,* "even, actually, in fact," *chrezvychaino,* "exceedingly"). Furthermore, there is this climactic syntax: "Everyone knew . . . but yet . . . such . . . such . . . interest in everyone, not only . . . but all over Russia." The very language of this description becomes an iconic sign, as it were, of the crowded, noisy, hysterical atmosphere of the trial.

5 624_{11}, $15:90_{19-20}$, "very smartly dressed"—translates *chrezvychaino razriazhennye,* "exceedingly dressed up," definitely

suggesting that it was in bad taste. The gaudy "carnival" atmosphere.

6   624_{13}, $15:90_{21}$, The translator understates. It should be "hysterical, greedy, almost morbid curiosity."

7   624_{16-17}, $15:90_{16-18}$, Note Dostoevsky's paradoxic psychology: his narrator takes for granted that most women would root for a suspected parricide, "chiefly owing to his reputation as a conqueror of female hearts."

8   624_{23-25}, $15:90_{34-37}$, "People said she intended . . ."—The translation misses the nuance which turns this sentence into a grotesque. It reads, literally: "and to be married to him [*obvenchat'sia* specifically signifies the marriage ceremony] somewhere in the mines, underground."

9   624_{29}, $15:90_{40}$, "hetaera"—sarcastic, of course: inspired by their sudden fame, the good people of Skotoprigonievsk elevate their mayor's kept woman to the rank of a "hetaera."

10   624_{34}, $15:90_{44-45}$, "a very common, ordinary Russian woman" —translates *samuiu obyknovennuiu . . . russkuiu meshchanku,* where *meshchanka* means "a woman of the lower middle class." The ladies in the audience are presumably of the nobility.

11   624_{42-44}, $15:91_{4-6}$, Both the men and the women are, of course, convinced of Dmitry's guilt. The men's condemnation of the parricide and the women's leniency thus become a matter of "sexual politics": the men identify with the father; the women sympathize with the son. It is easy to develop an archetypal pattern from this.

12   625_5, $15:91_{15}$, "legal"—translates *tak skazat', sovremenno-iuridicheskaia,* lit. "the so-to-say modern legal," a sarcastic dig at the pride of "modern" westernized Russia—its enlightened legal profession.

13   625_8, $15:91_{16}$, "Fetiukovich"—see Book Eleven, chap. iv, p. 562_{10}, and note 13.

14   625_{11-34}, $15:91_{19-44}$, "stories . . . about our prosecutor"—this rather detailed character sketch of what may seem to be a minor character is motivated both intrinsically and extrinsically, intrinsically because to a "local resident" (the narrator and his primary audience) he is a person of considerable interest, extrinsically because Dostoevsky makes him the mouthpiece of many of his own ideas. One is tempted to see in "this sickly man" (*etot boleznennyi chelovek,* translated by "with his delicate health") a partial self-portrait of Dostoevsky. As for the

fact that the honest Ippolit Kirillovich has all his facts wrong, while Fetiukovich, "the adulterer of thought," has most of them right, one of the messages of the novel is that in the face of God and His Truth, temporal truth becomes irrelevant.

15 625_{17-19}, $15:91_{25-26}$, "was keenly excited . . . and was even dreaming of rebuilding his flagging fortunes"—translates *voskres bylo dukhom . . . i mechtal dazhe voskresit' etim delom svoio uviadshee poprishche,* where the original and basic meaning of the verb *voskresit'* is "to resurrect," hence lit. "his spirit was resurrected . . . he was even dreaming of resurrecting. . . ." The repetition of this verb points to the terrible irony of the trial: it will be Ippolit Kirillovich's swan song, and his all-too-brief "resurrection" will be bought at the price of burying an innocent man alive.

16 625_{29-30}, $15:91_{39-40}$, ". . . his passion for psychology"—prepares us for the debunking of psychology in chapter ix. Cf. Book Nine, chap. ii, p. 427_{11}.

17 625_{42}–626_{1}, $15:92_{4-9}$, The presiding judge's attitude may be a "coded" comment on the novel itself.

18 626_{7-18}, $15:92_{14-27}$, The commentators of *PSS* observe that the Russian press of the 1870s often made fun of the excessive show of "material evidence" in criminal trials of that period—another aspect of Russian efforts to imitate progressive Western trial practices. See *PSS* 15:597. However, the catalog given here also serves as a quick recapitulation of some salient facts of the case.

19 626_{37-38}, $15:92_{48}$, "the composition of the jury"—it is significant that the accused parricide should be tried by a jury of fathers. The fact that Dostoevsky, through his narrator, is so very critical of the jury system presents a problem. On the one hand, trial by jury is another Western "import." But on the other, a believer in the moral integrity and good sense of the common people ought to have had some trust in the wisdom of a jury composed of "peasants."

20 627_{13-14}, $15:93_{22}$, "as I did as soon as I had looked at them . . ."—Dostoevsky takes care to place his narrator in the courtroom and to report the proceedings entirely from the narrator's personal vantage point.

21 627_{18}, $15:93_{27}$, "titular councilor"—the ninth rank (of four-teen) in the table of ranks of the Imperial civil service. It is characteristic of Dostoevsky's style that we discover something new about Fiodor Pavlovich even after his death: while this is a

low rank (the equivalent of a captain in the army), it still means that he must have spent some years in government service.

22   627_{21-25}, $15:93_{30-35}$,   Again, the narrator's personal impression. Dmitry's elegant clothes are bound to alienate the jurors: compare his clothes to those worn by the jurors (lines 10–12 above).

23   627_{27}, $15:93_{36-37}$,   "his yard-long strides"—a label of Dmitry's. Cf. Book Two, chap. vi, p. 59_{14-15}, and Book Eight, chap. i, p. 347_{41}.

24   627_{33-34}, $15:93_{43}$,   "curved into something between a sneer and a smile"—the "curve" is Fetiukovich's label (cf. chap. x, p. 689_{9-14}) and a symbol of the "adulterer of thought."

25   627_{38-39}, $15:94_{1-2}$,   "He was in evening dress and white tie."— Though this was appropriate garb for a trial at the time, one can imagine the impression it makes on the homespun jury.

26   628_7, $15:94_{13}$,   "stir and whisper"—translates *shevelen'e i shopot,* with onamatopoeic alliteration.

27   628_{12}, $15:94_{18}$,   "He was a dog and died like a dog!"— Translates *Sobake sobach'ia smert'!,* a formulaic expression and hence more likely to be blurted out spontaneously than the words of the English translation.

28   628_{32-38}, $15:94_{39-45}$,   Dmitry's vehement statement clashes not only with courtroom decorum, but also with the dispassionate tone of the narrative. Time and again Dmitry's ejaculations will remind us that there is a human being on trial here.

29   628_{41}, $15:94_{48}-95_1$,   "irrelevant exclamations"—there is an irony here: what could have been more relevant to the matter at hand than what Dmitry has just said?

Chapter ii

30   629_{26-28}, $15:95_{33-35}$,   "I imagine that even the ladies . . ."— Although Dostoevsky's narrator is of course overstating the paradox of the expected acquittal of a guilty man, his point is not without precedent in Russian reality. Some verdicts arrived at by Russian juries and opinions voiced in the Russian press were almost as frivolous. Cf. Book Eleven, note 45.

31   629_{33-35}, $15:95_{40-42}$,   "He is guilty, but he will be acquitted . . ."—We were introduced to a specific example of such reasoning in the person of Mme. Khokhlakov (Book Eleven, chap. ii, pp. 545–47).

32   629_{37-38}, $15:95_{43-44}$, "The men were more interested in the contest between the prosecutor and the famous Fetiukovich."—This, incidentally, describes the structure of this Book, a dramatic account of a forensic contest in which the question of guilt or innocence seems secondary and the jury's verdict anticlimactic.

33   630_{6-7}, $15:96_{13-14}$, "how cleverly he had 'taken down' all the witnesses for the prosecution"—one must realize that the practices and stratagems of a Western-style criminal trial were quite new in Russia at the time. Dostoevsky describes some of these stratagems (as used by V. D. Spasovich, defender of one Mr. Kroneberg, accused of child abuse) in *Diary of a Writer* (1876), 1:219-26.

34   630_{19-20}, $15:96_{25-26}$, "evidence about the open door"—in the original "about the open door into the garden" is set off by quotation marks, reminding the reader that the door was really closed at the time in question.

35   630_{33}, $15:96_{39}$, "devoured by lice"—the Russian *vshi by zaeli* is not a colorful exaggeration, but a matter-of-fact statement.

36   631_{4-6}, $15:97_{8-10}$, "were as effective as eloquence"—translates *vyshlo strashno krasnorechivo,* lit. "it came out terribly eloquent," where *strashno* is ambiguous, meaning both "very" and "awesomely."

37   631_{11}, $15:97_{13}$, "infidel"—translates *bezbozhnik,* "atheist, godless," which is then emphasized by "and that Fiodor Pavlovich and his elder son had taught him atheism [*bezbozhestvu*]."

38   631_{17}, $15:97_{19}$, We have heard these things before. Everything is true except the one thing that matters: his testimony about the open door.

39   631_{25-31}, $15:97_{27-33}$, "the envelope"—we know from Smerdiakov's account (Book Eleven, chap. viii, pp. 593_{30-36} and 597_{20-45}) that the version accepted by the prosecution is a fiction.

40   632_{10-11}, $15:98_{12}$, In the original, "the gates of heaven open" is set off by quotation marks, suggesting that Fetiukovich is thinking of Rev. 4:1, "A door was opened in heaven." Such irreverent use of the Scriptures labels him a modern liberal and agnostic.

41   632_{28-30}, $15:98_{32-34}$, "I am a servant . . ."—This unexpected comeuppance suffered by the "wise" lawyer at the hands of the "foolish" old servant falls into a pattern. See Introduction II. Ideas, note 7.

42　　633$_4$, 15:99$_8$, "Aesop"—cf. Book Three, chap. ix, pp. 128$_7$ and 131$_8$. Cf. Book Two, note 216.

43　　633$_{19}$, 15:99$_{23}$, "Captain Snegiriov's 'wisp of tow' "—it is important that the reader be reminded of this scene, just as of the beatings Dmitry gave Grigory and Fiodor Pavlovich. While the formal trial is a "miscarriage of justice," Dmitry's whole life is on trial. Cf. Introduction II.3.a. Fatherhood.

44　　633$_{24-27}$, 15:99$_{29-32}$, ". . . He was, in fact, allowed some latitude of speech."—Seals the irony: Rakitin's comments are obviously so much hogwash.

45　　633$_{34-35}$, 15:99$_{39-40}$, In the original: "independence of thought and the extraordinary nobility of his ideas," which is more sarcasm: Rakitin's ideas are of course hackneyed clichés.

46　　633$_{43}$, 15:100$_{1-2}$, " 'the kept mistress of Samsonov' "—we remember that he had spoken even worse of her in private (Book Two, chap. vii, p. 73$_{40}$). The surprising point of this little detail is yet to come: Rakitin is being set up.

47　　634$_{7-8}$, 15:100$_{11-12}$, The Life of the Deceased Elder, Father Zosima—this detail is taken directly from the biography of G. Z. Eliseev (1821–91), a radical journalist who early in his career had published works such as History of the Lives of the First Founders and Missionaries of the Church of Kazan, Saints Gurii, Varsonofii, and German (Kazan, 1847), which earned him a professorship of theology at Kazan Divinity School. The dedication to an archbishop is also authentic. Eliseev, over the years, had made some bitter attacks on Dostoevsky. See PSS 15:597 and V. S. Dorovatovskaia-Liubimova, "Dostoevskii i shestidesiatniki," in Dostoevskii (Moscow, 1928), pp. 14–16.

48　　634$_{15-16}$, 15:100$_{18-19}$, Fetiukovich's compliment is sarcastic, of course: he congratulates Rakitin on his ability to "take the widest view of every social question," meaning his total lack of principle.

49　　634$_{20}$, 15:100$_{23}$, "Svetlov"—the name, though common, may be symbolic. It is derived from svetlyi, "bright, luminous, serene."

50　　634$_{37-38}$, 15:100$_{44}$, "did you receive the twenty-five roubles from Miss Svetlov as a reward"—preparations for this punch line go back all the way to Book Two, chap. vii, p. 70$_{32-33}$. The reader remembers the payment of the twenty-five roubles from Book Seven, chap. iii, p. 331.

51　　635$_{8-12}$, 15:101$_{16-18}$, "Bernard"—Dmitry uses his private language even in court. Cf. Book Eleven, note 94.

52 635_{18}, $15:101_{23-24}$, "expert observation"—misses the irony of the original, which has *predvaritel'nuiu 'ekspertizu'*, lit. "preliminary 'expertise,'" meaning that the bailiff was instructed to examine witnesses for their sobriety.

53 635_{24-25}, $15:101_{29-30}$, "Daddy, daddy, how he insulted you!"— A leitmotif, cf. Book Four, chap. vii, p. 190_{26}, and Epilogue, chap. iii, p. 733_{21}. Cf. note 43 above.

54 635_{27-28}, $15:101_{32}$, "amidst the laughter of the public"—the reader knows better: Snegiriov, one of the three fathers injured by Dmitry, is a formidable witness, though not in a legal sense, of course.

55 635_{39-40}, $15:101_{45}$, "And if anyone did steal, he did not leave a receipt."—Another setup: little does Trifon Borisych know that he will be promptly exposed as a case in point.

56 636_1, $15:102_4$, "put aside in a little bag"—translates *otlozheny v ladonku*, where *ladonka* has been previously translated by "locket" and "amulet" (cf. Book Nine, note 160). The Russian word suggests a specific object, not any "little bag."

57 636_{29-30}, $15:102_{30}$, "seeing that this only increased his consequence in the eyes of the President and the prosecutor"— another sarcastic dig at the liberal jurists, this time at their lack of national pride.

58 636_{30-31}, $15:102_{31}$, "grew more and more pompous"—in the original, it is a sarcastic "now definitely elated in spirit."

Chapter iii

59 637_{15-16}, $15:103_{12-14}$, "The two latter appeared also as witnesses for the prosecution."—V. D. Rak has drawn attention to the fact that it was against the law for a person to function in this dual capacity in a criminal trial and that Dostoevsky knew it. In 1877 the case of Ekaterina Kornilov, in which Dostoevsky was deeply involved, had been reopened on account of an analogous technicality (*Diary of a Writer*, 1:459–65, 527–34, and 2:690–91, 913–35). Conceivably, Dostoevsky was creating an opening for a successful appeal by Dmitry in the sequel to the novel. See V. D. Rak, "Iuridicheskaia oshibka v romane *Brat'ia Karamazovy*," in *Dostoevskii: Materialy i issledovaniia*, 2 (Leningrad, 1976): 154–59.

60 637_{21}, $15:103_{18}$, "a Herrnhüter or Moravian brother"—it should be "Herrnhuter" (as it is in the original). Dostoevsky followed the activities of German Protestant sects in Russia with

a wary interest. See, for instance, *Diary of a Writer,* 2:566–68. Herzenstube is drawn in an exceptionally positive manner for a "foreigner." The name, a compound of *Herz,* "heart," and *Stube,* "chamber, room," would seem to be significant.

61   638_{7-15}, $15:103_{44}$,   Dr. Herzenstube's Russian is exactly as the narrator describes it: grammatically correct, yet very "peculiar" and with every phrase "in German style." The translation fails to catch this effect.

62    $638_{36ff.}$, $15:104_{26ff.}$,   "Aberration" once more translates *affekt,* "a fit of passion," used as a legal term equivalent to "temporary insanity" (cf. Book Eleven, note 45).

63   638_{42-43}, $15:104_{32-33}$,   "Promised" is not quite accurate for *prorochilo,* "presaged," but it catches very well the breezy tone in which the doctor makes such a terrible prediction.

64   638_{45-46}, $15:104_{35}$,   "All his actions are in contravention of common sense and logic"—Dostoevsky challenges the image of "normal" [behavior] as envisaged by positivistic psychology. Dmitry, precisely because he acts "in contravention of common sense and logic," is actively human. It was Smerdiakov who acted in accordance with "common sense and logic."

65   639_{3-4}, $15:104_{38-39}$,   The doctor has correctly observed these traits. Cf. Book Two, chap. vi, pp. 58_{36}–59_1.

66   639_{5-6}, $15:104_{40-41}$,   " 'Bernard!' 'Ethics!' "—Sophoclean irony: the reader knows the story behind these words; the doctor does not (see Book Eleven, chap. iv, pp. 556–57).

67   639_{44}, $15:105_{33}$,   "Bravo, apothecary!"—Translates *Bravo, lekar'!* where *lekar'* is the good-naturedly condescending term by which military officers referred to physicians, something between "surgeon" and "sawbone." Cf. Book Ten, chap. vii, p. 529_{24-29}.

68   640_{22}, $15:106_{11}$,   *spazieren*—German "to take a walk."

69   640_{36}, $15:106_{26}$,   "I've forgotten what it's called."—Dostoevsky gives us a truly classic example of effective use of retardation. Told without interruption, the story might have easily slipped by unnoticed; now it is unforgettable.

70   641_{3-6}, $15:106_{37-39}$,   *Gott der Vater . . . Gott der Sohn . . . Gott der heilige Geist*—The good doctor was playing the missionary a bit. The scene is symbolic in more ways than one. Herzenstube, by assuming fatherhood of the neglected boy, albeit only for a moment, plants the seeds of goodness ("the Holy Ghost") in his

heart. Then, too, it is important that the theme of fatherhood and sonhood be for once explicitly raised to a metaphysical level. That it is stated in a foreign language is a brilliantly conceived "foregrounding" device: it stops the reader and makes him think.

71 641_{30}, $15:107_{19}$, "witnesses *à décharge*"—"witnesses for the defense."

72 641_{34-36}, $15:107_{23-25}$, This chapter ending builds suspense.

Chapter iv

73 642_{24-26}, $15:108_{10-12}$, "He spoke to me once . . ."—Refers to Book Three, chap. v, p. 110_{35-40}.

74 642_{32}, $15:108_{17-18}$, "like a warhorse at the sound of a trumpet"—more sarcasm aimed at the prosecutor.

75 643_{20-21}, $15:109_{8-9}$, "certain moral convictions so natural in a brother"—one immediately remembers Ivan's "convictions" to the contrary.

76 643_{31-35}, $15:109_{20-24}$, Refers to Book Three, chap. xi, p. 143_{19-38}. We were reminded of this scene in Book Nine, chap. vii, p. 466_{16-18}.

77 644_{1-2}, $15:109_{37}$, "that little bag"—cf. note 56 above.

78 644_{15}, $15:110_3$, "he said *half* several times"—actually he said it only once.

79 644_{24-25}, $15:110_{12-13}$, "That's what brought it back to me just now."—Perfectly plausible psychologically. A careful reader should have remembered the detail for the same reason.

80 645_{5-9}, $15:110_{41-44}$, The massive concessions and qualifications in this sentence—"one fact at least . . . even though . . . only one tiny bit . . . a mere hint . . . it did go some little way"—are a hallmark of Dostoevsky's style. The idea seems to be to protect one's thesis by reducing it to infinitesimal proportions—something like Zeno's paradox, which will not let Achilles ever catch the turtle.

81 645_{24}, $15:111_{11-12}$, "particularly handsome"—understated by the translator: *udivitel'no* is "amazingly, strikingly, extremely."

82 646_{14}, $15:111_{47}$, "There was a note of defiance in her voice."—Here the mention of Katerina Ivanovna's voice serves as a transition to the approaching catastrophe.

83 646_{22}, $15:112_6$, "her 'bowing to the ground to him' "—this has

become a kind of shorthand notation for a whole episode, first
for Dmitry and Katerina Ivanovna, then for the narrator and his
readers as well. Cf. Book Three, note 96.

84    $646_{27ff.}$, $15:112_{11ff.}$,   "She   began   telling   her   story."—
Indiscretion is one of Dostoevsky's devices. Dmitry had in-
discreetly told the story to Ivan, to Grushen'ka, and to Aliosha.
Now Katerina Ivanovna commits the ultimate indiscretion.

85   646_{36}, $15:112_{19-20}$,   "It   was   something   tremendous!"—
"Tremendous" translates *potriasaiushchee*, "shattering, heart-
wrenching, deeply moving." The modern reader must consider
that, in an age of Victorian morality, Katerina Ivanovna is
ruining her reputation and social standing quite irreparably. The
strong words that follow—"sacrifice," "self-immolation"—are
quite literally apt.

86   647_1, $15:112_{31}$,   "but . . ."—this "but" is characteristic of
Dostoevsky's style: a notion will be developed with some
eloquence; then an antithesis will turn it around and deflate it
until nothing is left. Cf. Introduction III.1.a. The Narrator, note
17.

87   647_{31-34}, $15:113_{12-15}$,   Dmitry's outburst is well motivated. We
know that Dmitry believes Katerina Ivanovna is seeking revenge.
Cf. Book Nine, chap. vii, p. 463_{2-3}.

88    $647_{46}-648_1$, $15:113_{26-27}$,   We know Grushen'ka's black shawl
well. See Book Three, chap. x, p. 136_2, and Book Nine, chap.
viii, p. 476_{23}.

89   648_{4-9}, $15:113_{30-35}$,   The narrator shows that he has a mind of his
own: he contradicts the ladies on Grushen'ka's looks (cf. chap. i,
p. 624_{34-35}) and on the expression of her face. Cf. note 2 above.

90   648_{11-12}, $15:113_{38}$,   "There was an element of timidity, too, of
course"—the "of course" here is significant: Dostoevsky's
narrator takes the coexistence of aggressive pride and timidity to
be the thing to expect.

91   648_{15}, $15:113_{41}$,   "a sincere note"—intonation is particularly
important in this scene. Grushen'ka's impulsive manner is contrasted to Katerina Ivanovna's controlled behavior.

92   648_{42}, $15:114_{19}$,   "The woman who came between us"—
translates *razluchnitsa* (from *razluchit'*, "to separate"), a term
used by the people for the matchmaker, who "separates" the
bride from her family (this separation is perceived, in folk
tradition, as a lamentable event). Grushen'ka may be using the
word almost literally: had not Katerina Ivanovna been her own

matchmaker? Of course, she has also worked hard at separating Dmitry from Grushen'ka.

93   649_{1-2}, $15:114_{24-25}$, "Fascinate" translates *prel'stit'*, "to tempt, to seduce." Perhaps: "charm" (with a *double entendre*). The phrase "There's not much true shame about her" can also be read as a *double entendre:* Katerina Ivanovna had shown anything but "shame" in trying to "charm"—or "seduce"— Grushen'ka.

94   649_{21-22}, $15:114_{44}$, "He was always coming to me for money"— here Grushen'ka uses a slang expression: *kaniuchit'*, "to scrounge, to bum." One immediately thinks of Rakitin's lofty pronouncements.

95   649_{26}, $15:115_1$, "Why, he is my cousin."—This surprise is, however, well prepared for: see Book Two, chap. vii, p. 73_{30}.

Chapter v

96   650_{18}, $15:115_{37-38}$, "there was an earthy look in it"—translates *chto-to kak by tronutoe zemlioi,* lit. "something, as it were, touched by the earth." Dostoevsky does not mean simply "earthy, earth-colored, sallow" (there is a regular adjective for that: *zemlistyi*); he also means what he says: "touched by the earth"—by the grave, and by the netherworld, that is.

97   651_{20-24}, $15:116_{36-40}$, "I am like the peasant girl . . ."—An allusion to the wedding ritual of the Russian peasants, where the bride would go through a routine of wavering between joining her betrothed and refusing to do so. See *PSS* 15:598, where a wedding song of this type is quoted.

98   651_{37}, $15:117_5$, "Who doesn't desire his father's death?"— Launches one of the great metaphysical passages of the novel. See Introduction II.3.a. Fatherhood.

99   651_{41}, $15:117_8$, "and as all these . . . ugly faces"—"faces" translates *r-rozhi*, "mugs, snouts." Ivan must be seeing the faces in the courtroom as grotesque "mugs." Dostoevsky may have followed Act V, sc. viii, of Gogol's *Inspector-General,* where the mayor exclaims: "I see nothing. I see some sort of pig snouts instead of faces."

100   651_{45}, $15:117_{11}$, "One reptile devours another."—Ivan had said this before. See Book Three, chap. ix, pp. 129_1, 131_{6-7}.

101   652_1, $15:117_{13}$, "It's a spectacle they want!"—Ivan correctly senses the carnival atmosphere of the trial.

102   652_2, $15:117_{14}$,   The commentators of *PSS* suggest that "water"
is here a symbol of the "living water" of faith. See *PSS* 15:598.
Ivan, who has used the devil's name often throughout the novel,
here for the first time invokes Christ.

103   652_{8-11}, $15:117_{20-24}$,   In the original, both Dmitry's smile and
Ivan's laugh are called "twisted, distorted" *(iskrivlionnyi)*. The
parallelism is surely significant.

104   652_{21-22}, $15:117_{34-35}$,   "an envelope"—he means the envelope
mentioned on p. 651_{27}.

105   652_{25-26}, $15:117_{39}$,   *Le diable n'existe point!*—Repeats Book
Eleven, chap. ix, p. 608_{26}. The rest of Ivan's outburst likewise
consists of scraps from his nightmares of the preceding night
(Book Eleven, chap. ix): "the geological cataclysm" (see Book
Eleven, notes 369 and 370), "Van'ka went to Petersburg" (see
Book Eleven, notes 238 and 249), "a quadrillion quadrillions"
(see Book Eleven, chap. ix, pp. 610_{28}, 611_{36-37}). Dostoevsky likes
to recapitulate motifs of a novel in lyric monologues, which are
nevertheless well motivated psychologically.

106   652_{44}–653_1, $15:118_{11-12}$,   "He   screamed   furiously."—This
misses a nuance. In the original, *zavopil neistovym voplem* is
clearly biblical language, bringing to mind the screams of the
possessed healed by Jesus and the apostles (e.g., Luke 8:28, Acts
8:7).

107   653_{18-19}, $15:118_{29}$,   "It's a letter from that monster."—Katerina
Ivanovna's sudden loyalty to Ivan finds expression in her
repeating the ugly word which Ivan had applied to his brother.
Cf. Book Three, note 104.

108   653_{28-30}, $15:118_{37-39}$,   "that letter Mitia had written"—the
reader is familiar with this letter (see Book Eleven, chap. vii, pp.
585–86). "Mathematical proof" is of course openly ironic.

109   654_8, $15:118_9$,   "that creature"—Grushen'ka's label ever since
Book Two (see Book Two, note 158), much as "monster" has
been Dmitry's label.

110   654_{11-12}, $15:119_{18-19}$,   "And as I gave it to him, I looked him in
the face"—compare this account with Dmitry's version of this
scene in Book Three, chap. v, p. 107_{41-46}, where no mention is
made of any significant glances.

111   654_{25}, $15:119_{30}$,   "That's true, Katia"—Dmitry, impulsive and
perceptive, seals the truthfulness of Katerina Ivanovna's
description of the event. We know now that Katerina Ivanovna
has got her full measure of revenge, and more, for the

humiliation which she had suffered when she went to Dmitry's flat for the five thousand roubles.

112   655_{1-2}, $15:120_{1-2}$, "with venomous and malignant triumph"— "venomous" translates *ekhidno*, which is derived from *ekhidna*, "viper." Katerina Ivanovna has reached a nadir. But this is not the last of the peripeties in which she is involved.

113   $655_{26ff.}$, $15:120_{25ff.}$, "he has always despised me"—Dmitry's account of the "low bow" (Book Three, chap. iv) suggests that Katerina Ivanovna is quite wrong: she is projecting her own fears, suspicions, and hurts on the simple Dmitry. A masterpiece of psychology on Dostoevsky's part.

114   656_9, $15:121_6$, " 'the monster and murderer' "—in quotation marks even in the original: these are Ivan's words.

115   $656_{15ff.}$, $15:121_{11ff.}$, Katerina Ivanovna's account is a web of subtle half-truths. Cf. Book Eleven, chap. v, p. 567_{1-35}, where Katerina Ivanovna admits that she actually went to see Smerdiakov herself (line 31).

116   656_{32-33}, $15:121_{27-28}$, "that Smerdiakov was dead"—the euphemism is more obvious in the original, where she says "that Smerdiakov had died," instead of "that Smerdiakov had committed suicide." This little half-truth is symbolic of her whole testimony.

117   656_{32-35}, $15:121_{27-29}$, The word *izverg*, "monster," appears three times in a row here. It has fully established itself as a leitmotif.

118   $656_{36ff.}$, $15:121_{30ff.}$, The narrator breaks the tension of the court drama by a rather tense rhetorical digression of his own, from which he then gradually descends to a sober psychological analysis of Katerina Ivanovna's motives.

119   657_{5-6}, $15:121_{45-46}$, "was she lying in her description of her former relations with Mitia?"—cf. note 113 above.

120   657_{22-31}, $15:122_{13-21}$, "Hysterics began again . . ."—We can now see the reason for the narrator's digression (cf. note 118 above): with more exciting drama coming up, a moment of respite was indicated.

121   657_{28-31}, $15:122_{19-21}$, This pathetic little scene brings the *real* tragedy of it all back into focus.

122   657_{33}, $15:122_{23}$, "the spectacle had been a varied one"— translates *zrelishche bylo bogatoe*, lit. "the spectacle had been a rich one," which conveys the irony better.

123   657_{44-45}, $15:122_{32-33}$, We have heard nothing of Ivan's en-

counters with "persons . . . who were dead." Also, "every evening" is an overstatement, judging by what we know. Perhaps the doctor is enriching his testimony a bit. But the point is that a *real* experience of absolutely decisive importance for the life of a man is dismissed as a mere symptom of "brain fever," a medical term invented by doctors to designate a phenomenon which they could not understand.

Chapter vi

124 658_{23}, $15:123_{9-10}$, "his *chef d'oeuvre*"—note the irony: an aesthetic term, normally applied to a painting, musical composition, or novel, is applied to a legal effort, whose only legitimate purpose should be to determine the truth.

125 658_{24}, $15:123_{10-11}$, "his swan song"—equally ironic.

126 658_{28-30}, $15:123_{16-18}$, "And poor Ippolit Kirillovich . . ."— Literally: "revealed that both civic concern and even the 'accursed' questions, at least to the extent our poor Ippolit Kirillovich could make them his own, lay concealed in him." The "accursed" questions are the ones that tormented Dostoevsky himself: the existence of God, the human condition, the destiny of Russia. In fact, Ippolit Kirillovich treats some of these questions rather in the vein of Dostoevsky's *Diary of a Writer*. Ironically, Ippolit Kirillovich, who spends his effort in a miscarriage of justice, is right about some fundamental issues (from Dostoevsky's viewpoint, that is), while Fetiukovich, whose philosophy is odious to Dostoevsky, is right about the facts of the case.

127 659_{4-10}, $15:123_{33-41}$, "What are the causes . . ."—Dostoevsky had often asked the same questions, and in virtually the same language, in his *Diary of a Writer,* in connection with some notorious criminal cases. Thus, he commented on the conviction, on a charge of embezzlement, and subsequent suicide of one General Hartung in 1877: "One feels sorry for Hartung; but here it is rather a tragedy (very deep tragedy)—the destiny of Russian life, than an error on anyone's part. Or to put it better: here everybody is guilty: the habits and customs of our educated society; the characters which have developed and formed themselves, and finally, the habits and customs of our adopted, young and insufficiently Russified courts" (*Diary of a Writer,* 2:860).

128   659_{9-10}, $15:123_{40-41}$, "or is it, perhaps, a complete lack of such principles among us?"—the notion, advanced by P. Ia. Chaadaev (1794-1856) in his famous *Philosophical Letters* (1836), that Russian national consciousness was still in an unformed, infantile state, and Russian society still lacking in solid traditions, moral principles, and civic institutions, was heard often among Russian westernizers.

129   659_{16-17}, $15:124_{5-6}$, "the new jury courts"—trial by jury had been established by the judicial reform of 1864.

130   659_{23-30}, $15:124_{12-19}$, "a brilliant young officer of high society . . ."—the prosecutor is alluding to the murder case of one Karl von Landsberg, an ensign in the guards, who in 1879 was found guilty of a double murder. See *PSS* 15:598. The other miscreant mentioned by the prosecutor is unidentified or imaginary.

131   659_{41-42}, $15:124_{29-31}$, "that I am delirious"—it should be "that I am raving." This description might have been applied to Dostoevsky and his *Diary of a Writer*—and was, by his political opponents.

132   659_{45}-660_1, $15:124_{35-37}$, "Look, gentlemen, look how our young people commit suicide, without asking themselves Hamlet's question what there is beyond"—an echo of several articles on an alleged wave of suicides among young people in *Diary of a Writer* (1876). In the very first of these, Dostoevsky writes: "And in this connection—not a single Hamletian question: 'But that the dread of something after death . . .' " (*Diary of a Writer,* 1:158). In the original, "what there is beyond" is set off by quotation marks, even though it does not seem to be a direct quotation from any known Russian version of *Hamlet,* Act III, sc. i.

133   660_7, $15:124_{43}$, " 'he lived among us!' "—first line of an untitled poem (1834) by Pushkin, addressed to the Polish poet Adam Mickiewicz.

134   660_{11}, $15:124_{46-47}$, "tragic topsyturvydom"—an excellent translation of *tragicheskaia bezalabershchina.* The whole passage is written in an execrable journalese. It contains other expressions that are just as bad style as this one.

135   660_{22-26}, $15:125_{12-17}$, The prosecutor is referring to the concluding passage of Gogol's *Dead Souls* (1842). He misquotes it (of course Gogol's passage does not say "respectfully") and thus makes a travesty of it.

136   660_{29-30}, $15:125_{19-20}$, "in an access of childish and naïve op-

timism, or simply in fear of the censorship of the day."—
Dostoevsky parodies the style of progressive critics of the 1860s,
who blithely interpreted the works of Pushkin and Gogol in
terms of their own "advanced" ideas.

137 660_{31}, $15:125_{21-22}$, "Sobakevich, Nozdriov, Chichikov"—
characters in Gogol's *Dead Souls:* the first is a greedy boor, the
second a cheat and a brazen liar, the third a smooth swindler.

138 660_{32}, $15:125_{24}$, "heroes"—a misprint for "horses." Ippolit
Kirillovich's rather infelicitous metaphor continues.

139 660_{35}, $15:125_{26}$, "The liberal significance of this simile was
appreciated."—Lit. "They liked the liberalism of his depiction
of the Russian troika," a thrust at Russian liberalism: to be "liberal" is presumed to mean as much as to deprecate and mock
everything Russian. Dostoevsky had said that the surest way to
get applause from a Russian audience was to insult and make fun
of Russia. Cf. *The Possessed,* Pt. III, chap. 2, sect. iv (*PSS*
$10:374_{44-45}$).

140 660_{44}–661_2, $15:125_{36-38}$, "certain fundamental features . . ."—
Here the prosecutor's words become a suggestion for an interpretation of the novel.

141 661_3, $15:125_{39}$, " 'like the sun in a drop of water' "—a
quotation from G. R. Derzhavin's famous ode "God" (1784).

142 661_5, $15:125_{41}$, "vicious"—translates *razvratnyi,* "depraved,
dissolute."

143 661_6, $15:125_{42}$, "the head of a family!"—translates *'ottsa
semeistva,'* lit. "the father of a family," set off by quotation
marks, obviously to foreground the father motif.

144 661_{13}, $15:126_3$, "while his vitality was excessive"—translates *a
zhazhda zhizni chrezvychainaia,* lit. "yet an extraordinary thirst
for life": significant because it brings back the motif of the
Karamazovian "thirst for life" pronounced earlier by both Ivan
and Dmitry.

145 661_{18-21}, $15:126_{8-11}$, The maxims *après moi le déluge* ("after
me, the flood") and "The world may burn for all I care, so long
as I am all right" are attributed to Louis XV and Nero,
respectively. Fiodor Pavlovich would gladly have accepted them
for his own, especially the latter (cf. Book One, chap. iv, p.
17_{43-44}).

146 661_{20}, $15:126_{10}$, "malignant individualism"—translates
vrazhdebnoe ot'edinenie ot obshchestva, lit. "malignant

separation from society." Here *ot'edinenie* is not the same word
that is used by the mysterious visitor in Book Six, chap. ii (he
uses *uedinenie,* also translated by "individualism," p. 283$_{20}$).
The point is that the prosecutor is concerned about a negative
social attitude, while the mysterious visitor—and Dostoevsky—
think of man's alienation from God.

147   661$_{29-30}$, 15:126$_{19-20}$, "he has paid the penalty"—in the
original, a biblical "he has his reward" (after Matt. 6:5).

148   661$_{30-32}$, 15:126$_{20-22}$, "he was a father . . ."—the father theme
is foregrounded now. Note, however, that the prosecutor sees it
in pragmatic social terms.

149   661$_{35-39}$, 15:126$_{26-28}$, "Perhaps I am a pessimist, but you have
agreed to forgive me."—This kind of rhetoric would seem odd in
a modern courtroom. But Ippolit Kirillovich has received a
classical education and may actually be trying to imitate Cicero.

150   662$_3$, 15:126$_{36}$, "He never concealed his opinions"—we know
this from Book Two, chap. vi, p. 60$_{13ff.}$.

151   662$_{12-14}$, 15:126$_{45}$-127$_1$, Once more Ivan's leitmotif:
"Everything is lawful." See Introduction III.3.a. Motifs.

152   662$_{20-21}$, 15:127$_{7-9}$, "If there is one of the sons . . ."—We have
heard the same directly from Smerdiakov (Book Eleven, chap.
viii, p. 599$_{32-34}$). Ippolit Kirillovich demonstrates the absurdity of
his own contention that Smerdiakov was an "idiot."

153   662$_{25-28}$, 15:127$_{14-17}$, Deeply ironic. Ippolit Kirillovich does not
realize how literally right he is about "the direct force of truth."
But neither does he realize how different Ivan's motives were
from what he takes them to have been.

154   662$_{31-32}$, 15:127$_{20}$, " 'ideas of the people' "—translates
narodnym nachalam, where *nachalo* means "principle, foundation." In this passage, Dostoevsky engages in a parody of his
own ideas, whose bearer is Aliosha, of course. To the liberal
prosecutor these ideas must appear reactionary and rather absurd. See *PSS* 15:600 and U. A. Gural'nik, "Dostoevskii v
literaturnoestetacheskoi bor'be 60-kh godov," in *Tvorchestvo
Dostoevskogo* (Moscow, 1959), pp. 293–329.

155   622$_{39-40}$, 15:127$_{28}$, " 'native soil' "—Dostoevsky belonged to a
group of intellectuals of the 1860s who were called *pochvenniki*
(from *pochva,* "soil"), lit. "men of the soil." They accepted
most of the ideas of the Slavophiles and, specifically, advocated
a return to traditional values and beliefs of the Russian people,

particularly their Orthodox faith. They were, however, less anti-
Western, more democratic, and less inclined to see the landed
gentry as the bearer of Russia's destiny. The journals of the
Dostoevsky brothers, *Time* and *Epoch,* were the organs of
pochva in the early 1860s. Hence, letting the prosecutor make
fun of *'rodnaia pochva'* ("native soil") is a bit of self-parody on
Dostoevsky's part.

156   662_{39-40}, $15:127_{28}$, "to the bosom, so to speak, of their mother
earth"—Russ. *zemlia* is ambiguous, being "land" or "soil" as
well as "earth." Hence, "to the bosom of their native land" is
just as proper a translation. Either way, to the liberal prosecutor
it is but a sad self-delusion, even though he sees it as a mere
metaphor. We know it to be holy in a quite literal sense to
Aliosha and his teacher, Father Zosima. See Introduction III.5.f.
Mythical Symbolism.

157   $662_{46}-663_1$, $15:127_{35-36}$, "Mysticism" and "chauvinism" were
precisely the sins Dostoevsky was charged with by his progressive
critics. Thus, M. A. Antonovich dubbed *The Brothers
Karamazov* a "mystic-ascetic novel" in an essay of that title
(1881; see *PSS* 15:503).

158   663_{24}, $15:128_{9-10}$, "Russia"—translates *Rosseiushka,* which is
condescendingly deprecatory. The diminutive suffix is not in
itself derogatory: it might be tender, too. But the *-e-* in *Rosseia,*
instead of the "correct" *Rossiia,* suggests backward, crude,
uncivilized Russia.

159   663_{24-25}, $15:128_{10}$, "the very scent and sound of her"—
"sound" translates *slyshitsia,* which usually suggests "sound,"
but here it is "smell." Hence: "the very scent and smell." A
Russian reader knows the "smell" of Russia from a famous line
in Pushkin's *Ruslan and Liudmila* (1820).

160   663_{26}, $15:128_{12}$, "we are lovers of culture and Schiller"—
Schiller is a symbol of lofty ideals. But the prosecutor may mean
it literally, too: Dmitry may have quoted Schiller to others, as he
did to Aliosha (Book Three, chap. iii).

161   663_{27-40}, $15:128_{14-28}$, The prosecutor's characterization of
Dmitry, unsympathetic though it is (the rhetoric is a great deal
more caustic in the original), is obviously just. Dmitry will
acknowledge this in his final words (chap. xiv, p. 713_{29-30}).

162   663_{45-46}, $15:128_{33}$, "I am here to prosecute him, but to defend
him also."—Another rhetorical trick in the style of Cicero: he is
anticipating and defusing the moves of the defense.

163   664_{20}, $15:129_5$, "and will refrain from analysis"—more
Ciceronian rhetoric: he almost immediately goes on to perform
this analysis!

164   664_{24-25}, $15:129_{11-12}$, "That smile of mockery" is a product of
Ippolit Kirillovich's imagination: even Katerina Ivanovna had
not mentioned any such thing. This little detail shows how the
prosecutor misunderstands Dmitry's character.

165   664_{40}–665_1, $15:129_{28-35}$, Here Dostoevsky lets Ippolit
Kirillovich express a truly Dostoevskian conception, that of
man's infinite capacity for good as well as evil, and in truly
Dostoevskian terms, too: the "abyss" as a metaphor of man's
potential is most characteristic.

166   665_{5-6}, $15:129_{39-40}$, "they continually and unceasingly need this
unnatural mixture"—Dmitry had said something very similar
himself (Book Three, chap. iii, p. 97_{14-15}), only he had found
such a "mixture" to be proper to humanity at large, rather than
"unnatural."

167   665_9, $15:129_{43}$, "wide as mother Russia"—the notion that the
Russian national character, precisely because it was not as yet
fully formed, was "broad," capable of developing contradictory
traits, was a widespread one in Russia. Ippolit Kirillovich is
mouthing a popular cliché.

168    $665_{13ff.}$, $15:129_{46ff.}$, "Can you conceive that a man like that
. . ."—So far, Ippolit Kirillovich, apart from some minor
blunders, has been on fairly firm ground. But now the *quid pro
quo* of fact and fiction started in Book Nine continues. Ippolit
Kirillovich has made himself a model of Dmitry's mind, which he
trusts will explain its workings. He believes that this model is
anchored in reality. But it is only a fiction. Meanwhile, Dmitry's
story, which the prosecutor demolishes as a fiction, is in fact
true. This whole dialectic, which is yet to be amplified by its
inverted mirror-image in Fetiukovich's rebuttal, symbolizes
Dostoevsky's conception of his own fiction and its relationship
to reality. See Introduction III.3.d. Art of the Novel.

169   665_{16}, $15:130_2$, "a little bag"—cf. note 56 above. Further down
(line 29) it is called a "talisman" (which translates Russ.
talisman).

170   666_{22-23}, $15:131_{4-6}$, "legend of the little bag"—translates
legenda o ladonke, which sounds formulaic because of the
alliteration and because *ladonka* is a religious object. The
"legend" is of course true.

Chapter vii

171   667_{24-25}, $15:132_9$, "But such was the young person's 'game.' "—Grushen'ka's share of guilt is established. We know that Grushen'ka herself saw things that way (Book Nine, chap. iii, p. 431_{31-36}, and lines 29–31 below).

172   667_{27-28}, $15:132_{13-14}$, "stretching out hands that were already stained with the blood of his father and rival"—more rhetoric: the prosecutor implies that the charge of murder is proven.

173   667_{32-43}, $15:132_{18-31}$, Rakitin and Ippolit Kirillovich, here as elsewhere, see the psychological truth, but do not even suspect that beyond it there is still a deeper, spiritual truth. And so they misjudge Grushen'ka, as they misjudge Dmitry.

174   668_{20}, $15:133_4$, "(Then followed the anecdote about Captain Snegiriov.)"—We know that Dmitry did not beat up Snegiriov because the latter did not "take his part." But the prosecutor wholly misses one aspect of this episode which would have been grist to his mill: the heartless insult to a father in the presence of his son.

175   668_{40-41}, $15:133_{25-26}$, " 'it is the plan, the scenario of the murder!' "—Katerina Ivanovna had said "scenario" *(programma)*, but not "plan" *(plan)*. See chap. v, p. 655_6. Ippolit Kirillovich reveals the weakness of his argument by borrowing a phrase from a hysterical and biased witness. But he does a skilful job of covering up the weaknesses of his charge of premeditation.

176   670_1, $15:134_{30-31}$, "that Smerdiakov is in a fit"—details such as this remind us of the fact that Ippolit Kirillovich's version is false. We are treated to an exhibit of Dostoevsky's polyphony, where the "other voice" (Smerdiakov's) gives the true version of events.

177   670_{5-11}, $15:134_{34-40}$, Here the prosecutor once more lets his tongue run away with him: "judicious advice . . . to set off to Siberia to the gold mines" is of course ludicrous.

178   670_{17}, $15:134_{45}$, "the fatal influence of chance"—it is significant that while the prosecutor is of course right, Dmitry himself never blames "the fatal influence of chance" for his predicament. To the believer, there can be no accidents in life. Dostoevsky's novels are full of implausible concatenations of circumstances which in the end seem purposeful from a metaphysical vantage point. Cf. Lauren G. Leighton, "The

Crime and Punishment of Monstrous Coincidence," *Mosaic* 12, no. 1 (1978): 93–106.

179 670_{37-40}, $15:135_{16-19}$, "and the unhappy man would have us believe . . ."—here the translation deflates the prosecutor's sarcasm. In the original, the narration continues in the indicative mode: "and the unhappy man steals up to the window, peeps respectfully in, virtuously tempers his feelings, and discreetly withdraws, for fear that something terrible and immoral should happen." Only then comes: "And we are to believe this."

180 670_{40-41}, $15:135_{20-22}$, "us, who understand his character, who know his state of mind at the moment"—here the prosecutor veers into outright hubris: he claims command of the workings of a human being's mind.

Chapter viii

181 671_{21}, $15:136_{5-6}$, "the expression of his face"—this is set off by quotation marks in the original. Aliosha had said: "I saw from his face he wasn't lying" (chap. iv, p. 643_8, above).

182 671_{31}, $15:136_{16}$, "in a fit of insanity"—in the original we have lit. "in a fit of morbid mental derangement and insanity." This emphatic tautology again covers up the weakness of the prosecutor's argument.

183 671_{31}, $15:136_{17}$, "of weak intellect"—translates *slaboumnym,* "feeble-minded." The prosecutor is clearly stretching the truth, a fact blurred by the translation.

184 671_{33-34}, $15:136_{19-20}$, "certain modern theories of duty and obligation"—Ippolit Kirillovich's sarcastic circumlocution for "all things are lawful."

185 671_{38}, $15:136_{26}$, "feeling dull"—it should be "out of boredom."

186 672_{2-6}, $15:136_{31-36}$, Alludes to Book Nine, chap. v, pp. 448–49.

187 $672_{20ff.}$, $15:137_{3ff.}$, "He was naturally very honest . . ."—Here the prosecutor's words begin to verge on grotesque comedy, as we can hear Smerdiakov's own version in the background. Ippolit Kirillovich, who feels so superior to the "poor imbecile," is actually Smerdiakov's dupe (cf. Book Eleven, chap. viii, p. 597_{40-45}).

188 672_{24-29}, $15:137_{8-14}$, This observation on the mentality of an epileptic may be based on Dostoevsky's self-observation.

189 672_{45}–673_{11}, $15:137_{30-44}$, "Here I must mention . . ."—What

follows is *erlebte Rede* (see Introduction III.1.a. The Narrator), where we clearly hear Smerdiakov's voice through the prosecutor's words. The fact that it is the voice of a dead man enhances this effect.

190 673_{33}, 15:138_{16-17}, "the unhappy idiot"—the "feebleminded" Smerdiakov is now demoted even further, to "idiot."

191 673_{38-39}, 15:138_{22}, "for to charge Smerdiakov with that murder is perfectly absurd"—Ippolit Kirillovich believes he has carried his opponent's argument *ad absurdum*. The lesson from it all is, of course, that the truth is sometimes absurd.

192 673_{40}, 15:138_{23}, "let us lay aside psychology"—another rhetorical statement: he will be back to psychology within fewer than five lines.

193 $674_{3ff.}$, 15:$138_{33ff.}$, "And yet he tells another person . . ."—The prosecutor's argument from here on may be likened to the turning of a screw: Ippolit Kirillovich gives the screw several turns, never realizing that there is always another turn—or that he may have turned the screw one time too many.

194 674_{36-38}, 15:139_{17-19}, "Yet are we to believe . . ."—It all depends on how many turns you give the screw!

195 675_{6-10}, 15:139_{35-39}, "There, lying behind the screen . . ."— This is exactly how it was: see Book Eleven, chap. viii, pp. 593_7 and 597_{34-35}.

196 675_{16-17}, 15:139_{36-37}, ". . . and carry off the money"—this is exactly what would have happened if Dmitry had killed his father. In fact, Smerdiakov had counted on this contingency. See Book Eleven, chap. viii, p. 593_{28-34}.

197 675_{36-38}, 15:140_{17-19}, "what if they were in agreement"—the prosecutor sets up a dummy theory which he can easily demolish, thus creating the impression that all alternatives to his own theory are equally implausible.

198 676_{46}–677_3, 15:141_{23-25}, "What would it have cost him to add: 'I am the murderer, not Karamazov'?"—This seems to be a weighty argument. But the screw can be given another turn, as Fetiukovich will show (see chap. xii, p. 703_{24-31}).

199 677_{19-27}, 15:141_{42}–142_2, Note the irony of this situation: Ivan had obtained the money which discredits the evidence that would have exonerated his brother for the purpose of engineering his escape from prison (see Book Eleven, chap. iv, p. 564_{46}–565_2).

200 677_{42-43}, 15:142_{15-17}, "What if, finally unhinged by the sudden

news of the lackey's death, he imagined it really was so?''—The
screw gets another turn!

201   678_{6-7}, $15:142_{26-27}$, "We did not run respectfully and timidly''—this phrase has become a mocking echo of Dmitry's
assertion of his innocence; cf. chap. vii, p. 670_{38}, and chap. viii,
p. 675_{25-26}.

202   678_{18-21}, $15:142_{37-39}$, "Had he been an experienced murderer''—the observation which Smerdiakov has planted in the
prosecutor's mind. See Book Eleven, chap. viii, p. 597_{20-45}.
Ippolit Kirillovich does not suspect that here the screw has
another turn. And once again one can hear Smerdiakov's voice
through his words.

203   678_{39-41}, $15:143_9$, "All because it was Karamazov . . ."—Here
the turn of the screw is way ahead of Ippolit Kirillovich: it was
not that Karamazov "didn't think," but that Smerdiakov staged
this detail, first at the murder scene and later in the prosecutor's
mind, so that the latter might think that it was "Karamazov, not
Smerdiakov."

204   679_{1-3}, $15:143_{16-17}$, The prosecutor does not see the next logical
turn of the screw, which the counsel for the defense will point out
to him: "If he were so cold-hearted and calculating, why not hit
the servant on the head again and again with the same pestle so as
to kill him outright and relieve himself of all anxiety about the
witness?" (chap. x, p. 691_{29-32}).

Chapter ix

205   679_{18}, $15:143_{32}$, "Psychology at Full Steam"—the narrator's
irony is now quite open. Cf. Introduction II.6.a. Dostoevsky's
Psychology.

206   679_{30-31}, $15:144_{1-2}$, "Possibly he regarded him as a fiction."—
The key word has fallen: "fiction" is what the prosecutor's
speech is about, in more senses than he suspects. But his notion
of Dmitry's attitude toward Grushen'ka's former lover is
correct. Cf. Book Eight, chap. i, p. $343_{10ff.}$.

207   679_{39-40}, $15:144_{10-11}$, "a respect for woman and recognition of
her right to love"—Ippolit Kirillovich puts himself on the right
side of the feminism issue *(zhenskii vopros)*: one of the main
points of the Russian progressives' program for the emancipation of women was a woman's right to choose her own mate,

and to change mates, if she so desired. Chernyshevsky had advocated this in *What Is to Be Done?*

208   680_{20}, $15:144_{33-34}$, "To be sure, we are poets"—an ambiguity: Ippolit Kirillovich means this to be ironic, of course, but then, this is the one explicit statement in the novel of what is implicit throughout, namely that Dmitry *is* a poet.

209   680_{36-40}, $15:144_{48}-145_3$, "But *beyond* . . ."—Cf. note 128 above. Ippolit Kirillovich uses the occasion to make another deprecatory statement about Russia. The words "but we, so far, have only our Karamazovs!" may be read as a "coded" self-apotheosis on the part of Dostoevsky. The novel was even then referred to simply as *The Karamazovs (Karamazovy)*.

210   681_4, $15:145_{14}$, " 'Do you know, you are driving a murderer!' "—Alludes to Book Eight, chap. vi, p. $388_{41ff.}$, where the word "murderer" does not, however, fall.

211   681_{35}, $15:145_{46}$, "fascinating"—*obol'stitel'noi,* which is "seductive."

212    $681_{46}-682_{15}$, $15:146_{11-26}$, In the exercise of his "poetic license," Dostoevsky lets Ippolit Kirillovich appear to be a better "novelist" than he is credited with being. Here he allows him to veer into a fairly extended Homeric simile whose subject is one of Dostoevsky's favorites: the last moments of a condemned man, during which the questions of human existence acquire a dramatic urgency. This theme had been in the focus of *The Idiot.* See Michael Holquist, *Dostoevsky and the Novel* (Princeton, 1977), pp. 103–5.

213   682_{20-23}, $15:146_{29-33}$, This is the one obvious flaw in the whole argument. A man whose "soul was full of confusion and dread," and who was going to shoot himself anyway, is unlikely to have looked for a hiding place for half his money. Besides, the money was never found. Fetiukovich will make the most of this in chapter xi.

214   682_{43-45}, $15:147_{7-8}$, "Two extremes" translates *dve bezdny,* lit. "two abysses," a recurrent image. Cf. chap. vi, pp. 664_{46} and 665_{6-7} (where *bezdny* is also translated by "extremes"). Ippolit Kirillovich overestimates the depth of the "abyss": even if Dmitry had killed his father, he would not have been capable of cold-bloodedly hiding a part of the money.

215   683_{8-21}, $15:147_{17-31}$, A brilliant analysis on the part of the prosecutor, no doubt. Dostoevsky knew the accused criminal's

viewpoint only too well. In 1849, his resilient defense earned him this characterization from his interrogator: "Clever, independent, tricky, stubborn" (N. F. Bel'chikov, *Dostoevskii v protsesse petrashevtsev* [Moscow and Leningrad, 1936], p. 52). Ironically, all this brilliant psychology is in vain, because it does not apply to Dmitry.

216 683_{17}, $15:147_{28}$, "This torment of the soul"—translates *eto khozhdenie eio po mytarstvam,* where *mytarstvo,* "torment," is the expression that appears in the headings of chapters iii, iv, and v of Book Nine. The result is a deep irony: Ippolit Kirillovich sees the "torments of the soul" in a man's desperate, "animal-like" struggle for self-preservation, while the real torments of Dmitry's soul were caused by the painful death of his former self, and the birth of a new self.

217 683_{26-27}, $15:147_{36-37}$, "That was our fence for the moment and behind it we hoped to throw up a barricade of some sort."—This is where Ippolit Kirillovich's psychology really begins to pick up steam. Every fact is explained as another proof of Dmitry's guilt. But the alert reader can recognize the flaws in the prosecutor's argument, flaws which will be used by the counsel for the defense to reverse every single position of the prosecution.

218 684_{15-16}, $15:148_{21-22}$, ". . . and how he respectfully withdrew"—the old refrain again; cf. notes 179 and 201 above.

219 684_{24}, $15:148_{30}$, "romance"—translates *roman,* which means "romance" as well as "novel." At this stage, Ippolit Kirillovich becomes Dostoevsky's "dummy," used to present a theory of fiction which may very well apply to the novel at hand. See Introduction III.3.d. Art of the Novel.

220 684_{32-33}, $15:148_{38-39}$, "We had such a fact in readiness"—now Ippolit Kirillovich is simply bragging: he fancies that he has been in full control of things all along. The truth is that he was taken in by the false evidence of a stubborn and stupid old man, and duped by a clever murderer.

221 685_{7-13}, $15:149_{12-17}$, The key issue of Dostoevsky's theory of the novel: what is more important—accuracy of realistic detail or "grand invention as a whole"? Contrary to the theories of contemporary "realists," Dostoevsky believed that it was a novelist's power of vision that created truth in his art, rather than faithful copying of nature and writing "from the notebook." See, for example, *Diary of a Writer* (1873), 1:90–91.

222   $685_{14ff.}$, $15:149_{20ff.}$, Covers the same ground as Book Nine, chap. vii, pp. 469–70. It is one of the few links in the whole chain of events which the reader has been allowed to learn from hints and hearsay only, for reasons of novelistic composition (suspense and mystification).

223   685_{29-33}, $15:149_{35-39}$, "At the most terrible moments of man's life . . ."—These details may or may not be autobiographic. Dostoevsky himself had been taken to Semionovsky Square, the place of his anticipated execution on 22 December 1849, in a closed carriage. Cf. note 212 above.

224   685_{33-37}, $15:149_{39-43}$, The translation does not make it quite clear that this is *erlebte Rede*—Dmitry's thoughts, as imagined by the prosecutor and broken through the prism of the latter's ironic consciousness. Perhaps: "But wasn't he hiding from his landlord's family as he was sewing his little bag, doesn't he remember how he suffered from a humiliating fear that someone might come in and find him needle in hand," etc.

225   686_{17-19}, $15:150_{20-22}$, It is the irony of this passage that the author of this novel is himself a believer in holy Russia, "her principles, her family, everything she holds sacred." Now these principles are to be upheld by the conviction of an innocent man.

226   686_{24-27}, $15:150_{27-32}$, "Our fatal troika"—cf. chap. vi, p. 660_{22-33}, and note 135 above.

227   686_{29-36}, $15:150_{32-40}$, Ippolit Kirillovich's Cassandran message essentially coincides with warnings often voiced by Dostoevsky in his own name. Ippolit Kirillovich, a liberal westernizer, sees the danger in terms of Russia's relapse into barbarism and her subsequent chastisement by the civilized West. Dostoevsky believed that the Russian catastrophe would be resolved by a religious revolution. Cf. note 230 below.

228   687_{6}, $15:151_{6-7}$, " 'the Bernards!' "—see note 66 above.

229   $687_{18ff.}$, $15:151_{21ff.}$, Some internal commentary, allowing the reader to review highlights of the prosecutor's speech.

230   688_{24-26}, $15:152_{21-24}$, "Why, in the English Parliament . . ."— Alludes to p. 686_{29-36}. We have here another slight anachronism, as the political situation referred to is that of 1876, rather than that of a decade earlier. Relations between Britain and Russia were strained in 1876; the British were wary of Russian efforts to liberate the Balkan Slavs from Turkish rule, seeing this as a pretext for a move to Constantinople and the Mediterranean. In a political article of September 1876, Dostoevsky had written:

"And so Viscount Beaconsfield—an Israelite by birth (né Disraeli)—in an address at some banquet, suddenly divulges to Europe an extraordinary secret, to the effect that all those Russians, headed by Cherniaev, who rushed into Turkey to save the Slavs—that they all are Russian socialists, communists, communards—briefly, all those Russian destructive elements with which Russia is supposedly loaded . . . 'Europe should take notice of this threatening force.'—Beaconsfield stresses, menacing the English farmers with future socialism in Russia and in the East" (*Diary of a Writer*, 2:430–31).

Chapter x

231 688_{38-39}, $15:152_{35}$, "An Argument That Cuts Both Ways."—The Russian expression is lit. "A Stick with Two Ends."

232 $688_{41}-689_9$, $15:152_{37}-153_2$, Note once more Dostoevsky's careful attention to details of style, intonation, and verbal mannerisms.

233 689_{6-7}, $15:152_{45}-153_1$, " 'pierce the heart with untold power' "—a quotation from Pushkin's poem "Answer to an Anonymous Correspondent" (1830).

234 689_{9-14}, $15:153_{2-8}$, The "bending" into what seems an unnaturally distorted position is a suggestive symbolic detail. Cf. note 24 above.

235 689_{36-38}, $15:153_{31-33}$, "an overwhelming chain of evidence . . . and at the same time not one fact that will stand criticism"—a principle which the detective in *Crime and Punishment* states thus: "Thirty rabbits won't make one horse." The truth is indivisible. Fetiukovich will attack the prosecutor's fiction exactly the way the latter attacked Dmitry's alleged "romance": by demolishing its details. Cf. note 217 above.

236 690_{9-16}, $15:154_{1-9}$, We already know the lady who received Dmitry. Cf. Book Nine, chap. ii, p. $427_{6, 26-28}$.

237 690_{29-34}, $15:154_{23-29}$, "But there are things . . ."—Fetiukovich now launches into a parody of the prosecutor's sarcastic put-down of Dmitry's story, which he had called a "romance" (chap. ix, p. 685_4). This introduces another topic of Dostoevsky's theory of fiction: the work of fiction which has "vision," but a false vision. Such works are harmful because they propagate falsehoods in a convincing way. See, for instance, Dostoevsky's assessment of I. A. Goncharov's successful novel *The Precipice*

(1869), which Dostoevsky claimed was based on "such a decrepit, empty idea, and quite untrue besides" (letter to N. N. Strakhov, 26 February/10 March 1869, *Pis'ma* 2:169).

238    $690_{42ff.}$, $15:154_{38ff.}$, "The defendant, running away . . ."—Refers to chap. viii, pp. 678_{44}–679_{12}.

239   692_{6-11}, $15:156_{2-8}$, Dostoevsky uses Fetiukovich to express his own critical view of the powers of the science of psychology. See Introduction II.6.a. Dostoevsky's Psychology.

Chapter xi

240   692_{17}, $15:156_{14}$, "There Was No Money."—Legally speaking, Fetiukovich shows that the robbery charge is based on hearsay evidence. Symbolically, the treatise on fact and fiction continues. We reach the conclusion that what poses as fact is merely a "figure of fact," epistemologically of the same order as a "figure of fiction."

241   692_{42-43}, $15:156_{39-40}$, "the fine and spotless linen with which the bed had been purposely made"—this little detail once more calls back the mad excitement of Fiodor Pavlovich's last days.

242   694_{4-16}, $15:157_{44}$–158_{10}, This account is based on a real murder case, reported in the Petersburg papers in 1878–79. See *PSS* 15:600.

243   694_{32}, $15:158_{26-27}$, Ann Radcliffe's gothic romance *The Mysteries of Udolpho* (1794) was popular in Russia in Dostoevsky's youth. Here it is featured as a romance *par excellence,* totally a figment of the imagination.

244   694_{38-39}, $15:158_{33-34}$, "And we are ready to ruin a man's life with such romances!"—A figure of fiction can be just as potent as a strong fact: it can ruin a man's life.

245   694_{44}–695_1, $15:158_{39-40}$, "nothing can be more probable"—in the original, repeated negative markers (*ne* and *ni*) make for quite exaggerated emphasis: *nikogda nichego ne moglo i ne mozhet byt' veroiatnee.* Fetiukovich signals that he is determined to go one up on the prosecutor, who had called Dmitry's story "not only an absurdity, but the most improbable invention that could have been brought forward in the circumstances" (chap. ix, p. 685_{4-5}).

246   695_{10-12}, $15:158_{47}$–159_1, "What if you've been weaving a romance, and about quite a different kind of man?"—Another aspect of the figure of fiction: our image of another human being

is inevitably a fiction. The prosecutor's version of the course of events is necessarily based on his particular fiction of Dmitry's character.

247   695₃₄₋₃₅, 15:159₂₃₋₂₄, "I will not touch on it either, but will only venture to observe"—Fetiukovich shows that he can use the devices of Ciceronian rhetoric, too: he pretends that he is not taking advantage of a point in his client's favor, then calmly proceeds to exploit it to the hilt, and with some very unchivalrous reflections on Miss Verkhovtsev's character, too.

248   696₁₁₋₁₂, 15:159₄₆₋₄₇, "Karamazov is just such a two-sided nature, fluctuating between two extremes"—here the translation misses a philosophic point implicit in the original text: "two-sided nature" translates *natura o dvukh storonakh,* and "fluctuating between two extremes" translates *o dvukh bezdnakh,* where both expressions clearly parallel the expression featured in the heading of chapter x, *palka o dvukh kontsakh,* lit. "a stick with two ends" (translated by "An Argument That Cuts Both Ways"). Thus, a statement relating to psychological method has been expanded into a statement regarding the nature of man: psychology is inherently ambiguous, because man is.

249   697₃₇₋₃₈, 15:161₁₆, "Isn't that, too, a romance?"—One must remember that "romance" translates *roman,* which has a broader meaning than the English word (see note 219 above). Perhaps "fiction" should have been used all along.

Chapter xii

250   698₉₋₁₀, 15:161₃₀₋₃₁, "you will remember how a whole edifice of psychology was built on that pestle"—refers to chap. vii, p. 670₂₃*ff.*. "Edifice" is ironic, because Ippolit Kirillovich's attempt to prove premeditation from Dmitry's having armed himself with that pestle was a makeshift structure that would collapse if touched ever so lightly, which is exactly what happens now.

251   698₃₆₋₃₇, 15:162₁₂, "What reason have we to call that letter 'fatal' rather than absurd?"—Here "absurd" translates *smeshnoe,* "funny, droll, ridiculous, ludicrous" (from *smekh,* "laughter," hence also "laughable"), which is precisely the point. The word "fatal" (*rokovoe,* from *rok,* "fate") belongs to the domain of tragedy, while the "ludicrous," of course, belongs to comedy. The tragic and the comic are, certainly in Dostoevsky's aesthetics, different sides of the same coin. Once

again, a situation of "real life" becomes clear through the application to it of a literary model. Just as a figure of fact can always change into a figure of fiction, and vice versa, so tragedy can always change to comedy.

252   699_{7-8}, $15:162_{27-28}$, The original has lit. "if not respectfulness of feeling, so piety of feeling." Ironically, the presumably godless Fetiukovich, whom Dmitry had called a "Bernard" (Book Eleven, chap. iv, p. 562_{10}), comes up with this metaphysical version of the father-son theme: filial piety, it is suggested, is as innate a human quality as piety itself. The fact that Dmitry thought he had no reason to respect his father could not change this. See Introduction II.3.a. Fatherhood.

253   699_{18-19}, $15:162_{39}$, "the subtlest imagination"—translates *samogo tonkogo romanista,* lit. "the subtlest novelist." Dostoevsky repeats his leitmotifs and key words a great deal more often than the translation shows.

254   699_{42-45}, $15:163_{11-14}$, "And yet the prosecutor allowed him love . . ."—Refers to chap. ix, pp. 681_{46}–682_{15}.

255   699_{46}–700_1, $15:163_{14-15}$, "have you not invented a new personality?"—Once again a problem of novelistic technique is foregrounded. Critics of Dostoevsky's day (N. A. Dobroliubov, for example) had drawn attention to the fact that novelists pretend to know their heroes better than any person could ever hope to know a human being in real life. Hence there is the temptation to believe that the characters—in fact, the whole world—created by a novelist are objectively "real."

256   700_{40-43}, $15:164_{4-8}$, Here the translation misses a nuance. The original has, lit.: "But isn't it true that there are some others who accuse him, too: there is this certain ferment, in society, of a certain question, of a certain suspicion, a certain indistinct rumor is heard, there is a feeling that a certain expectation exists. Finally, there is evidence, too, of a certain combination of facts, most characteristic, though I admit inconclusive." There are as many as seven indefinite pronouns in this sentence. Fetiukovich has reached a weak spot in his argument and tries to slur over it. In fact, he appears to be mumbling for a moment.

257   701_{8-10}, $15:164_{21-23}$, In the original, there is a heavy accumulation of modal expressions here. Literally: "But nevertheless, Smerdiakov's name has still been pronounced, once again it is as though something mysterious were in the air. It is as if there were something here that hasn't been fully revealed,

gentlemen of the jury, nor completed.'' Fetiukovich is mumbling again. He knows that he is skating on very thin ice and tries not to commit himself in any decisive way.

258 701_{12}, $15:164_{25}$, "The court has resolved to go on with the trial"—an important legal point, perhaps the basis for an appeal (cf. note 59 above). The death of a key witness (Smerdiakov) and the severe illness of another (Ivan) apparently had caused Fetiukovich to plead for a postponement. A court of appeals may rule that the rejection of his motion was unreasonable.

259 701_{13-40}, $15:164_{26}-165_6$, It is tempting to see in Fetiukovich's character sketch of Smerdiakov an allegory of Russia's westernization on the level of the uneducated. The murder of Smerdiakov's natural father, instigated by his "legitimate" half-brother, the atheist intellectual Ivan, is then an allegory of the threatening social revolution. See Introduction II.1.b. The Apocalyptic Allegory.

260 701_{41-43}, $15:165_{7-9}$, "The destination of that sum . . . must have been hateful to him."—The three brothers, lovers of women like their father, could at least understand the old man's infatuation. Smerdiakov, who has the face of a eunuch and hates women, must have found his master's passion merely contemptible. Cf. Book Eleven, chap. viii, p. 596_{14}.

261 $702_{12ff.}$, $15:165_{22ff.}$, Here Fetiukovich patently allows his imagination to wander. He is not even pretending that things actually happened this way. But he zeroes in on the very truth of the event anyway, a triumph of the creative imagination. The moral of it all is that the fiction of a truly imaginative mind is more likely to hit upon the truth than the "scientific" speculation of a pedestrian mind.

262 $702_{43}-703_4$, $15:166_{5-11}$, ". . . I thought as I listened that I was hearing something very familiar . . ."—it is familiar to the reader, too: see Book Eleven, chap. viii, p. 597_{20-45}.

263 703_{26-31}, $15:166_{35-40}$, ". . . Despair and penitence are two very different things . . ."—Here Fetiukovich is not merely clever, but profound. Smerdiakov's suicide note ("I destroy my life of my own will and and desire, not to blame anyone") contains a diabolic irony: by destroying himself, he assures Dmitry's conviction and deprives Ivan of a chance to relieve himself of his guilt.

264 703_{36-38}, $15:166_{46-47}$, "I swear by all that is sacred . . ."— judging by Dmitry's impression (Book Eleven, chap. iv, p. 562_{10})

and by the following chapter, especially its heading, Fetiukovich
is perjuring himself: like everyone else, he believes Dmitry to be
guilty. But then, he has come so very close to seeing—and
showing—the truth of the case. He may believe in his version of
it, as an artist of genius believes in the truth of his own creation.
See Introduction III.3.d. Art of the Novel.

265　703$_{38-42}$, 15:166$_{47}$-167$_3$, "What troubles me . . ."—Once more,
Fetiukovich's dilemma illustrates a key problem of artistic
creation. According to the organic conception of the work of art,
in which Dostoevsky believed, the whole is more than the sum of
its parts. Yet it is also understood that if any part of the whole is
flawed, the whole must be faulty, too. The prosecutor, who
sincerely believes in the truth of his preconceived notion, is an
inferior artist: the flawed details of his fiction betray his whole
work. Fetiukovich may not have a sincere belief in anything, but
he is a gifted artist whose intuitive grasp of each detail produces
the truth. The inevitable corollary of this seems to be that it is
more important to be a true artist than an honest man!

266　704$_{2-3}$, 15:167$_{9-10}$, "the power to bind and to loose"—
Fetiukovich is alluding to Matt. 16:19, frivolously, it would
seem.

267　704$_{15-16}$, 15:167$_{24-27}$, "with a note of such sincerity"—this
clashes with the chapter heading immediately following.

Chapter xiii

268　704$_{32-33}$, 15:167$_{42}$, "But it's not an ordinary case of murder, it's
a case of parricide."—In Russian, *ottseubiistvo*, "parricide," is,
as it were, *ubiistvo*, "murder," in a higher power. This brings
out the metaphysical aspect of the crime. See Introduction II.3.a.
Fatherhood.

269　704$_{35-38}$, 15:168$_{1-3}$, "how can such a defendant be acquitted
. . ."—Precisely this kind of thinking had caused the—likewise
innocent—prototype of Dmitry, lieutenant D. N. Il'insky, to be
arrested and eventually sent to prison, even though there was no
conclusive evidence of his guilt. Tsar Nicholas I had personally
ordered that Il'insky be removed from the army and kept a
prisoner indefinitely, because it could not be tolerated that a
man under so terrible a suspicion remain in the army. See Introduction I.6.b. Il'insky and Dmitry Karamazov, and *PSS*
4:284-85.

270   704_{39}–705_2, $15:168_{3-10}$, The theme of fatherhood is foregrounded and hypostatized. Note that fatherhood is called a "great idea." See Introduction II.3.a. Fatherhood.

271   705_{36-37}, $15:168_{42-43}$, ". . . like a beast of the field"—echoes the story of the murderer Richard, one of Ivan's examples of innocent suffering. See Book Five, chap. iv, p. 220_{35}.

272   706_{5-9}, $15:169_{8-12}$, The idea of the psychological paradox is foregrounded. See Introduction II.6.d. Psychological Wisdom.

273   706_{24-25}, $15:169_{29}$, "however much the expression has been ridiculed"—by "progressive" positivists, such as the devil in Book Eleven, chap. ix.

274   706_{33-36}, $15:169_{37-40}$, "The Lover of Mankind" translates *raspiatyi chelovekoliubets,* lit. "the crucified lover of man(kind)," which is the secular verbiage of Renan and Strauss. The following quotation (John 10:11) is inappropriate and therefore frivolous. Cf. Book Two, chap. vi, p. 65_{11}, and note 165.

275   706_{42-43}, $15:169_{45-46}$, "Filial love for an unworthy father is an absurdity, an impossibility."—Fetiukovich now reduces "fatherhood" to a positivistic social and psychological concept: only a father who serves his children well deserves the name of a father. This thinking is analogous to Ivan's rebellion against God the Father: a God who does not serve men to their satisfaction, like a father who fails to satisfy the needs of his children, is rejected.

276   707_{42-43}, $15:169_{47-48}$, " 'Fathers, provoke not your children to wrath' "—Col. 3:21, which Fetiukovich quotes out of context. The verse continues: "lest they be discouraged." The preceding verse reads: "Children, obey your parents in all things: for this is well pleasing unto the Lord."

277   707_5, $15:170_3$, *vivos voco!*—the epigraph of Schiller's "Song of the Bell" reads: *Vivos voco. Mortuos plango. Fulgura frango.* "I call the living. I mourn the dead. I break lightnings." The words *Vivos voco* were the motto of *The Bell,* the revolutionary newspaper of Herzen and Ogariov.

278   707_{16-17}, $15:170_{13-14}$, " 'What measure ye mete . . .' "—These words (Luke 6:38), quoted out of context, pervert Christ's message. Fetiukovich gives them the meaning of a social contract, while Christ speaks of God's love and mercy to which man responds with filial love and with mercy toward his fellow men.

Note that Fiodor Pavlovich had misused the same biblical quote (see Book Three, note 163).

279   707_{33-34}, $15:170_{28}$, "Moscow merchants' wives who are afraid of 'metal' and 'sulfur' "—here, "sulfur" translates *zhupel,* the Russian equivalent of the biblical "brimstone," which makes the women's fear understandable. Fetiukovich is alluding to Alexander Ostrovsky's play *Hard Days (Tiazholye dni,* 1863), Act II, sc. ii, where a Moscow merchant's wife fearfully asks not to be told of "sounding metal" (1 Cor. 13:1) or "brimstone" (Luke 17:29 and elsewhere). Dostoevsky alludes to the same passage in *Diary of a Writer* (1881), 2:1044. The commentators of *PSS* suggest that Dostoevsky is taking a swipe at the liberal critic E. L. Markov (1835–1903), who had challenged Dostoevsky's pessimistic assessment of the bourgeois "ideal," saying that, unlike Ostrovsky's merchants' wives, he, Markov, was not afraid of the "sound of metal" and "brimstone." Cf. Dostoevsky's letter to E. A. Stakenschneider, dated 15 June 1879 (*Pis'ma* 4:63).

280   707_{38}–708_2, $15:170_{31-38}$, Fetiukovich's rejection of the "mystical meaning" of fatherhood now becomes an explicit allegory of the liberal atheists' rejection of the "mystical meaning" of godhood.

281   708_{23-30}, $15:171_{14-21}$, "The youth involuntarily reflects . . ."— This argument is taken from Schiller's drama *The Robbers,* Act I, sc. i, and Act IV, sc. ii. In connection with the trial of the Kroneberg child-abuse case of 1876, Dostoevsky wrote in his notebook: "I gave birth to you.—Franz Moor's answer. I consider the reasoning of this depraved man correct." See *The Unpublished Dostoevsky,* 2:123. *The Brothers Karamazov,* with its implied message of the absolute sanctity of fatherhood, is then a step forward from an earlier position. Cf. note 33 above.

282   708_{32-33}, $15:171_{23-24}$, " 'Drive nature out of the door and it will fly in at the window' "—a quotation from Lafontaine's fable "La Chatte métamorphosée en Femme" [The cat who was changed into a woman] in N. M. Karamzin's translation. See *PSS* 15:603. We have heard such enthusiastic acceptance of nature before: from the devil (Book Eleven, chap. ix, p. 614_{4-5}). Fetiukovich and the devil embrace precisely those sides of being "human" which Christianity teaches man to overcome.

283   708_{46}–709_1, $15:171_{38-39}$, Fetiukovich's smug positivism was the

modern and progressive thing in the 1860s. Hence the "frantic applause."

284   709_8, $15:171_{46-47}$, "old men with stars on their breasts"—major decorations were worn on the breast, so these men must have served the Tsar meritoriously in important positions. They are "fathers" in more than one sense—yet they, too, applaud.

285   709_{12}, $15:172_1$, "Fetiukovich, excited and triumphant"—a subtle signal of the orator's imminent downfall.

286   709_{36-37}, $15:172_{23-26}$, "It was an impulse of madness and insanity, but also an impulse of nature"—"impulse" translates *affekt* (see Book Eleven, note 45). Fetiukovich's version of the encounter between father and son may be read as anticipating Freud's Oedipal interpretation as stated in his essay "Dostoevsky and Parricide" (1928). Dmitry had himself given a somewhat similar version (Book Three, chap. v, p. 110_{35-40}). But his version is a fiction, never realized.

287   709_{45}–710_2, $15:172_{30-34}$, "Such a murder is not a murder . . ."—Here Fetiukovich's casuistry turns into a travesty. But Dostoevsky had seen Petersburg lawyers win acquittal for their clients with arguments as transparently frivolous, as in the Kroneberg child-abuse case, for instance. Cf. note 33 above.

288   710_{5-10}, $15:172_{36-40}$, Brings back the case of Richard (Book Five, chap. iv, p. $220_{30ff.}$), but without its conclusion. Dmitry's actual fate will bring the stories together even closer. Cf. note 271 above.

289   710_{8-10}, $15:172_{38-40}$, An obvious—and inappropriate—allusion to Matt. 25:35–36.

290   710_{16-17}, $15:172_{45-46}$, "the possibility of becoming a new man"—translates *vozmozhnogo eshchio cheloveka,* lit. "a still possible man." The empiricist Fetiukovich does not believe in innate good and evil but thinks that man is a product of his environment.

291   710_{19-22}, $15:172_{47}$–173_2, Fetiukovich's argument has degenerated into a travesty. It begins to remind one of Mme. Kokhlakov's tirade in Book Eleven, chap. ii, p. $546_{25ff.}$. The travesty is enhanced by the fact that Dmitry is, after all, innocent.

292   710_{34-35}, $15:173_{13-14}$, "I am guilty in the sight of all men and am more unworthy than all.' "—Suddenly, in the middle of Fetiukovich's unctuous harangue, we hear the voice of Father

Zosima. For a moment the lie becomes truth, for Dmitry is in fact willing to say these words, even though he is not guilty as charged.

293   710_{39-41}, $15:173_{19-21}$, "Better acquit ten guilty men . . ."—these words are found in Peter the Great's *Code of Martial Law* (1716). They are also found in the *Code of Laws of the Russian Empire* of 1876. See *PSS* 15:603.

294   710_{44-46}, $15:173_{22-25}$, "Let other nations think of retribution . . ."—This may sound like a sarcasm but is not. While Russia's penal system was certainly no better than that of other nations, and probably worse than most, her criminal code and criminal trial procedures were decidedly a bright spot in the record of postreform Russia. And Russian juries were often very lenient indeed.

295   711_{2-5}, $15:173_{26-29}$, The liberal Fetiukovich's version of the troika image introduced by the prosecutor (chap. ix, p. 686_{24-33}) is far more optimistic than the latter's.

Chapter xiv

296   711_{10}, $15:173_{34}$, "The Peasants Stand Firm"—translates *Muzhichki za sebia postoiali,* lit. "The Peasants Stood up for Themselves."

297   711_{16}, $15:173_{40}$, "something sacred"—blatant mockery, for the ladies' enthusiasm has been called forth by frivolous sophistry.

298   711_{33-35}, $15:174_{12-15}$, ". . . a romance in the Byronic style"— the commentators of *PSS* suggest that this may be a specific allusion to Byron's "Parisina" (1816), whose hero, Hugo, is the illegitimate son of Azo, Duke of Ferrara. Hugo develops a criminal love affair with Parisina, his father's young wife. They are discovered and condemned to death. Before bending his head to the ax, Hugo bitterly reproaches his father:

> "Thou gav'st, and may'st resume my breath,
>   A gift for which I thank thee not;
>   Nor are my mother's wrongs forgot,
>   Her slighted love and ruined name,
>   Her offspring's heritage of shame."

Obviously the rivalry of father and son for Parisina's love applies to Dmitry and Fiodor Pavlovich, rather than to Smerdiakov.

299 712$_6$, 15:174$_{26-27}$, "only a bogey"—in the original, *'zhupel,'* "brimstone," alluding to chap. xiii, p. 707$_{34}$ (see note 279 above).

300 712$_{7-11}$, 15:174$_{27-30}$, Here Dostoevsky lets the prosecutor say essentially what he himself had written in his article on the Kroneberg child-abuse case of 1876: "Yes, skillful defense lawyer, there is a limit to everything, and if only I had not known that you are saying all this purposively, that you are pretending to the best of your ability to save your client, I should have added, specifically for your own benefit, that there is even a limit to all sorts of 'lyres' and advocates' 'responsiveness,' and that the limit consists in that one should not be giving vent to the verbosity which has led you, Mr. Defense Lawyer, as far afield as the pillars of Hercules (*Diary of a Writer,* 1:232). Cf. note 33 above.

301 712$_{16-36}$, 15:174$_{36}$–175$_7$, "Religion and the Gospel are corrected"—here Ippolit Kirillovich becomes Dostoevsky's spokesman, without any admixture of irony. In his reportage on the Kairov case (1876), Dostoevsky had taken the counsel for the defense to task for frivolously bending the meaning of the Gospel to his own ends (*Diary of a Writer,* 1:329–30). Fetiukovich's "crucified lover of humanity" is clearly the Christ of Renan, and not the Christ of the Orthodox church. Ippolit Kirillovich is quite right when he accuses Fetiukovich of perverting the meaning of the Gospel quotation "What measure ye mete so it shall be meted unto you again" (cf. chap. xiii, p. 707$_{16-17}$, and note 278 above). The words "For Thou art our God!" appear in many prayers of the breviary.

302 712$_{45-46}$, 15:175$_{16-17}$, "Jupiter, you are angry . . ."—I have not been able to ascertain the source of this saying. It is called an "old saying" in chapter iii of Ivan Turgenev's novel *Rudin* (1855).

303 713$_8$, 15:175$_{25}$, "a personal insinuation"—the original has *insinuatsiiu* in quotation marks: it is a rare word in Russian and therefore more ominous than Eng. "insinuation." Here Fetiukovich is hitting below the belt: he is accusing Ippolit Kirillovich of what to every educated Russian was the lowest of actions—denunciation of a fellow citizen to the "authorities."

304 713$_{24-25}$, 15:175$_{40-41}$, "The hour of judgment has come for me"—Dmitry speaks of God's judgment, and before God he is guilty. No one in the courtroom save only Aliosha is capable of

seeing things in these terms. Dmitry has outgrown his human judges. The eloquence of prosecutor and defender alike pales before the power of his words.

305   713_{37-38}, $15:176_{3-4}$, "I'll break my sword over my head myself . . ."—breaking a sword over a condemned man's head was part of the ceremony called "civil execution," a ceremony to which Chernyshevsky had been subjected on 19 May 1864. By promising to kiss the broken sword, Dmitry accepts this extreme punishment.

306   714_{12-13}, $15:176_{21-22}$, "a dramatic moment or general enthusiasm"—"or" is a misprint for "of." To these people, the trial has been a spectacle which is now to reach its happy climax.

307   714_{19-23}, $15:176_{28-31}$, The "clever man" is about to get his comeuppance. The narrator does not try to conceal his glee at Fetiukovich's downfall.

308    $714_{46}-715_1$, $15:177_{4-5}$, "But it was a pity they dragged the lackey in . . ."—The *non plus ultra* of the *quid pro quo* of "fact" and "fiction": the truth has become an absurdity.

309   715_{3-4}, $15:177_{6-7}$, " 'What the hell!' "—In the original, lit. "go to the devil," reminding us that the devil is still around.

310   715_{7-8}, $15:177_{10-12}$, The case alluded to is that of the actress Kairov, who had attempted to cut the throat of one Mrs. Velikanov, wife of Kairov's lover, with a razor. She was acquitted on grounds of temporary insanity. Dostoevsky, in his reportage of the trial, was happy with the acquittal (although he found the "temporary insanity" plea laughable), but was critical of the defender's tactics of smearing Mrs. Velikanov in order to create sympathy for his client and, in effect, praising the latter for her crime. See *Diary of a Writer* (1876), 1:312–30.

311   715_{15-20}, $15:177_{18-23}$, "Think of Ippolit and his fate . . ."—bathos! We are witnessing a tragedy, yet there is so much comedy everywhere around it. We are familiar with the lady's dental troubles (Book Nine, chap. ii, p. 427_{26-28}).

312   715_{26-28}, $15:177_{29-31}$, "The devil's bound to have a hand in it."—Deep irony: the joker does not know how true this is.

313   716_{25}, $15:178_{22}$, "and broke into a terrible sobbing wail"—lit. "and broke into sobs, loud, terribly." This terrifying acoustic image seals the notion, carefully prepared by a number of earlier images, that Dmitry, too, is one of those innocently suffering children of whom Ivan had spoken in Book Five, chap. iv.

314   716_{35}, $15:178_{31}$, "He'll have a twenty years' trip to the
mines!''—Dostoevsky let Dmitry be sentenced to twenty years at
hard labor, apparently because his prototype, Il'insky, had been
serving twenty years, overlooking the fact that, according to the
criminal code then in force, the premeditated murder of a parent
carried a mandatory life sentence. See B. G. Reizov, "K istorii
zamysla *Brat'ev Karamazovykh*," in *Iz istorii evropeiskikh
literatur* (Leningrad, 1971), p. 135.

315   716_{37}, $15:178_{33}$,   The correct translation is: "Well, our peasants
stood up for themselves" (cf. note 296 above). It is difficult to
imagine a more ambiguous ending. The voice of the people has
spoken. The "peasants" have turned back Fetiukovich. They
have stood up for themselves, for fatherhood, and for traditional
morality. But in so doing they have been instrumental in a
miscarriage of justice. If the saying *vox populi, vox dei* is
correct—and there is every reason to assume that Dostoevsky
believes it is—a miscarriage of justice and Dmitry's innocent suffering is what God has willed.

Epilogue

Chapter i

1 717_{20-21}, $15:179_{21-22}$, "they could not yet give them positive hopes of recovery"—this is as much as we will hear of Ivan's fate, but some earlier hints suggest that he will recover. See Introduction III.3.e. Expository Novel.

2 717_{32-33}, $15:180_{1-2}$, "that hero of honor and conscience"— Katerina Ivanovna stubbornly clings to a fiction which she has created for herself.

3 717_{40}, $15:180_{8-9}$, We now learn the "secret" of Book Eleven, chap. iv.

4 718_{3-4}, $15:180_{13-14}$, Refers to Book Eleven, chap. v, p. $566_{35ff.}$

5 718_{12}, $15:180_{23}$, "with that creature"—"that creature" is the only way in which Katerina Ivanovna will refer to her rival. In the original, *tvar'*, "creature," appears five times within a little over ten lines. This sets up a sudden counterpoint on p. 719_{43-44}.

6 718_{28-31}, $15:180_{41-42}$, "Then he left me money . . ."—This suggests that Katerina Ivanovna ought to know that the three thousand roubles which Ivan Fiodorovich had shown in court had indeed come from Smerdiakov. But, much as Ivan had suppressed the truth until finally breaking down, so Katerina Ivanovna stubbornly refuses to see it.

7 718_{35-41}, $15:180_{46}-181_5$, The perverseness of Katerina Ivanovna's enthusiastic approval of Ivan's perverse actions is signalled by her grotesquely inappropriate verbiage ("self-sacrifice") and hysterical overstatement ("kissing his feet").

8 719_{1-3}, $15:181_{13-14}$, Refers to Book Eleven, chap. v, p. 567_{31-32}.

9 719_{16-17}, $15:181_{26-27}$, "it would have been for some reason too painful to him"—what is meant is "but for some reason he felt that it would be too painful to him." "Sloppy" syntax often appears in emotion-laden passages. We are dealing with what

438

may be called a syntactic metaphor reflecting the mood of the
moment: its pain and embarrassment are enhanced by a tortured
syntax.

10   719_{35}, $15:181_{45-46}$, "viciously"—translates *s iadom,* lit. "with
venom." Also, "sanction" translates *sanktsiia,* a bookish word
which smacks of Ivan. Anyway, it enhances the irony.

11   719_{37-38}, $15:181_{47}-182_1$, The motif of the "hymn" is reintroduced. Cf. Book Eleven, chap. iv, p. 560_{35}.

12   719_{40-41}, $15:182_{3-4}$, "how he loved that wretched man"—this is
new: there has been no evidence of Ivan's love for Dmitry
anywhere before; hence, we must assume that it is all in Katerina
Ivanovna's mind.

13   719_{43-44}, $15:182_{6-7}$, "It is I who am the creature, me."—A
surprise, but her self-abasement is as much of a lie as everything
else she has said and done: she is not guilty before Ivan at all.

14   $719_{44}-720_4$, $15:182_{7-15}$, Katerina Ivanovna's words and feelings
are perceived through Aliosha's consciousness. "And it was she
who had betrayed him" must be understood as *erlebte Rede.*

15   720_{7-9}, $15:182_{18-19}$, ". . . unchristian, perhaps?"—reintroduces
a motif from Book Eleven, chap. iv, p. 564_{22-23} ("I would have
run away from crucifixion!"). This will be a key issue in the next
chapter (pp. 723–24).

Chapter ii

16   721_{20}, $15:183_{27}$, "For a Moment the Lie Becomes Truth"—This
chapter heading, as it were, establishes an antithesis to the
preceding chapter, which had dealt mainly with Katerina
Ivanovna's stubborn refusal to see the truth.

17   721_{26-27}, $15:183_{33}$, "the one where Smerdiakov had been"—
Dostoevsky uses every opportunity to establish links with other
parts of the novel.

18   722_{42-43}, $15:184_{43-45}$, The translation is somewhat ambiguous
here. "Does she?" refers to "She understands now," not to
"Katia . . . loves Ivan."

19   723_{3-4}, $15:185_{3-4}$, "That means that she is convinced he will die
. . ."—Dmitry knows the movements of Katerina Ivanovna's
perverse mind.

20   723_{18-19}, $15:185_{17}$, "They speak to me rudely as is."—
Translates *Storozha mne ty govoriat,* lit. "the guards say 'thou'

to me," i.e., they use the disrespectful second person singular, instead of "your honor," to which Dmitry the officer is accustomed.

21 723_{22}, $15:185_{19-20}$, "but if a guard speaks to me"—in the original lit. "but if a guard says 'thou' to me."

22 723_{39}, $15:185_{36}$, "The advocate was right about that."—Refers to Book Twelve, chap. xiii, p. 710_{10}. So great is Aliosha's love for his brother he is willing to turn "Jesuit" (cf. p. 724_{10} below), or "Fetiukovich," for his sake.

23 723_{40}, $15:185_{38-39}$, "Such heavy burdens are not for all men."— The commentators of *PSS* suggest that this is an echo of Matt. 23:4 and Luke 11:46.

24 724_{7-11}, $15:186_{3-7}$, "Mit'ka" is the disparaging and condescending form, while "Mitia" is the affectionate one. Dmitry thus expresses his contempt for himself if he should "run away from crucifixion" (cf. note 15 above).

25 724_{10}, $15:186_6$, "That's how the Jesuits talk, isn't it?"—The argument which Aliosha has advanced is exactly the one he had heard from Smerdiakov in Book Three, chap. vii, p. 116_{8-14}. Fiodor Pavlovich had called Smerdiakov a "stinking Jesuit" for it (p. 118_{12}).

26 724_{21}, $15:188_{18}$, "I hate that America"—a Russian's attitude toward America and what it stood for ("Americanism") pretty well determined his ideological position. Chernyshevsky's hero Lopukhov (in *What Is to Be Done?*) goes to America and is happy and successful there. Dostoevsky's attitude toward America is necessarily negative. Cf. Book Ten, note 128.

27 724_{38-39}, $15:186_{35}$, James Fenimore Cooper's *Last of the Mohicans* (1826) was very popular in Russia. Dmitry, though, knows that America is no longer the land of Cooper's romantic novel (which is set in colonial America).

28 724_{40}–725_2, $15:186_{36-41}$, This pipe dream of Dmitry's is a parody of the conclusion of *What Is to Be Done?* whose hero Lopukhov returns to Russia as Mr. Beaumont, an American citizen.

29 725_{28}, $15:187_{17}$, "It's the headstrong, evil Karamazov spirit!"—Translates *Bezuderzh karamazovskii, nechestivyi!* "Impious Karamazov abandon!" The word order suggests that *bezuderzh,* "abandon, lack of restraint, lack of discipline," is the cardinal evil. Dmitry now realizes that letting oneself go, as he has done all his life, is impious (*nechestivyi*).

30   725_{31-32}, $15:187_{20}$,   A reenactment of Katerina Ivanovna's first
     appearance at Dmitry's door (Book Three, chap. iv, p. 102_{8-9}),
     and the second epiphany of her noble and exalted soul. She will
     immediately relapse into the woman we know from most of the
     novel. See Edward Wasiolek, *Dostoevsky: The Major Fiction*
     (Cambridge, Mass., 1964), p. 185.

31   726_{24-26}, $15:188_{13-15}$,   ". . . but at that moment it was all true
     . . ."—as suggested even by the chapter heading, this sentence
     signals one of the highlights of the novel. The "romance" of
     Dmitry and Katerina Ivanovna has been a web of fictions,
     pretenses, and lies. For a moment, "the lie becomes truth," and
     this even though the words spoken here are "perhaps not even
     true." Dostoevsky's point is that truth is above and beyond
     differences of "fact" and "fiction," and independent of the
     meaning of human words.

32   726_{40-42}, $15:188_{30-32}$,   "but suddenly uttered a loud scream
     . . ."—in a dramatic scene such as this, Dostoevsky will often
     sustain the tension by discharging it into a new and even more
     explosive collision. Cf., for example, Book Three, chap. viii, p.
     126, where Aliosha's dramatic fit of hysterics has barely subsided
     when Dmitry bursts into his father's house.

33   727_{29-34}, $15:189_{18-23}$,   "I can't go with you to the funeral . . ."—
     Note the smooth transition to the *finale* of the novel.

Chapter iii

34   727_{43}, $15:189_{32}$,   "There were about twelve of them"—an
     allusion to Christ's twelve apostles. Dostoevsky had no qualms
     about using blatant biblical symbolism at strategic junctures of
     his novels.

35   728_{1-2}, $15:189_{33-34}$,   "Dad will cry, be with dad"—Iliusha's
     words are the words a father might have spoken on his deathbed.
     See Introduction II.3.a. Fatherhood.

36   728_{17}, $15:190_{7-8}$,   "an innocent victim for truth"—"truth"
     translates *pravda,* which also means "justice." As in some other
     instances, "truth and justice" may be the appropriate trans-
     lation. Cf. Book One, note 130.

37   728_{26}, $15:190_{12}$,   It should be "May our names perish." Kolia
     quotes the Girondist Pierre Victurnien Vergniaud (1753–93), who
     had said in the Convent, in 1792: *Perissent nos noms, pourvu que
     la chose publique soit sauvée!* There may be a touch of irony here

nevertheless. The phrase is quoted (in French) in Turgenev's note "Concerning *Fathers and Sons*" (1868–69). See I. S. Turgenev, *Sochineniia,* 14:105. Dostoevsky had mercilessly parodied several passages of this piece in *The Possessed.*

38 728_{28-31}, $15:190_{14-17}$, "the boy who . . . knew who had founded Troy . . ."—cf. Book Ten, chap. v, p. 520_{2-16}. Bringing in a set of familiar minor details helps establish the credibility of the whole scene.

39 728_{34-35}, $15:190_{20-21}$, "there was practically no smell from the corpse"—this detail may be a counterpoint to "The Odor of Corruption" of Book Seven, chap. i.

40 729_{4-7}, $15:190_{37-40}$, "old man"—translates *batiushka,* lit. "father, daddy." The word is often used in addressing males other than one's father. But this detail has been so clearly foregrounded here that its symbolic meaning will be obvious to most readers. See Introduction II.3.a. Fatherhood.

41 729_{26-28}, $15:191_{11-13}$, The stone used to be the Snegiriovs' favorite spot (Book Four, chap. vii, p. 189_{1-2}).This little episode creates a suitable transition to "The Speech at the Stone."

42 729_{32}, $15:191_{17}$, "by an unholy stone"—translates *u kamnia poganogo,* where *poganyi* has the original meaning of "pagan, heathen." The large boulder, a landmark, may very well have seen heathen rites before Christianity came to Russia. In a way, it is symbolic of the sacrament of fatherhood and sonhood, which is also older than the Church.

43 $730_{9ff.}$, $15:191_{39ff.}$, Dostoevsky had highlighted his debut as a writer with the moving description of a father's grief at his son's funeral. Now he finishes it with another version of the same scene. Old Pokrovsky in *Poor Folk* (1846) has a great deal in common with Snegiriov.

44 730_{20}, $15:192_1$, "And the crust of bread, we've forgotten the crust!"—A skilful transition to the "Franciscan" birds-of-heaven motif. Cf. Book Six, chap. ii, p. 268_{37-38}. Dostoevsky makes Snegiriov think he forgot the bread so that the detail can be brought up before the actual burial.

45 $730_{32ff.}$, $15:192_{14ff.}$, This passage is one of very few in all of Dostoevsky in which the beneficial effect of institutionalized religion and its ritual on a troubled human soul is shown.

46 731_{30}, $15:193_7$, "Flowers" has become a leitmotif of the scene, occurring in several different contexts.

47 731_{44-45}, $15:193_{20-21}$, "the boy who discovered about Troy"—in

the original: "the boy who had discovered Troy." By "correcting" Dostoevsky the translator spoils the effect.

48   731_{45}–732_2, $15{:}193_{22-24}$, Irony: this is perhaps the very same flock of sparrows which will keep Iliusha company over his grave.

49   732_{26-27}, $15{:}193_{47}$–194_2, Dostoevsky, a master of tear jerking, knows that an emotional effect is enhanced if attached to a concrete object. Iliusha's little boots belong with Sonia Marmeladov's green plaid shawl (*Crime and Punishment*) or Sof'ia Andreevna's white-and-blue checked handkerchief (*A Raw Youth*).

50   732_{40-41}, $15{:}194_{14}$, "if it were only possible to bring him back"—"to bring him back" translates *voskresit'*, "to resurrect." The leitmotif of the chapter, resurrection, comes in through the back door, as it were.

51   732_{44}, $15{:}194_{18}$, "He'll be drunk, you know."—The inevitable anticlimax.

52   733_{7-8}, $15{:}194_{7-8}$, "such sorrow and then pancakes . . ."—the "funeral dinner" (*pominki*), with the traditional pancakes, must predate Christianity: another motif, along with the "pagan stone" and breadcrumbs for the birds, establishing the idea of the interpenetration of the everyday world with religion.

53   733_{20-21}, $15{:}194_{40-41}$, ". . . Daddy, daddy, how he insulted you"—the reference is to Book Four, chap. vii, p. 190_{26}.

54   $733_{29ff.}$, $15{:}195_{1ff.}$, This is Aliosha's first sermon. It recapitulates the whole message of the novel.

55   733_{33}, $15{:}195_5$, "Iliusha's stone"—the commentators of *PSS* suggest that the stone is the symbolic foundation of "the edifice of a new harmony" started by Aliosha and his disciples, with Matt. 16:18 serving as the model. See *PSS* 15:586.

56   733_{45-46}, $15{:}195_{20}$, "My little doves"—the dove is a symbol of the Holy Ghost (Matt. 3:16, John 1:32), as well as of apostleship. Cf. Matlaw, *"The Brothers Karamazov,"* p. 30.

57   734_{5-7}, $15{:}198_{25-28}$, "some good memory"—Father Zosima's memory of his brother Markel immediately comes to mind. Iliusha's brief life, suffering, and death have not been in vain or senseless, much as Markel's was not. This is one part of the refutation of Ivan's argument in Book Five, chap. iv.

58   734_{15}, $15{:}195_{38-39}$, " 'I want to suffer for all men' "—from a double of Ivan's, Kolia has become a double of Dmitry's.

59   734_{40}, $15{:}196_{19}$, "he discovered the founders of Troy"—again

the translator has corrected Dostoevsky. In the original it is "he discovered Troy."

60   735_{15-16}, $15:196_{40-42}$,   "don't be afraid of life . . ."—the positive side of Karamazovism: love of life.

61   735_{26-31}, $15:197_{4-9}$, This confident assertion of faith in Resurrection is a proper conclusion for a novel whose author had only a few months to live.

BIBLIOGRAPHY
AND
INDEX

Bibliography

Dostoevsky's Works, Letters, and Notebooks

Dostoevskii, F. M. *Polnoe sobranie sochinenii v tridtsati tomakh.* [abbr. *PSS*]. Vols. 1–17. Leningrad, 1972–76.

Dostoevsky, Fyodor. *The Brothers Karamazov.* The Constance Garnett translation revised by Ralph E. Matlaw, with backgrounds and sources, essays in criticism. Ed. Ralph E. Matlaw. New York, 1976.

_____. *The Diary of a Writer.* Tr. and ed. Boris Brasol. 2 vols. New York and London, 1949.

_____. *F. M. Dostoevskii: Novye materialy i issledovaniia.* V. R. Shcherbina, chief ed. Literaturnoe nasledstvo, vol. 86. Moscow, 1973.

_____. *Neizdannyi Dostoevskii: Zapisnye knizhki i tetradi 1860–1881 gg.* V. R. Shcherbina, chief ed. Literaturnoe nasledstvo, vol. 83. Moscow, 1971.

_____. *The Notebooks for "The Brothers Karamazov."* Ed. and tr. Edward Wasiolek. Chicago and London, 1971.

_____. *The Notebooks for "Crime and Punishment."* Ed. and tr. Edward Wasiolek. Chicago and London, 1967.

_____. *The Notebooks for "The Idiot."* Ed. and with an introduction by Edward Wasiolek. Tr. Katharine Strelsky. Chicago and London, 1967.

_____. *The Notebooks for "The Possessed."* Ed. and with an introduction by Edward Wasiolek. Tr. Victor Terras. Chicago and London, 1968.

_____. *The Notebooks for "A Raw Youth."* Ed. and with an introduction by Edward Wasiolek. Tr. Victor Terras. Chicago and London, 1969.

_____. *Pis'ma.* Ed. A. S. Dolinin. 4 vols. Moscow and Leningrad, 1928–59.

_____. *The Unpublished Dostoevsky: Diaries and Notebooks, 1860–81.* Ed. Carl R. Proffer. 3 vols. Ann Arbor, 1973–76.

448 Bibliography

Other Works

Adrianova, V. P. *Zhitie Alekseia Cheloveka Bozhiia v drevnei russkoi literature i narodnoi slovesnosti.* Petrograd, 1917.

Al'tman, M. S. "Eshchio ob odnom prototipe Fiodora Pavlovicha Karamazova." *Voprosy literatury* 14, no. 3:252–55.

———. "Proobrazy startsa Zosimy." In *Dostoevskii i ego vremia,* ed. V. G. Bazanov and G. M. Fridlender, pp. 213–16. Leningrad, 1971.

Amend, V. E. "Theme and Form in *The Brothers Karamazov.*" *Modern Fiction Studies* 4:240–52.

Anderson, Roger B. "Mythical Implications of Father Zosima's Religious Teachings." *Slavic Review* 38:272–89.

Antonii, Preosviashchennyi. *Slovar'k tvoreniiam Dostoevskogo: Ne dolzhno otchaiavat'sia.* Sofia, 1921.

Askol'dov, S. "Religiozno-eticheskoe znachenie Dostoevskogo." In *Dostoevskii: Stat'i i materialy,* ed. A. S. Dolinin, pp. 1–32. Peterburg, 1922.

Bakhtin, Mikhail. *Problemy poetiki Dostoevskogo.* 2nd rev. ed. Moscow, 1963. In English as *Problems of Dostoevsky's Poetics.* Tr. R. W. Rotsel. Ann Arbor, 1973.

———. *Voprosy literatury i estetiki.* Moscow, 1975.

Belinskii, V. G. *Polnoe sobranie sochinenii.* 13 vols. Moscow, 1953–59.

Belknap, Robert L. "Dostoevsky's Nationalist Ideology and Rhetoric." *Review of National Literatures* 3, no. 1:89–100.

———. "Memory in *The Brothers Karamazov.*" In *American Contributions to the Eighth International Congress of Slavists, Zagreb and Ljubljana, September 3–9, 1978,* vol. 2, *Literature,* ed. Victor Terras, pp. 24–41. Columbus, O., 1978.

———. "The Origins of Alësa Karamazov." In *American Contributions to the Sixth International Congress of Slavists, Prague, August 7–13, 1968,* vol. 2, *Literary Contributions,* ed. William E. Harkins, pp. 7–28. The Hague, 1968.

———. "The Rhetoric of an Ideological Novel." In *Literature and Society in Imperial Russia, 1800–1914,* ed. William Mills Todd III, pp. 173–201. Stanford, 1978.

———. "The Sources of Mitja Karamazov." In *American Contributions to the Seventh International Congress of Slavists, Warsaw, August 21–27, 1973,* vol. 2, *Literature and Folklore,* ed. Victor Terras, pp. 39–51. The Hague and Paris, 1973.

———. *The Structure of "The Brothers Karamazov."* The Hague and Paris, 1967.

Bem [Boehm], A. L. "*Faust* v tvorchestve Dostoevskogo." Fascicle 5 of *Russkii Svobodnyi Universitet v Prage: Zapiski nauchno-issledovatel'skogo ob"edineniia*, pp. 109–43. Prague, 1973.

Berdiaev, Nikolai. *Mirosozertsanie Dostoevskogo*. Prague, 1923.

Berlin, P. "Dostoevskii i evrei." *Novyi zhurnal* 83:263–72.

Bitsilli, P. M. "K voprosu o vnutrennei forme romana Dostoevskogo." In *O Dostoevskom: Stat'i*, ed. Donald Fanger, pp. 1–72. Brown University Slavic Reprints, 4. Providence, 1966.

――――. "Pochemu Dostoevskii ne napisal 'Zhitiia velikogo greshnika'?" In *O Dostoevskom*, ed. A. L. Bem, 2:25–30. 3 vols. Prague, 1929–36.

Blagoi, D. "Put' Alioshi Karamazov." *Izvestiia Akademii Nauk* 33: 8–26.

Bocharov, S. G. "O dvukh pushkinskikh reministsentsiiakh v *Brat'iakh Karamazovykh.*" In *Dostoevskii: Materialy i issledovaniia*, 2:145–53. Leningrad, 1976.

Borshchevskii, S. S. *Shchedrin i Dostoevskii: Istoriia ikh ideinoi bor'by*. Moscow, 1956.

Børtnes, Jostein. "Aleša." In *Dostoevskijstudier*. Oslo, 1968.

Braun, Maximilian. "*The Brothers Karamazov* as an Expository Novel." *Canadian-American Slavic Studies* 6:199–208.

――――. *Dostojewskij: Das Gesamtwerk als Vielfalt und Einheit*. Göttingen, 1976.

Camus, Albert. *The Rebel: An Essay on Man in Revolt*. Tr. Anthony Bower. New York, 1956.

Chaitin, Gilbert D. "Religion as Defense: The Structure of *The Brothers Karamazov.*" *Literature and Psychology* 22:69–87.

Chetverikov, Sergii. *Moldavskii starets Paisii Velichkovskii: Ego zhizn', uchenie i vliianie na pravoslavnoe monashestvo*. Paris, 1976. In English as *Starets Paisii Velichkovskii: His Life, Teachings and Influence on Orthodox Monasticism*. Belmont, Mass., 1977.

Chicherin, A. V. "Rannie predshestvenniki Dostoevskogo." In *Dostoevskii i russkie pisateli: Traditsii, novatorstvo, masterstvo*, ed. V. Ia. Kirpotin, pp. 355–74. Moscow, 1971.

Chulkov, Georgii. *Kak rabotal Dostoevskii*. Moscow, 1939.

――――. "Poslednee slovo Dostoevskogo o Belinskom." In *Dostoevskii*, pp. 61–82. Moscow, 1928.

Cox, Roger L. "The Grand Inquisitor." In *Between Earth and Heaven: Shakespeare, Dostoevsky, and the Meaning of Christian Tragedy*, pp. 192–214. New York, 1969.

Čyževs'kyj, D. "Schiller und die *Brüder Karamazov.*" *Zeitschrift für slavische Philologie* 6:1–42.

Dal', Vladimir. *Tolkovyi slovar' zhivogo velikorusskogo iazyka.* 4 vols. 1880–82. Reprint ed., Moscow, 1955.

Danow, David K. "Structural Principles of *The Brothers Karamazov.*" Ph.D. dissertation, Brown University, 1977.

Dolinin, A. S. "K istorii sozdaniia *Brat'ev Karamazovykh.*" In *F. M. Dostoevskii: Materialy i issledovaniia,* ed. A. S. Dolinin, pp. 9–80. Leningrad, 1935. Reprinted as "Posledniaia vershina: K istorii sozdaniia *Brat'ev Karamazovykh,*" in *Poslednie romany Dostoevskogo: Kak sozdavalis' "Podrostok" i "Brat'ia Karamazovy"* (Moscow and Leningrad, 1963), pp. 231–306.

Dorovatovskaia-Liubimova, V. S. "Dostoevskii i shestidesiatniki." In *Dostoevskii,* pp. 5–60. Moscow, 1928.

Dostoevskii, A. A., ed. *Vospominaniia Andreia Mikhailovicha Dostoevskogo.* Leningrad, 1930.

Dostoevsky, Anna. *Dostoevsky: Reminiscences.* Tr. and ed. Beatrice Stillman, with an Introduction by Helen Muchnic. New York, 1975.

―――. *Vospominaniia.* Moscow, 1971.

Drouilly, J. "L'Image du soleil couchant dans l'oeuvre de Dostoievski." *Etudes slaves et est-européennes* (Quebec) 19:3–23.

Dunlop, John B. *Staretz Amvrosy: Model for Dostoevsky's Staretz Zossima.* Belmont, Mass., 1972.

Durylin, Sergei. "Ob odnom simvole u Dostoevskogo: Opyt tematicheskogo obzora." In *Dostoevskii,* pp. 163–98. Moscow, 1928.

Egorenkova, G. I. "Poetika siuzhetnoi aury v romane F. M. Dostoevskogo *Brat'ia Karamazovy.*" *Filologicheskie nauki* 14, no. 5:27–39.

Engelhardt, B. M. "Ideologicheskii roman Dostoevskogo." In *F. M. Dostoevskii: Stat'i i materialy, Sbornik vtoroi,* ed. A. S. Dolinin, pp. 71–105. Moscow and Leningrad, 1924.

Evnin, F. "Dostoevskii i voinstvuiushchii katolitsizm 1860–70kh godov (K genezisu 'Legendy o velikom inkvizitore')." *Russkaia literatura* 10, no. 1:29–41.

Fasting, Sigurd. "Ierarkhiia 'pravd' kak chast' ideino-khudozhestvennoi struktury romana *Brat'ia Karamazovy:* K voprosu o 'polifonichnosti' romanov Dostoevskogo." *Scando-Slavica* 24:35–47.

Fedotov, George P. *The Russian Religious Mind.* 2 vols. Cambridge, Mass., 1946–66. Reprint ed., Belmont, Mass., 1975. (Vols. 3–4 of the *Collected Works* of George P. Fedotov.)

_____. *A Treasury of Russian Spirituality.* Belmont, Mass., 1975. (Vol. 2 of the *Collected Works* of George P. Fedotov.)

Florenskii, Pavel. *Stolp i utverzhdenie istiny: Opyt pravoslavnoi teoditsei v dvenadtsati pis'makh.* Moscow, 1914.

Freud, Sigmund. "Dostoevsky and Parricide." In *Dostoevsky: A Collection of Critical Essays,* ed. René Wellek, pp. 98–111. Englewood Cliffs, N.J., 1962.

Gessen, S. I. "Tragediia dobra v *Brat'iakh Karamazovykh* Dostoevskogo." In *O Dostoevskom: Stat'i,* ed. Donald Fanger, pp. 197–229. Brown University Slavic Reprints, 4. Providence, 1966.

Gibian, George. "Dostoevsky's Use of Russian Folklore." *Journal of American Folklore* 69:239–53.

Gibson, A. Boyce. *The Religion of Dostoevsky.* Philadelphia, 1974.

Girard, René. *Dostoïevski du double à l'unité.* Paris, 1963.

Goldstein, David I. *Dostoïevski et les Juifs.* Paris, 1976.

Goldstein, Martin. "The Debate in *The Brothers Karamazov.*" *Slavic and East European Journal* 14:326–40.

Golosovker, Ia. E. *Dostoevskii i Kant: Razmyshlenie chitatelia nad romanom "Brat'ia Karamazovy" i traktatom "Kritika chistogo razuma."* Moscow, 1963.

Gorodetzky, Nadejda. *Saint Tikhon of Zadonsk: Inspirer of Dostoevsky.* New York, 1976.

Grigor'ev, A. "Dostoevskii i Didro: K postanovke problemy." *Russkaia literatura* 9, no. 4: 88–102.

Grigorieff, Dmitry F. "Dostoevsky's Elder Zosima and the Real-Life Father Amvrosy." *St. Vladimir's Seminary Quarterly* 2:22–34.

Grossman, Leonid. *Biblioteka Dostoevskogo po neizdannym materialam: S. prilozheniem kataloga biblioteki Dostoevskogo.* Odessa, 1919.

_____. "Dostoevskii i pravitel'stvennye krugi 1870-kh godov." *Literaturnoe nasledstvo* 15:83–162.

_____. *Poetika Dostoevskogo.* Moscow, 1925.

_____. *Seminarii po Dostoevskomu: Materialy, bibliografiia i kommentarii.* Moscow and Petrograd, 1922.

Guardini, Romano. *Religiöse Gestalten in Dostojewskijs Werk.* Munich, 1947.

Hall, Vernon. "Dostoevsky's Use of French as a Symbolic Device in *The Brothers Karamazov.*" *Comparative Literature Studies* 2:171–74.

Hingley, Ronald. *The Undiscovered Dostoyevsky.* London, 1962.

Holquist, Michael. *Dostoevsky and the Novel.* Princeton, 1977.

Hugo, Victor. *Oeuvres poétiques.* Ed. Pierre Albouy. 3 vols. Paris, 1967.

Isaac of Niniveh. *Mystic Treatises.* Tr. from Bedjan's Syriac text with an introduction and registers by A. J. Wensinck. Leiden, 1923. Reprint ed., Wiesbaden, 1969.

Ivanov, Vyacheslav. *Freedom and the Tragic Life: A Study in Dostoevsky.* New York, 1971.

Jackson, Robert L. "Dmitrij Karamazov and the 'Legend.'" *Slavic and East European Journal* 9:257–67.

————. *Dostoevsky's Quest for Form: A Study of His Philosophy of Art.* New Haven and London, 1966.

————. "The Triple Vision: Dostoevsky's 'The Peasant Marey.'" *Yale Review,* Winter 1978, pp. 225–35.

————. "Vynesenie prigovora Fiodoru Pavlovichu Karamazovu." In *Dostoevskii: Materialy i issledovaniia,* 2:137–44. Leningrad, 1976.

Jones, Malcolm V. *Dostoevsky: The Novel of Discord.* New York, 1976.

————. "Dostoyevsky's Conception of the Idea." *Renaissance and Modern Studies* (University of Nottingham) 13:106–31.

Karlova, T. S. *Dostoevskii i russkii sud.* Kazan, 1975.

Karsavin, L. "Dostoevskii i katolichestvo." In *Dostoevskii: Stat'i i materialy,* ed. A. S. Dolinin, pp. 35–66. Peterburg, 1922.

Kashina-Evreinova, Anna A. *Podpol'e geniia: Seksual'nye istochniki tvorchestva Dostoevskogo.* Petrograd, 1923.

Khomiakov, A. *Neskol'ko slov pravoslavnogo khristianina o zapadnykh veroispovedaniiakh.* Leipzig, 1853.

Kiiko, E. I. "Iz istorii sozdaniia *Brat'ev Karamazovykh:* Ivan i Smerdiakov." In *Dostoevskii: Materialy i issledovaniia,* 2:125–29. Leningrad, 1976.

Komarovich, V. "Nenapisannaia poema Dostoevskogo." In *Dostoevskii: Stat'i i materialy,* ed. A. S. Dolinin, pp. 177–207. Peterburg, 1922.

Komarowitsch, W., ed., *Die Urgestalt der "Brüder Karamasoff": Dostojewskis Quellen, Entwürfe und Fragmente.* With comments by W. Komarowitsch and an introduction by Sigmund Freud. Munich, 1928.

Kubikov, I. N. "Obraz Smerdiakova i ego obobshchaiushchii smysl." In *Dostoevskii,* pp. 199–215. Moscow, 1928.

Kudriavtsev, Iu. G. *Bunt ili religiia: O mirovozzrenii F. M. Dostoevskogo.* Moscow, 1969.

Lapshin, I. I. "Kak slozhilas' legenda o velikom inkvizitore." In *O Dostoevskom*, ed. A. L. Bem, 1:125–39. 3 vols. Prague, 1929–36.

Lauth, Reinhard. *Die Philosophie Dostojewskis in systematischer Darstellung*. Munich, 1950.

Leont'ev, K. *Sobranie sochinenii*. 9 vols. Moscow, 1912.

Likhachov, D. S. " 'Nebrezhenie slovom' u Dostoevskogo." In *Dostoevskii: Materialy i issledovaniia*, 2:30–41. Leningrad, 1976.

_____. " 'Predislovnyi rasskaz' Dostoevskogo." In *Poetika i stilistika russkoi literatury: Pamiati akademika Viktora Vladimirovicha Vinogradova*, pp. 189–94. Leningrad, 1971.

Linnér, Sven. *Starets Zosima in "The Brothers Karamazov": A Study in the Mimesis of Virtue*. Stockholm, 1975.

Lord, R. "Dostoyevsky and Vladimir Solov'yev." *Slavonic and East European Review* 42:415–26.

Losskii, N. *Dostoevskii i ego khristianskoe miroponimanie*. New York, 1953.

_____. "O prirode sataninskoi (po Dostoevskomu)." In *Dostoevskii: Stat'i i materialy*, ed. A. S. Dolinin, pp. 66–94. Peterburg, 1922.

Lotman, L. M. "Romany Dostoevskogo i russkaia legenda." *Russkaia literatura* 15, no. 2:129–41.

Lukashevich, Stephen. *N. F. Fedorov (1828–1903): A Study in Russian Eupsychian and Eutopian Thought*. Newark, Del., 1977.

Lyngstad, Alexandra H. *Dostoevskij and Schiller*. The Hague and Paris, 1975.

Macarius, Starets of Optino. *Russian Letters of Direction, 1834–1860*. Ed. and tr. Iulia de Beausobre. New York, 1975.

Maceina, Antanas. *Der Grossinquisitor: Geschichtsphilosophische Deutung der Legende Dostojewskijs*. Heidelberg, 1952.

Maloney, G. A. *Russian Hesychasm: The Spirituality of Nil Sorsky*. The Hague, 1973.

Matlaw, Ralph E. *"The Brothers Karamazov": Novelistic Technique*. The Hague, 1957.

_____. "Recurrent Imagery in Dostoevskij." *Harvard Slavic Studies* 3:201–25.

Merezhkovskii, D. S. *Prorok russkoi revoliutsii*. St. Petersburg, 1906.

Miller, Orest. *Russkie Pisateli posle Gogolia: Chteniia, rechi i stat'i*. 6th ed. Vol. 1. St. Petersburg and Moscow, 1913. (Contains "Deti v sochineniiakh F. M. Dostoevskogo," pp. 300–337, and "Karamazovshchina i inochestvo," pp. 227–99.)

Mochulsky, Konstantin. *Dostoevsky: His Life and Work*. Tr., with an introduction, by Michael A. Minihan. Princeton, 1967.

Neifel'd, Iolan [Jolan Neufeld]. *Dostoevskii: Psikhoanaliticheskii ocherk pod redaktsiei prof. Z. Freida.* Tr. from the German by Ia. Druskina. Leningrad and Moscow, 1925.

Oates, Joyce C. "The Double Vision of *The Brothers Karamazov." Journal of Aesthetics and Art Criticism* 27:203–13.

Onasch, Konrad. *Der verschwiegene Christus: Versuch über die Poetisierung des Christentums in der Dichtung F. M. Dostojewskis.* Berlin, 1976.

Panichas, George A. "Dostoevski and Satanism." *Journal of Religion* 45:12–29.

Peace, Richard. *Dostoyevsky: An Examination of the Major Novels* Cambridge, 1971.

Perlina, Nina M. "Quotation as an Element of the Poetics of *The Brothers Karamazov."* Ph.D. dissertation, Brown University, 1977.

Pletniov, R. V. "Serdtsem mudrye: O startsakh u Dostoevskogo." In *O Dostoevskom,* ed. A. L. Bem, 2:73–92. 3 vols. Prague, 1929–36.

Pomerants, Grigorii. " 'Evklidovskii' i 'neevklidovskii' razum v tvorchestve Dostoevskogo." *Kontinent,* no. 3 (1975), pp. 109–50.

Proust, Marcel. *A la recherche du temps perdu.* Vol. 3. Ed. Pierre Clarac and André Ferré. Paris, 1954.

Radlov, E. L. "Solov'iov i Dostoevskii." In *Dostoevskii: Stat'i i materialy,* ed. A. S. Dolinin, pp. 155–72. Petersburg, 1922.

Rahv, Philip. "The Legend of the Grand Inquisitor." *Partisan Review* 21:249–71.

Rak, V. D. "Iuridicheskaia oshibka v romane *Brat'ia Karamazovy."* In *Dostoevskii: Materialy i issledovaniia,* 2:154–59. Leningrad, 1976.

Rehm, Walther. *Jean Paul—Dostojewski: Eine Studie zur dichterischen Gestaltung des Unglaubens.* Göttingen, 1962.

Reinus, L. M. *Dostoevskii v Staroi Russe.* Leningrad, 1969.

Renan, Ernest. *Vie de Jésus.* Paris, 1863.

Roseberry, Robert L. "Schillerean Elements in the Works of Dostoevsky: A Review of Recent Criticism." *Germano-Slavica* 3:17–35.

Rosen, Nathan. "The *Book of Job* in the Structure of *The Brothers Karamazov."* (Ms.)

———. "Style and Structure in *The Brothers Karamazov:* The Grand Inquisitor and the Russian Monk." *Russian Literature Triquarterly* 1:352–65.

———. "Why Dmitrii Karamazov Did Not Kill His Father." *Canadian-American Slavic Studies* 6:209–24.

Rowe, William Woodin. "*Crime and Punishment* and *The Brothers Karamazov:* Some Comparative Observations." *Russian Literature Triquarterly* 10:331–42.

_____. *Dostoevsky: Child and Man in His Works.* New York and London, 1968.

Rozanov, Vasily. *Legenda o Velikom Inkvizitore.* St. Petersburg, 1902. In English as *Dostoevsky and the Legend of the Grand Inquisitor.* Tr. with an afterword by Spencer E. Roberts. Ithaca and London, 1972.

Sandoz, Ellis. *Political Apocalypse: A Study of Dostoevsky's Grand Inquisitor.* Baton Rouge, 1971.

Schmid, Wolf. *Der Textaufbau in den Erzählungen Dostoevskijs.* Munich, 1973.

Semionov, E. I. "K voprosu o meste glavy 'Bunt' v romane *Brat'ia Karamazovy.*" In *Dostoevskii: Materialy i issledovaniia,* 2:130–36. Leningrad, 1976.

Shein, Louis J. "An Examination of the Kantian Antinomies in *The Brothers Karamazov.*" *Germano-Slavica* 2:49–60.

Shestov, Lev. *Athens and Jerusalem.* New York, 1966.

Slochower, Harry. "The Pan-Slavic Image of the Earth Mother: *The Brothers Karamazov.*" In *Mythopoesis: Mythic Patterns in the Literary Classics,* by Harry Slochower, pp. 246–83. Detroit, 1970.

Solov'iov, Vladimir Sergeevich. *Sobranie sochinenii.* 12 vols. St. Petersburg, 1901.

[Strakhov, N. N., ed.] *Biografiia, pis'ma i zametki iz zapisnoi knizhki F. M. Dostoevskogo.* St. Petersburg, 1883.

Struve, Gleb. "Notes on the Language and Style of Dostoevsky." (Résumé.) *Bulletin of the International Dostoevsky Society,* no. 7 (1977), p. 76.

Szylkarski, Wladimir. "Messianismus und Apokalyptik bei Dostojewskij und Solowjew." In *Der Grossinquisitor: Geschichtsphilosophische Deutung der Legende Dostojewskijs,* by Antanas Maceina, pp. 247–334. Heidelberg, 1952.

Tarasjev, Andrej. "Apokrif 'Hod Bogorodice po mukama' u okvirima idejnog plana *Braće Karamazovih.*" In *Zbornik Vladimira Mošina,* pp. 287–94. Belgrade, 1977.

Tikhon Zadonskii. *Tvoreniia izhe vo sviatykh ottsa nashego Tikhona Zadonskago.* 2 vols. St. Petersburg, 1912.

Tikhonravov, Nikolai. *Pamiatniki otrechennoi russkoi literatury.* 2 vols. St. Petersburg and Moscow, 1863.

Tiutchev, F. I. *Politicheskie stat'i.* Paris, 1976.

Trubetzkoy, N. S. *Dostoevskij als Künstler.* The Hague, 1964.

Verkhovskii, Starets Zosima. *Zhizneopisanie i zapisi.* Platina, Calif., 1977.

Vetlovskaia, V. E. "Literaturnye i fol'klornye istochniki *Brat'ev Karamazovykh:* Zhitie Alekseia cheloveka bozhiia i dukhovnyi stikh o niom." In *Dostoevskii i russkie pisateli: Traditsii, novatorstvo, masterstvo,* ed. V. Ia. Kirpotin, pp. 325–54. Moscow, 1971.

———. *Poetika romana "Brat'ia Karamazovy."* Leningrad, 1977.

———. "Razviazka v *Brat'iakh Karamazovykh.*" In *Poetika i stilistika russkoi literatury: Pamiati akademika Viktora Vladimirovicha Vinogradova,* pp. 195–203. Leningrad, 1971.

———. "Tvorchestvo Dostoevskogo v svete literaturnykh i fol'klornykh parallelei: 'stroitel'naia zhertva.'" In *Mif—fol'klor—literatura,* pp. 81–113. Leningrad, 1978.

Vivas, Eliseo. "The Two Dimensions of Reality in *The Brothers Karamazov.*" In *Dostoevsky: A Collection of Critical Essays,* ed. René Wellek, pp. 71–89. Englewood Cliffs, N.J., 1962.

Volynskii, A. L. *Tsarstvo Karamazovykh.* St. Petersburg, 1901.

Wasiolek, Edward. *Dostoevsky: The Major Fiction.* Cambridge, Mass., 1964.

Wharton, Robert V. "Evil in an Earthly Paradise: Dostoevsky's Theodicy." *The Thomist* 41:567–84.

Zakiewicz, Zbigniew. "Polacy u Dostojewskiego." *Twórczość 24,* no. 6:75–89.

Zander, L. A. *Taina dobra: Problema dobra v tvorchestve Dostoevskogo.* Frankfurt am Main, 1960.

Zedergol'm, Ieromonakh Kliment. *Optinskii starets Leonid, v skhime Lev: Zhizneopisanie i zapisi.* Platina, Calif., 1976.

Zen'kovskii, V. V. "Fiodor Pavlovich Karamazov." In *O Dostoevskom,* ed. A. L. Bem, 2:93–114. 3 vols. Prague, 1929–36.

Zenkovsky, V. V. "Dostoevsky's Religious and Philosophical Views." In *Dostoevsky: A Collection of Critical Essays,* ed. René Wellek, pp. 130–45. Englewood Cliffs, N.J., 1962.

Zundelovich, Ia. O. "Obraz mira Dostoevskogo v ego sotsial'no-filosofskom romane *Brat'ia Karamazovy.*" In *Romany Dostoevskogo: Stat'i,* pp. 180–242. Tashkent, 1963.

Index

Names of authors and of characters in *The Brothers Karamazov* that are of negligible importance to the interpretation of the novel are not included in this index. Characters of works other than *The Brothers Karamazov* are also not included in the index, but can be located by looking under the title of the work in question; for instance, to find references to Stavrogin, look under Dostoevsky, Fiodor Mikhailovich, *The Possessed*.

457

the father-son relationship, 61;
psychological metaphors, 252 *n62*,
291 *n132*, 331 *n175*, 372 *n146*,
417 *n165*; of minor characters,
312 *n4*; from the outside in, 79,
151 *n97*; of poverty, 203 *n139*;
psychoanalytic, 81–82, 400 *n11*,
433 *n286*; of the self-styled buffoon, 344 *n71*. *See also* Paradox,
psychological

Pushkin, Alexander, Russian poet
and writer, 3, 9, 11, 18, 160 *n189*,
172 *n67*, 292 *n148*, 310 *n316*,
352 *n131*, 361 *n42*, 414 *n136*
—"Answer to an Anonymous Corre-
spondent," 425 *n233*
—*Boris Godunov*, 294 *n174*
—"The Bridegroom," 159 *n175*
—"Budrys and his Sons," 301 *n236*
—"Chill Winds Still Blow," 44,
217 *n78*
—"City of Luxury," 369 *n111*
—*The Covetous Knight*, 18,
157 *n159*, 235 *n282*
—"The Demon," 205 *n157*
—"Dubrovsky," 225 *n161*
—*Eugene Onegin*, 18, 190 *n256*,
351 *n125*, 352 *n131*
—"Get Treated," 393 *n355*
—"He Lived among Us," 413 *n133*
—"The Hermit Monks," 392 *n352*
—"In the Depth of Siberian Mines,"
277 *n10*
—"A King Was Told," 218 *n88*
—*Little Tragedies*, 18 *n38*
—"The Prophet," 309 *n309*
—"Reminiscence," 238 *n321*
—"Ruslan and Liudmila,"
289 *n113*, 416 *n159*
—"The Stone Guest," 18, 230 *n229*
—"Table Talk," 285 *n78*
—"Tale about the Fisherman and
the Fish," 171 *n51*. *See also*
Dostoevsky, Fiodor Mikhailovich,
"Discourse on Pushkin"

Radicals, 33–34, 37, 341 *n42*,
342, *nn48, 49*, 346 *nn90, 92*,
351 *n123*, 352 *n131*, 368 *n109*,
396 *n372*; their ideology, 157 *n164*,
162 *n204*, 165 *n237*, 182 *n169*,
232 *nn247, 248*, 347 *n95*,
348 *n107*, 350 *nn117, 121*,
351 *n126*, 421 *n207*
Rakitin, author of a vita of Father
Zosima, 53, 404 *n47*; his background, 161 *n199*; his comeuppance, 268 *n72*, 404 *nn46, 50*,
409 *n95*; a Darwinist, 160 *n191*,
367 *n98*; dislikes God, 54,
368 *n104*; and Grushen'ka,
160 *n194*; his ideas, 162 *n204*,
395 *n370*, 404 *nn44, 45*; and Ivan
Karamazov's idea, 53–54,
161 *n198*, 273 *n121*; "not indifferent to Katerina Ivanovna,"
162 *n205*; and Mme. Khokhlakov,
360 *nn34, 37*; his language,
159 *n177*, 161 *n198*, 163 *n213*,
170 *n46*, 267 *n58*, 268 *n67*,
270 *n91*, 271 *n98*, 272 *n107*; his
prototypes, 30, 30 *n83*; the seminarian, 158 *n169*, 369 *n111*; and
Smerdiakov, 367 *n99*; a stock
character, 63, 159 *n175*, 162 *n203*;
mentioned, 49, 58, 67, 68,
75 *n122*, 77, 82, 96, 97, 102, 104,
107, 109, 122, 143 *n18*, 159 *n183*,
268 *n69*, 341 *n47*, 343 *n64*,
371 *n131*
Reader, the, 87, 92, 169 *nn36, 40*,
187 *n210*, 222 *n134*, 252 *n66*,
267 *n54*, 277 *n9*, 322 *n93*,
324 *n106*; his role in developing
subtexts, 96–97, 98, 99–100,
285 *nn81, 82*, 315 *n27*
Realism, 63, 78, 80, 88, 100, 210 *n1*,
282 *n48*, 283 *n61*, 284 *n65*,
288 *n107*; concern with realistic detail, 8, 9, 9 *n10*, 41, 78 *n130*,
170 *n43*, 175 *n95*, 203 *n139*,